Property Claim Practices

Property Claim Practices

1st Edition • 2nd Printing

The Institutes
720 Providence Road, Suite 100
Malvern, Pennsylvania 19355-3433

1st Edition • 2nd Printing • December 2013

Library of Congress Control Number: 2011961689

ISBN 978-0-89463-532-8

Foreword

The Institutes are the trusted leader in delivering proven knowledge solutions that drive powerful business results for the risk management and property-casualty insurance industry. For more than 100 years, The Institutes have been meeting the industry's changing professional development needs with customer-driven products and services.

In conjunction with industry experts and members of the academic community, our Knowledge Resources Department develops our course and program content, including Institutes study materials. Practical and technical knowledge gained from Institutes courses enhances qualifications, improves performance, and contributes to professional growth—all of which drive results.

The Institutes' proven knowledge helps individuals and organizations achieve powerful results with a variety of flexible, customer-focused options:

Recognized Credentials—The Institutes offer an unmatched range of widely recognized and industry-respected specialty credentials. The Institutes' Chartered Property Casualty Underwriter (CPCU®) professional designation is designed to provide a broad understanding of the property-casualty insurance industry. Depending on professional needs, CPCU students may select either a commercial insurance focus or a personal risk management and insurance focus and may choose from a variety of electives.

In addition, The Institutes offer certificate or designation programs in a variety of disciplines, including these:

- Claims
- Commercial underwriting
- Fidelity and surety bonding
- General insurance
- Insurance accounting and finance
- Insurance information technology
- Insurance production and agency management
- Insurance regulation and compliance
- Management
- Marine insurance
- Personal insurance
- Premium auditing
- Quality insurance services
- Reinsurance
- Risk management
- Surplus lines

Ethics—Ethical behavior is crucial to preserving not only the trust on which insurance transactions are based, but also the public's trust in our industry as a whole. All Institutes designations now have an ethics requirement, which is delivered online and free of charge. The ethics requirement content is designed specifically for insurance practitioners and uses insurance-based case studies to outline an ethical framework. More information is available in the Programs section of our website, www.TheInstitutes.org.

Flexible Online Learning—The Institutes have an unmatched variety of technical insurance content covering topics from accounting to under-writing, which we now deliver through hundreds of online courses. These cost-effective self-study courses are a convenient way to fill gaps in technical knowledge in a matter of hours without ever leaving the office.

Continuing Education—A majority of The Institutes' courses are filed for CE credit in most states. We also deliver quality, affordable, online CE courses quickly and conveniently through our newest business unit, CEU.com. Visit www.CEU.com to learn more.

College Credits—Most Institutes courses carry college credit recommendations from the American Council on Education. A variety of courses also qualify for credits toward certain associate, bachelor's, and master's degrees at several prestigious colleges and universities. More information is available in the Student Services section of our website, www.TheInstitutes.org.

Custom Applications—The Institutes collaborate with corporate customers to use our trusted course content and flexible delivery options in developing customized solutions that help them achieve their unique organizational goals.

Insightful Analysis—Our Insurance Research Council (IRC) division conducts public policy research on important contemporary issues in property-casualty insurance and risk management. Visit www.ircweb.org to learn more or purchase its most recent studies.

The Institutes look forward to serving the risk management and property-casualty insurance industry for another 100 years. We welcome comments from our students and course leaders; your feedback helps us continue to improve the quality of our study materials.

Peter L. Miller, CPCU
President and CEO
The Institutes

Preface

Property Claim Practices is one of the textbooks for the Property and Multi-line tracks in The Institutes' Associate in Claims (AIC) designation program.

Assignments 1 and 2 of this text discuss property insurance concepts in a general way. Assignments 3 and 4 review the loss adjustment process and loss investigation. The remaining assignments of this text concern specific types of losses:

- Good-faith investigation and coverage defenses
- Fraud investigation
- Estimating and residential construction fundamentals
- Merchandise losses
- Business income losses
- Specialty property losses

The Institutes are thankful to the individuals who contributed to the development of previous forms of this content, including manuscript reviewers and various advisory committee members. In particular, The Institutes would like to thank Richard C. Kelly, Esq.

For more information about The Institutes' programs, please call our Customer Service Department at (800) 644-2101, email us at customerservice@TheInstitutes.org, or visit our website at www.TheInstitutes.org.

Donna J. Popow

Contributors

The Institutes acknowledge with deep appreciation the contributions made to the content of this text by the following person:

Richard C. Kelly, Esq.

Contents

Segment A

Direct Your Learning ▶▶

Property Insurance Basics

Educational Objectives

After learning the content of this assignment, you should be able to:

▷ Explain the extent and importance of an insurable interest in a given loss situation.

▷ Explain how the rights of those with insurable interest are protected.

▷ Describe the differences in insurance coverage for real property, personal property, fixtures, and improvements and betterments.

▷ Explain the evolution of covered perils.

▷ Explain the difference in the coverage analysis of a specified-perils policy and a risk of direct physical loss policy.

▷ Explain how the burden of proof for a specified-perils policy differs from the burden of proof for a risk of direct physical loss policy.

▷ Describe how definitions and additional coverages affect covered causes of loss in a policy.

▷ Describe the various perils typically insured under property insurance.

▷ Explain why various exclusions are included in property policies and what the common exclusions are.

▷ Explain the concept of concurrent causation and the various approaches used to deal with it.

Property Insurance Basics

1

INSURABLE INTEREST

Insurable interest in property at the time of a loss is an underlying principle that makes the property insurance system work. It helps to determine who should recover in a loss situation.

This section begins the analysis of property loss adjusting with a general discussion of who and what are covered under property insurance policies. Insurance protects people, not property. Although every policy limits its coverage to specific property or types of property, property loss adjusters should focus on who is insured and what the insured's interests are in the property to determine coverage. This is a key part of the property loss adjusting process.

Property Loss Adjusting

Property losses are featured prominently in the news, with reports detailing cases ranging from mild property damage caused by inclement weather or vandalism to devastating accidents, catastrophes, and natural disasters.

The news does not always show such losses' aftermath, but most of the people whose property is damaged are insured and receive payments for their losses from insurers, often within days. The insurance industry fulfills its promises and obligations to its insureds through the work of property loss adjusters. Property loss adjusting is one of the most gratifying, and one of the most demanding, careers in the property-casualty insurance industry.

Property loss adjusters must have a detailed understanding of insurance policies; a vast knowledge of property values, costs, and repair methods; and at least a working knowledge of accounting and construction methods and materials. Additionally, property loss adjusters must be tactful and sensitive in dealing with insureds who have suffered great stress and anxiety from their losses. Adjusters must also detect and prove fraudulent claims.

This section presents one of the major property loss adjusting principles, insurable interest. Although it does not require a student's prior knowledge of property loss adjusting, the section develops this key concept to a substantially expert level.

Insurable Interest

Insurable interest

An interest in the subject of an insurance policy that is not unduly remote and that would cause the interested party to suffer financial loss if an insured event occurred.

An **insurable interest** exists when someone derives a monetary benefit or advantage by the property's preservation and continued existence or would suffer a monetary loss from its destruction. In other words, if a person will suffer a financial loss if a piece of property is damaged or destroyed, that person has an insurable interest in that property. Additionally, to recover the loss amount resulting from the property damage, that person must have an insurable interest in the property at the time of loss.

What Are the Purposes of the Insurable Interest Requirement?

The insurable interest requirement in property insurance policies serves three purposes. See the exhibit "Three Purposes of Insurable Interest Requirement."

Three Purposes of Insurable Interest Requirement

1. To indemnify the proper people for the proper amount
2. To prevent wagering on losses
3. To deter people from committing fraud or intentionally causing a loss

---

[DA03759]

Each of these purposes is discussed next.

Indemnification

Contract of indemnity

A contract in which the insurer agrees, in the event of a covered loss, to pay an amount directly related to the amount of the loss.

An insurance policy is a **contract of indemnity**. It is designed to restore an insured who has suffered a loss to the same financial condition as before the loss. A person who has no insurable interest would, by definition, not suffer any financial loss if the property were damaged. Insurable interest is not acquired by simply paying the policy premium. Furthermore, someone who has an insurable interest should recover no more than the value of his or her interest. However, a policy that indemnifies the insured based on current replacement cost allows the insured to collect more than the property's value at the time of the loss. While this technically violates the indemnity concept, the insured does pay a premium to obtain this extra coverage.

Wagering

Preventing wagering is important for legal as well as ethical reasons. Insurance differs from gambling because when a person places a bet, he or she hopes to win more than the amount wagered. Gambling results in one of two possible outcomes: the bettor either loses money or wins money. With insurance, an insured pays the premium, then either has a loss during the policy period or does not. After a loss, the insured receives just enough money from the insurer to pay for the loss, and no more. Insureds should not make a profit from insurance. However, replacement cost coverage can be viewed as a means of profiting from a loss, so adjusters must be vigilant for the potential for fraud when handling losses involving replacement cost coverage. The insurable interest requirement prevents wagering by removing the possibility for gain. If the insured has no loss, the insurance company uses his or her premium to help pay for other policyholders' losses. Even when no loss occurs, the insured pays for, and receives, protection and peace of mind.

Suppose that John could purchase a policy on Richard's house. John has no insurable interest in Richard's house, but he thinks buying a policy might be a good investment because Richard's house might burn down. In this situation, John is wagering his premium in the hope that Richard has a loss. Without the insurable interest requirement, a loss would allow John to collect money on the claim, and John would have no duty to use the money to repair the house. The entire payment would be profit, or winnings on his bet. Without the insurable interest requirement, many people could profit in such a manner from others' losses.

Fraud

The insurable interest doctrine discourages insureds from committing fraud or intentionally causing a loss. In the case of John and Richard, if John had paid premiums on Richard's house for a few years but never had any claims to file, he might start a fire just to make money.

If this scenario seems far-fetched, it is because the insurable interest doctrine makes it rare. The insurable interest requirement, established centuries ago, still works well. Without the insurable interest requirement, such crimes would be common. Yet adjusters must remain alert for potentially fraudulent claims and investigate insurable interest in each loss.

Who Has an Insurable Interest?

An insurable interest is not limited to the property owners. Also, the named insured on a particular policy does not automatically have an insurable interest at the time of the loss. Only four types of interest are considered insurable interests. See the exhibit "Four Types of Insurable Interests."

Ownership Interests

Ownership interests can exist in various forms for both personal and business personal property and for real property.

Personal ownership means that the person who owns the property has the right to use it, change it, sell it, rent it, or dispose of it in any way that he or she chooses.

Four Types of Insurable Interests

People with the following types of interest in property have insurable interests:

1. Ownership interests
2. Occupancy interests
3. Custody interests
4. Security interests

[DA03760]

Businesses also own property, but ownership rights depend on the type of business.

Personal Ownership—A homeowner often has a home mortgage, but the homeowner's insurable interest is for the property's full value, including equity and the mortgage amount. A homeowner is entitled to purchase enough insurance to protect both equity and debt because, in case of a serious loss, the homeowner would still be personally responsible for repaying the mortgage debt, or balance. Thus, a homeowner has an insurable interest for the portion of the home owned free and clear (equity) and the portion on which the bank has a lien (the mortgage balance).

Property is often owned in some form other than full individual ownership. Other types of ownership include joint owners, tenancy in common, and life tenants. Note that joint tenants, those in a tenancy in common, and life tenants are not tenants under a lease, as described later in the section on occupancy interests.

Joint owners/tenants

Two or more persons each having a full interest in the property. Each tenant has an insurable interest to the full extent of the property value.

Tenancy by the entirety

A joint tenancy between husband and wife.

Tenancy in common

A concurrent ownership of property, in equal or unequal shares, by two or more joint tenants who lack survivorship rights.

Life tenant (life estate)

A person entitled to exclusive possession of real property and to all income the land produces for the duration of that person's or someone else's life; terminates on the death of the life tenant and does not pass to his or her estate.

- Joint owners. **Joint owners, or joint tenants,** are two or more persons each having a full interest in the property. On the death of any joint tenant, the remaining tenant or tenants continue to have full ownership of the entire property. Each joint tenant has an insurable interest to the full extent of the property value. However, an adjuster making settlement should include all joint tenants on the settlement draft. In the case of a husband and wife, joint tenancy is known as **tenancy by the entireties.**

- Tenancy in common. When two or more persons own a piece of property, but each has a distinct fractional, or percentage, interest, they are a **tenancy in common.** Collectively, these tenants have an insurable interest to the full extent of the property value, but each tenant's interest is limited to his or her respective fractional value. Loss settlement should be made with all members of the tenancy in common collectively.

- Life tenants. Someone entitled to a piece of real property's full use and possession for his or her life is known as a **life tenant.** That person is said to have a life estate in the property. Upon the life tenant's death, the full interest in the property passes to someone else. Life tenants may not leave any interest by will to their heirs. Life tenants have a legal duty to preserve the property for the party with the future interest. This legal duty plus the life tenancy itself confer upon life tenants an insurable interest to the full extent of the property value.

Business Ownership—The most common types of business ownership are sole proprietorships, partnerships, and corporations.

- Sole proprietorship. In a **sole proprietorship**, one person owns the business's assets and is personally liable for the business's debts.
- Partnership. A **partnership** exists when two or more people voluntarily join in business. They share in both the business's profits and losses. All partnership property is owned in common by the partners, all of whom have an interest in the property. Most states provide a statutory distinction between general and limited partners. General partners' personal assets can be liquidated to pay the partnership's debts. In contrast, limited partners' liability would be limited to the partners' individual investments.
- Corporation. A corporation is a legal entity created for the purpose of conducting business, either for profit or as a not-for-profit organization. As legal entities, corporations can own and transfer property, sue, and be sued in their own names. Executive officers, members of the board of directors, other officers, and even stockholders all have a role in the business's operation. A corporation's daily operation is usually managed by the officers, but all other parties stand to gain or lose depending on the business's success.

The main difference between a corporation and a partnership or a sole proprietorship is the so-called **corporate veil**. This veil insulates the assets of the corporation's owners in case the corporation goes bankrupt. The corporation's owners, the stockholders, are not personally liable for the corporation's debts.

A corporation that owns property is, in many ways, like a private citizen who owns a home. The corporation has the right to sell, change, rent, improve, or dispose of the property as it sees fit. The corporation can also purchase enough insurance to cover its interest in the property.

The **limited liability corporation (LLC)** is becoming a more prevalent business entity. Each state has a law that either allows or forbids the formation of a limited liability corporation. The LLC is attractive because it insulates its members from creditors and lawsuits brought against the business while having a partnership's tax advantages. The LLC has the same ability to own, sell, rent, change, or improve property as a regular corporation.

Occupancy Interests

Someone who pays to use, possess, or occupy property belonging to another is a **tenant**, or lessee. Tenants usually sign a contract, or lease, for a certain time period. The insurable interest arises out of the property's use value for the time remaining on the lease or rental agreement.

Sole proprietorship

A form of business in which one person owns the business assets and is personally liable for the business's debts.

Partnership

A for-profit business entity jointly owned by two or more persons who share ownership and profits (or losses), although not necessarily on an equal basis.

Corporate veil

A doctrine that insulates the assets of the owners of the corporation in case the corporation goes bankrupt. The corporation's owners, the stockholders, are not personally liable for the corporation's debts.

Limited liability company (LLC)

A form of business entity that provides its owners the limited liability of a corporation and the tax advantages of a partnership.

Tenant (lessee)

Someone who pays to use, possess, or occupy property belonging to another.

If a tenant signs a lease for twenty years at a rent of $1,000 per month, and the building burns down before the lease is up, the tenant must find another building. The new rent for a comparable building might increase to $2,500 per month. Thus, the tenant bears the risk of losing $1,500 per month if the original lease is terminated.

Many lessees sublease all or part of the property to another tenant for a profit. Under these circumstances, the lessee would potentially lose income as a lessor if the building were to become damaged and untenantable.

Tenants who lease buildings for an extended time period often make improvements and betterments to the building. These improvements are at the tenant's (lessee's) expense and, according to most leases, would remain in the building when the tenant leaves. If the improvements are damaged or if the building is damaged and the lease is terminated, the tenant would lose either the money invested in the improvements or the use of those improvements for the remainder of the lease.

For example, suppose XYZ TV, a television retail business, rents space from a landlord. To store and display its TVs, XYZ must install shelves and counters. Interior walls must also be built, and extra electrical outlets must be added. All of these improvements cost $50,000, and XYZ must pay for them. XYZ has signed a ten-year lease and plans on using the building and the improvements for at least that much time. If a fire damages the building, XYZ would have to pay at least $50,000 to rebuild the improvements. If the lease is terminated, XYZ would have to relocate and make improvements in the new premises.

Custody Interests

Custody interests include those of bailees, consignees, common carriers, and trustees.

Bailee

The party temporarily possessing the personal property in a bailment.

Bailees are people and businesses who take possession of others' property for a specific purpose and for a limited time. Examples include repair shops, cleaners, and printers. A bailee has interest in the property up to the value of the material, labor, storage, or other unpaid charges incurred by the bailor. (The bailor is the party who hands over the goods to the bailee. In most, but not all, situations, the bailor is the property owner.) For example, someone who repairs computers might spend time and buy materials fixing a computer for a customer, but a fire might damage the computer before it is returned to the customer. The bailee cannot receive payment for the work because the computer has been damaged. The bailee needs insurance protection for the amount of time and money that he or she invested in the computer. Moreover, the bailee might be legally liable to financially compensate the customer for the computer's full value. Liability for replacing the computer is another interest of the bailee handled by insurance.

Consignee

The person or organization that receives property being transported by a carrier.

A **consignee** is a person or a business holding property owned by someone else or the party to whom goods are delivered (usually for the purpose of selling that property). When the sale is made, the consignee earns a percentage of the sale or another fee for this service. If the property is damaged before it can be sold, the consignee loses the fee. This loss represents an insurable interest of the consignee. Furthermore, consignees might be legally liable to the owner for the property's value and should protect themselves against such liability.

Bus lines, airlines, and other transportation businesses that are required by law to convey passengers and property for a price are called **common carriers**. If property is damaged on a common carrier before it is safely delivered, the carrier might lose its freight charges for services rendered. Additionally, common carriers might be legally liable for damage to property in their possession and must protect themselves against such liability.

Property or assets belonging to minors or incompetent people are sometimes placed in the care of a trustee, or guardian. This **trustee**, or **guardian**, has the legal title to the property but is responsible that it be used, handled, and transferred solely for the beneficiary's benefit. The trustee or guardian has an insurable interest up to the full extent of the property value because he or she would be required to compensate the trust or estate if the property were damaged. Likewise, administrators and executors of deceased persons' estates have an interest to the full extent of the property value.

Security Interests

Security interests involve those who hold a mortgage or another type of lien on property, such as a mechanics lien or a judgment lien.

A **mortgage** transfers an interest to a mortgagee. The **mortgagee** is the bank, financial institution, or person who lends money to the buyer to finance the purchase of the property. The mortgagee takes the mortgage as security for the loan. The loan's unpaid balance is the extent of the mortgagee's interest. Once recorded on city or county records, mortgages give the mortgagee priority over all other subsequently secured interests and creditors if a foreclosure occurs. A security interest in the mortgagor's personal property is called a chattel mortgage. Mortgagees receive additional protection in property insurance policies. A mortgagee is entitled to make a claim even if the insured's claim is denied.

A **loss payee** is a person or an entity, other than a mortgagee, who will be paid if a property loss occurs. The loss payee can be named in the declarations or by endorsement. Loss payees are usually owners of equipment leased to the insured, or they are the purchasers/sellers under a contract of sale. They do not receive the additional protection afforded by the policy to mortgagees.

Like a mortgage, a **lien** provides the lienholder with security in the event of property foreclosure. The lienholder's interest must be protected before any general creditor can benefit from a foreclosure. Liens can arise out of the operation of the law or because the owner has granted a lien.

The law grants a **mechanic's lien** to anyone who works on or repairs a specific piece of property. Liens can be held on real property (for example, a roofer

Common carriers
Airlines, railroads, or trucking companies that furnish transportation to any member of the public seeking their offered services.

Guardian
A person appointed by a probate court to safeguard and distribute the estate assets for a minor's or incompetent's benefit.

Trustee
Someone who has the legal title to a property but is responsible that it be used, handled, and transferred solely for the benefit of the beneficiary.

Security interest
An interest in property (real or personal) that allows the property to be sold on default to satisfy the debt for which the security interest was given.

Mortgage
An interest in land created by a written document that provides security for the payment of a debt.

Mortgagee
A lender in a mortgage arrangement, such as a bank or another financing institution.

Loss payee
A party entitled to share in whatever loss payment an insured receives.

Lien
A creditor's legal right or interest in another's property, usually lasting until satisfaction of the specific debt or duty that the lien secures.

Mechanic's lien
A lien, granted by law to anyone who repairs a specific piece of property, that secures payment for the repairs.

Tax lien
A type of lien held by local, state, and federal governments through operation of law in the amount of unpaid taxes and interest.

Judgment lien
A lien, in favor of the holder of a judgment, that attaches to the property of the one who owes the judgment.

Purchase money security interest
A type of security interest that gives the holder priority in foreclosure over subsequent lienholders or general creditors.

would have a mechanic's lien on a house on which he or she has worked) or on personal property (an auto mechanic who has worked on an auto would also have a mechanic's lien). The lien is for the value of the work performed. Local, state, and federal governments might have **tax liens** in the amount of unpaid taxes and interest on a property through operation of law. **Judgment liens** arise out of court verdicts. Property owners do not voluntarily incur any of these types of liens; they all exist by operation of law.

A property owner might, however, voluntarily grant a lien on his or her property to borrow money from a lender who insists on such security. A mortgage is this type of lien. Such security liens are also commonly associated with expensive personal property, such as autos and machinery. Often, the party that sells the property provides the financing for the purchase and obtains a **purchase money security interest**. This is a lien with special priority in certain circumstances. The holder of a purchase money security interest would have priority in a foreclosure over subsequent lienholders or general creditors. A second mortgage is a security lien on real property, but with a lower priority in foreclosure than a first mortgage.

Although most liens arise out of credit transactions, a general creditor does not automatically have a lien against any specific property and therefore has no insurable interest. Unless the owner has granted a security interest or the creditor has obtained a judgment lien, a general creditor has no interest in any specific property of the debtor.

Who Does Not Have an Insurable Interest?

Before a loss, an insured's rights under an insurance policy cannot be assigned without the insurer's consent. However, after a loss, the insured may assign its right to collect on the claim. The assignee does not have insurable interest in the property. Instead, the assignee has a contractual right to the claim payment. For example, when an owner sells property, the rights or benefits due on a claim but not yet received can be assigned by contract agreement. A homeowner who is selling his or her home with a damaged roof may assign the anticipated claim payment from the insurance company to pay for a new roof. In the sales agreement, the seller gets full value for the house but assigns the policy benefits to the buyer. Therefore, the buyer must rely on the insurance coverage to pay for the roof, which was damaged before the sale took place. The **assignee** did not have an interest in the property at the time of the loss and would have had no claim for the damage, except for the assignment of benefits.

Assignee
The individual or entity to whom property, rights, or interests have been transferred.

HOW ARE THE RIGHTS OF THOSE WITH INSURABLE INTERESTS PROTECTED?

Insurance policies normally protect the rights of those with insurable interests by listing them as named insureds, mortgagees, or loss payees.

Mortgagees have rights under insurance policies separate from the named insureds' rights. Loss payees do not. Lienholders, assignees, and other security interest holders do not have the same protection as mortgagees. Most policies have no special clauses designed for them, but they can be protected by appearing on the policy as a lienholder, a loss payee, or an additional insured. If named, they should be included on all payments of claims and notified if the policy is canceled.

Those who have an insurable interest are responsible for ensuring that they are appropriately named or qualify for coverage under the proper policies. Those who handle claims should verify the various interests in the property as part of the initial investigation and protect all the interests when payments are made.

The homeowners HO-3 form, 2000 edition, and the commercial property Building and Personal Property Coverage Form (BPP), 2002 edition, from Insurance Services Office, Inc., (ISO) are used in the section as representative policies. Other forms exist, from ISO, from other rating bureaus, and from specific insurers, so a property loss adjuster must learn to review the policy on each loss.

Named Insureds

When a policy is purchased to protect certain property, the property owners should be listed on the policy as named insureds. Their interest is primary and provable by the title. The insured or the insured's agent should be especially careful to list the property owners' names on the policy in exactly the same way as they appear on the title to avoid any misunderstanding should a claim arise.

Occupants have several ways to insure their interests. For example, tenants often carry coverage on their personal property only and leave the landlord to cover the building. A common alternative occurs when the owner/landlord requires the tenant to insure the building and to list the owner/landlord as an additional insured. This practice prevents duplicate coverage for the building while still protecting the interests of both owner and tenant.

Special policies are written for bailees and other custodians of property that protect the bailee for legal liability or for the labor and materials invested in the property. The property owner is not protected unless the bailee is legally liable for the loss. In contrast, bailees' customers policies, storekeepers policies, and other similar policies cover the interest of the owner as well as the bailee without regard for the bailee's legal liability. Common carriers have their own types of policies to cover the liability imposed on them by statute. Furthermore, shippers can obtain coverage for their property that is in a carrier's possession.

Trustees who have a long-term responsibility for the care of property are usually named on the policy as named or additional insureds.

The Mortgage Clause

The most common security interest is that of the mortgageholder. A special mortgage clause, which gives the mortgagee rights and duties independent of the named insured, is included in all property policies written for buildings. The BPP has language similar to the mortgage clause of the HO-3 that reads in part as shown here:

> 2. If we deny your claim, that denial will not apply to a valid claim of the mortgagee, if the mortgagee:
>
> a. Notifies us of any change in ownership, occupancy or substantial change in risk of which the mortgagee is aware;
>
> b. Pays any premium due under this policy on demand if you have neglected to pay the premium; and
>
> c. Submits a signed, sworn statement of loss within 60 days after receiving notice from us of your failure to do so. Paragraphs E. Appraisal, G. Suit against us and I. Loss Payment under Section 1—Conditions also apply to the mortgagee.
>
> 3. If we decide to cancel or not to renew this policy, the mortgagee will be notified at least 10 days before the date cancellation or non-renewal takes effect.
>
> 4. If we pay the mortgagee for any loss and deny payment to you:
>
> a. We are subrogated to all the rights of the mortgagee granted under the mortgage on the property; or
>
> b. At our option, we may pay to the mortgagee the whole principal on the mortgage plus any accrued interest. In this event, we will receive a full assignment and transfer of the mortgage and all securities held as collateral to the mortgage debt.[1]

In summary, a mortgagee is entitled to make a claim even if the insured's claim can be denied. For example, an insured who is guilty of arson for profit could not collect any insurance proceeds. However, the mortgagee can comply with all of the mortgage clause's provisions and collect up to the balance owed on the mortgage loan, even if the claim resulted from arson committed by an insured.

TYPES OF PROPERTY

Property loss adjusters must determine not only who, but also what, is covered under property insurance policies. Part of the property loss adjusting process concerns the different types of property insured under the policy. They must therefore know property characteristics and property-related insurance principles.

Real property is distinguished from personal property under both the law and insurance contracts. See the exhibit "Real Property and Personal Property."

Real property (realty)

Tangible property consisting of land, all structures permanently attached to the land, and whatever is growing on the land.

Personal property

All tangible or intangible property that is not real property.

Real Property and Personal Property

Generally, land and anything attached to land are considered real property. Buildings and all of the construction materials and elements incorporated in and attached to them are real property.

Everything else is personal property:

- Furniture

- Intellectual property (which is not insurable under a property policy), such as copyrights, trademark rights, and other intangibles such as the value of a business's goodwill

- Machinery

- Merchandise

[DA03766]

The distinction between real and personal property is usually obvious. This section discusses the importance of that distinction for adjusters and highlights cases in which that distinction is not as clear.

Certain types of property are not clearly real or personal. Such property, including fixtures, trade fixtures, and improvements and betterments, is also discussed, along with a brief description of how policies treat such property.

Distinction Between Real and Personal Property

The distinction between real and personal property is important to insurance adjusters for several reasons, including:

- The possibility of overlapping coverages
- The different valuation methods involved
- The effect on coinsurance requirements

Overlapping Coverages

More than one policy might cover a loss. This overlap happens infrequently with real property. Occasionally, an owner or the owner's insurance agent mistakenly causes two policies to be in effect simultaneously, or a mortgage lender might purchase its own policy during a foreclosure in fear that the owner will allow coverage to lapse. Otherwise, overlapping coverage on real property is unusual.

With personal property, overlapping coverage, though hardly the norm, is much more common. Because of its movable nature, personal property can be located anywhere, including away from the real property in which it is usually housed and/or used. In such situations, coverage might be provided by both the owner's policy and the policy covering the real property where the personal property is located when the loss occurs. Overlapping coverage also occurs with improvements and betterments, further detailed later in this section.

Valuation

All insurance policies stipulate how the covered property is to be valued when a loss occurs. Under many policies, valuation methods differ for real and personal property. For example, the ISO HO-3 homeowner policy values real property at replacement cost and personal property at actual cash value. This difference makes the adjustment process substantially different for real and personal property.

Coinsurance Requirements

Coinsurance
An insurance-to-value provision in many property insurance policies providing that if the property is underinsured, the amount that an insurer will pay for a covered loss is reduced.

Coinsurance requirements cause the insured to bear a portion of every loss unless adequate insurance has been purchased. The adequacy of the amount of insurance purchased is measured against the value of the property insured. Sometimes the insured property's value does not include personal property; coinsurance compliance is then measured only against the real property's value. In these cases, the adjuster must be able to ignore personal property and its value when testing coinsurance compliance. Policies can have coinsurance requirements ranging from 0 to 100 percent. The most common percentage is 80 percent. For a loss to be paid in full, with 80 percent coinsurance, the amount of insurance purchased must be equal to 80 percent of the property's value at the time of the loss.

The Law of Fixtures

Personal property can become real property by becoming so attached or adapted to real property that it becomes a part of it. In such a case, the property is known as a building fixture. By definition, building fixtures (or just **fixtures**) are part of the real property. All of a building's elements are fixtures, but all construction materials and elements are considered personal property until they are incorporated into a building.

Fixture
Any personal property affixed to real property in such a way as to become part of the real property.

Despite this definition, the term "fixture" is normally applied to a type of property that seems to retain its separate identity. A brick that has been incorporated into a building is legally and technically a fixture but is not normally called by that name. For insurance purposes, the term "fixture" is applied to something that has been added to a building after its original construction, such as a utility sink added by a tenant. A sign on a building might also be considered a fixture.

Some property can be considered as either personal property or fixtures (real property). Drapes, drapery hardware, carpets, shelves, lights, large appliances and machinery, and building ornamentation can be either personal property or fixtures, depending on the circumstances of installation, construction, ownership, and so on.

No single factor determines whether an object is personal property or a fixture, but the three important considerations in making such a determination are (1) attachment, (2) adaptation, and (3) intent. See the exhibit "Attachment, Adaptation, and Intent."

Attachment, Adaptation, and Intent

Attachment

Any property's physical attachment to a structure strongly indicates that the property is a fixture and has become part of the real property.

- However, the attachment would have to be more permanent and secure than, for example, a plug connecting an electrical appliance to an outlet.
- A building's rain gutters, which rest on support brackets, are real property, while a picnic table bolted to the ground to prevent it from being stolen or blown over is probably still personal property.

Adaptation

Whether an item is especially adapted to the use of the real property is important in distinguishing between real and personal property. See the following example:

- If property is incorporated into the building or structure and defines the building or structure, it becomes part of the building for insurance purposes. The relationship between a tennis court (which is clearly real property) and the net exemplifies this concept.

Without the net, the tennis court cannot be used appropriately. The net is incorporated into the court and helps to define the structure as a tennis court. It is specially adapted to the real property's use. As such, it is considered a fixture and thus part of the real property.

Although it is possible to argue that the net is personal property because the net can be moved easily, the net would more likely be considered part of the real property. This is because the net's function as an integral part of the court is probably more important than its ability to be moved.

Intent

Although subjective, the owner's intent might determine whether certain property is a building fixture. See the following example:

- A restaurant owner might select carpets, drapes, and ornamentation to suit her operation. When she moves to a new location, she might intend to move this property. In this type of case, the intent might be sufficient to deem these objects personal property. The intent to move property from one location to another might qualify an item as personal property even though it is bolted to the structure.

[DA03856]

Trade Fixtures

Property installed in a structure and used in a business is often referred to as **trade fixtures**. Trade fixtures can include items such as:

- Cabinets
- Cases
- Counters
- Display windows
- Racks
- Shelves

This property might or might not be a fixture in the legal sense. For example, property that is attached to the building but intended only for the tenant's (businessowner's) use and that serves the business rather than the building is personal property. The term "trade fixtures" is firmly entrenched in industry usage and is generally synonymous with "personal property" in insurance policies. As long as the adjuster knows the legal difference between legal fixtures and trade fixtures and knows how a policy applies to all types of property, referring to personal property as a "trade fixture" is appropriate.

Trade fixtures

Fixtures and equipment that may be attached to a building during a tenant's occupancy, with the intention that they be removed when the tenant leaves.

Improvements and Betterments

Improvements and betterments are changes made by a tenant to a structure to suit the tenant's purposes. In commercial leases, tenants commonly rent bare space in which all interior walls, finishes, and furnishings must be added. All improvements and betterments are fixtures because they are added to the structure after it was constructed. The term "improvements and betterments" exists because in lease and insurance agreements, treating these types of fixtures separately is important.

Improvements and betterments

Alterations or additions made to the building at the expense of an insured who does not own the building and who cannot legally remove them.

All leases that allow tenants to install improvements and betterments usually provide (1) that the items can or must be removed at the end of the lease or (2) that ownership of the items will transfer to the landlord at the time of installation or at the end of the lease. The lease provisions determine the extent of the tenant's "use" interest in improvements and betterments. The lease specifies how many years of use the tenant has and whether the tenant can renew the lease.

Because the tenant has a use interest in improvements and betterments, insurance policies have specific provisions for covering such property. Coverage might exist under the landlord's policy or the tenant's policy, or both. In any case, the adjuster must understand the nature and extent of the different interests in improvements and betterments.

DETERMINING COVERAGE: COVERED PERILS

Reviewing a policy for coverage requires a systematic approach. After an adjuster determines who is insured and what is insured, the next step is to determine if the cause of loss is covered. Property coverage has evolved from the original fire policy to the Extended Coverage Form to the Broad Form, each adding additional covered perils to the policy.

To determine coverage for a given loss, property loss adjusters should systematically analyze the applicable policy. The exhibit indicates the steps to determine coverage. Although the steps appear sequentially in the exhibit, coverage analysis does not always follow this sequence. Depending on what is being analyzed, adjusters may find themselves moving from definitions to conditions and then to perils and exclusions. The policy drives the analysis. Yet, regardless of the order of the steps, each of these policy sections is included in the analysis. This discussion assumes that coverage verification (meaning that the policy is in force for the date of loss and that the location is covered by the policy) has already occurred. See the exhibit "Steps in Determining Coverage."

Steps in Determining Coverage

1. Determine whether the loss is a direct physical loss.
2. Determine whether the loss was caused by a covered cause of loss.

2a. Review policy definitions for clarification.

3. Determine whether any additional coverages apply to the loss.
4. Determine whether any exclusions apply to the loss.
5. Determine whether all policy conditions have been met.

[DA03767]

Determine Whether the Loss Is a Direct Physical Loss

The first step in determining coverage for a particular loss is to review the insuring agreement and determine whether the loss is a **direct physical loss**. This section explains the meaning of this threshold requirement of policy coverage. An adjuster must next determine whether the policy coverage is specified perils or special form. An adjuster must also review the definitions to see whether they expand or limit the coverage. With a special-form policy (formerly known as an "all-risks" policy), the adjuster must determine whether any exclusions apply. With specified-perils coverage, the adjuster must determine whether any of the listed perils cover an insured's loss and then check to ascertain whether any exclusions apply. Additional coverages

Direct physical loss

A loss that is physical (not just financial) and results immediately from the occurrence.

might provide coverage that is otherwise excluded or not provided by a policy. Finally, compliance with the policy conditions is as significant to determining coverage as is any other part of the policy.

Property insurance policies (other than those for time element losses) protect against direct physical loss only. Any loss that is not a direct physical loss is not covered. This is true under both special-form and specified-perils policies. To be covered, a loss must be *both* a direct loss and a physical loss caused by a covered peril. To further identify a direct physical loss, as well as to clarify the meanings of other insurance policy terms, see the box. See the exhibit "Identifying a Direct Physical Loss."

Identifying a Direct Physical Loss

Policy forms do not define the phrase "direct physical loss." However, policies do define the meanings of many terms in an insurance policy. To determine or clarify a term's meaning, the following four sources should be consulted in order of priority:

1. Definitions listed in the policy
2. Definitions given to the term by previous court decisions
3. Definitions found in dictionaries or other references
4. Meanings from common usage

[DA03769]

Because "direct physical loss" is not defined in insurance policy forms, a definition must be found elsewhere. *Black's Law Dictionary* defines "direct loss" as "one resulting immediately and proximately from the occurrence and not remotely from some other consequences or effects thereof."[2] One dictionary definition of "direct" is "marked by absence of an intervening agency, instrumentality, or influence."[3] An example of a direct loss is a store burning down. An indirect loss associated with the fire would be the loss of market resulting from the store's being closed for six months to rebuild.

Direct Loss

All losses must be "direct" (as defined above). Indirect losses, if covered by insurance, are separate from direct losses. The most important type of indirect loss is the loss of use of property. Whenever property is damaged or destroyed, it cannot be used. Property insurance covers only the value of the damaged or destroyed property, not the loss of use of it while it is repaired or replaced.

Physical Loss

A loss is "physical" if it involves tangible property's damage, destruction, or disappearance. Nonphysical losses, if covered by insurance, are separate from physical losses. Nonphysical losses include all kinds of *financial* loss, such as loss of value to an inventory caused by changes in fashion or obsolescence, loss of value to a financial investment such as stocks or bonds, loss of income from an interruption in a business's operation, or loss to a business of customers' goodwill. Likewise, embezzlement, swindling, and other forms of financial fraud are not physical losses and would be covered, if at all, only by special fidelity policies.

Evolution of Covered Perils

Because much of the logic of current insurance policy coverage stems from the historical predecessors of today's policies, this section provides a brief overview of what causes of loss were originally covered and how such coverage evolved. In this discussion, the section uses the terms "causes of loss" and "perils" synonymously.

Among the first types of insurance coverage was fire insurance for commercial and private real property. Only building structures were covered for the peril of fire. Lightning coverage was added later, however, because it became extremely difficult, if not impossible, to separate damage caused by lightning from damage caused by the resulting fire. The so-called standard fire policy legislatively mandated in many states protected against fire and lightning. Because of its historic origins, property insurance is still often referred to as fire insurance.

Other perils were gradually added over the years and formed two types of broader coverages called extended coverage and broad-form coverage.

The Extended Coverage endorsement and the Broad Form endorsement only covered losses that were caused by the perils specifically listed in the policy.

Extended Coverage

In the late 1930s and early 1940s, the Extended Coverage endorsement was developed. It added seven additional perils to the two (fire and lightning) already covered. These additional perils were:

- Windstorm
- Hail
- Explosion
- Riot or civil commotion
- Vehicles
- Aircraft
- Smoke

This package of covered perils forms the foundation of the most basic coverages available today.

Broad-Form Coverage

A new form called the Broad Form endorsement added these covered perils to the Extended Coverage endorsement:

- Vandalism or malicious mischief
- Breakage of glass in a building, storm door, or window
- Falling objects
- Weight of ice, snow, or sleet
- Collapse of buildings
- Damage resulting from a steam or hot water heating system
- Accidental discharge or overflow of water or steam
- Freezing of plumbing, heating, air conditioning systems, or domestic appliances
- Sudden and accidental damage from artificially generated electrical current

The package of covered perils available under the Broad Form endorsement is very similar to the Broad Form specified-perils policies available today.

Special-Form Coverage

A Special Form endorsement that provided "all-risks" coverage on fixed real property, covering all losses unless specifically excluded in the policy, arose among inland marine underwriters who offered "all-risks" coverage for property in transit or connected with transportation (bridges and tunnels).

This Special Form endorsement and homeowners policies originally insured "against all risks of physical loss to the property," but the current forms insure "against risks of direct physical loss to the property." The word "all" has been eliminated, although the coverage is intended to be essentially the same as that of the previous forms. The word "all" was eliminated because various courts ruled that if an insurance policy covered "all risks," then that is exactly what the policy must do, regardless of exclusionary language. This text uses the term "special form" to refer to policies that insure against risks of direct physical loss. Some insurers may refer to these types of policies as open-perils policies. If the term "all-risks" is used in the text, it means that the policy specifically states that it is all risks, as some inland marine policies do. Adjusters should be cautious about using the term "all-risks" because it might mislead an insured.

Most of the early stock insurance companies that wrote fire coverages belonged to a rating bureau that represented a group of insurers from designated territories. Rating bureaus developed standard policy forms and set the specific coverage rates. The insurance companies had to send copies of their fire policies (dailies) to their specific bureau, where they were reviewed to make sure that the proper premium was charged and that the correct forms were used.

While this system was being used, each peril was separately coded, a loss history was developed for that peril, and a pure premium was established for the peril. Once special forms were used, however, determining the loss history of any specific peril covered by a special form became almost impossible. Eventually, the various local rating bureaus ceased to exist, and in 1971, a single advisory organization, ISO, replaced them. ISO still develops standard forms and calculates and disseminates loss cost information for most types of insurance.

The coverage comparison chart shows the evolution of the coverage forms with the additions of new covered perils. See the exhibit "Coverage Comparison Chart."

Coverage Comparison Chart

Fire Policy	Extended Coverage	Broad Form	Special Form
Fire	Fire	Fire	Risk of direct physical loss unless excluded
Lightning	Lightning	Lightning	
	Explosion	Explosion	
	Windstorm	Windstorm	
	Hail	Hail	
	Smoke	Smoke	
	Vehicles	Vehicles	
	Aircraft	Aircraft	
	Riot	Riot	
	Civil commotion	Civil commotion	
		Vandalism and malicious mischief	
		Sprinkler leakage	
		Sinkhole collapse	
		Volcanic action	
		Falling objects	
		Weight of snow, ice, or sleet	
		Water damage	

[DA03771]

SPECIFIED-PERILS VERSUS SPECIAL-FORM COVERAGE

Coverage is fundamentally different under specified-perils policies and special-form policies.

With a special-form policy (formerly known as an "all-risks" policy), the adjuster must determine whether any exclusions apply. With specified-perils coverage, the adjuster must see whether any of the listed perils cover an insured's loss. (The terms "specified perils" and "named perils" are used synonymously throughout the text.)

Specified-Perils Coverage

In specified-perils policies, a loss is covered only if the policy identifies the cause of loss (or peril). Both the Basic Form and the Broad Form are specified-perils policies. For example, if the policy states that it provides coverage for fire and lightning, the loss must be caused by either fire or lightning. Any other cause of damage is not covered. When investigating coverage under a specified-perils form, an adjuster must verify an identified peril that caused the loss before paying the loss.

Special-Form Coverage

Special-form policies cover any loss unless the loss is specifically excluded or limited by the policy. Although special-form policies generally have many more exclusions than do specified-perils policies, their coverage is still broader than even the most generous specified-perils policies. The exhibit illustrates the application of special-form coverage. See the exhibit "Illustration of Special-Form Coverage."

Illustration of Special-Form Coverage

Assume that a building's interior suffers water damage because rain during a windstorm entered through a defective or worn-out roof.

The building's interior damage would be covered under an HO-3 policy because the policy insures the building "against risk of direct physical loss to the property" and the policy has no exclusion for this type of damage. However, because the HO-3 policy provides only specified-perils coverage for contents, water damage to personal property from this same loss would not be covered. The windstorm or hail peril does not cover loss caused by rain unless "the direct force of wind or hail damages the building causing an opening in a roof or wall and the rain . . . enters through this opening."[4] In this case, the roof was already worn and open.

If this same damage occurred to a commercial building having special-form coverage, no exclusion would apply, but a limitation reads,

> We will not pay for loss of or damage to . . . the interior of any building or structure caused by or resulting from rain, snow, sleet, ice, sand or dust, whether driven by wind or not, unless: (1) the building or structure first sustains damage by a Covered Cause of Loss to its roof or walls through which the rain, snow, sleet, ice, sand or dust enters....

Again, because the roof was already worn and gradual wear is excluded, the rain damage would not be covered.

Form CP 10 30 04 02, Copyright, Insurance Services Office, Inc., 2001. [DA03772]

DETERMINING PROPERTY COVERAGE: BURDEN OF PROOF

An important consequence of the distinction between the specified-perils and the special-form approach is its effect on the burden of proof.

A party has the **burden of proof** when it is his or her duty to prove the truth of information that is in dispute. The burden of proof is crucial in doubtful and difficult-to-determine cases.

Burden of proof

In a trial, the duty of a party to prove that the facts it claims are true.

Specified Perils

An adjuster's approach when investigating a loss depends on the type of coverage provided. When the insured has a specified-perils policy, the insured is obligated to determine which peril applies to the damage to his or her property. Thus, the insured has the burden of proving that one of the specified perils was the cause of the loss. When the insured has the burden of proof and cannot prove what caused the loss, there is no coverage. See the exhibit "Burden of Proof: Specified Perils."

Burden of Proof: Specified Perils

The HO-3 covers personal property for theft including "loss of property from a known place" when the property has likely been stolen. An insured who reports a piece of jewelry missing must at least prove that the jewelry was likely stolen.

Unless the insured was robbed or there is evidence of burglary at the insured's house, the fact that the jewelry is missing is not, by itself, sufficient to prove theft.

[DA03773]

Special Form

Conversely, to avoid paying a claim under a special form, the insurance company must prove, on the basis of a policy exclusion, that the policy does not cover the cause of the damage. Proving that a loss resulted from a cause excluded in the policy is difficult. When the insurer has the burden of proof and cannot prove that an exclusion applies, coverage is afforded for the loss.

DETERMINING PROPERTY COVERAGE: DEFINITIONS AND ADDITIONAL COVERAGES

In specified-perils forms, the statements about and definitions of the specified perils are important in determining what is *not* covered. A section of coverages called "additional coverages" distinguishes those coverages from the rest of the policy.

In specified-perils forms, the statements about, and definitions of, the specified perils are as important in determining what is *not* covered as are the exclusions.

Drafters of insurance policies frequently include a section of coverages called "additional coverages." Certain coverages are distinguished from the rest of the policy for various reasons.

- Anything not contained within the definition of a specified peril is not part of that peril and is not covered.

- Certain additional coverages, such as fire department service charges, differ from the main coverages and could not exist at all except as additional coverages.

- Some additional coverages are created to reinstate coverage that has otherwise been eliminated by exclusions.

Role of Definitions

Anything not contained within the definition of a specified peril is not part of that peril and is not covered. For example, in the Causes of Loss—Broad Form, vandalism is defined as "willful and malicious damage to, or destruction of, the described property."[5] Any damage not fitting this definition would not be vandalism and would not be covered unless it was contained within some other peril. Another example from the same form is water damage, which is defined in such a way as not to cover some of the most common types of water damage, such as floods or gradual seepage.

Exceptions From Definitions

In addition to explicit statements that define a peril, most of the specified-perils forms include explicit exceptions as part of a definition. For example, the definition of windstorm or hail in the BPP with the Basic Form and Broad Form is almost entirely phrased as an exception to coverage. It reads, "Windstorm or Hail, but not including. . . ." The remainder of this definition of a specified peril concerns what is not windstorm or hail.

Supplement to Limits

Some additional coverages increase the available limit. For example, the additional coverage for debris removal under the HO-3 provides an additional 5 percent of the underlying limit for debris removal. Debris removal would be covered as part of the underlying loss, but this additional coverage increases the available limit.

New Types of Coverage

Certain additional coverages differ from the main coverages and could not exist at all except as additional coverages. For example, fire department service charges are not direct physical loss to covered property. They might arise out of such direct physical losses, but they are by nature strictly financial obligations. Likewise, the additional coverage for trees and shrubs under the HO-3 would not exist otherwise because trees and shrubs are not within the underlying coverages for the dwelling, other structures, or personal property.

Reinstatement of Coverage

Some additional coverages are created to reinstate coverage that has otherwise been eliminated by exclusions. This approach clarifies that the only available coverage is that contained in the additional coverage. For example, the HO-3 excludes collapse as a covered peril, except to the extent provided in the additional coverage for collapse.

PERILS TYPICALLY INSURED UNDER PROPERTY INSURANCE

This section discusses the essential considerations in the definition and investigation of specific causes of loss that are commonly found in property insurance policies.

Whether an insurance policy covers a particular loss depends on the specific cause of the loss. Property loss adjusters must therefore investigate the cause of the loss and determine whether it falls within the coverage defined by the policy.

A specified-perils policy contains a list of covered perils, such as fire; lightning; windstorm; hail; explosion; riot and civil commotion; vehicles; smoke; vandalism and malicious mischief; theft; falling objects; weight of snow, ice, or sleet; water; glass breakage; collapse; and volcanic action.

Fire

Property insurance was created to provide coverage against the peril of fire. The damage and destruction caused by fire are unmistakable. When a fire has caused damage, all damage caused by smoke, water, and firefighting activity is considered to arise out of the fire and is therefore covered.

Insurance Definition of Fire

Fire is the rapid oxidation of combustible material, releasing heat and flame. Without flame, there is no "fire," for insurance purposes. Slower types of oxidation and other chemical reactions might release heat or cause heat buildup.

However, heat alone is not considered fire. A scorch on a countertop from a hot pot is not fire damage. No one needs to witness the flame if an expert can attest to its presence or if its presence is obvious from evidence such as charring. In the absence of a flame, damage from heat and smoke is not covered as fire. Smoke, however, is a separately specified peril, and certain types of smoke and heat-related losses might be covered depending on the policy form.

Friendly Fire Versus Hostile Fire

The distinction is sometimes made between "friendly fire" and "hostile fire." A **friendly fire** is deliberately created in a place designed to contain fire, such as an oven, a heater, or a fireplace. A **hostile fire** is any other fire. Only losses from hostile fires are covered within the fire peril. This distinction is made primarily with regard to losses from the attendant heat and smoke of friendly fires—they are not covered under the fire peril, although smoke damage is a separate and standard covered peril. Should a friendly fire escape its container, it would become a hostile fire, and any resulting damage would be covered.

Lightning

Lightning is a natural electric discharge in the atmosphere that can cause damage in its flow to the ground.

Types of Lightning Losses

Three main types of lightning losses are:

- A direct hit
- A near miss
- A ground surge

Direct Hits and Near Misses—Lightning damage to a building following a direct hit usually consists of shatter or blast-like damage or resulting fire damage. The blast or shatter damage is obvious at the point of contact. Likewise, fire damage is obvious, although lightning might not have caused the fire.

When hit by lightning, some buildings ignite. Others do not because of differences in the combustibility of materials used in the structure and the extent of grounding afforded by lightning rods and metal roofs. Some engineers have offered the explanation that although all lightning is high-voltage electricity, some bolts are of high amperage (large flow of electricity), but others are of low amperage (small flow of electricity), and that the high amperage electricity causes ignition. These bolts are called "hot" and "cold," respectively. This distinction also explains why lightning can come into a building on power lines without blowing a fuse. Metal roofs offer protection only if the metal is 3/16 of an inch thick or more, and only if installed so that they are electrically continuous and adequately grounded. Otherwise, they can attract lightning

Friendly fire

A fire that stays in its intended place, such as a fire in a fireplace.

Hostile fire

A fire that leaves its intended place, such as a spark that escapes a fireplace and sets the carpet on fire.

and provide little protection. Near misses do not usually cause physical damage but can disturb electrical equipment's functioning.

Ground Surge—The type of lightning loss most difficult for an adjuster to handle is alleged ground surge damage to the wiring of a house, a business property, or an electrical appliance. A ground surge travels through the ground, usually only a few hundred feet, creating a burrow, before entering a building. The only evidence of a lightning strike might be nonfunctioning electrical equipment. Large losses justify an electrical expert's services, but most losses are not large. Weather records might establish that lightning was or was not a possibility in the area when the alleged loss occurred. Under a specified-perils form, the insured has the burden of proof to show that a specified peril caused the damage.

Coverage for Lightning Losses

Lightning losses were originally covered in early insurance forms as a type of loss from fire. Lightning is now a separate peril because it can cause damage separate from that caused by ordinary fire.

If lightning causes a fire, the resulting damage caused by the fire will be covered under the fire peril—if for any reason the damage will not be covered under the lightning peril, such as if the policy has an exclusion for the lightning peril specifically applicable to the type of property damaged.

Damage to wiring, allegedly caused by lightning, might involve various exclusions. Losses sometimes occur when wiring in a building shorts out and a claim is submitted to rewire the building, or at least the wiring that shorted out. The cost of bringing the entire wiring in the building up to code is usually excluded under all policy forms. The cost of repairing wiring that has shorted out might be restricted or excluded by the wear and tear exclusion found in most property forms. However, damage caused by a resulting fire is covered. Most property forms also have an exclusion for any loss resulting from any power failure off the premises.

Explosion

Most explosions are obvious events, yet explosion is difficult to define. An explosion is usually considered to occur if a sudden and violent release of pressure or energy has caused a bursting or breaking and a noise. To be an explosion, the breaking must be caused by the pent-up force of confined air or gases, which finally burst into the open, such as a steam boiler explosion. An explosion does not have to be accompanied by fire.

Nonexplosions

When something breaks by itself, whether or not accompanied by noise, an explosion has not occurred. The sheer weight of grain in a bin might cause the sides of the bin to break. This is not an explosion. However, if a bin is airtight and the grain ferments, creating heat and gas, the expansion of the gas with its resulting increase in air pressure might cause the bin to explode. Other forces that are not explosions are sonic booms, electric arcing, rupture of water pipes, and rupture or bursting of rotating parts of machinery caused by centrifugal force.

Windstorm

Property insurance policies provide protection against windstorm. They do not specify the wind velocity needed to constitute a windstorm. The definition usually accepted for windstorm is a wind velocity having sufficient force to cause damage. Although wind is not a covered peril, damage from windstorm is usually referred to as wind damage.

A tornado is certainly a windstorm, but so are many storms of much lesser velocity. In doubtful cases, local weather records should be checked, and surrounding property should be checked for damage.

Wind Versus Water Damage

Occasionally, a covered loss, such as a windstorm, occurs, and at the same time, another loss occurs that is not covered, such as a flood. This can happen along the Atlantic and Gulf coasts, where floods frequently accompany hurricanes. The windstorm peril, under both specified-perils and special-form policies, covers the wind damage, but it does not cover the damage caused by flood, surface water, waves, tidal waves, high water, or overflow, whether driven by wind or not.

The flood exclusion is particularly troublesome in the case of beachfront property during hurricanes and other severe windstorms accompanied by high waters. The policy wording is clear as to what is covered and what is excluded. The difficulty arises in trying to segregate the wind damage from the excluded water damage.

In beachfront areas, flood insurance coverage is available only through the National Flood Insurance Program at a price that the property owner often is not willing to pay. In many cases, the losses are disastrous. Therefore, property owners commonly try to collect under windstorm insurance. These cases are challenging to adjust and require considerable investigative and persuasive abilities to resolve satisfactorily.

Hail

Hail is precipitation in the form of small, hard pellets that can cause damage on impact. Icy precipitation, such as sleet or icy snow, is not considered "hail" and is not covered under the hail peril. Damage caused by ice storms, snow, or weight of snow is not covered under the hail peril, but it might be covered by a separately specified peril, as discussed next.

In some parts of the United States, hail can be the size of a golf ball and has been known to cause serious damage to real property. Hail can dent metal mobile homes and other steel or aluminum structures. In some cases, the dent repairs require reskinning the damaged structure. In other cases, an appearance allowance (a claim settlement based on loss of value caused by appearance rather than cost to repair, since repair is usually impractical) might be the best type of adjustment.

Smoke

Smoke damage must result from a sudden, accidental cause. The damage cannot result from an accumulation over time. It does not include loss from agricultural smudging or industrial operations.

Smoke damage from a friendly fire is covered if it is sudden and accidental.

Vehicles

Coverage for vehicle damage differs depending upon the policy form. Some policies cover damage to personal and real property. Some policies exclude damage caused by an insured's vehicle. Most policies require physical contact with the vehicle to trigger coverage.

Aircraft

Aircraft includes not only airplanes and helicopters but also self-propelled missiles and spacecraft. This peril includes loss caused by objects falling from aircraft.

Riot or Civil Commotion

The personal insurance specified-perils forms include riot or civil commotion as a peril. However, the forms provide no definition to indicate what the peril includes. Commercial insurance policies give a better description but still do not completely define the terms.

Generally, a riot is defined as a violent breach of the peace by three or more persons assembled together. A riot need not result from conspiracy; it can be spontaneous. Some states' criminal codes require only two people in defining the action as a riot, and others require that there must be as many as five. The rioters' act or acts must be of an unlawful nature. Any loss caused by a rioter is covered regardless of whether the loss is caused by fire, breakage, theft, looting, or vandalism.

Vandalism or Malicious Mischief

Vandalism

Willful and malicious damage to or destruction of property.

Vandalism is the willful or malicious destruction or defacement of public or private property. It is sometimes called malicious mischief.

Element of Intent

Damage alone does not indicate vandalism. The insured, in submitting the claim, must be able to show that the damage was willfully or maliciously caused. Usually, vandalism does not have eyewitnesses; however, intent can be established by circumstantial evidence. Paint spilled on a floor is not conclusive, but the same paint used to write graffiti on floors or walls is evidence of vandalism. A broken window can be accidental, but a pattern of broken windows indicates an intentional act. Other similar damage in a neighborhood, notification to the police, and recurrences of the same type of damage all indicate vandalism.

Damage caused by domestic animals is not covered. Claims are often submitted for carpets damaged by a dog or drapes damaged by cats climbing up them. These losses are not covered. Animals cannot form the intent necessary for vandalism. Additionally, policies have exclusions for damage caused by animals.

Coverage Suspension

Coverage for vandalism and malicious mischief is suspended once a property has been vacant for more than a certain time period. The amount of time varies among policies, with thirty to sixty days being common. A building under construction is generally not regarded as vacant. Vacancy has been interpreted to mean that the building does not contain any contents pertaining to the building's customary occupancy.

Theft

Coverage for theft varies according to the policy form. Theft is generally defined as the fraudulent taking of personal property belonging to another without consent, with the intent to deprive the owner of its value. The contrast between the homeowners and commercial BPP approaches to theft coverage is unmistakable. Homeowners policies provide substantial coverage for theft because it is a major risk for homeowners' personal property. The BPP provides no coverage, or much more limited coverage, by design. To fill this void, the commercial crime coverages provide theft coverage in a commercial setting.

Falling Objects

Much of the damage caused by falling objects is covered under the vandalism, windstorm, aircraft, and lightning perils. Any other damage from falling objects is covered only under a special-form policy or a policy in which falling objects is a specified peril. The falling object must make a hole in the structure's exterior for coverage to apply.

Weight of Snow, Ice, or Sleet

Most policy forms cover damage caused by the weight of snow, ice, or sleet that accumulates on the roof of a main dwelling, an appurtenant structure such as a garage, or a commercial building. The peril for weight of snow, ice, or sleet should be considered in connection with the collapse coverage.

Water Damage

Water that damages a structure can come from several different sources. The adjuster must therefore consider how the water entered or flowed into the property.

Often, policies that provide protection against water damage are primarily designed to cover only damage by water escaping from broken pipes and appliances. Generally, all other causes of water damage are excluded.

Seepage

Although not specifically mentioned as an exclusion, water damage resulting from seepage or leakage over time is excluded.

Flood

Both the HO-3 form and the BPP with the Causes of Loss—Special Form exclude water damage caused by "flood, surface water, waves, tides, tidal waves, overflow of any body of water, or their spray, all whether driven by wind or not."[6]In fact, the majority of personal insurance and commercial first-party policy forms excludes these types of water damage.

Sewer Backup

When sewer systems are unable to carry away extensive runoff and surface water, flood water starts to flow backward through the sewers, causing water and sewage to back up through toilets, sinks, and drains. The water might even be strong enough to lift steel sewer covers off the streets. This floodwater can carry raw sewage, contaminating both buildings and contents.

Water that backs up from sewers or drains is excluded in both the HO-3 and the BPP with the Causes of Loss—Special Form. Insurers differ as to whether water that backs up from a clogged toilet or drainage system on the insured premises is, in fact, excluded. Some insurers argue that the water is not backing up out of the sewage system but that the sewage system cannot accept the water that is flowing into it, so the insurer should cover the loss. Other insurers do not cover any water damage caused by water that backs up from a toilet, a sink, an automatic dishwasher, or a sewage system. All insurers exclude any damage resulting from water backing up from a drainage or sewer system because of blockage off the premises.

Other Water Damage

Water damage caused by a mudslide or mudflow and damage caused by subterranean water that exerts pressure or seeps or leaks through a building, sidewalk, driveway, foundation, swimming pool, or another structure is excluded under both the personal insurance and commercial special-form policies. These exclusions refer to water under the ground surface.

Glass Breakage or Damage

Glass damage is actually a consequence of other perils rather than a peril itself. Nevertheless, some policies list it among covered perils. This, in effect, becomes "all-risks" coverage for glass, except to the extent otherwise restricted. However, glass damage caused by any other specified perils is still covered. That is, glass can be broken or damaged by fires, windstorms, explosions, and other perils. If so, it is covered without regard to the glass-breakage peril. This coverage is important because the glass-breakage peril only applies to glass that is part of the real property (including storm doors and storm windows), and coverage under that peril might have dollar limitations.

Almost all property forms have an exclusion stating that the insurer will not pay for the added cost of making necessary repairs because of the enforcement of any ordinance or law. However, this provision does not restrict the added cost of replacing glass with safety glazing material if required by law. Building code agencies have changed their requirements for the type of glass that can be used in buildings. Therefore, if an ordinance does not allow the replacement of the glass with glass similar to that which existed at the time of the loss, the added cost might appear to be excluded by the ordinance or law provision. However, both personal and commercial insurance forms have provisions allowing for the replacement of glass with safety glazing material if required by ordinance or law.

Collapse

The older forms included collapse as an insured peril. Current personal and commercial insurance forms now include collapse as an additional coverage.

Covered Causes of Collapse

Collapse coverage is unusual because the insurers agree to pay for collapse of the insured building, or any part of the building, caused by those perils listed in the form. Also covered is collapse caused by hidden decay; hidden insect or vermin damage; weight of people or personal property; weight of rain that collects on a roof; and use of defective materials or methods in construction, remodeling, or renovation if the collapse occurs during construction, remodeling, or renovation.

Generally, special-form policies exclude damage caused by hidden decay, hidden insect or vermin damage, or use of defective materials or construction methods. However, collapse caused by these perils is covered.

Extent of Collapse

A building in danger of falling down or caving in is not a "collapse." The part of a building left standing after another part has collapsed is not part of the collapse loss. A building that is standing but has evidence of cracking, bulging, sagging, bending, leaning, settling, shrinkage, or expansion is not a collapse.

How much of the property must collapse for collapse coverage to apply? Both the HO-3 and the BPP with the Causes of Loss—Broad Form define the extent of **collapse**. According to the policies:

> Collapse means an abrupt falling down or caving in of a building or any part of a building with the result that the building or part of the building cannot be occupied for its intended purpose.

Collapse

An abrupt falling down or caving in of a building with the result that the building or any part of the building cannot be occupied for its intended use.

Volcanic Action Coverage

Volcanic action coverage was added because of the 1980 Mount St. Helens eruption in southwest Washington, which scattered ash over thousands of square miles. It covers damage caused by shock waves, ash, dust, or particulate matter and lava flow. The peril defines any volcanic action occurring within a seven-day period as a single occurrence. The time period is used so that multiple deductibles are not applied.

DETERMINING PROPERTY COVERAGE: POLICY EXCLUSIONS

All insurance policies list exclusions, the exposures for which underwriters do not allow coverage. These are found in both specified-perils and special-form coverages.

In specified-perils policies, a loss is covered only if it is listed as one of the perils in the insurance agreement. The coverage is specific, and relatively few exclusions apply. However, the perils themselves might also include definitions that limit the coverage or that exclude a certain aspect of the peril. Special-form policies, conversely, have very broad coverage (every loss is covered unless it is listed in the exclusions or limitations), so many exclusions apply. A good rule to remember is that policies with narrow insurance coverage have few exclusions, whereas policies with broad coverage have many exclusions.

Reasons for Exclusions

This section discusses some reasons for exclusions. Remembering the general rationale for exclusions is easier than trying to remember the exact wording of every exclusion in various policy forms.

Uninsurable Loss Exposure

To be insurable, a loss exposure must have an element of predictability, and it should be noncatastrophic. Therefore, exclusions are written to eliminate such exposures as war; nuclear hazards; and, to a certain extent, earthquake and flood. These exposures are generally uninsurable because of the difficulty of spreading risk, the events' unpredictability, and their potential for catastrophic loss.

Gradual Hazards

Other exclusions eliminate gradual, inevitable physical hazards such as:

- Wear and tear, smog, rust, mold, and wet or dry rot
- Settling; cracking; shrinking; bulging; or expansion of pavements, patios, foundations, walls, floors, roofs, or ceilings
- Damage by birds, vermin, rodents, insects, or domestic animals

These hazards are considered uninsurable because of their gradual and unavoidable nature.

Moral and Morale Hazard

Moral hazard

A condition that increases the likelihood that a person will intentionally cause or exaggerate a loss.

Morale hazard (attitudinal hazard)

A condition of carelessness or indifference that increases the frequency or severity of loss.

Some exclusions, such as those for intentional loss and for failure to perform necessary maintenance, reduce moral and morale hazards. **Moral hazard** refers to some people's mindset that leads them to exaggerate, fabricate, or cause losses. **Morale hazard (or attitudinal hazard)** is some people's disposition to be less careful because they are insured than they would be if they did not have insurance.

Specialized Coverages

Exclusions can eliminate coverage that would duplicate other specialized policies that the insured could obtain. Coverage for earthquake, flood, boiler and machinery exposures, and crime exposures, though important to certain insureds, is not needed by most and is therefore excluded in standard policies and made available through specialized policies.

Specific Exclusions

This section lists specific exclusions common to property policies.

1. *Ordinance or law.* An increase in construction or demolition costs result-
    ing from a local law or ordinance is excluded except as provided by
    additional coverages or by endorsement. This exclusion can generate
    significant disagreement during the adjustment process. The term "law"
    can be broadly interpreted to include government-issued codes, rules, or
    regulations. An adjuster must check case law in the loss jurisdiction to
    understand what the term "law" means there. From a practical standpoint,
    this exclusion does not require special enforcement from the govern-
    mental body. Simply rebuilding in compliance with the code is sufficient
    to trigger the provision. An adjuster valuing the loss must complete two
    estimates to determine what the increased costs are. One estimate would
    be to rebuild or repair as the building existed before the loss. The other
    estimate would be to repair or rebuild in compliance with the codes. The
    increased costs associated with this exclusion can appear in several areas.
    The cost of debris removal can increase if the debris contains hazardous
    material requiring special disposal procedures. An increase can occur in
    the length of time it takes to restore the building to pre-loss condition due
    to the code requirements. Hiring an engineer or an architect to redesign
    the building to comply with the regulations might be necessary. These
    costs would result solely from the regulations and would not be covered.
    Despite that fact that this is a common exclusion in property policies, the
    HO-3 gives limited coverage for increased costs due to ordinance or law.

2. *Earth movement.* Earth movement is defined as earthquake, including
    shock waves or tremors before or after a volcanic eruption; landslide;
    mine subsidence; mudflows; and earth sinking, rising, or shifting, whether
    caused by humans, animals, or nature.

3. *Water damage.* Water damage from flood, surface water, sewer backups,
    subsurface water, and waterborne material (sewage) is usually excluded.

4. *Power failure.* A power failure to the insured premises from a lightning
    strike is covered. However, a power failure occurring off the premises is

not covered. A covered cause of loss that results from a power failure is covered.

5. *Neglect.* Neglect is defined as the insured's failure to use all reasonable means necessary to preserve and protect property from further damage at and after the time of a loss.

6. *War.* The war exclusion includes undeclared and civil war; warlike actions by a governmental military force; and acts of insurrection, rebellion, revolution, or usurped power.

7. *Nuclear hazard.* This exclusion eliminates coverage for loss or damage from nuclear reaction, radiation, or contamination, regardless of the cause. Ensuing fire damage would be covered.

8. *Governmental action.* Property destruction by an act of government authority is not covered unless the property is destroyed to prevent the spread of a fire that would have otherwise consumed the property.

9. *Exceptions to exclusions.* The phrasing of some of the exclusions in the special form leaves coverage in place rather than excludes it. For example, the Causes of Loss—Special Form contains an exclusion for water damage from freezing pipes "unless (1) You do your best to maintain heat in the building or structure; or (2) You drain the equipment and shut off the water supply if the heat is not maintained."[7] Therefore, an insured who took these steps would be covered for water damage caused by freezing pipes.

DETERMINING PROPERTY COVERAGE: CONCURRENT CAUSATION

Concurrent causation (concurrent causation doctrine)

A legal doctrine stating that if a loss can be attributed to two or more independent concurrent causes—one or more excluded by the policy and one covered—then the policy covers the loss.

Concurrent causation is defined as a single loss that was caused by two or more perils occurring simultaneously or in succession. Concurrent causation becomes an issue when one of the perils is a covered peril and the other is not.

Both the HO-3 and the Causes of Loss—Special Form begin with the wording that a loss is excluded "regardless of any other cause or event contributing concurrently or in any sequence to the loss."[8] This language was the insurer's attempt to clarify whether a loss caused by concurrent causes would be covered.

Much debate over how to handle concurrent causation claims occurred before the introduction of policy language. Even with the policy language change, courts still interpret the policy language differently from one jurisdiction to another. The insurance industry's position is that a loss is excluded if caused by an excluded cause, whether or not that excluded cause is the predominant one.

Three Concurrent Causation Approaches

The courts have used three approaches when considering concurrent causation. See the exhibit "Three Concurrent Causation Approaches."

Three Concurrent Causation Approaches

1. Efficient cause approach: If the loss is caused by a covered peril and a noncovered peril, the loss is covered if the "dominant," "efficient," "prime," or "moving" cause is a covered peril.

2. Liberal approach: The entire loss is covered as long as one of the causes is a covered cause of loss.

3. Conservative approach: If a covered cause of loss and an excluded cause of loss combine to produce the loss, then the loss is not covered.

Adapted from Steven Cozen, ed., Insuring Real Property (New York: Matthew Bender & Co., Inc., 2002), 48.01[6], pp. 48-8 to 48-10, with the permission of Matthew Bender & Company, Inc., a member of the Lexis Nexis Group. All rights reserved. [DA08200]

Burden of Proof

Another important aspect of concurrent causation is how the burden of proof shifts, depending upon the approach followed and what type of policy is involved. For an "all-risks policy," jurisdictions following the efficient cause approach put the burden of proof on the insurer to prove that the policy excluded the dominant cause. The jurisdictions using the liberal approach and the conservative approach have not fully addressed the issue of burden of proof. If a specified-perils policy is involved, the jurisdictions following the efficient cause approach will require the insured to prove that the covered cause of loss was the dominant cause. The burden then shifts to the insurer to prove that it did not. With a specified-perils policy, a jurisdiction that follows the liberal approach makes the insurer rebut the insured's evidence that the covered cause of loss contributed to the loss, as well as give its own proof that the dominant cause of the loss was excluded. Finally, the conservative approach requires the insured to prove that a covered cause of loss was the dominant cause but then allows the insurer to show that an excluded or noncovered cause contributed to the loss.[9]

SUMMARY

Property loss adjusting begins with determining who and what a policy insures. The insurable interest requirement must be investigated and resolved. To prevent wagering and fraud, insurers developed the principle of insurable interest. Insurable interest represents the financial harm that one would sustain if a loss occurs. Because insurance policies are contracts of indemnity, they will pay only if the insured has suffered a financial loss.

Insurable interest can be held by the property owner as well as others who might have a financial interest, such as an occupancy interest, a custody interest, or a security interest. Financial interest can be based on a contract, such as in the case of a mortgagee or a loss payee; based on occupancy, such as in the case of a tenant; or based on custody, such as in the case of a motor truck carrier. A security interest can result from a judgment, such as a tax lien or a mechanic's lien. Property can be owned by a single person, by joint owners who each have a full interest, by a tenancy in common with a percentage interest, or by life tenants whose interest ends at death. Property can be owned by a business as a sole proprietorship, a partnership, or a corporation.

Insurance policies normally protect the rights of those with insurable interests by listing them as named insureds, mortgagees, or loss payees.

Property insurance protects two kinds of property: real and personal. Real property is land and anything attached to it, such as a building. Everything else is personal property. Understanding the distinction between real and personal property is important because coverages might overlap. The valuation of real and personal property differs so that miscategorization could affect coinsurance requirements and policy limits.

The policy makes the insured a coinsurer of the property through a coinsurance clause. If the insured fails to purchase sufficient insurance to meet the coinsurance clause, the insured will be penalized if a loss occurs. Only the value of real property is used in the coinsurance calculation.

Not all property is easily categorized into real and personal property. Some personal property additions become attached or adapted to the real property and become a building fixture. Building fixtures are usually items added to the building after its original construction. A tenant's improvements and betterments are considered a fixture. The tenant's lease specifies whether the improvements and betterments are to be removed or must remain at the lease's expiration.

Reviewing a policy for coverage requires a systematic approach. After an adjuster determines who is insured and what is insured, the next step is to determine if the cause of loss is covered. Property coverage has evolved from the original fire policy to the Extended Coverage Form to the Broad Form, each adding additional covered perils to the policy. The final evolution occurred when the Special Form (formerly the "all-risks" form) was devised to cover direct physical loss unless excluded.

A policy's definitions section does not define "direct physical loss." "Direct" is understood to mean resulting from the occurrence without an intervening agency. "Physical" means tangible property's damage, destruction, or disappearance.

In specified-perils policies, a loss is covered only if the policy identifies the cause of loss (or peril). Special-form policies cover any loss unless the loss is specifically excluded or limited by the policy.

When the insured has a specified-perils policy, the insured is obligated to determine which peril applies to the damage to his or her property. To avoid paying a claim under a special form, the insurer must prove, on the basis of a policy exclusion, that the policy does not cover the cause of the damage.

A property policy also contains additional coverages, some of which increase the available policy limit and some that grant coverage distinct from the main policy. Others are meant to reinstate, in a limited way, previously excluded coverage.

A specified-perils policy contains a list of covered perils, such as fire; lightning; windstorm; hail; explosion; riot and civil commotion; vehicles; smoke; vandalism and malicious mischief; theft; falling objects; weight of snow, ice, or sleet; water; glass breakage; collapse; and volcanic action.

Both a specified-perils policy and a special-form policy contain a list of exclusions. Exclusions usually concern loss exposures that are considered to be uninsurable because of the difficulty in spreading risk, the events' unpredictability, and their potential for catastrophic loss. They eliminate exposures such as war; nuclear hazard; and, to a certain extent, flood and earthquake.

Gradual, inevitable physical hazards such as wear and tear; smog; rust; wet or dry rot; settling, cracking, or sinking of foundations and walls; and damage caused by birds, vermin, rodents, insects, and domestic animals are excluded.

Other exclusions are meant to deal with moral and morale hazards, such as the ordinance or law exclusion and the neglect exclusion.

Determining coverage can be difficult when two or more causes of loss occur in a single event. If one of the two causes of loss is not a covered cause of loss, it is often impossible to determine which caused the damage that might be covered under the policy. To prevent such a concurrent causation dilemma, policies such as the HO-3 and the BPP with a specific causes of loss form have language stating that if an excluded cause of loss occurs, the event is excluded regardless of any other cause or event contributing to it. However, courts are still interpreting this language.

Another important aspect of concurrent causation is that the burden of proof shifts depending upon the judicial interpretation given to the concurrent causation language.

ASSIGNMENT NOTES

1. Form HO 00 03 05 01, Copyright, Insurance Services Office, Inc., 2000.
2. Black's Law Dictionary, 5th ed. (St. Paul, Minn.: West Publishing Co., 1979).
3. Webster's Ninth New Collegiate Dictionary (Springfield, Mass.: Merriam Webster, Inc., 1990).
4. Form HO 00 03 05 01, Copyright, Insurance Services Office, Inc., 2000.
5. Form CP 10 20 04 02, Copyright, Insurance Services Office, Inc., 2001.
6. Form CP 10 30 04 02, Copyright, Insurance Services Office, Inc., 2001.
7. Form CP 10 30 04 02, Copyright, Insurance Services Office, Inc., 2001.
8. Form CP 10 30 04 02, Copyright, Insurance Services Office, Inc., 2001.
9. Adapted from Cozen, 48.04[3], pp. 48-76 to 48-78.

Direct Your Learning ▶▶

2

Property Insurance: Valuation, Limits and Conditions

Educational Objectives

After learning the content of this assignment, you should be able to:

▷ Explain the difference between replacement cost and actual cash value (ACV) and, given a loss to a specific piece of property, calculate:

- ACV

- Market value

▷ Explain the application and effect of valued policy laws.

▷ Explain the repair or replace option and its appropriate use.

▷ Given a loss, explain the settlement to be made under the following provisions:

- Stated or agreed value

- Selling price

- Original cost

- Warranty services

- Pair or set

▷ Given a loss, calculate an adjustment that includes the following:

- Policy limits and special limits of liability

- Deductibles

- Coinsurance

▷ Given a loss involving other insurance, calculate the settlement using the following:

- Pro rata share method

- Payment by equal shares method

▶▶

2

▸ Describe the following methods of resolving a disagreement among insurers regarding their obligations for payment when overlapping coverage exists:

- Compromise

- Resolution in court

▸ Explain how waiver and estoppel can occur and can be avoided with respect to the insured's duties following a loss and, given a proof of loss, determine whether it is properly completed, and if not, explain how and why it should be rejected.

▸ Explain the purpose and operation of the appraisal procedure.

Property Insurance: Valuation, Limits and Conditions

2

PROPERTY VALUATION: REPLACEMENT COST AND ACTUAL CASH VALUE

Property is almost always valued either at replacement cost or at actual cash value (ACV). Replacement cost is the cost of replacing lost or damaged property with new property of like kind and quality, or its functional equivalent, at current prices. Actual cash value (ACV) is a method of determining amounts payable for a property loss; it is calculated as the replacement cost minus depreciation, market value, or a valuation determined by the broad evidence rule. This section presents property valuation and details replacement cost and actual cash value.

All insurance policies specify the valuation basis for lost or damaged property. Insurers can repair or replace lost or damaged property, but they usually make a settlement with money. The insurance policy states, in general terms, how much the property is worth for loss settlement purposes. Property is almost always valued either at replacement cost or at actual cash value (ACV). See the exhibit "Property Valuation Methods."

Replacement Cost

As stated, **replacement cost** is the cost of replacing lost or damaged property with new property of like kind and quality, or its functional equivalent, at current prices. Even if property is several years old, or if its replacement cost now exceeds its original purchase price, the insured is entitled to the current cost to replace the property. However, policy provisions and legal requirements can limit valuation.

Replacement cost
The cost to repair or replace property using new materials of like kind and quality with no deduction for depreciation.

Like Kind and Quality

Replacement cost can still be determined even if the item of property is no longer manufactured. Sometimes, a particular model or style of an item is no longer made and has, in a strict sense, become irreplaceable. But this does not make the object's value unlimited. If the object can no longer be purchased, the replacement cost for property of **like kind and quality** should be paid. For example, if a particular style of an armchair or appliance with certain features is discontinued, an item of like kind and quality will probably be available, often from the same manufacturer. The original item's replacement cost can be based on the existing model's cost. Settlement on this basis is usually

Like kind and quality
A method of determining replacement cost valuation using a comparable model or item.

Property Valuation Methods

- Replacement Cost
    - Usually, the current cost of replacing damaged or destroyed property with property of like kind and quality.
    - Replacement cost is determined by the current cost of the damaged or lost property's functional equivalent.
    - Policy provisions and legal requirements can limit the valuation amount.
- Actual Cash Value (ACV)
    - Usually, replacement cost minus depreciation.
        - Depreciation methods
            - Straight-line depreciation: An item steadily and predictably deteriorates.
            - Accelerated depreciation: An item depreciates rapidly when first purchased and then more slowly.
            - Decelerated depreciation: An item hardly deteriorates until a certain time and then rapidly deteriorates.
        - Depreciation causes
            - Physical wear and tear
            - Age
            - Obsolescence
    - Some courts have ruled that ACV is fair market value.
    - Other courts have a broad evidence rule stating that factors such as economic, technological, or fashion obsolescence—in addition to depreciation and market value—should determine ACV.

[DA03776]

acceptable to the insured, as long as the adjuster does not try to settle on the basis of an inferior object.

Functional Equivalent

Functional valuation approach

A valuation method in which the insurer is required to pay no more than the cost to repair or replace the damaged or destroyed property with property that is its functional equivalent.

Some policies may be written using a **functional valuation approach** to provide replacement on a functional equivalent basis. This type of replacement cost coverage is used on older, more ornate buildings. To insure them for actual replacement cost would be very expensive because of outdated construction methods and materials. Functional equivalent replacement cost provides coverage for the cost to repair or replace using current construction methods and materials. For example, Victorian-style homes have plaster walls and ceilings. The current replacement for such homes' walls and ceilings would be drywall.

Functional equivalent coverage can also be purchased for personal property (other than stock). It is particularly useful when old machinery or equipment is to be insured, because it might no longer be available for purchase. Therefore, if damaged beyond repair, such a machine could be replaced by the closest equivalent property available through this coverage.

Limitations on Replacement Cost Recovery

Replacement cost provisions technically violate the principle of indemnity. According to the **principle of indemnity**, insurance policies should only indemnify (compensate) the insured for losses; they should not allow the insured to profit from losses. An insured that has sustained a loss to old, used property and replaces it with new property has indeed profited. For this reason, virtually all replacement cost policies provide replacement cost only after the insured has actually replaced the damaged or destroyed property or when the loss is small. Until insureds have replaced the property, they are entitled to, and receive, only an ACV settlement. A loss settlement condition from the homeowners HO-3 policy illustrates this concept:

> We will pay no more than the actual cash value of the damage unless:
>
> (a) actual repair or replacement is complete; or
>
> (b) the cost to repair or replace the damage is both:
>
> (i) less than 5% of the amount of insurance in this policy on the building; and
>
> (ii) less than $2,500.[1]

Thus, computing actual cash value is important, even with policies requiring replacement cost settlement.

Principle of indemnity
The principle that insurance policies should provide a benefit no greater than the loss suffered by an insured.

Actual Cash Value

Loss settlements based on **actual cash value (ACV)** are common with personal property under homeowners policies and with both personal property and buildings under commercial policies. Although the term "actual cash value" is undoubtedly one of the most important terms in property insurance, no policy defines it. Various explanations of the term exist, and the courts have had a major role in defining it. The many explanations of actual cash value (discussed below) are, however, consistent with one another.

Actual cash value (ACV)
Cost to replace property with new property of like kind and quality less depreciation.

Replacement Cost Minus Depreciation

Most property has its highest value when new. It thereafter loses value, mainly because of age and use. In this context, actual cash value is best expressed as, and is usually determined by, replacement cost minus depreciation. Determining depreciation is more difficult than determining replacement cost. Depreciation represents any loss of value, and numerous factors affect the rate and amount of loss of value.

Straight-line
depreciation method

An accounting method of
calculating depreciation
by taking an equal amount
of an asset's cost as an
expense for each year of the
asset's expected useful life.

One method of calculating depreciation is **straight-line depreciation**. This method measures a piece of property's steady, predictable deterioration. An example of straight-line depreciation is a refrigerator's depreciation over its useful life. If the refrigerator's current cost is $500 and has a useful life of ten years, it will depreciate $50 per year ($500 divided by 10 years). If the refrigerator is three years old at the time of the loss, the depreciation amount is $150 (3 × $50). A graph of the depreciation amount over ten years shows a straight line. See the exhibit "Straight-Line Depreciation."

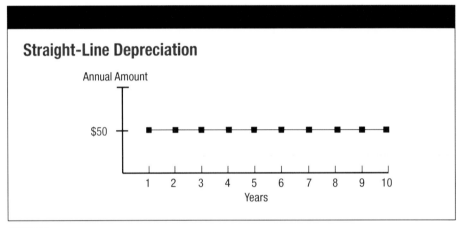

[DA03778]

Accelerated depreciation

Depreciation that occurs
more rapidly when an item
is first purchased and then
more slowly in subsequent
years.

The **accelerated depreciation** method is used for items that depreciate at a more rapid rate than that indicated by straight-line depreciation. Accelerated depreciation may be applied when an item depreciates rapidly when first purchased and then more slowly in subsequent years. Motor vehicles, electronics, computer equipment, and power tools all depreciate on an accelerated basis. A graph of accelerated depreciation shows a spike in the early years and then a slower rate of depreciation. See the exhibit "Accelerated Depreciation."

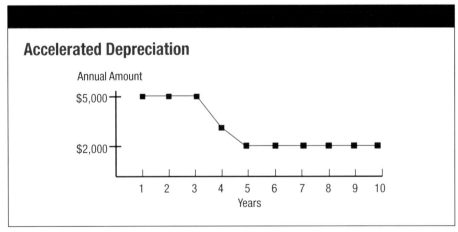

[DA03779]

Some items do not depreciate but instead appreciate or gain in value. Other items may depreciate little, if at all, until a given time period has passed and then lose value rapidly. This is called **decelerated depreciation**. Items subject to decelerated depreciation usually have an expiration date and do not depreciate until that date has passed, and then they depreciate rapidly. A graph shows this depreciation as occurring at the end of a calendar's useful life. See the exhibit "Decelerated Depreciation."

Decelerated depreciation

Depreciation that occurs slightly for a given time period and then increases rapidly.

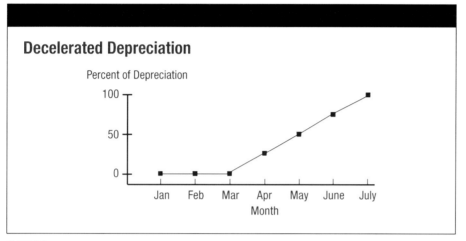

Decelerated Depreciation

[DA03780]

Film, food, medicine, and batteries are examples of items subject to decelerated depreciation. Some items are so new at the time of loss that depreciating them is inappropriate.

Physical wear and tear causes loss of value, but other factors such as age and obsolescence can result in loss of value and should be identified in computing depreciation. This section provides specific examples of how actual cash value can be determined according to different causes of loss of value and different types of deterioration.

Physical Wear and Tear

Physical wear and tear is the most obvious cause of loss of value. Physical wear and tear usually occurs at a steady rate throughout an item's life and can be calculated as a fixed amount, or a percentage, per year. For example, if a television is expected to last eight years, it would lose one-eighth of its value, or 12.5 percent, every year. At five years of age, it will have lost five-eighths, or 62.5 percent (5×12.5 percent), of its value. This amount of depreciation is subtracted from the current replacement cost to determine actual cash value. If the television's current replacement cost is $1,000, a five-year-old television's actual cash value is $375 ($1,000 minus $625 depreciation).

In straight-line depreciation, an adjuster can point out to the insured that depreciation represents the amount of use that the insured has already gotten from the property. If the insured had already enjoyed five-eighths of the television's expected use, five-eighths of the value of a new television should be deducted.

The rate at which a particular item is depreciated depends on what it is and how it is used. For example, clothing depreciates faster than furniture. Also, buildings' structural elements have widely different life spans. A roof might predictably wear out every twenty years, whereas an element of the frame carpentry might last indefinitely.

Most insurance companies publish guides for their adjusters that indicate various items' average expected life. These guides are useful as long as they are used as guidelines only. They present an average life for various items, but variation does occur. When using such guides, adjusters must also consider the circumstances under which the particular property has been used. These circumstances might indicate a much longer or much shorter expected life than the average life. For example, an adjuster might reasonably determine that carpeting, under different circumstances, might last either a few years (such as wall-to-wall carpeting with extremely heavy use or abuse) or indefinitely (such as a treasured Oriental carpet subject to little wear and excellent care). Insurance companies also have guidelines established for the maximum amount of depreciation to be taken on an item. Generally, most contents items are not depreciated at more than 50 percent as long as they were still in use at the time of the loss. However, exceptions occur, so adjusters should ask for their company's guidelines on this issue.

Age

An object's age usually corresponds closely to its extent of physical wear and tear, but age might be considered as a separate factor affecting depreciation. Age alone, however, should not cause an object to lose a large percentage of its value. If the object is functionally sound, it should retain most of its full value.

Obsolescence

Although age alone should not disproportionately affect depreciation, obsolescence might cause some objects to lose their value. **Obsolescence** is the loss of value caused by changes in technology or fashion. An object can lose value through obsolescence even though it has incurred no real wear and tear. Additionally, obsolescence can occur suddenly, regardless of an object's age. For example, fashions change overnight. Likewise, advances in technology and reductions in manufacturing costs have quickly rendered items only a year or two old obsolete.

A common term to use to explain depreciation is betterment. An object's amount of depreciation is identical to the amount of how much better, or more valuable, a new object is compared to the older object. Generally, an insured who receives a new object would be better off than would someone who has an older model of the same object. When the property is insured for actual cash value, the amount of the loss settlement reflects the betterment

Obsolescence

The loss of value caused by changes in technology or fashion.

that would exist were replacement cost values used. Explaining actual cash value as betterment can often help the insured understand why depreciation is calculated and applied against replacement values. Using the term "betterment" is not misleading. Quantitatively, betterment and depreciation are always equal. The term "betterment" expresses a different way of looking at the same situation.

Explanations of actual cash value in terms of betterment and the use already derived from the property can help the insured understand the concept of depreciation. Nevertheless, even after the insured understands the concept, the adjuster and the insured might disagree about how depreciation is applied to a piece of property. The adjuster must carefully listen to the insured's arguments and negotiate in good faith. Although the insured has obvious interests in the matter, the insured is also the party most familiar with the property and the circumstances of its use.

Except when replacement cost cannot be determined, calculating actual cash value as replacement cost minus depreciation is usually appropriate. This approach includes all information that would be considered in any other formulation of actual cash value. Nevertheless, two other approaches to actual cash value are important because of the support they have received from the courts. They are (1) the market value approach and (2) the broad evidence rule.

Market Value

Some courts have ruled that actual cash value means fair market value. An item's **market value** is the amount at which a knowledgeable buyer under no unusual pressure would be willing to buy an item and a knowledgeable seller under no unusual pressure would be willing to sell it. Buying a house is a good example of market value. The house's price will fluctuate depending on the supply and demand in the area. Having a market for an object depends on having a sufficient number of buyers and sellers and a complete flow of information regarding products, prices, and buyers and sellers. For many items, the market is irregular, imperfect, or even nonexistent. These conditions occur when there are not enough potential buyers or sellers or when information is too difficult to obtain. The courts that have criticized the market value approach have invariably done so when the market is not functioning properly. Any time that a commodity becomes controlled by a small number of sellers or a small number of buyers, the market value is artificial and therefore may not be a true indicator of actual value. This has occurred with diamonds, gold, and silver when a limited number of sellers has controlled the amount of the commodity available for sale at any one time (despite vast reserves) to drive up the price. Under such circumstances, the market value approach is inappropriate.

Perfectly functioning markets use the information contained in the actual cash value formula of replacement cost minus depreciation. No market would value an object for more than the cost to replace it. A market would also

Market value

The price at which a particular piece of property could be sold on the open market by an unrelated buyer and seller.

consider the depreciation factors previously discussed. When the market for an object is functioning well, that object's market price accurately reflects the value obtained by using replacement cost minus depreciation. Property loss adjusters should cite market prices as support for, and proof of, depreciation amounts.

Market valuation is particularly useful when an object has no real replacement cost; that is, when no other object of like kind and quality exists, as with antiques, works of art, and other collectibles. Additionally, market valuation can be useful with older buildings made from construction materials and methods that are no longer in use. Some features of older construction add to the property's value, but other features detract from it. A market valuation of the property would include both types of features.

Real property's market valuation includes both the land's value and the structure's value. Property insurance policies apply only to the structure, making the land's value irrelevant. Fortunately, eliminating the value of the land from loss calculations is easy. Generally, damage to, or destruction of, the building does not affect the land's value. Therefore, any change in the property's value following a loss must result from changes in the buildings' value. The market value determination of loss to a building can be calculated using this formula:

$$\begin{array}{c} \text{Market value of loss} \\ \text{to the building} \end{array} = \begin{array}{c} \text{Market value of entire} \\ \text{property before loss} \end{array} - \begin{array}{c} \text{Market value of entire} \\ \text{property after loss} \end{array}$$

This quantity is likely to equal the cost to repair when a minor portion of a building is damaged.

The previously mentioned formula applies when the value of the land is unaffected by loss to the building. Sometimes, however, the land's value increases after a loss, and sometimes it decreases. When the damaged structure does not make the best use of the property to begin with, its destruction might actually increase the land's value. For example, if an old warehouse is located in an area suitable for an office park or apartment development, the warehouse's destruction might increase the land's value, at least to the extent that demolition costs are reduced. Conversely, the destruction of a building that enjoyed privileged use of the land might reduce the land's value. For example, local building and zoning codes typically exempt properties that existed before the codes were enacted. However, an exempt structure's destruction renders any replacement structure subject to the codes. Because complying with building and zoning codes typically increases construction costs, the land's value might decrease.

In some states, most notably California, the courts require the use of market value to determine actual cash value. Except when replacement cost is indeterminable, the market value approach should yield the same results as the replacement cost minus depreciation approach.

Requiring the use of market value in the absence of a real functioning market can harm the insured by artificially devaluing the property. Most items of personal property immediately and dramatically lose market value when they are taken from the retail store where they were purchased. Soon they have no market value. For example, the market for used clothing is small, compared to the market for new clothing. However, a property loss adjuster cannot maintain that a one-year-old suit bought for $250 and still in good condition has virtually no value, even though it has no true market value. Obviously, the replacement cost minus depreciation value is much fairer to the insured and should be used to evaluate the suit.

The Broad Evidence Rule

The **broad evidence rule** has resulted from court-determined case law and explicitly requires property loss adjusters to consider all relevant factors when determining actual cash value. Adjusters should, however, already be considering all relevant factors when determining actual cash value by market value in a well-functioning market or by appropriately applying the replacement cost minus depreciation formula. The broad evidence rule arose when courts stipulated that adjusters must consider more than just depreciation or market value when determining actual cash value. See the exhibit "Broad Evidence Rule."

Broad evidence rule
A court ruling explicitly requiring that all relevant factors be considered in determining actual cash value.

Broad Evidence Rule

Factors that must be considered, in addition to depreciation and market value, in calculating actual cash value include the following:

- Replacement cost

- Economic, technological, or fashion obsolescence

- The circumstances of the property's use

- Income that might be derived from the property

- Any other related factors

[DA03786]

The broad evidence rule might appear to be the most flexible and complete approach to determining actual cash value. However, both the market value and the replacement cost minus depreciation approaches, when properly understood and applied, can be just as accurate and fair. In effect, all three approaches accommodate the same valuation information.

STATE-SPECIFIC VALUED POLICY LAWS

Valued policy laws dictate the amount of money that the insured can expect in settling certain claims. Some states have adopted such laws to protect insureds after loss.

Valued policy law
A law that specifies that insureds may recover the policy limit for certain losses regardless of the actual value of the property.

Valued policy laws require insurance companies to pay the policy's face amount for a total loss. If a valued policy law applies, a property loss adjuster must offer to settle the loss for the policy's face amount, even if a building was overinsured at the time of loss. In the absence of valued policy laws, an adjuster determines the building's value at the time of loss. If the value is less than the amount of insurance, the settlement will be based on the building's value, not the policy limit.

State-Specific Valued Policy Laws

Valued policy laws were enacted to ensure a fair settlement amount based on the total dollars of coverage on which the insured's premium was based. The theory is that if the insured is paying the premium for $200,000 worth of coverage, then $200,000 should be paid for a total loss.

Application

Valued policy laws usually apply only to a total loss to a building, not to partial losses. They also apply only to buildings and structures, not to personal property losses. Valued policy laws apply only to certain causes of loss, such as fire, but some states add other causes of loss. The exhibit is a sample of a valued policy law. See the exhibit "Sample Valued Policy Law."

Jurisdictions With Valued Policy Laws

Because valued policy laws vary, adjusters must check the law in the jurisdiction where a specific loss occurs. Valued policy laws are in effect in Arkansas; Florida; Georgia; Kansas; Louisiana; Minnesota; Mississippi; Missouri; Montana; Nebraska; New Hampshire; North Dakota; Ohio; South Carolina; South Dakota; Texas; West Virginia; Wisconsin; and, if the insured chooses to pay an additional fee for such coverage, in California.

Incentive for Fraud

Valued policy laws violate the principle of indemnity whenever the coverage exceeds the insured property's value because insureds can emerge after a loss in better financial condition than they were in before the loss. Insurers are deeply concerned about the increased potential for fraud whenever valued policy laws are in effect. Under such laws, for example, an insured might have greater financial incentive to commit arson. To counteract this possibility, insurers must be careful not to overinsure.

Sample Valued Policy Law

State of New Hampshire
Title XXXVII
Chapter 407
The Fire Insurance Contract and Suits Thereon

@ 407:11. Policy Value

I.   If a building insured for a specified amount, whether under a separate policy or under a policy also covering other buildings, is totally destroyed by fire or lightning without criminal fault on the part of the insured or his assignee, the sum for which such building is insured shall be taken to be the value of the insured's interest therein unless overinsurance thereon was fraudulently obtained.

II. If an insured building is only partially destroyed by fire or lightning, the insured shall be entitled to the actual loss sustained not exceeding the sum insured.

III. Nothing contained in paragraphs I and II of this section shall be construed as prohibiting the use of coinsurance, or agreed amount.

IV. When a building is insured not for a specified amount but under a blanket form with one amount covering 2 or more buildings or one or more buildings and personal property, the provisions of paragraph I of this section shall not apply.

HISTORY: 1885, 93:2. PS 170:5. PL 276:8. RL 326:8. RSA 407:8. 1959, 163:1, eff. Jan. 1, 1960.

[DA03790]

SETTLEMENT PROVISIONS: REPAIR OR REPLACE OPTION

Most claims are settled for cash. In some claims, the insurer has the repairs performed by a contractor or repairer or replaces lost or destroyed property.

The option to repair or replace the property is contained in virtually all property insurance policies, and it is strictly the *insurer's* option. The insured cannot insist that the insurer repair or replace property.

Repair or Replace Option

Because insurers reserve the option under many policies to repair, rebuild, or replace the property with other property of like kind and quality, insurance companies have for many years worked with camera dealers, furriers, jewelers, and similar merchants and often offer to replace property for insureds. The volume of business they do with these stores enables them to obtain discounts. For certain types of property, such as cameras, insurers can replace items with used equipment of like kind and quality. In addition to merchants, many large replacement service companies serve the insurance industry and stock most items of personal property. The higher the markup on an item, such as jewelry, and the more frequent the type of loss for the insurer, the greater the likelihood that the insurer will elect to replace the property through one of these services.

Insurers exercise the repair or replace option under these circumstances:

*   Settling the claim using this method is less expensive.
*   The insured is suspected of trying to profit from the claim.

The first condition might exist when the insurer has standing arrangements with wholesale suppliers to replace items of lost property. The insurer might be able to obtain attractive prices because of volume and because it can deal on the wholesale level.

The repair or replace option makes the insured's profiting from a loss very difficult. Insureds who falsify or stage a claim are usually interested in cash. Even if a falsified claim has been submitted, the repair or replace option limits the insurer's exposure on the loss.

MISCELLANEOUS LOSS SETTLEMENT PROVISIONS

Various policy provisions determine how much recovery an insured may receive from the insurer.

The two standard loss settlement alternatives are (1) settlement for cash, at replacement cost or actual cash value, and (2) repair or replacement of the property. Other settlement provisions, described in this section, apply to special cases.

Stated or Agreed Value

A stated value settlement provision requires the insurer to pay a previously agreed-on amount for a total property loss. This provision is not the same as the valued policy laws, which are legislatively imposed. Instead, the stated, or agreed, amount is determined by agreement between the insured and the insurer. This approach is very common with property floaters (which are usually inland marine policies or endorsements) because they are designed to cover a specific piece or type of property. A stated value settlement is also preferable when determining the replacement cost or actual cash value of an object is difficult, as with a piece of fine art.

Selling Price

A manufacturer or retailer can endorse its policy to be covered for the selling price of its inventory. Normally, the inventory would be insured for replacement cost or actual cash value (which, for current unused stock, might be equivalent). Selling price includes the normal business markup above replacement cost.

Original Cost

An item's original cost is usually irrelevant for claim-settling purposes. However, one exception occurs during loss settlement on a tenant's improvements and betterments. These losses are sometimes settled based on the unused amount of the original cost of the improvements or betterments. For example, a tenant who has spent $25,000 on improvements to a property on which he or she had a ten-year lease would enjoy $2,500 worth of use every year (the improvements become the landlord's property at the end of the lease). If the property were destroyed in year seven, the tenant would lose three years' worth of use of the improvements. This loss is calculated as 3 × $2,500 = $7,500. The dollar value of loss of use is based on the original cost of the improvements, prorated over the life of the lease.

Warranty Services

Similar to the replacement service is a newer service that provides warranties for repaired property. Generally, insurers replace warranties for machinery in a factory, for example, that has been damaged and is considered repairable. Manufacturers are rarely required to continue the original warranty of such damaged items, so insureds have reasonable concerns about the sufficiency of repair. The insurer's warranty service continues the manufacturer's original warranty on the machinery after the repair is complete. This service allows the insurance company to save the cost of a new machine and helps the insured to get back in business faster than if it had to order new machinery. The insurance company might pay a large premium for the warranty, but it will realize a savings on the entire adjustment.

Pair or Set Clause

The **pair or set clause** in policy forms is a traditional concept in property adjustments. This clause states that the insurer has the option (1) to repair or replace any part of a pair or set to restore it to its value before the loss or (2) to pay the difference between the property's actual cash value before and after the loss. Often, the value of property is severely diminished when a part of a set is damaged or lost. If the jacket of a suit is damaged, the adjuster will probably be unable to locate a matching jacket. If one of four three-year-old pairs of drapes in a dining room is damaged, a match could be difficult to make. However, if a creamer in a silver tea set is damaged, it might be a stock

Pair or set clause

A policy provision that indicates how values will be determined when part of a pair or set is lost, damaged, or destroyed.

item that is easily replaceable, and the adjuster should invoke the pair and set clause. Replacing the damaged item would restore full pre-loss value to the set. Adjusters should not consider a pair or set a total loss simply because a portion is damaged. They must investigate possibilities of restoring the pair or set to its pre-loss condition by replacing the damaged or lost item.

RECOVERY LIMITATIONS

Most insurance property coverages have specified limits of what can be paid for a claim as a limitation on the insurer's liability.

Most insurance property coverages have specified limits of what can be paid for a claim. These limits are usually actual dollar amounts. Other limits are based on specific policy provisions that limit recoverable amounts. For example, the cost to repair or replace damaged property is usually expressed as a limitation on the insurer's liability.

Policy Limits

Policy limits

The maximum that can be paid on the claim, regardless of the actual value of the property damaged.

Virtually all property coverages carry a policy limit. **Policy limits** are also referred to as "amount of insurance," "limit of insurance," or "limit of liability." Policy limits are normally the maximum that can be paid on the claim, regardless of the actual value of the property damaged. For example, assume that the policy limit for Coverage A—Dwelling in a homeowners policy is $150,000 and that the home suffers a total loss from a fire. Because of the limit of liability, or policy limit, the most that could be paid to the insured for the claim for the home is $150,000, even if rebuilding the home would cost $155,000.

Policy limits are normally inviolable, with some exceptions. Some policies can have an endorsement or provisions that provide for payment of the full cost to replace the structure or the contents, even if payment exceeds the policy limit, assuming that certain conditions are met. An Insurance Services Office, Inc., (ISO) homeowners policy can have an endorsement called Additional Limits of Liability for Coverages A, B, C, and D, which increases the limits when there is a total loss to the dwelling and the limit shown in the declarations is insufficient to replace the dwelling. It applies, if the insured has maintained a Coverage A limit equal to 100 percent of the dwelling's full replacement cost as determined by the insurer. Other policies may have an endorsement that guarantees replacement cost.

These endorsements can be important in catastrophe situations. For example, the costs to replace buildings may skyrocket because of the demand for competent contractors and a limited supply of construction materials.

Special Limits of Liability

Many insurance policies carry internal dollar limits on certain specified classes of property. In the homeowners policies, these are called **special limits of liability**. Commercial property policies also have internal policy limits. These limits can be found in several sections in the commercial policies, including Coverage Extensions and Limits of Insurance.

Special limits of liability
Internal dollar limits on certain specified classes of property that apply regardless of the overall policy limit.

Deductibles

Deductibles are included in most property insurance claims, whether personal or commercial. One important purpose of a deductible is that it requires the insured to share in the loss. By sharing in the loss, the insured has added incentive to prevent and to minimize losses. Deductibles also eliminate the insurer's obligation for small losses, those below the deductible amount. The insurer benefits because it does not have the administrative costs of small claims. The insured simultaneously benefits by having lower premiums.

Buying coverage for small losses is generally a poor decision for the insured. Because of the insurer's overhead costs of handling small claims, a much smaller percentage of the insured's premium dollar can be expected to be paid out in claims. The insured can save the premium expense of low levels of coverage and absorb the losses through the deductible. Most insureds should select the highest deductible that they can comfortably afford. As deductibles increase, premiums decrease.

Straight Deductibles

Homeowners policies typically have a deductible in the amount of $100, $200, or $250. Most homeowners policies have a **straight deductible**, which means that if a $100 deductible is selected, that would be the deductible whether there is a claim for windstorm, theft, fire, or any other covered cause of loss.

Straight deductible
A specified dollar amount that the insured must pay toward a covered loss.

Split Deductibles

An adjuster might occasionally encounter a **split deductible**. For example, a policy might carry a $250 theft deductible and a $100 deductible on all other covered losses. A higher deductible on theft gives the insured a greater incentive to guard against it. Additionally, the insurer is spared the economic impracticality of investigating small claims. Many questionable claims are alleged thefts. Conducting a thorough fraud investigation in such cases is not warranted unless substantial values are involved.

Split deductible
A deductible provision that applies one deductible for most causes of loss but a different, higher deductible for other specified causes of loss.

Deductibles on Commercial Policies

Commercial property policies commonly have a standard $250 deductible. With an adjustment in premium, the $250 deductible can be raised or lowered. Frequently, the deductible is raised to $500, $1,000, or $5,000.

No Deductible

Some specific coverages do not have a deductible. In commercial coverage, no deductible applies to the fire department service charge. The homeowners policy deductible does not apply to the fire department service charge or to the credit card, fund transfer card, forgery, and counterfeit money coverages. These claims are generally small, and their coverage limits are restrictive.

Absorbing a Deductible

Absorb a deductible

To apply the deductible to the actual loss before applying any coverage limits.

To **absorb a deductible** means to apply the deductible to the actual loss before applying any coverage limits. A deductible can sometimes be absorbed in the property loss settlement. If the loss exceeds the coverage limit by at least the deductible amount, then the insured could collect the full coverage limit without further application of a deductible. See the box for examples that illustrate this principle. See the exhibit "Absorbing a Deductible."

The principle of absorbing a deductible applies to both commercial property and homeowners coverage. Whenever a claim exceeds the policy limits, the excess loss can be applied to the deductible to absorb part or all of the deductible. To absorb all of the deductible in a claim, the excess loss amount must exceed or equal the deductible amount.

Absorbing deductibles is common in insurance, although the practice is never specifically stated in an insurance policy. Most property loss adjusters regard the practice as part of correct claims adjusting because the policy usually states that the deductible is to be applied to the loss, not to the policy limit. The only justification for handling the deductible otherwise would be if a policy clearly stated that the deductible was to be applied to the covered loss, rather than to the loss itself. Such a policy would never pay the full amount of its stated coverage limits.

Coinsurance

Coinsurance is a condition of the property insurance policy that can affect the recovery amount. Insurers include coinsurance clauses in their policies to encourage insureds to carry adequate insurance. The coinsurance clause requires the insured to carry an amount of insurance equal to or greater than a specified percentage of the property's total insured value. An insured who does so is considered adequately insured for a partial loss. For example, in a policy with an 80 percent coinsurance requirement for buildings, the insured must have an amount of insurance equal to or greater than 80 percent of a building's replacement cost to be considered adequately insured. The replacement cost is determined using the policy valuation provisions.

Coinsurance Examples

Jones Hardware Store has a policy with $90,000 coverage on the structure and an 80 percent coinsurance requirement. A partial loss to the building occurs.

Absorbing a Deductible

Example 1. Jane Rogers has a homeowners HO-3 form with a $100 deductible and a special limit of liability for cash in the amount of $200. A theft occurs at her residence. The following are stolen:

Television	$220 (ACV)
Cash	350
VCR	250 (ACV)
Total loss	$820

The total actual loss that Jane sustained is $820. Because of the special limit of liability for cash, $820 cannot be paid on the claim. The adjusted loss is as follows:

Television	$220 (ACV)
Cash	200
VCR	250 (ACV)
Total loss	$670

Jane has suffered a $150 uninsured loss of cash ($350 stolen minus $200 for the coverage limit), which cannot be paid under the insurance policy. Because she has already shared in the loss, no deductible would be applied. She should be paid $670 for her claim. Her $100 deductible is absorbed by the excess $150 cash loss.

Example 2. The Carr family has an HO-3 policy with a $250 deductible and a $1,000 special limit on jewelry. A theft occurs, and the following are stolen:

Diamond necklace	$1,200 (ACV)
Camera	300 (ACV)
Rifle	500 (ACV)
Stereo	1,200 (ACV)
Total loss	$3,200

The total loss suffered by the Carr family on this claim is $3,200. According to policy provisions, the following should be paid on their claim:

Diamond necklace	$1,000 (special limit)
Camera	300 (ACV)
Rifle	500 (ACV)
Stereo	1,200 (ACV)
Total loss	$3,000

The Carrs have an excess loss of $200 ($1,200 loss minus $1,000 coverage) on the jewelry. However, they carry a $250 deductible. The $200 excess loss allows $200 of the deductible to be absorbed because this is the insured's share of the loss. The remaining $50 of the deductible must be subtracted from the $3,000 subtotal above. The Carr family should be paid $3,000 minus $50, or $2,950, for their claim.

[DA03792]

At the time of the loss, the structure's replacement cost was $100,000. Jones met its coinsurance requirement by having more than the required minimum $80,000 (80 percent of $100,000) coverage. For a partial loss to the structure, Jones has adequate insurance, so the property loss adjuster will pay the full adjusted loss. If Jones Hardware had not met the coinsurance clause requirement, Jones would be paid only a portion of the adjusted loss.

Assume that Jones Hardware had carried only $60,000 worth of coverage on the structure to save premium, because more premium is charged for higher levels of coverage. With an 80 percent coinsurance requirement, Jones is inadequately insured. The minimum amount of insurance required is 80 percent × $100,000 (the property's replacement cost), or $80,000. If Jones were to suffer a loss under this set of circumstances, the amount paid would be calculated using this formula:

$$\text{Amount paid} = \frac{\text{Amount of insurance carried}}{\text{Amount of insurance required}} \times \text{Amount of loss.}$$

This is the shorthand version of this formula:

$$\text{Amount paid} = \frac{\text{Did}}{\text{Should}} \times \text{Loss.}$$

If Jones Hardware has a $10,000 windstorm loss:

$$\frac{\$60,000 \ (\text{Amount carried})}{\$80,000 \ (\text{Amount required})} \times \$10,000 \ (\text{Loss amount}) = \$7,500 \ (\text{Amount paid}).$$

Because of inadequate insurance, Jones Hardware must partially insure the loss, forgoing the benefit of the insurer's paying all of the loss. Therefore, Jones Hardware and the insurer are coinsurers.

Adjuster Tip—A common error when performing this coinsurance calculation is to use the wrong number in the "amount required." The amount required is not 100 percent of the replacement cost but is the coinsurance percentage amount stated in the policy, or 80 percent in this example. Therefore, the amount required is 80 percent of the replacement cost.

Application of Deductibles With Coinsurance

Deductibles must still be applied even when the insured bears a coinsurance penalty. The insured benefits by applying the deductible to the loss first, then applying the coinsurance penalty. In the second Jones Hardware example, this would work like this:

Deductible Applied First

$$\$10,000 \text{ loss} - \$100 \text{ deductible} = \$9,900.$$

$$\frac{\$60,000}{\$80,000} \times \$9,900 = \$7,425.$$

Coinsurance Applied First

$$\frac{\$60,000}{\$80,000} \times \$10,000 \text{ loss} = \$7,500.$$

$$\$7,500 - \$100 \text{ deductible} = \$7,400.$$

The first method should be used unless the policy indicates that the deductible takes effect after the coinsurance clause has been applied. The second method is prescribed in most commercial policies. The coinsurance provision and the deductible provision of the policy form involved in the loss should be reviewed to ensure the correct application of the deductible.

Determining Values for Coinsurance Purposes

When determining whether coinsurance requirements are met, adjusters must determine the insured value of *all* property, both damaged and undamaged. This effort can seem unwarranted for small losses. Fortunately, several sources of information can aid adjusters.

Replacement cost guides and services are available in both printed and computerized form. These enable the adjuster to quickly approximate structures' replacement cost based on square footage, use, and construction method. An insured's records of inventory can usually be accepted as an accurate approximation of the inventory's value.

With small losses, the adjuster might be satisfied to see that the insured has *apparently* complied with coinsurance requirements, rather than to precisely determine compliance. In such cases, any coinsurance penalty would be a small percentage of the loss.

POLICY CONDITIONS: SETTLEMENTS INVOLVING OTHER INSURANCE

As in any other contract, the conditions are an integral part of the insurance contract

Conditions are qualifying agreements that state who is to do what, as well as when and how it is to be done, for the contract to become effective. Conditions explain the rights and duties of the parties to the contract. This section focuses on conditions found in most property policies.

Condition

Any provision in an insurance policy that qualifies an otherwise enforceable promise of the insurer.

Other Insurance

In property insurance, more than one insurance policy sometimes covers a loss. Such a situation is usually referred to as overlapping coverage. Overlapping coverages might exist for part of a claim or even for the entire claim. Overlapping coverage usually occurs inadvertently. For example, an insured might forget to cancel an existing policy after a new one has been acquired. Coverage for property covered under a specific floater might also exist under general policies, such as the HO-3 or the Building and Personal Property Coverage Form (BPP). Sometimes, a mortgage company and a property owner separately insure the owner's property. However, these situations are uncommon. Another possibility is that the insured has intentionally obtained multiple coverages, which strongly indicates attempted fraud. Adjusters should thoroughly investigate these situations.

In investigating a claim, an adjuster should identify overlapping coverages. The first place to check is with the insured. The adjuster should ask the insured whether more than one policy covers the loss. If other insurance is inadvertently involved, most insureds will report it. If the adjuster believes that the insured is not being honest, the adjuster must investigate further. The adjuster can contact others associated with the claim (such as contractors or—as another example—a jewelry appraiser and employees of the retail store where a piece of jewelry was purchased) to question whether another insurance company has contacted them about the same claim. If so, overlapping coverages are likely.

A claims investigation might reveal other indicators that lead the adjuster to suspect other insurance. One indicator would be if the insured's property were grossly underinsured by one policy. Another indicator might be if the insured incorrectly indicates which agent or broker is servicing the policy. For example, the insured might indicate an agent not associated with the adjuster's company. If these indicators appear, the adjuster should investigate the case to determine what other insurance might be involved.

If the property loss adjuster discovers other insurance, he or she should review the policy's other insurance conditions. These conditions usually deal with overlapping coverages through primary/excess insurance or proportional (pro rata share) insurance.

Primary/Excess

Primary coverage provision

An other-insurance provision that specifies that the policy pays the loss amount before other applicable policies until its own limits have been exhausted.

Insurance policies might indicate that one coverage is primary. **Primary coverage** means that the claim will be paid from that policy first until the limits are exhausted. Excess coverage pays the amount over the primary coverage.

For example, Sharon Mitchell has property insured under two policies. Policy A, with a $6,000 limit, states that it is primary coverage; Policy B, which has a $10,000 limit, states that it is excess. Sharon has a $10,000 loss covered by both policies. Policy A will pay its $6,000 policy limit of coverage; Policy B will then pay the $4,000 amount of the loss over $6,000.

Excess of other insurance

Insurance that pays an amount over the primary layer of coverage.

Excess insurance, in this context, means insurance that is excess over other valid and collectible insurance. An **excess-of-other-insurance clause** is distinct from a true excess policy. A true excess policy covers losses only over some large deductible amount, usually in the six- or seven-figure range, and does not cover smaller losses, regardless of whether they are covered elsewhere. A policy with an excess-of-other-insurance clause is a primary policy, which pays only after the coverage of other primary policies is exhausted.

Few insurance policies explicitly state that their coverage is primary. Therefore, the general rule is that coverage is primary unless the policy states otherwise. Without an "other insurance" condition indicating that the coverage is excess or pro rata, the property loss adjuster should treat existing coverage as primary. If one policy states that it is pro rata and the other policy states that it is excess, the excess clause is effective and the pro rata policy becomes primary.

Adjusters must also apply primary/excess deductibles. With primary/excess coverage, the excess coverage can occasionally pay the difference in the deductibles. See the exhibit "Deductibles Example."

Deductibles Example

Suppose that ABC Insurance Company's policy states that its coverage is excess and has a $100 deductible. XYZ Insurance Company's policy does not have the other insurance condition, and its policy has a $250 deductible. For a loss, XYZ's coverage would be primary, and its obligation would be to pay the adjusted claim minus the $250 deductible. ABC's obligation would be to pay the difference in the deductibles, $250 minus $100, or $150. ABC would be obligated to pay only the difference in the deductibles when, as in this example, ABC's deductible is smaller than XYZ's. If XYZ has a smaller or an equal deductible, ABC would have no obligation to pay any part of the claim.

[DA03799]

Proportional (Pro Rata) Share Method

A common method of dealing with overlapping coverages is **proportional** or pro rata share. With this method, insurers contribute to the loss payment in the proportion to which they contribute to the total amount of coverage purchased. See the exhibit "Proportional (Pro Rata) Share Method Examples."

This method is traditionally called payment by policy limits.

Two other less common methods of proration are (1) payment by equal shares and (2) payment by amounts payable. These methods apply only when the other insurance clause indicates.

Payment by Equal Shares

Under **payment by equal shares**, the loss is paid equally by both policies until one policy is exhausted; then the other policy alone pays. Consider the Wilkinsons' coverage for losses of $40,000 and $60,000. The $40,000 loss would be shared equally ($20,000 each) by Company C and Company D. On a $60,000 loss, the two companies would equally share the loss up to

Proportional share (pro rata share)

An approach to other insurance by which the insurers contribute to the loss payment in the proportion to which they contribute to the total amount of coverage purchased (their limits of liability).

Payment by equal shares

An approach to other insurance by which the loss is paid equally by both policies until one policy is exhausted; then the other policy alone pays.

Proportional (Pro Rata) Share Method Examples

- Suppose that Insurance Company A has a policy with $40,000 coverage and that Insurance Company B has a policy on the same property with $60,000 coverage. The insured suffers a covered loss of $10,000. Insurance Company A would owe

$$\frac{\$40,000}{\$100,000} \quad \begin{array}{l}\text{(Insurance Company A's amount of coverage)}\\\text{(Total amount of coverage: \$40,000 + \$60,000)}\end{array}$$

or

40%, 4/10, or .40 of the loss

40% × $10,000 = $4,000.

Insurance Company B would owe

$$\frac{\$60,000}{\$100,000} \quad \begin{array}{l}\text{(Insurance Company B's amount of coverage)}\\\text{(Total amount of coverage: \$40,000 + \$60,000)}\end{array}$$

or

60%, 6/10, or .60 of the loss

60% × $10,000 = $6,000.

The combined payment of the companies equals the total payable claim of $10,000. The insured would not collect more than the amount of the loss.

- Suppose that Mark and Cindy Wilkinson are insured by two homeowners insurance policies. Both policies have other insurance conditions indicating that losses must be adjusted using the proportional share method. The Wilkinsons have $75,000 worth of coverage with Company C and $25,000 worth of coverage with Company D. Both insurance policies cover a $12,000 claim.

Company C owes

$$\left(\frac{\$75,000}{\$100,000}\right) \times \ \$12,000 = \$9,000.$$

Company D owes

$$\left(\frac{\$25,000}{\$100,000}\right) \times \ \$12,000 = \$3,000.$$

[DA03800]

Payment by amounts payable

An approach to other insurance by which each insurer pays a portion of the loss equal to the amount that one insurer would separately pay, divided by the total of the separate amounts payable by all insurers.

$50,000 ($25,000 for each), at which point Company D's coverage would be exhausted. Company C would then pay the remaining $10,000 of the loss.

Payment by Amounts Payable

When the **payment by amounts payable** approach to other insurance is used, each insurer pays a portion of the loss equal to the amount that one insurer would separately pay, divided by the total of the separate amounts payable. Using the example of the Wilkinsons, Company C and Company D would share the loss in these proportions:

Amount Company C would pay separately is $40,000.

$$\frac{\$40,000}{\$40,000 + \$25,000} \times \$40,000 = \$24,615.$$

Amount Company D would pay separately is $25,000.

$$\frac{\$25,000}{\$40,000 + \$25,000} \times \$40,000 = \$15,385.$$

Total: $24,615 + $15,385 = $40,000.

When both insurers fully cover the loss, this method results in an equal split.

In addition to loss payment, policy deductibles are proportionally split in cases of overlapping coverage. If Company C has 3⁄4 of the coverage, it would subtract 3⁄4 of the deductible amount from its claim payment. Company D would subtract 1⁄4 of the deductible amount when it carries 1⁄4 of the total coverage.

The deductible application follows the straight proportional method unless the two companies have different deductible amounts. See the exhibit "Prorating Deductible Example."

Despite these examples, applying the proportional share method to two different deductibles is uncommon.

Two insurance policies applying to the same claim sometimes contain the other insurance condition stating that their coverage is excess. In that case, the coverage reverts to a proportional share method of contribution.

Prorating Deductible Example

Suppose that the insured has a policy with Company X with a $100 deductible and a policy with Company Y on the same property with a $250 deductible. Both policies have other insurance conditions calling for a proportional share settlement. The Company X policy has $10,000 of coverage; the Company Y policy has $90,000 of coverage. Now assume that the insured sustains a $10,000 covered loss.

Begin the calculations by subtracting the largest deductible from the loss. Company Y has the $250 deductible, so the loss payable is $10,000 − $250 = $9,750. This loss is the common loss shared by both companies. The loss is apportioned between them as follows:

Company X $$\frac{\$10,000}{\$100,000} \times \$10,000 = \$1,000.$$

Company Y $$\frac{\$90,000}{\$100,000} \times \$10,000 = \$9,000.$$

The two companies would then calculate a proportional share of the common deductible. The common deductible is the smallest deductible amount that the two companies share. In this case, the common deductible would be $100; both companies have a deductible of at least this amount. The adjuster would apply the proportional share computation as earlier computed.

Company X's deductible would be as follows:

$$\frac{\$10,000 \text{ (Company X's coverage)}}{\$100,000 \text{ (Total coverage: \$90,000 + \$10,000)}} = 10\%.$$

or

1/10, or .10
10% of the common $100 deductible = $10.

Company Y's deductible would be as follows:

$$\frac{\$90,000 \text{ (Company Y's coverage)}}{\$100,000 \text{ (Total coverage: \$90,000 + \$10,000)}} = 90\%.$$

or

9/10, or .90
90% of the common $100 deductible = $90.

In addition to Company Y's proportional share of the common deductible, Company Y would also subtract the additional unshared deductible amount from the loss. The additional deductible amount for Company Y would be as follows:

$250 (Company Y's total deductible) − $100 (common deductible) = $150.

Company Y would then have a total deductible applicable to the claim of $240 ($90 + $150).

Company X would apply a $10 deductible to its claim payment. The insured would be subject to the total deductible of $100, an amount equal to the smallest deductible on any policy. Note that the $150 difference in Company Y's deductible calculation is still not accounted for. This $150 difference is added into the claim payment made by Company X. Company X pays this portion of Company Y's deductible because it is an insured loss under Company X's policy. By doing this, the insured is only charged the smaller of the two deductibles ($100) for the loss, while the $250 deductible is apportioned between the two companies. The loss payment calculation would then look like this:

Co. Y: $10,000 × 90% = $9,000 − $240 (deductible) = $8,760.

Co. X: $10,000 × 10% = $1,000 − $10 (deductible) = $990 + $150. (the difference between the two deductibles) = $1,140.

Total loss payment to the insured: $8,760. + $1,140 = $9,900.

[DA03802]

DISAGREEMENTS OVER OTHER INSURANCE

Insurers do not always agree on how to apply policy terms when more than one policy provides coverage for a loss.

Policy conditions affect the amount recoverable under a policy. If more than one policy applies to a loss, each policy's Other Insurance condition determines how coverage from the additional policy is applied. For example, one of the policies may state that its coverage is pro rata or excess if another policy is applicable to the loss.

When overlapping coverage exists and insurers disagree on the amounts each must pay, the disagreement is most often resolved through compromise. If compromise is not successful, insurers will litigate in court to reach a resolution.

Compromise

The most common approach used to resolve insurer disagreements regarding overlapping coverage is compromise. In most circumstances, informal negotiation can resolve disagreements. Regardless of the amount of time negotiations may take, it is important to consider the insured while the negotiations are in progress. The primary insurer or all applicable insurers could agree to pay the disputed amount to the insured and then reconcile the amounts due to each insurer at the conclusion of negotiations.

When informal agreement cannot be readily reached, the **Guiding Principles** should be used. The Guiding Principles were adopted in the 1960s by key insurance associations and were considered binding for insurers that were signatories to an agreement to be governed by these principles. Although many companies are no longer signatories, claims representatives continue to use the Guiding Principles to resolve coverage disputes.

Guiding Principles

A set of industry-agreed-upon principles designed to resolve situations of overlapping coverage.

The Guiding Principles operate only when more than one policy covers a loss and the policies' Other Insurance conditions do not resolve how coverage applies. The Guiding Principles resolve which policy is primary or what the pro rata distribution should be when there are no Other Insurance conditions in the policies or when the applicable conditions are contradictory. The principles contain guidelines for two different situations:

- When the policies cover the same property and the same interest—for example, when there are two homeowners policies that cover the same insured and the same property.
- When the policies cover the same property and different interests—for example, when a homeowners policy and a dry cleaner's policy cover the same damaged clothing.

When policies overlap, the policy that provides specific coverage for the property at issue at specified locations takes priority over more general policies. Courts will sometimes use the Guiding Principles in deciding coverage disputes, but often do not.

Resolution in Court

Because of the expense associated with litigation, it is preferable for insurers to resolve overlapping coverage disagreements through compromise. However, when there is a significant amount in dispute and the Other Insurance conditions are contradictory or nonexistent, informal compromise may not be possible.

The first step in a formal resolution of overlapping coverage disagreements is usually arbitration. Arbitration can be either binding or nonbinding. The policies involved may specify which type of arbitration is to be used in coverage disagreements. If binding arbitration is used, the insurers will be bound by the arbitration decision and the disagreement will be resolved. If arbitration is nonbinding and if one or more insurer does not accept the result, then litigation will proceed toward a court resolution.

The court cases that developed from the property loss at the World Trade Center in New York City on September 11, 2001, provide highly publicized examples of the types of litigation that can develop when there are multiple policies covering the same loss. More recent trends of litigation in overlapping coverage disputes can be found in coverage for builders' risks (particularly in Chinese drywall claims) and in cyber risk and other intellectual property coverages.

INSURED'S DUTIES AFTER LOSS

The insured's duties after a loss are explicitly stated in a policy's provisions. Adjusters must proceed carefully, however, because waiver and estoppel can affect the insured's duties.

A policy outlines certain duties of the insured and the insurer after a loss has occurred. The adjuster must be aware of these duties so that waiver and estoppel do not occur.

One of the conditions that the insured must comply with after a loss is the submission of a proof of loss. Once the proof of loss is submitted, the insurer must respond to it within a time period that is designated by the policy, state insurance code, or case law. The insurer can accept the proof of loss or can reject it. If it is rejected, the rejection must be timely and must state the reasons for the rejection.

Waiver and Estoppel

Waiver involves voluntarily and intentionally relinquishing a known contractual right. **Estoppel** prohibits a party to a contract from enforcing certain conditions of the contract because that party's behavior or words caused a breach of contract. Estoppel results when one party's behavior or words cause another party to rely detrimentally on that behavior or those words. Estoppel prevents one party from enforcing contract conditions. Adjusters often waive the need for a proof of loss on small property losses. For example, estoppel occurs when an adjuster tells an insured to throw out a damaged carpet before it is inspected. The adjuster is estopped from denying the claim for the coverage because it is not available for inspection.

If the insurer wishes to invoke any condition in the policy, the insurer or adjuster must advise the insured by either a **nonwaiver agreement** or a **reservation of rights letter**. Either one of these instruments preserves the insurer's rights to invoke a condition at a later time. The adjuster must be alert to coverage problems in a loss adjustment and must protect the insurer's interest with a nonwaiver agreement or reservation of rights letter whenever the possibility of waiver exists.

Proof of Loss

The **proof of loss** is a document describing the details of the loss, property values, and interests in the property for which the insured is making a claim under the policy. The insurer usually provides the insured with the proof of loss form. In some states, insurers are required to provide the form. In other states, no particular form is required, as long as all necessary information is included.

Proof of Loss Requirement

To be meaningful, the proof of loss should be required early in the adjustment process. The proof of loss is a powerful adjusting tool that commits the insured under oath to a specific set of facts.

Waiver

The intentional relinquishment of a known right.

Estoppel

A legal principle that prohibits a party from asserting a claim or right that is inconsistent with that party's past statement or conduct on which another party has detrimentally relied.

Nonwaiver agreement

A signed agreement indicating that during the course of investigation, neither the insurer nor the insured waives rights under the policy.

Reservation of rights letter

An insurer's letter that specifies coverage issues and informs the insured that the insurer is handling a claim with the understanding that the insurer may later deny coverage should the facts warrant it.

Proof of loss

A statement of facts about a loss for which the insured is making a claim.

Some insurers require a proof of loss at the end of the adjustment process. By that time, however, the adjuster has presumably agreed on the settlement, and the proof of loss accomplishes little, except to document the claim file. For routine or small claims, many insurers intentionally (or by inaction) waive the proof of loss requirement, which can facilitate the adjustment process. Many insurers simply disregard the proof of loss requirement on most losses and enforce the requirement only by exception. Others invoke the proof of loss requirement on losses such as total losses, questionable losses, or losses over a certain dollar figure. Some insurers invoke the requirement on all losses. Adjusters must know the requirements of the insurance company or companies for which they are handling claims so as not to waive rights under the policy.

Changes in or Waiver of Proof of Loss

If the insured wishes to change a proof of loss or file an amended proof of loss, the adjuster will consider these alterations after he or she thoroughly reviews the situation with the insurer's management. Any agreement considering a change or amended proof of loss might serve as a waiver by the insurer should it later want to deny a claim based on the original proof of loss. Courts freely permit changes to proofs of loss to correct honest errors.

Rejection of Proof of Loss

After the insurer has invoked the proof of loss requirement and the insured has filed the proof of loss, the insurer must, within a designated time set by either the policy, state insurance code, or case law, make a decision. The insurer can choose one of these actions:

- Accept the proof of loss as submitted
- Reject the proof of loss, using specific language as to why it is not acceptable, and give the insured an opportunity to refile a corrected proof of loss
- Reject the proof of loss, giving specific reasons for the rejection, and allow the insured to make the next move without any further direction

If the proof of loss is rejected for any reason, the rejection must be timely. Promptly rejecting the proof of loss protects the insurer in policies with language stating that payment will be made within a certain time after receiving proof of loss. Therefore, if the insurer does not reject a proof of loss immediately, the insurer might be compelled to pay even if the proof is believed to be deficient. After an insurer receives the proof of loss, state insurance codes allow a time period either to pay the claim or to reject the proof. In any case, an adjuster must check the state statutes or state-mandated insurance policy provisions or forms before rejecting a proof of loss.

If the proof of loss is rejected, it must be rejected for specific reasons, and with the consent of the insurer's management. Typical reasons for a rejection are as:

- The proof of loss does not contain sufficient documentation to support the amount claimed.
- The proof of loss was incomplete on its face.
- The proof of loss was not filed within the time required by the policy.

Examination Under Oath

Examination under oath (EUO) can be valuable to the insurer when arson is suspected or committed either by the insured or by collusion with an insured; when fraud is suspected; or when the adjuster has been unable to obtain information regarding how a loss occurred. Although it generates some expense, the savings gained can often offset the costs. Examinations under oath enable the insurer to obtain sufficient documentation from the insured either to support or refute the claim. Comparing the oral testimony from an examination to records supplied by the insured is also an ideal way to support or refute a claim.

Any question about the purpose and validity of the examination under oath has been answered by the United States Supreme Court in the case of Claflin v. Commonwealth Insurance Company:

> The object of the provisions in the policy of insurance requiring the insured to submit himself to an examination under oath, to be reduced to writing, was to enable the company to possess itself of all knowledge, and all information, as to the other sources and means of knowledge, in regards to the facts, material to their rights, to enable them to decide upon their obligations, and to protect them against false claims. A false answer as to any matter of fact material to the inquiry, knowingly and willfully made, with intent to deceive the insurer, would be fraudulent. If it accomplished its results, it would be a fraud effective; if it failed, it would be a fraud attempted. And if the matter were material and the statement false, to the knowledge of the party making it, and willfully made, the intention to deceive the insurer would be necessarily implied for the law presumes every man to intend the natural consequences of his acts.

According to this statement, the EUO gives the insurer a means to determine whether it will deny or provide coverage on a claim.

Examination under oath (EUO)

A statement given by a person who has sworn to tell the truth before an officer of the court.

THE APPRAISAL PROCEDURE

Almost all property insurance policies have a condition providing a method for resolving differences between parties.

The appraisal provision is used in most property policies. Any party that wants to preserve its rights must adhere to this provision.

This sections covers these topics:

- The purpose of appraisal
- The demand for appraisal
- The appraisal process

Purpose of Appraisal

The appraisal provision provides a means to resolve disputes regarding value without one party having to sue another. The provision has no role in resolving any questions of coverage or policy language interpretation. The provision's language is clear on that point. For instance, if the damaged property will be repaired and not replaced, one of the factors that can create differences concerning the loss amount is the repair method. The repair method, as well as the extent of repair, affects the repair's cost, which, in turn, affects the amount of loss. Many contractors or engineers consider tearing down sections of a building and rebuilding less expensive than repairing the structure as it stands. The appraisal provision can be invoked when the insured, insurer, and appraiser differ about repair methods and the amount of loss.

Nothing in the appraisal clause provides for resolving any other disagreements between the parties. Generally, coverage questions are not resolved through the appraisal process. Courts vary in their decisions, but the provision is intended to determine only the amount of loss. When what may or may not be covered in a loss is questioned, the parties involved must pursue avenues other than the appraisal provision.

Demand for Appraisal

The appraisal provision uses the word "demand," which means that if either party makes a demand, the other has no choice but to submit to the appraisal. If the insurer sends a letter to the insured "demanding" an appraisal, the insured cannot refuse. To do so would be considered a violation of a policy condition, and the insurer could deny the claim based on that violation. However, an insurer that denies coverage altogether waives its right to appraisal.

Some states have amendatory endorsements that have made the appraisal process voluntary or nonbinding, or have completely removed it from the policy. Adjusters should check the rules of the jurisdiction before invoking the appraisal clause.

Appraisers' and Umpire's Qualifications

The appraisal provision addresses the appraisers' qualifications in terms of competence and economic interest, as well as the selection of an umpire.

Appraisers' Competence

The appraisal provision states that each party will choose a competent appraiser within a specific time frame. Either party could plausibly question an appraisal award if the other party chooses an incompetent appraiser. If a dispute arises about the amount of loss on an extensive fire claim and the insured selects a friend who is an unlicensed carpenter as the appraiser, the insurer might have a reasonable basis to challenge the appraiser's competence and to contest the selection of that appraiser.

If one of the appraisal parties objects to the competency of the opposition's appraiser and that party continues to retain that appraiser until the appraisal is completed, the other party could contest the appraisal award through the courts. To avoid this possibility, each party to the appraisal must select an appraiser carefully.

Appraisers' Interest

Another area that should be considered is the appraiser's interest in the outcome of the appraisal. An appraiser with a strong conflict of interest should never be selected. In some policies, the appraisal provision states that the appraisers named by the parties must be disinterested. An example of an appraiser who is not disinterested is a contractor who was chosen by the insured but who had already agreed to perform the repairs on the insured's property. An insured's employee is another example.

The insurer should also be careful to choose a disinterested appraiser. This does not mean that the insurer and the appraiser have never dealt with each other in the past—only that the appraiser not be economically dependent on the insurer. All dealings between an adjuster and an appraiser should be professional. An adjuster should never select an appraiser because of personal favors. If the particular policy's language states that the appraiser must be disinterested, the insurer should name a disinterested appraiser to avoid jeopardizing its position or waiving its rights.

Umpire Selection

The appraisal provision states that the two appraisers should choose the umpire. This is usually accomplished without a problem, and the appraisal can proceed. When no agreement on the umpire can be reached, the selection goes to a court having jurisdiction over the dispute for resolution.

The Appraisal Process

The procedure required by the appraisal clause is not overly detailed, allowing some flexibility for the appraisers. A formal hearing is not required to complete an appraisal.

Separate Appraisals

The policy stipulates that each appraiser "separately set the amount of loss." The appraisers should go to the loss site, review the damage, and provide their own figures on what they determine to be the amount of loss. Different appraisers will probably select different repair techniques and will determine different costs. However, following their reviews, the two appraisers should try to agree on the scope of the damage—whether property should be repaired or replaced and its quantity (dimensions and amount) and quality. Separate appraisals act as competitive bids in keeping costs in line. Nevertheless, two appraisers commonly work together to resolve the scope of the damage.

Umpire's Role

Appraisers often disagree considerably about the amount of loss. The appraisal provision indicates procedures for handling such cases. Most policies contain language that requires the appraisers to submit their differences to an umpire. In this case, the appraisers submit only differing figures. According to some policies, the appraisers submit all of their figures on the amount of damage for the umpire to consider. The adjuster must carefully read the policy before proceeding with the appraisal process.

Appraisal Decision

Generally, in the appraisal provision, any agreement between two of the three parties sets the amount of loss. This language might differ in other policies, but it usually states that if any two agree, whether it is two appraisers or the umpire and one of the appraisers, then the appraisal is set and completed.

Challenges to the Decision

Once an appraisal has been set, it is binding on all parties. This is not to say that an appraisal cannot be challenged, but usually only fraud, collusion, and mistake of law are valid grounds to challenge and perhaps overturn an appraisal. Sometimes, a challenge is based on the contention that the appraiser was incompetent or that coverage issues were involved. In most cases, if the appraisers and the umpire are properly selected, the award stands.

Expenses

The final consideration in the appraisal relates to costs and expenses. The provision requires each of the parties to the appraisal to bear their own appraiser's costs. The parties equally share the umpire's cost and expenses.

Waiver and Estoppel

The adjuster should advise the insured throughout the adjustment of any condition that the insurer might invoke. The adjuster's action or lack of action could waive the insurer's rights to invoke that condition later. If an appraisal is being considered and the decision is made to invoke it, the insurer must advise the insured in a demand letter using exact policy language. The insurer must then follow all rules of the appraisal promptly and professionally. Any violation of the rules in the appraisal provision might result in an estoppel against the insurer to enforce the provision.

For example, if the insurer demands an appraisal and the insured properly names its appraiser within the twenty-day limit, but the insurer does not name its appraiser in the time allowed, the insured could refuse the appraisal because of the insurer's violation of the condition.

Precondition to Lawsuit

Because the appraisal provision is one of the policy conditions, this provision's requirement must be observed before a lawsuit can be filed. For instance, assume that the amount of loss is disputed and that the insurer demands an appraisal. However, the insured refuses appraisal and proceeds to file a lawsuit for contractual damage against the insurer. Each state has different laws, and courts typically differ in their findings, but the policy conditions must generally be complied with before a lawsuit is filed. In this example, the insured would lose. Alternatively, if the insurer denies coverage, the insurer will be deemed to have waived the appraisal right. An insured could initiate suit immediately after a coverage denial.

The Adjusters Role in the Appraisal Process

The appraisal provision is not used often, but when it is used, the adjuster must be prepared to follow the procedure through to a conclusion. The adjuster must also be thoroughly familiar with how the procedure operates, ensuring that it is followed according to the policy and that the appraisal conforms to the insurance code of the state in which it is being conducted.

Sometimes, the appraisers or the adjuster might testify. If an appraisal involves a large loss, the insured and insurer will usually be represented by counsel and will have their own appraisers. In such cases, the umpire can receive testimony from the appraisers, the attorneys, and the adjuster. The adjuster's knowledge of the procedure and the expectations of each party to the appraisal help the process to move smoothly.

SUMMARY

Actual cash value (ACV) has been defined in many ways. A commonly used definition is replacement cost minus depreciation. Depreciation can be straight-line, accelerated, or decelerated. Some items will not depreciate at all but instead will appreciate over time. The amount of depreciation taken is based on physical wear and tear, age, and obsolescence. Some courts have held that ACV means market value.

Market value is often described as what a willing buyer would pay to obtain an item from a willing seller. Market value can be useful for unique items or for older buildings that contain materials and construction no longer in use. When determining a building's market value, the land's value must be eliminated from the calculation.

Some courts have determined that depreciation and market value are not sufficient to ascertain actual cash value. These jurisdictions adhere to a broad evidence rule stating that many factors, such as economic, technological, or fashion obsolescence, should be considered in determining ACV.

Some states have valued policy laws. These laws require the insurer to pay the face amount of the policy if a total loss occurs. These laws apply only to buildings and structures, not to personal property. Like replacement cost coverage, valued policy laws violate the principle of indemnity.

Insurers have the option to repair or replace damaged property or to pay the cash value.

The two standard loss settlement alternatives are (1) settlement for cash, at replacement cost or actual cash value, and (2) repair or replacement of the property. Other settlement provisions, described in this section, include stated or agreed value, selling price, original cost, warranty services, and pair or set clause.

Policy limits are the maximum amount payable on a loss. However, homeowners policies can have endorsements that provide for payment of the full cost to replace the dwelling even if the loss exceeds the policy limit. Property policies also contain internal limits or special limits for specified classes of property, such as money, jewelry, and precious metals.

Property policies contain deductibles. The application of the deductible amount is specified by the policy. Most policies apply the deductible to the loss and then apply the policy limit. This practice is called absorbing the deductible.

Property policies contain a coinsurance provision that encourages insureds to purchase adequate insurance. The provision requires the insured to carry an amount of insurance equal to or greater than the specified percentage of the property's total value. If the insured fails to do so, the amount recoverable under the policy is reduced.

Policy conditions affect the amount recoverable under the policy. If more than one policy or coverage applies to the loss, the other insurance provision must be used to determine how the loss will be paid. Most policies are primary, meaning that they will pay first. Some policies specifically state that they are excess of other insurance, meaning that they pay after the primary policy coverage has been depleted. Other policies may state that they pay on a pro rata basis with other policies.

When more than one insurance policy applies to a loss, there may be disagreement between the insurers regarding their obligations under their respective policies. These disputes are usually compromised by using the policies' Other Insurance conditions or the Guiding Principles. When a compromise cannot be readily reached, arbitration is often used to reach a resolution. In complex and high-value losses, the insurers may litigate their disagreement in the courts.

A policy outlines certain duties of the insured and the insurer after a loss has occurred. The adjuster must be aware of these duties so that waiver and estoppel do not occur. One of the conditions that the insured must comply with after a loss is the submission of a proof of loss. Once the proof of loss is submitted, the insurer must respond to it within a time period that is designated by the policy, state insurance code, or case law. The insurer can accept the proof of loss or can reject it. If it is rejected, the rejection must be timely and must state the reasons for the rejection.

Another duty of the insured after a loss is to cooperate with the investigation of the loss. The insurer can demand that the insured be examined under oath. This procedure is often used when fraud is suspected or a question exists concerning the coverage for the loss. The examination under oath (EUO) enables the insurer to obtain information to support or refute the claim.

If the insured and the insurer disagree as to the value of the loss or damage, a property policy has an appraisal provision that will resolve the dispute. Appraisal must be attempted before the filing of any lawsuit. Either the insured or the insurer can invoke the appraisal provision. It is usually a binding decision on all parties, but some states have made it voluntary or nonbinding or have eliminated the language completely from the policy.

Both the insured and the insurer each pick a competent appraiser. Competent is interpreted to mean someone with property damage expertise as well as someone who has no interest in the final outcome. The two appraisers appoint a third person to act as umpire. The appraisal process can be as formal or informal as the umpire desires. Each side is responsible for the expense of their chosen appraiser, and both sides split the cost of the umpire. Any agreement between two of the three parties sets the amount of the loss.

ASSIGNMENT NOTE

1.   Form HO 00 03 05 01, Copyright, Insurance Services Office, Inc., 2001

Direct Your Learning ▶▶

3

Loss Adjustment Process

Educational Objectives

After learning the content of this assignment, you should be able to:

▷ Describe and explain the steps in the loss adjustment process after a loss notice is received.

▷ Describe public adjusters' role in the adjustment process.

▷ Explain how to verify losses through the use of the following:

- Statements

- Documentation, such as books, records, or photographs

▷ Describe the uses of various experts in a given claims situation.

▷ Identify the potential for subrogation in a given claim, and explain how experts and arbitration would facilitate recovery.

▷ Describe how to issue claim payments to account for all interests.

▷ Describe a denial letter's contents.

Loss Adjustment Process

3

STEPS IN THE LOSS ADJUSTMENT PROCESS

Adjusters must properly investigate, document, and report their activities and claim settlements.

Every investigation should determine the facts about what caused the loss, how coverage applies, and the amount of the loss.

When a loss occurs, several steps must be taken before the insurer can begin the adjustment process. Normally, the insured notifies the agent or broker of the loss or contacts the insurer directly. An agent or a broker notes some basic information about the loss, such as the date it occurred, its location and type, the extent of damage, and any other special details. With this information and additional information from his or her files, the agent or broker completes a loss notice such as the one shown in the exhibit and electronically submits the loss to the insurer. The completed loss notice form states details of the loss; the coverage that applies, including the insurer, the policy number, the policy's effective dates, the amounts of coverage, and the deductibles or coinsurance; and the form numbers and edition dates. Mortgagees or loss payees are also listed on the loss notice form. The agent/broker may also advise the insured about emergency repairs as well as assign an adjuster to inspect the loss. If the insured calls the insurer directly to report a loss, the insurer will obtain the same information that an agent or a broker would obtain. See the exhibit "ACORD Property Loss Notice."

After the loss notice is received, the insurer begins the loss adjustment process. The insurer's claims department assigns the claim to an adjuster. The adjuster acknowledges the assignment and initiates contact with the insured.

A property loss adjuster follows the same loss adjustment process regardless of the coverage involved in the loss. The adjuster follows six steps to resolve a property claim. See the box. See the exhibit "Loss Adjustment Process."

Step 1: Acknowledgment and Assignment to an Adjuster

After the agent reports a loss to the insurer, a claims department manager or supervisor decides which adjuster will handle the claim and assigns that adjuster. For an independent adjuster, the insurer often calls the adjuster with the assignment, giving the adjuster the information on the property loss notice along with any other relevant policy data or special handling instruc-

ACORD Property Loss Notice

ACORD®	**PROPERTY LOSS NOTICE**		DATE (MM/DD/YYYY)	8-25-X0

AGENCY	INSURED LOCATION CODE	DATE OF LOSS AND TIME		AM
Small Agency Malvern, PA		8-24-X0	2	X PM

	PROPERTY / HOME POLICY	
	CARRIER Atwell Insurance Co.	NAIC CODE 00-000

CONTACT NAME: Debbie Jones	POLICY NUMBER 99-23456	

PHONE (A/C, No. Ext): 610-555-1111		
FAX (A/C, No):	**FLOOD POLICY**	
E-MAIL ADDRESS: sagency@ins.com	CARRIER	NAIC CODE
CODE: 555 SUBCODE:		
AGENCY CUSTOMER ID:	POLICY NUMBER	
	WIND POLICY	
	CARRIER	NAIC CODE
	POLICY NUMBER	

INSURED

NAME OF INSURED (First, Middle, Last) Susan Reed	INSURED'S MAILING ADDRESS Kids Science Kits, Inc. 111 Street Malvern, PA

DATE OF BIRTH	FEIN (if applicable)	MARITAL STATUS	

PRIMARY PHONE # ☒ HOME ☐ BUS ☐ CELL 610-555-4444	SECONDARY PHONE # ☐ HOME ☒ BUS ☐ CELL 610-555-6666	PRIMARY E-MAIL ADDRESS:
		SECONDARY E-MAIL ADDRESS:

NAME OF SPOUSE (First, Middle, Last) (if applicable)	SPOUSE'S MAILING ADDRESS (if applicable)

DATE OF BIRTH	FEIN (if applicable)	MARITAL STATUS	

PRIMARY PHONE # ☐ HOME ☐ BUS ☐ CELL	SECONDARY PHONE # ☐ HOME ☐ BUS ☐ CELL	PRIMARY E-MAIL ADDRESS:
		SECONDARY E-MAIL ADDRESS:

CONTACT   ☐ CONTACT INSURED

NAME OF CONTACT (First, Middle, Last)	CONTACT'S MAILING ADDRESS

PRIMARY PHONE # ☐ HOME ☐ BUS ☐ CELL	SECONDARY PHONE # ☐ HOME ☐ BUS ☐ CELL	

WHEN TO CONTACT	PRIMARY E-MAIL ADDRESS:
	SECONDARY E-MAIL ADDRESS:

LOSS

LOCATION OF LOSS	POLICE OR FIRE DEPARTMENT CONTACTED
STREET: 111 Street	Local
CITY, STATE, ZIP: Malvern, PA	REPORT NUMBER
COUNTRY:	

DESCRIBE LOCATION OF LOSS IF NOT AT SPECIFIC STREET ADDRESS:

KIND OF LOSS	X FIRE	☐ LIGHTNING	☐ FLOOD	☐	PROBABLE AMOUNT ENTIRE LOSS
	☐ THEFT	☐ HAIL	☐ WIND		$15,000

DESCRIPTION OF LOSS & DAMAGE (Attach ACORD 101, Additional Remarks Schedule, if more space is required)

Fire started in kitchen and spread to another room. Science kits damaged.

REPORTED BY Susan Reed	REPORTED TO agent

Loss Adjustment Process

1. Acknowledging receipt of the insured's report of loss and assigning the loss to an adjuster
2. Verifying coverage
3. Initiating contact with the insured
4. Investigating the facts
5. Determining the cause of loss and the extent of loss to insured property
6. Concluding the loss adjustment

[DA03887]

tions. Most insurers follow up with written confirmation of the assignment, and they send the independent adjuster any claims documents that they have received or special policy forms involved. Both the staff adjuster and the independent adjuster need to review the policy to ensure that neither adjuster inadvertently commits waiver or estoppel. Upon receipt of the assignment, the adjuster assigned must promptly call the insured. During this telephone conversation, the adjuster questions the insured to learn essential facts about the loss and the extent of damage. The adjuster might have to direct the insured to protect the property from further damage, such as instructing the insured to board up windows following a serious loss. The adjuster can also make an appointment to inspect the loss site or advise the insured of who will be out to inspect the loss.

Most, but not all, adjusters handle losses within a specific geographic area. Some adjusters handle losses on a global basis. Adjusters handling only a specific geographic territory in the United States should be familiar with the adjuster licensing laws of those states. Noncompliance with these laws can result in fines levied against the insurer. These laws may apply to the insurer's staff adjuster, to independent adjusters, or to public adjusters, depending upon the state. If an independent adjuster is hired to handle a loss on the staff property loss adjuster's behalf, the independent adjuster must provide proof of a valid license if one is required in that state. Many insurers have centralized the responsibility for regulatory compliance, so it may not be necessary to have proof of a valid adjuster license in every claim file. Adjusters should check with their manager to determine what the insurer's policy is regarding adjuster licensing. Also, most adjuster licensing laws exempt catastrophe adjusters.

Step 2: Coverage Verification

Usually, a property loss adjuster is able to quickly verify that a policy is in force. However, if the actual paper policy is required to thoroughly review the forms and endorsements, the adjuster may need additional time to obtain the policy and perform the review. The adjuster usually accomplishes the policy review before contacting the insured and inspecting the loss, but this may not always be the case. If the coverage verification and review cannot be completed before contacting the insured, the adjuster must take care not to say or do anything that might waive any policy defenses.

The exhibit lists some of the questions that an adjuster should have in mind when reviewing a policy. See the exhibit "Key Questions When Verifying Coverage."

Key Questions When Verifying Coverage

After receiving a loss notice, an adjuster reviews the policy and determines the answers to the following questions:

- Does the loss fall within the policy's effective dates?
- Who is the insured in the policy?
- What is insured in the policy?
- What caused the loss, and is that cause of loss covered by the policy?
- Do any exclusions apply to the loss?
- How is the loss to be valued?
- Is the amount of recovery limited by the policy?

[DA03888]

The adjuster should read the applicable policy forms carefully, mindful of obvious coverage questions. For example, is a theft claim being filed under a named-perils policy that does not include theft? Is the insured a tenant who is claiming building damage under a personal property form? The adjuster should examine limitations and exclusions. Perhaps an insured homeowner has just reported a theft of $5,000 cash during a break-in, but a review of the standard HO-3 reveals a $200 limit on money. A nonwaiver agreement might be necessary if policy violations are known, such as late reporting or discarding of the damaged property before inspection.

Verifying coverage, the adjuster sometimes must consult with an expert to determine issues such as cause of loss. Perhaps an extensive computer network broke down shortly after a thunderstorm, and the adjuster must determine whether it was damaged by lightning or suffered a coincidental mechanical breakdown. The typical adjuster may not have the expertise to make such determinations, but an expert can expedite the adjustment process. If an expert is needed, the adjuster should schedule the first meeting with the insured so that the expert can attend.

An adjuster's final consideration before going to the loss site should be the information that the insurer will expect in the adjuster's reports and how such information will be gathered. The preparation time spent before the meeting allows the adjuster to establish credibility. That time will not be wasted—the preparation ultimately speeds the adjustment process to the benefit of all concerned.

Step 3: Contact With the Insured

After receiving the claim assignment and reviewing the initial loss report and policy, the adjuster should contact the insured and make an appointment to meet at the loss location, either on the same day or within the next few days. During this initial contact, the adjuster should get information about the extent of the loss and how the loss occurred. The adjuster will then be able to make some preliminary decisions about the need for outside vendors, such as a restoration company, to assist with the loss adjustment. During this initial contact, the adjuster may also learn that the insured has retained a public adjuster. The first trip to the loss site, together with the first meeting with the insured, sets the tone for the adjustment. The adjuster should listen to the insured. The insured probably considers the loss a major disruption; he or she might never have made a claim under the policy before. The adjuster might be the first representative of the insurer that the insured has met, and the insured might be apprehensive about what will occur during the adjustment of his or her claim.

Most insureds do not understand their coverage thoroughly. The adjuster must explain the policy and its meaning in relation to the loss.

Perhaps the most important information that the adjuster must convey is any possible policy violation, exclusion, or limitation that might affect coverage. The adjuster must be honest. Withholding this type of information might be construed as a breach of the adjuster's duty to deal fairly. Furthermore, because the adjuster is acting as an agent of the insurer, the insurer is liable for any of the adjuster's unfair acts or practices. At the initial meeting, the adjuster should explain the adjustment process and perform these steps:

1. Explain what inspection, appraisal, and investigation the adjuster will be conducting.
2. Tell the insured what is required to protect the property and to present the claim.
3. Supply the insured with blank inventory forms, a blank proof of loss form, and any necessary written instructions.
4. Note potential coverage questions or policy limitation or exclusions, and obtain a nonwaiver agreement (when necessary). Be prepared to tell the

insured what additional investigation is needed to resolve potential coverage issues.

5. Explain the time involved to process and conclude the claim.

6. Assist the insured in protecting the property by arranging for board-up, storage, and restoration and cleaning firms (when appropriate).

7. Be prepared to make emergency advance payments to the insured for clothing, living expenses, food, or other expenses, and obtain an appropriate receipt for the payment when the circumstances support such a payment.

8. Assist the insured by arranging for temporary housing (when necessary).

The insurer's adjuster must ensure that requests for documentation and the need for compliance with policy conditions are communicated to the insured in writing. This is a good policy to follow whether a public adjuster is involved or not.

Step 4: Investigation

Following the preliminary interview and discussions, the adjuster investigates, inspects, and appraises the loss. Good investigation is the basis of every claim settlement. Property loss adjusters are responsible for determining what investigation is appropriate in individual claims. The adjuster receives direction from his or her company's claims handling guidelines and supervisor as to how much investigation is appropriate. The adjuster's goal is to investigate enough to make the appropriate decision. A loss's dollar value does not necessarily indicate the amount of investigation needed to arrive at a decision. Every investigation should determine the facts about what caused the loss, how coverage applies, and what the amount of the loss is. The insured's duties following loss and statements from the insured and witnesses are key tools in the property loss adjuster's investigation.

The Insured's Duties

Almost all of the insured's duties in the event of loss, as described in the property coverage forms, are designed to aid the adjuster's investigation. According to the insurance policy, the insured must prove these elements:

•   That a loss is covered by the policy

•   The amount of the loss

•   That the insured has complied with all duties and conditions specified in the policy

After a loss, the insured's duties are the essential conditions of the insurance policy. Property loss adjusters should review those duties with the insured to remind the insured of what is expected. Nevertheless, insurers and claim adjusters aim to provide good service to their customers, especially after a loss. Unless they suspect fraud or lack of coverage for the loss, adjusters should work with insureds to accomplish the insured's duties. Review of these duties also helps the adjuster to organize his or her own investigation and specify what is needed from the insured.

Reporting

Although property loss adjusters often make oral reports about a claim's status by telephone or in person at the office, most reports are written.

Following the reporting procedures within an adjuster's own organization is crucial. An insurer's reporting requirements, including form samples, format, content, and time for submission, are commonly detailed in the insurer's claims operating and procedures manuals made available to all adjusters. Such manuals establish the standards of performance for adjusters. Because reports are the product of the adjuster's work and are used by the adjuster's supervisor to measure job performance, adjusters must provide clear, concise, and timely reports.

Although reports primarily communicate to and document for the insurer what was done to investigate, adjust, settle, and otherwise resolve a claim, they also document for others, such as state insurance authorities or juries, an insurer's good-faith investigation. An insured's attorney can obtain files from the insurer through discovery in litigation that deals with allegations of improper claims handling or bad faith, so the files must reflect:

- Clear, concise, accurate information
- Timely handling of the claim
- A fair and balanced investigation regarding the interests of the insured and insurer
- The absence of derogandatory or inflammatory comments regarding the character of the insured or anyone connected with the claim
- A thorough good-faith investigation

Reports can be as brief as a handwritten memo or very detailed and lengthy, especially when written for larger, more complex claims. The three types of reports used in the investigation phase of the loss adjustment process are these:

- Preliminary
- Status (or interim)
- Summarized (or captioned) reports

These reports usually have attachments such as claims documents, official reports, diagrams, photos, statements, and correspondence.

Preliminary reports are usually filed within the first twenty-four hours or up to seven days following assignment of the claim, depending on the insurer's reporting requirements. Many insurers provide preprinted, fill-in-the-blank-type forms or electronic templates that adjusters use to acknowledge receipt of the assignment, inform the insurer about initial activity on the claim, suggest reserves on certain coverages, advise the insurer of coverage questions, and request assistance and guidance from file supervisors as to the handling of coverage questions or any aspect of the claim. Preliminary reports can also include a scope and preliminary estimate of damages. Additionally, the preliminary report can serve as a closing report when claims are small and uncomplicated and the loss has been adjusted and payment has been made.

Status, or interim, reports inform the insurer of a claim's progress and can be filed periodically, generally every fifteen to thirty days following assignment, depending on a particular insurer's reporting requirements. Their purpose is to keep the insurer advised of the status of an investigation or adjustment, to make reserve change recommendations, and to request assistance and settlement authority when the amount payable exceeds the adjuster's authority. Status reports also confirm that the adjuster is giving appropriate attention to the claim and that the work is progressing in a timely manner.

Summarized, or captioned, reports are typically very detailed narrative reports that follow an established format. They are usually filed within thirty days of the assignment's date. They are generally required whenever a claim must be reviewed by regional or home office claim personnel. Summarized reports might be required when the size of loss and settlement authority exceed the local office's authority. When coverage might be denied, many insurers require regional or home office review and approval. Some insurers require summarized reports on certain types of claims so that the regional or home office can keep abreast of what is happening in certain types of business. Claims involving suspected arson or insurance fraud are typically reported to regional and home office personnel because of their sensitive nature. Regional or home office claim personnel can respond by extending the authority to settle the loss, by giving authority to deny a claim, or by suggesting further investigation or documentation before a decision is made. Summarized reports have captioned headings, which usually specify the information indicated in the Summarized Claim Report exhibit. See the exhibit "Summarized Claim Report."

The Investigation Report exhibit shows another format, which is more concise and very effective. See the exhibit "Investigation Report."

Step 5: Determining Cause of Loss and Extent of Damage

After an adjuster has completed his or her investigation, a decision as to the cause of loss and extent of loss must be made. Using the investigation as a basis for an opinion, the adjuster must communicate to the insured whether the loss was caused by a covered cause of loss and, if it was, how much of the loss is recoverable. Negotiations as to the extent of the loss often occur at this time.

Summarized Claim Report

Insured:_____   Date of Report: _____

Policy No.: _____   Adjustment Firm: _____

Date of Loss: _____   Adjuster: _____

Producer: _____

1.   Assignment Date

Give date notice of loss received and how.

Give date insured first contacted and how (phone or personal).

2.   Enclosures

List items attached (photos, estimates, fire/police reports, etc.).

3.   Activity Requested

List special request (expense payments, coverage questions, etc.).

4.   Suggested Reserves

Suggested reserves should be shown net, by coverage, after any advances.

Show scheduled items separately.

Example: Cov. A $22,000
                      Cov. C   10,000

5.   Abstract of Coverage

Give forms applicable and amounts; state deductibles; identify other contributing insurance, if any; identify any limiting clauses.

6.   Ownership/Encumbrances

List title holder, mortgagee, loss payees, additional named insureds, contract sellers, and liens. Indicate source of information. Also include opinion as to current solvency, cash flow, receipts.

7.   Location and Cause of Loss

Give date-time-place of loss. State cause as determined by authorities. If an outside expert has been employed, identify that expert and give his or her findings. State the adjuster's opinion.

8.   Insured/Employee Version of Loss

Give insured's version—indicate if statement was secured. Indicate manager, guards, and service personnel on premises at time of loss.

9. Witness's Version of Loss

Give witness's version—indicate if statement(s) secured. Indicate other parties present at time of loss.

10. Scope of Loss/Estimates of Damage

Describe property insured. Detail extent of damage. Cover any problems that might be encountered in reaching a settlement. List estimates received. Has an agreement been reached with the insured as to scope and procedures?

11. Salvage/Subrogation

Identify salvage, and give estimate of worth. Give details on your theory of subrogation and what steps have been taken to protect our interests.

12. Work To Be Done/Forecast of Closing

Itemize work to be done. Give your forecast of closing. Estimate hours needed for completion of each step.

13. Risk

Give your impression of the risk.

14. Remarks

Give comments on assistance of insured or insured's employees in completing investigation. Identify attorney or public adjuster if involved.

DATE OF NEXT REPORT

[DA03889]

Step 6: Concluding the Loss Adjustment

When the adjuster has compiled the documentation and all of the adjuster's questions have been answered, the adjuster should assemble the claim and submit it to the insurer for review and for advice as to settlement authority. In many cases, the claim is submitted to the insurer in the form of a statement of loss. This statement is an accounting overview of the adjustment. It is generally a three-column listing that tells the value of the property, the amount of loss to the property, and the amount claimed under the policy. The exhibit shows an example of a statement of loss. The statement should clearly indicate what the recommended payment is and why that figure is appropriate. The adjuster should also attach all supporting documents (so that the examiners can see where the figures came from) and should also outline the proposed adjustments in the closing report. See the exhibit "Statement of Loss."

Investigation Report

INSURED:

COVERAGE:

FACTS OF LOSS:

ORIGIN AND CAUSE:

OFFICIAL REPORTS:

COINSURANCE:

EMERGENCY REPAIRS OR ADVANCES:

SCOPE OF LOSS OR EXTENT OF LOSS:

A.   Structure

B.   Contents, equipment, or merchandise

C.   ALE or business income losses

SUGGESTED RESERVES:

RISK ADVICE:

FURTHER HANDLING/WORK TO BE DONE:

Attachments:

[DA03890]

Statement of Loss

	Value	Loss	Claim
One-story bowling alley, masonry-constructed building			
Repairs to vandalism damage.			
Remove and replace solid core door w/three lights, framing, and paint to lounge.			
Remove and replace hollow core door and paint to liquor storage room.			
Remove and replace exterior metal double-door set and paint.			
Remove and replace door to manager's office.			
Repair door, frame, and paint to diner area.			
Repair door, frame, and paint to service area.			
Remove and replace door, frame, and paint to storage room.			
Emergency repairs by Argo locksmith			
Safe:			
Repair dial.			
Repair corner of safe.			
Repair cement pier.			
Total loss			
Deductible			
Net claim			
Value, Loss, and Claim			

[DA03891]

Closing, or final, reports are made whenever the adjuster has completed the assignment by claim settlement or denial or whenever the adjuster's claims handling has been discontinued or transferred to another adjuster. Some final reports use preprinted forms that can be simple memoranda. These reports might include recommendations regarding subrogation, advice to the underwriting department, and suggestions or requests for further administrative handling within the office.

PUBLIC ADJUSTERS

Property loss adjusters can expect public adjusters, contractors, service providers, and certain experts to be involved in adjusting many claims.

Public adjusters are active in some states and metropolitan areas. They help insureds present claims to insurers for a fee. Although some claims lead to disputes between public adjusters and insurer-employed adjusters, the goal of both is the proper adjustment of the insured's claim.

Public adjuster

An outside organization or person hired by an insured to represent the insured in a claim in exchange for a fee.

Public Adjusters' Role

Public adjusters are most often involved in presenting fire claims to insurers, but they also handle property claims caused by flood, water, wind, burglary, and theft. The fee for their services is typically 10 to 15 percent of the amount paid under the policy.

Public adjusters perform many of the duties required of insureds in presenting and documenting claims. They analyze the scene and prepare a scope of the loss and damages, prepare inventories, and obtain repair or reconstruction estimates in connection with personal property and structure losses. They also assist insureds in documenting and presenting claims for loss of earnings, business interruption, and loss of rent. Finally, they are involved in settlement negotiations and sometimes act as appraisers when differences arise regarding the amount recoverable in accordance with policy conditions. Because of public adjusters' knowledge of property policies and experience in claims, they can help insureds by:

- Presenting claims in an organized manner, which may expedite settlement
- Compiling and documenting claims to fulfill the insured's obligations under the policy and to allow the insured to focus on other tasks
- Reassuring the insured that the claim settlement is fair

Because most states require public adjusters to be licensed, they meet certain minimum qualifications based on experience and education. Most public adjusters have worked as property adjusters for one or more insurers. They generally have extensive knowledge of property policies and insurers' claims procedures. Many public adjusting firms belong to the National Association of Public Insurance Adjusters (NAPIA). The association was founded in 1951 and seeks to establish ethical and professional standards for representing insureds before insurers.

Dealing With Public Adjusters

Public adjusters can help or hinder efficient claims processing, depending on the adjuster or public adjusting firm with whom the insurer is dealing and the claim's circumstances. Problems with public adjusters are usually related to how public adjusters procure business from insureds and the manner in which they evaluate and present claims for insureds.

Public adjusters may obtain business by monitoring police and fire calls and appearing on the scene immediately after a loss. Unfortunately, some public adjusters take advantage of the insured's vulnerable position by stating or implying that the claims handling process is highly technical and legalistic. They might also cause the insured to distrust the insurer by indicating that a fair settlement cannot be reached unless a public adjuster is retained. The insured's resulting anxiety might cause him or her to hire a public adjuster. Most insurance company adjusters proceed in good faith and do not treat insureds in an overly legalistic or unfair manner.

Public adjusters are usually paid a percentage of the amount paid to the insured by the insurer. This fee arrangement may encourage some public adjusters to overstate or exaggerate, and in some cases to misrepresent, the extent and/or amount of loss to increase the amount of recovery. For example, disputes might occur over the cost to repair or replace structures. Public adjusters also may submit bids from contractors who routinely work with them, which can make reaching an agreement on scope and price more difficult.

During claims adjusting, some public adjusters resist or delay the submission of documentation, books and records, and inventories, and object to other requests to which the insurer is entitled under the policy. Such public adjusters must be reminded that compliance with all policy conditions is a prerequisite to payment. Public adjusters might also appear at examinations under oath to try to object to questions posed to the insureds by claims personnel and the insurer's attorneys even though they have no contractual or other legal right to do so.

Claims involving public adjusters should be handled no differently than if an insurer-employed adjuster were dealing directly with the insured, meaning expediently and professionally.

VERIFICATION OF LOSSES

Every investigation should determine the facts about what caused the loss, how coverage applies, and the amount of the loss.

Taking a statement from the insured serves to establish the insured's version as to ownership of the property, the cause of loss, the facts surrounding the loss, and the extent of loss, and to determine whether any third party is responsible for the loss.

For loss to personal property, the documentation an adjuster might expect to receive from an insured includes bills, purchase receipts, charge card records or monthly statements, photos, appraisals, instruction manuals, or warranty paperwork.

Statements of the Insured and Witnesses

The insured's statement is often waived in connection with smaller or uncomplicated claims; the facts of a loss are typically clear, and coverage applies. In larger or more complicated losses, especially those involving a coverage question or suspected insurance fraud, the insured's statement is an essential part of the investigation.

The statement's purposes are to establish the property's ownership, the cause of loss and facts surrounding the loss, and the extent of loss, and also to determine for subrogation purposes whether any third party is responsible for the loss. Statements can either be written or recorded. The statement usually follows this format:

1. The identity of the insured

2. The ownership of, or interest in, the property

3. The existence of other insurance

4. The existence of mortgages or encumbrances

5. The facts and cause of the loss, including the insured's location at the time, the presence of any witnesses, and the involvement of the police or the fire department

6. A description of the damaged property, including the nature and extent of the loss or damage to personal and real property, plus information regarding other losses that the policy might cover, such as loss of rent or business income loss

7. The establishment of a basis for subrogation, including identifying individuals or organizations who might be responsible for the damage

Some property loss adjusters use statement outlines, which can be useful guides, but they should not be the sole source of questions. They can be too restrictive to resolve a particular claim's problems. Additionally, a statement outline can cause the adjuster to fail to ask appropriate follow-up questions to an unusual or a curious statement. The adjuster must review the initial report and analyze all of the information at hand, including the policy, and should formulate areas of investigation or specific questions that fit the particular claim.

In some states or jurisdictions, obtaining a statement might waive the insurer's rights to an examination of the insured under oath; it might also waive the required filing by the insured of a sworn statement in a proof of loss. This waiver is based on the theory that the insurer has been fully informed of all the information that would normally be supplied by compliance with these conditions. A nonwaiver agreement avoids the problem of waiving any conditions. The adjuster should incorporate into the insured's statement the insured's understanding that the insurer will or might require the insured's full compliance with the policy conditions.

The adjuster needs witness statements when gathering information regarding the cause of loss, especially if fraud is suspected. Statements also give the adjuster information regarding the potential for subrogation. Witnesses can be identified through official reports, information provided by the insured or the agent, and by a witness canvass. A witness canvass involves contacting residents of the neighborhood, people living around the insured's residence, or persons or businesses surrounding the loss location. In making such contacts, the adjuster must avoid any comments implying that the insured was responsible for the loss. The adjuster should fully identify him or herself, state that the purpose of the contact is to locate anyone with knowledge regarding the occurrence, and obtain a statement when appropriate. Whether or not the witness canvass is helpful should be recorded in the file to document the adjuster's activity and the insurer's good-faith investigation.

Documentation

Adjusters must document the extent of loss or damage for these reasons:

- To identify the property for coverage and possible coinsurance concerns
- To inform the insurer of the magnitude of the loss so that proper case reserves can be established
- To establish the cost of repairs or replacement for ultimate settlement
- To avoid disputes with the insured as to the amount payable
- To assist contractors in preparing bids for repair or reconstruction

Documenting a loss can involve gathering records, photographing and videotaping the loss site, drawing floor plans and diagrams, preparing scopes of the damage and estimates, preparing inventories, and reviewing financial records. The type of documentation required varies depending on the type of loss. Most insurers have claims handling guidelines that outline the many possible ways to document a loss.

Records

Books and records are useful in documenting loss to stock, inventory, and personal property. In most cases, the insured does not have all the information that the adjuster needs at the first meeting. The insured must often organize and submit bills or invoices to substantiate purchases and values later. Complete loss inventories also take time. The adjuster can help the insured by explaining specifically what is needed. For example, in a theft from a residence, some of the documentation that the adjuster might request includes bills or purchase receipts for the claimed items. If these are not available, a credit card record or monthly statement can prove the existence and ownership of the property, its age, and its purchase price. Photo albums can also help. A photograph might show a stolen television set in the background. If jewelry is involved, an appraisal might be available. For higher-value items, obtaining a copy of the receipt from the retailer might be possible. If an appliance is missing, the instruction manual or warranty paperwork might be available.

Photography and Videotaping

During the initial property inspection, photos should be taken or videotapes should be made to document the type of property, the nature and extent of the damage, the presence or absence of damage to the structure and contents, and the types of construction material used, as well as the overall condition of the premises. The number of pictures that the adjuster takes depends on the size of the loss. More pictures probably need to be taken in a large loss.

As to the structure, the adjuster should start by taking pictures of the exterior of the building or residence, including the roof in appropriate cases, and by photographing all sides. The adjuster should then move to the interior, usually starting with the main entrance to the building or residence, and take enough photos in each room to document the damage.

The photos of the structure might include pictures of the contents, merchandise, and equipment. Close-ups of the damaged property might be necessary. Extremely close photography is sometimes needed to depict nameplates with an item's manufacturer's name, model, and serial number. Documenting the absence of damage is not always warranted unless the adjuster receives some indication from the insured that a dispute will arise or when the insured claims damage that appears to be the result of wear and tear, deterioration, or something other than the reported cause of loss.

With videotaping, the adjuster should document the same items and structures, moving in the same pattern as in photography, and add narration that includes the date, identifying information, and comments regarding the videotaped property.

Adjuster Tip—When photographing or videotaping a loss site, an adjuster should include a ruler or a yardstick in the shot to indicate property's size and scale.

Floor Plans and Diagrams

Diagrams and floor plans are helpful in depicting a structure's size, the areas affected by damage, and the extent of the damage. Diagrams enable the adjuster to calculate repair costs and inform the insurer of the extent of loss. In smaller losses, the entire structure is not normally diagrammed, but for larger losses, a complete floor plan is essential. An example of a floor plan prepared for a kitchen grease fire appears in the exhibit. See the exhibit "Example of a Floor Plan."

The adjuster typically starts by measuring and diagraming the structure's entire exterior perimeter. The adjuster then measures the interior rooms, usually noting the amount of damage on a scope sheet as well as each room's measurements. In addition to a floor plan diagram, side elevation diagrams are sometimes drawn to illustrate gable ends and unusual or oddly shaped structures so that repair costs can be estimated.

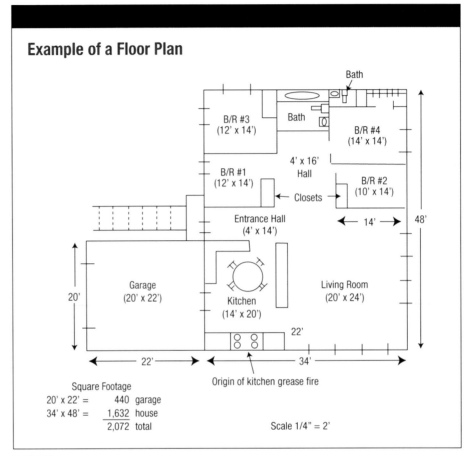

Example of a Floor Plan

[DA03898]

Scope and Estimate

A **scope** or scope sheet is a list of the areas damaged, which includes the type
of damage, a description of the proposed type of repairs, and the measurements of those areas. The exhibit shows an example of a scope sheet for a
kitchen grease fire. See the exhibit "Example of a Scope Sheet."

A preliminary scope is normally provided to the insurer with initial reports,
but it is also commonly provided to contractors who have been asked to
submit repair or reconstruction bids. The preliminary scope allows the contractor to prepare a bid that covers the same items as the adjuster's scope.

Property loss adjusters can also use the scope to prepare an estimate that
they can then use for proper reserving, to reach agreement directly with the
insured when contractors' bids are not required, and to compare with contractors' bids when appropriate. In the last case, a line-by-line comparison
of items can be made to ensure that the contractors have included all of the
areas requiring repairs and to confirm that the contractor's cost of repair is
fair and reasonable. If the contractor's repair costs appear to be too high or
too low, the adjuster could discuss that particular item with the contractor

Example of a Scope Sheet

Property Loss Worksheet

Page No. _____1_____   Claim No. _____524 BL 101_____

Preliminary Estimate ___10/19/20XX___   Insured _____J. Smith_____

Final Estimate _____Date_____   Claimant _____Insured_____

Date   M. Boyer

        Adjuster

1 Item	2 Description	3 Quantity	4 Units	5 Unit price	6 Cost	7	8	9
			Age	Orig. cost	Repl. cost	Deprec.	A.C.V.	Loss & Damage
1.	Permit (if required)							
2.	Demolition							
	Remove range hood							
	Remove cabinets (4 LF)							
	Remove drywall (above cabinet) (5' × 10' = 50 SF)							
	Remove Formica countertop (12 LF) (est. 2 men × 5 hrs. = 10 hrs.)							
3.	Cartage							
	1 pickup & driver (1.5 hrs.)							
	Dump fee ($10.00)							
4.	Clean range (est. 1.5 hrs.)							
5.	Install new range hood (Sears 30", est. 1 hr.)							
6.	Install upper cabinets Paint grade plywood of 4 LF × 3' tall (est. 1.5 hrs.)							
7.	New Formica countertop							

	Property Loss Worksheet
Page No. _____2_____	Claim No. _____524 BL 101_____
Preliminary Estimate _____10/19/20XX_____	Insured _____J. Smith_____
Final Estimate _____Date_____	Claimant _____Insured_____
Date	M. Boyer
	Adjuster

1 Item	2 Description	3 Quantity	4 Units	5 Unit price	6 Cost	7	8	9
		Age	Orig. cost	Repl. cost	Deprec.	A.C.V.		Loss & Damage
8.	Drywall (above range) 5' × 10' = 50 sq. ft. Tape and texture (splatter finish)							
9.	Painting							
	Kitchen — wash and paint (14' × 8') × 2 = 224 SF (20' × 8') × 2 = 320 SF 1 coat high gloss latex 2 coats on new cabinets							
	Living Room — wash and paint 1 coat flat latex (20' × 8') × 2 = 320 SF (24' × 8') × 2 = 384 SF							
	Entrance Hall (4' × 8') = 32 SF (14' × 8') × 2 = 224 SF							
10.	Shampoo carpets LR and halls (200 sq. yds.)							
11.	Clean vinyl tile in kitchen (280 SF)							
12.	Clean furniture (per estimate)							
13.	Contractor overhead & profit (OH/P 15% or 20%)							

[DA03899]

and adjust the cost up or down. The goal is to achieve an agreement with the contractor or contractors so that settlement can be reached with the insured.

Inventory

After the insured understands what information is required to support the claim and after a timetable has been set for submitting the evidence, the adjuster must examine the damaged property. An inventory should be taken and should include as much pertinent information about the property as is available. The property's manufacturer, serial and model numbers, size, color, age, and pre-loss condition are all helpful in determining value. The adjuster should note any property that might be obsolete or no longer available. To the insured, these items might have had some value, but they have relatively low actual cash value.

USE OF EXPERTS IN CLAIMS SITUATIONS

Experts are commonly used to determine facts, to verify the extent of loss or damage, and to estimate the value of loss to real and personal property. The ultimate purpose of using experts is to assist the adjuster in determining whether and to what extent coverage should apply, that is, whether the claim is payable and how much should be paid. In subrogation cases, experts are consulted to ascertain and establish facts that would show whether the insurer has the right to seek reimbursement from a third party for the amount paid on the loss.

Several types of experts can be used in connection with the adjustment of property losses. They include origin and cause experts, private investigators, accountants, restoration specialists, salvors, attorneys, engineers, architects, appraisers, and contractors. Any conflicts of interest among the adjuster, the insured, and any experts should be avoided.

Origin and Cause Experts

Origin and cause experts have an extensive background in fire science and arson investigation. They determine whether a fire was accidental or intentionally started and the identity of the person, organization, or entity that might have been responsible for the fire. The origin and cause expert's work includes investigating the scene at which the loss occurred and sometimes contacting witnesses. Private investigators and engineers can assist origin and cause experts when such expertise is required.

Origin and cause experts
Experts who independently determine how and where a fire began.

Private Investigators

Private investigators are typically employed when insurance fraud is suspected. They can also be used in connection with other intensive investigations. In most states, they must be licensed. They have the knowledge and skills required to obtain information for their clients from witnesses, public records, and law enforcement agencies. Insurers can use the information gathered by private investigators to reach coverage decisions, determine whether insurance fraud is being attempted, and document potential subrogation. Private investigators can work with origin and cause experts to establish facts that would determine whether an insured or someone at the insured's direction is guilty of arson. In personal property losses, private investigators can contact witnesses and retailers to confirm ownership. Generally, private investigators can be employed to ascertain the facts related to the insurance or the claim.

Accountants

Adjusters should have some knowledge of accounting, especially in connection with the handling of business losses. Nevertheless, accountants specializing in claims and legal matters are occasionally needed to resolve financial issues related to property claims. Claims accountants are often used to verify the extent of business merchandise or stock losses as well as business interruption losses. An accountant can help resolve cases in which the insured might have overstated or exaggerated the amount of a loss in the claim. Accountants can also determine the financial condition of the insured's business and whether the insured actually had the funds to purchase the property that was purportedly stolen or destroyed. For example, an insured might claim that a large amount of property was purchased within six months to a year before the date of loss. An accountant, using books and records and sometimes testimony obtained through an examination under oath (EUO), can determine whether the insured had the funds to purchase the items claimed to have been destroyed or stolen.

Restoration Specialists

Restoration specialists are firms specializing in cleaning structures, equipment, stock, merchandise, and personal property following a loss caused by fire, smoke, water, windstorm, or another peril. Property loss adjusters usually consult restoration specialists immediately after receiving the initial report so that steps can be taken to limit the amount of damage and protect the property from further damage. Household goods, personal property, merchandise, stock, and equipment are often moved to a restoration firm's plant or warehouse for further processing and cleaning. The removal of such items also facilitates the structure's cleaning, repair, and reconstruction. Restoration specialists can remove, clean, and dry carpets that have been damaged by smoke or water; they also clean and prepare interior walls and floors for painting and other repair work.

Salvors

Specialists who separate damaged merchandise from undamaged merchandise, prepare inventories of damaged and destroyed property, and establish values of damaged or destroyed business property.

Salvors

Salvors are mainly used in connection with business losses to separate damaged from undamaged merchandise, supplies, and equipment; to prepare inventories of damaged and destroyed property; and to establish values of damaged or destroyed business property. They can also inventory the entire stock of merchandise or supplies so that the insurer can determine whether a coinsurance penalty should apply or to confirm that the claimed amount of loss (by theft or burglary, for example) is accurate. Salvors are also employed to sell salvage or, by arrangement, to purchase salvage. Salvors are rarely used on homeowners claims except when the amount of loss is large.

Attorneys

Attorneys commonly provide advice and counsel to insurers on coverage issues and on investigations of complex claims. Insurers often retain attorneys to help direct investigations. They might conduct an investigation by formally requesting the insured's books and records and by conducting EUOs in these circumstances:

• Coverage might be in question

• The amount of loss payable is in dispute

• Insurance fraud is suspected

Attorneys provide accountants with copies of books and financial records as well as transcripts of testimony given during an EUO so that coverage and settlement disputes can be resolved. Attorneys also offer legal opinions and make recommendations to insurers regarding a claim's ultimate disposition. Of course, attorneys can also file suit on the behalf of the insurer to pursue subrogation, to resolve coverage disputes through declaratory relief actions, and to defend insurers against suits by insureds.

Engineers

Electrical engineers, mechanical engineers, and other engineers are occasionally needed to resolve issues related to the cause of loss. However, they are usually employed to document for subrogation purposes whether a third party or manufacturer is responsible for a fire or another cause of loss. An electrical engineer, for example, is sometimes used along with an origin and cause expert to establish whether a fire was accidental or whether it was caused by a defective or malfunctioning electrical device.

Architects

Architects are sometimes needed to draw plans and provide specifications for partial and complete reconstruction of structures. Plans are needed so that contractors can calculate accurate estimates or bids and can obtain remodeling or building permits. Architects can also be consulted to formulate engineering specifications for special equipment.

Appraisers

Appraisers are needed to establish the value of personal property, merchandise, equipment, and real property for settlement or for resolving disputes about the amount of loss. An appraiser can be anyone who has specialized knowledge of the kinds of property involved and their values. Some might be certified as appraisers in certain fields by professional organizations, such as the International Society of Appraisers. Others, such as real estate appraisers, are usually licensed by the state in which they do business. In connection with fire and windstorm claims, real estate appraisers can establish structures' actual cash value (usually the market value).

Contractors

Building contractors are often asked, sometimes on an emergency basis, to repair structures damaged by fire, water, windstorm, and other covered perils. However, in a dispute over the amount payable, building contractors can also act as appraisers.

Conflicts of Interest

Conflicts of interest can arise between an expert, an adjuster, and/or an insured whenever anyone receives gratuities or when a relationship is so close that there is an appearance of impropriety. When an appraiser (the expert) is needed to establish the amount recoverable in connection with a fire loss, that appraiser, whether a contractor or an antique dealer, should be impartial. The word "impartial" means that any appraiser must not be closely related to, a friend of, or economically dependent on, the insurer, insured, or adjuster. If the appraiser is not impartial and a conflict of interest exists, the appraisal award might not be binding and might be voided by either party unless the other party agrees to waive any objection before the proceedings. Therefore, the adjuster must choose experts carefully and keep the relationship on a professional level.

SUBROGATION AND REINSURANCE

After a loss adjustment is complete, the adjuster must conscientiously pursue the insurer's right of recovery against any responsible third party and report the claim settlement properly and adequately. In addition to conducting the loss adjustment process, adjusters must be able to deny claims and deal with reinsurance, depending on the details of a claim.

An insurer that pays a covered claim has the right, to the extent of the payment, to seek reimbursement and recover the amount paid from a third party who is legally liable for the loss or damage. This is called the right of **subrogation**. The insurer is said to be subrogated to the rights of the insured who is the party who would normally have the right to receive payment for damages. Subrogation is the substitution of one person or entity for another in a claim.

A property loss adjuster needs to recognize when a policy is subject to reinsurance so that the proper notices and reports can be distributed.

Subrogation

The process by which an insurer can, after it has paid a loss under the policy, recover the amount paid from any party (other than the insured) who caused the loss or is otherwise legally liable for the loss.

Subrogation

Subrogation rights are established by insurance policies and by law. Included in insurance policies are provisions regarding (1) the insured's role in the subrogation, (2) the waiver of subrogation, and (3) the subrogation's amount. The insurer's right to subrogation is established and expressed in the policy under a condition entitled "Transfer Of Rights Of Recovery Against Others To Us." This condition is often referred to as the subrogation clause. This clause or provision is listed in the conditions of all property insurance policies. For example, the transfer of rights of recovery clause of the ISO commercial property conditions reads:

> If any person or organization to or for whom we make payment under this Coverage Part has rights to recover damages from another, those rights are transferred to us to the extent of our payment. That person or organization must do everything necessary to secure our rights and must do nothing after loss to impair them. But you may waive your rights against another party in writing:
>
> **1.** Prior to a loss to your Covered Property or Covered Income.
>
> **2.** After a loss to your Covered Property or Covered Income only if, at time of loss, that party is one of the following:
>
> **a.** Someone insured by this insurance;
>
> **b.** A business firm;
>
> **(1)** Owned or controlled by you; or,
>
> **(2)** That owns or controls you; or
>
> **c.** Your tenant.
>
> This will not restrict your insurance.[1]

Additionally, the insurer has a right of subrogation implied in law regardless of whether the policy expresses such a provision.

Insured's Role in Subrogation

Most subrogation clauses require the insured to cooperate with the insurer by executing assignment of rights to the insurer, also known as a subrogation agreement. The sworn statement in proof of loss often contains the subrogation agreement, or assignment. Additionally, the subrogation agreement typically requires the insured to give testimony and appear in court, when necessary, so that the insurer can establish the legal basis to recover.

An insured might breach the subrogation condition by impairing or interfering with the insurer's right of subrogation, by failing to cooperate in preserving evidence, by giving or failing to give testimony, or by releasing the responsible party from any liability following the loss. In case of a breach by the insured, the insurer would have a right to collect damages from the insured in the amount that would have been recoverable from the responsible third party.

Some policies permit the insured to waive rights of recovery *before a loss.* In those cases, the insurer waives its right of subrogation. Lease agreements between landlords and tenants typically contain waivers of liability or subrogation. Construction contracts often contain waivers of subrogation clauses in them. The insured might also release a third party before a loss in connection with bailment situations. For example, if the insured has placed personal property in the custody of other parties as a condition of the bailment, the insured might be required to waive the claim or release liability. If the insurer has not permitted a release of liability by the insured before a loss and the insured has executed a release or waiver before a loss, the insurer will not be liable for the loss claimed under the policy. It is very important for the adjuster to determine early in the loss adjustment process whether waivers of subrogation have been granted.

Amount of Subrogation

The insurer has the right to receive only the amount that it has paid. The insurer would have no right of recovery for losses that the insured absorbs because of lack of coverage, exclusions, or limitations of coverage under the policy. Thus, both the insurer and insured might have rights to recover damages against a responsible third party or parties. When insureds absorb only a deductible amount, insurers commonly pursue recovery of that deductible amount on their behalf.

The decision to pursue subrogation usually includes consideration of the cost involved and the likelihood of success. This is especially true if litigation is needed to pursue subrogation. Therefore, there may be times when the insurer decides that pursuing subrogation is not cost-effective. However, the insurer's decision does not preclude the insured from pursuing a third party for the unpaid portions of his or her claim.

Typical Claims Situations

Property loss adjusters encounter many situations in daily claims handling in which a third party is legally liable for damages, such as these:

- Negligent operation or malfunctioning of equipment, such as automobiles, trucks, heavy equipment, and airplanes
- Fire, explosion, and water losses caused by the negligence of tenants occupying apartments or business complexes
- Fire, explosion, and water losses caused by construction workers at a building site or adjacent to a structure
- Losses resulting from poor workmanship of contractors or subcontractors that occur after work has been completed, such as malfunctioning sprinklers or alarms
- Losses caused by defective or poorly designed products such as electrical appliances

- Water and fire losses caused by owners or landlords failing to maintain plumbing and heating systems
- Losses caused by a government entity's failure to properly maintain public works, such as sewer and water systems
- Losses caused by a utility company's negligent installation of, or failure to maintain, gas and electrical lines

All of these situations have the potential for subrogation. The likelihood of success depends on the thoroughness of the claims investigation and the existence of contract provisions that might negate the pursuit of subrogation.

Preservation of Evidence

During the initial investigation into the cause of a loss, the adjuster should be mindful of potential avenues of subrogation. After a potentially responsible third party is identified, the adjuster should investigate this part of the loss at the same time that the insured's loss is being investigated. This ensures that evidence will not be discarded or destroyed.

Preserving evidence for use in subrogation proceedings and subsequent litigation is an important aspect of claims investigation. Without the physical evidence of the cause of the loss, the chances of successfully pursuing a subrogation claim against a third party are significantly diminished.[2] An insurer can be denied recovery if evidence is intentionally or negligently lost or destroyed. Similarly, an insurer defending a first-party coverage suit might be found liable if evidence is intentionally or negligently lost or destroyed. This is often referred to as spoliation of evidence. The property owner, the adjuster, and the origin and cause expert share the responsibility for preserving evidence.

Use of Experts and Attorneys in Subrogation

Property loss adjusters must recognize claims situations that have subrogation potential and must take steps to document the right to recovery through the use of experts, whenever warranted. Experts can be employed to gather and preserve evidence, to analyze and report on the cause of loss, and to testify in litigated cases. Any expert retained should have a set protocol for collecting and preserving evidence.

If an expert is not hired, then it will be the adjuster's responsibility to collect and preserve the evidence. It is advisable to get the property owner's permission in writing before taking any evidence from the scene. Photographs or a videotape should be taken of the evidence as it is found. This should document the surrounding area as well. Evidence collected should be clearly marked with the date and time of collection, where it was found, and by whom. Evidence should be stored in a clear container and kept in a locked storage area or compartment. Care should be taken if evidence must be refrigerated or heated. On some losses, many parties will be interested in the evidence. Whenever an adjuster takes possession or relinquishes possession of a piece of evidence, a written receipt should document the transfer of possession, and each party should retain a copy.[3]

After a coverage suit or subrogation action has ended, the evidence may be disposed of as long as no other litigation is pending. If the property owner's permission was given to take the evidence, the owner should be given notice that it will be destroyed. If other litigation is pending, then all interested parties should be advised that the evidence will be disposed of on a specific date and allowed the opportunity to take possession of the evidence. If an interested party requests that the evidence not be destroyed but does not wish to take possession of it, the insurer could recover reasonable storage fees.

In larger losses, attorneys might be enlisted from the start to help coordinate and direct the adjuster, investigators, and experts. After a loss is paid, an attorney can evaluate the evidence that has been gathered and give opinions on which party or parties should be pursued to recover the amount paid. The attorney can also handle the litigation. Many law firms specialize in subrogation; they typically handle cases on a contingent-fee basis for a percentage of the recovery, plus expenses.

Intercompany Arbitration

When an individual or another responsible party has liability insurance, the first-party insurer who has paid a loss can present a subrogation claim for payment. In most cases, the liability insurer responds by paying the entire loss or by making an offer to compromise on the claim, depending on how the liability insurer assesses liability. When liability is questioned, arbitration can resolve disputes between the insurers.

Many insurers are members or signatories of the Property Subrogation Arbitration Agreement, which appears in the exhibit. This agreement was created by Arbitration Forums, Inc., so that insurers would have a means of resolving subrogation matters without resorting to litigation. A local office of Arbitration Forums, Inc., can advise an adjuster whether another company subscribes to this agreement. That agreement is a mandatory arbitration program for certain claims. Member insurers must use arbitration when liability or the amount payable is in dispute. It is not used to resolve coverage issues between insurers. The main benefits of the arbitration program are the savings in litigation expenses and the quick resolution of disputes. See the exhibit "Property Subrogation Arbitration Rules and Agreement."

Intercompany arbitration is accomplished by having the arbitrator(s) review the written submissions of the applicant (the party who applied for arbitration) and the respondent (the party who must respond to the applicant's allegations). Although it is possible to present the case in person, it does not often occur that way. Therefore, the claims material presented should be legible and in chronological order. The arbitration file should be self-explanatory, but it is a good practice to highlight or tab specific documents for the arbitrator's benefit. A well-written arbitration statement, outlining the party's

Property Subrogation Arbitration Rules and Agreement

WHEREAS, it is the object of companies which are now or may hereafter be signatories to arbitrate disputes among themselves, the undersigned hereby accepts and binds itself to the following Articles of Agreement for the arbitration of property damage claims arising from fire and losses other than automobile:

ARTICLE FIRST

Signatory companies are bound to forego litigation and in place thereof submit to arbitration any questions or disputes which may arise from:

(a) any fire subrogation or property damage claim not in excess of $100,000;

(b) any extended coverage subrogation or self-insured additional extended coverage claim not in excess of $100,000;

(c) any additional extended coverage subrogation or self-insured additional extended coverage claim not in excess of $100,000;

(d) any inland marine subrogation or self-insured inland marine claim not in excess of $100,000;

(e) any first party property subrogation or self-insured claim not in excess of $100,000 that is not within the compulsory provisions of other industry inter-company arbitration agreements, except for subrogation or self-insured claims arising from accidents on waters subject to the International Rules of the Road, the United States Inland Rules of the Road, or the Great Lakes and Western Rivers Rules of the Road, provided the accident occurs on a body of water within the geographic limits of one state.

This Article shall not apply to:

(a) any claim for the enforcement of which a lawsuit was instituted prior to, and is pending, at the time this Agreement is signed;

(b) any claim as to which a company asserts a defense of lack of coverage on grounds other than

　(1) delayed notice

　(2) no notice

　(3) noncooperation;

(c) subrogation claims involving policies written under Retrospective Rating Plans, Comprehensive Insurance Rating Plans, or War Risk Rating Plans unless prior written consent is obtained from the companies in interest.

ARTICLE SECOND

Any controversy, including policy coverage and interpretations, between or among signatory companies involving any claim or other matter relating thereto and not included in Article First hereof or which involves amounts in excess of those stated therein may also be submitted to arbitration under this Agreement with the prior consent of the parties.

For matters within Article First, if the law on the issue is in doubt and has not been interpreted by the courts of the jurisdiction, a party to the controversy may petition AF's Board of Directors to authorize the disputing party to proceed through litigation rather than arbitration. The Board's validation will be influenced by effect on the industry through litigation to clarify the law. The decision to waive the mandatory provisions of the Agreement and proceed through litigation will be at the sole discretion of the Board.

ARTICLE THIRD

Arbitration Forums Inc. representing signatory companies is authorized:

(a) to make appropriate rules and regulations for the presentation and determination of controversies under this Agreement;

(b) to select the places where arbitration facilities are to be available, and adopt a policy for the selection and appointment of arbitration panels;

(c) to prescribe territorial jurisdiction of arbitration panels;

(d) to make appropriate rules and regulations to apportion equitably among arbitrating companies the operating expenses of the arbitration program;

(e) to authorize and approve as signatories to this Agreement such insurance carriers, self-insurers or commercial insureds with large retentions as may be invited to participate in the arbitration program and also to compel the withdrawal of any signatory from the program for failure to conform with the Agreement or the rules and regulations issued thereunder.

ARTICLE FOURTH

Arbitration panels, appointed by AF from among full-time salaried representatives of signatory companies, shall function in the following manner:

(a) Arbitration panel members shall be selected on the basis of their experience and other qualifications. They shall serve without compensation;

(b) No panel member shall serve on a panel hearing a case in which his/her company is directly or indirectly interested, or in which he/she has an interest;

(c) the decision of the majority of an arbitration panel shall be final and binding upon the parties to the controversy without the right of rehearing or appeal.

ARTICLE FIFTH

Any signatory company may withdraw from this Agreement by notice in writing to Arbitration Forums Inc. Such withdrawal will become effective sixty (60) days after receipt of such notice except as to cases then pending before arbitration panels. The effective date of withdrawal as to such pending cases shall be upon final settlement.

Arbitration Forums website: www.arbfile.org/webapp/pgStatic/content/pgDownloadRules.jsp (15 July 2003).
[DA03904]

contentions, should accompany the file. Under the rules of intercompany arbitration, the decision of the arbitrator(s) is final and binding with no right of rehearing or appeal except under very limited circumstances, such as lack of jurisdiction.

Reinsurance

Many property risks are subject to reinsurance. Reinsurers assume the financial consequences of a loss otherwise payable by the original insurer. Each insurer has its own reinsurance procedures, by which it flags a policy as being subject to reinsurance. Each insurer also sets a dollar threshold for the amount of the loss that will require notice to the reinsurer. The property loss adjuster needs to recognize when a policy is subject to reinsurance so that the proper notices and reports can be distributed.

Notice to the reinsurer can be given in several ways. Many insurers set a threshold of 50 percent of the retention as the point at which the reinsurer needs to be given notice of a potential claim. The issue of who actually puts the reinsurer on notice can be handled in several different ways. The handling adjuster can put the reinsurer on notice, but most insurers have a reinsurance accounting department that performs this function. Insurers may have a flag on the policy in their underwriting and claims processing systems, which automatically notifies the reinsurance accounting department when a claim over a specified amount is set up. The reinsurance accounting department would then provide notice to the reinsurer.

Reinsurers have the right to participate in a claim's investigation and settlement. The adjuster may have to work with the reinsurer, or the reinsurer may be satisfied with periodic updates from the adjuster. Claim payments and reserve changes often trigger a request for an update on a loss. Because a fiduciary relationship exists between the insurer and the reinsurer, the adjuster must be prepared to share relevant information with the reinsurer.

ISSUING CLAIM PAYMENTS

After the claim has been concluded, the adjuster must issue the claim payment.

When making any payment, the adjuster must ensure that the proper parties are being paid. Because of the various parties who can have a financial interest in the property in addition to the insured, the adjuster must verify the payee before check issuance.

Before paying a large structural loss, a property loss adjuster must check whether any tax liens are on the property.

Payments

Claim payments are made either by check, draft, or electronic transfer. A **draft** is distinguished from a check by the fact that when it is presented to a bank to be cashed, the bank must verify that it is authorized for payment by the issuing entity before disbursing any funds. A draft is not a problem if the payee is merely trying to deposit the draft. Usually, the funds will not be available immediately. It does cause a problem for a payee who does not have a bank account in which to deposit the draft, because the funds are not immediately available. The timing of claim payments is an important issue. Many states have regulations regarding the time period in which an insurer issues a claim payment. Additionally, the policies themselves have a time frame for payment in them. The BPP states that payment must be issued within thirty days of receipt of a valid proof of loss and agreement with the insured as to the amount or receipt of an appraisal award. The HO-3 has a sixty-day time frame.

Property loss adjusters are often called on to make advance payments to an insured. These advance payments are usually issued to help the insured make repairs quickly or to resume business operations quickly. On large property losses, advance payments may go directly to a contractor or repair firm on the insured's behalf. When an advance payment is made, the insured should sign an **advance payment receipt** that acknowledges an understanding that the insured will have to pay the advance amount back if the loss is not a covered loss and that the payment is part of the overall loss.

A mortgage or finance company often has a financial interest in the property and appears as a payee in the policy. But not all potential payees are named in the policy. An adjuster must be aware that other parties not named in the policy may have an interest in the claim payment.

When the insured has assigned the policy proceeds to someone else, the adjuster must include that other party as a payee. One example of this is when the insured has retained a public adjuster or an attorney to represent the insured in the claim. The insured might also assign the claim's proceeds to a repair firm so that no delay occurs in the repair of the insured's vehicle or piece of equipment. When an assignment is made, the adjuster must be given notice of the assignment. This notice is usually in writing and supported by a copy of the contract between the parties.

Tax Liens

Before paying a large structural loss, a property loss adjuster must check whether any tax liens are on the property. Some states require that such checking be performed based on a dollar threshold, such as $5,000 for a homeowners loss and $25,000 for a commercial property loss. Also, many insurers' claims handling guidelines require checking for liens. If an adjuster fails to check for tax liens and makes a payment to the insured, the insurer may be forced to pay the outstanding tax lien as well. This would amount to a dupli-

Draft (check)

A type of commercial paper containing an unconditional order by the drawer (person making out the draft), requiring the drawee, usually a bank, to pay a certain sum to the payee or to the bearer.

Advance payment receipt

A document that helps keep track of payments made under certain coverages, helps comply with unfair claim practices laws, and clarifies to the insured that the advance payments will be applied against the final claim.

cate loss payment. Checking for tax liens can usually be accomplished at the local municipal hall or at county offices.

DENIAL OF A CLAIM

Not every claim is closed by payment. Adjusters are often called on to deny a claim because of lack of coverage or because of a breach of a policy condition. Many insurers have strict guidelines regarding claims denial, often requiring an underwriter and a claims manager to approve the issuance of a denial.

Before denying a claim, the adjuster must have thoroughly investigated the loss, carefully analyzed the coverage, and fairly and objectively evaluated the claim. The insured is usually given the benefit of any doubt or ambiguity in cases of questionable coverage. Internal guidelines for issuing a denial must be followed. If any of these criteria are missing, the adjuster may be found to have acted in bad faith.

Denial Letter's Contents

Upon receiving the authority to deny a claim, the property loss adjuster ensures that the denial letter is prepared on a timely basis. Denial letters are often drafted by attorneys to ensure compliance with that jurisdiction's legal requirements. Generally, a denial letter must state all the known reasons for the denial. Specific policy language should be quoted, and the location of the language in the policy should be cited, such as "p. 2 of 14 of the BPP, A. Coverage, 2. Property not covered, c. Automobiles held for sale." The policy provisions should then be related to the facts of the loss. Insureds who disagree with the denial should be invited to submit additional information that might cause the claim to be reevaluated. A general reservation of rights paragraph is also included in the letter.

Mailing Protocol

The denial letter should always be signed by the adjuster, even if an attorney drafts it. The adjuster who signs the letter is likely to be called as a witness in the event of a coverage lawsuit. Denial letters are usually sent by certified mail, return receipt requested, restricted to the addressee only. It is a good practice to also send the letter by regular mail, marked personal and confidential, in case the certified mail is not claimed. These procedures help ensure that the letter reaches the correct party. They also help insulate the adjuster from any allegation made by the insured that the letter is public defamation.

SUMMARY

The claims adjusting process begins when an insured, or his or her agent or broker, reports a loss to the insurer. The insurer acknowledges receipt of the loss and assigns an adjuster to it. The adjuster verifies coverage, reviews the policy, and contacts the insured to begin the investigation of the loss.

The six steps an adjuster follows to resolve a property claim are these:

1. Acknowledging receipt of the insured's report of loss and assigning the loss to an adjuster
2. Verifying coverage
3. Initiating contact with the insured
4. Investigating the facts
5. Determining the cause of loss and the extent of loss to insured property
6. Concluding the loss adjustment

The initial contact with the insured begins the investigation of the loss. The insured may be represented by a public adjuster. If that is the case, the public adjuster will do much of the work required to present the claim to the insurer. Public adjusters are usually paid a percentage of the amount of the claim settlement. This may lead some public adjusters to inflate the claim in an attempt to generate a higher fee. A property loss adjuster should handle a claim involving a public adjuster no differently than if the adjuster were dealing directly with the insured.

During the initial visit, the adjuster reviews the circumstances of the loss with the insured or the insured's representative and advises the insured of what steps will be necessary to investigate and document the loss. Following this initial contact, the adjuster investigates the loss in depth. The adjuster may take statements of the insured and witnesses, may examine books and records, may photograph or videotape the loss scene, may draw diagrams, and may create a scope of the loss.

It may be necessary to call in experts to help determine the cause of the loss or to help quantify the extent of the loss. Several types of experts can be used in connection with the adjustment of property losses. They include origin and cause experts, private investigators, accountants, restoration specialists, salvors, attorneys, engineers, architects, appraisers, and contractors.

During the investigation, the adjuster considers any potential source of subrogation against a third party. The adjuster will need to preserve evidence if it is determined that a responsible third party exists and it is cost-effective to attempt recovery.

Furthermore, during the course of the investigation, the adjuster prepares several reports. These reports serve to inform supervisors and managers about the loss. Other reports may be required if reinsurance is covering the loss.

After the investigation is completed, the adjuster concludes the loss adjustment and issues a final report. The loss can be concluded by payment or by a denial of the claim.

After an investigation is completed, the adjuster concludes the loss adjustment and issues a final report. The loss can be concluded by payment or by a denial of the claim.

ASSIGNMENT NOTES

1. Includes copyrighted material of Insurance Services Office, Inc., with its permission. Copyright, ISO Properties, Inc., 1983, 1987.

2. Brian Marx, "Preserve the Evidence," *Claims Quarterly*, 20, no. 1 (Feb. 2002), pp. 1–6.

3. Email of Michael P. Griffin, training specialist, Liberty Regional Agency Markets, Keene, N.H., November 2001.

Direct Your Learning ▶▶

4

Loss Investigation

Educational Objectives

After learning the content of this assignment, you should be able to:

▷ Describe the basic loss investigations for losses caused by fire.

▷ Describe the basic loss investigations for losses caused by smoke.

▷ Describe the basic loss investigations for losses caused by lightning.

▷ Describe the basic loss investigations for losses caused by explosion.

▷ Describe the basic loss investigations for losses caused by theft.

▷ Describe the basic loss investigations for losses caused by water damage.

▷ Explain the causes of mold claims and possible ways to handle these losses.

▷ Describe the physical environment and the loss adjustment environment created by a catastrophe.

▷ Describe pre- and post-loss adjustment procedures for a catastrophe.

▷ Explain the purpose and operation of the National Flood Insurance Program (NFIP); explain the types of losses covered under the NFIP policy; and explain the loss adjustment procedures under the NFIP.

▶▶

Loss Investigation

4

LOSS INVESTIGATIONS: FIRE LOSSES

Property loss adjusters encounter a wide variety of loss types in their work, such as fire losses, which can be as simple as a small grease fire on a kitchen stove and as complex as a multialarm arson fire in a warehouse.

Regardless of the extent of a fire loss, the adjuster must be able to articulate where the fire originated (origin) and what caused the fire (cause). The adjuster might need an origin and cause expert's services to determine the answers. Sometimes, witness statements suffice to determine origin and cause. Local fire officials issue origin and cause reports, and these might be sufficient. If it is suspected that accelerants were used, then obtaining the services of a chemical analysis expert may be necessary. If an appliance such as a coffee maker or toaster is identified as the source, the appliance should be sent to a testing lab. The adjuster must exercise good judgment as to how extensive (and costly) the origin and cause investigation must be to properly document the claim file. The exhibit outlines the elements of an origin and cause report. See the exhibit "What Is A Good Origin And Cause Report?."

Picture Evidence

Fire losses can require photos, video, and diagrams. Good judgment will dictate the quantity and quality of such materials to support the claims. In property loss adjusting, a picture really can be more compelling than a thousand words.

Scope and Estimate of Damaged Areas

Every fire loss requires a list of the damaged areas, or scope. An adjuster can obtain a scope and estimate in several ways. The adjuster can go to the loss and prepare them. An independent adjuster can be dispatched to perform this task. For a simple homeowners claim, the insured might be permitted to supply the adjuster with estimates.

Commercial Fire Losses

Commercial fire losses provide certain challenges that homeowners fire losses do not. A commercial fire might produce hazardous material that requires the services of special containment companies to clean up. There may be stock that can be dried and cleaned (requiring a restoration company's expertise)

What Is A Good Origin And Cause Report?

Taken from a presentation to the New Hampshire Adjusters Association
by Stephen W. Houghton

While the focus of this presentation is on fire investigation reports, most of the principles stated here should apply in general to any report on cause.

GROUND RULE

Before beginning, it is necessary to review a basic ground rule that can get overlooked. This is an investigation being done for you so you are the "boss." Tell your expert what you want done and be sure he or she understands your needs. If you don't, you should not be surprised if you don't get what you expected. Most technical experts do not read minds. This is especially true if you have a budget in mind. It is extremely difficult to adhere to financial needs that are never stated. If the expert can't do the job for what you want to spend, you have two choices; find a new expert or change what you want him or her to accomplish. Remember the expert is working for you—you owe it to yourself and to the expert to establish your needs from the beginning.

WHO IS IT FOR?

As you read the report you should keep in mind whom the report is finally intended for. Who is the most important person who will read the report? The obvious answer is the potential members of the jury whether or not the file ends in litigation. If the report shows that the expert, and therefore your position, is ready for trial, the probability that you will end up there is diminished a great deal.

Expect that this report will have to stand up to scrutiny by opposing experts. It may also have to stand up to changes in testimony since fact witnesses' memories often play tricks as the years go by. There is also the possibility that some of the physical evidence gathered in support of the opinion in the report may be inadmissible in court. In short, the report should not hinge on any one element in the investigation but should be supported by all of the facts as they are known. That means you do not dismiss the observations of the fact witnesses simply because they don't fit your theory. If you do dismiss them, have good solid reasons for doing so or expect the opposing expert to throw them in your face.

FOUR ELEMENTS

Fire investigation reports should have four elements: 1) they should document the damage patterns; 2) they should reconstruct the scene; 3) they should eliminate all other sources of ignition; and 4) they should show the mechanism of ignition clearly.

DOCUMENT: This is usually done with photographs, videotape and a short narrative. One thing to check here is that the photographs match their captions and/or the descriptions in the narrative. Photographs should show conditions before the scene is disturbed as well as how the investigator put things together if they were able to put things together. There should also be references to any evidence taken from the scene.

RECONSTRUCT: Photographs and sketches are the most useful tools for preserving scene reconstructions. A narrative describing the scene before the fire accomplishes the same end. The important thing is that there is justification for identifying the area and point of origin and the probable cause of the fire.

ELIMINATE: This element is sometimes overlooked as unimportant. Our experience has shown that in origin and cause investigations, if other ignition sources are soundly and positively ruled out, the probability of an opposing opinion is reduced. It is difficult to dissent if there is no room for dissension.

DEMONSTRATE: One of the greatest keys to success is the clear demonstration of the mechanism of ignition. To demonstrate clearly requires an explanation of how the offending unit that caused the fire is supposed to work. It is then necessary to identify what the malfunction was and how that malfunction led to the fire. In other words, it is not enough to say "the compressor did it." An effort should be made to explain how the compressor normally works, then what part of the compressor failed and finally, how that failed part generated the heat that caused the fire. An explanation of how the fire spread from the unit to the surrounding area is also a part of this element.

KEEP IT SIMPLE

This is possibly the most important rule and it defines the adjuster's or attorney's most important role in assuring their company has a good report with which to work. Your ability to understand the reasoning in the report is critical. Your familiarity with the subject of the report is probably many times the understanding of the people who may be sitting on the jury. If you are confused by the report, won't they be also?

Often, an expert who is not sure of his or her opinion makes a report vague or complicates things with jargon and technical language. If you think you are getting the runaround, you may be right. Ask your expert to explain and, if necessary, to rewrite the report. It is your report, and you are paying for it.

Read the report, evaluate it, and be sure it meets your expectations. If it does not, find out why not. It may make the difference between recovery and simply adding expert fees to the loss.

and then sold as salvage (requiring a salvor's services). Repackaging and relabeling might be an issue. If a loss occurs to stock and inventory, it may be necessary to employ an accountant, who will review the business's books and records to verify the loss amount.

Businesses suffering a loss want to resume operations quickly, so the adjuster should be prepared to discuss options for relocating, retooling, and obtaining products from other sources to meet delivery deadlines.

Extensive fire losses may require the services of architects, engineers, general contractors, and many subcontractors if the building is to be repaired or replaced. Also, zoning issues, permit issues, tax issues, and increased costs stemming from ordinances or laws will arise.

Homeowners Loss

A homeowners fire loss can be even more challenging to handle because of the complex and sensitive issues involved in the loss of a home and the insured's personal possessions. Collectibles, fine arts, and items with sentimental value can be difficult to adjust. It may be necessary for the adjuster to employ an appraiser to get appropriate values for some of these items. Moreover, specialists who restore artwork, photos, and oriental rugs can be used to restore property to pre-loss condition. If items cannot be restored, replacement services can assist the adjuster in replacing contents at a reasonable cost.

A family displaced from its home because of a fire needs temporary housing. The adjuster should know what is available and appropriate under the circumstances. Temporary housing services can assist the adjuster. Relocating dogs, cats, birds, and even horses as part of the loss might also be necessary. Understanding the family's lifestyle is key to managing this portion of the loss.

LOSS INVESTIGATIONS: SMOKE LOSSES

Property loss adjusters encounter a wide variety of loss types in their work, including smoke losses. In small fires, smoke can cause more damage than the fire itself.

The type of smoke resulting from a fire depends on the fire's intensity, the material consumed in the fire, and the amount of oxygen consumed. Heavy smoke develops when burning material is shut off from an adequate supply of oxygen, thus preventing complete combustion.

Types of Smoke

Two types of smoke cause damage: (1) hot smoke and (2) cold smoke. Hot smoke is usually found closer to the fire's source and can penetrate the surfaces it contacts. Smoke cools as it moves away from the fire—this cold smoke rests upon, rather than penetrates, the surfaces it contacts. Hot smoke damage is more severe than cold smoke damage.

Hot smoke can deeply stain masonry. For example, ceramic tile has hairline cracks that are not readily visible but that appear when exposed to hot smoke. Once exposed to hot smoke, those cracks cannot usually be cleaned. An appearance allowance can be made when the tile or grout cannot be cleaned to the insured's satisfaction, or the tile might have to be replaced. Stonework, brick, and cement surfaces are also difficult to clean after exposure to hot smoke, but they can sometimes be cleaned with steam or boric acid.

Cold smoke is easier to remove from surfaces, but it can still extensively damage such items as wallpaper, drapes, and carpeting. Both cold and hot smoke residue should be removed from aluminum windows, metal fixtures, and ceramic kitchen and bathroom fixtures as soon as possible because the residue is usually acidic and can eat into these surfaces.

Damage to Metal and Ceramic Fixtures

Metal and ceramic fixtures should be test-cleaned before the insurer and the insured reach an agreement for replacing all items in the smoke-damaged area. Cleaning alone might be sufficient. Cold smoke can travel some distance from the source of the fire before it reaches the surface on which it will settle, and this cold smoke comes to rest in the form of soot. Vacuuming, brushing, or washing the area can often remove it. Cold smoke does not usually leave a pungent odor, so the damaged area can be effectively cleaned.

Fire Restoration Companies

Fire restoration companies specialize in working with insurance companies and adjusters to perform early cleaning and prevent further damage caused by hot and cold smoke. All fire loss adjusters should keep a list of fire restoration companies so that they can call such a company immediately after notification of a fire loss.

LOSS INVESTIGATIONS: LIGHTNING LOSSES

Property loss adjusters encounter a wide variety of loss types in their work, including lightning losses. A bolt of lightning is a release of electrical charges that have built up inside a cloud. A bolt of lightning is actually several strokes (from five to twenty-five) strung together. A lightning strike can carry the equivalent of 2.9 billion kilowatts of power (which is roughly six times the electrical generating capacity of the United States). Because of their height, the most frequent targets of lightning are roofs, chimneys, church steeples, power lines, antennas, and trees.

Approximately 30,000 homes and buildings are struck every year in the United States.[1] Direct strikes by lightning can have an explosive effect or start a fire. But direct strikes are not the only way that lightning can reach property and cause damage. If a lightning strike occurs near a utility line, an induced surge or spike of voltage will result. This surge can dissipate before it reaches a building, or it can be strong enough to overcome the safety devices on the power line and enter a building through the electric or phone service lines. The intense voltage can melt wiring and circuitry.[2]

Verifying a Lightning Loss

The loss adjuster's challenge in handling a lightning loss is to determine that the damage was caused by lightning and not some other type of failure. The first step is to confirm that lightning occurred in the area at the time of the loss. The National Weather Service, lightning reporting services, local TV stations, and power companies are all good sources for this information.

Physically inspecting the damage is another means of verifying a lightning loss, but this is useful only up to a point. Certainly an adjuster can see damage on a building or to an appliance's exterior. Evidence of burning or scorching will appear on wood and siding. Block walls and chimneys can be split or shattered. Roof flashing, gutters, and siding may be twisted or melted. Roofing nails may have popped up. Stucco may explode. Light bulbs can shatter or burn out. Several fuses can blow or trip breakers. Wall switches and wall outlets will have evidence of arcing. If a ground surge occurs (when the lightning travels along the ground surface or just below it), a burrow will appear along the ground.

Adjusters should not attempt inspections such as examining electrical products' internal workings. Such inspections should be left to competent repair people or consultants. Because repair personnel are aware that lightning is a covered cause of loss, they will often state lightning as the cause whether it is or not. One way to combat such a practice is to use an affidavit of lightning damage. This is a notarized statement from the repairperson. The fact that this statement is notarized helps to ensure the statement's veracity.

Pattern of Lightning Damage

At times, an affidavit is not enough, so the adjuster should be aware that lightning destroys electrical equipment and its components in an expected order. Lightning does not damage parts such as pipes or rotors. It damages more fragile parts before the more sturdy components. So if it is alleged that lightning damaged an electric dryer, for example, the repairer should state that there is damage to the timer (which has the smallest gauge wire) and not just damage to the heating coils (which have the heaviest). Similarly, the picture tube of a TV is one of its strongest components and is very far downstream in the TV set's electrical path. Therefore, if the picture tube is the only component damaged, it is unlikely that the cause is lightning. See the exhibit "Adjuster Tips."

> **Adjuster Tips**
>
> - Telephone systems are modular, so lightning damage is usually limited to the initial circuit board.
> - Computer systems usually sustain damage only to the first and second components in the series. If the modem and the motherboard are damaged, the disc drive and monitor should be unaffected.
> - Well water pumps are commonly claimed to be damaged by lightning. Barring a direct strike, the only damage to a pump should be the motor, not the entire pump.
> - Air conditioning units, unless hit by a direct strike, usually suffer damage only to the condenser and minor electrical components.
> - Burglar and fire alarm systems usually sustain damage only to a circuit board, not to the detectors, control boxes, and other parts.

Adapted from Inland Marine Underwriting Association (IMUA) Loss Prevention and Control Committee, "Lightning Protection," 1996. [DA03915]

LOSS INVESTIGATIONS: EXPLOSION LOSSES

Property loss adjusters encounter a wide variety of loss types in their work, including explosion losses. Most explosion losses show evidence of shattered glass, broken or displaced masonry, splintered timbers, and widely scattered debris.

An adjuster cannot always deduce from the evidence that an explosion has occurred. Such cases might raise these questions:

- Does evidence of sudden and rapid combustion or another similar process exist? (Not all instances of combustion by which other property is ignited are considered an explosion. The suddenness and rapidity of the process are important.)
- Did a violent expansion of the air occur?
- Was loud noise reported along with the occurrence?
- Did a sudden and violent outbreak of physical forces occur?
- Did a sudden or violent bursting or a breaking up from an internal force occur?

Determining the Type and Cause of an Explosion

Determining the type and cause of an explosion can be difficult at times, and adjusters must often arrive at a logical conclusion by using the process of elimination. Adjusters should also consider several related questions:

- Were any explosive materials normally used or housed in the building?
- If so, where were they used or housed in the building?
- In what kind of containers were they kept?

- What safety precautions were taken in using and storing these materials?
- What are the chances that the containers might have accidentally been broken and materials accidentally spilled or that fumes accidentally escaped?

Explosion Versus Cracking

Claims are often submitted under the explosion peril when construction activity is nearby and explosives are being used. Although the alleged blasting damage can include several items, the principal complaint is about cracked plastering.

When construction and blasting are performed near a residential area, the activity can annoy residents and become a topic of neighborhood conversation. Someone might suffer actual plaster damage as a result of the blasting, and word of it might spread. Then those living near the site of the damage might examine their plastered walls and ceilings, looking for cracks. Many of them are likely to find some plaster cracks because, regardless of nearby construction, few buildings are free of such cracks. However, many of those cracks result from normal shrinkage or expansion of building materials completely unrelated to any blasting explosions.

Another source of plaster damage is the heavily loaded vehicles on a street or highway close to a building. Such trucks produce greater vibrations in the earth and shock waves to nearby houses than do blasting operations at reasonable distances from the house.

Adjusters must distinguish the results of explosion and cracking from other sources. Newly occurring cracks should look fresh and be free of dust and dirt. The adjuster investigating these claims should also check with the party conducting the blasting for seismic information. Those who do blasting work should know the likelihood of damage at various distances from a blast.

LOSS INVESTIGATIONS: THEFT LOSSES

Property loss adjusters encounter a wide variety of loss types in their work, including theft, which is the taking of personal property from its rightful owner, without the owner's consent, with the intent to deprive the owner of its value.

The broad definition of theft encompasses burglary, robbery, fraud, and deception. Regardless of the type of theft, loss adjusters take certain actions to investigate a theft claim.

Investigating a Theft Claim

To begin an investigation, the adjuster ascertains whether theft is covered under the policy; then the adjuster determines whether any policy limitations apply. The adjuster confirms who owns the property and who has an insurable interest in the property. Depending upon his or her company's claims guidelines, the adjuster takes statements from the parties involved and from any witnesses. The adjuster obtains a police report of the incident. If the loss or security report concerns theft of an auto, a boat, or mobile equipment, the adjuster reports it to the appropriate index bureau, such as one of these:

- National Insurance Crime Bureau (NICB)
- Insurance Services Office, Inc., (ISO) Claim Search®, which encompasses the Marine Index Bureau (MIB), the Property Insurance Loss Register (PILR), and the Central Index Bureau (CIB) used for bodily injury claims
- National Equipment Register (NER), for contractors' equipment
- Art Loss Register (ALR), for works of art

Evidence of Theft

Theft claims often leave physical evidence to support them. The adjuster should confirm signs of forced entry, disabled or malfunctioning alarm systems, and—for example—even dust rings or scratch marks on the surface of the cabinet where a stolen TV once stood. If evidence of a malfunctioning or nonfunctioning alarm exists, the adjuster must investigate those circumstances. Did someone forget to set the alarm? Was the alarm broken, and if so, for how long? Did the alarm have a maintenance contract? Had the alarm been recently serviced? Was the alarm installed properly? Thinking along these lines will ensure that subrogation possibilities and potential fraud indicators are uncovered.

Documenting a Theft Claim

To document a theft loss as part of a claim investigation, an adjuster might request the insured to prepare an affidavit of theft, a proof of loss, or an inventory. Bills, receipts, credit card statements, warranties, instruction manuals, books and records, photos, or any other documents that tend to prove ownership and value should support the inventory. The best type of document is the original bill or receipt. The least credible is a photocopy of such a document. If the retailer makes up a duplicate receipt for the insured, a phone call to the retailer can verify the information supplied on the duplicate receipt.

Recovery of Stolen Property

With theft claims, there is always the possibility that the stolen property might be recovered. The adjuster should remember to place the investigating law enforcement agency on notice of the payment of the claim so that the insurer will be notified if recovery occurs. This notice will also be useful if an arrest and a conviction occur, because the court can order restitution as part of the penalty. It is also a good practice to remind the insured to contact the insurer if recovery occurs because the police might fail to do so. Also, the adjuster should recall that both homeowners forms and the Building and Personal Property Coverage Form (BPP) have provisions regarding recovered property.

Inflation of Theft Claims

One final word of caution regarding theft claims. They are, by far, the easiest to inflate or fabricate. So while the adjuster should be empathetic, he or she should also be skeptical when dealing with theft losses. For example, an adjuster should wonder whether all of the items that the insured claims were stolen from the trunk of his or her car could have actually fit in it. If the circumstances of the loss are questionable, the adjuster should investigate further and even enlist the assistance of the insurer's special investigations unit to confirm or deny suspicions.

LOSS INVESTIGATIONS: WATER DAMAGE LOSSES

Property loss adjusters encounter a wide variety of loss types in their work, including water damage loss.

Regardless of water damage's cause, the key to successfully adjusting a covered water damage loss is speed. Whether it is a leaking shower pan in someone's home, a burst water pipe flooding a basement, sprinklers saturating the contents of a retail clothing store, or the roof torn off a warehouse during a hurricane, the faster the water is stopped from flowing and the earlier the drying process is begun, the better. So an adjuster should be familiar with what water damage is and is not covered under the policy. The adjuster must be able to dispatch contractors and restoration companies to the scene of covered losses to mitigate the damages.

Finding the Source of Water

If a hurricane has torn a hole in a roof and rain is coming in, finding the source of the water is easy. Finding the source when a water stain is noticed in the middle of the living room ceiling, for example, is not as easy. Water does not necessarily travel in a straight line, so finding a leak within walls and ceilings can be difficult. Visual inspection will show only the result of a leak, be it a water stain, a puddle, or mold growth. It is usually necessary to do some tear-out before the source of the leak can be found.

This is why both the HO-3 and BPP provide coverage for the cost of tearing out and replacing of a part of a building or structure when necessary to repair a leaking system or appliance.

CAUSES OF MOLD CLAIMS

Property loss adjusters encounter a wide variety of loss types in their work, including mold losses. Although every loss investigation follows the same basic steps, different types of losses require different types of investigation.

Mold is one of the possible byproducts of water damage. The proper handling of, and communication about, mold damage claims are growing challenges that require property loss adjusters' special attention.

Mold Losses

Despite the fact that most mold does not cause serious problems, mold claims are having a significant effect on the insurance industry. Both the volume of mold claims reported to insurers and the bad-faith verdicts for improperly adjusted water damage claims involving mold have significantly cost the insurance industry in both dollars and bad publicity. In 2001, a Texas jury leveled a $32.1 million bad-faith award (which was substantially reduced on appeal) against an insurer in a case that has come to be known as the "Ballard Case" (Ballard, et al., v. Fire Insurance Exchange, et al., No. 99-05252, 345th Judicial District Court, Travis County, Texas). The bad-faith lawsuit was brought against the insurer for the wrongful denial of the water damage claim and for failing to notify the Ballards that a form of toxic mold had been discovered in their house.

Not all molds are harmful. Some are actually useful, such as those in penicillin and blue cheese. Humans have coexisted with various types of mold for many years with little or no serious effects. Understanding what causes mold to grow, what damage mold can cause, and how to remediate or clean up mold helps a property loss adjuster to correctly handle losses involving mold.

What Causes Mold Growth

Molds are a group of fungi that live by feeding on other organisms. They grow from spores and reproduce on a wide variety of natural and synthetic surfaces. Mold spores and particles continually drift through indoor and outdoor air. When the spores land on damp surfaces, they begin to grow by digesting the surface material, gradually destroying it. Mold spores can go dormant for many years until the conditions again support growth and reproduction.[3] While mold colonies can exist only on damp surfaces, they can extend a short distance through dry materials in search of moisture and digestible materials. When conditions are favorable, wet drywall can be covered with millions of spores per square inch within a week or two.

Water is the essential ingredient needed to grow mold. There are three types of water found on residential and commercial properties:

- Clean
- Gray
- Black

Clean water escapes from sources such as broken or leaking pipes, from an overflowing sink or tub, and from a leaky roof or window. Thoroughly drying these areas within forty-eight hours helps eliminate the risk of mold. The exhibit offers specific cleaning recommendations for clean-water saturation as provided by the United States Environmental Protection Agency (EPA). See the exhibit "Water Damage—Cleanup and Mold Prevention."

Gray water sources can include dishwasher, washing machine, or toilet overflow; broken aquariums; leaking waterbeds; and stagnant seawater. The gray color results from food, dirt, or other particles in the water. These particles contain high levels of bacteria that offer food for mold growth. Cleanup of gray water requires drying and the use of disinfectant cleaners to avoid mold growth. Gray water that sits for more than seventy-two hours can become black water.

Black water sources include sewage, seawater, and water that has flowed over organic materials, where it collects numerous contaminants. Bacteria thrive in black water and can cause illness in people exposed to it.[4] Professional remediation is usually necessary for black water damage.

Clean water

Water that comes from pipes, sinks, or bathtubs, or that leaks through a broken window or roof.

Gray water

Water that comes from a dishwasher rinse cycle, a washing machine, a toilet, an aquarium, or a stagnant pool of seawater.

Black water

Water that is filled with bacteria; sources include sewage, seawater, and water that has flowed over organic materials.

Physical Damage to Property

Property damage from mold claims can range from minor to extensive. Mold can collect on the surface of walls and look like an accumulation of black dirt. Such accumulation can usually be cleaned with disinfectant cleaner, but this will not remove the spores. This seemingly harmless condition could provide telltale signs of mold growth between the walls. Mold decay of a building's structural components can require that the building be condemned and demolished.

What Loss Exposures Can Result in Mold Damage?

Mold problems are common in areas where moisture manages to seep or run through building components. Mold accumulates around improperly fit windows and doors. Mold thrives where roofing is damaged and repairs have been postponed. Ice dams in gutters can cause moisture to leak into attics and can go undetected while mold and mildew flourish.

Other water damage that can cause mold growth include plumbing leaks, appliance failure (such as freezers, water softeners, or distillers), sewage intrusion, weather-related water intrusion (floods, windstorms, hurricanes), sprinkler leakage, and fire-suppression efforts.[5] Shoddy construction practices,

Water Damage—Cleanup and Mold Prevention

Guidelines for Response to Clean Water Damage Within 24–48 Hours To Prevent Mold Growth*

Water-Damaged Material†	Actions
Books and papers	• For non-valuable items, discard books and papers. • Photocopy valuable/important items, discard originals. • Freeze (in frost-free freezer or meat locker) or freeze-dry.
Carpet and backing—dry within 24–48 hours§	• Remove water with water extraction vacuum. • Reduce ambient humidity levels with dehumidifier. • Accelerate drying process with fans.
Ceiling tiles	• Discard and replace.
Cellulose insulation	• Discard and replace.
Concrete or cinder block surfaces	• Remove water with water extraction vacuum. • Accelerate drying process with dehumidifiers, fans, and/or heaters.
Fiberglass insulation	• Discard and replace.
Hard surface, porous flooring§ (Linoleum, ceramic tile, vinyl)	• Vacuum or damp wipe with water and mild detergent and allow to dry; scrub if necessary. • Check to make sure underflooring is dry; dry underflooring if necessary.
Non-porous, hard surfaces (Plastics, metals)	• Vacuum or damp wipe with water and mild detergent and allow to dry; scrub if necessary
Upholstered furniture	• Remove water with water extraction vacuum. • Accelerate drying process with dehumidifiers, fans, and/or heaters. • May be difficult to completely dry within 48 hours. If the piece is valuable, you may wish to consult a restoration/water damage professional who specializes in furniture.
Wallboard (Drywall and gypsum board)	• May be dried in place if there is no obvious swelling and the seams are intact. If not, remove, discard, and replace. • Ventilate the wall cavity, if possible.
Window drapes	• Follow laundering or cleaning instructions recommended by the manufacturer.
Wood surfaces	• Remove moisture immediately and use dehumidifiers, gentle heat, and fans for drying. (Use caution when applying heat to hardwood floors.) • Treated or finished wood surfaces may be cleaned with mild detergent and clean water and allowed to dry. • Wet paneling should be pried away from wall for drying.

*   If mold growth has occurred or materials have been wet for more than 48 hours, consult Table 2 guidelines. Even if materials are dried within 48 hours, mold growth may have occurred. Items may be tested by professionals if there is doubt. Note that mold growth will not always occur after 48 hours; this is only a guideline.

These guidelines are for damage caused by clean water. If you know or suspect that the water source is contaminated with sewage, or chemical or biological pollutants, then Personal Protective Equipment and containment are required by OSHA. An experienced professional should be consulted if you and/or your remediators do not have expertise remediating in contaminated water situations. Do not use fans before determining that the water is clean or sanitary.

†   If a particular item(s) has high monetary or sentimental value, you may wish to consult a restoration/water damage specialist.

§   The subfloor under the carpet or other flooring material must also be cleaned and dried. See the appropriate section of this table for recommended actions depending on the composition of the subfloor.

"Mold Remediation in Schools and Commercial Buildings," United States Environmental Protection Agency, February 20, 2002, www.epa.gov/iaq/molds/intro. html (accessed February 20, 2002). [DA 03920]

such as failure to use flashing around windows; the misapplication of synthetic stucco exteriors or other materials; faulty heating, ventilating and air conditioning (HVAC) systems; and improper grading along foundation walls can also foster mold growth.[6]

Mold growth resulting from covered water damage becomes part of that damage unless it is specifically excluded. Many personal and commercial policies exclude damage due to mold growth in clauses that are specifically aimed at avoiding coverage for deterioration of the property through natural causes or poor maintenance. However, these exclusions might not be applicable to all mold damage claims or upheld in every jurisdiction.

Investigating and Adjusting Mold Losses

Property loss adjusters should investigate potential mold losses as they would any other water damage loss. Timeliness is vital in investigating losses in which mold might be a factor. Carefully reading the policy and mold-related exclusions can avoid improper claim denial or settlement. When mold is identified, the choice of a remediation firm affects the final damages. (Selection of a remediation contractor will be discussed later.) Communication with building owners and inhabitants of dwellings with confirmed or suspected mold growth is crucial, regardless of whether coverage is provided for the claim. Mold can cause allergic reactions, so it is important to recognize it as a potential health hazard while investigating property damage.

Importance of Proactive Adjustment—Recognizing the potential for mold growth in water damage claims and promptly adjusting those claims is important to insurers for two reasons:

- Early recognition and remediation of potential mold growth minimizes damage costs.
- Prompt identification and communication of mold growth can minimize or avoid health risks for building occupants.

These recommendations focus on proactive adjustment of potential mold claims:

- Recognize the types of losses that result in conditions supporting mold growth, and inspect them quickly.
- Use good photos and diagrams to document and identify locations of mold.
- Be alert for preexisting damage that could have supported mold growth. Uncorrected hurricane and flood damage are common culprits. Take statements to document any preexisting conditions that might have encouraged mold growth.
- Work with the insured to hire a well-trained remediator. Remediation of mold damage has become a thriving business for contractors willing to accept the risks. Issues peculiar to remediating mold damage make selecting a contractor a crucial decision for insureds.

Identification of Mold Hazard—Careful visual inspection is required to identify mold growth. Early mold growth can resemble dirt on the surface of walls, flooring, carpets, and other materials. Any telltale signs of mold require further inspection. Many times the problem is worse than it appears because mold can migrate through materials and affect both sides. The unexposed side of the material often reveals extensive mold growth and damage. Removal of a portion of the material for a visual inspection of the back might be appropriate. Ventilation systems should be visually inspected especially when damp filters are observed. A boroscope can be used to view spaces in ductwork and behind walls to check for mold growth. A moisture meter can be used to detect moisture in building materials. The meter can help identify hidden mold growth and aid in assessing the extent of water damage.[7] Property loss adjusters should continue inspection, even after a source of the water has been found. More often than not, multiple sources will be found.

Indications that mold likely exists in a water-damaged area include:

- Color changes in linoleum or wallpaper
- Discoloration, cupping, or warping of wood floors
- Discoloration of drywall or blotches on the surface
- Discoloration of fabrics, carpets, and draperies
- Earthy odors
- Noticeable humidity
- Rot on baseboards and carpet backing, and around windows and doors

Whether or not the visual inspection reveals mold, if the building's occupants report symptoms of a mold-related illness, further investigation is warranted. This could include air-quality testing and the retention of an expert. The exhibit presents a mold-prevention flowchart that can be helpful to property loss adjusters investigating mold claims. See the exhibit "Preventing Microbial Contamination."

What Is the Effect of Preexisting Damage?—A challenge with mold claims is the difficulty in fully remediating the problem. Strong cleansers can sanitize a moldy surface, but unless every microscopic mold spore is removed, the spores go dormant and then flourish again when a new water source is presented. This creates problems for insurers who must determine the mold growth's cause. Suppose that mold damage existed previously, as from natural causes such as humidity in a basement. Then a covered cause of loss exacerbates the mold growth. How does a property loss adjuster properly assess the insurer's liability for the mold growth without risking a bad-faith suit? Careful investigation into preexisting conditions and knowledge of the law in the jurisdiction would help resolve this issue.

Remediation of Mold Damage—The New York City Guidelines (the full title is New York City Department of Health, Bureau of Environmental and Occupational Disease Epidemiology's Guidelines on Assessment and Remediation of Fungi in Indoor Environments) have been used by some states

Preventing Microbial Contamination

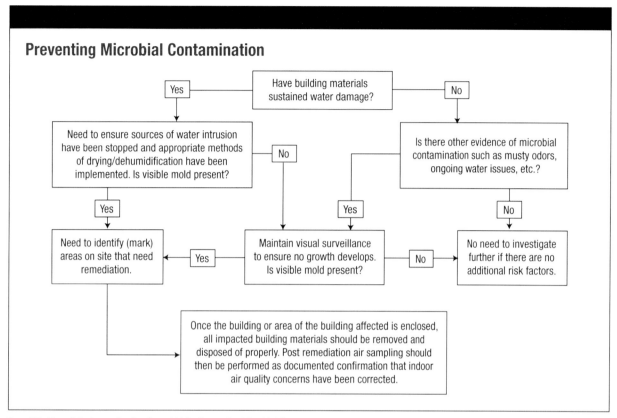

Russell S. Nassof, Environomics Southwest, LLC. "Preventing Microbial Contamination During New Construction." Phoenix, Arizona: Environomics Southwest, LLC, 2002. [DA03921]

as a standard for remediating mold. This document identifies five levels of mold damage and appropriate methods of remediation for each. Generally, the first step in remediating any mold damage is to immediately dry any moisture and correct the source of water infiltration. Repairs to buildings, pipes, or appliances will prevent recurrence of mold growth. Cleaning and drying the affected area, removing water-damaged materials, and maintaining humidity levels below 60 percent will prevent mold growth. Under the Guidelines, the scope of remediation escalates based on the square footage to be remediated. [8]

The EPA has also published recommendations for mold remediation in schools and commercial buildings. See the exhibit "EPA Checklist for Mold Remediation."

Selection of a properly trained, reputable remediation contractor is an important decision for the insured. Some opportunists have responded to the publicity associated with mold claims by offering mold remediation services without obtaining the necessary skills and equipment. If mold is not properly remediated, recurrence of the problem will be likely, and individuals who occupy affected buildings will be exposed to further health risks. Adjusters should use caution in recommending remediation contractors to the insured.

EPA Checklist for Mold Remediation

Investigate and evaluate moisture and mold problems

- ❏ Assess size of moldy area (square feet)
- ❏ Consider the possibility of hidden mold
- ❏ Clean up small mold problems and fix moisture problems before they become large problems
- ❏ Select remediation manager for medium or large size mold problem
- ❏ Investigate areas associated with occupant complaints
- ❏ Identify source(s) or cause of water or moisture problem(s)
- ❏ Note type of water-damaged materials (wallboard, carpet, etc.)
- ❏ Check inside air ducts and air handling unit
- ❏ Throughout process, consult qualified professional if necessary or desired

Communicate with building occupants at all stages of process, as appropriate

- ❏ Designate contact person for questions and comments about medium or large scale remediation as needed

Plan Remediation

- ❏ Adapt or modify remediation guidelines to fit your situation; use professional judgment
- ❏ Plan to dry wet, non-moldy materials within 48 hours to prevent mold growth
- ❏ Select cleanup methods for moldy items
- ❏ Select Personal Protective Equipment—protect remediators
- ❏ Select containment equipment—protect building occupants
- ❏ Select remediation personnel who have the experience and training needed to implement the remediation plan and use Personal Protective Equipment and containment as appropriate

Remediate moisture and mold problems

- ❏ Fix moisture problem, implement repair plan and/or maintenance plan
- ❏ Dry wet, non-moldy materials within 48 hours to prevent mold growth
- ❏ Clean and dry moldy materials
- ❏ Discard moldy porous items that can't be cleaned

"Mold Remediation in Schools and Commercial Buildings." United States Environmental Protection Agency, February 20, 2002. www.epa.gov/iaq/molds/intro.html (accessed February 20, 2002). [DA03923]

Untrained remediation staff who fail to take the necessary precautions are also exposed to health hazards.

The lack of government regulation or guidelines for health risks and the remediation of mold cases make mold damage claims ripe for litigation. The New

York City Guidelines have been adopted in some states, but they are only recommendations, not statutes. The United States EPA and the California Department of Health Services (DHS) have issued nonbinding guidelines to homeowners and business owners to assist in evaluating mold existence, effects, prevention, and cleanup. [9] Research to determine mold's health effects continues. Regulation is difficult when research is not conclusive.

Fraud Potential—Mold claims have created an environment in which disreputable remediation contractors and dishonest insureds can flourish. Remediators can prolong the amount of work they do by dragging it out for months or doing their own testing, only to determine that the remediation is not complete and that the work must continue. Price gouging for materials is common, as are phantom charges such as the use of water extraction equipment that was not actually used. [10]

Insured's mold fraud scams entail buying a home, insuring it, furnishing it with cheap property, living in it, and then cracking the pipes or turning on a faucet to saturate the premises. The scam artists then turn on the heat and seal the doors and windows. The scammers then try to collect for the damage to the building, the replacement cost of the contents, and additional living expenses.

Insured's Duty To Protect the Property From Further Damage—Following any loss, an insured has a contractual duty to protect the property from further damage. In a water damage loss, the insured and the insurer must attempt to reach agreement on the steps to be taken to protect the property and preserve any evidence as to the cause of the loss. The insurer can protect itself from a breach of good claims handling practices by advising the insured on the appropriate steps to protect the property from additional damage due to mold growth. Any verbal instructions given to the insured should be immediately followed in writing. The appropriate policy form numbers should be cited, along with quotations from the forms that describe the insured's duties after a loss. The letter should provide suggestions for preventing mold growth or accumulation. The letter should clearly state that the insured's failure to take actions to prevent mold growth could result in denial of coverage for further damages.

CATASTROPHES: PHYSICAL ENVIRONMENT AND LOSS ADJUSTMENT ENVIRONMENT

Property loss adjusters encounter a wide variety of loss types in their work. Although every loss investigation follows the same basic steps, different types of losses require different types of investigation.

Catastrophes are single events that cause massive losses. ISO Property Claim Services (PCS) of American Insurance Services Group officially recognizes and assigns a catastrophe serial number to any single event that causes more

Catastrophe
A single event that causes widespread losses.

than $25 million in insured damage. Catastrophic events cause suffering to those who experience losses and place great strain on insurance adjusting resources. But insurers' financial support of covered losses and professional and compassionate treatment of insureds suffering losses in catastrophes demonstrate insurance's value and importance.

Many different types of events cause catastrophes. Each type presents special challenges, but catastrophes also share common characteristics, including geographic concentration, disruption of services, political sensitivity, and great emotional stress. Insurers have learned to respond to catastrophes by planning ahead and by adapting their standard loss adjusting procedures. Hail, wind, and tornadoes are the most frequent causes of catastrophes. However, hurricanes, floods, and earthquakes cause more widespread damage. Fires and riots can also cause catastrophic losses. The nature of the losses and the demands on claims adjusters vary by type of catastrophe.

Hail

Hailstorms do not receive the same publicity in the national media as do other catastrophes, but every year they cause numerous catastrophes. Hailstorms can occur anywhere, but they are especially common in the Great Plains and Rocky Mountain states. The amount of damage caused by hail in 2000 was $446 million for property and $124.9 million for crops.[11] Adjusting hail losses is challenging, especially when the damage is minor to moderate. Severely damaged property can be repaired or replaced, just as when property is severely damaged by any peril. A claim for minor or moderate hail damage often raises two issues:

- Whether the property needs to be repaired at all
- Whether the claimed damage existed before the hail

Minor hail damage can include barely perceptible scratches and dings in siding and roofing. Such damage might be irreparable because of matching issues, and the property might need to be replaced. An insurance policy that measures loss as the cost to repair or replace might require the insurance company to pay for replacement. For example, the HO-3 measures loss to the building at the cost to repair (provided adequate limits of coverage exist and the insured actually makes repair). If an insured with an HO-3 suffers superficial scratching of the siding on his or her house, he or she will be entitled to the cost to repair or replace the property. Unless the repairs are satisfactory, the homeowner is entitled to the cost to replace. The cost of replacement can be extraordinary compared to any decrease in the market value of the home caused by the hail damage. Indeed, many homeowners in this situation prefer an actual cash value (ACV) settlement, an option that is always available and that does not require the insured to make repairs. In catastrophes, unfortunately, this dilemma occurs frequently.

An equally difficult problem with hail claims is the possibility of preexisting damage. Virtually all homes show some wear and tear. Scratches, chips, dings, and marks can come from innumerable sources. Following a hailstorm, homes typically have some new damage in addition to old damage. Moreover, some insureds might use the opportunity of a hailstorm to make a claim for old damage. Adjusters who handle hail claims regularly must become familiar with how normal wear on buildings and vehicles appears.

When settlements are made for ACV, distinguishing preexisting damage is crucial.

Adjuster Tip—When adjusters are doubtful about the circumstances of a hail-related loss, they should look for hail damage to exposed condenser coils of an HVAC (heating, ventilating, and air conditioning) unit because they are easily damaged by hail.

Wind and Tornadoes

Loss due to violent, severe winds and tornadoes can devastate a community. These losses usually occur in a specific geographic area. The extent of damage, injuries, and loss of life make adjusting such losses difficult. These losses share many of the characteristics of hurricane losses and are similarly handled.

Hurricanes

Hurricanes can arise in the tropical regions of the Atlantic Ocean and the Gulf of Mexico during summer and autumn. Once developed, hurricanes are hundreds of miles wide with sustained winds in excess of seventy-five miles per hour. They characteristically move westward and northward out of the Tropics. The Gulf and Southeastern states of the United States are especially vulnerable to hurricanes, but the mid-Atlantic and New England states have also suffered hurricane damage. In addition to their powerful winds, hurricanes deliver enormous amounts of rain and cause tides to surge well beyond normal.

Most structures can withstand, with minor damage, a relatively low-velocity hurricane with winds between seventy-five and ninety miles per hour. However, as wind speeds increase, hurricane destruction becomes severe. In August 1992, Hurricane Andrew crossed southern Florida with sustained winds in excess of 130 miles per hour, obliterating homes and essentially causing the same damages as a thirty-mile wide tornado. Most hurricanes bring down trees and power lines and flood low-lying areas, making immediate travel dangerous.

Sustained rainy weather often follows a hurricane, when many homes have damaged roofs. Most homeowners are eager to comply with their insurance policy's requirement to mitigate damage after a loss, because they want to save their personal property. However, tarpaulins and repair materials are almost always in short supply following a hurricane. Insurers and adjusters should enforce the insured's duty to mitigate damage only to the extent that mitigating measures are feasible.

Property insurance policies cover damage from wind and wind-driven rain but generally do not cover damage from floods or tidal surge. Only flood insurance policies from the National Flood Insurance Program cover flood and tidal surge. Adjusters handling claims under ordinary property insurance policies must first determine whether wind or water caused the damage. Wind damage is covered, but water damage is covered only if it results from wind-driven rain. If the water that caused the damage rose up from the ground, then it was a flood, and the damage is not covered. If the water came from the sky, the resulting damage is covered.

Floods

Floods can result from melting snows, rising rivers and lakes, hurricanes, or heavy rains.

Except for certain specialized commercial policies, all flood insurance comes from the National Flood Insurance Program (NFIP). The NFIP has its own policy provisions and its own requirements for who can adjust flood claims. Flood insurance policies are relatively expensive, so many property owners choose to do without them. Thus, lack of insurance coverage is a serious problem in beachfront areas and in any area that suffers flood damage. Floods invariably result in a great amount of uninsured losses.

Earthquakes

California is known for its susceptibility to earthquakes, but other states are also at high risk, including Alaska, Hawaii, and Washington. Earthquakes strong enough to cause damage might occur in any state.

Earthquake damage is excluded from standard property insurance policies, but it is available by endorsement. Insureds in earthquake-prone areas are most likely to have such coverage. In California, homeowners insurers must offer earthquake coverage. Nevertheless, following an earthquake, most property owners are uninsured. Communities suffering earthquakes absorb much more of the financial loss than does the insurance industry.

Unless it strikes a rural area, an earthquake strong enough to cause damage can damage thousands or tens of thousands of properties at once. In this respect, earthquakes are similar to hurricanes. An entire community can be damaged and traumatized. In such an earthquake, thousands of people will need the same services at once. Immediately after an earthquake, highways, water pipelines, gas lines, and electric lines might be severed. Firefighters might be overwhelmed and lack adequate water. Fires might destroy buildings that survived the quake. Following a major quake, aftershocks continue for days or weeks, possibly inflicting significant damage on already weakened structures.

As with hail damage, the most challenging claims following an earthquake are for buildings with minor to moderate damage. Damage might be hidden inside walls and under floors. Separation of major structural elements might initially appear only as cracks in stucco or plaster. Even moderate earthquake damage to an ordinary house can cost $50,000 or more to repair. Unfortunately, relatively few people are qualified to assess earthquake damage properly. Only structural engineers or highly qualified contractors can determine the proper scope of repairs for the most difficult earthquake losses. After a serious earthquake, they will be in great demand. All of these issues may contribute to delays in closing files after an earthquake.

Fires

Fires are usually limited to one owner's property, but some are extensive enough to cause a catastrophe. In the United States, the West is much drier than the East and is consequently prone to fire following long droughts. Moreover, although cities throughout the United States have extensive and sophisticated firefighting forces, the concentration of properties clustered close together in cities can result in widespread conflagration.

Rural fires usually involve uninsured property, such as trees in national parks and forests or property that is self-insured by timber companies. Growing timber is not a type of property insured under most property insurance policies. Nevertheless, rural areas can contain significant insured property, both residential and commercial. Insurers might have difficulty providing prompt service to insureds in rural areas if they do not have preexisting relationships with independent adjusters and contractors in those areas.

A fire severe enough to cause a catastrophe will incinerate the property involved. Many homeowners who returned to their homes following the Oakland, California, fires of 1991 found nothing but the brick chimney still standing, surrounded by ashes. Under these circumstances, even the owner would have difficulty recreating the detailed plans of a home's construction. Nevertheless, insurance policies require the insured to prove the amount of any loss and to include all documentation specified in the proof of loss. Insurers differ in the type and extent of proof they require of insureds in these circumstances. Adjusters should not subject fire victims to an additional trauma, but they need to know the amount of every loss.

Riots

Riot losses include damage caused by fire, vandalism, and looting. Commercial structures and property are damaged disproportionately more than residential property by riots. Commercial insurance policies that otherwise limit coverage for theft losses often cover losses incident to a riot, even if the thief is not identified as a rioter. For example, the BPP with the Causes of Loss—Broad Form defines the peril of riot to include looting occurring at the time and place of a riot. The "time and place of a riot" are not specifically defined but would certainly include any place where riot activities required police intervention.

A riot in a declining urban area represents a perfect opportunity for a would-be arsonist. A commercial structure in such an area might be unsalable, and the owner might prefer an insurance settlement to the existing building. A property loss adjuster assigned a fire claim following a riot should investigate with neighbors to see whether anyone saw how the fire began. Neighbors are likely to be extra vigilant during a riot. They might be very cooperative with a claim investigation because they might be angry with the wrongdoers. However, unless an eyewitness is available, an arson investigation might be hopeless. In the context of a riot, proof of an incendiary fire does not necessarily implicate the insured. Even proof of a motive and an incendiary fire might not carry much weight.

The Catastrophe Environment

The environments of almost all catastrophes have certain common characteristics that are interrelated: the losses are geographically concentrated; necessary services are disrupted or in short supply; response to catastrophes is politically sensitive; and the claims adjusters who must operate in this environment and the people with whom they deal are under great stress.

Geographic Concentration

Catastrophes strike in one community or within a relatively limited geographic area. Even hurricanes, the geographically largest type of catastrophe, usually hit hard an area of just a few hundred square miles. After a catastrophe, thousands of people in a relatively small area need the same services. Existing services in that area, even if they survived the catastrophe, are inadequate to meet the sudden great need.

In particular, not enough property loss adjusters are in an area following a catastrophe. Most insurers set up catastrophe teams to augment the regular adjusting staff in a catastrophe area. The "cat team" adjusters and processors leave home for at least a few weeks to work fourteen-hour days out of cars and motel rooms. Many experienced personnel go from one catastrophe site to another with only brief periods of time off to return home. Unfortunately, this pattern of work exhausts all of the claims staff who participate in settling catastrophe claims. To keep errors to a minimum, the cat team is usually rotated out of the area after a few weeks or after having handled a specified number of claims.

Contractors are also in short supply following a catastrophe. The construction industry can have chronically high unemployment, so catastrophes attract contractors from out of state. This influx helps enormously in rebuilding a community, but it also raises potential problems. Unlicensed or incompetent contractors can take advantage of insureds who suddenly and simultaneously have large amounts of money and a significant need for contractors' help. An unscrupulous contractor might take an assignment of the insured's claim settlement, then disappear from the state. An incompetent contractor might be indifferent about correcting poor work because a great amount of other work is available. Legal remedies against contractors are of dubious value even under normal circumstances. Thus, property loss adjusters can provide valuable advice to insureds who are naive about their situation. Claims adjusters should advise insureds to select contractors carefully.

Interruption or Shortage of Services

In addition to claims adjusters and contractors, just about every other necessary service or supply is in shortage or unavailable following a catastrophe. Immediately after a catastrophe, essential utilities such as electricity, water, gas, and telephone might be disrupted. Such disruptions make an area unlivable and dangerous. Fortunately, public authorities usually have the most pressing and dangerous situations resolved in a few days.

Hotels and motels even a significant distance from the catastrophe area will be filled to capacity. Rental cars in the area will be quickly obtained. (However, cars can quickly be moved into a catastrophe area.) If the roads are blocked or severed, supplies of goods in supermarkets might run low.

Building supplies are often unavailable immediately following a catastrophe. Supplies usually become available within a few weeks, but prices are high and may remain so for months. Adjusters preparing estimates in catastrophe environments must be aware of prevailing prices. Estimating losses based on prices that prevail only during normal times is unrealistic.

Political Sensitivity

Public authorities and elected political officials face as much challenge from catastrophes as does the insurance industry. They are more responsible than the insurance industry for the immediate response, including control of threats to personal safety. Public authorities decide whether an area must be evacuated or kept off-limits until safe.

After the initial danger passes, public officials must process an enormous number of licenses and building permits stemming from repair work. As construction progresses, they must inspect and issue occupancy permits for a great number of properties. They also enforce building code provisions for new construction. Public authorities are not staffed to handle the unusual amount of work caused by catastrophes, which is an additional source of frustration and stress for insureds who have suffered a loss.

Most public officials recognize the importance of insurance settlement funds to rebuilding their community. They cooperate with property loss adjusters as much as possible. However, tensions can result when public officials involve themselves in the claim settlement process when they believe that their constituents are not being treated properly. After a catastrophe, community members, community leaders, and public officials may talk about perceived obstacles to insureds' recovery.

Nevertheless, public officials are usually not qualified to resolve specific differences that arise in claim settlements. Some public officials, who in their official capacity never thought about insurance, might make highly publicized pronouncements about how claims should be settled. These pronouncements are usually not legally binding and often are not even helpful. However, such adverse publicity following a catastrophe would not be surprising given the thousands of frustrated insureds concentrated in a single community.

State insurance department officials are more knowledgeable about insurance than are other public officials, but they are under just as much political pressure to show results. A catastrophe environment is an obvious opportunity to enforce an unfair claims practices act. Insurers with significant losses in a catastrophe often designate a liaison to the state insurance department to facilitate communication of complaints and concerns. After a catastrophe, state insurance department officials know which insurers performed well and which did not.

Emotional Stress

Virtually everyone involved with a catastrophe is subject to great emotional stress, including community members, public authorities, contractors, and property loss adjusters. Stress affects people differently. Some people become visibly agitated and unable to concentrate. Other people become vacant-looking and depressed. People subject to stress are less able to control their emotions or to communicate effectively.

Property loss adjusters who work in catastrophe environments are aware of the emotional climate. Nevertheless, because they are also subject to stress, property loss adjusters might sometimes be impatient, impersonal, distracted, or unreasonable. Monitoring staff morale is a key challenge for claims managers in catastrophe environments. Major catastrophes command the attention of senior claims officers, who realize that the insurer's reputation is at stake in a catastrophe situation. Claims officers and managers understand that the volume of work, emotional stress, and separation from home caused by a catastrophe require adjusters to be relieved on a regular basis.

Adjusters experienced with catastrophe environments know that listening to insureds is valuable. Insureds who have suffered great loss need an outlet for their feelings. Most experienced adjusters have encountered insureds who seem to need sympathy more than cash. Adjusters who regard catastrophe work as relieving human suffering are much more motivated, and often find more professional satisfaction, than adjusters who regard the work as primarily closing files.

CATASTROPHES: PRE- AND POST-LOSS ADJUSTMENT PROCEDURES

Catastrophes are single events that cause massive losses. ISO Property Claim Services (PCS) of American Insurance Services Group officially recognizes and assigns a catastrophe serial number to any single event that causes more than $25 million in insured damage. Catastrophic events cause suffering to those who experience losses and place great strain on insurance adjusting resources.

Every major catastrophe teaches the insurance industry something new about the inadequacies of existing catastrophe plans. Property loss adjusters and managers must be prepared to improvise following any major disaster. Nevertheless, planning is essential to an effective catastrophe response. Insurers must have plans for providing the equipment, services, and staff necessary to adjust claims in catastrophe environments.

Equipment

A catastrophe requires that a huge number of adjusters and supplies be brought to the catastrophe area. Catastrophe planners must arrange for office supplies and major office equipment, such as furniture, copiers, files, manuals, and computers, to be available. Planning for computers is especially important because offices are increasingly automated and the types of computers needed in a catastrophe environment might not be the same as in normal circumstances. Adjusters might rely heavily on laptop computers because they are constantly in the field in places without electricity.

Communication equipment is important because normal communications in the catastrophe environment might be disrupted. Catastrophe planners must arrange for telephones, cellular telephones, pagers, and even satellite dishes. A catastrophe plan should also address an insurer's internal communications so that all company employees are clear about who should respond and within what time after a catastrophe.

Most insurers try to be fully operational within two or three days after a catastrophe. To do so, major insurers prepackage equipment on pallets for immediate airlift or trucking into the catastrophe site. They also package jackets, badges, and licenses or license information so that adjusters can be properly identified and authorized to work. Catastrophe kits usually include briefcases, cameras, film, batteries, flashlights, tape measures, and first-aid supplies.

Services

Catastrophe planners must prearrange various services. Property loss adjusters brought into a catastrophe area must have hotel or motel rooms, rental cars, office space, and telephones. Many major insurers have price arrangements with motel and car rental chains.

More important are the services necessary to adjust claims. Catastrophe planners prearrange prices and service with contractors, salvage companies, replacement services, engineering and architectural firms, and independent adjusters. When a catastrophe occurs, planners must be ready with detailed maps of the affected area. Insurers must also arrange reliable means for property loss adjusters to verify coverage. Agents' offices in the catastrophe area might be destroyed or nonfunctioning. Computerized coverage information is usually a listing of policy form numbers only, so adjusters must also have access to actual policy forms.

Staffing

Providing adequate staff is the most challenging aspect of a catastrophe. Unless an insurer is exceedingly overstaffed during normal times, it will have a shortage of qualified staff for a catastrophe. Major national insurers draw staff from around the country to work in a catastrophe, but doing so leaves the rest of the country with inadequate staff to handle normal claims volume. Leaving less-experienced staff to handle normal claims volume elsewhere in the country is not always satisfactory because normal claims volume includes major losses that inexperienced personnel cannot handle. Many insurers use retirees to cover normal claims volume in offices throughout the country.

Staff assigned to catastrophe duty must be rotated out after a certain time period or number of claims. Traditionally, insurers assigned "storm troopers" to a catastrophe for two to four weeks, then allowed them to return home. The effect of this practice was that insureds with major claims faced a parade of adjusters, each of whom had to become acquainted with that insured's claim. Those adjusters did not always deal consistently with the claim or the insured, resulting in the insured's dissatisfaction. Many insurers now assign an adjuster to a certain number of claims that the same adjuster handles to conclusion.

Independent adjusters are an essential resource for handling catastrophes. Independent adjusting firms have a great number of personnel experienced in the fieldwork integral to catastrophe claims adjusting. However, an insurer's staff cannot expect independent adjusters to give the insurer's needs in such cases top priority if the insurer never uses independent adjusters except for catastrophes. Independent adjusters give top priority to insurers that are regular customers.

An often overlooked aspect of catastrophe planning is the need for adequate support staff. Insurers do not usually move support staff from around the country to the same extent that they move adjusters. Nevertheless, catastrophe situations require support staff. Qualified adjusters should be focused on the adjusting work. Other staff should handle as much of the paperwork of a claim file as possible. Personnel from local agents' offices can answer phones and take loss reports. Help from temporary agencies can perform routine tasks. Although all insurers vie for temporary help after a catastrophe, insurers should also consider hiring additional workers for a specified time period. Such help might not be difficult to obtain because a portion of the local workforce might be looking for such employment or might be temporarily unemployed and available.

Catastrophe Loss Adjusting

Adjusting catastrophe claims is markedly different from adjusting typical claims. Aspects of claims adjusting handled differently in a catastrophe include the initial response and reserving practices, communications with insureds, price increases and settlement costs, and adjusting standards.

Initial Response and Reserving Practices

Immediately after a catastrophe, insurance companies typically send an initial survey team to the area to determine the geographic scope of the damage. A survey team can identify affected areas by ZIP code. Computer searches can identify every insured in a given set of ZIP codes. The initial survey should also identify the degree of damage typical of properties in the affected area. This information can help identify the level of expertise needed of catastrophe team adjusters and the extent to which the insurer can rely on telephone adjusters.

Information from the initial survey and from PCS is used to set proper reserves for the catastrophe. PCS provides not only serial numbers for recognized catastrophes but also estimates of the total insured losses. PCS serial numbers and loss estimates are used to activate reinsurance treaties and to help primary insurers estimate their exposure in a catastrophe. Insurers typically set loss reserves for catastrophes in bulk. Bulk reserves are gross estimates of losses; individual loss reserves are determined claim by claim. An insurer's senior management must know that the catastrophe loss reserves are accurate. Without accurate reserves, senior officers are unaware of the insurer's true financial state and might make improper underwriting and reinsurance decisions. Senior officers do not appreciate surprises, such as loss reserves being continually revised upward for a year after a catastrophe occurs. Correct reserves also help claims department managers determine proper staffing for a catastrophe.

Another important aspect of an insurer's initial response is hiring specialists to provide restoration services. Restoration companies perform a variety of tasks valuable to mitigating losses after a catastrophe, including drying, dehumidifying, decontaminating, cleaning, removing soot, inventorying, and packing away property. Restoration companies can work with salvage companies to save and recover as much of the damaged property's value as possible. Every year, the technology used by restoration companies improves. Property damage once deemed hopeless can now be repaired. Restoration work's success depends on timely retention of services. Insurers that wait until after disaster strikes to look for restoration contractors are unlikely to find any available.

Communications With Insureds

After a catastrophe, insureds are in shock. They need an outlet to express their loss and a source for specific advice about recovery. Claims adjusters should be both. Effective communications with insureds is as important to claims adjusting as is verifying coverage or preparing estimates. Nevertheless, several obstacles hinder good communications in a catastrophe environment.

Telephone service might be disrupted by a catastrophe or might be jammed immediately after a catastrophe. Agents' offices might be destroyed or overwhelmed with calls. Local claims offices might be shut down. Fortunately, most insurers can arrange with their telephone service to have calls redirected to an undamaged office. Insureds in the catastrophe area who can make an outgoing call should succeed in reaching their insurer. An insurer's catastrophe operation should inform affected insureds how to reach claims adjusters in the catastrophe area, providing insureds with all new or temporary telephone numbers that the local adjusters are using.

Insureds whose homes are unfit to live in can be hard to reach. They sometimes move elsewhere without leaving a new telephone number for their insurer. Such insureds eventually contact their insurer, but they should be told their duties following loss as soon after the loss as possible. Insurers operating in a catastrophe area have resorted to billboards, radio messages, and even banners towed by airplanes to let insurers know how to contact them.

Price Increases and Settlement Costs

Prices of many goods and services increase after a catastrophe, especially building supplies and contractor services. The local, regional, and national economies are organized to provide a flow of goods and services that meets a predictable, normal demand. Catastrophes result in unpredictable, abnormal demand. For example, the rebuilding after Hurricane Andrew in August 1992 caused high lumber prices throughout the country well into 1993. High prices can actually be beneficial to the extent that they encourage additional output that hastens recovery.

Claims adjusters can make two different mistakes when prices are high. The first is insisting that normal prices should prevail and refusing to settle claims for a higher amount. Normal prices are unlikely to return until most damaged properties have been repaired, but insureds should not wait that long to repair their property. The delay might also be irrational, from the insurer's point of view, if it causes increased living expense or business interruption claims.

The second mistake adjusters can make is paying any amount to close claims. Not every significantly damaged structure is a total loss or policy limits claim. Even in a catastrophe environment, adjusters must evaluate losses and pay an amount that indemnifies, not enriches, the insured. Adjusters need not pay exorbitant prices that appear because of acute shortages immediately after a catastrophe, nor must they accept at face value estimates from contractors so busy that they unapologetically quote clearly unreasonable prices.

Adjusting Standards

Adjusters face some tradeoffs among the cost of claim settlements, the speed of claim settlements, and the thoroughness of their adjusting work in catastrophes. Painstaking adjusting work is ideal for controlling the cost of claim settlements, but it is very slow. In a catastrophe environment, rapid, efficient work is essential. Thus, claims adjusters are likely to be less thorough in their adjusting procedures and more flexible about settlement cost. Adjusters' challenge in catastrophe environments is to be less thorough and more flexible in ways least likely to harm the insurer. For example, if adjusters do not require sworn proofs of loss, an alternative would be to require realistic estimates or damage inspections.

Some documentation or verification of the extent of loss is essential to know what settlement amount is appropriate and to discourage fraud. Insurers' special investigation units (SIUs) should have catastrophe capability so that catastrophes do not become an open invitation to fraud. However, property loss adjusters must recognize that severely damaged buildings are susceptible to fires and looting. Owners are required to protect their property from further damage, but adjusters can enforce this duty only to the extent feasible under the circumstances. Repair materials, generators, and pumps might not be available at any price shortly after a catastrophe, so the adjuster would not require them.

Adjusters may have to reopen numerous files from a catastrophe. They make many settlements at actual cash value, pending repair of the insured's property, and conclude the claim later with a replacement cost settlement. Reopening files might also occur because the initial adjusting work was too hasty or because hidden damage was not apparent until repairs began. Redoing adjusting work is inefficient, but it is predictable with certain catastrophes, such as earthquakes.

Coverage Defenses

A property loss adjuster performs an investigation to determine whether a loss should be paid and how much should be paid. Regardless of the type of coverage involved, insurers do not pay every claim presented by insureds. The adjuster's investigation may show that the insurance policy does not cover a claim. Claims can be denied because of the insured's improper behavior. Insurers can deny coverage in the event of the insured's fraud, but they can also do so for various reasons not involving any serious wrongdoing by the insured, including simple absence of coverage or the insured's failure to comply with a policy condition.

Insurer Not Obligated Under the Policy

The insurer may not be contractually obligated to pay a claim as a result of one or more of the following:

- Some change in conditions, ownership, or interest in the property before a loss that breaches an ongoing promise
- A cause of loss or type of property not covered or specifically excluded by the policy
- The insured's breach of policy conditions following a loss

Change in Property: Ongoing Promises

Promissory warranty

A policy provision in which the assured guarantees or negates the existence of a fact or state of facts at policy inception or promises that something will be done, or will not be done, during the policy period.

An ongoing promise, also known as a **promissory warranty**, is the insured's agreement made at the time of the application for insurance to do or refrain from doing certain things during the policy term. Under a property policy, such a promise might include the agreement to provide a burglar or fire alarm system, deadbolt locks, and fire extinguishers. In exchange for the insured's promise to provide these safeguards, the insurer usually provides a discount of the premium. For business property policies, such promises sometimes include the insured's agreement to provide guard services, burglar/fire alarm systems, sprinkler systems, and certain kinds of safes. A breach of a promissory warranty by the insured that causes a loss or increases the risk of loss might be a basis for the insurer to deny liability under the policy.

Excluded Causes of Loss or Property

A loss might not be covered because the cause of loss is not within the perils listed in the policy or is excluded in the policy. The policy might also specifically exclude coverage to certain kinds of property. In such cases, the claim might be denied, or questions about coverage might be raised and need to be answered.

Policy Conditions Following Loss

All property policies include conditions requiring the insured to do certain things following a loss. In the HO-3 policy and the BPP, these requirements are listed under "Your Duties After Loss." Included is the insured's obligation to give prompt notice of the loss to the insurer; protect the property from further damage; file a sworn statement in proof of loss; provide an inventory of stolen, damaged, or destroyed personal property; submit books and records to document the facts and loss; and submit to one or more examinations under oath. The insured's failure or refusal to comply with these policy conditions is a breach of the policy and would preclude payment of the claim or a suit by the insured to enforce policy rights until the insured has complied.

Fraud, Concealment, and Misrepresentation

Although providing prompt claims service to insureds is a property loss adjuster's primary task, ensuring fair and equitable claim payments is equally important. Adjusters should pay no more than a fair and reasonable amount for covered claims while being vigilant for fraudulent activity. Unfortunately, insurance fraud is a reality that creates a special challenge for adjusters. The Insurance Information Institute estimates that property-casualty fraud costs insurers about $30 billion annually.[12] Yet it is almost impossible to determine the number of claims industry-wide that are fraudulent. Part of the difficulty comes from the lack of uniform definitions throughout the industry. Almost every claim may have an element that is termed a "fraud indicator," but that does not mean that the claim is fraudulent. Many claims that are fraudulent but not provable will be paid. Therefore, finding a uniform way to measure the number of fraudulent claims is difficult.

The opportunity for fraud can appear at many different places in the insurance process. The potential insured may misrepresent or conceal information during the application process. False information may be given to the underwriter about a risk's nature. Claims may be staged or exaggerated. Adjusters, attorneys, and insureds might conspire to obtain fraudulent claim payments. It is important to be aware of the opportunities but be mindful that most people do not accept the opportunity to commit fraud when presented with it.

Definitions

Although the terms "fraud," "concealment," and "misrepresentation" might seem to be synonymous, they are different and have distinct legal meanings.

Fraud is a general term encompassing all types of acts by one or more persons intended to deceive another person. **Fraud** is an intentional deception, by word, deed, or concealment, to cause another to part with something of value or to surrender a legal right. For fraud to be actionable, the deceived party must suffer legal injury from having relied on the deception.

Concealment is the withholding of information by one who knows that he or she has a duty to disclose. Concealment in the application for insurance is the intentional withholding of any fact material to the risk, which the insured, in honesty and good faith, ought to communicate to the agent, underwriter, or insurer.

Misrepresentation is the statement of something as fact that is false. Misrepresentation includes statements that are only partially true. For example, an insured would misrepresent his or her loss history by revealing only one loss if several have occurred.

Fraud

An intentional misrepresentation resulting in harm to a person or an organization.

Concealment

An intentional failure to disclose a material fact.

Misrepresentation

A false statement of a material fact on which a party relies.

Policy Provisions

All property insurance policies provide that the policy will be void or that coverage will not be provided to an insured when the insured engages in fraud, concealment, or misrepresentation.

The HO-3 homeowners policy states the following in Section I—Conditions:

> Concealment or Fraud. We provide coverage to no "insureds" under this policy if, whether before or after a loss, an "insured" has:
>
> 1. Intentionally concealed or misrepresented any material fact or circumstance;
>
> 2. Engaged in fraudulent conduct; or
>
> 3. Made false statements;
>
> relating to this insurance.[13]

One purpose of the fraud and concealment condition in any policy is to prohibit payment of fraudulent claims. To pay such claims would be against public policy. The concealment or fraud condition applies to fraud in the application for insurance as well as to claims fraud.

Materiality and Intent

Misrepresentation in the application occurs when an insured has concealed or misrepresented some material fact that the insurer has relied on in issuing the policy. Common misrepresentations concern the insured's true loss or claims history, insurance history, interest in the property, and concealment of concurrent or duplicate coverage. In an insurance application, fraud, concealment, or misrepresentation is deemed material if knowledge of the facts would have influenced an underwriter in accepting a risk or charging a higher premium. In other words, if the insurer had known the truth about the insured's ownership, the insured's interest, encumbrances on real property, or the insured's actual insurance and loss history, the policy would not have been issued or would have been issued only at a higher price. In claims, a misrepresentation or concealment is material if the fact or matter misrepresented or concealed would have made a difference to the insurer in its investigation or in the amount paid under the policy.

To void the policy, the insurer must prove that the misrepresentation or concealment was willful. Concealment or misrepresentation is considered willful or intentional when the insured knows that his or her statements are false, swears falsely with reckless disregard of the truth, or swears to matters as true when he or she knows little or nothing about the facts. An intent to defraud can be inferred whenever the misrepresentation is both material and willful. In contrast, slight or trivial exaggerations, innocent or inadvertent mistakes in computation, or statements of opinion, made in good faith, regarding the property's value do not provide the requisite intent to void the policy.

The burden of proving fraud and concealment for the purpose of voiding the policy is on the insurer. When an insurer documents fraud or concealment, the policy can be voided.

Fraudulent Claims

Adjusters assigned to investigate suspicious claims must do so responsibly. They must have an in-depth knowledge of the policy, proper investigative methods, and the law applicable to insurance fraud. Adjusters must also guard against being overzealous and must conduct the investigation fairly, being careful not to reach premature conclusions about a claim's legitimacy.

Fraudulent claims come in many forms. **Hard fraud** usually refers to staged or invented losses. **Soft fraud** is a fraud of opportunity such as padding or exaggerating an otherwise legitimate loss. Arson for profit is probably the best example of how insureds create losses. It is probably the most common and well-known type of property insurance fraud. However, dishonest insureds can create losses by explosion, water, or almost any other peril. Staged burglaries and thefts are also common—the insured merely creates circumstances indicating that a theft or burglary has occurred. The property supposedly stolen is simply stored off premises or hidden. In commercial losses, the allegedly stolen merchandise might have been sold before a purported burglary or might not have existed at all. Fake or altered receipts and other fraudulent documents might be submitted as proof of purchase. In some cases, dishonest insureds purchase duplicate insurance to increase the recovery amount. Such insureds conceal the existence of duplicate coverage from both insurers.

Hard fraud
Actions that are undertaken deliberately to defraud.

Soft fraud, or opportunity fraud
Fraud that occurs when a legitimate claim is exaggerated.

A legitimate loss can become the opportunity for soft fraud if the insured grossly exaggerates the extent of the loss. The insured might exaggerate the amount and value of personal property that was destroyed or stolen. Some insureds might claim loss of property that was not on the premises at the time of loss. Others might claim the destruction of property that was not owned or never existed. With building losses, some insureds misrepresent the type and value of building materials to increase their recovery.

NATIONAL FLOOD INSURANCE PROGRAM (NFIP)

Except for certain specialized commercial policies, all flood insurance comes from the National Flood Insurance Program (NFIP). The NFIP has its own policy provisions and its own requirements for who can adjust flood claims.

Because of the problems associated with flood insurance in the private market, the government has made flood insurance widely available through the **National Flood Insurance Program (NFIP)**.

National Flood Insurance Program (NFIP)
A government-sponsored flood insurance program for communities in designated areas.

Beginning in 1983, the Federal Insurance and Mitigation Administration (FIMA), of the Federal Emergency Management Agency (FEMA), invited private insurers to participate in a Write Your Own (WYO) program to increase the base and geographic distribution of flood insurance and to improve service and claims handling.

A WYO company sells flood policies under its own name, collects premiums, services the insureds, adjusts the claims, and pays the losses. FEMA reinsures 100 percent of these losses. FEMA pays commissions on premiums and reimburses expenses and costs. If an insurer loses money on the program, FEMA makes up the difference. Any profits are returned to the government.

NFIP Coverage

The NFIP has three policy forms:

- A dwelling form (DF) insures a one- to four-family residential dwelling or condominium unit and residential contents.
- A general property form (GPF) insures other residential and nonresidential buildings and contents.
- Another form insures residential condominium building associations (RCBAP).

Under the regular NFIP program, the insurance limits for property are:

Building Coverage	
Single-family dwelling	$250,000
Two- to-four-family dwelling	$250,000
Other residential	$250,000
Nonresidential	$250,000
Contents coverage	
Residential	$100,000
Nonresidential	$500,000

Definition of Flood

The NFIP policies cover the described property from direct loss by or from flood. Flood is defined in both policies as a general and temporary condition of partial or complete inundation by water of two or more acres of normally dry land or of two or more properties caused by any of these:

- The overflow of inland or tidal waters.
- The unusual and rapid accumulation or runoff of surface waters from any source.
- Mudflow, which is defined as a river of liquid and flowing mud on the surfaces of normally dry land, as when earth is carried by a current of water or collapse or subsidence of land along the shore of a lake or similar body of water as a result of erosion or undermining caused by waves, or currents

of water exceeding anticipated cyclical levels that result in a flood, as defined previously.

Dwelling Form: Property Covered

In this discussion of NFIP coverage, the text refers to the Dwelling Form. However, adjusters are reminded that other forms are available and that the coverages may differ. Building coverage (Coverage A) under the Dwelling Form is written similar to that under other property forms. Coverage is provided for the dwelling at the described location and the extensions and additions to the buildings, detached garages, building materials and supplies, and certain specifically described fixtures. Automatic coverage applies for a separate garage for up to 10 percent of the overall building coverage limit. If the detached building's value exceeds 10 percent, a separate policy should be obtained on that building. The 10 percent extension is not an additional amount of insurance, so using this coverage reduces the limit otherwise available for the dwelling. There is also an extensive list of items— such as built-in appliances, permanently installed bookcases, wallpaper, and paneling— that are considered to be part of the building. And there are limitations for items below the lowest elevated floor of the building or in a basement.

Contents coverage (Coverage B), if purchased, applies to direct physical loss by or from a flood to personal property inside a building at the described location if owned by the insured or by household family members. Property must be contained in a fully enclosed building on the residence premises or secured against floating out of a partially enclosed building. There are limitations on coverage for personal property in a basement or below the lowest elevated floor. The insured has the option to include the personal property of guests and servants. The policy also contains a list of items such as air conditioning units, carpeting, and grills that are deemed to be personal property.

Similar to the HO-3 policy, the Dwelling Form has a $2,500 limit for any one loss to high-value items such as artwork, jewelry, furs, and business personal property. It also has provisions for debris removal and loss-avoidance measures.

The policy also provides coverage for the cost of complying with a state or local floodplain management law or ordinance that affects the structure's repair or reconstruction. This coverage is called Increased Cost of Compliance (Coverage D). Activities such as elevation, floodproofing, relocation, and demolition are covered. The coverage applies to nonresidential structures and residential structures with basements that meet certain FEMA standards. The maximum amount payable is $20,000. This limit is in addition to the Coverage A limit; however, the combined total amount payable cannot exceed $250,000 for a dwelling or $500,000 for a commercial structure.

Property Not Covered

The Dwelling Form lists the types of property not covered by the policy. Generally, property that is out in the open, such as trees, shrubs, decks, and fences, are excluded.

Exclusions

Consequential or indirect loss is excluded. Loss of use, additional living expenses, and business income losses are indirect losses resulting from flood and are thus not covered. Increased costs of construction resulting from ordinance or law are not covered. A loss already in progress at the inception of the policy is not covered.

The policy also excludes the perils usually covered by a homeowners policy, such as fire or theft.

Several exclusions explain that a flood must be a general, not an individual, condition. Flood policies exclude water, moisture, mildew, or mold damage confined to the insured property, or any damage resulting from conditions within the insured's control. This exclusion applies to any design, structural, or mechanical defects, or any failures, stoppages, or breakage of water or sewer lines, drains, pumps, fixtures, or equipment. Any property or premises modifications by the insured that increase the hazard of flooding can exclude subsequent losses from coverage. Any intentional act by the insured is also excluded. Testing or monitoring of pollutants is not covered unless required by law. Finally, there is no coverage for loss to any building or personal property located on land leased from the federal government caused by a flood, where the lease holds the federal government harmless under flood insurance issued by a federal government program.

General Conditions

Like other property policies, the dwelling form has a list of familiar conditions: a pairs and sets clause, a concealment or fraud clause, and an other insurance clause. The other insurance clause makes the NFIP policy primary over all other policies that state that they are excess. If the other policy does not specifically state that it is excess, then the NFIP policy is primary up to the other policy's deductible, and then the coverage becomes pro rata. After a loss, the insured must comply with requirements such as giving prompt notice of the loss, separating the damaged property from the undamaged property, making an inventory with backup documentation, submitting a proof of loss, cooperating with the investigation, allowing inspection of the damaged property, and submitting to an examination under oath if required. The insured cannot abandon property to the insurer. The amount of the loss can be reduced by salvage. Either party may demand an appraisal. Mortgagees' interests are protected.

The NFIP policy also has some unique conditions, such as a special condition for continuous lake flooding. If the structure has been flooded by lake water for ninety continuous days and it is reasonably certain that the structure will be a total loss, the insurer will make a settlement without waiting for further damage to occur. Naturally, there is a requirement for a release so that the insurer does not have to pay twice for the same property. There is a similar provision for flooding from a closed basin lake (a natural lake from which water leaves primarily by evaporation). However, this provision does not require ninety days of continuous flooding. Lastly, the NFIP policy does not allow a structure to be covered by more than one NFIP policy.

Loss Settlement Provisions

Like all property policies, the Dwelling Form has a limit of liability and deductibles. Separate deductibles apply to the building coverage and the personal property coverage. The deductibles do not apply to loss avoidance measures, condominium loss assessments, or increased cost of compliance coverage.

Losses under the Dwelling Form can be settled in one of three ways:

- Replacement cost
- Special loss settlement
- Actual cash value

Replacement cost and ACV are handled similar to the ISO HO-3. Special loss settlement involves the replacement cost to a manufactured (mobile) home or travel trailer.

Adjustment Procedures

The adjustment of flood losses involves numerous special procedures, most of which are dictated by NFIP requirements.

NFIP Authorization

All independent adjusters must have NFIP authorization to handle losses, or they will not be paid for their work. NFIP sets standards for adjusters in five categories:

- Residential
- Commercial
- Large commercial
- Manufactured and mobile homes
- Residential condominium building association (RCBA)

The standards require an adjuster to have a number of years' experience and the ability to write estimates.

Loss Settlements, Denials, and Rejections

Only NFIP personnel can accept or deny claims or reject proofs of loss, based on the investigating adjuster's recommendations. An NFIP proof of loss is required on every claim with payment recommended. On claims up to $7,500, the adjuster's final report will be accepted in lieu of a proof of loss. NFIP has its own forms for the purpose of loss settlement and reporting.

SUMMARY

Property losses vary by the type of peril that causes the loss and the type of building and contents involved in the loss. A fire loss often needs an origin and cause expert to determine where and how the fire started. If a piece of equipment or personal property is found to be the cause, the adjuster must undertake a subrogation investigation. This often requires the use of another expert to test the item alleged to be the cause of the fire.

Smoke damage can be a difficult loss to clean up. Successful restoration often requires specialists and depends on whether the smoke was hot or cold and what type of surface is involved.

Lightning is commonly alleged to be the cause of many losses, but some-times lightning is not the real cause. Confirming the presence of lightning in the area of the loss is an important aspect of handling a lightning damage claim. Lightning often leaves distinctive damage on certain types of property. Inspection and testing can be performed to confirm that lightning caused damage.

Determining whether an explosion has occurred can be difficult because other sources of ignition can cause the same type of damage. Property loss adjusters often have to use a process of elimination to determine that an explosion is the cause of loss.

Additionally, claims for blasting damage, such as cracked plaster, are often submitted as explosion damage. Cracked plaster can result from various causes, so the property loss adjuster should thoroughly investigate the circum-stances surrounding the loss before accepting the claim as damage from an explosion.

Theft claims can result from burglary, robbery, fraud, or deception. Property loss adjusters investigate the circumstances of the loss and determine coverage for the loss. Theft claims usually are reported to an index bureau containing a comprehensive database of stolen property, which can aid in detecting fraudu-lent claims.

Water can cause extensive damage in a short period of time. Often the source of the water is difficult to locate. And not all water damage is covered by insurance. Adjusters must always be on guard for maintenance issues when handling a water damage claim.

Property losses vary by the type of peril that causes the loss and the type of building and contents involved in the loss. Mold can complicate water damage losses. Adjusters must be alert to the possibility of a mold claim in every water damage claim.

A single event that causes insured property damage in excess of $25 million is designated a catastrophe and assigned a serial number. For reinsurance purposes, all of the insured losses are aggregated at this serial number.

Catastrophes present a challenge for adjusters. Large numbers of adjusters and support staff must be mobilized and sent to the area of the catastrophe. Essential services may not be functioning. Contractors and suppliers may be extremely busy and not easily available. Add to all of this the emotional stress being suffered by insureds, and the environment can be draining for all involved.

Despite the expansive property coverage available, not every claim is paid. Insurers can assert exclusions; changes in conditions, ownership or interest in the property; or breach of a policy condition to deny a claim. Fraud, concealment, and misrepresentation are grounds for denial of coverage. The fraud, concealment, or misrepresentation may occur during the application process, during the loss itself, or during the claims process. The adjuster must always be alert for the potential of fraud in a claim.

The National Flood Insurance Program (NFIP) was created to provide flood insurance to communities in flood-prone areas. The program covers residential and commercial buildings and contents. It can also insure residential condominium building associations. The NFIP has its own set of qualifications for an adjuster and its own set of claims handling guidelines.

ASSIGNMENT NOTES

1. Adapted from Dave Matana and Steve DiPilla, "Lightning Causes Electrifying Losses," National Underwriter (April 29, 1996), p. 9.

2. Adapted from Property Loss Research Bureau (PLRB), "Lightning and Electrical Losses, An Adjuster's Guide," 1994.

3. United States Environmental Protection Agency (EPA), "Mold Remediation in Schools and Commercial Buildings," www.epa.gov/iaq/molds/intro.html (accessed February 20, 2002).

4. J. Brian Tuttle, "General Overview," Toxic Mold: A Growing Risk, seminar report, Guy Carpenter & Company, 2001, p. 6.

5. Cliff Zlotnik, presentation for Property Loss Research Bureau Claims Conference, February 14, 2001, p. 4

6. Patrick J. Wielinski, "Mold: Is There Coverage in Your CGL?" (Dallas: International Risk Management Institute, Inc., October 29, 2001), p. 23.

7. New York City Department of Health, Bureau of Environmental & Occupational Disease Epidemiology, "Guidelines on Assessment and Remediation of Fungi

in Indoor Environments," www.ci.nyc.ny.us/html/doh/html/epi/moldrpt1.html (accessed February 20, 2002).

8. New York City Department of Health and Mental Hygiene, "Guidelines on Assessment and Remediation of Fungi in Indoor Environments," www.ci.nyc.ny.us/html/doh/html/epi/moldrpt1.html (accessed February 20, 2002).

9. California Department of Health Services, "Indoor Air Quality Info Sheet, Mold in My Home: What Do I Do?" www.cal-iaq.org/mold0107.pdf (accessed March 5, 2002).

10. Adapted from Daniel Hays, "Mold Insurance Fraud Could Spread Nationwide," National Underwriter (September 9, 2002), pp. 28–29.

11. World Wide Web: http://www.nws.noaa.gov/om/severe_weather/sum.00.PDF.

12. III Fact Book 2002 (New York: Insurance Information Institute, 2002), p. 120.

13. Includes copyrighted material of Insurance Services Office, Inc., with its permission. Copyright, ISO Properties, Inc., 2010

Segment B

Direct Your Learning ▶▶

5

Good-Faith Investigation and Coverage Defenses

Educational Objectives

After learning the content of this assignment, you should be able to:

▷ Explain how waiver and estoppel can occur and how they can be avoided.

▷ Explain the bases for bad-faith claims and damages.

▷ Explain the purpose of an examination under oath (EUO).

▷ Explain how an EUO should be demanded and conducted.

▷ Explain how to resolve various problems that arise with an EUO.

Good-Faith Investigation and Coverage Defenses

GOOD-FAITH INVESTIGATIONS: WAIVER AND ESTOPPEL

Coverage issues must be resolved correctly and promptly to avoid waiver, estoppel, and bad faith. Many situations that present coverage questions require further investigation to determine whether the claim should be denied or paid.

While attempting to resolve these coverage issues, adjusters must continue to look for facts that will confirm coverage as well as facts that will result in coverage denial. And adjusters must continue to quantify the loss so that payment will not be delayed, should coverage be confirmed. Until these matters are resolved, the adjuster and insurer must avoid any conduct that would lead the insured to believe that the claim will be paid. Otherwise, a waiver of coverage defenses and policy conditions may occur.

Waiver

Waiver is the voluntary and intentional relinquishment of a known and existing right. This surrender of a known right can be made expressly or by implication. It can be oral, written, or inferred through any conduct of the adjuster or insurer inconsistent with a particular right.

The circumstances under which a waiver can occur are varied. For example, whenever the adjuster or insurer makes an unconditional offer to pay a claim after becoming aware of a coverage defense or a basis for denying liability, the insurer waives its right to deny the claim. This is true regardless of whether the coverage defenses concern a right to rescind the policy because of misrepresentation in the insurance application, a cancellation of coverage before the loss, or the lack of coverage for the loss. Payment or an offer of settlement waives a defense based on fraud and concealment.

Waiver can also occur following a claim denial. The insured might allege that the insurer, upon denial of the claim, breached its obligations, thereby waiving the continued application of the policy conditions. The insured would therefore be relieved of any further obligation to comply with the conditions.

The adjuster or insurer can waive the insured's compliance by offering to pay the loss before the insured has complied with the conditions. In some jurisdictions, the insurer waives the proof of loss condition by failing to provide or request a proof of loss within the time limits established by the insurance code. In some jurisdictions, a claim investigation in which the adjuster obtains a detailed statement from the insured covering the facts and extent of loss waives the proof of loss and examination under oath conditions. The insurer is deemed to be fully informed of the information required to be produced by these conditions.

A waiver of the insurer's option to repair or replace the property can occur when the insurer elects to pay the claim in money or enters into a formal appraisal of the amount of the loss. Making payment or initiating appraisal also waives any coverage defenses unless the insurer expressly advises the insured that it is reserving its rights to investigate further and assert policy conditions.

Estoppel

An adjuster's or insurer's conduct might result in estoppel. For estoppel to occur, the insured must rely on the insurer's conduct. The insured might change his or her position about the policy, might incur some expense, or might be led into breaching a policy condition as a result of relying on the representations or conduct of the adjuster or insurer. This situation is called **detrimental reliance**. To permit an insurer to assert a coverage defense in such cases would be improper. Estoppel prevents an insurer from claiming its right, privilege, or defense if it would be inequitable to do so because of the insurer's conduct toward the insured.

Detrimental reliance

A situation in which an insured relies on the words or actions of an insurer and that reliance harms the insured's financial position.

For example, when an adjuster tells an insured to repair a structure or to replace or repair some personal property, causing the insured to incur expense, the insurer will be estopped from raising any coverage defense or exclusion. The insurer will be estopped from claiming a breach of the proof of loss condition when the adjuster has told the insured that the proof of loss need not be filed until settlement is agreed upon. The insurer waives its rights to have the insured show or exhibit the property or to take all or part of the damaged property as salvage if the adjuster has advised the insured to discard or sell the damaged property. In these circumstances, there have been a waiver and an estoppel; the insurer is estopped from asserting that the insured breached the policy because the insured relied on the insurer's direction. Anything said or done by an adjuster or insurer that causes the insured to conclude reasonably that coverage applies or that nothing more is required to collect under the policy can constitute a waiver and can estop the insurer from asserting coverage defenses or policy conditions.

All standard property insurance policies contain provisions (or general conditions) against a waiver or change of policy provision, unless the insurer consents to waive or change a provision in writing. However, the courts have consistently held that an adjuster, as the insurer's agent or apparent agent, can waive the policy conditions, either orally or through behavior.

Avoiding Waiver and Estoppel

Property loss adjusters can avoid waiver and estoppel with timely nonwaiver agreements or reservation of rights letters, followed by prompt investigation and, when appropriate, by a carefully considered denial of coverage or a retraction of the reservation of rights. Whenever an adjuster makes advance payments while a coverage issue is pending, he or she should include nonwaiver language in the advanced payments receipt. Because of jurisdictional differences, adjusters should check the law to determine the proper nonwaiver language.

Nonwaiver Agreements

Nonwaiver agreements and reservation of rights letters both serve these general purposes:

- To advise the insured that any action taken by the insurance company in investigating the cause of loss or in ascertaining the amount of loss is not intended to waive or invalidate any policy conditions
- To clarify that the agreement's intent is to permit an investigation of the claim and that neither the insured nor the insurer will thereby waive any of its respective rights or obligations

The two types of nonwaiver agreements are general and specific. A general nonwaiver agreement includes the two items previously mentioned. This type of agreement is commonly used in daily claim adjusting whenever the insurer is concerned about investigating a claim before the insured has substantially complied with the policy's duties after loss conditions. The exhibit shows an example of a general nonwaiver agreement. See the exhibit "General Nonwaiver Agreement."

A specific nonwaiver is used whenever the insurer becomes aware of a specific coverage problem or defense. This might occur because of information provided in the initial report, during initial contact with the insured, or during an inspection of the damaged property. The Specific Nonwaiver Agreement exhibit illustrates a specific nonwaiver agreement. It contains the same provisions as a general nonwaiver agreement, but it includes a blank space for the adjuster to enter the specific reasons for the coverage question after the words: "Specifically, your policy. . . . " The adjuster should fill in the specific policy provisions or exclusions that raise questions regarding coverage. The adjuster should then explain to the insured the reasons for requesting a nonwaiver agreement, request that he or she sign it, and provide the insured with a copy of the agreement. See the exhibit "Specific Nonwaiver Agreement."

Reservation of Rights Letters

Reservations of rights letters serve the same purpose as nonwaiver agreements, but they are in letter form. They contain the same general provisions and might include a more specific reason for the coverage question. Like a specific

General Nonwaiver Agreement

NONWAIVER AGREEMENT—FIRE LINES

Insurance Company (hereinafter called the "Company") agrees with _____

(hereinafter called the "insured") as follows:

1. The Company has heretofore issued to the insured policy No. _____

2. The Insured has reported to the Company a loss said to have occurred as a result of _____
    on or about _____ at _____ by reason whereof the insured claims
    damage to the property insured by policy No. _____

3. That any action taken by the Company in investigating the cause of loss, or investigating and ascertaining
    the amount of the actual cash value of the property or the amount of the loss and damage, shall not waive or
    invalidate any of the terms or conditions of the policy and shall not waive or invalidate any rights whatever of
    either of the parties to this Agreement.

4. Neither the examination of the insured or of any other person, the examination of the books of account, bills,
    invoices or other vouchers of the insured or of any other person, the request of any other information, or the
    furnishing thereof, or the incurring of any trouble or expense by the insured shall waive or invalidate any of
    the terms and conditions of the policy or policies, or any defense thereunder.

5. The intent of this Agreement is to preserve the rights of all parties hereto, and to permit an investigation of
    the cause of the loss, the investigation and ascertainment of the amount of actual cash value, or the amount
    of loss or damage, or any of them without regard to the liability of the Company.

6. Execution of this Agreement shall not be taken as a waiver or surrender by the insured of any claims or rights
    under said policy and no representations have been made by the Company to induce the insured to execute
    this Agreement, except as herein contained, and the insured affirms that he has read this Agreement and fully
    understands the terms and effect thereof.

Executed in triplicate this _____ day of _____ 20 _____ .

Witnesses: INSURANCE COMPANY

_____   By _____

_____   Insured _____

[DA03930]

nonwaiver, a reservation of rights letter should list the specific coverage part, provision, or exclusion that applies to the situation in question. Some claims supervisors attach photocopies of the specific policy provisions at issue so that the insured understands the insurer's concerns. Reservation of rights letters also include wording through which the insurer reserves the right to raise other coverage issues later if they become known.

Specific Nonwaiver Agreement

NONWAIVER AGREEMENT

IT IS HEREBY UNDERSTOOD AND AGREED by and between the parties signing this agreement that any action taken by the hereinafter named Insurance Company or Companies in investigating the cause of loss, or investigating and ascertaining the amount of sound value, or the amount of loss and damage which occurred on _____, 20 _____, shall not waive or invalidate any of the terms or conditions of any policy or policies, and shall not waive or invalidate any rights whatsoever of either of the parties to this agreement.

IT IS FURTHER UNDERSTOOD AND AGREED that neither the examination of the insured or of any other person, the examination of the books of account, bills, invoices, or other vouchers of the insured or any other person, the request of any other information, or the furnishing thereof, or the incurring of any trouble or expense by the insured shall waive or invalidate any of the terms and conditions of the policy or policies, or any defense thereunder.

Specifically, your policy_____

_____

_____

_____

_____

_____

THE INTENT of this agreement is to preserve the rights of all parties hereto and to permit an investigation of the cause of loss, the investigation and ascertainment of the amount of sound value, or the amount of loss and damage, or any of them without regard to the liability of the named Insurance Company or Companies.

WITNESS our hands in duplicate this _____ day of _____ 20 ____ .

_____   _____
                                                         INSURANCE COMPANY
_____   BY: _____

_____   _____

[DA03931]

Reservation of rights letters are usually sent to all named insureds (sometimes with copies to loss payees) by certified mail and are return receipt requested. Some are hand-delivered so that the insurer has evidence of the insured's receipt of the letter. They are used whenever face-to-face contact cannot be made to obtain a nonwaiver agreement or whenever the insured has refused to sign a nonwaiver agreement. A reservation of rights letter is as effective as a nonwaiver agreement as long as receipt by the insured can be shown. Some claims managers prefer to use both nonwaiver agreements and reservation of rights letters to ensure that notice to the insured of coverage questions is clearly documented.

Further Investigation

Once the insured has signed a nonwaiver or acknowledged receipt of a reservation of rights letter, the adjuster can investigate the cause and extent of the loss without concern about waiving either party's rights. The information obtained through the investigation can then be provided to claims management so that an informed decision can be made regarding coverage. Many adjusters treat nonwaiver agreements and reservation of rights letters as ends in themselves. This is a mistake. Both are tools that enable an adjuster to further investigate and evaluate a claim. The coverage issue must be resolved as quickly as possible, and the insured must be informed of the resolution.

Denial Procedures

Most insurers have established guidelines and strict procedures for the denial of claims not covered under the policy. The adjuster's supervisor or a file examiner might review smaller claims before the adjuster is authorized to deny them. Other claims, depending on the insurer's procedures, require review at the level of branch office claims manager. More serious claims and claims involving certain types of policies or types of business are typically referred to regional claims managers or are reported to home office claims staff.

To assist claims staff with difficult or questionable claims, many insurers have established claims committees within their branch, regional, and home offices. These committees are made up of personnel with extensive experience in claims, usually supervisors and claims managers. Adjusters handling doubtful claims present their claim at a committee meeting at which the claim file can be reviewed and discussed. If the claims committee thinks additional information is necessary to reach a decision regarding the claim, the adjuster will be given suggestions for further investigation. The claims committee might also require a legal opinion from an attorney before making a final recommendation.

Declaratory
judgment action

A legal action in which the insurer (or insured) presents a coverage question to the court and asks the court to declare the rights of the parties under the applicable insurance policy.

The claims committee might decide that coverage is in order and that the claim should be paid. Or it may decide that denial is appropriate. The insurer then has two options: (1) the claim can be denied by letter, specifying the reasons for the denial and citing specific provisions of the policy, or (2) the insurer may file a declaratory judgment action. In a **declaratory judgment action**, the insurer requests a court to review the evidence and determine the parties' duties and obligations under the policy. Determining coverage through this type of legal action is usually done only when the law is unclear or undecided or when the exposure on the claim is high.

Advance Payment Receipts

Partial payments of claims are sometimes advanced to insureds when they demonstrate the need for, and request an immediate payment for, emergency reasons. In homeowners losses, insureds and their families might need temporary housing or money for food and clothing. In commercial property losses, insureds might need funds for emergency repairs to the structure or to replace destroyed or stolen equipment so that the business can operate and thereby minimize business income loss. Advance payments are usually made during the first few days after a loss before the insurer can fully investigate the cause of loss and before the insured has fully complied with policy conditions. Because the courts have held that payment waives coverage defenses, including the insured's failure to comply with policy conditions, the insurer must act to avoid a waiver. This is accomplished with an Advance Payment Receipt— Reservation of Rights Form. See the exhibit "Advance Payment Receipt."

The receipt is essentially a nonwaiver agreement, but it also serves to advise the insured that:

- The insurer has neither accepted nor denied the claim.

- Payment is not an admission of liability.

- Payment is made in response to the insured's good-faith representation regarding the loss and request for payment.

- The insurer does not waive any conditions and expects full compliance under the policy.

- If the claim is not covered or is invalid, the insured agrees to repay the insurer the amount advanced.

- If the claim is valid, the advance will be deducted from or credited against any covered claims.

Advance payment receipts are routinely obtained even when the policy clearly covers the cause of loss and circumstances surrounding the loss. As a practical matter, they help to keep track of payments made under certain coverages, help comply with unfair claims practices acts, and clarify to the insured that the advance payments will be applied against the final claim. Such receipts are essential when handling losses involving suspected arson and insurance fraud; without them, payment of such claims would waive any defense against the insured's breach of conditions regarding false swearing, fraud, and concealment. Although advance payments demonstrate the insurer's good faith, they should not be made unless the property loss adjuster obtains a receipt.

Advance Payment Receipt

Advance Payment Receipt and Reservation of Rights

I, the undersigned, hereby acknowledge the receipt of _____ Dollars ($ _____) in partial payment of the claim for insurance benefits which I have asserted in connection with a policy of insurance issued by _____ (herein the Company) and bearing Policy Number _____. The claim I have made pertains to a _____ loss which I reported as having occurred on or about the _____ day of _____ , 20___.

I understand and acknowledge that the Company is continuing to investigate, in good faith, the claim I have made, that my claim has neither been accepted nor denied, that the advance payment is not an admission of liability whatsoever on the part of the Company, and that the payment should not be considered payment under the policy.

I further understand that the Company is making this advance payment in good-faith reliance upon the claim I have made, the representations I made to the Company in support of that claim, and my express request for an advance payment.

I further understand that the Company reserves its rights under the policy and will require full compliance with all the conditions of the policy including, but not limited to, my submission of a proper Sworn Statement in Proof of Loss, the submission of receipts, invoices, books and records, and that the Company may exercise its right to require me to take an examination under oath, if deemed necessary.

I further understand that if the policy or the claim is not valid and payment is not required by the Company, I will repay the advance to the company.

I further understand that if the policy and claim are deemed valid that the advance will be applied against any benefit due under the policy.

TO BE SIGNED BY ALL NAMED INSUREDS

_____   Coverage paid under _____
Named Insured   (specify)

_____
Spouse or Partner

State of _____

County of _____

Subscribed and sworn to before me this _____ day of _____ , 20 _____ .

Notary Public for _____   My Commission Expires: _____

[DA03932]

BAD-FAITH CLAIMS AND DAMAGES

Coverage issues must be resolved correctly and promptly to avoid bad faith. Many jurisdictions have enacted rules, regulations, and laws to control conduct involving claims handling and settlements.

Adjusters' good-faith duties stem from three sources:

- The policy or contract
- The law of bad faith
- Unfair claims practices acts

A breach of these duties might be the basis for an insured's bad-faith lawsuit against the insurer. A bad-faith lawsuit seeks damages beyond those available in a breach of contract lawsuit. An insurer found to have committed bad faith might have to pay damages far beyond the claim amount. This payment would have to come from the insurer's own assets. Claims and corporate management are highly sensitive to any bad-faith suit because of the negative effect it can have on the insurer's reputation and financial status.

Contractual Duties

Insurance contracts contain conditions obligating each party to perform certain duties following the loss. The insured must report the claim promptly, file a sworn statement in a proof of loss, and do other things before the insurer is obligated to pay covered claims. The insurer must investigate the claim promptly and appraise and pay covered claims in a timely manner, either within the time limits specified in the policy or by the time limits set in the applicable unfair claims practices statutes. If an insurer fails to pay a covered claim or negligently denies liability under the policy, the insurer might be liable for breach of contract damages and/or extracontractual damages. Depending on the jurisdiction, contract damages might include prejudgment interest, court costs, other penalties prescribed by statute, and attorney fees, as well as the amount of the loss that should have been paid.

The Law of Bad Faith

In addition to a policy's contractual duties, the insurer has a duty implied by law to act in good faith. If the insurer has behaved otherwise, the insured may allege breach of the duties of good faith and fair dealing. In property claims, this is commonly called **first-party bad faith**. In most jurisdictions, the misconduct must go beyond ordinary negligence or breach of contract to be bad faith. The insured must usually plead and prove that the insurer *intentionally* breached its duty of good faith or was guilty of oppression, fraud, or malice. However, other states may have different standards. If the insured prevails in such cause of action, he or she might recover **extracontractual damages**. These are punitive damages and damages for things such as emotional distress, lost profits, or consequential damages awarded in addition to compensatory and statutory damages. An insurer's breach of its good-faith duties generally falls within one of five areas:

- Inadequate investigation
- Improper denial of coverage

First-party bad faith

The insurer's mishandling of a first-party claim that can result in extracontractual damages.

Extracontractual damages

A payment awarded by a court that exceeds the usual contract damages for a breach of contract.

- Unreasonable delay in payment
- Unreasonable compromise
- Withholding payment of undisputed portion of the claim

An insurer cannot reasonably and in good faith deny payment to an insured without thoroughly investigating the facts of the case. This means that the adjuster and insurer must conduct a fair and unbiased investigation, giving as much consideration to the insured's rights under the policy as to their own. An insurer must also pay covered claims within a reasonable time after the insured has fully complied with policy conditions. An unreasonable delay in paying the claim can expose the insurer to extracontractual damages. Most policies and many state laws specify the time period in which the insurer must make payment or deny liability. Also, an insurer must not force an insured to accept a compromise settlement by alleging fraud or by threatening legal action or other consequences. The insurer may also pay that portion of the claim in which the coverage and amount of loss are undisputed, depending upon the jurisdiction. The insurer can then proceed to resolve disputes as to any remaining portion of the claim, such as by invoking the appraisal procedure.

Unfair Claims Practices Acts

Almost all states have enacted some form of unfair claims practices statutes. The acts are designed to prohibit certain unfair and deceptive claims practices. Some states have specific regulations that establish time limits (usually fifteen to thirty days) within which an insurer must pay, respond to, or deny claims following receipt of a proof of loss.

When an insurer has engaged in prohibited conduct with such frequency as to make the behavior a general business practice, the acts provide for fines or penalties, as well as administrative sanctions by the state insurance commissioner. In a few states, insureds may use violation of the act as a basis to sue the insurer and recover damages. However, in most states, only the department of insurance has the power to enforce the unfair claims practices act.

Most of the provisions in these acts deal with four major areas of unfair or deceptive claims practices:

- Delays
- Failures to act
- Failures to communicate
- Denials

Delays that are considered unfair and prohibited by law include delays in responding to claims or communications, delays in settling claims by requesting formal proof of loss, and delays in payment of claims when liability is reasonably clear. Failing to conduct a timely or an adequate investigation is considered an unfair claims practice by most acts. However, the acts usually have a mechanism by which an adjuster can obtain extensions of time to complete an ongoing investigation. Failing to communicate to the insured the specific coverage under which a payment was made is usually an unfair claims practice. Adjusters must also explain any denial or offer of a claim compromise with reference to the policy, the facts, and any applicable law. Unjustified denials, which include denying a claim without conducting a reasonable or an adequate investigation, are also considered an unfair claims practice.

EXAMINATIONS UNDER OATH

An examination under oath (EUO) can be a valuable tool for an insurer when a fraudulent claim is suspected.

The EUO often clarifies issues sufficiently for the adjuster to recommend acceptance of the claim as submitted. The examination can provide new avenues of investigation for the adjuster to pursue. Or the EUO can reinforce the adjuster's suspicions regarding the fraudulent nature of the claim.

When to Use an Examination Under Oath

The adjuster should conduct an EUO as early as possible in the investigation if the claim's validity or value is in question or if the facts are unclear. The insurer can use the EUO to resolve serious questions about a claim, doubts about whether a loss actually occurred, or questions about who is covered under a policy.

Adequate Prior Investigation

Although the EUO should occur as early as possible in the investigation, the adjuster should have sufficient information for the examination to be useful. The adjuster should obtain statements of the parties involved and should receive, verify, and fully review bills, receipts, records, and other documentation *before* the EUO. The insurer's right to an EUO is not waived by the adjuster's taking informal statements from the insured, provided that the adjuster has issued a reservation of rights letter. Likewise, statements by the insured to fire marshals or other public officials do not eliminate the insurer's right to an EUO.

An effective examination also requires that whoever is conducting the examination has thoroughly established the questions that must be asked. Before the EUO, the adjuster and the insurer's attorney must review the entire claim file and agree on the areas of questioning as well as on the EUO's objectives.

Before or After Proof of Loss

Opinions vary about whether an EUO should be taken before or after a sworn statement if proof of loss is submitted. Although an EUO does not waive an insurer's right to a signed, sworn proof of loss, most adjusters prefer that a signed, sworn proof of loss be submitted before the EUO is scheduled. The rationale is that filing a proof of loss is a policy condition. The claim is considered submitted when the insurer receives the proof of loss. The insured is therefore committed to the facts sworn to in the proof of loss.

DEMANDING AND CONDUCTING EXAMINATIONS UNDER OATH

An examination under oath (EUO) can be a valuable tool for an insurer when a fraudulent claim is suspected.

The examination is a condition of the policy and can be *demanded* at any time by the insurer. If an insurer decides that an EUO is necessary, the person to be examined must be told that it is a *demand* by the insurer, not a request. An attorney usually conducts the EUO.

Those Subject to Examination Under Oath

The insurer has the right to examine certain parties and can request an examination of others. The insured is required to give an EUO. Anyone claiming benefits under the policy is also subject to a demand for such an examination. This discussion concerns the ISO HO-3 policy, but some policies differ as to who is subject to an EUO, and the policy language also varies by state and insurer. Therefore, adjusters should examine the policy covering the person and property before arranging or demanding an examination.

In addition to those who are *required* to give an EUO, the insurer can request an EUO of anyone it chooses.

Date, Time, and Place

The insurer demanding the EUO must include a specific date, time, and place in a demand letter. Court cases have relieved an insured of the obligation to complete an EUO when the letter demanding an EUO did not state a definite date, time, and place and person before whom the insured should appear. [1]

The date, time, and place must be reasonable for the person being examined. An insurer cannot arbitrarily set a date and time that would make it impossible for the person to comply and cannot select a place that is an unreasonable distance from the examinee. The person being examined must also be given a reasonable amount of time to gather any documentation required for the examination.

Demand Letter

To be legally binding, a demand letter must contain these elements:

- A demand clearly stating that the insurer is intent on conducting the EUO with the insured (or other examinee)
- A definite time and place for the examination as well as the name of the person who will be conducting the examination for the insurer
- The records or documents that the examinee must produce and bring to the examination
- The name, telephone number, and address of the person to contact if the examinee cannot, with good reason, be present for the examination

If the demand letter is not properly written, or if the time and place are unreasonable, the demand might not be enforceable. A second chance at obtaining the EUO might not be possible.

Procedures for Examinations Under Oath

The procedures for the EUO vary by area and company. Generally, the examination is conducted in an attorney's office. Although an adjuster can conduct the examination, insurers usually choose an attorney who is well trained in this area to conduct the examination.

Formalities

An insured required to give an EUO must appear in person and give oral testimony. Providing written answers to written questions is not sufficient. The insured need not submit to a polygraph (lie detector) test. The person examined under oath is sworn in by a court reporter that records every word said during the examination. The person examined might or might not be represented by an attorney.

Types of Questions

The insurer's attorney or the adjuster questions the person being examined. The examiner can ask anything relating to the loss. If an attorney is representing the examinee, the attorney can raise objections only to the materiality of a question. Questions are material if they might lead to information about the cause or amount of the loss, any possible contractual defense, or the insured's motives.

Thus, questions about the insured's financial condition at the time of loss, the insured's whereabouts at the time of loss, the source of funds to buy the damaged property, or previous losses would all be material. The attorney cannot object to anything else and has no right to offer evidence or cross-examine the examinee. The person being examined must answer any question material to the loss and, for such a question, cannot invoke the Fifth Amendment right against self-incrimination.

Continuances

Every effort should be made to allow enough time to complete the examination in one sitting. When the examination is arranged, all parties should understand that the time allowed should be adequate for the entire examination to be completed, without having to continue or conclude prematurely. An EUO's results can change dramatically if the examination is continued.

If the EUO is not completed in one sitting, the record should state that the examination is incomplete and will be continued. The time and date for the continuance of the examination should be stated on the record. Although plausible reasons for continuances exist, they should be avoided whenever possible. A plausible reason for a continuance would be if the insured's story were much more involved and complicated than the initial evidence indicated. The attorney or another person conducting the examination should not neglect any relevant evidence just because the evidence is extensive or complex.

Signing and Swearing to Transcript

When the EUO is completed, the court reporter transcribes the statement. Next, the person who conducted the interview reviews it. The attorney or adjuster sends the document to the examinee to review and sign. Only then is the exam completed. The policy says that the examinee must "sign and swear" to his or her statements under oath.

POTENTIAL PROBLEMS WITH AN EXAMINATION UNDER OATH

An examination under oath (EUO) can be a valuable tool for an insurer when a fraudulent claim is suspected.

What happens if the examinee does not appear for the examination or appears without the demanded documents? What if more than one person must be examined? What if the insured faces criminal charges? These situations require the adjuster to proceed firmly but carefully.

Failure to Appear

When an examinee does not request that the examination be rescheduled and does not appear at the EUO's appointed date and time, the insurer has three options:

- Do nothing further. In states in which an adjuster must respond to a proof of loss with a prescribed period, this is not an option if a proof has been filed.
- Send a letter requesting that the examinee contact the adjuster to reschedule the examination.
- Send a reservation of rights letter stating that because the examinee failed to appear, coverage for the loss may be denied.

Each insurer has different procedures for handling this situation. No further investigation with the insured should be conducted until management has been informed of the situation and has decided on a course of action.

Failure to Bring Documents

When an examinee appears for examination but does not have the demanded documentation, the insurer has two options:

- Proceed with the examination without documentation and continue on a later date when the examinee must return with the documents.
- Record that the person appeared but did not bring the demanded documents and reschedule the EUO for another date and time.

In either case, exactly what occurred and exactly what documents were to have been and are to be produced must be recorded. The record must state the exact date, time, and place of the rescheduled examination. The meeting should not end without recording the rescheduled examination.

Separate Examinations

When more than one person is to be examined and the adjuster wants separate examinations, the attorney representing the parties might reject the demand and insist on the presence of all parties. Before demanding individual exams, the adjuster must check the law of the applicable state. Courts vary widely on this issue. Also, current Insurance Services Office, Inc. (ISO) policies allow the adjuster to exclude any other "insured" from the examination. Thus, case law based on earlier policy forms should not determine this issue when a current ISO form applies.

Insured Facing Criminal Charges

An adjuster can demand an EUO from an insured who is being prosecuted or who is suspected of arson or fraud. If the insured refuses the EUO until after the fraud or arson charges have been decided and the insurer refuses to wait and denies the claim for violating the EUO condition, the insurer could become guilty of bad faith. Management must be involved in any decision to give an EUO under these circumstances. Although criminal charges against the insured do not eliminate the insured's contractual obligation to appear for an EUO, it is better for the insurer to wait, if possible. Unless the adjuster's investigation will be prejudiced by delay, the claim investigation should be suspended until the insured can cooperate.

SUMMARY

Every claim must be adjusted through a good-faith investigation. Adjusters must be careful not to waive any rights under the policy or engage in any conduct that would result in the insurer's being estopped from asserting its rights under the policy. One method used to avoid waiver and estoppel situations is a nonwaiver agreement.

Nonwaiver agreements clarify the insurer's intent to investigate the claim without waiving any of its rights. A reservation of rights letter can also be used for this purpose. In certain circumstances, the adjuster, in consultation with counsel, may decide that filing a declaratory judgment action is an alternative to denying a claim outright. Before a declaratory judgment action is filed or a claim is denied, many insurers have the claim reviewed by a claims committee of more experienced claims handlers to ensure that an appropriate course of action is chosen.

Many states have enacted rules and regulations regarding claims handling. The policy also establishes some requirements, and case law interprets the regulations and policy language. An insurer's breach of its good-faith duties usually occurs as a result of inadequate investigation, improper denial of coverage, unreasonable delay in settlement, unreasonable compromise, or withholding payment of the undisputed portion of the claim. If an insurer is found to have acted in bad faith, it can be subject to extracontractual damages.

One investigative tool that can aid in the resolution of a questionable coverage claim is the EUO. This tool should be used to verify the claim's validity. Many adjusters prefer to have a signed proof of loss before demanding the EUO.

One investigative tool that can aid in the resolution of a questionable coverage claim is the EUO. An attorney usually conducts the EUO. The insured is required by the policy to appear with requested documents and give sworn testimony. The EUO is recorded by a court reporter, and the typed transcript is later signed by the examinee.

Problems can occur with an examination under oath. These situations require the adjuster to proceed firmly but carefully.

ASSIGNMENT NOTE

1.   *Citizens Ins. Co. et al. v. Martin Herpolsheimer et al.*, 77 Neb 232, 10 NW 160.

Direct Your Learning ▶▶

Fraud Investigations

Educational Objectives

After learning the content of this assignment, you should be able to:

▷ Describe the federal and state laws regarding fraud.

▷ Given a claims situation:

- Identify indicators of fraud.

- Identify industry resources and state and local resources used in fraud investigations.

▷ In an arson claim:

- Explain under what circumstances an arson defense would be successful.

- Identify the policy provisions used to support an arson defense.

- Distinguish between the burden of proof in a civil lawsuit and a criminal lawsuit.

▷ Explain how a fire's origin and cause are determined.

▷ Explain the role of the members of an arson team.

▷ Explain how to evaluate suspicious burglaries and thefts.

▷ Explain the purpose of a special investigation unit (SIU) and the appropriate use of the SIU in a claims investigation.

Fraud Investigations

FRAUD PREVENTION LAWS

Fraud prevention laws can assist an adjuster who suspects that a claim is fraudulent.

Insurance fraud not only costs insurers and insureds billions of dollars each year, but it is also a crime. Both the federal government and state governments have enacted laws regarding fraud. Additionally, various insurance industry organizations, such as the Coalition Against Insurance Fraud and the National Association of Insurance Commissioners, create model laws relating to insurance fraud and actively campaign for their enactment.

Federal Laws

Various federal laws relate to fraud. The **Violent Crime Control and Law Enforcement Act of 1994**, 18 U.S.C. § 1033, makes insurance fraud a federal crime when it affects interstate commerce. (See the box for tips on reading a legal citation.) The **Federal Mail Fraud Statute**, 18 U.S.C. § 1341, prohibits the use of the U.S. Postal Service for the purpose of defrauding or obtaining money or property by means of false or fraudulent pretenses, representations, or promises. The **Racketeer Influenced and Corrupt Organization Act**, 18 U.S.C. § 1961, is commonly referred to as the RICO statute. This law specifies these acts as a racketeering activity: arson, theft from interstate shipments, mail fraud, wire fraud, bank fraud, and interstate transportation of stolen vehicles or property. Prosecution under the RICO statute requires at least two acts of racketeering activity. See the exhibit "How To Read a Legal Citation."

State Laws

Additionally, all fifty states and the District of Columbia have laws on various fraudulent activities. The states have reporting statutes and immunity statutes. Reporting statutes outline what types of activities must be reported to authorities and to whom the report must be made. The immunity statutes grant immunity to those who provide information to public authorities investigating a suspected fraud. In some states, immunity exists only when public authorities have initiated the request for information, but in most states, immunity also exists for those who initiate contact with the authorities. In most states, the immunity is limited in the sense that no immunity exists for malicious or fraudulent communications. Some states grant immunity from civil suits only, such as suits for defamation, false arrest, or infliction of mental

Violent Crime Control and Law Enforcement Act of 1994

A statute that makes insurance fraud a federal crime when it affects interstate commerce.

Federal Mail Fraud Statute

A statute that prohibits the use of the U.S. Postal Service for the purpose of defrauding or obtaining money or property by means of a false or fraudulent pretense, representation, or promise.

Racketeer Influenced and Corrupt Organization (RICO) Act

A statute that permits prosecution under federal law of two or more acts of racketeering activity, including arson, mail fraud, wire fraud, bank fraud, interstate transportation of stolen vehicles or property, and theft from interstate shipments.

How To Read a Legal Citation

A legal citation begins with the name of the case (Smith v. Jones) or the name of the law (Racketeer Influenced and Corrupt Organization Act). The name is followed by the citation, which lists the volume of the series of books in which the case or law is found, the name of the series (called the reporter), and the page or section. An index of the reporter abbreviations usually appears at the beginning of any legal case reporter.

A citation looks like this:

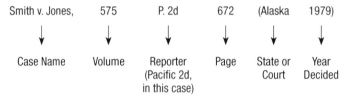

| Smith v. Jones, | 575 | P. 2d | 672 | (Alaska | 1979) |
| Case Name | Volume | Reporter (Pacific 2d, in this case) | Page | State or Court | Year Decided |

Note that the court's name and the year of the decision appear.

A citation to a law looks like this:

| 18 | U.S.C. | § 1961 |
| Volume | Reporter (United States Code, in this case) | Section |

[DA03933]

distress. Most states grant both civil and criminal immunity. Adjusters must become familiar with the laws in the states in which they operate.

As an example, the reporting statute from the state of California says that an insurer that believes a claim is fraudulent shall report the claim within sixty days of such determination to the Bureau of Fraudulent Claims and that the insurer may also report the claim to law enforcement officials or licensing officials governed by the Business and Professionals Code. The California code grants immunity from civil lawsuits if the report is made without malice. [1]

California also has similar statutes concerning the reporting of fraudulent motor vehicle thefts, incendiary fires, and fraudulent workers compensation claims.

In many insurance companies, the special investigations unit does the actual reporting of suspected fraud, not the property loss adjuster. Even so, adjusters should be familiar with the reporting requirements and the immunity statutes in the states in which they adjust claims because they may specify the good-faith practices for claims handling in a particular situation.

FRAUD DETECTION AND INVESTIGATION

Property loss adjusters must be vigilant for signs of fraud during the claims-adjusting process while at the same time conducting a good-faith investigation.

The adjuster is primarily responsible for detecting and investigating fraud. Therefore, the adjuster must be on the lookout for facts and circumstances that might signal a fraudulent claim. The adjuster should be familiar with fraudulent schemes that are common to insurance fraud but that could be carried out in different ways. Although part of the adjuster's job is to discover such schemes, the adjuster must investigate all claims fairly and thoroughly.

Fraudulent Schemes

Fraudulent schemes can be simple or complex. They can involve one person or many people. Adjusters who work in property claims become attuned to elements of a claim that might indicate a fraudulent scheme. Fraudulent schemes usually involve one or more elements. See the exhibit "Typical Elements of Fraudulent Schemes."

Typical Elements of Fraudulent Schemes

- Deliberately causing an accident or a loss

- Claiming that a loss or an event occurred when it did not

- Exaggerating the amount of a loss

[DA03935]

Detection

When reviewing a claim, a property loss adjuster might notice one or two indicators of fraud that might or might not mean that the claim is fraudulent. The adjuster must use common sense: for example, how likely is it that a homeowner would have a receipt for every item claimed to have been stolen, or how likely is it that a business owner would not have any receipts or invoices to document his or her loss? The adjuster must consider all of the circumstances and then test any suspicions within that environment.

To be prepared to thoroughly investigate a claim, a property loss adjuster should be aware of some common fraud indicators. See the exhibit "General Indicators of Property Insurance Fraud."

Some insurers are using technology to enhance the fraud-screening process. They are using software packages that screen claims data for specific indicators and then assign them a score or weight. A particular score or weight designates a claim as potentially fraudulent. These systems search the insurer's own

General Indicators of Property Insurance Fraud

Note: Adjusters should familiarize themselves with the following general indicators of insurance fraud, which may apply to more than one type of fraud scheme. After review of the general indicators, the adjuster can then refer to the more specific fraud categories which follow. The following categories of fraud are separated merely to facilitate your understanding of that type of fraud. However, multiple forms of fraud may appear in a single claim.

- Insured is overly pushy for a quick settlement.

- Insured is unusually knowledgeable regarding insurance terminology and the claim settlement process.

- Insured handles all business in person, thus avoiding the use of the mail.

- Insured is willing to accept an inordinately small settlement rather than document all claims losses.

- Insured contacts agent to verify coverage or extent of coverage just prior to loss date.

- Insured is recently separated or divorced.

- Suspiciously coincidental absence of insured or family at the time of the incident.

- Losses occur just after coverage takes effect, just before it ceases, or just after it has been increased.

- Losses are incompatible with insured's residence, occupation and/or income.

- Losses include a large amount of cash.

- Commercial losses that primarily involve seasonal inventory or equipment, and that occur at the end of the selling season, for example, a ski inventory loss in the spring or a farm machinery loss in the fall.

claims data to find similar patterns. Links are possible to third-party databases, which increase the number of claims reviewed for potential matches.

Investigation

An adjuster has a good-faith obligation to conduct a fair and adequate investigation to determine whether a loss is legitimate and whether coverage exists for the loss. Likewise, an insured should expect to document his or her loss and that this documentation will then be verified. How far can an adjuster go in a fraud investigation without crossing over the line into invasion of privacy? Local law can vary, so an adjuster should consult with counsel to determine whether his or her investigative techniques are acceptable within the jurisdiction.

Once an adjuster has suspicions regarding a claim, it is best to involve the insurer's special investigation unit (SIU). Early involvement preserves the investigation's integrity and facilitates additional investigation. It also allows the adjuster to continue to work on the loss while the parallel SIU investigation is conducted. Industry and government resources can assist an adjuster in identifying and investigating potentially fraudulent claims.

Industry Resources

Industry resources that can assist in identifying and investigating potentially fraudulent claims include (1) index systems, (2) investigative support organizations, and (3) educational organizations. Various index systems are available to research individual claimants and specific properties that are involved in claims. These indexes are so important that they should be an integral part of every claim investigation, even for claims that do not initially appear to be suspicious. These systems can identify previously fraudulent claimants and can detect multiple claims for the same property.

Insurance Services Office, Inc., (ISO) provides an extensive database for its client companies. As of this writing, the ISO ClaimSearch® database contains information on 300 million claims and receives approximately 250,000 new claims each day.[2] Insurers, self-insurers, third-party administrators, and other participants submit claims reports on a daily basis. The database can match reports to other claims based on the same individuals or businesses, addresses, Social Security numbers, vehicle identification numbers, driver's license numbers, tax identification numbers, and parties to the loss. This database now includes information on bodily injury claims, property claims, and auto theft and physical damage claims. It allows for the search of public criminal and civil records by partnering with various federal, state, and local databases.

The Art Loss Register (ALR) can be found on the Internet at www.artloss. com. This is a private database of stolen artwork that can aid in its identification and recovery.

The National Equipment Register (NER) on the Internet at www.nerusa. com contains information on heavy equipment, construction equipment, and agricultural equipment. Insureds are encouraged to register their equipment at this site so that if a piece is stolen, the ownership can be traced. This site also provides for a used equipment search in case the adjuster is trying to find a replacement for a stolen or damaged piece of equipment. Both the ALR and NER are allied with ISO ClaimSearch®.

The National Insurance Crime Bureau (NICB) fights all types of insurance crime, including arson. The NICB's full-time field agents investigate potential criminal activity in insurance claims. The NICB sponsors a Special Investigation Academy to educate claims personnel in all aspects of fighting fraudulent claims.

The Insurance Committee for Arson Control (ICAC) is composed of more than twenty of the leading insurers in the United States and includes participation from organizations such as the NICB and the Independent Insurance Agents and Brokers of America. ICAC is an educational and communication organization dedicated to fighting arson. It sponsors an annual National Arson Investigation Training Seminar, a training program for adjusters in the law, investigative techniques, and scientific principles of fighting arson. ICAC also sponsors an annual National Arson Forum, dedicated to coordinating the efforts of all parties interested in fighting arson, including the insurance industry, law enforcement authorities, public interest groups, and legislators.

The International Association of Arson Investigators grants the Certified Fire Investigator (C.F.I.) designation to those dedicated to investigating fire origin and cause and who meet education and experience requirements. It also publishes the quarterly *Fire & Arson Investigator*. This publication includes articles on the law and the investigation of arson as well as listings for educational programs on arson.

Various educational programs are specifically devoted to detecting and proving fraud, including arson. These include the Fraud Claim Law Associate (FCLA) program of the American Educational Institute and the fraud examiner program of the National Association of Certified Fraud Examiners.

Local and State Information

In addition to insurance industry resources, an adjuster can access information from many local and state government sources as well as the federal government. Some of these sources may require written authorization before releasing information. A special investigator or local counsel can help in determining what can and cannot be obtained without a written authorization.

Financial information may be obtained from the United States Federal Bankruptcy Court and from credit reporting agencies. Adjusters should be aware of what they can and cannot obtain under the Fair Credit Reporting Act and individual state acts. Because of the many privacy issues involved in obtaining financial information, adjusters should strictly adhere to their company's guidelines regarding the acquisition and use of such information. Some of these agencies may require written authorization before releasing any information. See the exhibit "Information Sources for Property Adjusters."

Information Sources for Property Adjusters

- County registrar of deeds
- Local building permit department
- Local city recorder or clerk
- Local and county street department or department of public works
- Retailers
- State division of motor vehicles
- State division of vital statistics
- State and local tax assessor/collector
- State office of corporate registrations
- Telephone companies
- Utility companies

[DA03938]

ARSON CLAIMS

Arson is one of the most significant types of fraud by insureds.

Arson is deliberately setting fire to a building, car, boat, or other property for a fraudulent or malicious purpose. Arson is not only a property crime, but it also can involve fatalities of civilians, firefighters, and even the arsonist.[3]

Intent to defraud an insurer is not the leading cause of arson; vandalism is the leading cause. About one-quarter of arson fires are drug-related. Minors are responsible for almost half of the arson fires in the United States. The leading cause of church fires is arson, usually motivated by vandalism, revenge, or racial bias.[4]

Arson

The deliberate setting of fire to property for a fraudulent or malicious purpose.

The Arson Defense

The insurance industry pays most arson losses because (1) insureds do not commit many of the arsons and (2) proving insured involvement is often not possible. Generally, the insured is not the arsonist. Proving that the insured was involved in the conspiracy to start the fire is much more difficult than proving that the fire was intentionally started.

Arson is a defense to an insurance policy claim only if it is committed by the insured or at the insured's direction. Arson against an insured's property committed by someone else with whom the insured has not conspired is simply a covered fire. Thus, the insurance industry pays such arson losses. However, the industry also pays many claims when the insurer suspects that the insured committed arson but cannot prove those suspicions. The outcome of cases of suspected arson depends on the quality of the evidence. The quality of an arson investigation depends on the timeliness and alertness of the adjuster first assigned to the claim.

Policy Provisions

Property insurance policies have no specific arson exclusion or defense. The coverage defense for arson arises when an insured represents an arson fire as an accidental fire and seeks coverage for the loss. Such a representation violates the fraud or misrepresentation clauses that are part of every property insurance policy.

Neither the HO-3 condition concerning concealment and fraud nor the Common Property Conditions attached to the BPP, quoted next, specifically mention arson. The Common Property Conditions state:

> This Coverage Part is void in any case of fraud by you as it relates to this Coverage Part at any time. It is also void if you or any other insured, at any time, intentionally conceal or misrepresent a material fact concerning:
>
> 1. This Coverage Part;
>
> 2. The Covered Property;
>
> 3. Your interest in the Covered Property; or
>
> 4. A claim under this Coverage Part. [5]

Representing an arson as an innocent or accidental fire violates these conditions. The true cause of a loss is certainly a material fact. Additionally, adjusters can use these conditions to void the insurance for material misrepresentations made before a loss or concerning the property in any way. Adjusters should remember the broad scope of these anti-fraud provisions when proving the cause of loss is difficult. Fraud of any type can be grounds for voiding the policy.

Other policy conditions might also be relevant to cases of suspected arson or fraud. Changes in the occupancy or use of a property are material and are usually addressed specifically in property insurance policies. For example, a substantial change in the risk covered by an HO-3 allows the insurer to cancel the policy. However, the policy remains in effect until canceled. Under the BPP, if the property is vacant for more than sixty consecutive days, the insurer need not pay at all for losses caused by vandalism, sprinkler leakage (if the insured has not protected against freezing), building glass breakage, water damage, theft, or attempted theft. The settlement amount for other losses will be reduced by 15 percent. Therefore, a fire loss would still be substantially covered.

Both the HO-3 and BPP provide that a mortgagee may submit a claim and be paid to the extent of its interest, even if the insured's claim can be denied. If a mortgagee is paid after an insured's claim has been denied, the insurer would be subrogated to the mortgagee's rights under the mortgage.

In such a situation, the insured/owner would be responsible to the insurer for the mortgage amount because, under most mortgages, the entire balance of the mortgage becomes due upon destruction of the premises.

Burden of Proof

With a specified-perils policy, the insured has the burden of proving that the cause of a loss is covered. If there is a covered cause of loss, such as fire, the insurer will then have the burden of proving any coverage exclusion, defense, or breach of policy conditions. For example, to succeed with an arson defense in denying coverage, the insurer must prove both that a fire was deliberately set and that it was set by, or at the direction of, the insured.

The arson defense is asserted in one of two contexts:

* The insured sues the insurer for the amount allegedly due on the claim plus, usually, extra damages for bad faith, and the insurer defends on the grounds of arson.

* The insurer initiates a declaratory judgment action in which it asks the court to declare that the insurer has no liability under the insurance policy because of the insured's arson.

The legal standard of proof by which the insurer must prove its case is the preponderance of evidence. This is the same standard of proof applicable to any party with the burden of proof in a civil lawsuit. Preponderant evidence is the more believable evidence; it need only be slightly more believable than the evidence to the contrary. Believability is not the same as the greater quantity of evidence. Evidence in a case of suspected arson might include oral testimony, business records, tangible physical evidence, and expert analysis. The evidence might be circumstantial and might depend on inference for its meaning. In any case, properly preserved, legally admissible evidence is crucial. No amount of suspicion, conjecture, or conviction on the adjuster's part substitutes for evidence. Unless an adjuster can prove his or her suspicions with evidence, the claim is valid and should be paid.

The burden of proof in a civil suit between an insured and an insurer is easier than the burden of proof in a criminal case. Prosecutors must prove crimes beyond a reasonable doubt; a defendant should be acquitted whenever reasonable doubt exists. Unless the evidence is overwhelming, an insured might be acquitted of criminal charges of arson or might never be prosecuted. These circumstances do not prevent an insurer from asserting an arson defense to an insurance claim. A jury might believe an insured committed arson even if it is not convinced beyond a reasonable doubt. Nevertheless, an insurer considering an arson defense must recognize that some jurors will regard the insured's acquittal on criminal charges as favorable for the insured. In contrast, because of the higher standard of proof in criminal cases, an insured's conviction on criminal charges of arson is a conclusive defense to an insurance claim.

THE COURSE OF AN ARSON INVESTIGATION

A property loss adjuster's detection of a suspicious claim and the evidence gathered in the resulting investigation are crucial to fighting arson.

An investigation into possible arson is time-sensitive and can have various outcomes. Upon initial assignment to the claim, an adjuster knows only that an insured has had a serious fire loss and expects to be paid. Adjusters must respond promptly and courteously to all initial reports of serious fire losses.

Adjusters usually become suspicious of a fire loss because of the fire's physical circumstances or because of the insured's behavior. The exhibit lists some of the circumstances that the National Insurance Crime Bureau identifies as indicators of possible arson. However, these circumstances are only indicators and do not prove arson. See the exhibit "General Indicators of Arson-for-Profit or Fire-Related Fraud."

The Course of an Arson Investigation

In any significant loss, especially one that might involve arson, the adjuster should obtain a nonwaiver agreement or issue a reservation of rights letter to preserve the insurer's rights while the investigation is conducted. The adjuster should preserve all of the insurer's rights as soon as there is any indication of the existence of a coverage issue.

Upon obtaining a nonwaiver agreement or issuing a reservation of rights letter, the adjuster should immediately begin parallel investigations. The adjuster should simultaneously (1) involve all supervisors, experts, and other resources needed to prove an arson case and (2) devote an equal effort to proving the insured's innocence and determining the amount of the claim. Failing to pursue one or the other of these avenues might result in the claim being improperly resolved. If the claim does involve arson and the adjuster tries to handle it alone or with belated assistance, the important evidence could be lost, the claim could have to be paid, and the insurer could face a bad-faith lawsuit. However, developing evidence of the insured's innocence is an excellent outcome for an arson investigation. Unfortunately, some insurers have become so fixated on evidence of a deliberate fire that they have completely overlooked that the insured had no motive to commit arson and would suffer significant financial harm even with a full insurance settlement.

The exhibit illustrates the importance of developing evidence carefully and not leaping to conclusions. Determining that a fire was deliberately set does not mean that the claim will not be paid, because the insured might not have set it. Determining that a fire was accidental does not end the need to preserve evidence because subrogation possibilities might exist. Many accidental fires and other losses result from some other party's negligence. See the exhibit "Course of a Fire Investigation."

General Indicators of Arson-for-Profit or Fire-Related Fraud

Note: While arson-for-profit is unquestionably the most vicious and costly economic assault on the property insurance industry, claims personnel should also be alert to fraud which occurs when an insured takes criminal advantage of an accidental fire.

- Building and/or contents were up for sale at the time of the loss.

- Suspiciously coincidental absence of family pet at time of fire.

- Insured had a loss at the same site within the preceding year. The initial loss, though small, may have been a failed attempt to liquidate contents.

- Building and/or business was recently purchased.

- Commercial losses include old or nonsaleable inventory or illegal chemicals/materials.

- Insured or insured's business is experiencing financial difficulties, e.g. bankruptcy, foreclosure.

- Fire site is claimed by multiple mortgagees or chattel mortgagees.

Indicators at the Fire Scene

- Building is in deteriorating condition and/or located in a deteriorating neighborhood.

- Fire scene investigation suggests that property/contents were heavily over-insured.

- Fire scene investigation reveals absence of remains of noncombustible items of scheduled property or items covered by floaters, e.g. coin or gun collections or jewelry.

- Fire scene investigation reveals absence of remains of expensive items used to justify an increase over normal 50 percent contents coverage, e.g. antiques, piano, or expensive stereo/video equipment.

- Fire scene investigation reveals absence of items of sentimental value; e.g. family Bible, family photos, trophies.

- Fire scene investigation reveals absence of remains of items normally found in a home or business. The following is a sample listing of such items, most of which will be identifiable at fire scenes except in total burns. Kitchen: major appliances, minor appliances, normal food supply in refrigerator and cabinets. Living Room: television/stereo equipment, record/tape collections, organ or piano, furniture (springs will remain). Bedroom: guns, jewelry, clothing and toys. Basement/Garage: tools, lawn mower, bicycles, sporting equipment, e.g. golf clubs (especially note if putter is missing from otherwise complete set). Business/Office: office equipment and furniture, normal inventory, business records (which are normally housed in metal filing cabinets and should survive most fires).

Indicators Associated With the Loss Incident

- Fire occurs at night, especially after 11 P.M.

- Commercial fire occurs on holiday, weekend or when business is closed.

- Fire department reports fire cause is incendiary, suspicious or unknown.

- Fire alarm and/or sprinkler system failed to work at the time of the loss.

Course of a Fire Investigation

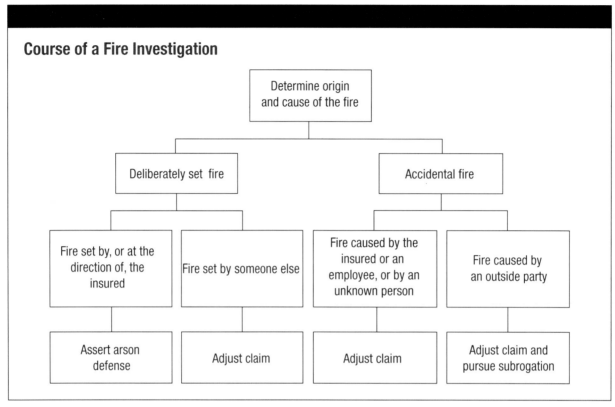

[DA03944]

Arson investigations explore four areas: (1) proof of incendiary fire, (2) proof of opportunity, (3) proof of motive, and (4) other miscellaneous evidence.[6] An adjuster who becomes suspicious must act immediately. Because most adjusters do not conduct the actual fire-scene investigation, experts must be retained as soon as arson is suspected. Generally, a good practice is to hire an origin and cause expert on any substantial fire loss. An origin and cause expert can assist in identifying subrogation possibilities. The experts whom an adjuster enlists in an arson investigation must also act promptly. Physical evidence from a fire scene might be bulldozed and carted away in a matter of hours. The expert must ensure that his or her techniques for sampling, collecting, and testing will stand up to scrutiny at trial. After an insured has performed the duties following loss, he or she expects to be paid. In many states, an insurer has a certain number of days following receipt of a sworn proof of loss in which to pay a claim or to explain why it will not do so. Ideally, an insurer should have its arson investigation completed, or nearly completed, upon receipt of the sworn proof of loss. Submission of the proof of loss is likely to be only a month or two after the loss.

Duties Following Loss

The insured's duties following loss are crucial in cases of suspected arson. In a suspected arson, the adjuster must remind the insured that these duties are conditions to the policy and that the claim will not be adjusted unless these duties are performed. The adjuster should specify the need to perform these duties in the initial nonwaiver agreement or reservation of rights letter.

A proof of loss must be signed and sworn to and must state the cause of the loss. Thus, the proof of loss is a crucial document in a suspected arson. A false statement about the fire's cause is grounds to void the policy. The adjuster should also check the proof thoroughly for fraud with respect to any other matter included in the proof of loss, such as the nature of the insured's interest, the existence of other insurance, and the amount of the loss.

An insured will probably list the cause of a suspected arson as "fire." After reviewing the contents of an insured's proof of loss and supporting documentation, the adjuster should require the insured's examination under oath (EUO). If arson is suspected, an experienced examiner, perhaps an attorney who is experienced in arson investigations and arson trials, should conduct the EUO. An insured's failure to appear for an EUO, failure to bring requested documents, or refusal to answer questions is grounds to not adjust the claim any further until the insured complies. Most policies require the examinee to write his or her signature after providing answers to questions. The signature is a formality that the insurer should insist on so that a judge or jury eventually faced with the statement will have no doubt about its authenticity or materiality.

Was the Fire Incendiary?

An **incendiary fire** is an intentionally set fire. To prove that a fire was set intentionally, an investigator must determine where and how the fire began. These circumstances are known among fire investigators as the fire's origin and cause. Adjusters, or experts working for them, should determine the origin and cause of every fire, including fires that appear to be accidental. As mentioned previously, a fire might have subrogation possibilities. Fire investigators thoroughly explore the known accidental causes of fires either to rule out such causes or to verify that they played a role in the fire in question.

Incendiary fire
An intentionally set fire.

Origin and Cause of Suspicious Fires

In almost all cases, intentionally set fires do not begin or progress like accidental fires. Investigators can identify these fires as intentionally set by how they begin and progress. The **origin** of a fire is the place where it ignited. Whatever provided the heat and combustible material that led to ignition is the **cause** of a fire. Intentionally set fires usually present suspicious circumstances as to both the origin and cause. Nevertheless, a fire investigator must prove the origin and cause of any suspicious fire before an adjuster can assert an arson defense.

Origin
The location of a fire's ignition.

Cause
The mechanism or event that provided heat and fuel for a fire.

Arsonists usually intend to destroy the structure they target. To be successful, they cannot generally rely on matches and paper alone to start the fire. Small, relatively low-heat fires are easily contained and exterminated. Arsonists often use accelerants, such as gasoline or other highly flammable chemicals, to accelerate the heat and spread of the fire. A structure soaked with gasoline will be consumed in flames before firefighters arrive. Other signs that a fire was deliberately set include unusual ventilation, such as all windows open, or evidence that fire alarms and sprinklers were disabled.

A fire's origin is important. Accidental fires originate in typical places, such as electric wiring, kitchen appliances, and heating equipment. Intentionally set fires often have multiple points of origin. Multiple points of origin are powerful evidence of an incendiary fire. Accidental fires virtually never have more than one origin. Also, a fire that originates in the middle of a floor is odd and inexplicable. Such an origin likewise indicates an incendiary fire. Fires that begin around, but outside of, electrical appliances are also suspicious.

Tracing a Fire's Origin

Determining a fire's origin is not always easy or even possible. When a fire reduces everything within the four walls of a building to debris, the physical evidence from one part of the debris might be indistinguishable from another part. However, a fire that is thorough and intense is not typical, and determining the cause of such a fire might be sufficient evidence of an incendiary fire, even if the origin is never determined. Less-thorough fires leave evidence of their origin for an investigator to study.

All fires begin as a small flame. A small flame must grow and spread before it can destroy a structure. As a fire grows and spreads, the origin usually remains in the flame. Thus, a fire's point of origin usually burns longer and more intensely than does any other point. After a fire is extinguished, investigators trace the spread of a fire from its perimeter to its origin by examining burn patterns and by following basic principles of fire transmission.

Fires require combustible material to burn. After the combustible material is consumed, the fire will go out unless it has spread to, or been fed, additional combustible material. The structure itself might be a source of combustible material, but most structures do not burn readily, especially commercial structures of concrete, masonry block, and steel. Structures burn only after a hot fire has otherwise developed.

Fires spread upward much more readily than they spread horizontally. Firefighters characteristically open the roof of a burning building to relieve the built-up heat inside. Once the heat and flames can escape upward, the fire's intensity subsides considerably. A fire will not spread horizontally except in these situations:

- It is trapped from moving upward by a ceiling or roof.
- A great deal of combustible material, such as trash or inventory crowded closely together, is present.
- An accelerant is present.

Investigators looking for the origin of a fire with significant horizontal spread try to explain such spread in terms of the factors listed above. A fire trapped by a structure's ceiling or roof will burn the ceiling or roof intensely. Thus, a fire should not traverse the floor of a room unless the ceiling is severely burned. Inspection of the debris usually confirms the presence or absence of crowded combustible property, such as inventory. Lack of these factors suggests the presence of an accelerant.

Many types of witnesses can provide information regarding a fire. A complete fire investigation includes interviews with firefighters, police, the property's owners, the property's occupants, neighborhood witnesses, the caller who raised the alarm, and the person who discovered the fire. The adjuster should obtain the police report and the fire marshal's report regarding the loss. When interviewing any potential witness, the adjuster must not mention that arson is suspected or make any suggestion as to what he or she thinks caused the fire. The exhibit lists important questions to ask witnesses. An investigator must compare the statements of witnesses to physical evidence for consistency. See the exhibit "Questions for Fire Witnesses."

Questions for Fire Witnesses

- Who discovered the fire?
- Who initiated the alarm?
- How did the witness happen to observe the fire?
- Where was the witness when he or she first observed the fire?
- Was the alarm given by an alarm or by telephone?
- Did the witness go near the building?
- Did the witness enter the building?
- What did the witness see?
- In what room or portion of the building was the fire burning when the witness first saw it?
- How large was the fire?
- What color were the flames?
- If the witness was close enough to observe, specifically what was burning?
- How rapidly did the fire spread to other portions of the building and the contents?
- Whom else did the witness observe around the building in the early stages of the fire?
- Was anyone observed in the building?
- Was anyone observed leaving the building when or just before the fire was observed?

[DA03946]

Identifying a Fire's Cause

Physical evidence of the cause of a fire can usually be found at its point of origin. Accidental causes of fires that begin in heating equipment, stoves, chimneys, or electric wiring can usually be identified. These devices are designed to handle fuel, heat, or electricity safely, but they can malfunction because of age, abuse, overuse, or poor maintenance. When a fire originates at one of these devices, an expert can examine the physical evidence and determine whether the fire began within the device or outside of it. A device burned from the inside shows different characteristics than one burned from the outside.

When an investigator cannot confidently identify the point of origin, the investigator must methodically examine all possible causes. In addition to examining all devices that handle heat, fuel, or electricity, the investigator should check for lightning, careless smoking, mischief by children, and vandalism. An adjuster should consider all possible innocent or accidental causes before concluding that the insured committed arson. Proving that a fire had an innocent cause is a favorable outcome of an arson investigation.

Detecting and Preserving Evidence of Accelerants

When the spread of a fire suggests the presence of accelerants or when all innocent explanations of a fire are disproved, an investigator must search for and preserve any evidence of accelerants. Fire consumes accelerants, but traces of unburned or partially burned accelerant usually survive the fire. Detection devices or trained dogs can locate accelerants in fire debris. Experts are needed to remove or document any surviving substances properly.

Sometimes, accelerants' presence can be proven indirectly. For example, if the depth of the charring on the floorboards is more than can be explained by the known heat of the fire, an accelerant was likely spread over that floor. Also, the burn pattern on the floor might show a telltale splashing pattern.

Investigators and adjusters should not leap to conclusions without adequate evidence. An insured might legitimately have gasoline, paint thinner, or similar substances stored on the premises that could catch fire. A wide variety of substances can serve as accelerants, and other materials, such as synthetic carpets, upholstery, and plastics, can have a chemical signature similar to accelerants. Thus, an expert's testimony must establish the exact nature of the substance in question and must show that the pervasiveness or pattern by which the substance was spread has no innocent explanation.

Did the Insured Cause the Incendiary Fire?

An incendiary fire is a covered loss unless it was committed by, or at the direction of, the insured. Proving the insured's involvement is an essential aspect of the arson defense. However, the insured's involvement is not necessarily likely just because an incendiary fire has occurred.

Sometimes, eyewitnesses see the insured start the fire, or the insured suffers burns while starting the fire. However, there is usually no direct evidence of who started the fire. An insured's involvement or noninvolvement in a fire is usually proven through circumstantial evidence. Some actions that the insured may have taken before, during, or after the loss can give rise to suspicion. These actions might include:

- The insured is the only one at the property at the time of the loss or is the last person to be at the property before the fire.

- In a residential loss, the insured and his or her family and pets are staying elsewhere for a short period of time.

- The insured has a copy of the insurance policy and other records that would normally have been on the premises at the time of the fire.

- The insured is having financial or marital difficulties.

- The insured applies pressure for a quick settlement and is willing to take less than the policy limits so that he or she does not have to supply the adjuster with additional documentation.

- The insured avoids using the U.S. Postal Service.

The Insured's Motive

The insured's motive for starting a fire is sometimes included as an essential element of the arson defense. Strictly speaking, the arson defense only requires proof that the insured deliberately caused the fire. Motive is not strictly necessary. However, in the absence of direct evidence of who set the fire, the insured's motive or lack of motive becomes the key circumstance. An adjuster should diligently investigate both an insured's motives to burn property and motives not to do so. Indeed, a conspicuous motive to commit arson might be the initial reason for thoroughly investigating origin and cause. Conversely, a conspicuous lack of motive is often a sufficient basis for an insurer to disregard an arson defense.

Financial need is the usual motive for an insured to commit arson. Property insurance policies are intended only to indemnify an insured for covered losses; that is, the loss settlement should return the insured to the same financial position that he or she was in before the loss. However, a loss settlement substitutes a liquid sum of cash for an illiquid, and sometimes unsalable, asset. An adjuster investigating an insured's financial motives to commit arson must examine whether the insured would be better off with cash than with the insured property. To do so, the adjuster must become familiar with the insured's financial condition. When the adjuster is investigating a fire at an insured's business site, expert accountants can inform the adjuster about the business's profitability, cash flow, and trends.

Financial motive to commit arson can arise when an asset is losing value, cannot be sold, or is overinsured. Out-of-season or obsolete merchandise is an example of property losing value. Certain other property might retain intrinsic value but be very hard to sell, such as a building in a glutted real estate market. Overinsuring property, unless done inadvertently, is suspicious. Insureds might be unaware of other insurance and other clauses of policies that prevent recovery for more than the property is worth. However, if aware of the significance of such policy clauses, an arsonist would not be likely to inform his or her insurer of other coverage.

Financial motives are not the only motives to commit arson. An incendiary fire committed by an insured is an arson even when the insured acts irrationally or harms himself or herself financially. An insured might act out of motives of revenge or hatred towards a spouse or business partner, especially during a difficult divorce or dissolution.

The Insured's Opportunity

Along with the motive to commit arson, the insured's opportunity to commit arson is powerful circumstantial evidence of involvement. The opportunity to commit arson can be demonstrated by the lack of an alibi, by behavior that enables another to commit arson, or by behavior demonstrating knowledge that arson was going to occur.

Alibi

An assertion that the party in question was elsewhere at the time the crime occurred.

An **alibi** is an assertion that the insured was elsewhere when the fire started. It is a strong defense if supported by unbiased witnesses. An adjuster should thoroughly explore an alleged alibi, including the relationships and motives of the insured's supporting witnesses. However, an insured can have a strong alibi even if he or she started the fire or enlisted someone else to start the fire. An apparent alibi can be meaningless if, for example, the remains of a timing device are found at the fire scene. A timing device can start a fire hours after being set. In such a situation, an insured with no verifiable alibi might be innocent, but that person would still have to be investigated as to having had the opportunity to commit the arson.

If, contrary to all previous practice, the premises where an arson occurred were apparently unlocked and burglar alarms were disabled, allowing access for the fire setter, an inference could be made that the insured was involved. Likewise, if an incendiary fire is set inside premises that are securely locked and have not suffered a break-in, an inference could be made that someone with keys to the premises started the fire. Proof of an incendiary fire in such circumstances is evidence supporting the allegation of the insured's involvement. However, following a major fire and firefighting activity, proving that a break-in did not occur is often impossible.

The insured's involvement can be inferred when the insured apparently knew that arson was about to occur. Following a fire, debris of personal property should be present throughout the premises. The debris should reflect the usual contents of similar premises. A business location should contain inventory, office equipment, and extensive business records. A residence should have the furniture, appliances, clothes, and other items typical to a home. The absence of a great deal of expected contents suggest these contents were removed before the fire, especially if the missing items are high-value or sentimental objects. If items seem to be missing, the adjuster should canvass neighbors for witnesses who saw their removal.

THE ARSON TEAM

An adjuster investigating and proving arson should not act alone.

The adjuster should involve various experts as soon as he or she suspects arson. Such experts include these:

- A professional investigator
- An origin and cause expert
- A forensic chemist
- Public authorities, such as the police, the fire marshal, and prosecutors
- An attorney
- An accountant

The Adjuster and Investigator

The adjuster or the supervisor, claims examiner, or claims manager directing the outside adjuster acts on the insurer's behalf. The insurer has promised to pay covered claims but is not obligated to pay intentionally caused losses. The adjuster must fulfill the insurer's promise but must protect the insurer's rights to deny fraudulent claims. Thus, the adjuster faces the fundamental issue in any arson investigation: Should the claim be paid or resisted? That decision has enormous consequences for both the insurer and the insured. The adjuster has an ethical obligation to deny claims that involve arson and pay claims that do not.

Adjusters must be familiar with the circumstances that might indicate arson. The adjuster's failure to recognize signs of arson could cause the insurer's rights to be waived. An adjuster who sees signs of a possible arson must know how his or her employer responds to suspected arsons and must involve the people and resources necessary to conduct a thorough and correct arson investigation.

The adjuster might serve as an investigator, or the insurer might hire an independent professional investigator. An insurer's adjuster can usually identify relevant sources of information and take statements from witnesses. Adjusters should also check industry resources for information on past claims. A professional investigator might be preferable for obtaining background information on the insured, such as financial, legal, and personal records.

The adjuster must coordinate the efforts of all others involved in the arson investigation, give clear instructions on the scope of an assignment, respond promptly to all inquiries and other issues that arise, and reserve for himself or herself the ultimate decision on the claim. An adjuster can make good decisions in cases of suspected arson by gaining experience and education in the elements of arson. Adjusters must develop a sophisticated sense of the credibility and persuasiveness of various types of evidence and should always approach an arson investigation with the attitude that proving an insured's innocence is preferable to proving arson.

Origin and Cause Expert and Forensic Chemist

Origin and cause experts are often former fire department investigators. They typically have much more experience studying fire scenes than even the most experienced adjusters do. Additionally, they usually have specific training and education in fire-scene analysis. An adjuster, even one with extensive experience, is not the best choice to determine origin and cause. Origin and cause experts must often testify in court. As the insurer's employee or agent, an adjuster would be seen as a biased witness. An origin and cause expert is crucial to proving that a fire was incendiary and thus essential to proving an arson.

To be an effective witness, the origin and cause expert must be able to demonstrate that his or her conclusions are based on specific scientific, technical, or specialized knowledge. Others must respect the methods and techniques used to support the expert's findings and conclusions in the field. An adjuster should select the origin and cause expert in consultation with senior claim staff and legal counsel so that the potential for a confrontation over the expert's methods and qualifications is minimized. Origin and cause experts should not rely solely on the fire marshal's investigation. An insurer that hires an origin and cause expert should expect an independent determination of how and where a fire began.

A forensic chemist plays a specific role in an arson investigation by detecting, identifying, and preserving chemical residue from a fire scene that is relevant to determining the cause of a fire. A forensic chemist must be trained in preserving evidence in a legally admissible manner. Also, the chemist is likely to have to testify in court and should be clear and well-spoken, especially when explaining scientific instruments and procedures. A forensic chemist might also serve as an origin and cause expert. However, the expertise of each job is distinct enough that insurers should get the best person for each element.

Public Authorities

A city or county fire marshal may investigate the fire. Some communities require all structural fires to be inspected. Others inspect only suspicious fires. The adjuster should ascertain the fire marshal's identity and scope of authority. When a fire is not investigated by a fire marshal, the adjuster must make his or her own determination as to the origin and cause, relying on the insurer's own expert.

A fire marshal has different goals than an adjuster has. The fire marshal's conclusions are used to prevent future fires, strengthen building codes with respect to fire protection, and identify suspects for criminal prosecution.

Adjusters are interested in criminal prosecutions, but they cannot defer their investigation on the assumption that the public authorities will investigate the cause of the fire and prosecute those involved. Public authorities might decline to prosecute because the evidence is insufficient for a criminal conviction or because no injuries or deaths resulted from the fire. Also, public authorities vary widely with respect to their ability, resources, and motivation to investigate and prosecute arson.

Adjusters should interview the firefighters who worked at the fire in question. These interviews should occur as soon as possible following the fire while the firefighters' memories are fresh and the public authorities are still organizing or conducting their own investigation. Property loss adjusters should determine what firefighters observed with respect to the fire's origin; whether the premises were locked and secured; whether fire alarms and sprinklers functioned; whether unusual smoke or odors were present; whether the owner appeared during the firefighting; and, if so, how the owner behaved. Firefighters might not have any special training in determining origin and cause, but their opinions about whether the fire seems suspicious are valuable. The adjuster should also interview the personnel in the fire department or fire marshal's office who are responsible for determining origin and cause.

When public authorities investigate a suspicious fire, they usually obtain a statement from the property owner. This statement should be available to the adjuster investigating the same fire. The owner's statement to the public authorities does not relieve the insured of the obligation to submit to an examination under oath (EUO). The examiner conducting the EUO should look for discrepancies between the EUO and the statement given to the public authorities.

Attorneys

A claim denied as arson is likely to result in a lawsuit. Adjusters must foresee having to prove their position to a judge or jury. Adjusters who handle suspected arsons must learn the rules of court evidence and develop their investigations accordingly. They might have to appear in court as witnesses. Attorneys experienced in arson cases help prepare adjusters for court and can answer legal questions.

Defending an arson claim has three key elements. First, a good investigation with proper documentation and qualified experts is essential. Second, the denial of the claim has to have been accomplished in a timely and effective manner. Third, a declaratory judgment action should be filed shortly after the denial is issued. Attorney involvement in all of these elements helps to ensure a successful defense.

Part of an adequate investigation is the EUO. An attorney usually conducts the EUO because experienced attorneys are familiar with the style and scope of questioning required in these examinations. Also, the adversarial nature of EUOs requires someone other than the adjuster to be the examiner because the adjuster must continue to communicate with the insured. An EUO is an excellent opportunity to see what kind of witness the insured will make. An arson defense's success or failure depends heavily on the insured's credibility. Adjusters should attend EUOs as often as possible.

Adjusters should also involve an experienced trial attorney in suspected arson cases as soon as possible. Attorneys with the right experience can advise adjusters about what evidence is essential, what evidence is persuasive, and what evidence is favorable to the insured. If they follow an experienced attorney's advice, adjusters should go to trial with an arson defense only with solid cases. A solid case is protection against bad-faith liability.

Accountants

Because one of the most common motives for arson is financial, involving an accountant in an arson investigation is important. By the time of an examination under oath, an adjuster should know as much about the insured's financial condition as the insured does. Few adjusters have sufficient training in accounting to do this by themselves. Upon first becoming suspicious of an arson, the adjuster should immediately request complete financial records from the insured. The Building and Personal Property Coverage Form Duties In The Event Of Loss specifically provide, "As often as may be reasonably required, permit us to … examine your books and records. Also permit us to … make copies from your books and records."[7] An adjuster should request at least the insured's tax returns, records from suppliers, all evidence of indebtedness, all regularly prepared financial statements during the past year, and all bank statements from the past year. The adjuster should also consult with an expert accountant to determine what other records are important and likely to exist.

An accountant might want several years' worth of records to look for trends in the insured's business. The insured's business might have natural seasonal or annual trends. Apart from such natural trends, an accountant can discern the overall trend for the insured's company. Is the insured's business failing, or has it recently lost some revenue? Have the owners tried selling the business recently? An accountant can answer these questions and can spot other telltale signs of trouble. For example, a business that fails to pay the Internal Revenue Service (IRS) the withholdings from its employees' pay is in both legal and financial trouble. An accountant can address the ultimate question about the insured's financial motive: Would the insured be better off with an insurance settlement than with an intact building?

STAGED BURGLARIES AND THEFTS, PADDED CLAIMS, AND MULTIPLE POLICIES

Arson is one of the most serious types of property loss fraud, but adjusters should be alert for other types of property loss fraud, including staged burglaries and thefts, padded claims, and claims under multiple policies.

As with arson, the two keys to fighting any type of fraud are (1) detection and (2) proof. Adjusters must be alert for indicators of fraud and, once alerted, must diligently gather evidence that proves the fraud.

Following a burglary or theft, the insured property is gone and is rarely recovered. Thus, burglaries and thefts are easy to stage. An insured staging a burglary might break a door or window lock with a crowbar to simulate a burglar's break-in. A damaged lock can be included in the claim, but there need not be any physical evidence of the event. Most homeowners cannot document the vast majority of their personal property.

Staged Burglaries/Thefts

The exhibit lists circumstances that the NICB has indicated would be suspicious in burglary or theft claims. Adjusters should remember these circumstances but must also remember that any of them can arise in legitimate losses. These circumstances are only indicators and not proof of fraud. An adjuster who is suspicious about the circumstances of any loss must gather solid evidence to prove fraud. As with arson investigations, adjusters must reserve the insurer's rights, must require the insured to perform all duties listed in the policy, and must move rapidly in the investigation. See the exhibit "Burglary/Theft Fraud and the Claims Process."

Adjusters must exercise judgment with burglary and theft claims. Although most homeowners cannot document most of their personal property, they are more likely to have evidence of high-value items. They might have owners' manuals, checks, or receipts, or they might remember where they bought the items. Many stores have records of purchases that go back several years by individual customer name. If the property was alleged to have been a gift, the donor should be able to identify the store where it was purchased. Nevertheless, some homeowners who suffer genuine burglaries or thefts cannot produce documentation or remember how they obtained their property. Adjusters should be creative and reasonable regarding documentation. Photos, videos, boxtops, and labels can be useful in documenting ownership when the receipt is no longer available. However, just about anything can be created to document a fraudulent claim, so adjusters should scrutinize all information about the loss.

Adjuster Tip—The NICB has the technology to analyze receipts or documents to determine whether they are forgeries or whether alterations have been made to them.

Burglary/Theft Fraud and the Claims Process

Indicators of Burglary/Theft Fraud

- Losses include total contents of business/home including items of little or no value.

- Losses are questionable, e.g. home stereo stolen out of car, fur coat stolen on trip to Hawaii.

- Losses include numerous family heirlooms.

- Losses include numerous appraised items and/or items of scheduled property.

- Extensive commercial losses occur at site where few or no security measures are in effect.

- No police report or an over-the-counter report in situations where police would normally investigate.

Indicators Associated With the Claims Process

- Insured over-documents losses with a receipt for every loss and/or receipts for older items of property.

- Insured's loss inventory differs significantly from police department's crime report.

- Insured cannot provide receipts, canceled checks or other proof of ownership for recently purchased items.

- Insured provides numerous receipts for inexpensive items, but no receipts for items of significant value.

- Insured provides receipt(s) with incorrect or no sales tax figures.

- Insured provides receipt(s) with no store logo (blank receipt).

- Loss inventory indicates unusually high number of recent purchases.

- Insured cannot recall place and/or date of purchase for newer items of significant value.

- Insured indicates distress over prospect of an examination under oath.

- Insured cannot provide bank or credit card records for recent purchases of significant value.

- Insured provides receipts/invoices from same supplier that are numbered in sequence.

- Insured provides receipts from same supplier with sequence numbers in reverse order of purchase date.

- Insured provides two different receipts with same handwriting or typeface.

- Insured provides single receipt with different handwriting or typefaces.

- Insured provides credit card receipts with incorrect or no approval code.

Adjusters must evaluate the plausibility of every reported burglary or theft. Is the type and amount of property allegedly stolen consistent with the insured's standard of living? Does the claim include items such as artwork, antiques, jewelry, guns, or musical instruments that often have individual floater coverage and are individually underwritten? Were all items supposedly purchased recently? Does the claim include high-value items that burglars might not take because of their bulk or weight, such as large Oriental carpets or large power tools? Does the claim include items that burglars virtually never target, such as clothes, kitchen utensils, books, sofas, or washing machines?

Alleged burglaries to commercial insureds present different challenges than do homeowner claims. Commercial insureds should have complete records of their property, including types, amounts, quality, and sources and dates of purchase. Adjusters should be able to document the property's existence. With commercial insureds, a typical fraudulent burglary involves relocating the "stolen" property. Adjusters should canvass the neighborhood for witnesses of extensive moving operations, especially during irregular hours. The adjuster should try to interview employees, alone and separate from each other, about the alleged event. As with arsons, adjusters need information about the financial condition of the insured's business. A successful business with good current inventory is much less likely to stage a burglary than is a failing business with unsalable inventory.

Adjusters should require all insureds to report all burglaries or thefts to the police. Among the duties after loss in the HO-3 is that the insured must notify the police in case of loss by theft. The Business and Personal Property Coverage Form requires the insured to notify the police if a law may have been broken. Adjusters should require a signed, sworn proof of loss with every burglary or theft claim.

Padded Claims

A legitimate loss can be the occasion for an insured to inflate the claim by including items that were not part of the loss or by inflating the value of items that were. Insureds who engage in this behavior rationalize it in terms of recovering their deductible or premium payments. Some in the insurance industry even regard this "soft" fraud as less objectionable than the "hard" fraud of completely fabricated claims. Nevertheless, an insured who intentionally misrepresents a material fact commits fraud. Items that are the subject of a claim and their value are material facts to which the insured must swear in a proof of loss. The circumstances listed in the exhibit might also be present when an insured pads a claim.

Requiring the insured to prove his or her claim is crucial to fighting padded claims. Adjusters should insist that insureds submit sworn proofs of loss and all required supporting documentation in all cases of suspected padding. As with suspicious burglaries, adjusters should consider the inherent plausibility or implausibility of the insured's claim. Unfortunately, padding can be difficult to detect.

Multiple Policies

An insured who has two or more policies covering the same loss and who does not disclose the multiple coverages to all insurers has almost certainly intended fraud from the outset. An insured might inadvertently have two or more policies in effect at once but should disclose these policies to all affected insurers when a loss occurs. The other insurance clauses of the various policies will then result in the insured's receiving only an amount that indemnifies the loss. An insured should not collect multiple recoveries for the same loss. However, if the various insurers do not know about the multiple policies' existence and if the insured has submitted a fraudulent proof of loss to each insurer, swearing in each that no other coverage exists, there is the potential for duplicate recovery.

An insured who submits the same claim to several insurers has probably staged the claim. Any indicators that a claim might have been staged should also alert the adjuster to the possibility of multiple insurance policies. By using one of the index systems, the adjuster can detect multiple claims from the same loss or multiple claims involving the same property. Adjusters should make a habit of submitting all claims to an index system, even those that seem completely legitimate.

SPECIAL INVESTIGATION UNITS

Insurers have established units specially dedicated to investigating suspicious claims and other possible frauds. These units are usually known as **special investigation units (SIUs)**.

Special investigative unit (SIU)
A division set up to investigate suspicious claims, premium fraud, or application fraud.

Insurers have an obvious interest in resisting fraudulent claims, but most ordinary claim units are staffed in a way that assumes almost all claims are routine. To have staff with the time and expertise to investigate suspicious claims, insurers created SIUs. Personnel selected for SIU work are carefully trained. They perform investigations that are infeasible for claims representatives and property loss adjusters handling routine claims.

The Need for SIUs

Most claims departments are staffed on the assumption that all claims are routine. Such staffing makes devoting more time or effort to suspicious claims difficult. The appropriate investigation of suspicious claims is time-consuming. Furthermore, since the 1970s, insurers have relied more on telephone contact than on in-person meetings to resolve claims.

State legislatures and insurance departments have been aware for years of fraud and its cost. Most states make insurance fraud a crime. Before the 1990s, only a few states had bureaus within the state government devoted to fighting insurance fraud. Today, forty-one states have some type of fraud bureau.[8] Additionally, several states require insurers to maintain SIUs. State requirements have increased the already existing incentive for insurers to create and operate SIUs.

The Mission of SIUs

SIUs do not exist simply to deny claims. Claims representatives could deny claims in much greater volume and at much less expense. Likewise, SIUs do not exist simply to prove fraud. SIU investigations often prove that a claim is legitimate and should be paid. SIUs exist to determine the facts about suspicious claims, to prove fraud when it can be proven, to avoid improper and unfounded accusations that can cause bad-faith problems, and to pay claims that the evidence supports.

SIUs investigate more than just first-party property claims. Suspicious circumstances might also exist in workers compensation cases, auto accidents, auto theft claims, and bodily injury claims. In addition to addressing individual claims, SIUs investigate organized rings of professional claimants and any doctors, lawyers, and body shops that assist such rings. When the evidence supports a finding of fraud, SIUs also try to obtain criminal prosecutions through the state attorney general, local prosecutors, or the United States Attorney, in cases of violations of federal law. Successful criminal prosecutions require expert collection and preservation of evidence. Therefore, many SIUs employ former police or other law enforcement authorities.

Some SIUs investigate types of fraud other than claims fraud. For example, SIUs might be assigned to investigate:

- Misrepresentations on policy applications, including identity and use of vehicles; exposure base and classification of workers compensation; the applicant's financial condition; and claims history
- Agents' wrongdoing, including the appropriation of trust funds, the issuance of phony bonds, and the failure to place coverage
- Internal fraud, including collusion by claims personnel with outsiders, embezzlement, and kickback schemes

SIU personnel who investigate white-collar wrongdoing in the insurance industry must have different skills than those required by typical criminal investigations, and they must have a thorough understanding of the legal, contractual, and business relations among insureds, applicants for coverage, agents, company personnel, and insurers.

Insurer Interest in SIUs

Insurers have a significant self-interest in fighting fraud. Payment of fraudulent claims is extremely expensive. Because of the nature of fraud and the difficulty of estimating exaggerated claims, the precise number of paid fraudulent claims is impossible to state. The annual cost of fraud is undoubtedly comparable to the cost of the worst natural disasters. Consequently, all property-casualty insurers fight fraud, and nearly all have a formal fraud-control program.

The insurance industry supports collective resources for fighting fraud, such as the National Insurance Crime Bureau (NICB) Special Investigation Academy for training in fraud awareness and investigation. Also, the International Association of Special Investigation Units (IASIU) is a professional organization of SIU personnel. It has conducted an annual seminar on fraud awareness, investigation, and prosecution since 1986. Moreover, several insurers have joined the Coalition Against Insurance Fraud, a group of insurers, consumer organizations, and governmental bodies that tries to influence public policy through a united effort by the various organizations affected by fraud.

Antifraud programs' prevalence and size often depend on the insurer's size.[9] The lack of state requirements and specialization in types of insurance that are less prone to fraud are often reasons why a small- to medium sized insurer does not have a formal antifraud program.[10] The difficulty in performing a true cost-benefit analysis may be another reason. The costs of a formal antifraud program are usually quantifiable, but the benefits are far less easy to identify and quantify. Nevertheless, fighting fraud can result in these benefits to an insurer:

• Successful denial of fraudulent claims that can be quantified (for example, arson of a known dollar amount)

• Successful denial of fraudulent claims that cannot be easily quantified (for example, phony injury claims whose dollar amount cannot be precisely known)

• Reduction of exaggerated claims

• Discouragement to those considering submitting fraudulent or exaggerated claims

• Increased public awareness that fraud can and should be fought

Although all of these benefits are real, only the first can be quantified. In contrast, the costs of SIU operations are these:

• Direct salary, benefits, training costs, overhead, and support for the SIU. These costs are expended on a unit that is extremely inefficient in the sense of handling relatively few claims compared to ordinary claims operations.

• Increased legal expenses, even when the SIU is successful.

• Increased bad-faith lawsuits and legal expense to defend such suits, with occasional adverse results.

State Mandates

After hearing for years from insurers about the extent of insurance fraud, many state legislatures and insurance departments enacted laws making antifraud efforts mandatory. Although most states have antifraud bureaus within the insurance department or attorney general's office, a few states have gone further. A small but increasing number of states require antifraud plans from insurers, and a few require SIUs.

The exhibit is an excerpt from the Pennsylvania law requiring antifraud plans of auto insurers. This law is typical of the requirements contained in mandatory antifraud laws. Additionally, the Pennsylvania Department of Insurance has enacted extensive and detailed regulations to enforce this excerpted provision. In states with mandatory antifraud laws, insurers must have specific procedures in place to fight fraud. As of February 2000, Arkansas, California, Colorado, the District of Columbia, Florida, Kentucky, Maryland, Minnesota, New Hampshire, New Jersey, New Mexico, New York, Ohio, Pennsylvania, Tennessee (for workers compensation only), and Washington had laws mandating antifraud plans, and Delaware required insurers to report all suspicious claims to the state bureau. Many of these states require SIUs as part of the plan. California has detailed requirements in its regulations as to the organization, staffing, education, and training for SIUs, and the detection, investigation, prosecution, recording, and reporting of fraudulent claims. See the exhibit "Control of Plans."

Control of Plans

The anti-fraud plans of each insurer shall establish specific procedures:

- To prevent insurance fraud, including internal fraud involving employees or company representatives; fraud resulting from misrepresentation on applications for insurance coverage; and claims fraud.

- To review claims to detect evidence of possible insurance fraud and to investigate claims where fraud is suspected.

- To report fraud to appropriate law enforcement agencies and to cooperate with such agencies in their prosecution of fraud cases.

- To undertake civil actions against persons who have engaged in fraudulent activities.

- To report fraud-related data to a comprehensive database system.

- To ensure that costs incurred as a result of insurance fraud are not included in any rate base affecting the premiums of motor vehicle insurance consumers.

Title 75, Pennsylvania Consolidated Statutes Annotated, § 1812. [DA03958]

SIU Procedures

An SIU's chief purpose is to resolve claims correctly. In that respect, SIUs function like ordinary claims operations and perform many of the same tasks, such as building and maintaining claims files; communicating with insureds, claimants, and witnesses; and negotiating settlements. Nevertheless, the cases assigned to SIUs are suspicious ones that require much more investigation and scrutiny than the typical claims operation can perform. Most of the operating characteristics special to SIUs result from the nature of this work.

Staffing

Two backgrounds predominate among SIU personnel: prior claims work and law enforcement work. Both backgrounds provide valuable experience, but each must be supplemented with additional training.

Claims personnel selected for SIU work are usually among the best. They typically have several years of successful experience investigating and negotiating claims and have demonstrated the interest and energy necessary to take on special duties. Upon joining an SIU, claims personnel must acquire deeper expertise in investigating claims, collecting and preserving evidence in a legally admissible manner, and litigating policy defenses. They usually acquire expertise in particular areas, such as origin and cause analysis or examination of financial records.

Law enforcement personnel seeking career advancement and a stable work environment are often attracted to insurer SIUs. They might be police or fire marshal officers who have extensive training and experience in collecting and preserving evidence. However, not every former police officer is appropriate for SIU work. The orientation of claims work, even in SIUs, is to determine whether the insurance policy covers a given situation, while law enforcement authorities are interested in proving whether a person committed a crime. Although the coverage issue faced by SIUs is often whether an insured submitted a fraudulent claim, they should always try to resolve claims according to policy language. SIUs do not presume an adversarial attitude toward the subjects of their investigations. Once hired into an SIU, a former law enforcement officer must learn insurance policy coverages, insurance business relationships, and litigation in the civil courts.

Management of SIUs is usually directly under an insurer's senior claims officer, but, depending on an SIU's focus, it might be under other nonclaims corporate officers or decentralized into regional or local offices. In any case, the person to whom the SIU reports must be understanding and supportive of the SIU's mission and must be able to command adequate resources for the SIU to perform properly.

Detection and Review

SIU personnel and claims personnel throughout an insurance company must recognize fraud indicators. They cannot defend claims as frauds unless they first recognize the possibility of fraud. Claims representatives should be familiar with the fraud indicators for the types of claims they handle, because the indicators differ by type of claim. For example, the indicators of workers compensation fraud are very different from those for auto theft fraud or arson.

SIU personnel must develop more sophistication about those indicators than the typical claims representative has. In a well-functioning claims operation, claims representatives refer files for review by the SIU when fraud indicators are present. The indicators alone prove nothing. SIU personnel must develop judgment concerning which specific cases referred to them are candidates for intensive investigation and scrutiny. Such judgment is based on combinations of circumstances or the recognition that a single circumstance in a given case is compelling. In well-functioning claims operations, more files are referred to the SIU than the SIU selects for investigation.

Investigation

All property loss adjusters investigate, but SIU personnel investigate more thoroughly. Their investigations often include steps that ordinary adjusters do not take. For example, SIU personnel must learn to preserve physical evidence to criminal case standards, which involves obtaining signed waivers from owners for removal of evidence and maintaining a log showing the chain of custody of that evidence.

SIU personnel usually investigate in person. Those who would commit fraud are especially uncomfortable with direct scrutiny. When taking statements from insureds, claimants, and witnesses, SIU personnel are more likely than ordinary adjusters to verify previous names, previous addresses, Social Security numbers, spouse identification, fictitious business names, date of birth, and any other information useful in establishing the complete history of a person or business. SIU personnel establish the insurance coverage history of any insured or claimant, especially the dates of coverage and the agents who placed the coverage.

SIU investigators try to obtain original documents rather than copies. To invoke the federal mail fraud laws, SIU personnel save envelopes when they receive items in the mail. They also obtain written or recorded statements from the person who supplied or can verify the documents. In first-party losses, SIUs require insureds to complete proofs of loss, including all supporting documentation.

Insureds seeking insurance policy benefits must provide financial and medical releases upon the insurer's request. SIU personnel use these releases to obtain complete histories of the claimant's financial or medical condition. Professional accounting or medical review might be necessary to clarify a claimant's situation.

Databases and online services have greatly increased SIU investigative power. All fifty states can be searched at once for information on a claimant.

Antifraud laws enacted in many states require insurers to share their investigations with law enforcement authorities when a claim is suspicious. SIU personnel are usually eager to do so because a criminal conviction would be conclusive as to an insurance claim. However, SIUs must not depend on law enforcement authorities. Criminal investigation or prosecution might not be pursued because the authorities do not have the staff, training, budget, or motivation to pursue the crime or because they determine that the evidence is insufficient for criminal charges.

Training

SIUs devote significant resources to training both SIU staff and other claims personnel. SIU staff receive training from more experienced members and from formal programs run by the IASIU and the NICB. The National Association of Certified Fraud Examiners and the American Educational Institute also have fraud education programs for SIU personnel.

Education of typical claims personnel is essential to any SIU's success. SIUs receive claims only by referral from other claims personnel. Claims personnel must be educated to recognize signs of possible fraud and must know how to make referrals to the SIU. SIU personnel can conduct regular seminars and meetings with claim staff to create awareness and remind everyone of the SIU's role. Company newsletters can feature SIU activities.

Paying or Denying Claims

An SIU's objective is to resolve claims correctly. Some SIU claims are paid, and some are denied. Claims are paid when the SIU investigation proves that the claim is legitimate, or when the SIU believes it cannot prove fraud, even though the claim still seems suspicious. From the point of view of the insured and society, paying claims is preferable unless fraud can be proven. Allegations of fraud are an extremely serious matter and can result in criminal charges. However, claims staff can become discouraged from making SIU referrals when suspicious claims end up being paid, especially if the claims staff did a great deal of the investigation required by the SIU. SIU staff should be sensitive to this reaction and should explain why fraud cannot be proven in a given case. Such explanations preserve the SIU's goodwill among the claims staff and will reinforce the claims staff's fraud education.

When claims are denied, the SIU must be prepared for lawsuits. SIUs should have extensive working relationships with attorneys and law firms experienced in insurance defense work, both first party and third party. SIU personnel should be sophisticated about insurance litigation, including the persuasiveness of various evidence, the value of proposed discovery, and the need to present scientific or financial information clearly. When a claim denial is successful, whether before or after civil litigation occurs, the SIU should consider asking the law enforcement authorities to prosecute. Some SIUs are satisfied to deny a fraudulent claim, but others believe criminal prosecution is important as a matter of principle and is the best deterrent to fraudulent behavior by others.

SUMMARY

Both the federal government and state governments have enacted laws regarding fraud. These laws can assist an adjuster who suspects that a claim is fraudulent.

The adjuster has the primary responsibility for detecting and investigating fraud. As such, the adjuster must always watch for facts and circumstances that might signal a fraudulent claim.

Arson is one of the most serious types of first-party property claims fraud. The arson defense arises when an insured submits a loss caused by arson but swears its cause was accidental.

Property insurance policies have no specific arson exclusion or defense. The coverage defense for arson arises when an insured represents arson fire as an accidental fire and seeks coverage for the loss.

The burden of proving arson is on the insurer, but it is an easier burden of proof than in criminal prosecutions.

Adjusters should learn about and look for arson indicators. Arson is proven by showing that a fire was incendiary and was set by, or at the direction of, the insured. Both elements are crucial because juvenile vandals start many incendiary fires and because many insureds who have a motive for arson suffer an accidental fire. Proof of an incendiary fire is usually made through careful, scientific analysis of the fire scene. Proof of the insured's involvement is usually made through showing the insured's motive and opportunity to commit arson.

Many parties should be involved in arson detection and proof, including the adjuster, an investigator, an origin and cause expert, a forensic chemist, the fire marshal, public prosecutors, attorneys for the insurer, and accountants.

The most common first-party claims frauds, other than arson, are staged burglaries, padded claims, and duplicate claims under multiple policies. As with arson, the keys to defending such claims are detection and proof.

To fight both first-party and third-party claims fraud, most insurers have established special investigation units (SIUs). Insurers have an obvious interest in resisting fraudulent claims, but most ordinary claims units are staffed in a way that assumes almost all claims are routine. To have staff with the time and expertise to investigate suspicious claims, insurers created SIUs. Many state legislatures and insurance departments have required insurers to create detailed antifraud plans. Like other claims units, SIUs review, investigate, and settle claims. Their mission is not to deny claims, but to resolve them correctly. Because all of the claims that they handle are suspicious, SIU staff must be highly trained in proper investigation and legal procedures. SIU personnel also play a major educational role within insurance companies.

ASSIGNMENT NOTES

1. CA Insurance Code § 1872.5, 1872.5(a) and 1872.4(a).

2. Phone interview November 1, 2002, with Susan Black, assistant vice president, American Insurance Services Group (AISG).

3. Adapted from *Hot Topics & Insurance Issues*, "Arson," February 2003, Insurance Information Institute (III), www.iii.org/media/hottopics/insurance/test1/content (accessed August 1, 2003).

4. III, *Hot Topics & Insurance Issues*, "Arson."

5. Common Property Conditions, CP 00 90 07 88, Copyright, Insurance Services Office, Inc., 1983, 1987.

6. Arson Basics, www.interfire.org, "Motive, Means and Opportunity, a Guide to Fire Investigation," American Re-Ins. Co., 1996.

7. Building and Personal Property Coverage Form, CP 00 10 10 00, Copyright, Insurance Services Office, Inc., 1999.

8. *III Insurance Fact Book 2002* (New York: Insurance Information Institute, 2002), p. 121.

9. Insurance Research Council (IRC), *Fighting Insurance Fraud* (Malvern, Pa.: Insurance Research Council, 2001), p. 13.

10. IRC, *Fighting Insurance Fraud*, p. 14.

Direct Your Learning ▶▶

7

Fundamentals of Estimating

Educational Objectives

After learning the content of this assignment, you should be able to:

▷ Describe the type of building construction, fire detection and suppression systems, and intruder alarm systems in a given claim situation.

▷ Identify and describe the parts of the basic building structure.

▷ Describe the elements of, and correct procedure for, taking a scope.

▷ Explain how to determine each of the following elements of cost contained in an estimate:

- Materials
- Labor and employer's burden
- Tools and equipment
- Overhead and profit
- Direct costs

▷ Explain the labor and materials method of estimating and the unit cost method of estimating their application.

▷ Describe the advantages and disadvantages of computerized estimating services.

▷ Explain how estimates are calculated in situations involving demolition.

▷ Explain how estimates are calculated in situations involving debris removal.

▷ Explain how estimates are calculated in situations involving small losses.

▷ Explain how estimates are calculated in situations involving large losses.

▷ Explain two reasons for, and how to negotiate, differences in estimates with a contractor.

▷ Explain how various insurance policy provisions affect an estimate.

Fundamentals of Estimating

7

TYPES OF BUILDING CONSTRUCTION AND DETECTION AND SUPPRESSION SYSTEMS

To estimate property damage, property loss adjusters should be familiar with different types of construction and the kinds of damage that the construction can be subject to.

Knowing what type of building is involved in a loss helps an adjuster understand what is needed to repair or rebuild the building. It can also help with coverage analysis. The type of detection and suppression system installed in a building can also affect the loss.

Types of Building Construction

Two versions of the classification of buildings by type of construction are available as resources that adjusters can use. One version is by Insurance Services Office, Inc., (ISO) and is used primarily by underwriters to determine a particular risk's damage potential. The second version is by the National Fire Protection Association (NFPA). It classifies building construction based on damageability from fire and on life safety issues. Adjusters should be aware that these two versions, while similar, are not the same, because they serve different purposes and consequently can use the same terms with different contexts and meanings. Also, these resources may use terms differently than how an adjuster might expect. For example, in both versions of the building classifications, there is no such thing as a fireproof building. Buildings are classified by their resistance to fire. A **fire-resistance rating** is the resistance of a building to collapse or to total involvement in a fire.[1]

Fire-resistance rating
A rating given to a building that indicates the resistance of the building to collapse or to total involvement in a fire.

The discussion of construction types is based on the definitions used by ISO. Although primarily used to determine property insurance rates, these definitions provide an adjuster with basic knowledge of construction types.

Frame Construction

A building made of **frame construction** is one in which the exterior load-bearing walls are constructed of wood. Wood can be combined with brick or stucco and still be considered frame construction. Because the structure is made up of wood, it is highly susceptible to fire damage. See the exhibit "Frame Construction."

Frame construction
A class of construction that has load-bearing components made of wood or other combustible materials such as brick or stone veneer.

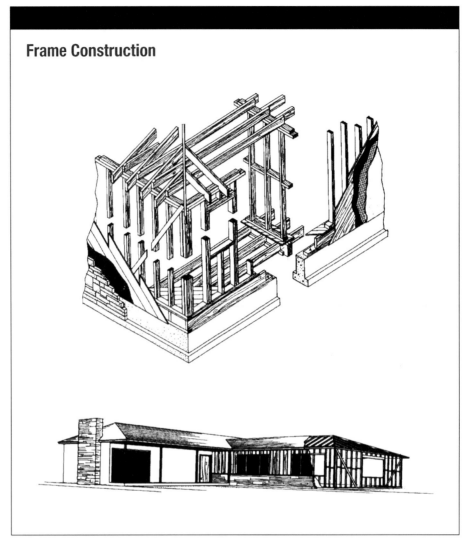

Frame Construction

Adjuster Tip—A load-bearing wall is any wall that bears its own weight as well as other weight and the force of wind. Partition and panel walls are not usually load-bearing. The term "load-bearing wall" is often shortened to "bearing wall."

Joisted masonry construction

A class of construction that has load-bearing exterior walls made of brick, adobe, concrete, gypsum, stone, tile, or similar materials; that has floors and roofs of combustible materials; and that has a fire-resistance rating of at least one hour.

Joisted Masonry Construction

Joisted masonry construction has the exterior load-bearing walls constructed of brick, stone, and concrete, while the joists and beams that support the roof and floors are wood. In a fire, the interior will burn, leaving behind the masonry shell. If the fire is extremely intense, the masonry can be damaged also. The exhibit shows joisted masonry construction. See the exhibit "Interior Detail of Joisted Masonry Construction."

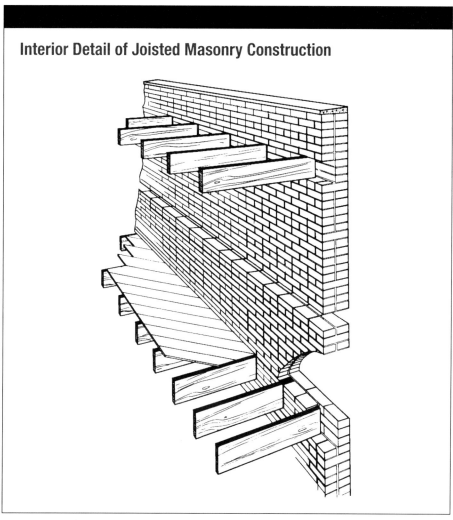

Interior Detail of Joisted Masonry Construction

Noncombustible Construction

Exterior load-bearing walls, floors, and the roof in **noncombustible construction** are made of and/or supported by steel, metal, gypsum, or other noncombustible materials. Even though they do not contribute to the fuel for fire, they can be extensively damaged from the intense heat of a fire and generally lose their weight-bearing ability very quickly during a fire. All-metal construction is common. In a fire, the structural members can twist, crack, or expand to the point of collapse unless protected with fireproofing material or sheathing. The exhibit shows noncombustible construction. See the exhibit "Light Noncombustible Construction."

Masonry Noncombustible Construction

In **masonry noncombustible construction**, the exterior bearing walls are constructed of self-supporting masonry. Floors and the roof are steel or another

Noncombustible

An ISO combustibility classification for occupancies with merchandise or materials that do not in themselves constitute an active fuel for the spread of fire.

Masonry noncombustible construction

Masonry construction or construction that includes exterior walls of fire-resistive construction with a fire-resistance rating of not less than one hour.

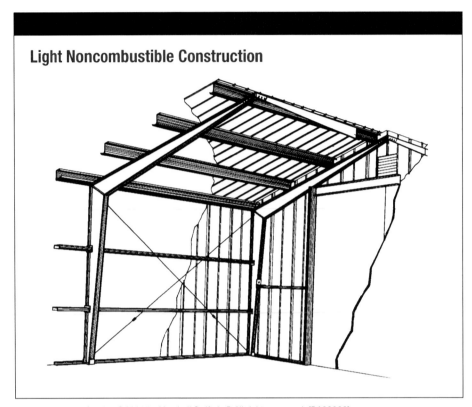

Light Noncombustible Construction

noncombustible material. The exhibit shows masonry noncombustible construction. This type of building would supply little fuel for a fire, but the structural members would lose their weight-bearing ability during an intense fire. See the exhibit "Masonry Noncombustible Construction."

Modified Fire-Resistive Construction

Modified fire-resistive construction has exterior bearing walls, floors, and roof made of masonry or fire-resistive material that has a fire-resistance rating of one hour but less than two hours.

Fire-Resistive Construction

A building with **fire-resistive construction** is one in which the exterior bearing walls, floors, and roof are made of fire-resistive material such as masonry, reinforced concrete, or protected steel. It has a fire-resistance rating of not less than two hours.

Although it is not essential that an adjuster know how a particular building is classified by the underwriter, it is valuable to know the various classes when evaluating the overall loss and considering use and occupancy issues as well as identifying potential avenues of subrogation.

Modified fire-resistive construction

A class of construction that has exterior walls, floors, and roofs of masonry or other fire-resistive materials with a fire-resistance rating of one to two hours.

Fire-resistive construction

A class of construction that has exterior walls, floors, and roofs of masonry or other fire-resistive material with a fire-resistance rating of at least two hours.

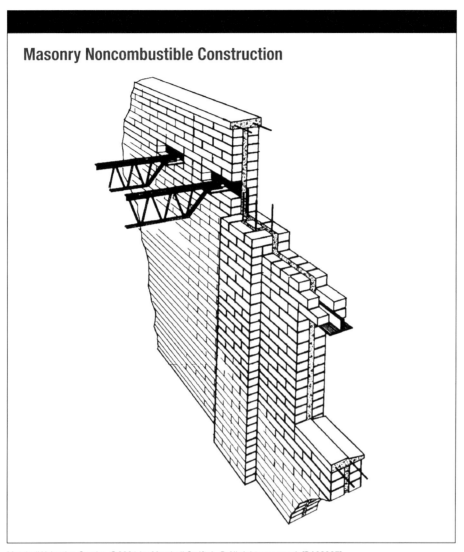

Masonry Noncombustible Construction

Detection and Suppression Systems

Detection and suppression systems encompass a wide variety of fire and smoke detectors, sprinklers, and intruder alarms. Commercial buildings often have complex devices that can detect and suppress fire, detect water leakage, or detect a break-in. Many homes have intruder alarms, and some have residential sprinkler protection.

Detection and suppression systems can affect a loss in many ways. Fire detection and suppression systems can mitigate the loss sustained as a result of fire. Intruder alarms, or burglar alarms, may scare off thieves. Quick police response may mean a significantly reduced loss or the potential of a recovery. Malfunctioning detection and suppression systems may even be a potential source of recovery through subrogation. The type of detection and suppression system used in a building is often dictated by the building's construction and use.

Fire Detection and Suppression Systems

Many types of fire detection systems are available. Most are tied into some type of fire suppression system as well as an alarm.

Wet pipe sprinkler systems

Automatic fire sprinkler systems with pipes that always contain water under pressure, which is released immediately when a sprinkler head opens.

Dry pipe sprinkler systems

Automatic fire sprinkler systems with pipes that contain compressed air or another inert gas that holds a valve in the water line shut until an open sprinkler head releases the gas and allows water to flow through the previously dry pipe to the sprinkler head.

Deluge system

A type of sprinkler system in which all the heads remain permanently open; when activated by a detection system, a deluge valve allows water into the system.

Halogenated agent extinguishing system

An automatic fire sprinkler system in which halocarbons are used to disrupt the chemical reaction of fire; commonly used in computer rooms and magnetic-tape storage vaults.

Dry chemical system

A type of fire suppression system in which finely divided powders are distributed through pipes to nozzles positioned to allow for full distribution over the fire exposure area.

Wet Sprinkler Systems—The most common type of sprinkler system is the **wet system**. It continuously has water in the pipes. Depending upon the type of sprinkler head installed, the system can be activated by heat, smoke, or flame. In a wet system designs, only the heads nearest the fire area will actuate. The sprinklers operate independently and do not actuate simultaneously unless a large area is involved in a fire. When a loss involves the actuation of a sprinkler, the adjuster asks questions concerning its installation and maintenance to determine if a malfunction caused the loss or made it worse.

Dry Pipe Systems—Sprinkler systems can also be designed as **dry pipe systems**. This means that the pipes remain dry until a sprinkler head is actuated. A sprinkler that actuates from heat in a dry pipe system releases air pressure maintained in the piping network, eventually enabling a dry pipe valve to trip and allow water to enter the piping system. Like the wet pipe system, water is only distributed from sprinklers that have actuated from heat in the local fire area. Dry systems are used in locations that are prone to freezing temperatures, like an unheated warehouse.

Deluge Systems—A variation of the dry system design is the **deluge system**. It differs from the regular dry system because it has the sprinkler heads open continuously. When heat or smoke triggers the system (through combined detection of infrared and ultraviolet light), the deluge valve receives the signal and trips, allowing water into the entire piping system. As the sprinkler heads in a deluge system are all open, the water immediately discharges into the area from every sprinkler head in the system.

A hybrid of both the wet system and the deluge system is the preaction system. In this design, a closed piping network uses a minimal amount of air under pressure. A deluge valve maintains the piping network in a dry state until receiving a signal from the actuating sprinklers or detectors. When it has received signals from two different sources, the deluge valve trips, allowing full water flow into the piping. Water is then distributed to the actuated sprinklers. This type of system is used in libraries and computer rooms, as it requires more than just sprinkler head activation to enable water flow to occur.

Foam and Chemical Systems—Other types of fire suppression systems include halogenated, dry chemical, foam, and carbon dioxide. The particular system used in a building depends on the building's use and occupancy. **Halogenated systems** are used in laboratories, art museums, and computer rooms because these buildings' contents should not be subjected to water. **Dry chemical systems** are often used in paint-spray booths, electric transformers, and in the deep fryer area of restaurants. These systems smother a fire rather than spread it around as water might. **Foam systems** have the same purpose as dry chemical systems and are used around flammable liquids and oil-storage facilities. Foam is used outside effectively because it will not blow around like dry chemical does. **Carbon dioxide systems** are used in dry cleaning plants, fur vaults, printing press rooms, and computer rooms. The carbon dioxide reduces the oxygen in the area to the point that combustion cannot be sustained.[2]

Foam system

A chemical foam system that is used in outside areas to smother a fire.

Carbon dioxide system

A type of fire suppression system in which carbon dioxide is stored as a liquid under pressure and is discharged as a gas through the pipes of the system to the fire site.

Intruder Detection Systems and Alarms

Many different types of intruder alarm systems exist. Both residential and commercial properties use them. The most familiar type of alarm is the sensor trigger alarm, whose circuit is normally closed. When the circuit is broken, the alarm is triggered. This type of alarm is recognizable by the strip appearing on the windows of the building. There is another type of sensor alarm in which the circuit is normally open. The trigger is usually a pressure mat. Once walked on, these mats close the circuit and trigger the alarm. There are also radio-controlled sensor alarms that can be mounted to doors and windows without wiring.

Alarms systems are usually tied into a police department or private security company. When investigating a loss involving a building that has alarm systems, the property adjuster obtains information regarding the alarm's installation and maintenance as well as how the alarm is set and by whom. Additionally, the alarm company or police department has vital information regarding the alarm's performance at the time of the loss.[3]

BASIC BUILDING STRUCTURE

To estimate property damage, property loss adjusters should be familiar with different types of construction and the kinds of damage that the construction can be subject to. Knowing what type of building is involved in a loss helps an adjuster understand what is needed to repair or rebuild the building.

A building has six essential parts:

- Foundation
- Framing
- Windows and doors
- Utilities (heating, cooling, plumbing, and electrical)
- Interior finishes (trim, drywall, and plaster)
- Exterior finishes (roofing and exterior wall coverings)

For the purposes of this section, a residential building is discussed in the examples.

Foundation

Houses sit on some form of foundation, such as a basement foundation, a slab, or a crawl space. Foundations can be made from concrete block or concrete poured into forms to create the walls or the slab. Poured concrete is often reinforced with reinforcing bars. See the exhibit. The shorthand term for these bars is "rebar." The amount of poured concrete to use is usually calculated by the cubic yard. Concrete blocks are calculated using the size of the block and the size of the desired foundation. See the exhibit "Foundation."

Foundation

Concrete
block walls

Reinforcing
bars

Photo courtesy of National Property & Casualty Claims Research Services, Inc. (NPCCRS). [DA03968]

Adjuster Tip—An inadequate foundation can cause uneven settling of a house and cracking of the interior plaster, and ill-fitting doors and windows evidence this.

Framing

Framing
The structural members that form the skeleton of a building.

Framing is the term used to describe the structural members that form the skeleton of the building. Floors, walls, roofs, and ceilings are all framed out to construct the building. Framing begins with structural members that are attached to the foundation.

Floor Framing

After the concrete foundation has properly cured, wooden sills are attached to it. These provide the base for attaching the wood frame of the house to the foundation.

Adjuster Tip—Framing lumber that has suffered fire damage does not always have to be replaced. If joists, rafters, and studs have suffered no structural damage, they can be scraped, sealed, and then covered. Determining whether the joist is structurally sound may require the use of a contractor or an engineer. Another possible repair technique is called "sistering." This entails attaching a new section of joist, rafter, or stud, to the damaged section, overlapping the damaged section with a new section, thereby reinforcing the damaged section.[4]

Floor joists are added next. The term **joist** is applied to a horizontal timber to which either the floor or ceiling is attached.

> **Joist**
> A horizontal timber to which either the floor or ceiling is attached.

Floor joists are usually 2" × 6", 2" × 8", 2" × 10", or 2" × 12". The floor joists are installed so that the center of one floor joist is 16" away from the center of the next floor joist. This is called on-center spacing. Note that the measurement is from the center of one joist to the center of another, not 16" from the side of one to the side of the other. Floor joists extend the entire length of the house. If the length of a joist exceeds 8', then bridging the joists will be necessary. **Bridging** means inserting a short piece of bracing (can be metal or wood) laterally between the joists. The exhibit shows an example of bridging. See the exhibit "Floor Framing."

> **Bridging**
> A short piece of bracing that is inserted laterally between joists.

After the floor joists are in place, a subfloor or rough floor is installed over them. This is the base for the finished floor. Subflooring is usually plywood sheets or particleboard.

On top of the subfloor, following the outline of the foundation, soleplates are attached. These are pieces of lumber that anchor the wall studs to the floor. Soleplates are usually 2" × 4".

Wall Framing

Wall studs are nailed to the soleplates to form the frame of the walls. Studs are usually 2" × 4" in a two-story house. Wall studs are usually placed using 16" on-center spacing. After the studs are all in place, a top plate is attached across the top of them to hold the studs and all the walls together. See the exhibit "Vertical Application of Plywood or Structural Insulating Board Sheathing."

Studs are doubled around both sides of any window or door and tripled at the corners of the house. Sheathing is installed on the exterior of the wall studs to enclose the structure. The exterior finish of the house will be attached to this sheathing. See the exhibit "Headers for Windows and Door Openings."

After the walls are up, the roof can be installed. Ceiling joists are installed, running in the same direction as the floor joists. They extend from the rafter

Floor Framing

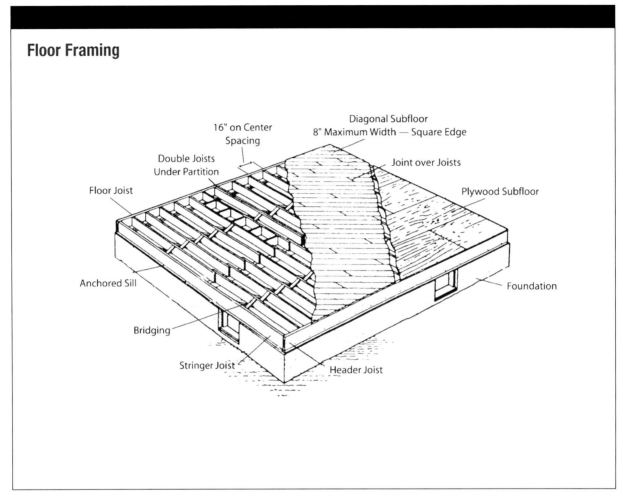

L. O. Anderson, Wood-Frame House Construction, U.S. Dept. of Agriculture Forest Service, Agricultural Handbook No. 73 (Washington, D.C.: U.S. Government Printing Office, July 1970), p. 27. [DA03974]

plate to the top plate of the wall studding. See the exhibit "Ceiling Joist Connections."

Roof Framing

Roof rafters are installed next. They run parallel to each other and can be 12 to 24 inches apart. The most common spacing is 16 inches. Rafters extend upward at an angle called a **pitch**. Roofs can be either flat or pitched. Flat roofs can have a slight slope in them to facilitate drainage. In a flat roof, the rafters serve as the ceiling joists. They attach at the top to a piece called the ridge board. See the exhibit "Ceiling and Roof Framing."

The ridge board runs the length of the roof, perpendicular to the rafters. After the rafters are in place, the roof sheathing is added to the exterior of the rafters. The sheathing serves as the base for the roof covering and adds strength to the roof frame. See the exhibit "Application of Plywood Roof Sheathing."

Pitch

The angle of the roof.

Vertical Application of Plywood or Structural Insulating Board Sheathing

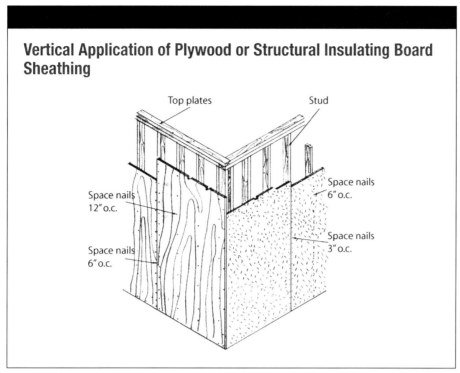

L. O. Anderson, Wood-Frame House Construction (Carlsbad, Calif.: Craftsman Book Company, July 1992), pp. 47, 71.
[DA03976]

Headers for Windows and Door Openings

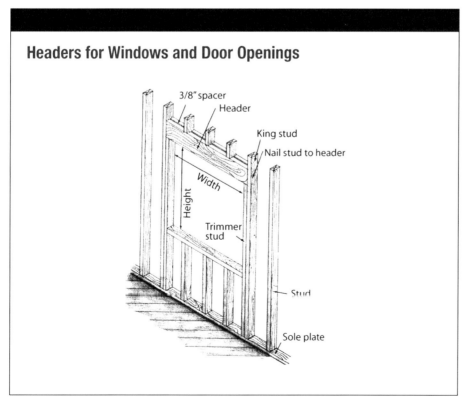

L. O. Anderson, Wood-Frame House Construction (Carlsbad, Calif.: Craftsman Book Company, July 1992), pp. 47, 71.
[DA03977]

Ceiling Joist Connections

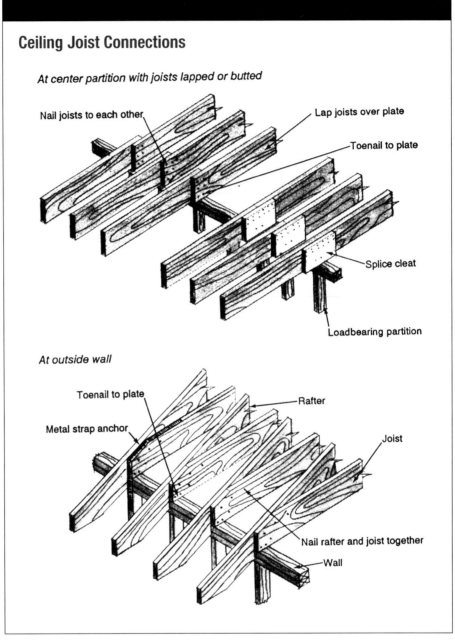

At center partition with joists lapped or butted

Nail joists to each other

Lap joists over plate

Toenail to plate

Splice cleat

Loadbearing partition

At outside wall

Toenail to plate

Rafter

Metal strap anchor

Joist

Nail rafter and joist together

Wall

L. O. Anderson, Wood-Frame House Construction (Carlsbad, Calif.: Craftsman Book Company, July 1992), p. 54. [DA03978]

Adjuster Tip—Using unseasoned wood as roof sheathing can cause buckling and lifting of shingles as the sheathing dries out.

Many roofs have dormers in them. A dormer is a gable in a pitched roof, usually containing a window. A gable is the triangular shape formed by the roofline of the dormer. See the exhibit "Dormer."

Ceiling and Roof Framing

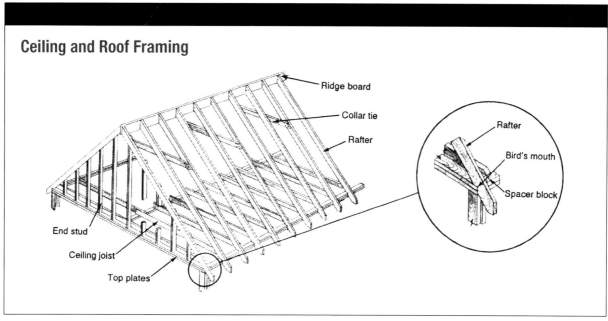

L. O. Anderson, Wood-Frame House Construction (Carlsbad, Calif.: Craftsman Book Company, July 1992), p. 60. [DA03980]

The intersection of the dormer roof and the main roof is called a valley. Valleys are formed whenever two sloping sides of a roof meet. Valleys have valley rafters and jack rafters as part of their structure to reinforce them. These are all basically the same piece of wood, usually a 2" × 10" or a 2" × 12", cut to different lengths and put to different uses in the structure. Their names derive from their use rather than from some significant difference in their composition. See the exhibit "Framing at Valley."

Interior Partitions

While the exterior walls and roof are being framed, interior partition walls are also erected. Interior partition walls can be **load-bearing** and non-load-bearing. Load-bearing walls run at right angles to the joists, and they help bear the weight of the above structure. Non-load-bearing walls merely define the room space. Doors and windows are framed out with studs, header beams, and sills.

Load-bearing wall

A wall that runs at a right angle to the joists and bears the weight of the structure.

Steel Framing

Framing can also be done in steel. Although steel framing is typically used for commercial buildings, some parts of the United States use steel as interior partition wall framing members for residential buildings and apartments. Steel framing is installed in much the same manner, and to the same specifications, as wood. Steel framing requires different insulation because of the ease in which heat is lost through steel framing. The most typical solution for this heat loss problem is to use full width batts of insulation (meaning that they cover the entire area in between the studs) or to use blown-in insulation. Steel can be an inexpensive, sturdy alternative to wood framing, but it does

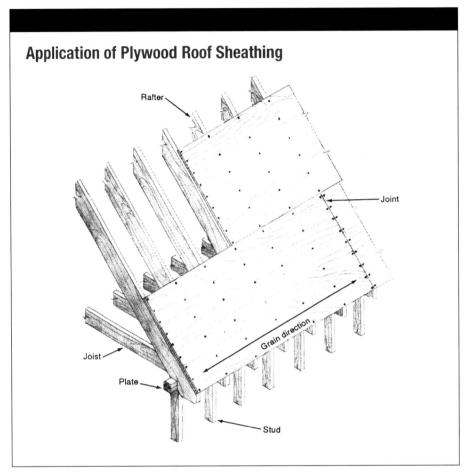

Application of Plywood Roof Sheathing

L. O. Anderson, Wood-Frame House Construction (Carlsbad, Calif.: Craftsman Book Company, July 1992), p. 79. [DA03981]

Dormer

Home Repair and Remodel: 2002 Cost Guide (Los Angeles: Marshall & Swift, L.P., 2002). [DA03983]

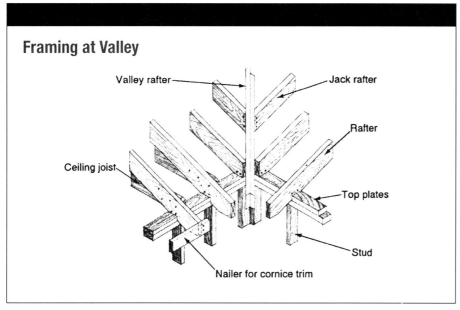

Framing at Valley

L. O. Anderson, Wood-Frame House Construction (Carlsbad, Calif.: Craftsman Book Company, July 1992), p. 61.
[DA03984]

have its drawbacks. Steel is susceptible to rust at the points at which it has been cut and at which fasteners have penetrated the piece.[5]

Windows and Doors

Windows and doors are inserted into the framed openings. Windows and doors are constructed of many different structural pieces. Unless an estimate is being prepared to repair a part of a door or window, estimating these structural pieces individually is not necessary. Most doors and windows arrive from the manufacturer with all of the component pieces already installed.

Utilities

As the framing nears completion, the plumbers **rough in** the pipes. Roughing in is the installation of the pipes that will ultimately be concealed within the walls and ceiling. Roughing in does not include the attachment of the fixtures or appliances. After the roof is on and the windows are in, the electricians usually do their roughing in of the wiring. See the exhibit "Roughing-In Pipes."

Rough in

To install the plumbing and electrical wiring that will ultimately be concealed within the walls and ceiling.

Interior Finishes

Following the rough in of the utilities, the insulation is put in and the walls are enclosed with drywall or plaster. Finished floors are installed, as are the fixtures and appliances. Installation of trim and molding usually completes the process.[6]

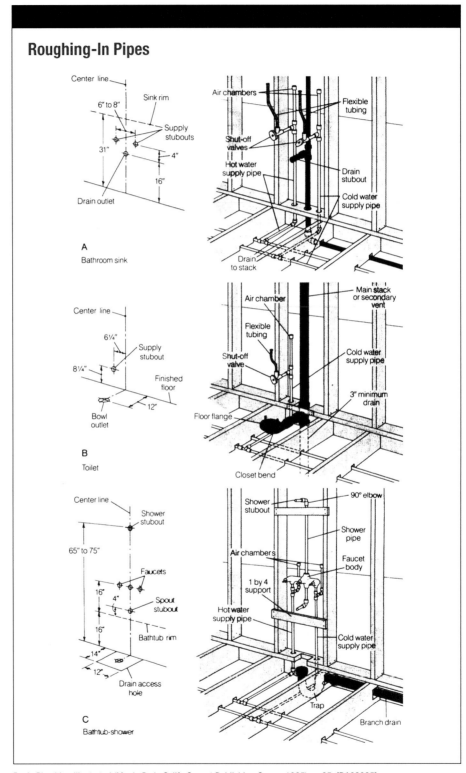

Roughing-In Pipes

A
Bathroom sink

B
Toilet

C
Bathtub-shower

Basic Plumbing Illustrated (Menlo Park, Calif.: Sunset Publishing Group, 1985), p. 65. [DA03985]

Exterior Finishes

After the wall sheathing and roof sheathing are completed, the exterior finish is installed. So many different types of exterior wall finishes and roof coverings are available that it is impossible for this text to fully discuss them all. Common exterior wall finishes are siding, shakes, stucco, and brick or another masonry product. Roofing material often is dictated by climate. For example, while asphalt shingles are used countrywide, Spanish tile is prevalent in the Southwest. Also, specialty buildings might have a slate or metal roof.

Adjuster Tip—Examining items in a local lumber store or home improvement store can make the terms used in this text more meaningful after seeing the items close up.

In the course of building a small house, which is the example used in this discussion of basic building structure, carpenters, electricians, masons, and plumbers are involved. Other trade professionals who could be involved are tile setters; counter installers; heating, ventilation, and air conditioning (HVAC) installers; painters; wallpaper hangers; and landscapers. Trying to schedule all of these trades can be difficult because some may not be able to begin work until others are finished. For large jobs, a general contractor (GC) does this scheduling and supervision. By definition, a GC has a contract directly with the owner. On large projects, the GC arranges for all of the other trades to perform specific parts of the project. The GC may perform part of the actual construction in addition to supervising the work done by the other trades. These other trades are referred to as subcontractors. Their contract is usually with the GC and they agree to perform some part of the GC's obligation to the owner. A GC may not be needed on a small job. In such a case, each trade professional contracts directly with the owner.[7]

TAKING A SCOPE OF A BUILDING LOSS

A property adjuster must know how to prepare an estimate as well as be able to evaluate an estimate prepared by someone else. Otherwise, it would be difficult to negotiate the extent of damage, the type of repair necessary, and the cost of labor and materials.

If the damage presented by the loss is significantly different from the expected damage, the adjuster will have to ask more questions about the loss. This section explains how to scope a loss.

Every estimate should contain this information:

- Specifications
- Material
- Labor
- Overhead
- Profit[8]

Specifications are the dimensions of the area that needs to be repaired, replaced, or built. The specifications also include special conditions like cramped workspace, the need for scaffolding, the weather, or the need to protect other areas from damage during the project.

Material specifies the quantity, quality, and size of the material needed to accomplish the work. Labor is the amount of time needed to complete each part of the job.

Overhead
The fixed costs to run a business.

Overhead encompasses the fixed costs for any business. Overhead has two varieties: (1) general and (2) specific. General overhead exists whether or not the contractor is working on a project. Some examples of general overhead items are the salaries of estimators, job supervisors, and office personnel; office rent; utilities; and business licenses. The contractor usually recovers these costs by charging a flat percentage on each estimate. Specific overhead is charged to a specific job. Examples of specific overhead are building permits, travel costs, equipment rental, and insurance. Depending on the location and type of job, the overhead can range from 5 percent to 20 percent. For example, if the fixed operating costs of the business are $100,000 per year and the contractor expects to do $1 million worth of work, then the contractor recovers the annual overhead by adding a 10 percent overhead charge to every job.

Profit is the amount over the costs of a job that the contractor expects to earn for his or her services. Profit varies depending on the job's size and complexity and how much competition there is for the job. Usually, the higher the estimate, the lower the percentage of profit charged. A large job or a competitively bid job can have a profit as low as 2 or 3 percent. Although the generally accepted amount is 10 percent, a small job consisting of only a few hundred dollars' worth of work can have a profit figure as high as 20 percent. If the insured elects to do the work himself or herself, profit is not usually included in the estimate.

When a general contractor is used to oversee the project, overhead and profit are included in the estimate. Note the distinction between "ten and ten," which is 10 percent overhead and 10 percent profit calculated off the total estimate, and the "ten on ten" method, which results in a total of 21 percent. The ten on ten method calculates the 10 percent overhead first, then adds it to the total estimate. Then the 10 percent profit is calculated using the new total. The exhibit shows the difference in the final estimate using these two methods. See the exhibit "Examples of Overhead and Profit Calculations."

In other areas, a flat 15 percent to cover both overhead and profit is common. Regardless of local practices, competitive pressures can dictate a different amount.

Adjuster Tip—The acceptable amount of overhead and profit can vary because of location, competitive bidding, and market conditions. Therefore, adjusters should verify what the acceptable amount of overhead and profit is for the loss location.

Examples of Overhead and Profit Calculations

	10 and 10 Method	10 on 10 Method
Estimate amount	$100,000	$100,000
10% overhead	10,000	10,000
	New total	$110,000
10% profit	10,000	11,000
Final estimate	$120,000	$121,000

[DA03987]

Local Practices

Estimates can vary among locations because of local practices. The terms used in the estimate can differ. Depending upon where the loss is, a wood sill can be called a sill, a soleplate, a shoe, or a mudsill. Roof sheathing might be called roof boards or roof decking.

Construction methods can also vary. Climate dictates what is the best local practice for a given trade. For example, if the loss is in the Southwest, stucco might be the preferred exterior finish and Spanish tile might be the preferred roofing material.

Estimating methods can also cause a difference in the bottom line. How waste is accounted for or whether the window and door openings are deducted from the measurements can affect an estimate's final cost. Market-driven conditions in an area might result in a local practice among tradesman so that they all charge the same labor rate.

Temporary Repairs

A substantial loss in a residential or commercial property may necessitate temporary repairs. These repairs protect the property from further damage. These repairs can include closing up openings with boards or tarpaulins, providing temporary heat or light, and even draining the plumbing to prevent the pipes from freezing. It may be necessary to pump out water, dry out contents, or fence off an area to keep it secure. All of these temporary repairs can appear on an estimate.

Scope of a Building Loss

An adjuster inspecting a loss creates a scope of the loss. The scope is broader than the specifications already discussed. The scope is a list of the damaged areas, a description of the damage, a proposed method of repair, and the measurements of the damaged area. See the exhibit "Scope Sheet."

Scope Sheet

Property Loss Worksheet

Page No. _____1_____

Preliminary Estimate ___10/19/0X___

Final Estimate _____Date_____
　　　　　　　　　　Date

M. Boyer
Adjuster

Claim No. ____524 BL 101____

Insured _____J. Smith_____

Claimant _____Insured_____

1	2	3	4	5	6	7	8	9
Item	Description	Quantity	Units	Unit price	Cost			
			Age	Orig. cost	Repl. cost	Deprec.	A.C.V.	Loss & Damage
1.	Permit (if required)							
2.	Demolition							
	Remove range hood							
	Remove cabinets (4 LF)							
	Remove drywall (above cabinet) (5' × 10' = 50 SF)							
	Remove Formica countertop (12 LF) (est. 2 men × 5 hrs. = 10 hrs.)							
3.	Cartage							
	1 pickup & driver (1.5 hrs.)							
	Dump fee ($10.00)							
4.	Clean range (est. 1.5 hrs.)							
5.	Install new range hood (Sears 30 ", est. 1 hr.)							
6.	Install upper cabinets Paint grade plywood of 4 LF × 3' tall (est. 1.5 hrs.)							
7.	Replace drywall (above cabinet) (5' × 10' = 50 SF)							
8.	Replace Formica countertop (12 LF) (est. 2 men × 7 hrs. = 14 hrs.)							

[DA03989]

The scope is used by the adjuster to create an estimate. The adjuster also uses the scope to reach an agreement with the contractor regarding the extent of the damage. How to scope a loss is discussed in greater detail later in this section.

Estimating is a two-step process. The first step is preparing the scope of damage at the loss scene. The adjuster itemizes the damage elements, or scopes the loss, to establish the extent of the insured's loss. The scope details the damage to each building component. (Some property adjusters substitute other terms for "scope." Common synonyms are "take-off," "survey," "specifications," or "field notes." Regardless of the name, the scope is the first and most crucial step in preparing a repair estimate.) The second step is pricing the work determined by the scope into a repair estimate. To properly price the estimate, the adjuster must know the quantity of material needed, the amount of labor that each task requires, what the overhead and profit margin will be, and what considerations must be taken into account.

For smaller losses, the adjuster prepares the scope and writes the estimate at the scene of the loss. For larger losses, trying to finish the estimate at the scene is impractical. Although completing the scope and estimate in a timely manner is important, the adjuster can use references to find labor and material usage rates and current prices.

Elements of a Proper Scope

The scope must contain enough detail to calculate loss restoration costs. For each damaged building component, the scope must describe three things:

- Degree of damage, usually stated as a method of repair
- Quality of the materials and workmanship of damaged property
- Raw counts or measurements needed to calculate quantities

For example, assume that an interior water loss has occurred. The entire ceiling in a small bedroom is bowed, and the walls are stained. The scope entries for the damage in that room are these:

Bedroom: 9 feet × 10 feet × 8 feet.

Replace 5/8 inch ceiling drywall, complete.

Seal and paint walls and ceiling, flat latex.

The room's dimensions provide the raw measurements needed to calculate the surface areas that determine the amount of material needed. Replacing the drywall and sealing and painting the surfaces are the repair methods that indicate the damage degree. Finally, the thickness of the drywall and the type of paint describe the quality of the damaged component.

Contrast to Finished Estimate

The scope differs from the finished estimate in two ways. First, the scope does not necessarily list any prices, although prices can be used to describe quality. Second, the scope does not list the calculated quantities. It includes just the raw counts and measurements needed to calculate quantities for the estimate. Calculators are not needed to prepare a scope. The quantities should be calculated as the adjuster extends and prices the scope into a finished estimate.

Suggested Sequence for an Inspection and a Scope

Following a set sequence in inspecting the loss and preparing the scope is important. The sequence suggested here works well for larger fire losses, and it can be tailored to fit other types of losses. For smaller losses, some of the steps can be combined or eliminated.

The steps in an inspection and a scope include:

Step 1—Conduct the initial survey

Step 2—Prepare diagrams and sketches

Step 3—Scope the damage

Step 4—Consider coverage

Step 5—Document with photographs

Step 1: Conduct the Initial Survey—The adjuster inspects the building to get an idea of construction type, damaged areas, condition before the fire, and any building hazards. The adjuster should enter the building below the lowest damaged floor to check the condition of the floors above. On some losses, it may be necessary to have an origin and cause expert accompany the adjuster during this initial inspection. Partly as a result of the initial inspection, coverage issues that demand immediate attention might become apparent. Whenever possible, the adjuster should finish the scope during the initial inspection.

Step 2: Prepare Diagrams and Sketches—After preparing a perimeter diagram, the adjuster can draw in the interior walls. Starting with the perimeter helps ensure that the interior dimensions will all fit. Next, the adjuster should measure and sketch exterior elevations, trusses, cabinets, doors, and windows. Thoroughness makes the final detailed scope easier to prepare.

Step 3: Scope the Damage—Conducting an organized scope of the damage ensures that nothing is missed. Whenever possible, the adjuster should complete the scope with the insured or with the insured's contractor. One of the purposes for preparing the scope is to agree on the extent of the damage. Insureds typically want to discuss every detail, so the insured and the adjuster should agree on anything that might become an issue. If the insured's contractor is present, he or she could be part of the agreement on the major unit costs and labor rates as well as on each repair item. Experts should resolve uncertainties or legitimate differences of opinion. See the exhibit "Scope the Damage."

Scope the Damage

A scope of damage should include examining the following five categories in the following order. The adjuster should consider only one category at a time, necessitating five complete tours of the loss scene:

1. Structural components

2. Exterior, including insulation

3. Room by room (architectural items, finishes, fixtures, and components of building systems completely contained within the room)

   a. Floor

   b. Walls

   c. Trim, doors, and windows

   d. Ceiling

   e. Fixtures, appliances, built-ins, and cabinets

4. Building systems that cross room boundaries (plumbing, electrical, and heating and air conditioning)

5. General considerations (debris removal, permits, access, and equipment rental)

[DA03990]

There are two reasons for beginning with the structural components. First, they are difficult to scope on a room-by-room basis. Second, structural component damage might require removing an undamaged component. Exterior items are next because they span room boundaries and cannot be seen from the inside. In the detailed scope of each damaged room, besides the finished ceiling, walls, and floors, the adjuster should also scope the fixtures, ducts, pipes, outlets, and wiring within the room. The next category, scoping the plumbing, electrical, and heating systems, is limited to the components that cross room boundaries. After these systems have been scoped, the adjuster should evaluate debris removal, permits, access items, and equipment rental.

For smaller or different losses, the individual situation often dictates a different sequence. For instance, if the insured reports a wind loss with interior water damage, starting on the inside to get an idea of where the roof is damaged is logical.

Common abbreviations found in a scope are as follows:

P&D	Paint and decorate	S&F	Sand and finish (usually floors and trim)
PL	Plaster		
R&R	Remove and replace	S&P	Seal and paint
REF	Refinish	T&C	Tear out and cart
REM	Remove	WW	Whitewash
REP	Repair		

Step 4: Consider Coverage—The adjuster should consider code requirements, damage from excluded causes, and damage to excluded property. The adjuster should also gather enough information to calculate the building's value before the loss to establish that the insured has complied with the coinsurance or replacement cost requirements.

Step 5: Document With Photographs—The final step is to photograph the items important to the adjustment. A photograph of the overall premises is recommended for general descriptive purposes. Photos of the damaged area help preserve the scene and document the scene as found. Photos can also assist in identifying the quality or grade of items used in construction. Identifying marks on cabinets, siding, and appliances can be preserved in this manner. If the loss is sizable, documenting the loss with photos is essential for the benefit of others within the claim department who may be reviewing the file.

PRICING AN ESTIMATE

The second step in the estimating process is pricing out the scope into a final repair estimate. The adjuster estimates the loss restoration cost on the basis of the damage as itemized in the scope document.

This section discusses construction costs. Any construction operation involves these types of costs:

- Materials
- Labor and employer's burden
- Tools and equipment
- Overhead and profit
- Miscellaneous direct costs, such as permits and sales taxes

Materials

Establishing the cost of materials is also a two-part process. First, the adjuster must identify the materials, their quality, and the quantities needed to make the repair. Second, the adjuster must obtain current local prices for those materials.

Several sources can identify the items and quantities needed. *Home Repair and Remodel Cost Guide* by Marshall & Swift, L.P. and *Walker's Building Estimators Reference Book* by Frank R. Walker Company are two recognized sources that are updated annually. For each construction or repair operation, these references identify the materials needed and provide usage factors to convert the sale unit into the units used for estimating. For example, these books reveal that a gallon of latex wall paint covers 450 to 500 square feet of smooth walls. Estimating software packages also contain this same information.

Waste

The material usage information is sometimes described as a "waste factor." There are two kinds of waste. The first is **cutting and fitting waste**, which can occur, for example, when installing a ceramic tile floor. The references indicate that an additional 5 to 10 percent of material should be added to the estimated quantity, allowing for breakage and cutting of tiles to fit the room. Cutting and fitting waste is also a factor in estimating required quantities of drywall, roofing, wallpaper, wood siding, paneling, and plywood.

Another way to handle cutting and fitting waste is to consider waste causes while determining the quantity needed. For example, some references state that the waste in drywall should be allowed by including door and window openings in the surface area measurements unless these spaces are larger than one full 4 ft. × 8 ft. sheet of drywall. If this method is used, adding a percentage of material might not be appropriate.

The second type of waste is more difficult to understand because it does not appear in the scrap pile. It is called **milling waste**. Milling waste is the difference between the actual size and the **nominal size** of a piece of material and is often associated with lumber. The nominal size of a piece of lumber is the size of the piece just after it was cut from the log. It then is dried out and planed to give it a more finished look. This causes it to lose some of its size. A piece of 1" × 3" oak flooring actually measures 25/32" thick by 2 1/4" wide.

The milling waste occurred because some of the board was removed when the tongue and groove were formed. The piece is called a 1 × 3, but it is actually smaller, which means that it will cover a smaller area. In this case, 33 1/3 percent more material is needed to cover the nominal width of 3 inches with 2 1/4 inches of material. As a result, a 33 percent milling waste factor should be added to the actual floor area when determining the quantity of material required.

Lumber that is planed on all four sides, such as a softwood, is stamped "S4S." This stands for "surfaced 4 sides." Redwood is an exception to this rule. It can be sold rough or unsurfaced. Rough wood stays close to its nominal size. Because of the surfacing or planing, the actual size of a surfaced piece of lumber is something less than 2" × 4". It is actually 1 1/2" × 3 1/2". The exhibit shows the nominal and actual size for common pieces of lumber. See the exhibit "Standard Dimensions of Surfaced Lumber."

Cutting and fitting waste
The amount of material that is left over after cutting and fitting to size for repair.

Milling waste
The difference between the actual size and the nominal size of a piece of material.

Nominal size
The size of a piece of lumber before it is surfaced or finished.

Standard Dimensions of Surfaced Lumber

Nominal Size	Actual Size
1 by 2	$\frac{3}{4}$" by $1\frac{1}{2}$"
1 by 4	$\frac{3}{4}$" by $3\frac{1}{2}$"
2 by 3	$1\frac{1}{2}$" by $2\frac{1}{2}$"
2 by 4	$1\frac{1}{2}$" by $3\frac{1}{2}$"
2 by 6	$1\frac{1}{2}$" by $5\frac{1}{2}$"
2 by 8	$1\frac{1}{2}$" by $7\frac{1}{4}$"
2 by 10	$1\frac{1}{2}$" by $9\frac{1}{4}$"
2 by 12	$1\frac{1}{2}$" by $11\frac{1}{4}$"

[DA03992]

Material Prices

The second part of estimating the cost of materials is to obtain local prices. Although reference sources exist, the best way to get current costs is to contact local suppliers. The adjuster should determine the contractor's price for the material delivered to the site. In many cases, this price is close to the price charged to the public without the delivery service. For small jobs, the contractor picks up the material at the lumberyard and pays the retail price.

Contractors who pay their bills on time might receive time payment discounts. On large jobs, a contractor receives an additional quantity discount. If a job requires a carload lot of one material type, there could be some discount. The type of material often dictates the discount. Construction materials range from commodity items such as lumber and nails to specialty items such as lighting fixtures and cabinets. Because of their generic nature, commodity items carry a relatively small markup, resulting in minimal discounts. However, specialty items often carry higher markups and, consequently, higher discounts. These discounts should be accounted for in the estimate.

Labor

Estimating labor costs consists of two steps similar to determining material costs: (1) determine the quantity of labor and (2) determine the price of labor. The quantity of labor is the number of hours needed to perform the operation. The price is the cost of work for each hour.

Quantity of Labor

The amount of labor required can be obtained from several reference sources. Some of the standard reference sources for estimating construction costs include *The Means Repair and Remodeling Estimator*, published by R. S. Means Company; the *Sweet's Repair and Remodel Cost Guide*, by Marshall & Swift Company; and *Walker's Building Estimators Reference Book* by Frank R. Walker Company. These sources give the amount of labor associated with any construction operation. For example, these references indicate that hanging, taping, and finishing 100 square feet of drywall require two and a half hours. Estimating software packages also contain labor rates and location modifiers.

Published production rates reflect the average labor required for a usual quantity of new construction. If the job is very large or very small, the production rates can be adjusted accordingly. On small jobs, the adjuster adds the additional time needed for setup, preparation, and cleanup. On large jobs, the highest productivity figure given in ranges is usually appropriate.

Some repair operations require two or more skills. For example, a job might require the skills of a plumber and an assistant. The labor times quoted might refer to the crew. In this case, the crew is two workers. The adjuster might accidentally overestimate a plumbing loss if the plumber's rate is allowed when half of the hours should have been figured at the helper's rate. The standard references indicate whether the operation requires more than one labor type and more than one worker.

Price of Labor

The contractor's price of a labor hour can be obtained from references or computed according to local rates. The most important part of accurately computing local labor costs is understanding and accounting for the difference between the worker's wage and the contractor's hourly price. This difference is a group of costs called **employer's burden**. The employer's burden costs are these:

Employer's burden

The difference between the worker's wage and the contractor's hourly rate; includes costs such as taxable and nontaxable benefits, unemployment tax, Social Security tax, and insurance costs.

- Taxable fringe benefits, such as vacation and sick leave
- Nontaxable fringe benefits, such as health insurance plans
- State and federal unemployment tax
- Employer's Social Security tax
- Workers compensation costs
- Liability insurance costs

To arrive at a local labor rate, add these costs to the base wage.

If a subcontractor is performing the work, the labor price might also be marked up to include the subcontractor's overhead and profit. The total costs to the general contractor produce the labor price to the public. The percentage of burden varies by trade and locale. An estimating reference book provides factors for each of these cost components.

Tools and Equipment; Overhead and Profit; Direct Costs

The cost of most tools and equipment is either borne by the worker or included in the contractor's overhead. However, some jobs require specialty equipment such as scaffolding, a floor sander, or heavy equipment such as a crane or a bulldozer. The best way to estimate the cost of specialty equipment is to allow a daily or hourly rental charge quoted by a local supplier. The labor associated with erecting scaffolding or using equipment comes from the same references as does any other labor factor. Overhead and profit and direct costs are then added to the estimate to complete it.

ESTIMATING METHODS

This section summarizes basic mathematical formulas that adjusters need to know to calculate quantities and estimate property losses.

The same process of scoping the loss scene damage and pricing the estimate always applies, but preparing the estimate itself can involve different methods, depending on the nature and size of the loss. Although some estimates must be developed by using the labor and materials method, the unit cost method is more efficient in other situations. Estimates themselves might differ because of differences in the scope of the loss or differences in the price, and the adjuster must reconcile the differences. Insurance policy provisions also affect estimate preparation. Finally, the adjuster might be able to apply computerized tools as well as standard mathematical formulas to prepare estimates.

Estimating Methods

Adjusters use two primary methods to estimate the repair cost. They are not mutually exclusive; in fact, most estimates use both approaches depending on the item. Neither method is inherently more accurate than the other because both methods rely on the same data. They use the same labor and materials usage factors and the same local labor and materials prices.

Labor and materials method, or time and materials method: Cost estimation with this method is based on the number of labor hours and the amount of material for each repair item. For instance, for a painting job, the estimate shows the number of hours and the gallons of paint required to paint each room. The labor and materials method is best for estimating the restoration cost of unique or unusual items such as elements of a house's frame, cabinets, fixtures, doors, and windows.

Unit cost method: A unit is the most common way of counting or measuring the quantity of material needed. Examples include square feet, cubic feet, or board feet. The unit cost shows the combined cost of material and labor needed to install one unit of material. For instance, for painting, the estimate

Labor and materials method

An estimating method based on the number of labor hours and the amount of material for each repair item.

Unit cost method

An estimating method based on a common unit of measure such as square feet, which combines the cost of the materials and the cost of the labor into one amount.

shows the square footage of an area to be repainted and the cost to paint one square foot.

Application of Estimating Methods

The best way to describe the two methods is to estimate an item of repair both ways. Ceramic tile is a good example. Ceramic tile can be set in mortar or set directly on smooth plywood, drywall, or concrete by using an adhesive. The latter method is called "thin set." How much will replacing a thin set, ceramic tile floor in a room that is 8 feet × 10 feet cost? Assume that the local labor tile setter's rate is $20 per hour and that the local material costs are these:

1 inch × 1 inch white ceramic tile, 1 square foot paper-backed sheets: $1.75

Tile adhesive, 1 gallon: $10.00

Grout, 25 pounds: $11.00

How much of each material is necessary?

The Labor and Materials Method

First, the repair is estimated using the labor and materials method from the data found in an estimator's reference book.

Materials—The area of the 8' × 10' floor is 80 square feet. Add 10 percent cutting and fitting waste to arrive at a quantity of 88 square feet. Because the tile is sold in square-foot sheets, 88 sheets are needed. The cost for 88 sheets at $1.75 per sheet is $154. For the adhesive, the reference book says that a gallon covers 40 to 50 square feet. Two gallons are needed to cover the 80 square feet. The cost for 2 gallons at $10 per gallon is $20. For the grout, 1 pound is needed for 4 square feet of 1" × 1" tile. Dividing 4 into 80 square feet results in 20 pounds to grout 80 square feet. If 25 pounds costs $11, how much would 20 pounds cost? A simple formula that works when the quantity needed and the quantity of sale are stated in the same units of measure is this:

$$\text{Cost of quantity needed} = \frac{\text{Quantity needed}}{\text{Sale quantity}} \times \text{Sale price,}$$

or, in this case,

$$\text{Cost} = \frac{20}{25} \times \$11 = \$8.80.$$

This example is for illustrative purposes only. Grout actually comes in 5-, 10-, 20-, and 25-pound bags, so in reality the estimate would use the actual price for a 20-pound bag and not go through this calculation.

Labor—For the labor in this job, the reference sources indicate that 8 hours of tile setter's labor are necessary to install 100 square feet of thin set ceramic tile. How many hours are needed for 80 square feet if 8 hours are needed to set 100 square feet? A version of the Cost of Quantity Needed formula can be used:

$$\text{Hours needed} = \frac{\text{Quantity needed}}{\text{Standard quantity}} \times \text{Hours required for standard quantity,}$$

or, in this case,

$$\text{Hours needed} = \frac{80}{100} \times 8 = 6.4 \text{ hours.}$$

The adjuster should allow for 6.4 hours at the tile setter's rate of $20. The labor cost to set 80 square feet is $128.

Final Estimate—The finished labor and materials estimate for this item is $310.80, as shown in the exhibit. Overhead and profit would then be added. See the exhibit "Labor and Materials Estimate."

Labor and Materials Estimate

	Quantity	Materials	Labor	Total
Replace 1" × 1" Ceramic Tile	88 sq. ft. × $1.75	$154.00	6.4 hrs. @ $20 = $128.00	$282.00
Adhesive	2 gal. × $10.00	$20.00		20.00
Grout	20 lbs.	$8.80		8.80
Total				$310.80

[DA03997]

The Unit Cost Method

If the adjuster must estimate the cost to repair or replace a ceramic tile floor a second time for another loss or in another room, he or she could repeat the labor and materials process or develop a unit cost to streamline the estimating process. From estimating the first job, the adjuster knows that replacing 80 square feet would cost $310.80. Dividing $310.80 by 80 provides the cost per square foot, $3.89. This is a unit cost that represents the labor and materials to replace one square foot of 1" × 1" white ceramic tile. The next time this tile is used in a repair, the adjuster can use the unit cost method. If the next room is 6 feet × 9 feet, the estimate would read:

Replace 54 square feet of 1" × 1" white ceramic tile @ $3.89 = $210.06.

The procedure used to estimate the floor repair can be used to estimate the cost of repairing base tiles around the perimeter of the room. Once the adjuster uses the labor and materials method, he or she can apply a unit cost for a linear foot of wall to determine the cost for that item.

In estimating the cost to repair a bathroom floor, the adjuster must allow for access time—in this case, removing and resetting the toilet to replace the tile underneath it. The access time should be stated as a separate item using the labor and materials method. The references estimate that the work would take 1 hour and that the only material required is a wax ring at $1.

The estimate would therefore include:

Remove and reset toilet, 1 hour at $20 + $1 material = $21.

The adjuster would not build that item into the unit cost for three reasons:

- The access cost does not vary with the room size.
- The cost might be used in rooms other than the bathroom.
- Including access or preparation time in the unit cost can lead to counting the cost to gain access twice. The best approach is to keep unit costs as simple as possible. The adjuster should separately estimate and show extra labor and materials needed to gain access in a particular work area.

Choice of Estimating Methods

Which estimating method is better? Unit costs work well with common generic items such as paint, drywall, and floor coverings. Unit costs do not work as well with uncommon items because developing the unit cost takes as much time as using the labor and materials method. The time to develop a unit cost for common items is justified by the long-term time savings realized by applying that unit cost to similar items in that particular project or in subsequent projects, thus eliminating the time needed to recompute labor and materials. However, no time savings can be realized in computing a unit cost for uncommon items such as the installation of a furnace, because differences in items make applying one item's unit cost to another item difficult. In this case, computing a unit cost simply adds to the time it takes to recompute labor and materials for each item.

For some components, such as framing, the labor and materials method is clearly more satisfactory. Although estimating a set of unit costs for different types of framing is possible, the unit costs do not help much because the labor factor depends on many variables. Rafters can help to illustrate the point. There are different factors for 2" × 6" rafters and 2" × 8" rafters. Installing rafters on hip roofs takes more time than installing them on gable roofs, which in turn takes more time than installing them on flat roofs. Depending on the design of the roof and the assessment of the job, some rafters are supported by collar beams. If the same variables were applied to the other framing components, the huge collage of unit costs would be more confusing than revealing. If the adjuster tried to simplify the unit costs for framing by developing an average cost, this average cost would be too much in some cases and too little in others. When properly used, the unit cost method is not an average cost method. Each unit cost should be tailored to a specific component, rather than to a class of similar components.

Unique items should also be estimated using the labor and materials method. Lighting fixtures, which come in various types and qualities, are a good example. However, the labor to install the fixtures is relatively constant. The most accurate way to estimate the cost to replace light fixtures is to price the fixture and add the labor to install it. The same holds true for cabinets, plumbing fixtures, and appliances.

The unit cost method should produce the same estimate as a pure labor and materials method, as shown in the tile calculation example. The only difference is that the adjuster does not spend the extra time calculating the number of gallons of paint or rolls of dry wall tape needed in each room. Unit cost estimating has fallen into disfavor with some insurers because some adjusters do not take the time to verify the unit cost quoted by a contractor. When presented with a unit cost estimate, the adjuster should determine if overhead and profit are included in the figure. The adjuster should also determine whether the figure has been rounded up. If it has, a substantial overpayment on a large loss could result.

ESTIMATING SOFTWARE PACKAGES

Adjusters can use computer estimating systems to prepare scopes. Those systems can produce easy-to-read printed estimates that are free of mathematical errors, but they cannot replace human judgment. Errors commonly occur in the use of these systems.

Estimates are now done electronically with stand-alone software on laptops and personal digital assistants (PDAs) or through web-based applications. An adjuster still scopes the loss at the scene but is able to enter the data directly into the estimating system, using codes for quality and grade. The system then calculates the time and material costs or the unit cost based on the information contained in its database.

The adjuster must have accurate measurements and descriptions when using one of these systems. The adjuster must also know when to override the system or to manually enter an item because of special circumstances.

Additionally, these systems also assist in preparing a personal property inventory and the cost estimate for restoration or replacement. They can also perform insurance to value calculations based on the data entered by the adjuster.

Cost Data

Most computer programs use unit cost data. Many create their unit costs from the labor and material costs method in much the same manner as the adjuster would do manually. In some systems, the adjuster uses location modifiers and does not research costs in every possible place. At the very least, a good system offers some breakdown, if not complete disclosure, of the prices and usage rates that make up the unit costs. Without this information, checking or negotiating individual items is difficult. Many systems use quality codes to indicate an item's relative cost and quality. However, more often than not, the adjuster must manually determine an unusual item's cost and then look for the quality code that produces that same cost. A more direct approach is to override the built-in costs for unusual items.

Estimators and those who review estimates must know what costs are included in the system's cost data. Does it remove door and window openings from the square foot calculation? What does the unit cost calculation include? Are overhead and profit included? If the adjuster does not know this information, a duplication in the estimate could occur.

Common Errors

Those who use estimating software programs must take some precautions in their use. The average unit cost in the system may not account for the conditions at a job site, such as adverse weather or limited road access. The unit cost may not take into account the productivity achieved because, for example, numerous rooms are having sheetrock applied. Some programs estimate removal or demolition by square feet or linear feet when the biggest cost is the hauling. Hauling cost varies by location, not by footage.[9]

Estimating systems may rely heavily on "remove and replace" rather than "repair or restore." They often fail to consider partial replacement as an alternative. It is also easy for an adjuster to allow for removal of sheetrock or drywall while at the same time removing wallpaper from the same wall. Keying errors can also occur, causing—for example—10 linear feet of cabinets to become 100 linear feet.[10]

Regardless of the estimating method used, the estimate should appear logical. Measurements must be accurate and correctly calculated. Material must be properly identified. There is an enormous difference in cost between manufactured stone and natural stone. The appropriate material grade must also be noted. The cost differential between stock cabinets and custom cabinets can add thousands of dollars to an estimate.

Other Features

One feature of a computerized system is the speed with which the adjuster is able to complete the scope and estimate. If the insured's contractor finishes his or her estimate first, the adjuster would need to negotiate from the contractor's figures. With an estimate in hand, the adjuster negotiates from his or her figures. In competitive bid situations, the system helps control the bids' form and format. Several programs print a scope that lists only the items and quantities, without pricing or extensions.

Another feature that helps negotiations is the automatic trade breakdown. Most programs print a trade estimate as well as a detailed room-by-room estimate. The trade estimate summarizes the detailed estimate by totaling the repairs for each trade. The trade estimate makes comparing the adjuster's estimate to a contractor's estimate that is itemized by trade easy.

ESTIMATES INVOLVING DEMOLITION

Demolition is the tearing out of damaged components from their original place in the building. Demolition yields debris, which must be removed from the site. Often, the size of the loss dictates how the estimate is to be prepared.

Demolition work is generally figured using a laborer's wage rate rather than a skilled worker's rate. The labor and materials method is the best approach to use for demolition. The demolition labor figures include the time needed to pile the debris on the premises.

Demolition and removal can vary from one estimate to another. Demolition is the tearing out of damaged components from their original place in the building. Demolition yields debris, which must be removed from the site. Demolition work is generally figured using a laborer's wage rate rather than a skilled worker's rate. The adjuster can estimate demolition on either a labor and materials basis (also called a time and materials basis) or a unit cost basis. The labor and materials method uses the cost of the labor (time) needed to complete the job and the cost of the materials. Unit cost is a way to stream-line the estimating process. If the labor and materials rate has been calculated once, it can be divided by the unit of measure (such as square feet) to calculate the unit of measure cost otherwise known as unit cost. Unit removal costs can be added to the unit item replacement cost to arrive at a remove and replace unit cost. Theoretically, the unit cost method should be as accurate as any other approach. Nevertheless, it can lead to serious overestimating, especially on larger losses, for these reasons:

- Some components are out of sight, requiring no tear-out.
- Demolition of one component often includes demolition of another. To estimate both with a remove and replace cost duplicates the cost of the demolition.
- The remove and replace cost tends to become the accepted norm and is often used when the repair option is more appropriate.
- On larger losses, unit cost fails to recognize economies of scale. A few hours with heavy equipment can replace days of manual labor.
- Many of the tear-out figures in the labor references are appropriate for careful remodeling demolition rather than for large-scale demolition involved in larger losses.

The labor and materials method is the best approach to use for demolition. If that method is used, the unit costs used in the rest of the estimate should not include removal.

Experience is necessary to estimate the number of work hours or days of demolition. The references contain enough information to get the adjuster started, but duplications are still possible. The tear-out time for the most significant item in a building assembly should be used. The labor factor usually includes secondary components. For instance, if 2.5 hours are allowed to tear out 100 square feet of partition wall, additional time to remove the drywall, wallpaper, switch plates, or heating vents should not be allowed.

One approach to checking the demolition portion of a contractor's estimate is dividing the amount by the local common labor rate. The result approximates the number of hours of demolition labor. If the hours seem excessive, negotiating time is usually easier than negotiating dollars.

ESTIMATES INVOLVING DEBRIS REMOVAL

Demolition yields debris, which must be removed from the site. Often, the size of the loss dictates how the estimate is to be prepared.

The debris removal cost represents the additional cost to remove debris from the site and properly dispose of it. The best approach to estimating the cost of debris removal is to estimate the number and size of boxes or trash bins needed to handle the debris and apply the fee quoted by a local waste disposal company.

Debris removal cost is the labor and expense involved in removing debris from the site. The two types of debris are these:

• The debris of the damaged property
• The waste produced by repairs

The demolition labor figures include the time needed to pile the debris on the premises.

Disposal companies quote a single price to place the bin on the site and to pick it up when it is full. Trying to estimate debris removal costs by truckloads, hours of driving time, mileage allowances, and dump fees is not feasible. Demolition and removal usually is a lump sum in the estimate. It can also be called tear-out and cart, demo and trucking, debris removal, or drayage.

Adjuster Tip—Because demolition and removal is usually labor cost plus the cost of a dumpster and truck, contractors might inflate this item to cover other contingencies.

ESTIMATES INVOLVING SMALL LOSSES

Often, the size of the loss dictates how the estimate is to be prepared. The economies of scale available on a large project do not exist in a small project.

One popular approach for estimating small losses is to allow a minimum charge that represents two to four hours of labor and a small amount of material, but adjusters can also use the labor and materials method or the unit cost method.

The labor tables in most references allow time for normal setup, preparation, and cleanup. For small jobs, this allowance might be inadequate. Drywall repair is a good example. Even if the damage is less than one square foot and the actual repair time is less than one hour, completing the repair is more time-consuming because the drywall compound has to dry between coats. Even the smallest repair might require an additional trip or two, unless other work can be performed while the compound dries. On a large job, the worker would have other things to do while waiting for the compound to dry or could return to the job site later without the extra travel time significantly affecting the cost.

One approach to estimating a small job is to allow for driving time in addition to the time required to do the work. The more popular approach is to allow a minimum charge. The minimum charge quoted by a contractor usually represents two to four hours of labor and a small amount of material. Minimum charges are convenient but should be used with caution. The adjuster should consider whether separate trades are necessary when a small job involves minimum charges for several trades. If there are several small items for a single trade, a better approach is to estimate the damage using the labor and materials or unit cost method. When the estimate is completed, the adjuster checks to see whether the total for that trade exceeds the usual minimum charge.

ESTIMATES INVOLVING LARGE LOSSES

Often, the size of the loss dictates how the estimate is to be prepared.

The adjuster analyzes the unit costs and production rates used on smaller losses and adjusts as needed for large losses.

An insurance adage states that the only difference between estimating a $10,000 loss and a $100,000 loss is one zero. Although those words might comfort a new adjuster, they are also misleading. Large jobs involve economies of scale. Subcontractors with specialized skills and equipment can produce significant savings. Material discounts for large quantities are possible. Finally, competition can play a greater role in larger losses.

If the loss involves painting the interior of an apartment building, the unit cost should be based on spray painting rather than brush or roller painting. Drywall specialists, who might be engaged for a large job, can work more efficiently than can the carpenter who only occasionally paints a room or two. Additionally, drywalling a large space is usually easier because it involves less cutting, fewer odd shapes, and more standard seams. The adjuster can check unit costs by talking with specialty subcontractors about pricing for the quantity of work involved. Finally, an adjuster might want to approach demolition as a single labor and materials item, avoiding the possibility of redundancy in remove and replace unit costs.

NEGOTIATING BUILDING LOSSES

Estimates of loss might differ because of differences in the scope of the loss or differences in the price, and the adjuster must reconcile the differences.

Estimators looking at the same loss would develop two different repair figures for only two reasons. The first reason is scope differences, including measurement and quantity errors, as well as divergent opinions on the quality and the type of repair. The second reason is price.

Resolving Differences in the Scope

Estimating is not an exact science, and legitimate differences are common. Negotiating a repair figure begins with the first inspection. If the scope is agreed on early, the pricing issues are relatively easy to resolve through negotiation or competitive bidding. The easiest way to reach an agreement on a scope is for the adjuster to prepare it jointly with the insured or the insured's choice of contractor. An adjuster should find a way to resolve any differences in a scope before an estimate is written.

Approaches to Resolving Scope-Related Issues

- If the adjuster is scoping with a contractor, each should keep separate notes and diagrams, which help to identify differences more quickly, unless the contractor wants to work from the adjuster's notes.

- The adjuster can resolve any question of hidden damage by arranging for some quick demolition or by doing a more complete inspection.

- Some scope questions require an expert, such as a structural engineer. A common question is the degree of fire damage to concrete, masonry, or steel. Although building inspectors usually have an opinion, they might not have the training and resources to make an accurate decision.

- Other differences in scope can be resolved by calling in a subcontractor. Most insurance repair contractors are general contractors who rely heavily on their subcontractors for technical expertise. Scope issues involving electrical, plumbing, and heating and air conditioning can be resolved by consulting a specialty subcontractor.

- Test repairs can be made on a small area to determine whether a repair option would work.

- Competitive bids can resolve scope problems in a few specific situations. If the insured has chosen a contractor who usually deals in remodeling or new construction, that contractor might want to tear out and replace everything. A more experienced contractor in damage restoration might be needed to identify more conservative yet equally effective alternatives.

Resolving Price Differences

Resolving price-related differences can begin only after the scope has been agreed on. Some contractors charge higher prices than others do. If a contractor with a reputation for quality work charges a higher price, the adjuster might decide to pay that price. Although no single price is correct, some ranges are acceptable. This section lists general guidelines for negotiating price.

Price Negotiation Guidelines

- Unit costs are difficult to negotiate. The adjuster can suggest the unit costs as the scope is prepared. Most contractors have a range of unit costs that they will accept. If the adjuster suggests a price on the lower side of the range, the contractor will be more likely to accept it during the scope phase than after the estimate is written. The same is true for labor rates. If the adjuster and contractor can agree on the price of labor in advance, they can then negotiate the labor production rates based on published sources.

- If unit costs are not agreed to in advance, the labor and materials methods could be used to analyze and negotiate the unit cost. For larger losses, the standard labor production rates are usually on the high side, just as they are on the low side for small jobs.

- For trades in which the involvement of a subcontractor is expected, the adjuster should ask the general contractor to confirm the price with the subcontractor. That gives the general contractor a chance to reduce the price without losing face. If the price still seems high to the adjuster, another subcontractor can be asked to bid on the repair. The difference might be an additional markup by the general contractor.

- As a general rule, negotiating from a known quantity such as the adjuster's detailed estimate is more effective than negotiating without an agreed scope. Simply comparing estimates from contractors can cause errors if there is no established norm. The electrical portion of two general contractors' bids could have been prepared by the same subcontractor who accidentally hit the wrong key on the calculator. The two amounts will be similar, but both will be wrong. Bid comparisons are effective as long as everyone works from the same scope and presents the bid in about the same format. In each bid, some items will be higher, and some will be lower. The adjuster should address the bigger discrepancies. Trying to get a contractor to agree to the lowest price for every item is rarely successful.

COVERAGE ASPECTS OF ESTIMATING

This section discusses how insurance policy provisions affect the preparation of estimates.

Insurance policy provisions affect the preparation of estimates in several important ways:

- Without an endorsement, most policies exclude the additional repair costs needed to bring a damaged building up to current codes.

- Generally, most adjusters estimate the cost of repairs using like kind and quality. The adjuster might suggest an alternative repair, but the insured must decide whether to accept that option. The usual policy language does not specifically address the issue of alternative repairs.

- Determining the actual cash value (ACV) of a repair estimate requires knowing the useful life of building components as well as the court decisions dealing with ACV in the jurisdiction.

- Confirming that a building meets coinsurance or replacement cost requirements involves a different sort of cost estimating.

Code Requirements

Without an endorsement, most policies exclude the additional repair costs needed to bring a damaged building up to current codes. These codes might require demolishing and replacing undamaged components, replacing obsolete components with new ones, or even adding new items. Determining the additional cost resulting from the codes involves determining the difference between the cost of replacing the damaged portion with items or material of like kind and quality and the cost of replacing with items or materials to meet the current code. In some situations, the amount is obvious. In others, it is not so clear. Because the insured will pay the extra cost, an expert opinion might be warranted.

Alternative Repairs

Generally, most adjusters estimate the cost of repairs using like kind and quality. Creative adjusters sometimes identify repair methods that add value to the insured yet cost less than the usual replacement with like kind and quality. Carpet damaged by a burning log rolling out of the fireplace is a good example. For wall-to-wall carpet, many companies pay to replace carpet in the damaged room and any area that cannot be closed from view. The insured, however, might choose to replace the burned area in front of the fireplace with quarry tile rather than replace several rooms of carpet. Installing drywall instead of plaster and using a butcher block to cover a small burned area on a countertop are other examples of alternative repairs. Although these approaches make sense, the usual policy language does not specifically address the issue of alternative repairs. The adjuster might suggest an alternative repair, but the insured must decide whether to accept that option. If necessary, the adjuster might rely on the policy provision of paying only the actual cash value until repairs are completed, which can prevent an overpayment.

Determining the Actual Cash Value of a Repair Estimate

Determining the ACV of a repair estimate requires knowing the useful life of building components as well as the court decisions dealing with ACV in the jurisdiction. Determining ACV involves examining each item of repair and quantifying the extent of betterment. The item's age, condition, and expected use affect the amount of depreciation. If the paint in a family room was badly worn before a loss and the loss required that the room be repainted, it would be subject to greater depreciation than the paint in a guest room, which would show little or no evidence of wear. The process of making an objective judgment on depreciation follows no set rules, only general principles.

In determining the ACV of an item to be repaired, the adjuster must understand what causes building components to lose value. Some reasons include these:

- Physical wear most frequently leads to loss in value. Paint, wall and floor coverings, roofing, and mechanical appliances wear out over time. The *Repair and Remodeling Quarterly* by Marshall and Swift contains a list of the expected life for some common building components. Another source of determining useful life is the manufacturer's warranty, although the useful life can be expected to be longer than the warranty period. These items are generally depreciated on a straight-line basis; therefore, if a component has a useful life of ten years, it will depreciate in value one-tenth per year. Items that do not wear out are rarely subject to depreciation. However, exceptions occur. For example, evidence of rot or termite damage in framing would justify depreciation if the loss was caused by fire and damaged components were to be replaced with new ones.

- Obsolescence also contributes to loss in value. As building materials and techniques change, older buildings' features lose value. An example is piping for gaslights in an old building. Although the lines might be functionally sound, they add no value to the building. However, obsolescence can be an elusive concept. The nine- and ten-foot ceilings that were becoming obsolete during the energy crisis of the 1970s are again considered a sign of superior construction as well as an aesthetic advantage.

- Partial repairs usually do not improve the insured's financial position. As a result, they are rarely subject to depreciation. Replacing a few shingles causes no betterment, but replacing the entire roof usually does. Between the extremes of partial repair and total replacement, the adjuster must decide each case on its merits. Replacing only the damaged slope of a roof might not increase a house's value. However, it would reduce the ultimate cost of replacing the rest of the roof at a later date.

- In large losses involving older buildings, the ACV of the entire building might be the measure of loss. The market eventually devalues building components that do not wear out. The old notion that the entire building's ACV should reflect the same reduction in value as the depreciated repair estimate is simply incorrect. The effective building age depends on factors beyond the simple deterioration of the components.

Estimating the Value at Risk

Confirming that a building meets coinsurance or replacement cost requirements involves a different sort of cost estimating. Most insurers use the Marshall & Swift/Boeckh (MSB) publications to verify the insured value. The simplest methods use square-foot costs for several classes and qualities of construction for each type of occupancy. The more complex methods come close to the detail of the stick-by-stick estimate. These publications can also be used to set reserves, settle total losses, and verify value.

The key to using these references is to identify the *class*, *quality*, and *occupancy* of the building correctly. The books define these three terms. Adjusters must study and apply these definitions rather than rely on what they think a term or terms might mean. For example, an office in a good-quality warehouse is different from a good-quality medical office. Another example of differences in definition is the case of an adjuster trying to determine whether the cost to replace a fitness club building includes the cost of a pool. The answer to this question depends largely on whether the publisher of the reference source defines a fitness club as including a pool. The adjuster must be sure to interpret this definition as the publisher intends.

SUMMARY

Knowing the type of building construction and the type of detection and suppression system (if any) involved in a loss gives a property loss adjuster an understanding of the type of damage to be expected in a loss and how best to repair or replace the damage.

Property loss adjusters must know how to estimate building damages. They should be able to identify the six essential parts of a building structure:

- Foundation
- Framing
- Windows and doors
- Utilities
- Interior finishes
- Exterior finishes

The two steps in the estimation process are (1) preparing the scope of damage at the loss scene and (2) pricing the work determined by the scope into a repair estimate.

A scope is a detailed list of damage to each building component. The scope consists of the raw counts of the materials necessary for the repairs, a description of the degree of damage to each component, and the quality of the materials of the damaged property. Unlike a finished estimate, a scope does not list any prices or the calculated quantities. This section described a recommended method for inspecting a loss site and preparing a scope.

Pricing an estimate involves estimating the loss restoration cost by using the itemized damage in the scope. Construction operations typically include costs for materials, labor and employer's burden, tools and equipment, overhead and profit, and other miscellaneous costs. Adjusters can use reference materials to identify the materials and quantities needed and to estimate other construction costs.

The two primary methods for estimating repair costs are (1) the labor and materials method (also called the time and materials method) and (2) the unit cost method.

The labor and materials method relies on data contained in various estimating reference books or software. These references list information such as the number of square feet that a gallon of paint will cover and how long a worker would need to paint a wall of a certain size. The unit cost method calculates the labor and materials necessary to repair one unit, such as installing one square foot of white ceramic tile. After the adjuster has determined the unit cost for a job, he or she can multiply that cost by the number of units that the job includes. Depending on the circumstances of the job, either the labor and materials method or the unit cost method might be the more appropriate estimating choice. Unit cost estimating can be quicker if properly used, but adjusters must understand its limitations to apply it correctly.

The adjuster should know what costs are included in the systems' cost data. The adjuster may have to take into account the adverse conditions at a job site. Productivity and duplication of effort may not be taken into account by the software package. Estimating systems often do not consider alternatives such as partial replacement. Keying errors are also a concern.

Demolition, the removal of damaged components from their original place in the building, can lead to overestimating, so the labor and materials method is usually the best approach for estimating the cost of demolition.

The best approach to estimating the cost of debris removal is to estimate the number and size of boxes or trash bins needed to handle the debris and apply the fee quoted by a local waste disposal company.

For smaller losses, some of the steps of the scope can be combined or eliminated.

- Estimates for small losses are usually done on a labor and materials basis.
- For small jobs, the allowance for normal setup, preparation, and cleanup might be inadequate.

- One approach to estimating a small job is to allow for driving time in addition to the time required to do the work.

- The more popular approach is to allow a minimum charge.

Large jobs involve economies of scale. The adjuster analyzes the unit costs and production rates used on smaller losses and adjusts as needed for large losses.

- Subcontractors with specialized skills and equipment can produce significant savings.

- Material discounts for large quantities are possible.

- Competition can play a greater role in larger losses.

Estimators studying the same loss might develop different repair figures either because of scoping differences or because of different opinions on the quality and type of repairs. The best way for an adjuster to resolve scoping differences is to prepare the scope jointly with the insured or the insured's contractor. After the scope has been agreed to, the adjuster can resolve the difference in price by using the methods described in this section.

Policy provisions could affect the preparation of estimates. For example, most policies exclude the additional repair costs needed to bring a damaged building up to current codes. Additionally, an adjuster might be able to identify repair methods that add value but that cost less than the usual replacement with like kind and quality. Although the insurance industry has historically considered actual cash value, the basis of estimating repairs, to be equal to replacement cost less depreciation, the courts have used the broad evidence rule to include market value factors that can affect the amount of the cost to repair.

ASSIGNMENT NOTES

1. Francis L. Brannigan, Building Construction for the Fire Service (Boston: National Fire Protection Association, 1971 and 1977), p. 8.

2. Sprinkler material adapted from Charles Bahme, "Fire Officer's Guide to Extinguishing Systems" (Boston: National Fire Protection Association, 1977).

3. Alarm information adapted from Vivian Cape, Security Systems and Intruder Alarms (Oxford: Newnes, 1999).

4. Paul I. Thomas, How to Estimate Building Losses and Construction Costs, 4th ed. (Englewood Cliffs, N.J.: Prentice-Hall, Inc., 1983).

5. "Using Steel for Optional Engineering of Framing Techniques," Property Damage Report, No. 501 (Newville, Pa.: National Property Casualty Claims Research Services, Inc., July 1994).

6. Adapted from Mutual Loss Research Bureau, 1969 Adjuster's Basic School Training Material.

7. Adapted from Paul I. Thomas, How to Estimate Building Losses and Construction Costs, 4th ed. (Englewood Cliffs, N.J.: Prentice-Hall, Inc., 1983), pp. 17–18.

8. Adapted from Paul I. Thomas, How to Estimate Building Losses and Construction Costs, 4th ed. (Englewood Cliffs, N.J.: Prentice-Hall, Inc., 1983), pp. 18–50.

9. Adapted from Curtis W. Driver, "Reality Estimating in the Property Insurance Industry," Claims Magazine, December 1999, pp. 60–66.

10. Adapted from "Estimating Errors," Property Damage Report, No. 532 (Newville, Pa.: National Property and Casualty Claims Research Services, Inc., September 1999).

Direct Your Learning ▶▶

8

Fundamentals of Residential Construction

Educational Objectives

After learning the content of this assignment, you should be able to:

▷ Give examples of causes of damage, explain the methods of repair and factors affecting repairs, and create a residential construction estimate for each of the following:

- Concrete and masonry
- Frame carpentry
- Drywall
- Roofing
- Painting and wallpaper
- Siding

▷ Create a gross area and net area estimate for painting a room.

▷ Describe the elements of, and damage that can occur to, the following systems:

- Electrical
- Plumbing
- Heating and cooling

Fundamentals of Residential Construction

RESIDENTIAL CONSTRUCTION ESTIMATES FOR DAMAGE AND REPAIR

Understanding basic construction principles helps an adjuster to evaluate a loss, whether it is a field adjuster who goes out to loss sites and prepares estimates of damage or a liability adjuster who receives estimates to repair damage caused by insureds.

This section follows a "ground up" approach to discussing construction, beginning with a building's foundation and ending with the exterior finish. Familiarity with such construction basics enables an adjuster to create, understand, and question construction estimates.

Concrete

Concrete is used as the foundation for most residences. It is used for patios, walkways, and driveways. Concrete is a fire-resistive material. Prolonged exposure to extreme heat causes concrete to lose its moisture. The surface then flakes off in thin pieces. This condition is called **spalling**. Spalling also results from repeated heating and cooling during firefighting activities. Concrete can also shrink as a result of fire, and that shrinkage causes cracks to form.

Fire-damaged concrete can be repaired by cutting out the damaged area and replacing it. Areas that have spalling can be scraped and resurfaced. Stained and smoke-damaged concrete can be cleaned with steam, sand, or chemicals. The concrete surface can also be painted to cover the stains.

Concrete comes in two forms: (1) ready mix and (2) mixed on site. Ready mix is delivered by large mixer trucks and is poured into waiting forms. Concrete mixed on site is prepared by stand-alone mixers and requires additional labor to mix it and haul it to the forms. Concrete also comes in various formulas to suit different purposes, although the essential ingredients are always cement, sand, and stone. There are concrete mixes for heavy-use locations, such as driveways and garage floors. There are also watertight mixes for foundations and pools. The cost varies depending on the mix.

Adjuster Tip—On smaller jobs using ready mix, there may be a minimum charge or a minimum amount, such as five cubic yards, that must be purchased.

Concrete is estimated by volume, and its unit of measure is cubic yards.

Spalling

The flaking of a concrete surface when exposed to prolonged extreme heat.

Concrete form

A temporary mold to support the shape of concrete while it sets and cures.

Estimating concrete work entails more than just determining the quantity of material. Slabs, sidewalks, patios, floors, and foundations need to have forms built. A **concrete form** is a temporary mold to support the shape of the concrete while it sets and cures. The estimate must therefore include the quantity of lumber needed to build these forms. The forms are usually built by carpenters and torn down by laborers.

Adjuster Tip—Some contractors reuse lumber from old forms, or they may have prefabricated forms that are reusable.

The amount of lumber needed for forms is based on the square footage of the concrete surface. An average is between two and a half to three board feet per square foot of concrete.

Masonry

Foundations can also be built from concrete block. Because concrete block, brick, and stone are similar in installation and estimation, this section discusses them together. A mason and helper usually install brick, concrete block, and stone. Brick is often the exterior finish to a house, but it can be used in a wall, in steps, in a walkway, in a patio, and in a fireplace. Concrete block is often used as a footing for another part of the structure. Stone has the same variety of uses as brick.

Masonry is most often installed using mortar to hold it in place. Mortar is a mix of cement, sand, water, and sometimes lime. Mortar is estimated on the basis of cubic feet or cubic yards needed. On average, 18 cubic feet or two-thirds cubic yards of mortar is used per 1,000 bricks. Forty cubic feet, or one and a half cubic yards, is used per 1,000 blocks. These numbers vary depending on the size of the brick or block used and how thickly the mortar is applied. [1]

Brick

A common brick is 4" × 8" × 2". Its actual size is 3.75" × 8" × 2.25". On average, there are 21 bricks to one cubic foot of masonry. One hundred bricks are called a strap, which is usually the minimum quantity available for purchase. A pallet is 500 bricks.

Many varieties of brick are available. The exhibit illustrates various types of bricks. Intended use determines whether a specialty brick is needed, such as for a fireplace. Brick can discolor, crack, or spall. It can develop white surface deposits, which are salt crystals leeching out of the brick. These salt crystals can usually be removed with linseed oil. Brick can be cut out and replaced; however, matching its color might be difficult. When preparing an estimate for brick repair, the adjuster might have to include scaffolding or bracing needed to keep adjacent walls in place. [2]

Block

Concrete block is available in two weights and several sizes. Lightweight block (referred to as cinder block) is 8" × 8" × 16" and weighs about 30 pounds. Its actual size is 7.625" × 7.625" × 15.625". Heavy block is also 8" × 8" × 16", but it weighs about 45 pounds. Concrete block can also be found in smaller sizes.

Concrete block is susceptible to the same damage as is concrete. Although concrete block does not spall under extreme heat, it can crumble. Cracks usually result from fire, earth movement, blasting, and vibration. Damaged concrete block can be cut out and replaced. If this is done, adjacent walls may need to be braced during such repairs.

Estimating Brick and Block

To estimate the amount of 8" × 8" × 16" concrete block needed, first calculate the square foot area of the wall and deduct all openings and corners. This is done by deducting the opening and by taking 8 inches off of 2 walls for a total of 16 inches when using 8" × 8" × 16" blocks to deduct for corners. Multiply the square foot area by 1.125 to get the required number of blocks.

Brick walls pose a challenge for an adjuster because he or she must know how thick the wall will be. A 1-brick-thick wall is a 4-inch wall; 2 bricks thick is an 8-inch wall. The way to estimate the number of bricks needed is to find the gross wall area and deduct the openings. Then multiply the square feet by the number of bricks per square foot of the desired wall thickness. As an example, suppose that the wall is 8' × 10' and that it is going to be 8 inches thick. A table in an estimating reference book would show that 14 bricks make 1 square foot of an 8-inch wall. So 8' × 10' = 80 square feet × 14 bricks per square foot = 1,120 bricks. See the exhibit "Common Brick Wall With Block Backup."

Frame Carpentry

To properly complete a scope and an estimate for frame carpentry, an adjuster must identify the quantity and quality of the lumber needed. Correctly identifying the quantity and quality helps to ensure an accurate estimate.

Lumberyard Terminology

With so many different types of lumber available, an adjuster's job is easier if he or she understands the various types of lumber available and their uses. How lumber is sized and how it is sold directly affects the estimate's accuracy.

About 80 percent of building construction involves carpentry work. When wood is damaged, identifying its type and quality is essential. Wood is either hardwood or softwood. **Hardwood** comes from deciduous, broadleaf trees. **Softwood** comes from coniferous, evergreen trees. The names are slightly

Hardwood

Wood that comes from deciduous, broadleaf trees such as maple and oak.

Softwood

Wood that comes from coniferous, evergreen trees such as pine and cedar.

Common Brick Wall With Block Backup

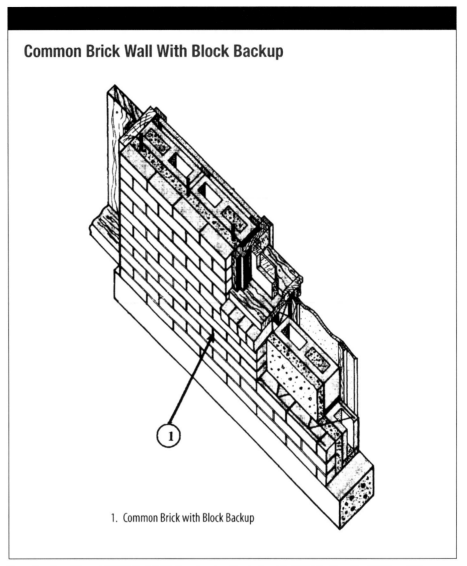

1. Common Brick with Block Backup

Home Repair and Remodel 2002 Cost Guide (Los Angeles: Marshall and Swift Publications Co., 2002), p. 410.
[DA04033]

deceiving because some hardwoods are actually softer in consistency than some softwoods. Generally, hardwoods are typically used in finish carpentry, and softwoods are used in framing. See the exhibit "Types of Wood."

Softwood lumber usually comes in 6- to 20-foot lengths. It is sold only in 2-foot increments, so an 18-foot length or a 20-foot length is available, but a 19-foot length is not available. Hardwood lumber is sold in random lengths based on availability. A strip is a small piece of lumber usually less than 1 inch thick and 3 inches wide. A board is normally 4 to 12 inches wide and less than 2 inches thick. Framing lumber ranges from 2 to 6 inches thick and is usually a minimum of 2 inches wide, so common sizes are 2" × 4", 2" × 6", or 4" × 6". Beams are 4 or more inches thick and are at least 2 inches wider than

Types of Wood

Softwoods	Hardwoods	
Cedar	Ash	Gum
Cypress	Aspen	Mahogany
Fir	Basswood	Maple
Hemlock	Beech	Oak
Pine	Birch	Poplar
Redwood	Cherry	Sycamore
Spruce	Chestnut	Walnut
	Elm	Willow

[DA04034]

their thickness. Posts and timbers are usually 4 inches by 6 inches, and their width should not exceed the thickness by more than 2 inches.[3]

Lumber is sold in two ways:

- Linear foot is used for small quantities.
- Board foot is used for large quantities.

The price for lumber is stated as the price per 1,000 board feet.

Frame Carpentry Damage and Repair

A house's frame can be damaged by various causes, including fire, smoke, windstorm, water, vandalism, earthquake, settlement, vehicle impact, and many other perils, some insured and others excluded. Serious losses might require replacing roof sections or completely reframing a room. Less severe losses might simply call for replacing a single rafter, stud, or floor joist.

Because framing members are the first elements to be constructed when a house is built, removing and replacing undamaged items are often necessary to repair damaged structural members, such as when an attic fire severely chars roof rafters. Even when only slightly damaged, the finished roof surface and roof sheathing must be removed and replaced to replace the rafters.

Exposure to extreme heat causes wood to lose moisture, so lumber might shrink, warp, or split. Exposure to excessive moisture causes wood to swell, and swelling will begin within hours of immersion. If left undisturbed, the swelling will stop within a few days.[4]

Damaged wood framing can be repaired by several methods. It can be replaced entirely, or it can be partially replaced, reinforced, concealed, or resurfaced. In some cases involving cracked, split, or charred framing members, the damaged parts do not need to be removed. Instead, they can be reinforced by **splicing (also called sistering or scabbing)** new framing members alongside them. Finished materials almost always cover framing members, so the change created by splicing has no cosmetic effect. Structural members that are only slightly charred or stained by smoke can be spray-sealed, painted, or covered by drywall. Most insureds simply want to be assured that the smell of smoke will not linger. Spray sealing is acceptable to most insureds and fire restoration contractors.

Splicing, sistering, or scabbing

A repair technique in which new framing members are placed alongside damaged members to reinforce them.

Frame Construction

The two basic types of residential frame construction are (1) platform (sometimes called "western") and (2) balloon. Platform construction is the common method employed today. Balloon construction is seldom used in new homes because of the cost of extra-long framing members. However, adjusters should be familiar with balloon construction because homes built before 1940 sometimes used this method of framing. These two types of frame construction are discussed here, followed by a description of the components that form the shell of a typical house. See the exhibit "Platform Frame Construction."

Platform Construction—In **platform construction**, each story of a house is built as a separate platform. Imagine each story as boxes stacked one on top of another. The wall framing in platform construction is built above the subfloor and extends to all edges of the building. A common method of building these walls is to prefabricate full sections of walls and tilt them up and into place. This method is not always possible if only sections of a wall damaged by loss are replaced.

Platform construction

A method of construction in which each story of a house is built on a separate platform, like boxes stacked one on top of another.

Balloon Construction—In **balloon construction**, the wall studs extend from the sill of the first floor to the top plate or end rafter of the second floor. In platform construction, the framed wall is complete for each floor. This is the major difference between balloon construction and platform construction. The construction of interior walls is the same for balloon framing as for platform framing. See the exhibit "Balloon Frame Construction."

Balloon construction

A method of construction that uses long wall studs that extend from the ground on up to the second floor.

Adjuster Tip—To tell what type of construction was used for a house, go into the basement or crawl-space and look for the mudsill on top of the foundation. If paired joists and studs are resting on the sill, the house was built using balloon construction. If only joists are visible below the subfloor, then the house was built with platform construction.[5]

Elements of Frame Carpentry

Frame carpentry, also called "rough carpentry," is the work done by a carpenter in erecting the basic shell of a house. Knowledge of frame carpentry is especially important because frame damage is not always visible after a loss. The easiest way to develop an understanding of frame carpentry is to study each of the basic elements of a house's shell separately.

Frame carpentry

The work done by carpenters to erect the basic skeleton of a house.

Floor Framing—The floor framing of a wood-frame house consists of the posts, beams, sill plates, joists, and subflooring. Together, these form the level plat-

Platform Frame Construction

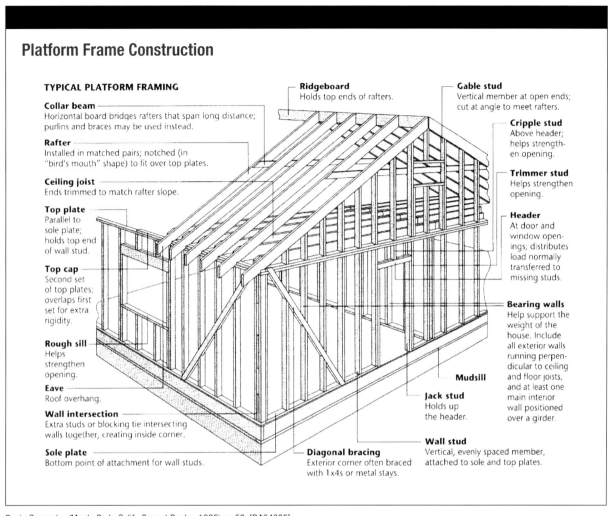

TYPICAL PLATFORM FRAMING

Collar beam
Horizontal board bridges rafters that span long distance; purlins and braces may be used instead.

Rafter
Installed in matched pairs; notched (in "bird's mouth" shape) to fit over top plates.

Ceiling joist
Ends trimmed to match rafter slope.

Top plate
Parallel to sole plate; holds top end of wall stud.

Top cap
Second set of top plates; overlaps first set for extra rigidity.

Rough sill
Helps strengthen opening.

Eave
Roof overhang.

Wall intersection
Extra studs or blocking tie intersecting walls together, creating inside corner.

Sole plate
Bottom point of attachment for wall studs.

Ridgeboard
Holds top ends of rafters.

Diagonal bracing
Exterior corner often braced with 1x4s or metal stays.

Mudsill

Jack stud
Holds up the header.

Wall stud
Vertical, evenly spaced member, attached to sole and top plates.

Gable stud
Vertical member at open ends; cut at angle to meet rafters.

Cripple stud
Above header; helps strengthen opening.

Trimmer stud
Helps strengthen opening.

Header
At door and window openings; distributes load normally transferred to missing studs.

Bearing walls
Help support the weight of the house. Include all exterior walls running perpendicular to ceiling and floor joists, and at least one main interior wall positioned over a girder.

Basic Carpentry (Menlo Park, Calif.: Sunset Books, 1995), p. 52. [DA04035]

form for the rest of the house. The posts and center beams support the inside ends of the joists. Wood or steel posts are generally used to support wood girders or steel beams.

Posts and Girders—Wood and steel posts, girders, and beams are used in residential construction. The most common steel beam is the I-beam, which spans the full length of the house. When wood girders are used, they are generally built up, meaning that they are composed of two or more 2" × 10"s or 2" × 12"s nailed together. Some new homes are constructed with plywood I-beams, which provide great support and are lightweight

Wood Sill—The exhibit shows that platform construction uses a box sill consisting of a two-inch sill anchored to the foundation wall, which provides support and fastening for the joists and box header at the end of the joists.

Adjuster Tip—Sills cannot be replaced easily because of the amount of the building that they support. In a fire, usually only a sill's edges burn because they are the only surfaces exposed. Replace sills only if the bulk of the building on top of them is destroyed.

Balloon Frame Construction

COMPONENTS OF BALLOON FRAMING

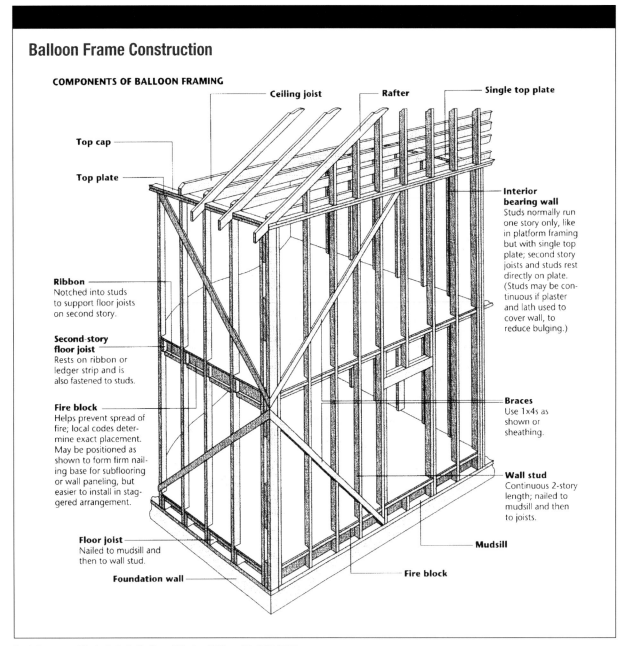

Basic Carpentry (Menlo Park, Calif.: Sunset Books, 1995), p. 53. [DA04036]

Floor Joists—Wood floor joists are generally 2" × 8", 2" × 10", or 2" × 12". They run perpendicular to the center beam and usually sit directly on it, with their ends slightly overlapping. They can also be attached directly to a wooden girder or steel beam by joist hangers or a supporting ledger strip. They are usually spaced 16-inch on center. Joists are attached to the sill, and the header joist is then attached to each stringer joist. Double joists are usually used under any area that will support additional weight, such as partition

Floor Joists

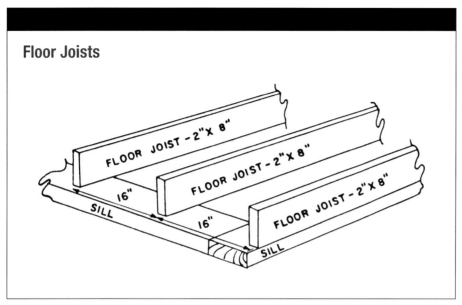

Adjuster Handbook (Denver: General Adjustment Bureau, Inc., 1972), p. 12. [DA04038]

walls, bathtubs, fireplaces, or openings for stairways. See the exhibit "Floor Joists."

Bridging—Cross bridging is placed between joists at various intervals to help transfer loads. Three types of bridging are commonly used in residential structures: (1) solid board, (2) wooden (usually using 1" × 2"s or 1" × 3"s), and (3) metal. Metal is rapidly becoming the most popular bridging material because it is strong, lightweight, and easy to install.

Subflooring—**Subflooring** is used over the floor joists to provide a working platform and base for finish flooring. Plywood is graded by letter. "C" and "D" grade are typically used for sheathing. The sheets are usually 4' × 8' and cover 32 square feet. Depending on the strength needed, thicknesses from one-half inch to three-quarters of an inch are used. Plywood is installed with the grain direction running perpendicular to the joists and is staggered so that end joints in adjacent panels line up over different joists. To avoid squeaky floors, carpenters both glue and nail most plywood subflooring. This practice varies, however, depending on the quality of construction. Plywood is purchased in full sheets, so it is necessary to round up when estimating it. If the area is 100 square feet, divide by 32 square feet, which equals 3.125 sheets. Round up to 4 sheets for the estimate. See the exhibit "Floor Framing."

Adjuster Tip—When subflooring is damaged, it is better to tear up and replace full sheets than to cut sheets to size unless it is necessary to cut because of a cabinet or another protrusion. Tearing up full sheets saves on labor because less cutting is involved.

Wall Framing—**Wall framing** includes the studs, sole plates, top plates, and window and door headers on interior and exterior walls. These walls support ceilings, upper floors, and the roof. The wall-framing members used in residential construction are generally 2" × 4" studs spaced 16 inches on center.

Subflooring

The working platform or layer that goes over the floor joists, providing a base for the finished floor.

Wall framing

The framing that provides the support for ceilings, upper floor, and roof; also provides the base to which wall sheathing is connected.

Floor Framing

Double Joists
Under Partition

16" on Center
Spacing

Diagonal Subfloor
8" Maximum Width — Square Edge

Joint over Joists

Floor Joist

Plywood Subfloor

Anchored Sill

Foundation

Bridging

Stringer Joist

Header Joist

L. O. Anderson, Wood-Frame House Construction, U.S. Dept. of Agriculture Forest Service, Agricultural Handbook No. 73 (Washington, D.C.: U.S. Government Printing Office, July 1970), p. 27. [DA03974]

New construction often uses 2" × 6" studs spaced 24 inches on center to allow for thicker exterior wall insulation. Top plates and sole plates are also 2" × 4" or 2" × 6", depending on the studs used. Headers over doors and windows are doubled 2" × 6"s or deeper members, depending on the opening's span. Double studding is used around window and door openings. See the exhibit "Studs."

Window and Door Framing—Headers are the members used to span over windows and doors. See the exhibit "Rough Framing for Wall Openings."

Wall sheathing

The outside covering installed over the wall framing, usually made of plywood.

Wall Sheathing—**Wall sheathing** is the outside covering installed over the studs, plates, and window and door headers. Various materials are used; half-inch plywood or chipboard is typically used in corners for reinforcement or when some form of continuous nailed exterior siding is planned. In some climates, plywood siding serves as both the sheathing and the exterior finish. With plywood, adding corner bracing to the walls is unnecessary.

Studs

Sole Plate   127 FBM

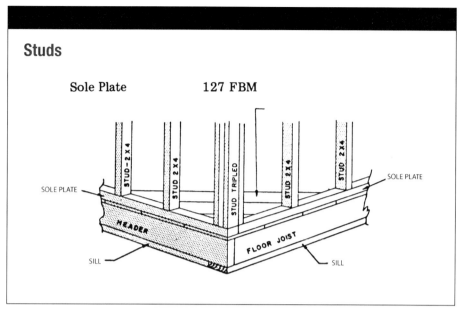

Adjuster Handbook (Denver: General Adjustment Bureau, Inc., 1972), p. 18. [DA04039]

Rough Framing for Wall Openings

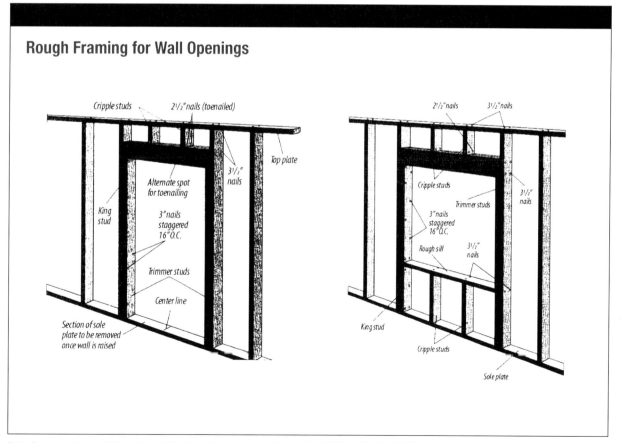

Basic Carpentry Illustrated (Menlo Park, Calif.: Sunset Books, Lane Publishing Co., 1995), pp. 65, 66. [DA04042]

Insulated sheathing, sometimes referred to as "blackboard," is composed of ground wood fibers supplemented by asphalt or other water-resistant products. It is not as structurally strong as plywood or chipboard, but it is less expensive and provides better insulation.

More new construction uses a rigid foam sheathing that has excellent insulating properties. It is generally one-inch thick and comes in 4' × 8' sheets. Because the foam lacks strength, metal let-in braces, plywood, or chipboard is used to strengthen the exterior wall corners. Foam sheathing costs about the same as plywood and is preferable in climates requiring substantial insulation.

Ceiling Joists—After the exterior and interior walls have been constructed, ceiling joists can be nailed into place. Ceiling joists are normally placed across the width of a house. The joists' sizes depend on the span, the spacing between joists, and the load anticipated on the second floor or attic. Ceiling joists are used to attach the ceiling to the room below and act as floor joists for the floor above. See the exhibit "Ceiling Joists."

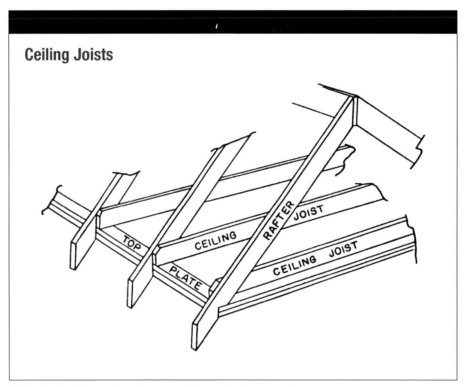

Ceiling Joists

Adjuster Handbook (Denver: General Adjustment Bureau, Inc., 1972), p. 21. [DA04043]

Rafters and Ridge Board—The type of rafter used in residential construction varies depending on the style of roof. The various styles are discussed later in this section. In a gable roof, all rafters are the same length and run from a ridge board to the top plate of the exterior wall (or beyond, depending on the overhang). The ridge board is usually a 1" × 8" or a 2" × 8", which provides support and a nailing surface for the upper rafter ends. The rafters are notched out to fit snugly on the top plate. See the exhibit "Wood-Frame House Construction."

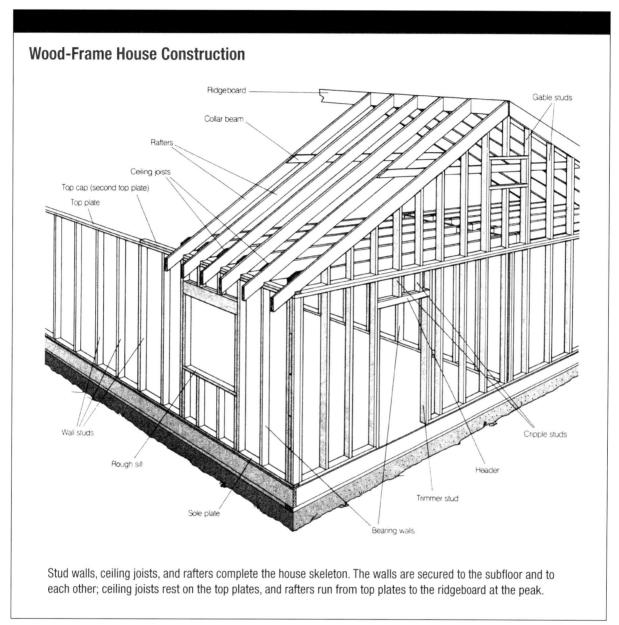

Wood-Frame House Construction

Stud walls, ceiling joists, and rafters complete the house skeleton. The walls are secured to the subfloor and to each other; ceiling joists rest on the top plates, and rafters run from top plates to the ridgeboard at the peak.

Basic Carpeting Illustrated (Menlo Park, Calif.: Lane Publishing Co./Sunset Publishing Group, 1984), p. 56. [DA04044]

Adjuster Tip—When estimating the number of rafters, use the entire roof length as the dimension, not the building's length. Using the roof's length includes the overhangs on a gable.

Trusses—**Trusses** are becoming very popular in the construction of new homes and are often recommended by contractors in the repair of existing homes whose roof-framing members have suffered significant damage. They take the place of the joists and rafters and are installed without a ridge

Trusses
Preassembled roof framing.

board. Most trusses are preengineered and assembled by a truss-fabricating plant, then delivered to the job site, where they are installed quickly, generally with the aid of a crane. They are usually placed on 24-inch centers. The three kinds of trusses used most often in residential construction are: (1) the W-type, (2) the king-post, and (3) the scissors. However, many other types of trusses are available. See the exhibit "Light Wood Trusses."

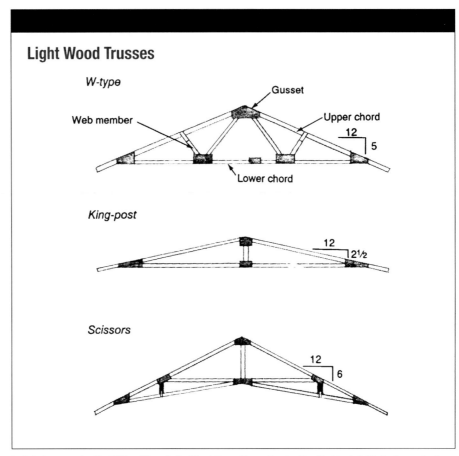

Light Wood Trusses

L. O. Anderson, revised by William Oberschulte, Wood-Frame House Construction (Carlsbad, Calif.: Craftsman Book Company, July 1992), p. 65. [DA04045]

Individual members of a truss can be replaced without replacing the entire truss. Replacing one or more members often becomes necessary when a rafter (known as a "rafter-cord") breaks as a result of either the weight of ice and snow or the impact of a fallen tree limb.

Roof Sheathing—Roof sheathing is the covering over rafters or trusses and usually consists of either half-inch plywood or seven-sixteenth-inch chipboard. Many roofs still have solid board sheathing, although its use in new construction is limited to homes that have wood shingles or shakes. Plywood is also an option for sheathing when wood shakes or shingles are to be installed. See the exhibit "Application of Plywood Roof Sheathing."

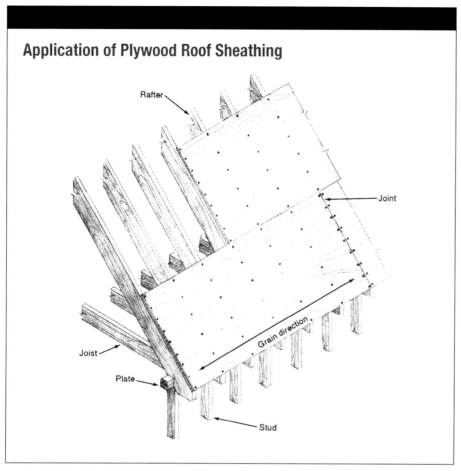

Application of Plywood Roof Sheathing

L. O. Anderson, Wood-Frame House Construction (Carlsbad, Calif.: Craftsman Book Company, July 1992), p. 79.
[DA03981]

Estimating Frame Construction

After the damaged area has been exposed and the demolition has been completed, estimating is similar to that for new construction. For example, if a tornado twists only the roof framing from a house, the adjuster needs to determine the cost to frame a new roof using materials and construction methods similar to those used for the previous roof.

Board Foot Calculations—Structural framing members such as joists, studs, rafters, headers, sills, and plates are sold by the board foot. Douglas fir is the most common material used for framing lumber, although Southern pine or larch is also used in some locations. Estimating the materials needed involves determining the number of pieces, their nominal dimensions, and their length. This formula is used to calculate the number of pieces (such as joists, rafters, or trusses) when counting the pieces is not possible:

$$\text{Number of pieces} = \frac{\text{Length of section (in feet)(measured perpendicular to framing pieces)} \times 12}{\text{On-center spacing (in inches)}} + 1$$

For example, if a foundation measures 16' × 24', and the joists are spaced 16" on center, the number of 16' joists that are needed is calculated as:

$$\frac{24' \times 12}{16''} + 1 = 19 \text{ joists}$$

The Board Foot Formula—The next step is to determine the number of board feet of joists. If 2" × 10"s are used, the number of board feet would be found by using the formula:

$$\text{Board feet} = \frac{\text{Number of pieces} \times \text{Length of each piece} \times \text{Nominal dimensions}}{12}$$

$$\frac{19 \times 16' \times (2'' \times 10'')}{12} = 507 \text{ Board feet}$$

Labor—Framing construction labor tables found in estimating reference books quote the number of man-hours necessary for a particular operation and the number of crew involved. In this example, 19 joists would be multiplied by 0.020 man-hours to arrive at the number of hours needed to make the repair, or 0.38 hours. See the exhibit "Framing Lumber Time Estimates (in Hours)."

Framing Lumber Time Estimates (in Hours)

Item Description		Output per Day	Manhours per Unit	No. of Crew
Studs	2" × 4"	120 sq. ft.	.133 manhours	2
Joists (12" oc)	2" × 8"	800 sq. ft.	.020 manhours	2
Rafters (16" oc)	2" × 12"	896 sq. ft.	.018 manhours	2
Sheathing, floor	3/4" plywood	1,230 sq. ft.	.013 manhours	2
Sheathing, roof	1/4" plywood	1,080 sq. ft.	.015 manhours	2
Trusses	20' to 24' span		1.609 manhours	3

Adapted from Sweets Repair & Remodel Cost Guide 2003 (New York: Marshall & Swift® McGraw Hill, 2003), pp. 116–118.[DA04051]

Total Estimate—The cost of replacing the joists in this example can be calculated given this information:

If 2" × 10"s that are 16' long cost $450 per 1,000 board feet, and the cost for labor is $1.57 per joist, then:

Materials:	$507 \text{ board feet} \times \dfrac{\$450}{1{,}000 \text{ bd. ft.}} = \$228.15$
Labor:	$19 \text{ joists} \times \$1.57 = \$29.83$
Total cost:	$\$257.98$

Profit and overhead should then be added.

Finish Carpentry

Finish carpentry is the work done by a carpenter to complete, or "finish off," a house's interior after the frame has been erected. It includes the installation of floors, windows, doors, cabinets, countertops, interior wood trim, stairs, and exterior wood trim.

Finish Wood Floors

The term "finish flooring" refers to the material used as a floor's top layer (sub-floor for carpeting or tile) or final wearing surface. A wide selection of wood materials can be used for finished flooring. Hardwoods, softwoods, and laminated wood are available as strip flooring in various widths and thicknesses and as random-width planks and block flooring. Because each kind comes in different grades, adjusters should be certain of the kind, size, and quality of the flooring material.

If the final floor is going to be some surface other than finished wood, only a subfloor will be put down. Wall-to-wall carpeting, vinyl tile, linoleum, and ceramic tile can be installed directly over a subfloor. A subcontractor usually installs these floor surfaces.

An estimate for flooring is based on the floor's area. The price of materials and labor varies according to the type of flooring that will be installed.

Floors are susceptible to all sorts of damage. Fire and water can damage most types of flooring. Carpets are susceptible to damage from caustic chemicals, smoke, and soot. Ceramic tile can be broken. Vinyl often gets torn when a refrigerator gets moved.

Repairing damaged flooring can be a challenge. Similar to the problem of matching wallpaper, finding the exact flooring material with the same dye lot may be next to impossible. Even if the homeowner has material on hand, the existing floor may have been worn or faded to the point that it no longer matches the unused material. While there is some benefit to being creative in attempts to repair a floor, sometimes there is no option but to replace it.

Windows

In the past, window building required the special skills of a master carpenter. Today, most windows are fully assembled at the factory and are shipped to the job site to be installed. They can be standard-size windows or custom-built windows. Although windows are factory-assembled, many manufacturers sell replacement parts, especially sashes that hold the glass.

Proper estimating requires identifying the type of window. The most common styles are double hung, casement, sliding, fixed, and awning. See the exhibit "Types of Windows."

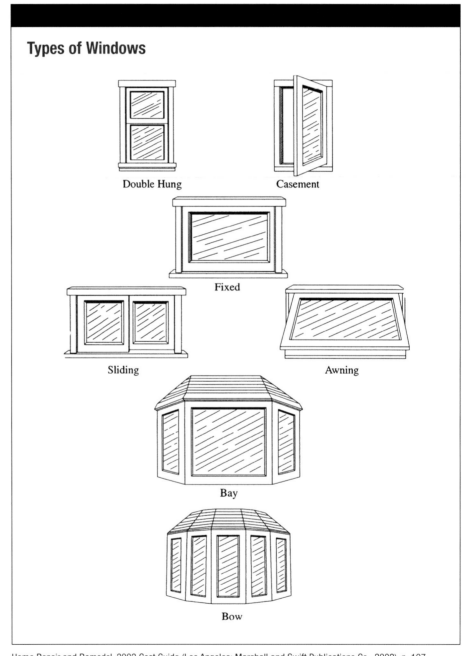

Types of Windows

Double Hung

Casement

Fixed

Sliding

Awning

Bay

Bow

Home Repair and Remodel, 2002 Cost Guide (Los Angeles: Marshall and Swift Publications Co., 2002), p. 107.
[DA04053]

Double-hung windows are probably the most common. They consist of an upper sash and lower sash that slide up and down in separate grooves in the side jambs. Small wood members called muntins can divide the sashes into several different lights (pieces of window glass). The screens are located on the outside. The hardware for double-hung windows includes sash locks and sometimes sash lifts.

Replacement windows use the existing window jamb as the rough opening. The old pulley, chain, and sashes are removed and replaced with new mechanism, sashes, and glass.

At one time, a single pane of clear glass was sufficient for a window. But these windows were a source of serious heat loss. As the need for energy efficiency and ease of maintenance have become primary concerns, various types of glazing material have become popular.

Tempered glass is heat-treated to give it strength. It crumbles into small fragments when broken, rather than breaking up into sharp pieces.

Safety glass consists of two or more lights of glass with a layer of vinyl sandwiched in between. Pressure is applied to this glass "sandwich" to form a single unit. Safety glass can crack, but it does not break up into pieces.

Insulating glass is also made from two sheets of glass, but a space is maintained in between the panels. The air space helps decrease the amount of heat loss through the window as well as keep condensation from forming. Some types of insulated glass have a gas such as argon fill the air space. Other types have the air from this space pumped out to create a vacuum.

Insulating glass is usually rated for its thermal conductivity. This is called the U-factor. For windows, a lower U-factor is better. The inverse of the U-factor is called the R-value. Good windows should have a high R-value.

Low E stands for low emittance. Low E glass allows short wavelength light to pass through it but reflects long-wavelength light back into a room. This means that natural light is allowed in while minimizing the damage to curtains, drapes, carpets, and furniture from ultraviolet light. Low E glass reflects heat back inside the home in the winter and reduces heat gain from the outside in the summer.

The key to estimating windows is to identify a window's type; size; and, if possible, the manufacturer. Windows can vary greatly in cost depending on the manufacturer and material, which can be wood, vinyl-clad wood, steel, or aluminum. The key to installing windows is taking proper measurements. The "rough" opening of a window (meaning the opening in the framing) is usually a quarter inch to a half inch larger on all sides than the window unit itself.

After the material cost is established, the labor time for tear-out and replacement is generally standard. An estimating reference guide states the amount of time allowed for installation and demolition.

Doors

The two types of doors commonly found in residential construction are exterior and interior. The parts that make up a door are the jambs; the door; the doorstop; casings; and hardware, including hinges and locksets. The parts can be purchased separately, but many doors come as complete units. Most interior door units are prehung (assembled at the factory) and are easy to install. See the exhibit "Anatomy of a Door."

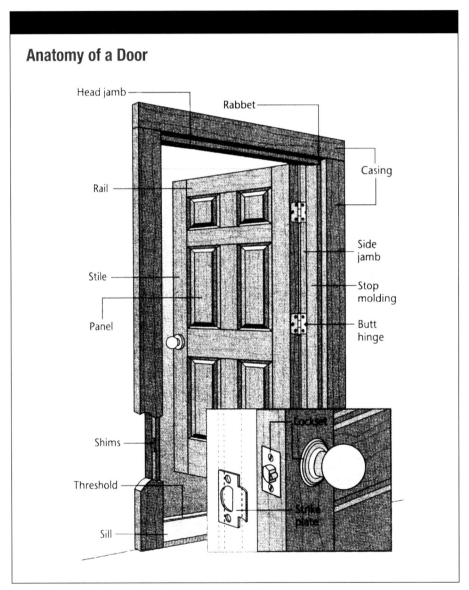

Anatomy of a Door

Head jamb · Rabbet · Casing · Rail · Side jamb · Stile · Stop molding · Panel · Butt hinge · Lockset · Strike plate · Shims · Threshold · Sill

Basic Carpentry Illustrated (Menlo Park, Calif.: Sunset Books, Lane Publishing Co., 1995), p. 90. [DA04054]

Exterior doors are available in many types and styles. The panel type consists of stiles (solid vertical members), rails (solid cross members), and filler panels. Exterior flush doors are usually solid-core to provide more insulation and to prevent warping. Many new homes are built with decorative steel doors, which are foam-filled for even greater insulation. Most exterior doors also come complete and ready to install, except that they are not predrilled for the locksets.

Adjuster Tip—The local building code usually governs the type of exterior door used on a structure.

The two most common types of interior doors are flush and panel. Flush interior doors are usually made with a hollow-core framework of plywood, hardboard, or even cardboard. Flush interior doors are available in several different woods, including oak, birch, and mahogany. Closets often have wood or metal doors, which slide on tracks or are folding units.

Like windows, doors are available in various styles, so adjusters must be able to describe the manufacturer; the kind of material that the door is made of; and the door's size, style, thickness, and type of casings. The hardware varies depending on type, material, and manufacturer. Often, as in a burglary loss, only a part of the door unit must be replaced. At other times, the complete unit must be replaced. Estimating reference guides provide the average time needed to install and remove different kinds of doors.

Assume that a burglar, in an attempt to gain entry, damages a front door and frame beyond repair. The door is a prehung panel door. The door unit costs $640. The carpenter's labor rate is $20 per hour. The estimate for the job would be prepared like this:

Demolition	1 hour × $20/hour (from estimating reference guide)	$ 20
Material cost	1 door unit, complete	640
Installation labor	3 hours × $20/hour (from estimating reference guide)	60
Reinstall lockset and deadbolt	.5 hour each × $20/hour	20
Total cost		$740

Profit and overhead should be added to this total.

Kitchen Cabinets

In estimating the cost to repair or replace cabinets, adjusters should consider the cabinet type, quality, type of damage, and repair methods.

Cabinet Types—Kitchen cabinets can often account for a sizable portion of a claim. The key to estimating cabinets is identifying their quality. Cost usually depends on the quality of materials used for doors, drawer fronts, and hardware. There are three basic classifications of kitchen cabinets:

• Base

• Wall

• Utility cabinets

Over the years, their sizes have become standardized.

Base cabinets rest on the floor and are covered with a countertop. They contain drawers and usually have shelves. They are generally 24 inches deep to allow for a 25-inch countertop to overlap by 1 inch.

Wall cabinets are about half as deep as base cabinets and are attached to the wall above the countertop. They have shelves but no drawers.

Utility cabinets come in several sizes. One of the most common utility cabinets is the broom cabinet, which runs from the floor nearly to the ceiling.

Identifying Cabinet Quality—This section provides some guidelines for identifying the cabinets' quality by examining economy-quality, average-quality, and premium-quality cabinets.

Economy-quality cabinets often have a photographic wood grain veneered to particleboard or other composition material rather than consist of real wood for doors and drawer fronts. The doors are usually flush-mounted and lack a more appealing recessed edge. The shelves are usually particleboard or hardboard. The front frames are generally pine. Economy-quality cabinets sometimes have no back and are attached to the wall by a 1" strip on the inside top and bottom. These cabinets only come in stock sizes. Drawer guides are usually plastic, and the drawers might not be removable.

Average-quality cabinets are the most common. The doors and drawer fronts are usually half-inch solid wood or raised panel. The front frames of cabinets are usually three-quarter-inch solid wood with a natural finish. The shelves and the rest of the cabinet are usually particleboard or plywood. The shelves are often fixed in place. Like economy-quality cabinets, these cabinets are available only in stock sizes. The drawer guides are metal with nylon rollers, and the drawers are usually removable.

Premium-quality cabinets are usually found in more expensive homes. They are often custom-made and can be ordered in special sizes. The doors are usually solid hardwood or raised panel. The front frames of cabinets are solid hardwood like birch, maple, or oak and are at least three-quarters of an inch thick. The shelves are usually plywood and adjustable on metal strips. Although very little particleboard is used in the construction of premium-quality cabinets, it is usually faced with some other material when it is used.

Damage and Repair—Fire, smoke, water, and vandalism are the most common perils causing cabinet damage. Kitchen grease fires might be the single most common cause of loss. Repair methods vary depending on the scope of damage, the cabinet's quality, and the insured's attitude. If all of an insured's cabinets are destroyed, the adjuster's job is simply to scope the damage to determine the replacement cost. However, if only one or two cabinets are involved in a loss, the adjuster would have several options, as in these three examples.

First, if the cabinets are economy or average quality, the manufacturer might still make the same style, so exact replacements would be easy to obtain. Second, if the cabinets are custom-made, a cabinetmaker might be able to duplicate the cabinets, but stripping and refinishing all of the undamaged cabinets might be necessary to match the new ones. A third approach is to replace the damaged cabinets with new cabinets and only replace the doors and drawer fronts of the undamaged cabinets.

Because of the cabinetry's high cost, the repair options available to adjusters are numerous; the cost to replace more expensive items is usually much higher than the cost to repair them. Some imagination is often required to arrive at the best method for handling the loss. The final choice must be acceptable both to the insured and to the insurer.

Estimating Kitchen Cabinets—Cabinets are usually estimated on the basis of cost per linear foot. Because of the differences in cabinet quality, doors, drawer fronts, and hardware, adjusters should consult a lumberyard, supplier, or cabinetmaker to establish material costs. Generally, the cost quoted for base units differs from the cost quoted for wall units, and special cabinets might be individually priced. Cabinetmakers might quote the price installed. The adjuster should take a sample with permission from the insured, such as a drawer front, when seeking prices.

Regardless of cabinet quality, the labor to tear out and replace cabinets is usually standard. Most labor guides indicate a quarter of an hour per linear foot for demolition and a range of between a quarter of an hour and half an hour per linear foot to install either base or wall cabinets.

Countertops

Base cabinets are generally covered with a countertop made from Formica, ceramic tile, stone, or a solid surface material such as Corian. Corian and Formica countertops can be assembled on site using flat stock; they also come preformed with rounded edges and a backsplash. They are usually laid over a three-quarter-inch-high density particleboard using contact cement. Ceramic tile is estimated and installed much like a tile floor. Stone such as granite or marble is cut and polished, then installed over the cabinets.

Countertops usually come in 25-inch widths so that they overlap the base cabinets by 1 inch, giving a more finished appearance and protecting the cabinet surface from spills. They are usually priced on a cost-per-linear-foot basis. Granite, marble, and other stone surfaces have a higher labor rate than do other surfaces. There is extra cost because of the weight of the pieces. There are also costs for transporting, cutting, and finishing the stone countertops.

Adjusters should inquire how these are handled if presented with a unit cost estimate from a contractor.

Interior Trim

Interior trim consists principally of base moldings, baseboards, ceiling moldings, picture moldings, chair rails, and door and window trim. They add a decorative and finished appearance to interior walls, floors, and ceilings and are available in hardwoods, softwoods, and prefinished plastic. The hardwoods include birch, maple, and oak. The softwood is usually ponderosa pine and is sometimes available prefinished.

Base molding can be made of one, two, or three separate members. The main baseboard is between two and eight inches high and up to three-quarters of an inch thick. Large and ornate base molding is often constructed of hardwood in older houses. See the exhibit "Base Moldings."

Base Moldings

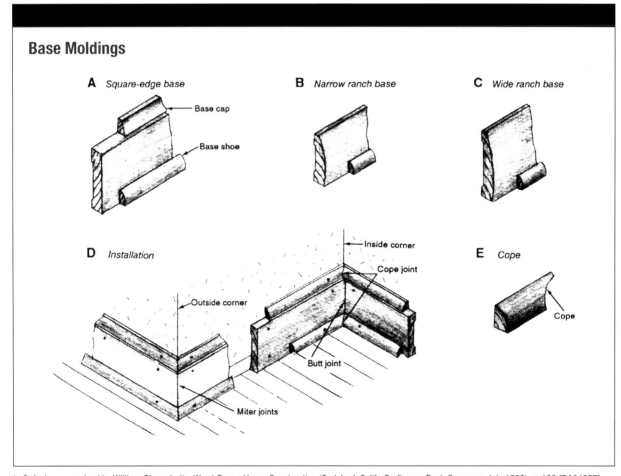

L. O. Anderson, revised by William Oberschulte, Wood-Frame House Construction (Carlsbad, Calif.: Craftsman Book Company, July 1992), p. 193 [DA04057]

Ceiling moldings are usually of a cove or picture type and are almost always one member. Chair rails are one-, two-, or three-member moldings that are applied around the room's perimeter at chair-back height. Door and window trim (or "casings," as they are commonly known) is generally made of the same material and is usually included in the estimate along with the windows or doors. See the exhibit "Ceiling Moldings."

Ceiling Moldings

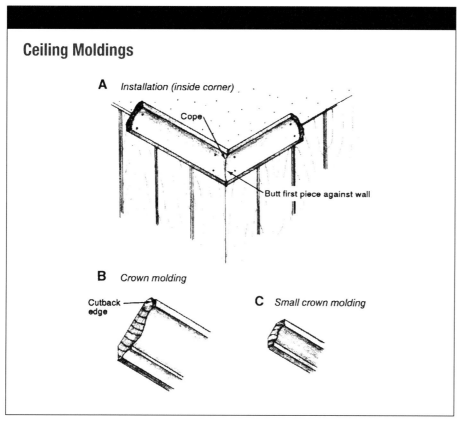

L. O. Anderson, revised by William Oberschulte, Wood-Frame House Construction (Carlsbad, Calif.: Craftsman Book Company, July 1992), p. 194. [DA04058]

Interior trim is estimated by the linear foot. Adjusters must determine the style and type of wood as part of the scope. If the trim is popular, a lumber-yard or supplier can give a material price per foot. Especially on older or more expensive houses, obtaining a bid to have the moldings specially milled to match the existing molding is sometimes necessary. A sample is needed for an accurate estimate. Tables are available to help adjusters calculate labor costs. These tables are usually based on hours per 100 linear feet.

Drywall

Common terms for **drywall** are "sheetrock," "wall board," "gypsum board," and "plaster board." It comes in 4-foot widths and 8- or 12-foot lengths.

Drywall

A sheet of plaster material covered on both sides with a fiber paper bond; usually comes in 4-foot widths and 8- or 12-foot lengths.

Drywall is plaster material covered on both sides with a fiber paper bond. It has many advantages over plaster, a building material common in old structures but rarely used now. For example, the cost of drywall is relatively low compared to the cost of plaster. Drywall can also have a finished design face instead of its paper bonding. Its use is limited to interior walls and ceilings. Paint and wallpaper are the most common coverings for drywall. For kitchens and bathrooms, where moisture is present, a product called "green board" is often used. This product is similar to drywall, but it has one side coated with a green water-resistant material instead of fiberpaper board.

Drywall Damage and Repair

Fire can consume drywall, and heat can scorch it, especially on ceilings and upper wall areas. In addition to direct fire and heat damage, vandalism or carelessness can puncture drywall. Opening a door forcibly can cause the doorknob to puncture or dent the wall surface. Small amounts of water generally do not affect drywall, but when drywall is exposed to water for a longer period, it tends to absorb the water like an ink blotter, resulting in brownish stains. If allowed to dry properly, it can be sealed and covered by paint or paper as long as the bonding of the exterior paper is not damaged.

Drywall is easily repairable. Even if punctured or pierced, drywall is repaired by spot patching another piece to the damaged area or by filling any area less than six inches with spackle or joint compound material.

Adjuster Tip—If water damage occurs, a portion of the drywall should be removed to permit the drying of the interior wall cavities. This would prevent mold and mildew from forming.

Drywall damage greater than six inches must be cut out. The drywall should be cut back with a utility knife to expose part of the vertical wall studs. Boards can be screwed to the vertical studs and the back of the existing drywall to provide a fastening surface for the new patch. After a patch of new drywall is screwed in place, it must be finished with drywall tape and joint compound.

Drywall Installation

Drywall can be nailed or screwed onto wall and ceiling studs, or screwed onto metal stud framing. Drywall can be installed with the long edges either parallel or perpendicular to the wall studs. The most common installation method is perpendicular. However, perpendicular installation is not used if the wall is higher than eight feet because of the extra cutting and taping that would be involved. The ceilings should be done first so that the drywall that forms the walls butts under and supports the ceiling sheets. Nailing is recommended every six to eight inches vertically along the length of the stud on walls and every five to seven inches on ceiling sheets. The sides of the drywall are tapered to form a wide "V" shape where sheets butt together. This technique provides an area for joint compound and tape, which is used to smooth over and to create a continuous wall or ceiling surface.

Tape and joint compound are used for inside joints. On outside corners, that is, where two walls meet at a right angle, metal strips are nailed in place over the corner, then covered by joint compound. This technique protects the outside edges from damage. After carpenters install the drywall, finish subcontractors or drywall specialists commonly do the taping and apply joint compound. At least two and possibly three coats of joint compound are applied, with at least a day allowed for each previous coat to dry.

Estimating Drywall

Drywall can be estimated with a gross area method or a unit cost method. The gross area method calculates the gross area of the room to estimate labor and materials needed.

Calculating Area—The gross area of the room can be used to estimate the amount of drywall needed. Only openings larger than fifty square feet should be excluded. Measuring in this way eliminates the need to apply a waste factor. Assume that a room measures 12' × 12'. The wall height is 8'. It has a window (3' × 4') and a door (3' × 7') that are excluded because they are less than 50 sq. ft. in total area. This room has a gross wall area of 384 square feet [(12' + 12' + 12' + 12') × 8'].

Materials—The three basic thicknesses for drywall are 0.375", 0.5", and 0.625". Prices vary by thickness. As mentioned, drywall comes in sheets 4-feet wide and 8- and 12-feet long. For this job, 4' × 8' sheets are used. To find the amount of drywall needed for this job, divide the total area of the room by the area of one sheet of drywall:

Ceiling	144 square feet
Walls	384
Total area	528 square feet
Amount of drywall	528 ÷ 32 = 16.5, rounded to 17 sheets

The amount of nails or screws needed for installation depends on the on-center spacing. Assume that the studs are 16" on center and that the nails will be placed 8" apart. An average is 1,625 nails per 1,000 square feet. Nails are usually sold to contractors by the pound. Five pounds of 1.5" drywall nails installs 1,000 sq. ft. of drywall. For the purpose of this example, five pounds of 1.5" drywall nails cost $7.49.

Rather than price the materials for taping and applying joint compound individually, adjusters can use a unit cost per square foot of drywall in calculating the total materials cost:

17 sheets of drywall @ $8 per sheet	$136.00
Nails for 528 square feet	7.49
Tape and compound for 528 square feet @ $0.07 per square foot	36.96
	$180.45

Labor—Labor is affected by the size of the job, by whether the drywall is installed horizontally or vertically, and by what will cover the drywall. Generally, the larger the job, the faster the rate of application. The common rate for installing drywall in a large area is 1.5 hours per 100 square feet; in a medium-size area (one to three rooms), 2.5 hours per 100 square feet; and in a small area where accessibility is a problem, 3.5 hours per 100 square feet. Taping and applying joint compound require 1.2 hours per 100 square feet. If the drywall is to be painted or wallpapered, it must be taped, and joint compound must be applied. However, tape and compound are not required on walls that are to be paneled or otherwise covered by decorator wood materials.

Total Cost—The room in this example is a medium-sized area. The calculations for labor are shown here:

528 square feet × 2.5 hours per 100 square feet	
5.28 × 2.5 hours	13.2 hours
5.28 × 1.2 hours (tape and compound)	6.3
Total labor time	19.5 hours
Labor: 19.5 hours @ $20 per hour	$390.00
Materials	$180.45
Total estimated cost:	$570.45

Unit Cost—Unit cost can be calculated by dividing the total cost by the area.

$$\frac{\$570.45}{495 \text{ square feet}} = \$1.15 \text{ per square foot}$$

The unit cost developed this way includes waste for openings. The example given did not state the size of any openings in the room, but it is assumed that there is at least a door. As an example, a 21 sq. ft. door would be subtracted from the area; otherwise, waste will be included in the cost twice.

Roofing

The most common residential roofing material is asphalt composition three-tab shingle. Estimates for these types of shingles are calculated on the basis of units equal to **one square**, or 100 square feet. Each square has three bundles.

A bare roof consists of wooden boards, or decking, called sheathing, nailed onto roof rafters. Roofing felt paper is placed onto the roof sheathing and sta-

One square

One hundred square feet of shingles.

pled, and shingles are then nailed over the roof felt paper. Shingles are usually installed with a five-inch exposure, and the remainder of the shingle is covered by the rows of shingles above it. In shingling a roof, a roofer starts at the bottom edge of the roof. The starter row is an "upside-down" row. Then the first row with the surface material showing is placed. This technique builds a slight incline that channels water into the gutter. It also prevents any leakage between the tabs of the first row of shingles. Subsequent rows of shingles are nailed in place, with each row overlapping about two-thirds of the previous row. Another double row is installed at the top (ridge), where shingles are cut and laid across the ridge joint to seal and join both sides of the roof surface at the top. See the exhibit "Shingle Installation."

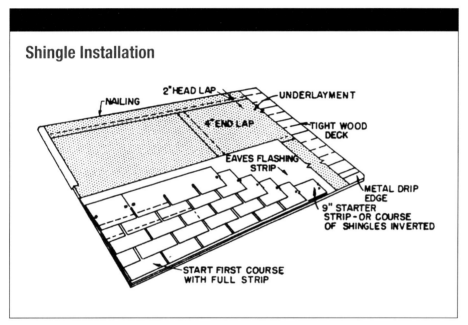

Shingle Installation

Adjuster Handbook (Denver: General Adjustment Bureau, Inc., 1972), p. 27. [DA04066]

Wood shingles (which are sold four bundles to the square) are usually made from western red cedar, but they can also be made of redwood and cypress. They are normally 16 inches long, with a 5-inch exposure. Thicker shingles may have a larger exposure. The roofing felt, which serves as a moisture barrier, is not applied with wood shingles. Wood shingles must instead have ventilation from the underside to properly dry out and space on either side for expansion.

Slate and tiles are laid over 30-pound felt and are never applied over existing roof materials.

Rolled roofing paper of 90-pound weight covers 100 square feet of area and is usually double-covered in areas of heavy snow accumulation. It is the least expensive roof covering and is used on flatter surfaces where shingling is not adequate to protect the interior from moisture of melting snow or ice. See the exhibit "Roofing Materials."

Roofing Materials

1. Asphalt Shingle (Low - $)
2. Roll (Low - $)
3. Built-up (Medium - $)
4. Preformed Metal (Low - $)
5. Standing Seam (Medium - $)
6. Wood Shingle (Medium - $)
7. Wood Shake (High - $)
8. Slate (High - $)
9. Spanish Tile (High - $)

Home Repair and Remodel, 2002 Cost Guide (Los Angeles: Marshall and Swift Publications Co., 2002), p. 410.
[DA04067]

Flashing is tin, aluminum, copper sheet, or rolled roofing material that covers any break on the roof surface. It is applied around chimneys and around plumbing vent pipes and can also be laid around the eave of the roof and where valleys are formed by intersecting roofs or dormers. Flashing is curled up along vertical surfaces and extends under the roof covering to seal any openings from moisture. Flashing on roofs extends up along the eave a distance of 18 to 20 inches; when ice forms at the eave and then melts, the water does not run up under the shingle and damage the interior walls or ceilings.

Adjuster Tip—A common site for leaks is the flashing around vents, chimneys, valleys, and abutting walls.

Built-up roofs are common on flat roof surfaces. Although much more common on commercial structures, they are also found on residences. In the installation of a built-up roof, the first step is to tack down a layer of red rosin sheeting over the roof board decking. This sheeting serves as a sealer or vapor barrier. A base covering of 30-pound felt roofing paper is then applied and mopped with tar sealer. This process is repeated three times for a three-ply covering and five times for a five-ply roof. Crushed stone can then be put over the top layer. This type of roof is called a tar and gravel roof surface.

Roofing Damage and Repair

Strong winds (generally in excess of 40 miles per hour); hail; and falling objects such as tree limbs are the usual insured causes of loss to roofs. Steep pitched roofs are less likely to sustain wind damage from significant wind. Slate and tile roofs are unaffected by wind unless it is hurricane or tornado force.

Exposure to heat from the sun and normal wear and tear exact a heavy toll on common roof coverings. The average life of an asphalt composition shingle roof is 15 to 30 years, depending on the roofing material's quality. Worn granular surfaces, curling of the shingle ends, and leaks into the interior are signs of age and damage that accumulates over time. Insurance does not cover wear and tear, but it might cover a new roofing job as part of an insurable loss to a home with replacement cost coverage. Because of their composition, asphalt roof shingles might sustain several slight incidents of damage that go unnoticed. The first indications of leakage usually signal the need for a new covering.

Adjuster Tip—South and west exposures deteriorate faster than north and east exposures. Also, steeper-sloped roofs last longer than flatter roofs.

A roof can sustain a great deal of damage from a hailstorm, depending on the roofing material and the size of the hail. Large hailstones can shatter Spanish tile and slate. Light gauge metal can be severely dented. Wood shingles can be dented or split. Even asphalt shingles can be dented by large hailstones.[6]

When inspecting damage to an asphalt roof, adjusters should, if possible, climb onto the roof. Wind might have broken the shingles, but unless the

Flashing

Tin, aluminum, copper, or other resistant material strip that is used to seal joints or other breaks on a roof surface such as chimneys, parapet walls, and skylights.

shingles are visibly torn, damage can be observed only by close inspection. Even if broken, the shingles will lie flat once the wind has subsided and will not appear to be damaged.

Roofs of slate, tile, fiber panels, or wood can be damaged if walked on. Adjusters can go up on a ladder to get a good vantage point for inspection and should take photos from the edge of the roof.

Most building codes allow only two layers of asphalt shingles on a roof. This amount is based on the roof structure's capacity to bear the cumulative weight of the material. Some adjusters believe that if the roof already has two layers, an allowance should be made to remove only the top damaged layer. The underlying layer, though, will almost certainly be damaged while the top layer is being removed, resulting in a need to replace parts of the underlying layer. The care needed to minimize underlying-layer damage can make the job take longer, increasing the labor cost. Whether both layers should be removed therefore becomes a matter of judgment.

Both asphalt composition shingles and built-up roofing can be repaired on a spot basis.

Individual shingles can be removed with a special tool. The nails of the next two layers are pulled up or cut off, exposing the entire shingle. The nails on the damaged shingle are then removed, and a new replacement shingle is inserted in place and nailed. The existing shingle or shingles above the new piece are renailed over that piece.

Shingles not only protect the interior, but they also contribute to the exterior appearance. Matching older shingles can be a problem. Reroofing an entire side might be necessary if damages appear so extensive as to warrant replacement of 50 to 60 percent of scattered, missing, and broken shingles. The labor involved in patching such a large area will exceed the cost of replacing one whole side. The best way to estimate individual spot-patch repairs is to use the labor and materials method. No unit price would accurately reflect such repairs. Built-up roofing is repairable by patching. Tar- and gravel-surfaced roof covering is usually affected little by hail or strong winds, but damage might occur nonetheless. The damaged area can be cut out, and the layers or plies can be removed down to the decking. Patches cut to the opening are put in with alternating tar, as when the roof was originally constructed. The top patch should overlap all sides by about two inches. It is nailed to the decking and then tarred over. Gravel stones can then be replaced on the patched area.

Roofing Estimates

The starting point for any roof estimate is determining the style of roof on the structure. The roof's style directly affects the level of difficulty of the roofing job, thereby increasing labor. The style also affects the net area calculation. The more intricate the roof, the more calculations will have to be done. Estimating for roof damages is based on net area, to which a waste factor is applied. Measurements can be made directly by someone taking the measurements on the roof or by counting rows of exposed roof shingles. Measurements can also be made by mathematical computation. Measurements obtained directly should be accurate, but the roof must be sturdy enough for the adjuster to climb onto it. Counting rows of shingles is based on a standard exposure per row. For example, if each row is exposed 5 inches and 36 rows are showing, the distance from the eave of the roof to the ridge is 5 inches × 36 = 180 inches, which, divided by 12 inches, equals 15 feet. The same distance can be determined if the geometry and measurements of a gable end are known. See the exhibit "Common Roof Styles."

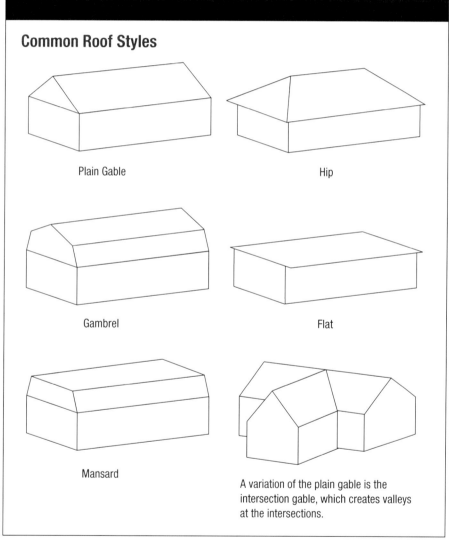

Common Roof Styles

Plain Gable

Hip

Gambrel

Flat

Mansard

A variation of the plain gable is the intersection gable, which creates valleys at the intersections.

[DA04070]

The roof's pitch also affects roof estimates. A roof's pitch is the degree of its inclination. It is calculated as the relationship of the rise in height of the roof angle to the run. For example, assume the rise is 8 feet and the run is 13 feet.

The pitch is eight thirteenths. The lower the number that the pitch is, the flatter the roof angle. See the exhibit "Pitch."

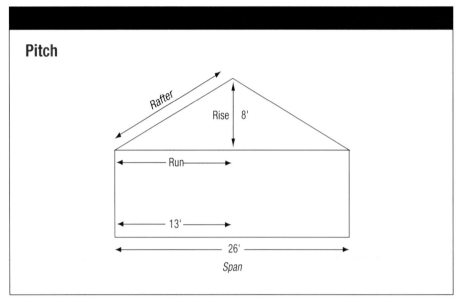

Pitch

[DA04071]

Roof Area—To calculate the area of a roof, the adjuster must know the rafter length. If the rafter cannot be measured, it is possible to calculate the length by using a formula, which the next section discusses.

Rafter Length—For this example, a gable roof is used. See the exhibit "Rafter Length of a Gable Roof."

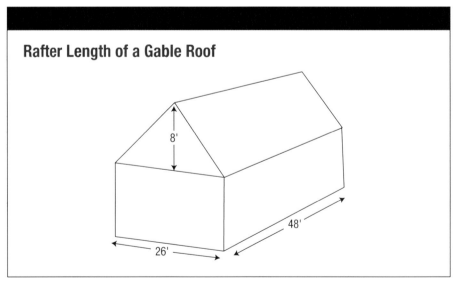

Rafter Length of a Gable Roof

[DA04072]

The rafter length for a gable end can be calculated by using this formula:

$$\text{Rafter length} = \sqrt{(\text{Run})^2 + (\text{Rise})^2}$$

This formula provides the length of the rafter in the example shown in the Rafter Length of a Gable Roof exhibit, as:

$$\text{Rafter length} = \sqrt{13^2 + 8^2}$$
$$= \sqrt{169 + 64}$$
$$= \sqrt{233}$$
$$= 15.26'$$

The roof in the illustration has no overhang. If it did, the overhang should be measured and added to 15.26'. The roof might also extend beyond the gable-end walls.

A calculated rafter length can be rounded to the next half foot. For the roof surface in the Rafter Length of a Gable Roof exhibit, a rafter length of 15'6" can be used.

Total Area—The area of this roof, which has no overhang, would be:

Rafter length of 15'6"	15.5 feet
Length of roof	48 feet
Area of one side	744 square feet (48' × 15.5')
Total area (both sides)	1,488 square feet (744 square feet × 2)

If the gable end overhangs, the extra length must be added to the overall length figure.

Material—In calculating the cost to remove damaged materials, adjusters should use the net area for removal labor. For calculating new felt and shingle materials, however, other factors might create a need for material beyond what the area alone indicates. For instance, in this case, the eave edge is double-layered, and a cap layer is on the ridge to seal both sides of roofing. Waste would also result from fitting materials around roof openings, dormers, and valley areas. The most common way to account for waste is to use percentage allowances. See the exhibit "Approximate Percentage Allowances for Waste for Asphalt Shingles."

For the example based on the Rafter Length of a Gable Roof exhibit (total area of a roof), 10 percent waste would be appropriate:

1,488 square feet × 10% = 148.8, rounded to 149 sq. ft. for waste allowance

1,488 + 149 = 1,637 square feet

Approximate Percentage Allowances for Waste for Asphalt Shingles

Roof Shape	
Gable	10%
Hip	15
Hip with dormers	20

Walker's Building Estimator's Reference Book, 26th ed. (Lisle, Ill.: Frank R. Walker Company, 1999), p. 7.45.
[DA04076]

Asphalt shingles are bought by the bundle, with three bundles per square. To determine the amount of material needed for the gable roof in the Rafter Length of a Gable Roof exhibit, divide the total area including waste by 100 square feet (because 1 square = 100 square feet), and then round up to the next 1/3 square:

$$\frac{1,637}{100} = 16.37 \text{ squares}$$

Total shingles = $16\frac{2}{3}$ squares = $(16 \times 3) + 2 = 50$ bundles

The underlying felt covers approximately 400 square feet per roll. It comes in a roll 3 feet wide and 144 feet long, or 432 square feet. The felt must overlap, so some waste is inevitable. An allowance for waste is already considered if a 432-square-foot roll is used to cover 400 square feet of roof area. If any more than one roll of felt is necessary, then another whole roll must be purchased. For the roof in this example, four rolls would be needed:

$$\frac{1,488 \text{ square feet}}{400 \text{ square feet per roll}} = 3.72, \text{ rounded to 4 rolls}$$

A generally accepted allowance for roofing nails is two pounds per square.

Labor—The labor rate per hour reflects several considerations. Features that disrupt the surface such as dormers, several openings, and valleys with flashing slow productivity. Labor for roofing is also affected by the workers' experience, the roof's slope, the height of the area to be worked on, and workplace safety rules from the Occupational Safety and Health Administration (OSHA). If the roof is too steep to be easily worked on, roof scaffolding brackets can be fastened under the shingles, and boards can be put across triangular brackets to provide a level standing and working area. Access scaffolding might have to be erected for high areas. Materials might have to be hoisted to the roof area. An allowance for these additional labor expenses is appropriate.

Like materials, labor is based on a per-square measurement. As an example, the labor for the roof in the Rafter Length of a Gable Roof exhibit would be:

Removal of 14.88 squares @ 1 hour per square	14.9 hours
Install 16.67 squares @ 2 hours per square	33.3
	48.2 hours
Labor @ $22 per hour	$1,060.40

The net area of the roof was used to determine the removal time because no waste removal is necessary. However, in the estimation of replacement time, a waste factor must be added because the roofer will handle all of the shingles, including the waste. Some estimators would not follow this practice but would estimate labor without consideration for waste. This approach would result in an estimate of 29.8 hours labor, which is 3.5 hours and $77 less.

Total Estimate—The total estimate for this job is shown here:

	Material	Labor
Removal is 14.9 hours @ $22 per hour	—	$ 327.80
Install 16 .67 squares @ $35 per square	$583.45	
Labor is 33.3 hours @ $22 per hour		732.60
Nails for 16 .67 squares × 2 pounds per square = 33.3 pounds @ $1 per pound	33.30	included
Felt paper for 1,488 square feet/400 square feet per roll = 3.72 = 4 rolls @ $15 each	60.00	included
Total materials and labor	$676.75	$1,060.40

Total cost (material + labor) = $1,737.15.

(Overhead and profit have not been included in this example.)

If the roof is cut up or if its height or access is a problem, the labor rate should be adjusted to allow more time per square. The labor to install individual shingles on several different areas of damaged roofing cuts productivity in half (4 hours per square). Additional allowances for hauling debris, scaffolding, and a steep pitch might be necessary.

Unit Cost—The unit cost is determined by dividing the total cost of the job by the number of squares:

$$\frac{\$1,737.15}{14.88} = \$116.74$$

The unit cost includes removal and felt paper because they were included in the estimate that resulted in the $1,737.15 figure.

Labor rates vary by area, and additional factors might cause a job to be more expensive than an average job, so adjusters should be wary about approaching every job on a unit cost basis. For an average residential roofing loss, a breakdown of labor and materials helps to resolve discrepancies between the adjuster's estimate and the contractor's estimate.

Painting

In adjusting losses involving damage to painted surfaces, adjusters determine how much area has been damaged and the cause of the damage (which often determines the type of necessary remedy). Then, an adjuster prepares an estimate for the painting by considering the preparation for painting, the type of surface to be painted, the materials necessary for the painting, and the labor. This section also discusses other considerations in adjusting painting losses: varnish, shellac, stains, and exterior painting.

Determining the Repair Method

Damage to painted surfaces can be repaired by cleaning, repainting, or sealing over and repainting. The degree of damage to interior finishes is closely related to their location relative to the cause of loss. Adjusters must be aware of this relationship when examining damages to interior painted surfaces. Water, heat, smoke, grease, soot, and fire can affect paint. In case of damage to interior paint surfaces, the cause of the damage, in many instances, determines the remedy.

Water Stains—Water stains to walls and ceilings are common. When water such as overspray from water hoses, fire extinguishers, or seepage of water from the outside damages painted surfaces, the result is generally a stain or multiple spots. Depending on the type of painted surface, the area might be cleaned with mild detergent. The adjuster should wipe the surface with a dampened cloth in an out-of-view area, a lower corner, or around a far window frame to determine whether the painted surface can be cleaned. With experience, adjusters will begin to recognize the relatively few times that such water stains or spots can be cleaned.

Water stains or spots on fiber material ceiling tiles such as acoustical tile have a brownish color. Most tiles discolored by water are not distorted or warped, but the stains cannot be removed. Covering the stained area with a sealer and painting the entire ceiling area can effectively hide the stains. A clear shellac or sealer additive in the paint prevents the stain from bleeding through the coat of paint. Unless such a sealer is used, the stain will continue to show no matter how many coats of paint are applied. As long as the tile itself is not bowed or warped, sealing and repainting the ceiling help to avoid extensive renovations.

Some areas are repeatedly affected by water seepage, such as from ice buildup along the eaves that forces water back into the interior or from rain driven under roof shingles by severe winds. In these cases, the tiles affected not only show several shades of brownish staining but also are probably bowed or warped. Replacement is the only appropriate solution for bowed or warped tiles.

Adjuster Tip—When confronted with what appears to be a repeated exposure to seepage or another water problem, adjusters should question the owner about previous occurrences. Insurance coverage excludes losses caused by repeated exposures.

Water Damage to Drywall—Unless continuously and repeatedly exposed to water or moisture, drywall ceilings and walls will dry and maintain their integrity. If the only damage is staining of the painted surface, sealing and painting the drywall can be effective. If an area of drywall must be replaced, the damaged area alone can be patch-repaired, smoothed, cleaned, and primer-sealed. The entire wall or ceiling area can then be painted to match the rest of the room.

Smoke Damage—In addition to damage by water, interior wall surfaces are subject to smoke damage. Smoke damage can occur from a fire, a furnace malfunction, or cooking grease fires. Smoke residue from sources other than grease fires or soot must be carefully examined and evaluated. Applying a light cleanser to an out-of-view area, such as over door trim, can determine whether the smoke residue can be removed. If the surface appears to clean readily, a cleaning allowance should be considered instead of repainting the surface. A professional cleaning service can provide an expert opinion when an interior cleaning appears possible. Generally, smoke from wood stoves and heating surfaces is cleanable. Because wood stoves and fireplaces are inherently dirty, their continued use deposits smoke on interior surfaces.

Soot—Greasy or oily soot deposits are generally not completely cleanable. Soot clings to drywall nailheads and settles in cracks and crevices and between ceiling tiles and paneling on the walls. Flat painted surfaces can be washed when rubbed briskly with detergents, but areas painted with semi-gloss paint and gloss paint are more resilient and might require industrial strength-detergent cleaning. Because over-wetted soot tends to smear and streak, the cleaning of soot is best left to professional cleaners. However, paneling, including marlite surfaces and ceramic tiles, can be cleaned easily.

Fire and Heat—Direct fire always severely damages painted surfaces, either by burning paint off or by blistering or scorching it. Damage from heat alone can also require repainting. Heat damage is most severe at the ceiling, on the upper walls, and especially around door and window openings. If the paint is bubbled or blistered, it must be completely removed, and the entire area must be thoroughly cleaned and then repainted.

Factors in Painting Estimates

The four important factors that adjusters must consider in preparing estimates for painting are (1) preparation before painting, (2) the type of surface to be painted, (3) materials, and (4) labor.

Examples of the types of preparation work and the estimated amount of work in square feet that can be done in an hour of labor are presented in the exhibit. Estimates of painting costs should show a separate breakdown for unusual amounts of preparation time, covering of walls, moving of furnishings, or cleaning. See the exhibit "Painting Preparation Estimates."

Painting Preparation Estimates

Approximate Number of Square Feet of Prepared Surfaces for Painting Completed Per Hour

Kinds of Work	Sq. Ft. Per Hour Per Coat
Sanding woodwork, preparatory	150–250
Sizing plastered walls	300–400

Paul I. Thomas, How to Estimate Building Losses and Construction Costs, 4th ed. (Englewood Cliffs, NJ.: Prentice-Hall, 1983), p. 327. [DA04084]

Paint should never be applied to any smoke- or soot-covered surface. The surface to be painted must be clean, dry, and smooth for best results. Nailheads should be spackled, and all drywall joints must be compounded and sanded. If new drywall has been applied, a sealer coat will be needed, followed by at least one and possibly two additional coats of paint. Cracked or peeling paint must be removed.

Interior surfaces to be painted are usually plaster, drywall, wood trim, or ceiling tiles. Generally, surfaces not previously covered by paint absorb the first coat, and subsequent coats are needed to achieve a more finished and color-rich appearance. When estimating materials, adjusters must remember that completely new surfaces require more paint because of their tendency to absorb it. The additional cost created by the need for more materials is offset by the ease of applying those coats, thereby reducing the time and the cost of labor to apply the paint.

Masonry, or block walls, textured finishes, and metal ceilings are more difficult interior surfaces to paint. The rougher and more absorbent the surface is, the more labor and material are required. Some masonry materials contain water-soluble salts, which, if not washed down by muriatic acid or a similar product and rinsed thoroughly, can form white or powdery deposits on the surface. Masonry surfaces are best restored with epoxy paint. It forms a strong bond and is less susceptible to bubbling and peeling as a result of moisture penetration. Existing high-gloss surfaces of some masonry might have to be sanded lightly to ensure better adhesion.

Depending on the type of paint covering, the materials for any job might range in price from $10 to $30 a gallon. Sale prices of paint are not relevant in cost estimates because losses do not always coincide with sales. Interior paint is generally less expensive than exterior paint. Color and gloss are important factors. Although color is a matter of personal preference, gloss affects both appearance and wear. Adjusters can determine the average price range for paint in a locale and can usually use that price in their estimate.

Adjuster Tip—Adjusters should be aware that for large jobs, contractors buy paint in five-gallon buckets. An estimate for such work should reflect the contractor's price, not the retail price.

The most commonly used paints are latex, oil, and alkyd for interior and exterior finishes; rubber base and cement paints for masonry; and epoxy and urethane for those surfaces subjected to the toughest treatment and requiring the most protection from moisture, such as hardwood flooring.

One coat is generally enough to paint over a cleaned surface. If a sealer is used to cover a stain, one coat is also typically adequate. For heavily soot-damaged areas, two coats are usually needed despite the initial cleaning of the surface. This fact might justify reducing the cleaning allowance because the cleaning has not removed the need for two coats. If the soot is not as heavy, the cost of more extensive cleaning might be justified because either paint will not be needed at all or, more likely, only one coat will be needed because cleaning has effectively repaired the damage.

Primers are used for the first coat over new woodwork or new drywall. The new woodwork or drywall will absorb some of the primer, so each gallon of paint used on those surfaces will cover less square footage than normal.

The exhibit presents the approximate number of square feet per hour for the application of paint or other materials to different surfaces. This exhibit is for illustrative purposes only. An estimating reference book would make the distinction between interior and exterior work, as well as the distinction between brushwork and the use of a roller or sprayer. There is also a difference in the labor rate for a primer coat and a finish coat. In the painting and decorating trades, labor represents approximately 70 percent of the total cost. One person can typically handle painting jobs, especially interior ones. In a given geographic area, wage rates are set by trade custom or by local economics. Wages per hour for a painter tend to be a few dollars less than for a roofer or general carpenter. In some areas of the country, union contracts might affect the number of workers hired for a job. See the exhibit "Painting Time Estimates."

In most small residential losses, the time for preparation, set-up, cover-up, and other elements should be included in the estimate. Also included should be any unusual circumstances, such as extraordinary travel distance, very high or inaccessible areas, special types of surfaces, or material that would increase the time for the job. Working on ladders reduces mobility, thereby reducing the area painted per hour. If a room has no furnishings, a quicker pace is possible. Moving and covering furnishings and removing draperies and wall decorations all require extra time. A spray gun is faster than a brush or roller, but the time

Painting Time Estimates

Approximate Number of Square Feet of Paint Application For Various Kinds of Work Completed Per Hour

Kinds of Work	Sq. Ft. Per Hour
Interior	
Painting primer on smooth walls	200–225
Painting, second coat	165–175
Painting wood floors, first coat	290–300
Exterior	
Painting primer on smooth walls	100–110
Painting smooth walls, second coat	115–125

Walker's Building Estimator's Reference Book, 26th ed. (Lisle, Ill.: Frank R. Walker Company, 1999), pp. 9.176, 9.183. [DA04086]

involved in properly covering and protecting areas not to be painted could offset the time saved by using such a device. Of course, the painter's experience also affects the rate of work.

Painting an area that is flat, smooth, and accessible requires less time than painting an area with windows, trim, cupboards, built-in shelving, and similar features. If the trim is a different color than the walls or needs to be covered with high-gloss paint as opposed to an alkyd or a latex paint, additional painting time is required. If an adjuster believes that a painting contractor's preliminary estimate figure is not justified, perhaps the adjuster has not fully considered the difficulties and limitations of the particular area involved.

Varnish, Shellac, and Stains

Clear finishes like varnish and shellac not only enhance wood's natural colorings, but they also provide needed protection. Stain enhances wood's grain by altering its color. The process of varnishing and refinishing solid wood surfaces is similar to painting, so the labor and material computations are identical to those used for painting.

Damage to Exterior Paint

Because exterior paint is exposed to weather, it can be damaged in ways that interior surfaces cannot be. Wind-driven rain, dust, and debris can chip or pit surface paint and can wear off its protective coating. Intense direct sunlight and heat and very cold temperatures and accumulations of ice and snow can peel and crack exterior paint and shorten its lifespan. Improper methods of construction, which prevent proper ventilation, can create a moisture build-up, causing wood siding to remain wet and paint to peel away from the surface. Problems such as these, caused by normal wear and tear, are not covered by insurance and are handled through regular maintenance.

The two basic adjusting considerations in handling damage to exterior paint are (1) distinguishing normal wear and tear and deterioration from insurable damages and (2) determining an allowance for appearance. Physical damage caused by fire or exposure to heat from fire at an adjoining property, hailstone damage, strong winds that propel objects into the exterior finish, and direct impact by vehicles are some of the causes of exterior paint damage that insurance might cover.

The complete exterior may be treated as one unit. Because paint can change color as it ages, new paint can rarely be perfectly matched to the old. Adjusters must carefully judge the situation after inspecting the property. Building interiors are segmented and are generally a variety of colors, but exteriors are usually one color and should present a consistent appearance. The adjuster must decide among painting only the damaged area, painting the entire side where the damage is present, or painting the entire building. Many states have claims-practices regulations that dictate how this situation should be handled.

The main considerations in estimating exterior painting are the same as in interior painting: the initial preparation, the type of surface involved, and the amount and cost of materials and labor.

Preparing exterior surfaces to be painted might include the removal and replacement of deteriorated wood siding. Adjusters should note areas that appear to be maintenance problems, take photographs to substantiate these findings, and communicate the problem to the insured and any contractor involved. No reputable contractor will paint a deteriorated exterior surface before replacing the rotted materials. Paint that is blistered, peeling, or cracked must be scraped, and the surface must be sanded and possibly filled with wood filler and then smoothed. Paint surfaces can be stripped to bare wood by heating the coating, but burning the paint might scorch the wood. Paint flakes off stucco or masonry for the same reasons that it peels from wood surfaces, but, in addition, masonry contains alkalis that affect the paint's ability to adhere to the surface. The damaged surface might have to be sandblasted or cleared by chemical strippers. Staining can be a problem on exterior surfaces. Rust and stains must be covered or removed so that paint will properly adhere to the surface.

For metal surfaces, paint adheres best to the bare metal. Painting over a previously painted metal surface is acceptable if the original coating is still firmly bonded. Both aluminum and steel should be prime-coated before a final coat of paint is applied. Masonite siding and clapboard sidings are the smoothest surfaces for paint coverage. Aluminum and masonry need more preparation and expertise in treatment. As with interior painting, the smoother the surface is, the better the result and the higher the productivity will be.

Materials for outside painting include alkyds, latex, epoxy, and oil. Because of weather exposures and the generally rougher surfaces to which exterior paints are applied, these paints contain additives that promote flexibility. Latex paint is the most versatile: it cleans in water, is the fastest drying, and allows water vapor to escape, reducing the chances of blistering. Latex might not, however, adhere over other types of paint. Although latex can be applied to masonry, an alkyd base or a rubber base coating is recommended for that type of surface. Oil- or alkyd-base metal paints are recommended for a direct application to metal siding.

Basic protection against moisture and expansion and flexibility characteristics needed for exterior finish materials are constantly being improved. An adjuster's knowledge of the proper use of these materials helps in assessing the reasons for preexisting conditions and enables the adjuster to make reasonable judgments regarding the distinction between direct physical damage and normal wear and tear.

The largest single factor to be considered in exterior paint estimating is the labor cost. Because of weather's effects and the special preparation for exterior surfaces, proper labor estimating requires that the surface be inspected. In estimating labor costs, an adjuster should list each distinct operation separately. Normal unit prices per square foot do not usually include preparation or scaffolding. Operations vary so much by job that a single unit cost is unlikely to apply to any particular job.

Wallpapering

Water, smoke, fire, or heat can damage wallpaper. Other types of losses to wallpaper are caused by vandalism, carelessness in moving furniture, or any striking or puncturing of the surface. Although these causes of loss affect wallpaper in different ways, the decision to repair a damaged section or to repaper a room is typically based on whether the existing paper can be matched. This section discusses the typical types of damage and repair options.

Water damage is the most common form of wallpaper damage. Water leakage from a shower, tub, or defective toilet seal in an upstairs bathroom can dilute the paste and cause the paper to loosen from the wall. In some cases, once the paper is dry, it can be carefully repasted with a small brush and laid back onto the wall. If the paper becomes stained or brittle, the only alternative is to replace the stained area. One advantage of papering is that it can often be repaired by applying a matching piece over the damaged area. The success of this approach depends on the paperhanger's experience, the type of paper and adhesive used, and the pattern design.

When confronted with stained wallpaper, an adjuster should ask the homeowner whether matching paper is available. Because people generally buy more paper than they need, if the paper was installed within the past several years, a roll might be stored in the attic or basement.

If there is no extra paper, a match might not be possible because wallpaper, although manufactured in long rolls, is often made in different dye lots. For this reason, even if a pattern is available that matches the damaged pattern, the colors might be different. If a match cannot be made, the paper must be completely replaced. Therefore, although some wallpaper losses are small, others are very large.

Wallpaper does not need to be *on* fire to be damaged *by* fire. A nearby fire can generate enough heat to scorch wallpaper. Smoke can be washed from some vinyl or fabric wallpaper. Untreated common vinyl-coated or cloth-backed papers can be washed. Professionals should handle these tasks, though, because pattern inks might run or the paper can tear if handled too roughly. Professional cleaning is also required for oily soot damage. If not properly treated, soot will streak wallpaper, as it does a painted surface. Foil, flocked, and felt coverings are not cleanable, so if they are damaged by soot, they must be replaced.

Factors Affecting the Costs of Wallpaper Losses

The main factors to consider in estimating wallpapering losses are (1) preparation, (2) the size and shape of the surface to be covered, (3) the quality of material to be replaced, and (4) labor.

Preparation—Like paint, wallpaper requires a smooth surface. The best surface on which to apply paper is a bare wall. Undercoats of paper, especially if the seams are overlapped rather than butted, result in a poor appearance. If the damaged layer is to be covered, any loose material must be removed before the new covering is applied. More than three layers of paper are not recommended because the weight of the newest layer and the moisture of its adhesive might loosen the layers beneath it. Additional time must be allowed to wet down, heat, or steam-remove underlayers; to patch the bare surface; and, in some instances, to properly size the bare wall area for adhesion. Sizing, the application of a thin coat of paste onto a bare surface, enables the paste or glue on the back of the wallpaper to adhere more securely.

Surface Features—As with painting, wallpapering can be accomplished most quickly over a flat, smooth, continuous surface. Door openings, built-in shelving, windows, and other features slow the process of application, especially for patterned wallpaper, for which the lengths of paper must be carefully aligned. That alignment might involve as much as 15 to 20 percent waste, even in average-sized rooms. Areas above and below large windows, where the pattern must be aligned both vertically and horizontally, create additional waste and delay.

Materials—Wallcovering materials include such items as cork, carpet-like deep-pile material, fabric-backed vinyl, felt, and grass cloth. Handprinted wallpaper, leather, and wood veneer laminates are also used. However, the most common covering is machine-printed paper, either plastic-surfaced or vinyl with paper backing. The variation in materials creates wide variations in costs. Consequently, adjusters must carefully identify the type of wallpaper to make an appropriate estimate. When possible, adjusters should take a sample from the damaged area and secure an opinion from a knowledgeable local supplier as to material cost.

These are three common types of wallpaper:

- *Vinyl.* Vinyl wallcovering is basically an elastic film on a backing of paper or fabric. Vinyl paper does not breathe, as most other wallcoverings do, so the proper antimoisture adhesive must be used to prevent mildew. Because fabric-backed vinyls are washable and durable, they are commonly used in the kitchens, bathrooms, and hall areas. The thickness and weight of the vinyl wall covering determine its ability to withstand grease, smoke, and dirt from contact with people's hands. Categories of vinyl range from decorative to industrial.

- *Fabric-backed foil.* Fabric-backed foils are installed in much the same way as vinyls, but more care is necessary to keep excess paste off the surface. If dried paste adheres to the foil facing, it can scratch it. Some foils have a plastic-coated covering that makes them more washable. Foils are difficult to work with, and their sheer surface magnifies any defects in the underlying wall surface. For this reason, lining paper is often used as a primer surface to reduce wall imperfections. Foil paper must be carefully applied so that the foil cover is not creased.

- *Flocked coverings.* Flocked wallcovering has part or all of the design made from short textile ends that are bonded to the wallcovering material. The textile material stands on end.

Standard double roll

Seventy-two square feet of wallpaper.

Wallcoverings are generally sold in a **standard double roll**, which measures 72 square feet, or in single rolls of 36 square feet. Similarly, a standard English bolt of wallpaper consists of 2 rolls and measures 72 square feet. A European bolt measures 57 square feet. Wallpaper designs include no pattern at all, random match patterns (which create an overall design effect, but which might not be the same design from roll to roll), straight-across matches, and drop matches. Drop is the length of movement needed to match a pattern. It is measured in inches. It literally means that the adjacent piece of wallpaper must be moved up or down by a certain number of inches to match the pattern. Determining the amount of coverage that a roll of wallpaper provides varies by manufacturer, by pattern, and by material. The only accurate way to estimate the area to be covered is to use the information given on the rolls themselves.

When estimating materials, adjusters can allow for the waste involved in a matching design by considering the area of coverage of a single roll to be 30 square feet and for a double roll to be 60 square feet. Use 46 square feet for a European bolt. This calculation is illustrated in the discussion of estimating.

Labor—The paperhanger's experience is the most important factor in estimating labor costs. Paperhangers can generally work alone. Their rate is typically about the same as the rate for painters. When checking estimates, adjusters should determine the trade cost averages for the particular area. An allowance should be made for difficult materials or work circumstances. The more intricate the pattern is, the more expertise is required for applying the wallcovering.

As mentioned, wallcoverings should be applied to dry, flat, and clean surfaces. Removing existing paper that is plastic-coated, foil type, or not strippable requires that it be hand-sanded, then wetted and scraped off. Additional labor is needed if there are multiple layers of wallpaper. Spackling cracks and gouges create porous surfaces that must be primed or sealed. Drywall is very porous and does not allow the proper application of wallpaper, so new drywall surfaces must be primed. Additionally, the drywall would be damaged if the covering were ever stripped off. Sizing the surface to be covered creates a uniform and smooth surface to ensure good adhesion.

Estimating Wallpaper

Wallpaper estimates can be based on the net area method or unit cost method.

Net Area Method—Assume that a room to be papered is 18' × 20' and has one door (3' × 7'), one window (4' × 5'), and a ceiling height of 8'. The wallpaper to be used is random match or small repeated pattern, so the anticipated average waste is between 15 and 20 percent.

If the amount of necessary materials is not estimated accurately, reordering at a later date might mean that the wallcovering is a different color or that the style is no longer available. Wallpaper comes in different widths, but each double roll always covers 72 square feet, and each single roll always covers 36 square feet. The most common width is 18 inches.

To determine the amount of materials necessary, the adjuster should measure the room's perimeter and multiply it by the height to determine the room's total wall area. This calculation includes two areas that will not be covered, a door and a window. Just as in the net area method for estimating paint jobs, the openings should be deducted to arrive at the net area to be covered.

Perimeter (20' + 20' + 18' + 18')		76 feet
Wall height	×	8 feet
Total wall area		608 square feet
Window (4' × 5')		20 square feet
Door (3' × 7')	+	21 square feet
Total openings area		41 square feet
Total wall area less openings area		608 square feet
	−	41 square feet
Net wall area		567 square feet

Assume that a single roll, allowing for 15 to 20 percent waste, covers thirty square feet. This project requires 19 single rolls (567 ÷ 30 = 18.9, rounded to 19). If the wallpaper pattern is larger or less regular, more waste should be allowed, resulting in a need for additional material. However, a good average net area per single roll is 30 square feet; a good average for a double roll is 60 square feet.

To calculate the amount of paste needed, assume that one pound of paste is enough to apply 10 single rolls. Therefore, two pounds would be needed for 19 single rolls (19 ÷ 10 = 1.9, rounded up to 2). The sizing material is a gelatin sealer, which is already added to the paste compound and does not need to be calculated separately.

The labor is based on the number of rolls of wallpaper to be applied. The rate to overlap paper is faster than when the edges are butted. Working with high-grade paper or wall coverings reduces the number of single rolls that can be applied per hour. See the exhibit "Wallpapering Time Estimates."

Wallpapering Time Estimates

Approximate Rate per Hour for Various Kinds of Paperhanging Work

Kind of Work	Quantity Per Hour
Remove wallpaper—single layer	150 sq. ft.
Remove wallpaper—several layers	100 sq. ft.
Hang wallpaper—butt joint—average grade	3 single rolls
Hang wallpaper—first grade	2 single rolls
Hanging borders	100 linear feet

Adapted from Paul I. Thomas, How to Estimate Building Losses and Construction Costs, 4th ed. (Englewood Cliffs, N.J.: Prentice-Hall, 1983), pp. 337–339, and Walker's Building Estimator's Reference Book, 26th ed. (Lisle, Ill.: Frank R. Walker Company, 1999), p. 9.210. [DA04087]

The room in this example requires 19 rolls for the walls. The average labor factor is 3 single rolls per hour for butt joint, average-grade material. Dividing 3 into 19 rolls shows that 6.33 hours of labor are required to hang 19 single rolls.

If the previous layer and several other layers must be removed, the labor hours estimate will change. As the Wallpapering Time Estimates exhibit shows, the rate to remove several layers of paper is 100 square feet per hour.

In the example, this rate adds 5.67 hours to the labor estimate. Total labor is then calculated like this:

Removing paper $\dfrac{567 \text{ sq. ft.}}{100 \text{ sq. ft./hr.}} = 5.67 \text{ hours}$

Applying paper $\dfrac{19 \text{ rolls}}{3 \text{ rolls per hour}} = 6.33 \text{ hours}$

Labor total   12 hours

These figures do not assume extensive preparation of the bare walls or sizing.

Total Cost—This breakdown shows the total estimated cost to remove the old paper and to hang new paper on walls only (no ceiling) at the price of $10 per single roll with butted edges, no extreme pattern matching, and two openings:

Net area of walls: 567 square feet	
19 rolls @ $10 per single roll	$190
2 pounds paste @ $1 per pound	2
Labor to strip old and hang new paper	
12 hours @ $20 per hour	240
Total cost	$432

As with paint estimating, the labor factor should include access time and any above-normal preparation of the surface. These extra items can be listed separately on an estimate sheet. Each additional allowance should be explained.

Because of the wide variation in the cost of materials, estimating a single unit cost for some jobs is difficult, but applying a unit cost to separate rooms in the same house is possible. As shown in the Wallpapering Time Estimates exhibit, even the labor hours differ with the grade of wallcovering being applied. The unit cost for the room in the example would be the total estimated cost for the job divided by the total net square feet, as calculated here:

$$\text{Unit Cost} = \frac{\$432}{567 \text{ sq. ft.}} = \$0.76 \text{ per square foot}$$

Any unusual preparation or accessibility problems should be figured separately and added to the unit cost estimate.

Exterior Siding

The extent of, and potential for, damage to exterior siding are affected very much by the type of siding material. Wood shingles or shakes of redwood and western red cedar normally have an excellent moisture-resistant composition. Nevertheless, weather-related losses are the main cause of damage to such shingles. Over time, wind-driven rains can seep behind siding and cause deterioration. Hail can split wood shingles and puncture or dent aluminum or vinyl siding. Hail can cause a range of damage, from minor cosmetic damage to moderate and severe losses. The same force of impact that would dent aluminum would cause little, if any, damage to more pliable vinyl or even to wood clapboard surfaces. Siding losses related to vandalism involve spray paint damage or tearing of siding.

Although aluminum can be repainted, it will also need to be painted several years later. Even though it dulls over time, the original baked-on surface will not peel or crack, as will paint. Many siding losses, especially to aluminum siding, can be adjusted with an allowance for appearance. When in doubt, an adjuster should secure photographs of the damage, note the kind of siding involved, and try to arrange an inspection by an expert familiar with this kind of damage.

Spot repairs can be made to wood clapboard and vinyl/aluminum siding. Repair of wood siding is discussed in the next section.

Siding Materials

The major types of siding material are wood exterior panels such as wood shakes; hardboard; aluminum; vinyl; seamless steel; and fiber cement. Masonry, stucco finishes, and composition asphalt coverings are also used.

The most common types of wood siding are bevel design and dropsiding. Wood siding is usually white pine, redwood, Douglas fir, or red cedar. It is usually applied horizontally and readily accepts paint or stain. The corners can be finished with vertical trim boards or covered by metal corner caps. High-quality installations have mitered corners, which require more time. See the exhibit "Wood Siding."

Wood drop or bevel siding is applied over felt paper, which serves as a vapor barrier for the back of the siding. The siding is nailed directly onto the sheathing of the framed building. The siding material can range up to 1 inch thick and 12 inches wide and typically comes in lengths of 8 to 20 feet.

Surface damage to wood siding can be filled and sanded, then painted. Broken boards, however, must be replaced. That replacement involves loosening the board strip above the damaged area, cutting the replacement boards to fit, and

Wood Siding

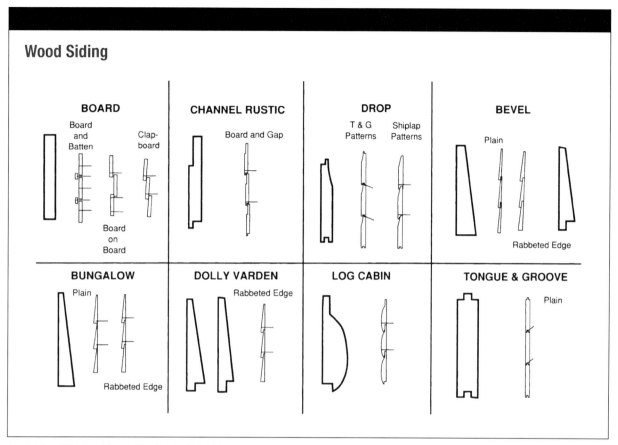

Adapted from "Wood and Composition Exterior Siding," Property Damage Repair Reports, No. 432 (Chambersburg, Pa.: National Property & Casualty Claims Research Service, Inc., formerly Vale Lab Research, January 1983), p. 1. [DA04092]

replacing all but the bottom board. The back lip of the bottom board must be cut away so that the board can be pressed against the siding and nailed in place. Wood siding can also be applied vertically.

Sheet Materials—Exterior sheet materials generally come in 4' × 8' panels, various patterns, and several different colors. Exterior grades of particleboard and plywood can be used when quality is not the primary concern. These materials can be easily painted and should have a good vapor barrier behind them. Batten strips should be nailed where the edges butt against one another to prevent leaking at the seams.

Wood shingles come in lengths of 16, 18, and 24 inches. Shingles are sold by the square, with four bundles per square. Four bundles cover 100 square feet with an exposure of 5 inches. (The exposure of a shingle is the amount that is exposed to the weather.) With a smaller exposure, such as 4 inches, the shingles cover less area. Larger exposures, some up to 8 inches, are used depending on the size of the wood shingle.

Aluminum siding is sold in cartons of 12 sheets, which cover 100 square feet of surface. They are interlocking and have an exposure of 8 inches. For a slightly higher cost, they can be backed with insulating material.

Vinyl siding might be an alternative to aluminum. Vinyl siding's color is part of the material and will not fade over time. It is pliable and not as prone to damage by hail or other minor impact. It can also be bought with or without insulation. Vinyl tends to stiffen in cold weather and can crack if bumped. Its surface is not adaptable to painting. Vinyl siding can be roll-formed at the work site so that it will be seamless when installed.

Seamless-steel siding is PVC-coated steel. It is manufactured on site, so it has no joints or endlap. It is a durable product that resists chipping and peeling.

Fiber cement siding is cement and sand mixed with cellulose to form planks that look like wood siding. It holds paint much better than wood and has a very long usable life. Fiber cement siding's disadvantage is that is heavy and takes two professionals to install. It is also very hard on power tools and should be cut with a masonry or diamond-tipped blade.

Estimating Siding

In estimating the amount and cost of siding, adjusters must consider waste as well as materials and labor. Unit costs for siding can be calculated.

Waste—In estimating beveled siding, adjusters should use the net area method and add a percentage for mill waste, cutting, and overlap. An estimating reference book or an estimating software package will have the percentage of waste for the type of siding involved in the loss.

Calculating Area—Regardless of the type of material used, the structure's exterior must be measured, and the area of all openings must be deducted. To determine the exterior surface area of a house, multiply the perimeter measure by the height of the walls under the roofed eave, then calculate and add on the area of the gable ends.

Assume that a house is 40' × 26' and thus has a perimeter of 132'. The height of the walls under the roof eave is 8', so the surface area is 1,056 square feet. The triangular area of each gable end is 104 square feet, (26' × 8') × 2. To determine the total *net* surface area, the adjuster must deduct the area of the openings:

Total exterior surface area		1,056 square feet
Total gable end area (2 × 104')	+	208 square feet
Gross surface area		1,264 square feet
Door (3' × 7')	–	21 square feet
3 windows (4' × 5' each)	–	60 square feet
Net area		1,183 square feet

Materials—The house in this example has 1" × 8" bevel cedar siding that costs $1.25 per board foot. A 35 percent waste factor should be added for bevel siding of that size. Multiply the net area by 1.35 (1,183 × 1.35 = 1,597 BFM) to determine the amount of siding needed to cover the exterior walls and gable ends.

Before wood siding is installed, a vapor barrier is installed over the wood sheathing material. Each roll of the vapor barrier material covers approximately 500 square feet. There is no waste factor for vapor barriers.

Labor—Labor for installing siding is based on 1,000 BFM of material. The first step in estimating labor is to determine the time needed to do the job. The exhibit indicates the labor hours per BFM for different types of siding and nominal material sizes. Because this job require 1,597 BFM of material, 57.5 hours of labor will be necessary:

$$1,597 \text{ BFM} \times \frac{36 \text{ hrs.}}{1,000 \text{ BFM}} = 57.49 \text{ hrs., rounded to } 57.5$$

The second step is to determine the labor rate per hour in the locality. At $20 per hour, the labor cost is $1,150 ($20 per hour × 57.5 hours).

Total Cost—The total cost for material and labor to install 1" × 8" beveled siding is broken down like this (the labor for the felt is included in the rate):

1,597 BFM @ $1.25 per BFM	$1,996.25
Vapor barrier: 3 rolls @ $16 per roll	48.00
Labor: 1,597 @ 36 hours per BFM 1,000 = 57.5 hours	
57.5 hours @ $20 per hour	1,150.00
Total material and labor	$3,194.25

Additional factors that might need to be considered are removing damaged siding; erecting and disassembling scaffolding or staging; removing outside trim such as shutters, gutters, and headers; and applying stain, varnish, or paint.

Unit Cost—A unit cost per square foot is determined by dividing the total cost by the total board feet:

$$\text{Unit cost} = \frac{\$3,210.25}{1,597 \text{ sq. ft.}} = \$2.01 \text{ per square foot}$$

This figure can be used as a basis for estimating the cost of other beveled wood 8" siding installations. No one unit cost applies to patch repair jobs, however. In siding, as in other trades, smaller jobs make establishing a feasible unit cost more difficult.

GROSS AREA ESTIMATING AND NET AREA ESTIMATING

In adjusting losses involving damage to painted surfaces, adjusters determine how much area has been damaged and the cause of the damage (which often determines the type of necessary remedy). Then, an adjuster prepares an estimate for the painting by considering the preparation for painting, the type of surface to be painted, the materials necessary for the painting, and the labor.

This section explains three methods of measuring areas that need repainting. The first two, the gross area method and the net area method, are based on the labor and materials method. The third method, the unit cost method, is appropriate for larger jobs.

Gross Area Method

The exhibit shows a room for which the gross area method can be used. The floor of the room in the exhibit is 28' × 15', and the ceiling is 10'. The door is 7' × 3' feet. The room has three windows: two are 3' × 5', and the third is 3' × 6'. See the exhibit "Example of Gross Area Method for Paint Estimates."

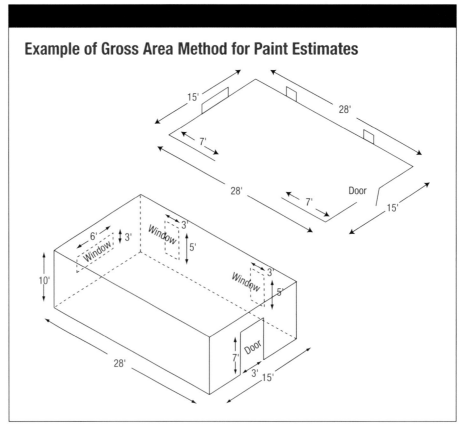

Example of Gross Area Method for Paint Estimates

[DA04098]

The gross area method does not deduct openings totaling less than 100 square feet from the room's total wall area. In effect, this method assumes that the door surface (21 square feet) and the three window areas (15 square feet, 15 square feet, and 18 square feet) are to be painted. This method therefore provides an allowance for the extra time needed to paint the trim around the windows and door, without requiring separate calculations.

These are the steps in calculating a painting estimate using the gross area of a room:

1. Calculate the surface area
2. Deduct openings when the total area of all of the openings is 100 sq. ft. or more
3. Estimate the materials
4. Estimate the labor
5. Total the estimate

This section details each of those steps.

Step 1: Calculate the Surface Area

For the purposes of painting, the surface area in any room is the sum of the wall area and the ceiling area. The wall area equals the perimeter of the room, which is simply the sum of the lengths of the four walls, multiplied by the room's height. In this case, the perimeter equals 86 linear feet (28 + 28 + 15 + 15), so the wall area is 860 square feet (86 × 10).

The ceiling area equals the ceiling's length (28') multiplied by the ceiling's width (15'), or 420 square feet. The total gross area is therefore the sum of 860 square feet and 420 square feet, or 1,280 square feet.

Adjusters must measure rooms precisely, and not simply pace them, guess, or even accept a homeowner's estimate. Even minor measurement errors can prove costly later. For example, an error of only two additional feet in this room's linear dimensions (30' × 17' room dimensions) would result in a wall area of 940 square feet and a ceiling area of 510 square feet, resulting in a gross area of 1,450 square feet, which equals approximately 13 percent more area. If this miscalculation were multiplied by several rooms and multiple claims files, the potential for distortion would be enormous. Adjusters must also remember to deduct nonpainted surfaces (such as those that are paneled or papered) from the total gross area.

Step 2: Deduct Openings Totaling 100 Square Feet or More

In this example, there is no deduction for openings, because the total of the door and three windows is less than 100 square feet.

Step 3: Estimate the Materials

Labels on most paint cans estimate approximately 400 square feet of coverage per gallon. Paint is available in gallons or quarts. This text rounds up to the next gallon. Given that estimate, 3.2 gallons of paint (rounded to 4 gallons) are necessary to paint the room in this example (1,280 square feet divided by 400 square feet per gallon). If two coats are required, 8 gallons of paint would be necessary (2 coats multiplied by 4 gallons per coat).

When several rooms will be painted the same color, a more accurate method for estimating the materials is to total the gross area of all of the rooms to be painted, divide by the number of square feet per gallon, then multiply by the number of coats before rounding up to the nearest gallon.

Step 4: Estimate the Labor

The exhibit presents the approximate number of square feet of painting material that can be applied per hour to different surfaces. According to that schedule, 165 square feet of paint can be applied per hour to cover smooth walls with one coat of paint. Based on this rate, the labor for the sample room can be estimated at 7.75 hours (1,280 square feet gross area divided by 165 square feet per hour). See the exhibit "Painting Time Estimates."

Painting Time Estimates

Approximate Number of Square Feet of Paint Application For Various Kinds of Work Completed Per Hour

Kinds of Work	Sq. Ft. Per Hour
Interior	
Painting primer on smooth walls	200–225
Painting, second coat	165–175
Painting wood floors, first coat	290–300
Exterior	
Painting primer on smooth walls	100–110
Painting smooth walls, second coat	115–125

Walker's Building Estimator's Reference Book, 26th ed. (Lisle, Ill.: Frank R. Walker Company, 1999), pp. 9.176, 9.183. [DA04086]

Included in the average rate is the time required for normal preparation such as dusting, sanding trim, and patching minor surface cracks. Not included, however, are any openings larger than 100 square feet and unusual items such as radiators and built-in bookshelves. Those items should be deducted from the gross area and considered as separate items. Also not included are preparatory tasks such as washing soot from walls and ceilings; removing furnishings such as draperies, light fixtures, and furniture; covering furnishings and wall-to-wall carpeting; and anything other than minor filling, sanding, and patching. Finally, ceilings and walls higher than nine feet might slow the rate of painting.

Step 5: Total the Estimate

The cost to apply one coat of paint to the room in the example is calculated like this:

4 gallons of paint × $18 per gallon	$ 72
7.75 hours of labor × $20 per hour	155
Remove/replace furnishings, cover floor, flooring, and fixtures as needed:	
1.2 hours × $20 per hour	24
Gross area method total	$251

For a small residential loss, the labor rate for the removal and replacement of furnishings will be the same as the painter's trade rate because the painter will be the only laborer on the job. For very large losses, those nontrade duties can be negotiated at a lower hourly rate.

Net Area Method

Most of the steps in the net area method of paint estimating are the same as the corresponding steps of the gross area method. The only difference between the two is that the net area method deducts the true size of all openings from the total actual area. The net area method uses the multiple system of measurement to calculate separately the size of all openings, and those areas are added to the adjusted area to estimate the materials. If a room has more than four windows and two doors, the net area method would probably be more appropriate than the gross area method.

Step 1: Calculate the Net Surface Area

The first step is to calculate the net wall and ceiling areas in the room. The room in this example is 28' × 15' × 10'. The gross area of the walls and ceiling is 1,280 square feet, but the room has four openings: a door and three windows. The door is 7' × 3', or 21 square feet. Two of the windows are 3' × 5', or 15 square feet apiece and 30 square feet combined. The third window is 3' × 6', or 18 square feet. Altogether, the openings represent 69 square feet of area. When that figure is subtracted from the 1,280 gross square feet of surface area, the result is 1,211 net square feet of area.

Step 2: Calculate the Openings

The multiple system of measurement adds a percentage or multiple of the actual size of a surface to the actual size to arrive at an effective size that reflects the time needed to paint such a surface. The adjustments to the actual openings can be considered a "difficulty factor." See the exhibit "Painting Difficulty Factors."

Painting Difficulty Factors

The factors are based on the time necessary to paint irregular surfaces compared to painting a simple wall or ceiling area. For example, the factor of 4 allowed for painting a picket fence indicates that four times as much time is necessary to paint a fence than is necessary to paint a wall area of the same dimensions.

All of these factors are for one coat of paint.

The actual measurements of the item should be shown in the Description column of the estimate. The Square Foot Equivalent should be shown in the quantity column of the estimate. For example, to paint a 50' section of 3½'-high picket fence, $50 \times 3.5 \times 4$ = 700 square feet is necessary.

Item	Square Foot Equivalent
Cabinets with doors	$L \times H \times 5$
Bookcase, shelves, cupboards	$L \times H \times 3$
Drop or bevel siding less than 5"	$L \times W + 20\%$*
Drop or bevel siding 5" or wider	$L \times W + 10\%$*
Eaves with open rafters	$L \times W \times 3$
Picket fence (both sides)	$L \times H \times 4$
Gratings/grille work	$L \times H \times 4$
Balustrade	$L \times H \times 4$
Stairs	No. of risers $\times$ W (in feet) $\times 8$
Masonry or stucco	$L \times H + 30\%$
Windows	Add 2' to both width and height of opening. Use 3' $\times$ 6' as minimum size window. Calculate all openings at a minimum of 40 sq. ft.

* Deduct for large openings greater than 100 SF (10' $\times$ 10')

Adapted from Estimating Guide, 14th ed. (Falls Church, Va.: Painting and Decorating Contractors of America), 1984, p. 15. [DA04100]

According to the multiple system of measurement, no opening should be calculated at less than 40 square feet. Therefore, the openings in the sample room would be calculated like this (the numbers in the parentheses are the adjustments made based on the dimensions presented in the Example of Gross Area Method for Paint Estimates exhibit):

2 Windows	$3' (+ 2') \times 5' (+ 2') = 5' \times 7' = 80$ (40 minimum × 2)
1 Window	$3' (+ 2') \times 6' (+2') = 5' \times 8' = 40$ square feet
Door	$7' (+ 1') \times 3' (+ 2') = 8' \times 5' = 40$ square feet

Total effective area for calculating labor and time is 160 square feet.

Step 3: Estimate the Materials

The difficulty factors added through the multiple system of measurement only affect labor, so the actual square footage is used for determining materials.

The method for estimating the materials involves dividing the total number of square feet by the number of square feet that one gallon of paint can cover, rounding that number to the next gallon, and multiplying that figure by the cost of a gallon of paint. In this example, one gallon of paint covers 400 square feet and costs $18, so the materials estimate is calculated like this:

$$\frac{1,211 \text{ square feet}}{400 \text{ square feet}} = 3.03 \text{ gallons, 4 when rounded to the next full gallon}$$

Total materials = $72 (4 gallons × $18).

Adjuster Tip—A separate calculation must be done for each type of paint to be used in a room.

Step 4: Estimate the Labor

The hourly rate to paint smooth walls only with a coat of paint is 165 to 175 square feet per hour, according to the Painting Time Estimates exhibit. The rate to paint windows, doors, and trim may only be 125 square feet per hour. Because the multiple system of measurement has already accounted for the difficulty of the trim, the rate for smooth walls can be used for the trim. Because the ceiling is higher than normal, the rate for smooth walls should be reduced to 150 square feet per hour. Based on these figures, the labor hours can be estimated:

Net area of walls:
$$\frac{791 \text{ square feet}}{165 \text{ square feet/hour}} = 4.79 \text{ hours}$$

Rate for windows, door (trim):
$$\frac{160 \text{ square feet}}{165 \text{ square feet/hour}} = 0.96 \text{ hours}$$

This comes from the multiple system of measurement calculation.

Ceiling:

$$\frac{420 \text{ square feet}}{150 \text{ square feet/hour}} = 2.8 \text{ hours}$$

Total labor: 8 hours × $20/hour = $160

Step 5: Total the Estimate

The estimate for the whole job is the sum of the cost of the materials ($72), the cost of the labor (8 hours at $20 per hour = $160), and the cost of removing and replacing the furnishings (1.2 hours at $20 per hour = $24). For this job, the estimate based on the net area method is $256.

Unit Cost Method

The unit cost method is most appropriate when several areas of damage or large areas of damage must be repaired. Once the cost per square foot to paint one room has been determined, that unit cost can be applied to similar rooms. Only one additional step is needed to determine unit cost once the time and material figures have been calculated. That step is to divide the total cost by the total area:

Gross area method totals $266/1,280 square feet = $0.20 per square foot

Net area method totals $238/1,211 square feet = $0.19 per square foot

The unit cost method might not be accurate for smaller jobs (that is, those requiring fewer than three working days or 24 labor hours). Although less time is needed to complete smaller jobs, contractors have fixed overhead costs, so a five- or six-hour job might not be calculated at less than an eight-hour job.

ELECTRICAL SYSTEMS, MECHANICAL SYSTEMS, AND INSULATION

Electrical systems have become complicated and difficult to repair because of the wiring that is now needed to support the various technologies included in many homes. The plumbing system is roughed-in during the framing of the house. Later, the cooling system is installed.

The mechanical systems discussed in this section include the electrical system, the plumbing system, and the heating and air conditioning systems.

Electrical Systems

Although residential electrical systems might appear complicated, the methods used in wiring homes are generally straightforward and follow strict guidelines. The National Electrical Code establishes those methods, and most local codes and electrical contractors follow them.

Entrance of Electrical Service

The wires that transmit electricity from the power company to residences are either above or below ground. Most homes use a weatherhead, which receives the wires from the utility pole. Many newer homes have an underground cable running through a pipe called a "conduit." In both cases, the wiring passes through the electric meter before running into the service panel.

Service Panel

After passing through the meter, the wires enter one of two types of service panels, a **circuit breaker** or a fuse box. The circuit-breaker panel and fuse box serve two purposes. First, they distribute electricity into several branch circuits. Second, they act as safety devices by breaking the circuit if an overload occurs, preventing the wiring from overheating and causing a fire.

These panels are rated by amperage. Adjusters need to identify the service panel rating when scoping the loss because it significantly affects the cost of the loss. The amperage of service is also often upgraded after a loss. The 60-amp fused service was standard before the invention and increased use of many modern electrical appliances. Today, new homes usually contain a 200-amp service using circuit breakers.

Circuit breaker (fuse box)

An electrical service panel that distributes electricity into several branches and acts as a safety device if an overload occurs.

Branch Circuits

Branch circuits are made up of wires running from the service panel to the outlets, switches, and fixtures located throughout the house. They can generally supply different amounts of electricity, depending on their amperage, which varies by the wire's size.

With the exception of heavy-duty appliances, which should have their own circuits, most residential branch circuits serve eight to ten outlets each. The National Electrical Code recommends one 20-amp circuit for every 500 square feet of living area for lighting. Appliances such as air conditioners, electric ranges, electric water heaters, and electric dryers often have their own 220-volt circuit as opposed to the 110-volt circuits used for lighting and general usage.

Ground Fault Circuit Interrupters

Electrical shocks can be minor to fatal. The **ground fault circuit interrupter (GFCI)** was designed to protect people from fatal electrical shocks. The National Electrical Code requires GFCI outlets for bathrooms, kitchens, basements, garages, and outdoors. The GFCI monitors a current's flow through a circuit. When it senses a leak (ground fault), it shuts the power off to the

Ground fault circuit interrupter (GFCI)

A device that monitors the flow of current through a circuit; when it detects a leak (ground fault), it shuts the power off to the circuit.

circuit. If a person has become the ground for the leaking current, the person will still get a shock, but the GFCI will prevent that shock from being fatal.[7]

Wiring Types and Methods

Wiring types and methods significantly affect the cost of materials and amount of labor required for repairs. These are the most common types of wiring used in residential construction:

- Rigid conduit
- Thin-wall conduit
- Nonmetallic sheathed cable
- Armored cable

Wiring comes in two types: 2 wire and 3 wire. In a 2-wire strand, there is no ground wire. There is only a black wire that has current in it (referred to as the "hot" wire) and a white wire that is neutral. In a 3-wire strand, there is a green or bare copper wire in addition to the hot wire and the neutral wire. The green or copper wire is the ground wire.[8]

Rigid conduit is similar to water piping and is usually used outside or underground. It comes in ten-foot lengths and various inside diameters. The pipe is threaded for coupling and connecting to boxes. Conduit systems are installed before the wiring is threaded through them.

Thin-wall conduit is similar to rigid conduit in many ways. It is available in ten-foot lengths and the same inside diameters. However, because it can be easily cut and bent and because it has compression fittings rather than threaded ones, thin-wall conduit is far more popular than rigid conduit for residential electrical applications. Another name for thin-wall conduit is electrical metallic tubing (EMT). Thin-wall conduit can also be nonmetallic.

Nonmetallic sheathed cable is one of the most popular methods of electrical wiring. It is both less expensive than conduit and less time-consuming to install. Unlike the conduit systems, in which wires are run after the tubing has been installed, nonmetallic sheathed cable is made up of individual plastic-coated wires and a bare ground wire all wrapped in a flame-retardant, water-resistant plastic sheath. Connections must be made in metal or plastic junction boxes. Many local building codes prohibit the use of nonmetallic sheathed cable in some types of residential construction.

Armored cable is commonly called "BX cable." Armored cable is not used as often as it once was because of nonmetallic sheathed cable's popularity. Armored cable consists of two or more insulated wires encased in a spiral steel sheath. Like the other forms of wiring described, BX has special connectors and fittings.

Structured Wiring

Most commercial buildings and many new homes are built with structured wiring to accommodate audio, video, and data technology. **Structured wiring** (also known as infrastructure wiring) consists of the wiring and components used for telephones, fax machines, computers, the Internet, audio equipment, security cameras, and video equipment such as cable or satellite TV. Commercial properties often use fiber-optic cables to transmit data. Some communities are installing fiber-optic cable so that residents can enjoy high-definition television.

Whatever type of wiring is used, structured wiring begins at a distribution box or panel, similar to the service panel found in most homes today. In addition to the electrical outlets are wall receptacles that contain jacks for telephones, fax machines, data lines, audio, and video. There may be control panels or keypads on walls to operate lighting, heating and air conditioning, and alarms. Repairs to structural wiring can be expensive because of the labor involved in "fishing" wire through enclosed walls.[9]

> **Structured wiring (infrastructure wiring)**
> The wiring built into a building to accommodate audio, video, and data technology.

Damage

Residential electric systems can be damaged by various causes, but fire, lightning, and power surges are the most common. The extent of damage varies by the type of electrical wiring. Plastic sheathed cable can withstand less heat than can metal conduit. Building inspectors often require complete rewiring after a loss when it is not necessary. Adjusters should consider employing an electrical engineer or qualified contractor for an expert opinion, thus resolving disputes and satisfying the building inspector. Likewise, upgrades may be required by code. If this situation occurs, the adjuster must be aware of the potential coverage issue that it raises.

Mechanical Systems

Several building trades are more specialized than carpentry, including plumbing, heating, and cooling. The purpose of this section is not to teach the detailed methods of estimating claims involving mechanical systems, but rather to stress that adjusters should have a working knowledge of the vocabulary and elements of those systems and should be able to evaluate the estimates prepared by subcontractors specializing in those trades. Although estimates are not always easy to obtain, adjusters should insist that these estimates be broken down into specifications, labor, and materials so that an analysis is possible. The labor rates paid to these specialists are much higher than those for carpenters and other laborers. A rule of thumb for approaching costs in these trades is that rates can be expected to be one and a half times the labor rate that carpenters charge.

Plumbing

The plumbing systems in residential construction use four distinct networks of pipes. The first two networks are made of the pipes that carry hot and cold water to faucets and appliances. The third network is the system of drain-pipes that carry away wastewater through the main soil stack, and the fourth network is a vent stack that allows for the equalization of air pressure needed for the drain system to function properly. All plumbing systems work similarly, but materials can differ considerably among various systems.

Plumbing work consists of rough plumbing and finish plumbing. Rough plumbing involves placing pipes and drains within walls and under floors. Finish plumbing involves the installation and repair of fixtures.

Galvanized steel piping, rigid and flexible copper tubing, and polyvinyl chloride (PVC) piping are the most common materials in use. Galvanized steel piping comes in various inside diameters, but one-half inch and three-quarters of an inch are most common in houses. The ends are threaded, usually at the job site, so that the pipes can be joined to prevent leaks. Various elbows, tees, and angles are available to complete the system.

Sweating a pipe

Sealing two pipes by heating and soldering the point of connection between them.

Copper tubing is the preferred and most common material used today. Joints are made through a process known as **sweating a pipe**, in which the point of connection between two pipes is heated and solder is applied and allowed to flow into the joint, thus sealing it. Because no threading is necessary, copper tubing is less time-consuming to install than is galvanized pipe. As with galvanized pipe, one-half inch and three-quarters of an inch are the most common sizes in residential plumbing.

Although not allowed by many building codes, plastic piping is gaining popularity because it is less expensive and easier to install than either galvanized pipe or copper tubing. Plastic pipe is rigid and is joined by cement designed specifically for this purpose. It can be joined to existing galvanized or copper systems.

In the past, cast iron was typically used for piping in these systems. The most common material used today is a plastic compound, acrilonitrile-butadiene-styrene (ABS). PVC might also be used in drain and waste systems.

Hot tubs and whirlpools, in addition to great variety among the more common plumbing fixtures such as sinks, bathtubs, toilets, and faucets, have changed the task of estimating plumbing losses. Adjusters must identify the quality of plumbing fixtures involved in the loss because prices vary considerably depending on brand, material, finish, and installation.

The most common losses affecting plumbing are fire damage and water damage, primarily from leakage and freezing. Galvanized pipes can usually withstand considerable heat without being significantly damaged. Copper tubing can withstand less heat because the copper and especially the solder melt at lower temperatures. Plastic pipes also melt at relatively low temperatures. Smoke from a fire is usually acidic and can etch the finish on plumbing fixtures unless the fixtures are cleaned shortly after the fire. The porcelain finish on fixtures such as sinks and bathtubs is porous, and hot smoke can stain it permanently. Porcelain can be reapplied to bathtubs, but the cost of the procedure cannot usually be justified for sinks, which are far less expensive to replace.

Most residential insurance policies do not cover the cost to repair leaking pipes, although the resulting water damage is often covered, as is the cost to locate the leaks. Freezing damage, covered by most policies, is common in many climates. Both leakage and freezing losses can involve cutting into walls, floors, or ceilings to locate the damaged plumbing.

A qualified plumber should inspect most plumbing losses. A pressure test is usually performed on extensive losses to help pinpoint the damage. Appliances should also be inspected and tested to determine whether repair is feasible.

Heating and Cooling Systems

Each of the many available heating and cooling systems works according to similar principles. For example, with heating systems, each must transfer energy from a fuel source to either water or air; circulate the warm water or air throughout the house, allowing the heat to dissipate; and then return the water or air to the energy source to be reheated.

All heating systems have a thermostat that controls temperature. The thermostat sends an electric signal to the furnace, signaling the fuel valve to open up when the air temperature in the house falls to a certain point. Either an electric igniter similar to a spark plug or a pilot light ignites the fuel.

Adjusters must understand how the various types of heating systems work to analyze, evaluate, and negotiate losses involving these systems.

Warm-Air Heating—The most common systems for warm-air central heating are forced air and radiant systems. Each system uses a furnace fueled by oil, gas, or coal. Some systems allow wood to be used alone or in conjunction with other fuels.

Forced warm-air systems have a blower at the cool-air entrance to the furnace to suck in the cool air while it blows out the warm air. The air flows through a system of warm-air ducts, and it exits through registers located in each room. Cool air is drawn through cold-air returns into ducts to be returned to the furnace. The cool air passes through a filter, which removes dust and other particles, and then flows through a heat exchanger that sits above the furnace's burners. Once heated, it enters the plenum, a chamber attached to the furnace where the duct runs begin. See the exhibit "Forced Warm-Air Heating System."

Radiant heating systems have ducts or tubes, rather than registers, contained within the floors or ceilings. When heated by the ducts or tubes, these surfaces

Forced Warm-Air Heating System

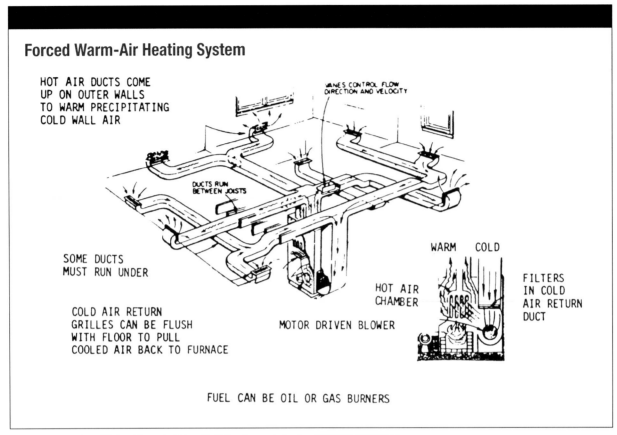

HOT AIR DUCTS COME
UP ON OUTER WALLS
TO WARM PRECIPITATING
COLD WALL AIR

VANES CONTROL FLOW
DIRECTION AND VELOCITY

DUCTS RUN
BETWEEN JOISTS

SOME DUCTS
MUST RUN UNDER

WARM   COLD

COLD AIR RETURN
GRILLES CAN BE FLUSH
WITH FLOOR TO PULL
COOLED AIR BACK TO FURNACE

HOT AIR
CHAMBER

MOTOR DRIVEN BLOWER

FILTERS
IN COLD
AIR RETURN
DUCT

FUEL CAN BE OIL OR GAS BURNERS

Used with permission of National Property & Casualty Claims Research Services (NPCCRS). [DA04105]

warm the air around them. The furnace and controls work like a forced warm-air system, although they are more difficult to access for repairs.

Steam and Hot-Water Heating Systems—Both steam and hot-water heating systems use a boiler rather than a furnace. Oil or gas usually fires the boiler. In a steam system, the water in the boiler is converted to steam and is circulated to radiators through pipes. The steam condenses in the radiators as it dissipates the heat and is then returned to the boiler either through the same pipes or in separate pipes connected to the opposite end of the radiators.

Hot-water systems circulate heated water rather than steam; otherwise, they work in the same manner as do steam systems. Hot water can also be used with copper tubing in a radiant heating system. See the exhibit "Hot-Water Heating System."

Electric Heating—Electric heaters burn no fuel on site; require no vents; and are quiet, durable, and easy to maintain. The simplest and most common electric system is the baseboard heater, which is available in various sizes. It contains a series of fins, which are heated by electric coils. Warm air rises and gradually heats the air. One of the advantages of electric heat is that each baseboard heating unit can be controlled by a different thermostat, allowing

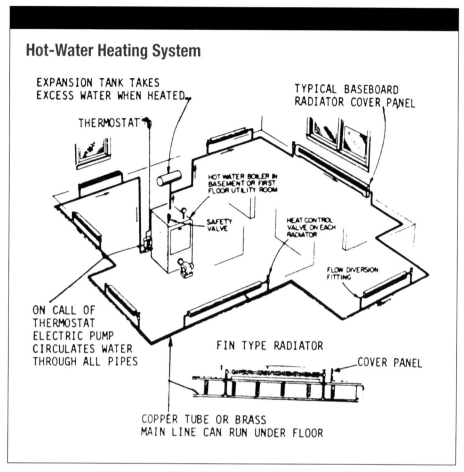

Hot-Water Heating System

EXPANSION TANK TAKES
EXCESS WATER WHEN HEATED

THERMOSTAT

TYPICAL BASEBOARD
RADIATOR COVER PANEL

HOT WATER BOILER IN
BASEMENT OR FIRST
FLOOR UTILITY ROOM

SAFETY
VALVE

HEAT CONTROL
VALVE ON EACH
RADIATOR

FLOW DIVERSION
FITTING

ON CALL OF
THERMOSTAT
ELECTRIC PUMP
CIRCULATES WATER
THROUGH ALL PIPES

FIN TYPE RADIATOR

COVER PANEL

COPPER TUBE OR BRASS
MAIN LINE CAN RUN UNDER FLOOR

Used with permission of National Property & Casualty Claims Research Services (NPCCRS). [DA04106]

each room to be heated to different temperatures and allowing individual units to be shut off.

Electric heaters can also be installed on walls or in ceilings. Some come with fans, which allow for greater air circulation. Electric heating units are generally installed by electrical contractors rather than by contractors specializing in heating and air conditioning.

Air Conditioning—Residences are generally air conditioned either by a central system or by room air conditioners installed in windows or in wall pockets. This section discusses only central air conditioning systems because losses involving room air conditioners are usually covered under the contents coverage section of a property policy. A typical system includes a condensing unit located outside the house, evaporator coils placed within the furnace plenum, and refrigerant tubing connecting the two. For the purpose of circulating air, air conditioning systems are typically used in conjunction with a forced-air furnace, thereby using the furnace's blower and duct system. See the exhibit "Typical Central Air Conditioning System Installation."

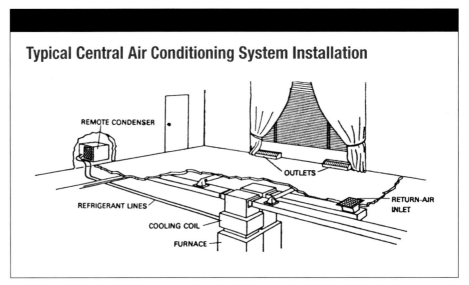

Used with permission of National Property & Casualty Claims Research Services (NPCCRS). [DA04107]

The furnace blower draws in warm air through the return ducts, filters it, and circulates it through the evaporator coils in the plenum to the supply ducts. Humidity removed in the cooling process runs down the coil and into a drain line running to a floor drain. A separate 240-volt circuit supplies the power that the compressor motor and fan in the condensing unit need. A thermostat controls the compressor and blower.

Miscellaneous Heating and Cooling Systems—Adjusters should be aware of several additional types of heating and cooling systems, including heat pumps and solar heating systems.

Heat pump

A unit that can act as an air conditioner and can reverse itself and draw heat from the outdoors to heat the inside of a house.

A **heat pump** is basically an air conditioner that not only draws heat from indoors and transfers it outdoors but also can reverse itself and draw heat from the outdoors to the interior of the house. Solar systems are used for a wide range of purposes, from preheating water for water heaters to heating swimming pools. In a typical solar system, water or another liquid is pumped through tubes to one or more solar collectors, where it is heated and returned to be circulated through copper coils. These copper coils might be located within a water heater or in a special solar tank. Because of the variety of solar collection systems, adjusters should consult with the original contractor or supplier when adjusting losses involving one of these systems.

Damage—Forced-air heating systems generally run for years with little trouble. Normal maintenance includes periodically changing the filters, lubricating the bearings, and cleaning. Fire is the most common cause of loss to these systems. When the smoke is heavy, the furnace often draws it in through the return ducts. Heat exchangers can crack when cold water is sprayed on them during firefighting activities.

Furnace puff-back

The sudden ignition of unconsumed fuel in the furnace, resulting in a heavy soot being spread throughout the building.

Furnace puff-back is caused by the sudden ignition of unconsumed fuel. As a result, heavy soot can be spread throughout the house, especially if the house contains an oil-fired furnace. A cracked heat exchanger can also cause soot deposits, but less gradually than a puff-back.

Steam and hot water systems are more likely to break down simply because they are more complicated than forced-air systems and have more parts. The most common claims for these heating systems are for freezing, which can crack radiators and boilers. These losses can be extensive because of the resulting water damage. Pressure tests are required to determine the extent of damage.

Claims for losses related to air conditioning are most often associated with the compressor, a hard-working unit subject to heavy wear. Lightning and power surge are the most typical causes of air conditioning failure. Adjusters should have experts check these units before committing to coverage.

Insulation

Insulation is found in exterior walls, floors, and ceilings. It is designed to be a poor conductor of heat. It can also be used as a sound barrier, so it is used around family rooms and bathrooms.

Insulation is rated by its thermal resistance. This rating is called an R-value. The higher the value, the greater and the better the insulating properties. The insulation may have a moisture barrier on one side, or it may not, depending on its intended use. Insulation's type and size depend on where in the structure it will be used and what the climate is in that particular building location.

Insulation can be purchased in batts or blankets. Batts come in two widths, 15 or 23 inches wide, to fit between joists and studs. They are usually 48 or 96 inches long. Blankets can be 24 feet to 40 feet long. Both blankets and batts are used to insulate finished attic floors, attic rafters, the underside of floors, and open sidewalls. Foam insulation is used to insulate finished walls or places with limited access. Rigid board insulation is used to insulate exterior wall sheathing and basement masonry walls. There is also loose fill insulation, which can be blown in or poured in. Loose fill is usually used in finished attic floors and framed walls.

Insulation can be made from many different materials. Fiberglass has been popular for many years and is now sold in an encapsulated form so that its fibers are prevented from becoming airborne.

Homes built before the 1960s usually contain mineral wool insulation. Mineral wool is made from natural stone or iron ore blast furnace slag. It is more water-resistant than fiberglass, provides better soundproofing, and can withstand higher temperatures. The disadvantage of mineral wool is that it uses density to boost its R-value; therefore, it is heavier than fiberglass and tends to be more expensive.

Rigid board insulation can be made from styrofoam or polystyrene. It is made in 4' × 8' sheets and is easy to install over interior walls or masonry surfaces. Rigid board is very susceptible to fire and can produce a toxic gas when burned.

Foam insulation is usually spray polyurethane. It can be obtained in aerosol cans that are good for sealing cracks around windows, doors, and fixtures. It is also blown in from trucks when large quantities are needed.

Insulation is susceptible to damage from fire, water, and smoke. Usually it cannot be dried or cleaned. Once it is damaged, it should be replaced.

Batt and blanket insulation are estimated using square footage of the area to be covered. It is precut to fit inside wall studs and joists, so a carpenter can easily install it. Rigid board also uses square footage of the wall area and is easily installed by one person. A subcontractor usually handles foam and blown-in insulation. The material is estimated by the square foot of the area.[10]

SUMMARY

This section provided construction basics along with estimating techniques for various types of losses affecting residences. Concrete foundations are the starting point for most residential construction. Frame carpentry is the work that a carpenter does in erecting the skeleton of the house. It includes the exterior and interior walls, the ceilings, the floors, and the roof. Various causes can damage the frame of a house, including fire, smoke, windstorm, water, vandalism, earthquake, and vehicle impact.

Finish carpentry describes the work done to install the top layer of the floor and the moldings around the rooms and openings. It also includes the installation of cabinets and countertops in the kitchen.

The amount of materials needed for a roof is estimated using the area of the roof. The area will differ depending on the roof's size and shape. The labor needed to install the roof can increase based on the roof's shape and pitch.

Various interior finishes are found in homes. Painting and wallpapering both use the area of the walls and ceilings to estimate the amount of labor and materials needed for a job. Unit costs can be developed for these elements and are time saving on large jobs.

The exterior finishes discussed in this section include the various types of siding and masonry products available to finish the walls of a home.

The gross area and the net area methods of estimating painting are based on the time and materials method. The gross area method does not deduct openings totaling less than 100 square feet from the room's total wall area.

Most of the steps in the net area method of paint estimating are the same as the corresponding steps of the gross area method. The only difference between the two is that the net area method deducts the true size of all openings from the total actual area.

The mechanical systems discussed in this section include the electrical system, the plumbing system, and the heating and air conditioning systems.

Electrical systems have become complicated and difficult to repair because of the wiring that is now needed to support the various technologies in many homes. The plumbing system is roughed-in during the framing of the house. Later, the fixtures and appliances are installed. The same is true for the cooling system.

ASSIGNMENT NOTES

1. Paul I. Thomas, How to Estimate Building Losses and Construction Costs, 4th ed. (Englewood Cliffs, N.J.: Prentice-Hall, Inc., 1983), pp. 134–155.

2. Adjuster Handbook: Estimating Small Dwelling Losses (Denver: General Adjustment Bureau, 1972).

3. Basic Carpentry Illustrated (Menlo Park, Calif.: Sunset Books, Lane Publishing Co., 1984), p. 35.

4. Paul I. Thomas, p. 234.

5. Basic Carpentry Illustrated, p. 59.

6. Paul I. Thomas, pp. 311–312.

7. "Ground Fault Interrupter," PDR, No. 467 (Chambersburg, Pa.: National Property & Claims Research Services, Inc., Nov. 1989).

8. "Wire, Wire Uses," PDR, No. 468 (Chambersburg, Pa.: National Property & Claims Research Services, Inc., Nov. 1989).

9. "Structured Wiring and Home Automation," PDR, No. 547 (Chambersburg, Pa.: National Property & Claims Research Services, Inc., March 2002).

10. "Insulation and Moisture Control," PDR, No. 521 (Chambersburg, Pa.: National Property & Claims Research Services, Inc., Nov. 1997).

Segment C

Direct Your Learning ▶▶

9

Merchandise Losses

Educational Objectives

After learning the content of this assignment, you should be able to:

▷ Distinguish between the coverage provided by the Building and Personal Property Coverage Form (BPP) and the Business Owners Policy (BOP) for merchandise and the insurable interest requirements of the BPP and the BOP for merchandise.

▷ Explain how replacement cost and actual cash value are determined for merchandise.

▷ Describe the information contained in a business's books and records and financial statements.

▷ Given a case, calculate the cost of goods sold by a business during a given time period.

▷ Given a case, calculate the book value of remaining inventory on a date of loss using books and records.

▷ Describe a salvor's services, and explain the operation of salvage contracts.

▷ Given a case, calculate settlements involving salvage proceeds.

▷ Explain a reporting form policy's purpose and operation; explain how reporting form policies treat underreporting and late reporting; and, given a claim involving reporting form coverage, calculate a loss:

- With proper reporting and no specific insurance

- With proper reporting and specific insurance applicable

- With underreported values and no specific insurance

- With underreported values and specific insurance applicable

▷ Explain what procedures an adjuster should follow and what information the adjuster should gather in the adjustment of loss to a large quantity of merchandise and loss to a small quantity of merchandise, and explain why percentage damage settlements of merchandise losses can be advantageous to both the insured and insurer.

Merchandise Losses

9

COVERAGE FOR MERCHANDISE LOSS

This section discusses the nature of losses sustained by a business when its stock or inventory is damaged. These merchandise losses present adjusters with different policy terms, definitions, conditions, and limitations. This section explains the basic coverage involved in claims for merchandise.

Merchandise, also called "goods" or "stock," includes manufactured and processed goods as well as goods held by merchants for sale and is found in many different locations and conditions. Any piece of merchandise begins as raw material or a combination of raw materials in a manufacturing or processing plant, progresses through the manufacturing operation as goods in process and emerges as finished goods. The terms "raw materials," "work in process," and "finished goods" are found in various commercial policies.

Some finished goods become part of another manufacturing process. An example is in the garment industry. Ribbed knit cuffs are manufactured by a supplier then shipped to another manufacturer that stitches them onto a sweatshirt. Other finished goods are sent in transit to the premises of the manufacturer's customers, such as distributors or retailers. Separate policy provisions can cover merchandise in each stage: during manufacture, in transit, and at the retail level. This section addresses merchandise claims in this last stage.

Damageability of Merchandise

In a retail establishment, merchandise is damaged most often by fire, smoke, water, firefighters' actions, flood, sprinkler leakage, leaking roofs, collapse, or windstorm. Merchandise can also be stolen. Damage to merchandise can be either total or partial. A total loss does not necessarily mean destruction. Merchandise can be damaged to the extent that it cannot be sold by the insured and is therefore treated as a total loss in the adjustment even though it has some remaining salvage value.

Smoke, heat, water, or odor can inflict partial damage. Many items in a retail establishment are packaged in such a way that smoke or water does not penetrate to the merchandise itself. In this case, a cleaning allowance is an appropriate settlement of the claim. **Hard goods**, such as glass, metal, and china, can often be cleaned after exposure to smoke or water. **Soft goods**, such as apparel, linens, and other items made of fabric, however, are not truly restored by cleaning. Because the insured is in the business of selling new

Hard goods

Merchandise made principally from glass, metal, and china, which can be cleaned after exposure to smoke or water.

Soft goods

Merchandise made principally from textile and fabric, which is not truly restored by cleaning.

merchandise, not cleaned or laundered merchandise, adjusters must work with insureds to adjust losses involving goods that cannot be cleaned appropriately. In adjusting a merchandise loss, the adjuster considers coverage, insurable interest, and valuation issues.

Coverage for Merchandise Losses

Adjusters encounter merchandise claims for retail goods under two general types of commercial property policies:

- The Building and Personal Property Coverage Form (BPP)
- The Business Owners Policy (BOP)

The BPP

The BPP extends coverage for personal property to "furniture and fixtures; machinery and equipment; stock; meaning merchandise held in storage or for sale . . . and supplies used in packing or shipping."[1] Coverage is for direct physical loss unless excluded or on a specified-perils basis. Stock valuation is typically at actual cash value, but the policy can be modified to provide replacement cost coverage. For stock the merchant has sold but not delivered, the BPP provides reimbursement of "selling price less discounts and expenses you otherwise would have had."[2] Coverage on personal property of others is included, but with strict limitations. A coinsurance clause usually applies.

The BOP

Stock coverage under the BOP is similar to the coverage in the BPP. Although the BOP definition of "business personal property" is not as detailed as the BPP's definition, it extends to all likely exposures, including owned property, property of others, and improvements and betterments. Two kinds of BOPs are available. See the exhibit "BOP Policies."

BOP Policies

- Standard BOP: covers specified perils and values stock at replacement cost
- Special BOP: provides coverage for direct physical loss unless excluded and also values stock at replacement cost

---

[DA04109]

All BOPs incorporate a seasonal automatic increase clause, which automatically increases business personal property coverage by 25 percent, providing for seasonal variations. This seasonal increase is effective only if insureds carry insurance equal to at least 100 percent of their average monthly value during the twelve months preceding a loss. BOPs do not contain a coinsurance clause.

Coverage Review

On any mercantile claim, the adjuster must review the applicable policy thoroughly. The adjuster cannot rely on coverage information recalled from previous claims. Policies can differ in many ways, including such areas as a coinsurance clause, the coinsurance percentage, the deductible, and other differences. An adjuster handling numerous homeowners claims might eventually memorize general coverage provisions, but adjusters cannot memorize the many variations in commercial policies.

Insurable Interest

Commercial property policies' intent is to cover only the named insured's interest in the property. The BPP states that its coverage extends to "your business personal property."[3] The BOP covers business personal property owned by the insured. Both the BPP and the BOP contain identical language: "We will not pay you more than your financial interest in the Covered Property."[4]

Certain property not owned by the insured is automatically covered under commercial property policies. The BPP describes this property as personal property of others in the insured's care, custody, or control and located in or on the described building. The BOP is more explicit, describing the covered property of others as property held by the insured and belonging to others, but not exceeding the amount for which the insured is legally liable, including the labor value, materials, and charges furnished, performed, or incurred by the insured. The property coverage of others in the BPP differs from that in the BOP. Under the BPP, coverage exists regardless of the insured's legal liability for the damage. For example, if an event entirely out of the insured's control destroyed the insured's property as well as property of others, the insured would not be legally liable to the other owners, but the BPP would cover such losses. The BOP would not. Despite these policies' different wording, their coverage is similar with respect to the types of property to which coverage extends. Merchandise such as layaways and items in the insured's custody for alterations or repairs is covered.

In adjusting a retail store loss, the adjuster must separate the claim from any merchandise not owned by the insured, such as merchandise in leased departments. In larger stores, this merchandise usually includes jewelry, cameras, and shoes. In smaller stores, items such as sales displays of hosiery and watches are generally not the property of the insured merchant, although the insured might be responsible for them under contract. If the insured claims legal responsibility, the adjuster should examine the contract between the insured and the manufacturer or distributor.

REPLACEMENT COST, ACTUAL CASH VALUE, AND SELLING PRICE OF MERCHANDISE

This section discusses the nature of losses sustained by a business when its stock or inventory is damaged. These merchandise losses present adjusters with different policy terms, definitions, conditions, and limitations. This section explains the basic methods of determining value and damage involved in claims for merchandise.

Commercial property policies normally insure retail merchandise for replacement cost or actual cash value (ACV). A policy might also base valuation on the selling price.

Replacement Cost

Replacement cost for merchandise is the insured's cost to buy stock from its suppliers, less any trade discounts or allowances, plus incoming freight. It can also include the cost of receiving, opening, tagging, marking, and arranging the goods in the insured's premises by the supplier. These additional costs reflect the different (usually greater) value that the merchandise has on the merchant's premises ready for sale to the public as compared to the value it has in the supplier's warehouse or factory. Determining replacement cost is not difficult if the adjuster has access to the insured's books and to records such as invoices.

Freight

Incoming freight charges

The amount that the insured pays to have goods shipped to the insured's premises from a supplier.

Incoming freight charges are the amounts that insureds pay to have goods shipped to their premises from suppliers. Any freight paid by the insured's suppliers is not counted.

Trade Discounts and Allowances

Trade discounts and allowances

Reductions from the stated purchase price, given by the supplier, for such reasons as purchasing in bulk or paying in a timely manner.

Trade discounts and allowances are stated purchase price reductions that suppliers grant the insured for purchasing in volume or for paying in a timely manner. Discounts and allowances represent reductions in the effective price paid by the insured for its merchandise, and they reduce the cost value of the insured's inventory. For example, 2 percent may be deducted from the price if the invoice is paid within ten days.

Handling Costs

There are two types of handling costs:

- Internal, which are the costs of the insured's own employees handling the items.
- External, which are the costs of a third party handling the item for the insured and adding a separate charge to the cost.

Handling costs incurred on the insured's premises are not always accounted for in the value of merchandise, but they represent a real cost and real value. These costs reflect the difference in value to the insured between goods on a receiving dock and those ready for sale to the public. **Internal handling costs** are not added to the cost of goods sold. If external handling costs are identified in the insured's accounting records, they can be included for adjustment purposes in the value of goods. Insureds, however, do not always want these costs counted. These costs increase the insured's stock value for settlement purposes but also increase it for coinsurance purposes. Higher value does not necessarily translate into a higher settlement if a coinsurance penalty is incurred. Handling costs should be treated the same for loss settlement and coinsurance purposes.

Internal handling costs

The insured's cost to have its own employees handle stock, such as pricing and arranging.

Actual Cash Value

Calculating merchandise's ACV is more difficult than calculating its replacement cost because no policy defines the term "actual cash value." ACV can equal replacement cost when there is no depreciation, markdown, or other loss of value. If so, determining ACV requires examining the insured's purchase records item by item in the same way that replacement cost is determined.

Depreciation Causes

Any retail stock of merchandise can suffer a reduction in value and selling price because of depreciation, even if it never leaves the merchant's premises. The possible causes of depreciation are innumerable, but the principal causes are physical damage and obsolescence. Careless handling, dust, fading, moisture or humidity, missing parts, infestation, excessive heat, freezing, and thawing can cause physical damage. The adjuster must inspect the goods to determine whether any physical damage to merchandise existed before the loss. Obsolescence means that an item has lost value because it is out of fashion, past its marked shelf life, a fad, or a seasonal item; because it shows evidence of slow turnover; or because it was offered in an incomplete size, color, or pattern range.

Market Value

In California, courts have ruled that ACV equals market value. The market is where the insured merchant obtains its stocks of merchandise. The insured is a buyer in the wholesale market. The insured's costs reflect the value of goods in this market, including incoming freight and handling costs, less trade discounts. Unless unusual circumstances are present, the insured's costs can be interpreted as an accurate reflection of market value in a given wholesale market. Any loss of value to the merchandise once it is on the insured's premises is not easy to detect. Goods are seldom resold on the wholesale market. The adjuster must judge whether goods on the insured's premises would sell as prime merchandise on the wholesale market. If not, some reduction in actual cash value is appropriate. Markdowns at retail strongly suggest that goods have lost value to the merchant and would likewise have less value at the wholesale level.

Markdowns

Most retail accounting systems operate on the premise that when the merchant reduces the selling price of a piece of merchandise because the item is not moving, is approaching the end of its season, or has become shop-worn, the item's original cost value automatically drops by the same percentage by which the merchant has reduced the selling price. For example, if an item's retail price is reduced 40 percent, from $100 to $60, then its cost value must likewise be reduced by 40 percent. If the original cost value was $50, it would drop (for ACV purposes) to $30 (40 percent less). Examples of this phenomenon are calendars and date books. These items rapidly lose value after January of every year. A retailer who suffers a loss in March would certainly have reduced the retail price of its remaining calendars and date books by then. In determining the ACV of that loss, the adjuster would value any damaged date books and calendars not according to their cost value when purchased, but on the basis of the marked-down price. Because these items are nearly worthless to the merchant in March, regardless of what was paid for them, their ACV would be extremely low. It is also possible to have circumstances that cause the retail value to drop, yet the wholesale value remains the same.

Adjusters should use the accounting method for determining value that mirrors the insured's accounting system of valuation. If the adjuster can show that he or she is using the same method as the insured's own accounting system for valuing merchandise, the argument for using such value determination would be strengthened. All retail merchants mark down merchandise at some time. If the insured's inventory system reveals that end-of-year inventory values are always devalued, then the merchant clearly subscribes to the retail method of accounting and inventory valuation. The **retail method of accounting** assumes a consistent profit percentage, so that goods marked down at retail also lose value as assets on the business's books. This system should be included in ACV determination.

An adjuster cannot automatically assume that all marked-down items have been reduced in price because of depreciation or obsolescence. Grocery markets commonly have weekly promotions during which certain popular items are marked down as loss leaders. At the end of the promotion, the unsold items are marked back up to their normal prices. This practice is also common in other retail establishments such as shoe stores, clothing stores, drugstores, and record stores. If a loss occurs during the promotion, the adjuster cannot realistically argue that an item only temporarily marked down for a sales promotion has actually been reduced in value and that its ACV should be reduced accordingly.

Retail method of accounting

An accounting procedure that assumes a consistent profit percentage so that goods marked down at retail also lose value as assets on the business's books.

Selling Price

Adjusters sometimes encounter policies that give merchants selling price coverage on their merchandise. The selling price is the tagged price on the merchandise at the time of the loss, whether it is the originally marked selling price or a marked-down price. Almost all value calculations begin with the selling price marked on each piece of merchandise at the time of the loss.

Layaways

Layaways are treated differently from merchandise held for sale. A layaway should be valued at the selling price, whether it has been completely paid for or not. Layaways are valued on the assumption that once the item has been put aside for a customer, the sale has been made, and a profit has been realized. This standard for layaway values must be used whenever total valuation of the insured's stock of merchandise is relevant, such as when a coinsurance clause applies. The insured's inventory figure ordinarily does not include layaways because they are considered to have been sold.

Universal Pricing Code

The universal pricing code (UPC) is the small box of bars of various widths appearing on an item of merchandise. As the item is scanned at a check-out counter, the UPC registers an electronic entry in inventory records and prints a price on the register tape. This method of checking out merchandise eliminates the need for a price tag on each item. It complicates the process of determining retail inventory values, however, because the absence of a price on each item makes verifying the price on the date of loss more difficult. The approach used in conducting a partial or total physical inventory with the UPC system must be different from the one used when each item is tagged with a price. Fortunately, computerized inventory systems using UPCs usually have detailed histories of retail price changes and physical inventory counts.

DETERMINING BOOK VALUE USING BUSINESS BOOKS, RECORDS, AND FINANCIAL STATEMENTS

Merchandise losses require the property loss adjuster to use the insured's books and records to ascertain the merchandise's value.

If merchandise has been partly or completely destroyed, its total value must be established. Merchandise has suffered a total loss if it has been destroyed, as by fire, or has been so badly damaged that the insured cannot be expected to try to sell it at a reduced price.

Merchandise damaged beyond recognition, called **out-of-sight merchandise**, poses a problem for adjusters because it cannot be inventoried or identified.

Out-of-sight merchandise
Merchandise that has been damaged beyond recognition.

One precaution that an adjuster should take when a loss involves out-of-sight merchandise is to determine by measurement that the quantity of merchandise claimed could have fit into the space in which it was supposed to have been stored or located. If a physical inventory is impractical because some merchandise has been destroyed or damaged beyond recognition, the only way to establish acceptable values is by using the insured's books and records.

Types of Financial Records

Income statement

The financial statement that reports an organization's profit or loss for a specific period by comparing the revenues generated with the expenses incurred to produce those revenues.

Balance sheet

The financial statement that reports the assets, liabilities, and owners' equity of an organization as of a specific date.

The fundamental financial records of any business are its **income statement** and its **balance sheet**. See the exhibit "Income Statement and Balance Sheet."

Income Statement and Balance Sheet

- The income statement is also called the profit and loss statement or earnings statement. It is an account of the operations of the business, from gross revenue to net profit before taxes, over a defined time period.

At a minimum, an income statement is prepared at the end of the insured's fiscal year. Income statements are commonly prepared monthly so that merchants have the opportunity to follow trends in the business. Year-end statements furnish adjusters with valuable reference material for handling property claims. They disclose the cost of goods sold and other merchandise-related costs that adjusters can use to value stock. They are also invaluable for handling attendant loss of earnings claims.

- A balance sheet provides values on a stated date of all assets, liabilities, and paid-in capital (also known as owner's equity). It is especially important for the property loss adjuster because it includes among the assets a physical inventory figure. A balance sheet is usually prepared only at the end of the fiscal year, and it furnishes an inventory figure for that date. This figure represents an actual physical inventory at values determined by the insured and the insured's accountant. To bring that inventory figure up to the date of loss, an adjuster must examine purchase and sales records since that physical inventory.

[DA04110]

Determining Book Value

The value of an inventory that is lost out-of-sight can be determined by using the information contained in most businesses' books and records. The basic method is straightforward. The inventory was accurately known the last time a physical count was made, usually at the end of the year or at the end of the business's fiscal year. Since then, the business has added to its inventory by making purchases from its suppliers. Suppose that a retailer selling men's suits had 500 suits in inventory on December 31 and purchased 900 suits between

December 31 and the date of loss. This retailer had a total of 1,400 (500 + 900) suits that it could have sold between December 31 and the date of loss.

The number of suits sold between December 31 and the date of loss is subtracted from the total number of suits that could have been sold. The remaining number is inventory unsold. In the example, suppose that 950 suits were sold between December 31 and the date of loss. The total remaining in inventory would be:

1,400 (500 + 900) (What could have been sold)

− 950 (What was sold)

450 (What remains in inventory)

This formula is useful when determining the amount of inventory that has been lost out-of-sight or damaged beyond recognition is necessary. The method for determining book value is summarized as:

Amount in last physical inventory

+   Amount added to inventory between last physical inventory and date of loss

=   Amount that could have been sold

−   Amount that was sold between last physical inventory and date of loss

=   Amount remaining in inventory on date of loss

The book value formula is presented in terms of the number of physical units. To determine inventory's true book value, dollar amounts must be used in the formula. All businesses maintain their accounting records in dollars; not all of them maintain records in physical units. The issue in claims adjusting is the dollar value of lost inventory; an insurer would not be obligated to replace 450 suits, but the insured value of those suits. If the insured value of the suits is $100 per suit, the book value of inventory would be calculated as:

	$50,000	(500 suits × $100 each)	(Value of beginning inventory)
+	90,000	(900 suits × $100 each)	(Value of additions to inventory)
=	$140,000	(1,400 suits × $100 each)	(Value of amount that could have been sold)
−	95,000	(950 suits × $100 each)	(Value of amount that was sold)
=	$45,000	(450 suits × $100 each)	(Value of amount remaining in inventory on date of loss)

In this analysis, the dollar figure for the amount of suits sold cannot be directly obtained from most businesses' records. Although all businesses can provide a dollar figure for the number of items sold, these sales figures are kept in terms of retail prices or values. To determine inventory's book value accurately, this amount must be reduced from the retail value to the business's cost of obtaining the suits. In this analysis, $100 is the cost to the suit retailer of obtaining suits from its suppliers. This cost must be used for two reasons:

- Sales figures and purchase figures are otherwise not comparable. Purchases to inventory worth $1,000 are not the same as retail sales of $1,000. Assume, for example, that the retail store actually sells the suits for $200. *Purchases* of $1,000 represents *ten suits*, but *sales* of $1,000 represents only *five suits*.

- Generally, the insured value of stock with a business is the cost to the business of replacing the stock, not its selling price.

DETERMINING COST OF GOODS SOLD

To determine inventory's book value accurately, the cost of goods sold must be used.

Cost of goods sold

An expense representing the cost of merchandise sold to customers during the period.

The historical relationship between the cost and the selling price of goods determines the **cost of goods sold**. This relationship is determined by examining a business's complete records for a year, or several years, in which no loss occurred.

Cost of Goods Sold Formula

The cost of goods sold during a year is determined using this formula:

> Beginning inventory
> + Additions to inventory
> = Amount that could have been sold during the year
> − End inventory (amount not sold during the year)
> = Cost of goods sold

Sample Calculation for Cost of Goods Sold

Assume that in the year *before* the loss, the suit retailer began with an inventory of $52,500 and made purchases to inventory of $110,000. The cost of goods sold for this retailer was:

> $52,500 (Beginning inventory)
> + 110,000 (Additions to inventory)
> = 162,500 (Amount available for sale)
> − 50,000 (End inventory on 12/31)
> = $112,500 (Cost of goods sold)

The $112,500 can be compared to the retail sales figure to determine the historical relationship between these two figures. If retail sales were $202,500, then retail sales are 1.8 times the cost of goods sold, because $202,500 ÷ $112,500 = 1.80. This represents an 80 percent markup, as when a business buys a suit for $100 and sells it to the public for $180. Markups by retail businesses can be any percentage.

Cost-to-Sales Ratio

In this example, the **cost-to-sales ratio** (cost of goods sold divided by retail sales) is approximately 56 percent ($112,500 ÷ $202,500). In the year of a loss, a business is not likely to have a figure for the cost of goods sold, and such a figure cannot be determined without an accurate ending inventory figure. When the inventory is lost out-of-sight, determining an accurate ending inventory figure is not possible. However, the business should know its historic cost-to-sales ratio and its retail sales figures for the year of the loss. The business should also know retail sales figures from the date of the last physical inventory to the date of loss. The cost-to-sales ratio multiplied by the retail sales figures is the cost of goods sold. For example, if retail sales were $84,000 and the cost-to-sales ratio is 60 percent, the cost of goods sold is $84,000 × 60 percent (or .60), which equals $50,400. The markup would be 67 percent ($84,000 ÷ $50,400 = 1.67).

Cost of sales

An income statement value that represents the cost to the company of merchandise sold or services provided during the year (the inventory at the beginning of the period adjusted for all purchases made during the period, less those goods on hand at the end of the period).

CALCULATING BOOK VALUE

When calculating book value, the adjuster must try to recreate the insured's records using information from the insured's accountant, bank statements, supplier records, and tax returns.

After a loss occurs, a business can provide its sales figures since its last physical inventory. The adjuster or an accountant working for the adjuster can determine the cost-to-sales ratio from historical data. These two figures (the sales since the last inventory and the cost-to-sales ratio) determine the cost of goods sold during the year of the loss. This cost of goods sold figure can be inserted into this formula:

> Beginning inventory
> + Additions to inventory
> = Amount that could have been sold
> − Cost of goods sold
> = Value of inventory remaining on date of loss

The inventory's value on the date of loss is the amount of the loss on which a settlement is based when the inventory is destroyed or lost out-of-sight. The Income Statement for Period 1/1/X1 Through 12/31/X1 exhibit uses an income statement to show the calculation of the cost of goods sold and the value of inventory on the date of loss. The Calculation of Book Inventory exhibit is a more elaborate example of the calculation of book inventory. See the exhibit "Income Statement for Period 1/1/X1 Through 12/31/X1."

Adjustment Difficulties With Book Inventory

The value of merchandise losses can in theory be determined from the insured's books and records, but practical difficulties can arise when adjusting a particular loss. These include the destruction of records, the phenomenon of shrinkage, and differences between perpetual and physical inventories.

Destruction of Records

The destruction of the insured's records at the time of the loss would make the adjuster's task difficult, but not impossible. If the insured has an outside accounting or bookkeeping service, year-end records will be available. If sales records have been destroyed, the adjuster could reconstruct sales history by referring to bank statements and to state sales-tax records. Purchase information can also be developed by referring to bank records and by requesting information from all known suppliers. Privacy laws may require the insured's permission to obtain this information. Tax returns are, in effect, profit and loss statements. They cover all salient points, including a total inventory figure. With the insured's permission, previous state and federal income tax returns can be obtained from the Internal Revenue Service (IRS) and the state tax department.

Shrinkage

Shrinkage

The reduction in stock on hand because of petty theft, breakage, unrecorded sales, and other mishaps.

The adjuster must also consider the phenomenon of **shrinkage**. All businesses suffer a reduction in stock on hand caused by petty theft, breakage, other mishaps, and unrecorded sales. This reduction, known as shrinkage, can be represented by a dollar figure. The total amount of shrinkage increases with the length of time that has passed since the last physical inventory. Shrinkage is not generally a large figure. The Calculation of Book Inventory exhibit shows shrinkage of about 1 percent. A deduction for estimated shrinkage could be included in the book value of inventory on hand, when it has been a regular pattern in past physical inventories.

Perpetual Inventories

Perpetual inventory

A method of continuously tracking inventory that may not have been reconciled to the actual physical inventory.

Insureds often present a **perpetual inventory** record. The insured might tell the adjuster that the perpetual inventory eliminates the need for all the accounting work of producing a book inventory or the time and effort involved in a physical inventory. The insured might be completely sincere in believing that the perpetual inventory record is accurate, but that sincerity does not guarantee its accuracy.

A perpetual inventory's accuracy depends on the accuracy and adequacy of the method of entering information into the inventory. This information

Income Statement for Period 1/1/X1 Through 12/31/X1

Good Times Merchandise Co., Inc.

Gross Sale		$240,000
Less:		
Returns and allowances	$ 2,500	
Discounts	2,800	
Bad debts	700	6,000
Net Sales		$234,000
Determination of Cost of Goods Sold		
Inventory 1/1/X1	$50,000	
Purchases	144,000	
Incoming freight	3,000	
	$197,000	
Less discounts received and returns	3,000	
Merchandise available for sale	$194,000	
Less ending inventory 12/31/X1	46,000	$148,000
Costs of Goods Sold	$148,000	
Gross Profit on Sales		
{36.75% of net sales, $234,000.00}	$86,000	$86,000
Expenses		
Payroll and taxes	$35,100	
Rent	18,000	
Advertising	2,000	
Utilities	6,000	
Supplies	2,000	
Telephone	1,000	
Depreciation	9,000	
Insurance	2,500	
Taxes and licenses	900	
Miscellaneous	500	$77,000
Net Income		$9,000

[DA04116]

Calculation of Book Inventory

Good Times Merchandise Co., Inc., Total Fire—12/20/X2

Last Physical Inventory 12/31/X1 From Income Statement		$ 46,000
Net Purchases		140,000
Available for Sale		$186,000
Less Cost of Goods Sold:		
Net sales, same period	$215,000	
Less gross profit % (36.75%) from income statement or tax return	79,012	135,987
Indicated Inventory 12/20/X2		$ 50,013

Note: Insured's perpetual inventory records indicate stock on hand as of 12/20 to be $50,500. Shrinkage for 51 weeks could account for the difference. The book inventory figure should prevail.

[DA04118]

consists of a record of each purchase of merchandise and a record of each sale of merchandise, at cost. Over time, errors of omission and commission occur, and normal shrinkage might not have been deducted. By the end of a fiscal year, a perpetual inventory figure is almost never equivalent to the results of the physical inventory taken on that date.

For this reason, adjusters should not depend on the accuracy of a perpetual inventory figure because a computer printout is only as accurate as the method of entering data into the computer. People enter this information, and people can make mistakes. If it is necessary to use a computer printout in a book inventory calculation, a certified public accountant (CPA) should test the accuracy of the insured's data-entry method.

SALVAGE

The salvor's role is to protect inventory, and, if necessary, sell damaged merchandise. The salvor should not assume or be asked to perform the adjuster's roles of determining coverage issues and settlement amounts.

Adjusters often use the services of an outside expert called a "salvor" on claims involving merchandise. Salvors are experts in preserving and realizing the value remaining in partially damaged merchandise. They are able to do this by preparing an inventory of the damaged items and then locating the best possible market for the goods.

Salvors' Services

If an adjuster anticipates that a salvage company will be needed, he or she should call the salvor in at the beginning of the adjustment process. A salvor can assist the adjuster in surveying the loss scene and can offer immediate advice on protecting remaining merchandise, minimizing further damage, and determining the feasibility of a physical inventory. A salvor can talk professionally with the insured about the insured's line of business. A salvor works with the insured's employees in separating damaged and undamaged goods, conducting a physical inventory, and checking invoices. A salvor can also offer the adjuster confidential and professional advice on merchandise's degree of damage.

Salvor's Role in Settlement

One of the most important decisions that an adjuster must make on a merchandise loss is the manner of settlement. The adjuster can choose to settle in any of these ways:

- Pay the insured the full value of the merchandise and take the salvage for the account of the insurer
- Sell the salvage on the account of the insured and pay the insured the difference between the salvage proceeds and the merchandise's insured value
- Agree with the insured on the merchandise's percentage of damage, paying the insured for that percentage of value and leaving the merchandise with the insured for disposal

The salvor can provide invaluable advice on the likely outcomes of these three choices. Even with the third option, in which the salvor does not sell the merchandise, the salvor's advice can be crucial.

Sale of Salvage

If the decision is made that the merchandise is salable, the salvor arranges a sale to dispose of the goods. This sale can occur at the insured's premises, or the salvor may take the goods to its own facility. The salvor can arrange for packing and shipping the merchandise or for an on-site, complete disposal of the merchandise in an "as-is, where-is" condition. A salvor knows the best people to contact if a sale is held and can ensure that the best possible price is obtained for the merchandise taken over by the insurer. The salvor is the adjuster's most important colleague in any sizable or complex merchandise claims adjusting.

In merchandise claims, certain types of damaged stock must be treated differently from ordinary stock. Examples are prescription drugs, for which there is practically no market, no matter how lightly they are damaged; alcoholic beverages, which can be disposed of only through licensed dealers; and highly perishable edibles, which should not be disposed of without the authority of local health and food inspectors. Salvors can assist adjusters in helping to realize some kind of return in disposing of these types of merchandise.

When necessary, the salvor must communicate with a health and food inspector. The salvor has the expertise to discuss in a professional manner the possible disposition of damaged edibles. For example, almost all granulated sugar can be re-refined at a reasonable cost, regardless of how it has been damaged. Contaminated salt and items not fit for human consumption but acceptable as animal feed also have markets. Salvors know of markets for merchandise of all kinds.

The Adjuster's Role

All insurers have a list of approved experts of all kinds, including salvors. An independent adjuster should not choose a salvor without first consulting the insurer, preferably by telephone. Staff adjusters should refer to their employer's list of recommended experts when choosing a salvor.

An adjuster who has engaged a salvor's services should not expect the salvor to substitute as an adjuster. The salvor should not argue any point with the insured. Professional salvors do not intercede in any dispute between the adjuster and the insured or the insured's representative. The adjuster must maintain control of the adjustment process and should not rely on others to negotiate with the insured.

Acting Without Salvor Assistance

Adjusters must be able to make on-the-spot field decisions during the adjusting of a merchandise loss. When certain types of merchandise become wet, they must be dried out to prevent mildew or staining damage. In such a case, an adjuster must work immediately with the insured to arrest the moisture damage. If an adjuster waits and submits a report asking for instructions, the merchandise affected by water might become worthless. Adjusters should realize when field decisions must be made and when the insurer must be consulted for instructions.

Salvage Contracts

Damaged merchandise is still owned by the insured and cannot be taken without permission. Salvors operate in a professional and legal manner and do not remove merchandise from an insured's premises until the insurer and the insured have signed a proper contract. See the exhibit "Agreement for the Removal of Stock."

Salvage Fees

The salvor's fees and commissions come out of the sale proceeds. The settlement with the insured is based on *net* proceeds. The salvor's fees and commissions become part of the loss indemnified by the insurer.

Agreement for the Removal of Stock

XYZ COMPANY

AGREEMENT FOR THE REMOVAL OF STOCK
FOR BETTER PROTECTION AND DISPOSITION

Insured: _____   Stock: _____

Insurance Company: _____   Location of Stock: _____

Date of Loss: _____   Stock No.: _____

BACKGROUND:

The Stock may have been damaged by fire, smoke, or other casualty, and it is to the benefit of all who may have an interest in the Stock that the Stock be handled with as little delay as possible and without waiting to determine the respective interests, rights, or liabilities under policies purporting to insure the Stock.

AGREEMENT:

1. XYZ Company ("XYZ") is hereby retained to take possession of the Stock and to place the Stock in the best possible order for sale and to sell the Stock in the interest of whom it may concern. The proceeds of any sale of the Stock, less XYZ's commissions and expenses, as set forth below, will be held by XYZ in trust until the loss is adjusted and will then be turned over to such party(ies) as may be entitled to receive those proceeds.

2. As compensation for its services, XYZ will receive an amount equal to (a)_____% of the gross proceeds of any sale of the Stock, plus (b) all costs and expenses (including labor costs) incurred by XYZ in connection with the removal, handling, maintenance, and sale of the Stock. XYZ may retain such amount from the gross proceeds of any sale of the Stock.

3. If XYZ at any time determines that the cost of the removal, handling, and maintenance of the Stock exceeds the estimated salvage value of the Stock (less XYZ's expenses and commissions, as set forth above), the responsibility of XYZ for continued custody of the Stock may be terminated.

4. The Insurance Company and the Insured will hold XYZ harmless from and against any claim made by any person or entity, other than the Insurance Company or the Insured, who or which may claim an interest in the Stock.

5. This Agreement is the entire agreement between the parties hereto and may only be changed in writing.

Date: _____, 20XX

XYZ COMPANY   INSURANCE COMPANY

By: _____   By: _____

    Its: _____   Its: _____

                                                  INSURED

                                                  By: _____

                                                      Its: _____

[DA04119]

Insured's Liability to Salvor

The insured is never directly liable for the salvor's fees, except possibly in one circumstance. The insured might want to use the salvor to separate, inventory, and protect the merchandise even though the insured ultimately retains the goods. This might happen when the insured's premises are in a physical condition that threatens the merchandise. Ordinarily, in this situation the policy covers the reasonable cost of removal for protection. An adjuster might disagree with the need for removal and might resist approving the expense. Because the insured owns the property, the insured is free to contract directly with the salvor. Although the insured would undoubtedly submit the salvage fees as part of its claim, the insured would bear the initial liability to the salvor. This situation is undesirable and should be avoided if possible. The salvor's expert advice should be sought to resolve any dispute between the adjuster and the insured over whether property should be removed. If the salvor believes it should be removed, the adjuster should approve the expense. If the salvor thinks that the property is safe on the insured's premises, the insurer bears the risk of the salvor's being wrong.

Sale Before Settlement

When goods must be sold quickly, as in the case of perishables, the adjuster and the insured do not have to settle the claim before the salvor can take over the goods. As long as the adjuster and insured agree that the goods must be sold, they can execute a contract to that effect with the salvor. The salvor will sell the goods on account of whom it may concern.

METHODS OF ACCOUNTING FOR SALVAGE PROCEEDS

Adjusters must be scrupulous in accounting for salvage sale proceeds.

Various ways of accounting for salvage proceeds are described in this section. The adjuster should be familiar with the law in the jurisdiction of the claim because the insured may be entitled to first-dollar recovery on salvage regardless of coinsurance.

Sale on Account of Insurer

The adjuster and insured agree on the merchandise's full insured value. The insurer pays the insured this full amount and takes the salvage for its own account:

Agreed full value of stock	$100,000
Insurer pays insured	$100,000
Net proceeds from salvage sale paid to insurer	$35,000
Insurer's net payment	$65,000

Sale on Account of Insured

The salvage sale is used to determine amount of loss:

Agreed full value of stock	$100,000
Net proceeds from salvage sale paid to insured	$35,000
Therefore, insurer pays insured	$65,000
Total payments to insured from salvage and insurance	$100,000

Sale on Account of Whom It May Concern

The salvage sale is made before agreement on the value of stock:

Net proceeds from salvage sale held by salvor pending agreement	$35,000
Agreed full value of stock	$100,000
Net proceeds paid to insured	$35,000
Insurer pays insured	$65,000

Sale in Which Insured Coinsures

If the insured has inadequate limits of coverage and is required to bear a coinsurance penalty, the insured will share in the net proceeds of the salvage sale in the same percentage as the loss. Assume a 25 percent coinsurance penalty:

Agreed full value of stock	$100,000
In light of coinsurance, insurer would pay no more than	$75,000
In light of coinsurance, insured might have to bear up to	$25,000
Net proceeds of salvage sale	$35,000
Shared 75 percent with insurer	$26,250
Shared 25 percent with insured	$8,750
Insurer's net payment ($75,000 − $26,250)	$48,750
Insured's net loss ($25,000 − $8,750)	$16,250

However, some jurisdictions mandate that the insured be made whole irre-spective of the coinsurance provision.

REPORTING FORM POLICIES

Reporting form

A form to periodically report fluctuating property values to an insurer.

A **reporting form** is a type of coverage for merchandise associated with risks in which the value of covered merchandise fluctuates by season or by month. A reporting form is used for such risks because it is designed to respond to what can be extreme fluctuations in merchandise's value.

Reporting form coverage is offered as an endorsement to a commercial policy. It affects the policy only by the method of determining compliance with policy conditions, such as the coinsurance clause. The Insurance Services Office, Inc. (ISO) Value Reporting Form is an example of a reporting form coverage. A reporting form can cover one or many locations and even covers property at newly acquired and incidental locations. The form incorporates a declarations page, which describes all locations at which coverage is to be provided and also establishes different limits at different locations.

A reporting form is designed to provide maximum dollar coverage when it is needed. For a merchant with a seasonal business, carrying commercial insur-ance throughout the year with a coinsurance clause based on the maximum possible value on hand at peak season would be very expensive. With report-ing form insurance, merchants can obtain coverage equal to full value, or the face amount of the policy, no matter how much the inventory fluctuates.

Operation of Reporting Forms

Reporting form coverage has certain conditions. First, a provisional amount of insurance is designated when the policy is written. This provisional amount becomes the maximum limit of liability and is also used for initial premium calculations. When reporting form insurance is in effect, the insured must report total values on hand at each of the designated reporting times during the policy's term. The insured must report the property as it is to be valued in the policy: selling price, replacement cost, or actual cash value. The reporting period is usually on a monthly basis, but it can be on a quarterly or semian-nual basis. The value report must be submitted to the company through the producer within thirty days of the end of any designated reporting period. Any submitted report is binding upon the insured and cannot be changed or corrected after a loss has occurred.

Full reporting clause

A clause that states that if the last report of values is less than the full value of the covered property at the time of the loss, then the insured participates in the loss in much the same manner as in coinsurance.

Reporting Full Values

The reporting form accomplishes its purpose by replacing the coinsurance clause with what is called a **full reporting clause**. Although the intent of reporting form coverage is for an insured to report full value at every insured location within thirty days of the designated reporting date, the form does not explicitly require the full value to be reported. Instead, the full reporting clause allows the insured to coinsure the losses when values have been under-reported. The full reporting clause replaces the coinsurance clause with:

COINSURANCE

a. If your report of values for a location where loss or damage occurs for the last "reporting period" before loss or damage, shows less than the full value of the Covered Property at that location on the report dates, we will pay only a proportion of loss. The proportion of loss payable, prior to application of the deductible, will not be greater than the proportion determined by:

(1) The values you reported for the location where the loss or damage occurred, divided by

(2) The value of the Covered Property at that location on the report dates.[5]

An adjuster should not regard an insured who has underreported values as willfully dishonest. Some insureds deliberately underreport by a certain amount, acknowledging that they will be in the position of a coinsurer in the event of a loss. The insured's premiums are reduced, and if no loss occurs during the policy term, a savings is realized.

Timeliness of Reports

Other restrictive conditions in the value reporting form address the insured's failure to submit reports on time. If an insured fails to make a report on a stipulated reporting date, thirty days after the end of the designated reporting period, the coverage at any insured location is limited to the amount of the last report made for that location, no matter how long before the date of loss it was made. If the insured is late in making a first report of value and a loss occurs before any report has been made, the coverage at any given location is limited to 75 percent of the amount that the insurer would have otherwise paid. That is not 75 percent of the amount of insurance shown for that location; it is 75 percent of what an adjusted claim would have been.

Specific Insurance

Another possible complication in adjusting a claim under a reporting form policy concerns the existence of what is referred to in the reporting form as **specific insurance**. Specific insurance is other insurance covering the same insured and at least some of the same property that the reporting form covers at the described location. The claim payable under the specific insurance, whether collectible or not, and after the deductible has been applied, must be calculated according to the terms of the specific insurance. The reporting form coverage applies to the balance of the claim. Specific insurance should be reported to the reporting form insurer along with each value report. This is often not done, so the adjuster must determine the existence of any specific insurance.

Specific insurance

Insurance that covers each building for a specific limit of insurance and personal property at each building for a specific limit of insurance.

Checking Reported Values

In adjusting a claim under reporting form coverage, an adjuster must check and verify certain values. The value of all stock on the date of loss is not important except for a total loss. The value figure that must be verified is the value of the stock on the date of the insured's last report of values. The adjuster should check these values against a copy of the last report received by the insurer or the producer. See the exhibit "Procedure for Determining Inventory Values for Last Report Date."

Procedure for Determining Inventory Values for Last Report Date

Date of Loss 10/1
Demonstration of Value Calculation for Last Reported Date
Under Reporting Form Policy

Last report of value, for 7/1	$173,000	
Last physical inventory as of 1/1		$160,000
Add net purchases—1/1 to 7/1		70,000
Available for sale		$230,000
Deduct net sales, at cost, same period		60,000
Indicated inventory 7/1		$170,000

Variation
Reverse Book Inventory Calculation

Complete physical inventory for 10/1 (Date of Loss)	$150,000
Deduct net purchases 10/1 back to 7/1	8,000
	$142,000
Add net sales, at cost, same period	28,000
Indicated value as of 7/1	$170,000

Both methods indicate that the insured fully reported values for the last report date, 7/1. The reported amount, $173,000, exceeds the actual amount.

[DA04125]

The adjuster must determine book inventory, perhaps with an accountant's assistance. A book inventory calculation can be worked either backward or forward. If establishing a precise total inventory value figure for the date of loss is possible, a reverse book inventory figure to a previous report date should be more accurate than one obtained by working forward from a past physical inventory figure, especially if the figure is from the distant past. The inventory's actual value on the date of the last report should be less than or equal to the value reported to avoid coinsurance. If the inventory's established value on the last report date exceeds the amount stated in the report, the insured must coinsure the loss. See the exhibit "Calculation of Book Inventory."

Calculation of Book Inventory

Good Times Merchandise Co., Inc., Total Fire—12/20/X2

Last Physical Inventory 12/31/X1 From Income Statement		$ 46,000
Net Purchases		140,000
Available for Sale		$186,000
Less Cost of Goods Sold:		
Net sales, same period	$215,000	
Less gross profit % (36.75%) from income statement or tax return	79,012	135,987
Indicated Inventory 12/20/X2		$ 50,013

Note: Insured's perpetual inventory records indicate stock on hand as of 12/20 to be $50,500. Shrinkage for 51 weeks could account for the difference. The book inventory figure should prevail.

[DA04118]

Often the reported value does not include items such as incoming freight, the cost of handling and tagging merchandise after its receipt, and trade discounts. These items should be included when they are identifiable in the insured's accounting records. The adjuster must ascertain whether the value that he or she calculated, as of the date of the last received report, is determined on the same basis as the value that the insured used in making the report. The calculation of value for claims purposes must be made on the same basis.

In calculating a book inventory figure, an adjuster must enter sales at cost, not at selling price. In some cases involving a claim under reporting form coverage, insureds have calculated value on hand on the date of each value report by taking the value figure from the previous report, adding purchases at cost, and subtracting sales at selling price. Because their policy had been in effect for several months, these insureds had been understating their values by an increasing amount with each report and would soon have been reporting no value at all had their mistake not been discovered.

Reporting forms might also cover furniture, fixtures, machines, and other personal property (even though their primary purpose is to cover stocks of merchandise). The reporting form is used to insure stock that might vary in total value each month. The insured is required to submit regular reports of values. The balance of nonstock items of personal property does not usually change much from month to month. Thus, the insured might overlook additions to personal property other than stock. The adjusters must carefully evaluate the nonstock portion of the values because new equipment purchased in the past few years might have been omitted from the monthly reports of values.

Value Reporting Form Examples

The exhibits show solutions to various problems arising under claims involving reporting form coverage, with and without specific insurance, in which values were either properly reported or underreported. In these illustrations, assume under the reporting form that:

- The limit indicated is either the original provisional amount of insurance or the amount of the last report of value received by the insurer before the date of loss.

- The insured is not delinquent in reporting.

Proper Reporting—No Specific Insurance

Bad Times Mercantile Co., Inc.
Date of Loss 10/1

Coverage: No specific insurance	
$175,000—Stock reporting form limit (provisional)	
Last report of value, for 7/31, new limit	$173,000
Actual value, 7/31	170,000
Agreed loss	26,000
Insured recovers entire loss subject to a deductible	$26,000

[DA04126]

Proper Reporting—Specific Insurance Applicable

Bad Times Mercantile Co., Inc.
Date of Loss 10/1

Coverage: $25,000 —Specific insurance on stock, 80% coinsurance
$175,000—Reporting form limit

Last report of value, for 7/31, to reporting form insurer

Total value, new limit	$173,000
Specific insurance	25,000
Actual value, 7/31	170,000
Actual value, 10/1	180,000
Agreed loss	26,000

Specific insurance pays: $\dfrac{\$25,000}{(80\% \times \$180,000)} \times \$26,000$	$4,514
Reporting form insurance pays balance of loss	21,486
Insured collects entire loss subject to deductibles	$26,000

[DA04127]

LOSS ADJUSTMENT

Adjusters should handle every merchandise loss with at least one visit to the insured's premises. On merchandise losses, the adjuster should not leave the determination of loss and damage to the insured. The adjuster should work with the insured to establish the facts of the loss and fair and accurate figures.

Adjusters should prepare a file and follow standard procedures for all large merchandise losses. Percentage damage settlements frequently arise with merchandise losses, and considerable negotiation might be required. Small losses do not require such elaborate procedures.

Preparation of File for Adjustment

To build an acceptable and reliable file, the adjuster must prepare to do everything in an orderly and complete manner. An adjuster should use a checklist, preferably a written one, beginning with the first visit to the insured's premises.

Values Underreported—No Specific Insurance

Bad Times Mercantile Co., Inc.
Date of Loss 10/1

Coverage: No specific insurance
$200,000—Reporting form limit

Last report of value, for 7/31	$150,000
Actual value, 7/31	170,000
Agreed loss	26,000
Deductible	250

Insurance pays:

$$\frac{\$150,000}{\$170,000} \times \$26,000$$

$22,941
−250 deductible
$22,691

Insured shares loss

$3,059
+250 deductible
$3,309

[DA04128]

Such a checklist includes at least these steps, not necessarily in order of importance:

1. Introduce and establish a satisfactory relationship with the insured. Gain an understanding of how the insured business operates.
2. Inspect the entire premises, including merchandise that is not involved.
3. Decide whether to use a salvor. If a salvor is to be used, the insured should be told because the salvor will probably arrive while the adjuster is not present.
4. Take photographs.
5. Inquire about the existence and availability of books and records and other insurance. Explain to the insured how he or she will have to document his or her loss through the use of books and records.
6. Identify the insured's independent accounting firm or bookkeeping firm. Obtain authorization from the insured so that the accounting firm can release financial information.
7. Discuss with the insured immediate steps to minimize damage, including board-up and general security.

Values Properly Reported—Existing Specific Insurance Not Reported

Bad Times Mercantile Co., Inc.
Date of Loss 10/1

Coverage: $25,000 —Specific insurance on stock, 80% coinsurance
$175,000 —Reporting form limit

Last report of values, for 7/31, no report of specific insurance	$173,000
Actual value, 7/31	170,000
Actual value, 10/1	180,000
Agreed loss	26,000

Although not reported, the existence of specific insurance is developed.	
Specific insurance pays	$ 4,514
Reporting form insurer pays	21,486
Insured collects entire loss subject to deductibles	$ 26,000

[DA04129]

8. Obtain the insured's explanation of the origin and cause of the loss. Inquire about whether a fire department investigator has already been to the scene.

9. Provide the insured with a general description of the normal procedure to follow during the adjustment process. Be specific as to what the insured must do and what the adjuster will do.

10. Be prepared to answer the insured's questions in a professional and cautious manner. Anticipate many questions.

11. Investigate thoroughly any possibilities of subrogation upon arrival at the scene of the loss. In many claims, the adjuster discovers that the damage resulted from equipment malfunction or from some third party's negligence. Evidence in proof of subrogation possibilities can disappear rapidly, especially if the person who furnished or installed equipment or the person whose negligent act caused the damage realizes the exposure to a possible subrogation action. The adjuster must determine by questioning both the insured and any possible investigative authority whether subrogation possibilities exist.

Values Underreported—Specific Insurance Applicable

Bad Times Mercantile Co., Inc.
Date of Loss 10/1

Coverage: $25,000 —Specific insurance on stock, 80% coinsurance
$175,000 —Reporting form limit

Last report of value, for 7/31	$150,000
Actual value, 7/31	170,000
Actual value, 10/1	180,000
Agreed loss	26,000
Specific insurance pays	$ 4,514

Reporting form insurer pays:

$$\frac{\$150,000}{\$170,000} \times \$21,486$$

	18,958
Insured collects less the deductible	$ 23,472
Insured shares loss	$ 2,528

[DA04130]

Large Losses

When damage to merchandise is severe and widespread but not total, the first visit by the adjuster involves inspecting the premises, taking photos, and guiding the insured, who has probably suffered his or her first major insured loss. On this visit, the adjuster must establish a rapport with the insured and develop mutual trust and confidence.

Preliminary Survey

The adjuster's inspection of the premises and the damaged merchandise should reveal whether a complete physical inventory is practical or even possible. Even when an appreciable amount of merchandise has been damaged beyond identification, a physical inventory of remaining merchandise can help provide an estimate of the out-of-sight loss (by subtracting the inventory of remaining merchandise from book inventory) as well as help provide information on pre-loss obsolescence or other loss of value.

The adjuster should use the first visit to gain a preliminary idea of the scope of damage and of the total value involved (perhaps a statement from the insured will suffice) and to assure the insured that he or she will be treated fairly and reasonably throughout the adjustment.

Discussions With the Insured

During the first visit with the insured, the adjuster must establish general procedures that will be followed during the entire adjustment process. The adjuster must notify the insured of the insured's duties in the event of loss as outlined in the policy. The adjuster should not, on the first visit, try to describe to the insured every aspect of an adjustment. The adjuster should also refrain from confusing the insured, who is probably already upset, with discussions of the coinsurance clause or other complex matters that can best be discussed during subsequent visits.

Also important during the adjuster's first visit is a thorough but courteous questioning of the insured about the conduct of the business before the loss. The insured knows more about his or her business than does the adjuster. By questioning the insured about marketing and merchandising methods, the adjuster can gain insight into how this particular business operates and can develop some ideas of how to prepare the claim file. Most insureds are eager to answer such questions and to demonstrate their own expertise regarding the business's conduct.

If a great deal of lightly damaged merchandise remains on the premises, during the first visit the adjuster should determine the insured's attitude about a fire sale after the adjustment is complete. The insured's answer to a question about a fire sale will guide the adjuster in deciding whether a salvor's services are necessary.

The adjuster should be prepared to answer questions that the insured is likely to ask concerning board-up and protection of the premises, expenses that must be incurred immediately to minimize damage, and possibly the use of a public adjuster. In larger cities, public adjusters often contact insureds after a serious fire, even before the insurer's adjuster arrives on the scene. An insured that has never heard of public adjusters might be confused. The insurer's adjuster should be prepared to politely answer questions about public adjusters' activities and reassure the insured that the claim will be properly adjusted.

Nonwaiver of Rights

During the first visit, the adjuster should exercise the insurer's right of access to all books and records of the insured's business. If an outside accountant possesses the records, the adjuster should get permission to contact the accountant directly to obtain the necessary information.

The adjuster should be cautious during this first visit not to make any commitments, such as these, that waive policy conditions:

* Giving permission to move merchandise before it has been inventoried
* Approving expenses that later prove not to be covered under the policy

- Approving expenses that, although possibly covered, might not be justified by the circumstances
- Making a decision on the property adjustment that might be prejudicial to adjusting the business income claim or that might inadvertently increase the business income claim

The insured's first impression of the adjuster is important. The adjuster should reflect an attitude of professionalism and competence and should proceed with authority and with prudence.

Percentage Damage Settlements

Merchandise damaged but still salable at the retail level is almost certainly worth more to the insured than to anyone else. If the insured is considering retaining the merchandise for a fire sale, the merchandise would only have to be moved within the store and repriced. Such expense would be much less than the cost of having an outside purchaser pack the merchandise, move it to another location possibly hundreds of miles away, unpack it, classify it, and reprice it. As an example, if a salvor estimates the net salvage return on merchandise after being taken over by the insurer to be 40 percent of cost, then the merchandise is likely to be worth more, perhaps between 50 and 60 percent of cost, to the merchant who retains it.

If, in the merchant's opinion, the stock has lost *at least* 40 percent of its value, the merchant could sell it for no more than 60 percent of its value. To the insurer, the stock has lost *no more* than 60 percent of its value. The insurer could reimburse the merchant 100 percent and take the stock for salvage. Because salvage is expected to yield 40 percent of value, it has suffered *no more* than a 60 percent loss. Settlement should be made at a loss figure between 40 percent (the least that the merchant would accept) and 60 percent (the most that the insurer would pay).

If both parties have accurately assessed the situation, any amount between 40 percent and 60 percent would be fair and advantageous to *both* parties. For example, assume a settlement at 50 percent. The insured receives 50 percent from the insurer and retains the stock, which the insured still believes has 60 percent of its value. The insurer would be satisfied to pay 50 percent because the only alternative would be to pay the insured 100 percent and take the stock as salvage, for a net loss of 60 percent. Sixty percent is the maximum, or break point, that an insurer should pay if the merchandise is left with the insured. Beyond 60 percent, the insurer would be better off paying the insured the merchandise's full value and taking the salvage for itself.

Use of Salvors in Percentage Damage Settlements

After a salvor is hired and has initially inspected the damaged merchandise, the adjuster and salvor meet. The salvor's advice should guide, but not control, the adjuster. The salvor offers opinions on the degree of damage and possible net salvage return and advises the adjuster on what the break point is likely to be.

If a large percentage of the insured's stock has been lightly or moderately damaged, the salvor might divide the stock into lots. The salvor can then assign a possible damage allowance percentage to each lot. Seldom is an entire stock subject to the same degree or percentage of damage.

Brands and Labels Clause

Certain policy conditions are sometimes added by endorsement, which makes merchandise's ultimate salvage value much less than might normally be expected. A brands and labels clause requires the manufacturer's label to be removed from all merchandise taken in salvage by the insurer. When the label is popular or prestigious, its removal certainly reduces the salvage's value to the insurer. The insured who keeps merchandise on a percentage-of-damage settlement need not remove labels. This increases the attraction of such settlements.

Negotiation

The adjuster's negotiation skills are especially important when adjusting serious merchandise damage claims. The adjuster's negotiating ability determines whether a satisfactory adjustment is possible. When the discussion focuses on damage allowances, the adjuster should inform the insured that a negotiated settlement of the damage allowance will be considered. During the process of negotiating an adjustment, the adjuster should maintain a confident but flexible attitude, depending on the insured's attitude. If the insured is inflexible about a percentage of damage allowance, the adjuster has the right to take over the damaged merchandise for salvage disposal. With the break point in mind, the adjuster will at some point realize that paying the insured the full insured value and taking the salvage for the insurer's account is less expensive than paying the percentage that the insured demands.

In negotiating a settlement for partial damage to merchandise, the adjuster is dealing in an area in which the insured is much more knowledgeable. The subject under discussion is the insured's own merchandise and the insured's ability as a merchandiser. The adjuster, in consultation with a salvor, should understand the goods' income potential if sold at a fire sale and should use this knowledge to bring the adjustment to a conclusion that is fair to both the insurer and the insured.

Small Losses

The preceding discussion outlined procedures and considerations for adjusters handling large, complicated merchandise claims. Most merchandise claims, however, are relatively small and uncomplicated. For such routine losses, following all of the preceding procedures can be contrary to the insured's and the insurer's interests. Adjusters should not overlook smaller merchandise claims. The adjuster should establish to the best of his or her ability, without bringing in outside salvors or accountants, the accurate measure of the insured's actual loss, and then apply policy conditions to readily conclude the matter.

SUMMARY

Merchandise includes goods or stock that is manufactured, processed, or held by a merchant for sale. A merchant's stock is insured under commercial property insurance policies whether the merchant owns the property or holds it in consignment. Adjusters encounter merchandise claims for retail goods under two general types of commercial property policies: the BPP and the BOP.

Merchandise can be valued at actual cash value or replacement cost. To determine value, adjusters must review records from the insured's suppliers and adjust the cost for freight, handling, and trade discounts. Settling losses to merchandise requires adjusters to follow procedures and make considerations not present in other claims.

An adjuster is not expected to have a professional accountant's expertise but must be able to follow financial records. Adjusters can use the information in the income statement and the balance sheet to reconstruct the value of an inventory destroyed or otherwise lost out-of-sight.

The value of inventory that was sold since the last physical count is determined by applying the cost-to-sales ratio to the retail value of sales. The retail value multiplied by this ratio provides the cost value of the items sold.

When calculating book value, the adjuster must try to recreate the insured's records using information from the insured's accountant, bank statements, supplier records, and tax returns. The value of merchandise losses can in theory be determined from the insured's books and records, but practical difficulties can arise when adjusting a particular loss.

Merchandise losses are the most frequent circumstances in which adjusters use professional salvors. Salvors perform a variety of services, including protection, removal, inventory, and sale of merchandise involved in a loss. Most important, salvors provide invaluable advice to adjusters on how a loss can be settled to everyone's satisfaction. Adjusters must be familiar with salvage operations and salvage contract provisions and must be scrupulous in accounting for salvage sale proceeds.

There are various ways of accounting for salvage sale proceeds. Adjusters must be scrupulous in accounting for salvage sale proceeds.

Reporting form policies sometimes apply to merchandise losses. These policies were designed so that merchants could adequately insure inventories that fluctuate widely in value. They require the merchant periodically to submit reports of value to the insurer. A merchant who complies with this requirement should have adequate insurance coverage for any merchandise loss.

When merchants are late with their reports or underreport inventory values, the merchant will coinsure the loss.

When negotiating merchandise losses, adjusters should have a clear understanding of:

- When to pay the insured a percentage of the inventory value for settlement and leave the damaged goods with the merchant for a fire sale.
- When the insurer would be better off to pay the merchant full value and to take the remaining stock for salvage sale.

Adjusters should also develop judgment about the degree of effort appropriate to settling small losses versus settling large losses.

ASSIGNMENT NOTES

1. Building and Personal Property Coverage Form CP 00 10 04 02, Copyright, Insurance Services Office, Inc., 2001.

2. Building and Personal Property Coverage Form CP 00 10 04 02, Copyright, Insurance Services Office, Inc., 2001.

3. Building and Personal Property Coverage Form CP 00 10 04 02, Copyright, Insurance Services Office, Inc., 2001.

4. Building and Personal Property Coverage Form CP 00 10 04 02, Copyright, Insurance Services Office, Inc., 2001.

5. Includes copyrighted material of Insurance Services Office, Inc. with its permission. Copyright, ISO Properties, Inc., 2001

Direct Your Learning ▶▶

10

Business Income Losses

Educational Objectives

After learning the content of this assignment, you should be able to:

▷ Explain the purpose of business income coverages.

▷ Explain the basics of accounting for organizations and how losses affect accounting statements.

▷ Explain the insuring agreement of the Business Income (and Extra Expense) Coverage Form (BIC) and explain the types of, and the extent of, extra expense coverage under the BIC policy.

▷ Given a loss, calculate the loss of business income.

▷ Explain how to determine the period of restoration.

▷ Explain the additional, optional, and extended coverages under the BIC.

▷ Explain the application of the coinsurance requirement or optional coverages instead of coinsurance for the BIC policy.

Business Income Losses

BUSINESS INCOME COVERAGES

Damage or destruction of tangible property might interfere with an organization's operations. That interference could cause loss of revenue or increased expenses. Businesses need to cover themselves against this eventuality.

With losses involving physical damage to, or destruction of, tangible property, adjusters normally indemnify insureds for the physical damage or destruction according to the terms of the insurance policy.

After an insured loss, and once the insured receives payment, he or she generally can repair or replace the property in question. Organizations, however, can suffer losses that go beyond tangible property's damage or destruction. For example, the damage or destruction of tangible property might interfere with an organization's operations. That interference could cause loss of revenue or increased expenses, both of which are harmful to organizations. Such losses of revenue or increased expenses, are called **business income losses** or **business interruption losses**. Property insurance policies did not originally cover these types of losses. However, coverage for loss of business income and increased expenses has become common in commercial policy forms. Loss of business income and increased expenses are also called **time element losses** because they occur over time. Because business income losses are purely financial losses, evaluating these losses involves examining business documents and financial records rather than inspecting tangible property.

BASIC ACCOUNTING FOR ORGANIZATIONS

To evaluate business income losses, property loss adjusters must understand basic accounting principles and the financial records of organizations that suffer direct physical losses.

Adjusters should be comfortable analyzing sales and expense figures as well as inventory records, production records, budgets, orders or contracts for products, and tax records. Simple losses can be efficiently evaluated with a basic spreadsheet program, but more complex losses may require the assistance of a **forensic accountant** who is experienced in evaluating business income losses and business records for insurance claim purposes. However, even if the adjuster will primarily rely on forensic accountants, he or she must understand fundamental concepts related to business income losses.

Business interruption

Loss of revenue that a business or another organization sustains because its operations are suspended as a result of physical injury to its property.

Business income loss

A financial loss that occurs when tangible commercial property is damaged or destroyed, resulting in a loss of revenue or increased expenses during the time that the property is being replaced or repaired.

Time element loss (indirect loss)

A loss that arises as a result of damage to property, other than the direct loss to the property.

Forensic accountant

An expert at evaluating business income losses.

The basic elements of accounting are essentially the same for all organizations, regardless of whether the organization is a for-profit business, a not-for-profit organization, a corporation, a partnership, a sole proprietorship, a large manufacturer, or a small retailer. The two basic financial statements for any organization are (1) the balance sheet and (2) the income statement.

Balance Sheet

An organization's balance sheet answers the question, "Where do we stand right now?" The balance sheet is a simultaneous listing of everything that the organization owns and everything that it owes at a particular moment in time. What it owns are called **assets**, and what it owes are called **liabilities**. See the exhibit "A Simple Balance Sheet."

Liabilities

Financial obligations, or debts, owed by a company to another entity, usually the policyholder in the case of an insurer.

Assets

Types of property, both tangible and intangible, owned by an entity.

A Simple Balance Sheet

ABC, Inc., Balance Sheet
December 31, XXX2

Assets		Liabilities	
Cash	$ 75,000	Accounts Payable	$ 50,000
Accounts Receivable	100,000	Bank Loan	150,000
Inventory	325,000	Mortgage	800,000
Plant and Equipment	1,500,000	Total	$1,000,000
Real Estate	1,000,000		
		Owner's Equity	$2,000,000
Total	$3,000,000		$3,000,000

[DA04131]

Owners' equity (net worth)

The balance sheet value that represents the difference between total assets and total liabilities as of the balance sheet date and that represents the value of the owners' interest in the business.

The difference between assets and liabilities in a for-profit business is called **owners' equity** or net worth. Owners' equity is shown on the liabilities side of the balance sheet because a business does not own its net worth. It "owes" its net worth to its owners. Owners' equity (net worth) is always the difference between assets and liabilities. Owners' equity is therefore calculated as:

$$\begin{array}{r} \text{Assets} \\ - \text{ Liabilities} \\ \hline \text{Owners' equity (net worth)} \end{array}$$

For example, the owners' equity for ABC, Inc., shown in the exhibit, is calculated as assets minus liabilities equals owner's equity ($3,000,000 –

$1,000,000 = $2,000,000). Owners' equity is negative whenever liabilities exceed assets. A business with negative owners' equity may be eligible for bankruptcy. Because of how owners' equity is calculated, the balance sheet always balances.

The Income Statement

An organization's income statement answers the question, "How did we do during a particular time period?" such as a year, month, or quarter. Whereas the balance sheet lists the organization's assets and liabilities at a given moment, the income statement describes the organization's experience over time. See the exhibit "A Simple Income Statement."

A Simple Income Statement

ABC, Inc., Income Statement
January 1, XXX2 to December 31, XXX2

Revenue From Gross Sales	$1,500,000
Cost of Goods Sold	700,000
Gross Profit	$ 800,000
Operating Expenses	
Employee Wages	$300,000
Depreciation	100,000
Interest	100,000
Utilities	50,00
Total Operating Expenses	$ 550,000
Net Income	$ 250,000

[DA04133]

Almost all organizations prepare annual income statements. Some organizations have a fiscal year different from the January-December calendar year. Their fiscal year is some other 365-day period of their choice. For example, a university or college might have a fiscal year of August 1 to July 31 that corresponds to the academic year.

This section is primarily concerned with a loss's financial consequences that affect the income statement. The important elements of the income statement are revenue and expenses. An organization's operations generate revenue, usually from sales, and incur expenses in creating such revenue. Normally revenue should exceed expenses. However, it is not unusual to find a business that shows minimal net profit annually. This is common in business structures that are closely held by an individual or a small group. The business may pay the owner a salary and may also pay operating expenses such as those for a company car, business travel expenses, and business entertainment expenses. Strictly speaking, if expenses consistently exceeded revenue, the organization would eventually run out of money and be forced to close. However, a business owner may continue and even support an operation that gathers minimal net income in some cases.

Revenue

The money generated by an organization's operations is its revenue. For a for-profit business, revenue usually comes from sales of its products or services. For a not-for-profit organization, revenue might come from dues, memberships, contributions, or sales. A business's revenue depends on the number of sales it makes and the prices it can charge, both of which are affected by competitive pressures.

Only money generated by the organization's *operations* is counted as revenue. Operations do not include the purchase or sale of major assets, investment activities, or other unrelated receipts and expenditures. So, for example, if a manufacturing business sold a piece of real estate, the money it received would not be part of its revenue. The proceeds from the real estate sale would appear on the manufacturer's balance sheet, but not on its income statement. The asset "real estate" would decrease from the previous balance sheet, and the asset "cash" would increase. Likewise, when a business settles an insurance claim, the money it receives from the insurer is not revenue. For accounting purposes, settlement of an insurance claim substitutes one asset, cash, for another asset, insurance claim receivable, on the business's balance sheet.

Expenses

Expense directly related to sales

An expense that increases or decreases in direct relationship to sales, such as cost of goods sold.

General operating expense

An expense that is necessary to run a business but bears no direct relationship to the volume of sales.

All organizations incur expenses in generating their revenue. The nature of these expenses depends on the organization's nature. For purposes of evaluating business income claims, every operating expense can be categorized either as a general operating expense or as an expense directly related to sales. An **expense directly related to sales** is one that increases or decreases in direct relationship to sales, such as the cost of goods sold, commissions, or the cost of the materials used to ship goods that have been sold. If there are no sales, these types of expenses are not incurred. A **general operating expense** is one that is necessary to run the business but bears no direct relationship to the volume of sales, such as a retail store's cost for heating or air conditioning. Whether sales are booming or nonexistent, the cost of heating or air conditioning is necessary each day. Understanding and recognizing this difference is important in evaluating coinsurance compliance and is useful in determining which expenses are likely to continue after a loss.

A key distinction among businesses is between those that sell services and those that sell goods. Professionals in service businesses, such as barbers, dry cleaners, insurance agents, physicians, and accountants, do not sell any significant tangible product. Thus, their businesses do not manufacture or purchase tangible goods for resale, and generally, their income statements do not show a specific cost of goods sold expense. But there are almost always some expenses directly related to sales even if they are not labeled as such (materials and supplies consumed, for example). Some businesses, such as auto repair shops, construction companies, and restaurants, sell significant goods in addition to services. These businesses incur some expense in acquiring the materials they resell. Other businesses, such as supermarkets, department stores, and manufacturers, are in business primarily to sell goods, and their income statements show a clear and substantial expense for cost of goods sold. These businesses have significant expenses for the cost to acquire or manufacture the goods that they sell.

Cost of Goods Sold—The cost of goods sold is an expense that deserves special note. Although the term "cost of goods sold" applies to any business, the type of business dictates the expenses that are included in it. In retail, the cost of goods sold is usually the business's cost to purchase its merchandise and shipping. In manufacturing, the cost of goods sold includes the cost of the materials to make the product, the labor involved, and the overhead to make the product. In a service business, the cost of goods sold is minimal because no physical product is being sold. Unlike most other operating expenses, the cost of goods sold corresponds directly to sales. Calculating cost of goods sold is an accounting method for appropriately recognizing as expense the cost of purchasing inventory. Inventory is an asset that appears on the balance sheet until it is sold. Directly showing the purchase of inventory as periodic lump sums to represent expense on the income statement would skew the income statement because the purchase of inventory and the resale of it are not perfectly timed. Businesses often stock up months in advance of a busy sales season and may not restock as their busy sales season nears an end. The cost of goods sold formula is a method of recognizing the expense of acquiring goods to sell and coordinating it directly with sales on the income statement. For this reason, the cost of goods sold expense that appears on the income statement is calculated according to this formula:

Beginning inventory

+ Additions to inventory
_____
= Amount that could have been sold

− Ending inventory
_____
= Cost of goods sold

If there are no sales, the ending inventory is equal to the sum of the beginning inventory plus all additions to inventory. Notice that under this formula there can only be a cost of goods sold if there has been a sale that lowers the ending inventory from the amount that could have been sold. Once an item of inventory is sold, its cost appears as an expense on the income statement by operation of the cost of goods sold formula.

Some small or simple businesses may list merchandise purchased as a general operating expense even though doing so is not strictly in keeping with generally accepted accounting principles (GAAP). If such a listing is found, the adjuster must account for the cost of goods sold according to the previously mentioned formula to properly evaluate the loss.

The adjuster should pay close attention to the inventory numbers in the cost of goods sold formula. The most likely sources of error in computing cost of goods sold are the beginning and ending inventory figures. Valuing an inventory in which goods have been added and withdrawn at various times and at various prices is complex. Accounting rules recognize several valid methods for valuing inventories under these circumstances. These methods are beyond the scope of this text, but adjusters must be sure that the same method was used to evaluate the beginning inventory and the ending inventory.

Gross profit

An income statement value that represents sales or operating revenue minus the cost of goods sold.

The difference between a business's revenue and its cost of goods sold is its **gross profit**. The A Simple Income Statement exhibit shows gross sales of $1,500,000, gross profit of $800,000, and net income of $250,000. Although the cost of goods sold is an expense, it is separated from the other expenses. This placement on the income statement of the cost of goods sold expense to arrive at the gross profit is sometimes referred to as the trading section of the income statement. Any item deducted from revenue to arrive at gross profit is said to be included in the trading section. This section has a relationship to expenses that is sometimes referred to as being placed "above the line" to arrive at a gross earnings value in computing a business income loss. This arrangement easily shows gross profit and is the starting point for the evaluation of continuing expenses and coinsurance.

Gross margin (gross profit margin)

The percentage of sales remaining after deducting the cost of goods sold from sales, calculated by dividing gross profit by sales.

Mark-up

Gross profit expressed as a percentage of cost of goods sold.

From gross profit, a business must cover all other operating expenses and try to earn net income. Gross profit expressed as a percentage of gross sales is sometimes called the **gross margin** ($800,000 ÷ $1,500,000 = 53%). Similarly, the gross profit expressed as a percentage of the cost of goods sold is sometimes called **mark-up** ($800,000 ÷ $700,000 = 114%). It could be said that the goods purchased by ABC, Inc., at wholesale are marked-up 114 percent for a retail price. It could also be said that 53 cents of every retail sales dollar is gross profit. Note, however, that the relationship between mark-up as calculated previously and the actual percentage that a business marks-up its merchandise is not exact because the income statement figures reflect discounts, returns, allowances, and similar items.

Similar to the treatment of revenues, not all money spent by a business is counted as operating expenses. Expenses must be incurred in the business's *ordinary operations* to be recorded as operating expenses. For example, if a manufacturing business bought a piece of real estate, the money spent on the purchase would not be an expense item on the manufacturer's income statement. The purchase would appear only on the manufacturer's balance sheet, as a reduction of one asset, cash, and an increase in another asset, real estate. The Effect of a $1 Million Mortgage Financed Real Estate Purchase on the Balance Sheet exhibit shows the effect on ABC's balance sheet of obtaining an additional mortgage to purchase a piece of real estate for $1 million (compare the Effect of a $1 Million Mortgage Financed Real Estate Purchase on the Balance Sheet exhibit to the A Simple Income Statement exhibit). See the exhibit "Effect of a $1 Million Mortgage Financed Real Estate Purchase on the Balance Sheet."

Effect of a $1 Million Mortgage Financed Real Estate Purchase on the Balance Sheet

ABC, Inc., Balance Sheet
After Receiving Mortgage but Before Real Estate Purchase

Assets		Liabilities	
Cash	$1,075,000	Accounts Payable	$ 50,000
Accounts Receivable	100,000	Bank Loan	150,000
Inventory	325,000	Mortgage	1,800,000
Plant and Equipment	1,500,000	Total	$2,000,000
Real Estate	1,000,000		
		Owners' Equity	$2,000,000
	$4,000,000		$4,000,000

ABC, Inc., Balance Sheet
After Real Estate Purchase

Assets		Liabilities	$ 50,000
Cash	$ 75,000	Accounts Payable	150,000
Accounts Receivable	100,000	Bank Loan	1,800,000
Invetory	325,000	Mortgage	$2,000,000
Plant and Equipment	1,500,000	Total	
Real Estate	2,000,000		$2,000,000
		Owners' Equity	$4,000,000
	$4,000,000		

[DA04135]

These large purchases of land, buildings, or equipment are called capital expenditures. These capital expenditures appear on the balance sheet but do not appear as one-time lump sums on the income statement. Although capital expenditures may seem to be simply very large operating expenses, showing such large expenditures as a one-time lump sum expense on an income statement would skew the income statement. Capital investments and expenditures are not operations. For this reason, capital expenditures appear on the income statement gradually over time, normally as a depreciation expense. A **depreciation expense** spreads out the expense of a large purchase over time and may be calculated based on the item's life expectancy or, more arbitrarily for accounting convenience, according to GAAP. Depreciation is a common operating expense. As an operating expense, depreciation also lowers the business's net income for tax purposes. The question of whether depreciation expenses continue after a loss depends on the nature of the depreciated item, method of depreciation, extent of damage to the item being depreciated, and the facts of the particular loss. This issue is fact-sensitive and is often hotly debated.

Depreciation expense

An accounting method that spreads out the expense of a purchase over the life expectancy of the item.

Net Income

The difference between all operating revenue and all operating expenses is called **net income**. Net income is often expressed using this formula:

Net income

The difference between revenues (such as money received for goods or services) and expenses (such as money paid for merchandise, rent, and insurance).

All operating revenue
− All operating expenses
─────────────────────
= Net income

Therefore, in the A Simple Income Statement exhibit, ABC's net income was computed as gross profit less total operating expenses ($800,000 – $550,000 = $250,000), which is all revenue less all expenses. The same result can be reached using the figures from the A Simple Income Statement exhibit and the previously mentioned formula. $1,500,000 – $700,000 – $550,000 = $250,000. Net income is colloquially known as the "bottom line" because net income appears as the bottom item in a listing of revenue and expenses.

Net income can be negative whenever expenses exceed revenue. Negative net income is known as a net loss. Positive net income for a for-profit business is often called net profit. The ability to earn net income is essential to a business's continuation. Anything that decreases revenue or increases expenses threatens a business's profit and its future.

For not-for-profit organizations, the difference between revenue and expenses might be called by a different name, such as "contribution to surplus" or "excess of revenue over expenses." Nevertheless, just like for-profit businesses, not-for-profit organizations must have revenue greater than expenses.

Net income is the most precise term to use for the difference between all revenue and all expenses. The adjuster should be careful not to confuse net income (all operating revenue less all operating expenses) with gross profit (all operating revenue less cost of goods sold). This section uses net income to mean the difference between all revenue and all expenses for all organizations, whether for-profit or not-for-profit.

What Happens to an Organization After a Loss?

All losses are troublesome, but some are so disruptive that they affect revenues, expenses, and net income. Therefore, organizations' risk managers recognize that insurance for direct physical losses alone might not be sufficient. Business income losses can threaten an organization's well-being as much as, or more than, direct physical losses. Adjusters who handle claims for business income losses must evaluate direct physical losses' effect on organizations' revenue, expenses, and net income.

Effects of Property Losses on the Balance Sheet

Direct damage to, or destruction of, physical property is the subject of most property insurance claims. For an organization, such losses affect the assets on the balance sheet.

An organization's typical assets include cash, inventory, machinery and equipment, and real estate and improvements. These are the items affected by insurance claims for direct losses. For example, suppose that an electronics merchant had $100,000 of electronic equipment stolen by burglars. Before the loss, the assets on the merchant's balance sheet included, "Inventory – $100,000." Immediately after the theft, the merchant's balance sheet would have to be adjusted to show "Inventory – $0," but it would include a new asset, "Insurance claim receivable – $100,000." Amounts that other persons or organizations owe to the merchant are *assets* to the merchant, including any amount that the merchant's insurer owes the merchant for a claim (this example ignores any deductible or possible problems with limits). After the claim is paid, the merchant's balance sheet would show "Insurance claim receivable – $0," but "cash" would increase by $100,000. See the exhibit "Loss Settlement for Theft of Merchandise."

An insured loss to a building would be accounted for in a similar way. Ignoring any possible coverage problems or limitations, insurance claims convert other types of assets on the balance sheet into cash. Thus, typical insurance claims for direct physical losses affect only an organization's balance sheet. However, physical damage or destruction of property can affect an organization's income statement if it disrupts the organization sufficiently to cause a decrease in revenue, an increase in expenses, or both. An adjuster can evaluate business income losses only by examining an organization's financial records.

Loss Settlement for Theft of Merchandise

Loss Settlement for $100,000 Theft of Merchandise

Before Loss

Assets		Liabilities	
Cash	$ 50,000	Accounts Payable	$ 75,000
Accounts Receivable	50,000	Bank Loan	50,000
Inventory	100,000	Mortgage	200,000
Building	500,000	Total	$325,000
		Owners' Equity	$375,000
	$700,00		$700,000

Immediately After Loss

Assets		Liabilities	
Cash	$ 50,000	Accounts Payable	$ 75,000
Accounts Receivable	50,000	Bank Loan	50,000
Inventory	0	Mortgage	200,000
Insurance Claim Receivable	100,000	Total	$325,000
Building	500,000		
		Owners' Equity	$375,000
	$700,000		$700,000

Immediately After Claim Settlement

Assets		Liabilities	
Cash	$150,000	Accounts Payable	$ 75,000
Accounts Receivable	50,000	Bank Loan	50,000
Inventory	0	Mortgage	200,000
Insurance Claim Receivable	0	Total	$325,000
Building	500,000		
		Owners' Equity	$375,000
	$700,000		$700,000

[DA04137]

Effects of Property Losses on the Income Statement

Because net income is the difference between revenue and expenses, either lower revenue or increased expenses can reduce net income. For example, when revenue goes down, most operating expenses do not automatically adjust downward in proportion, so net income is reduced. Likewise, after a property loss, a business might incur normal operating expenses at a higher rate that will lower net income or may incur expenses other than *normal* operating expenses just to continue operations.

Loss of net income would threaten any organization's survival. Insurance for business income loss responds to this exposure by covering an organization's loss of net income and continuing expenses during an interruption of operations. Business income insurance is meant to keep the organization in the same financial position as it would have been in had no loss occurred.

Effect of a Loss on Revenue—A direct physical loss will reduce revenue if it disrupts sales. Many types of direct physical losses can reduce sales, including loss of inventory, destruction of the organization's manufacturing plant, and destruction of its operating premises. The duration of any disruption of sales depends on how long it takes to repair or rebuild the physical damage and the extent to which customers have transferred their loyalties elsewhere during the repairs or rebuilding. An organization can continue to experience loss of income until (1) it has repaired any physical damage *and* (2) it has regained its old customers.

After a loss, sales typically decrease or stop for a period of time, depending on the extent of damage and type of business. Some businesses cannot operate while repairs to damaged property are made, so sales will stop completely after the loss and resume completely after repairs are complete. Other businesses may be able to resume limited operations while repairs are being made and may make some limited amount of sales, which is referred to as partial sales.

Calculating loss of revenue is simple when a business's sales are level and do not fluctuate. However, most businesses are dynamic. Product lines come and go, as do competitors. Some businesses have seasonal fluctuation, some have annual fluctuation, and some have monthly fluctuation. Most businesses also show some overall trend of rising or falling sales in addition to their regular fluctuations. These fluctuations and trends in sales are easily observed by analysis of gross sales over a period of days, weeks, months, or years. An adjuster with basic spreadsheet proficiency can evaluate the fluctuations and trends, or the adjuster may choose to hire a forensic accountant to assist in the evaluation of gross sales trends and projections.

Effect of a Loss on Expenses—Direct physical losses can affect expenses in various ways. A business's normal operating expenses will either (1) stop, (2) continue at a decreased rate, (3) continue at the same rate, or (4) continue at a higher rate during the period of restoration. The normal operating expenses that continue during the period of restoration are covered at the rate at which they are incurred (subject to policy limits and terms) during the period

Continuing expenses

Expenses that continue to be incurred during a business interruption.

Extra expenses

Expenses, in addition to ordinary expenses, that an organization incurs to mitigate the effects of a business interruption.

of restoration as **continuing expenses**. Additionally, the business may have **extra expenses** that are an increase over the *normal* operating expenses to continue business operations during the period of restoration. For example, a business that is burned out of a building it owns may rent other space temporarily while the fire-damaged building is being repaired. Hospitals may not be able to relocate their patients while a loss is repaired. Risk managers for such organizations must plan to continue operations after a loss or disaster, even at greatly increased expense. However, extra expenses are covered only if the organization has purchased a policy with extra expense coverage.

Adjuster Tip—Suppose that the insured purchases a large amount of office supplies to replace those destroyed in a fire. The expense of this purchase would be recorded, and upon examination of the records, this expense proves to be $5,000 more than normal. If the property insurer paid for these supplies as business personal property, then payment of the $5,000 as an extra expense would result in a duplicate payment to the insured. On large losses, in which this circumstance might occur, have the insured set up a special account designated for loss-related expenses. If the property insurer is another company, check with it to see what was included in its settlement.[1]

Some businesses are unable or unwilling to remain in operation after a loss. However, a business that shuts down temporarily is unlikely to eliminate its expenses completely, especially if the shutdown is expected to be brief. A business that expects to reopen soon is unlikely to lay off its workforce, because the cost of hiring and training new employees would exceed any savings from a layoff. Even a business that expects a prolonged shutdown usually retains its key employees on its payroll and incurs some amount of other expenses, such as those for utilities, professional services, and insurance.

Some expenses like the cost of goods sold and commissions are directly related to sales. Accordingly, these expenses will stop or continue at a rate directly related to sales. Expenses directly related to sales are not counted as continuing expenses. The cost of goods sold expense and expenses directly related to sales are sometimes referred to as "uninsurables" because there is no need for business income insurance to cover them. By their nature, these kinds of expenses cannot continue unless there is a sale, and if there is a sale, it pays for these kinds of expenses, so they cannot be claimed as part of the loss. The gross revenue from partial sales will pay for the cost of the uninsurable expenses incurred.

The adjuster need only consider other normal operating expenses when evaluating the continuing expenses that are part of a business income claim. The adjuster must also be aware that an insured may present a claim for continuing expenses that actually includes items of extra expense, contents damage, building damage, or other items that are generally not expenses covered under the standard business income coverage (BIC) form but may be covered elsewhere.

There is no definitive list of expenses that will or will not continue. Therefore, the adjuster must understand the insured's business to determine if an expense will likely continue or not. The adjuster will often have to examine the insured's business records to make this distinction. For example, a contract for advertising services may continue even though the business is closed. The only way to know is to examine the contract. Identifying expense fluctuations can often be done from a simple review of business records, but adjusters facing a large or complex loss may hire a forensic accountant. The Components of a Business Interruption Loss exhibit is an example of the components of a business income loss that were used in the adjustment of losses resulting from the Cerro Grande fire in New Mexico. See the exhibit "Components of a Business Interruption Loss."

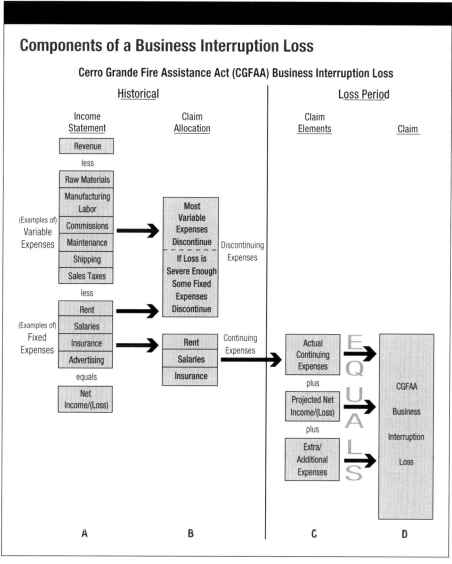

www.fema.gov/pdf/cerrogrande/handbook022801.pdf (accessed July 15, 2003). [DA04139]

An adjuster must keep in mind that the replacement of damaged inventory (ending inventory) is covered under Business and Personal Property Coverage Form (BPP), not under the BIC form.

Adjuster Tip—*Another situation in which duplicate payments may occur is the insured's use of its employees to clean and make repairs. Usually these costs are paid for by the property damage insurers and would not be covered expenses on the business income claim.*[2]

Possible Business Income Losses—The amount of a business income loss can be calculated using two different methods. First, start with gross revenues lost and subtract noncontinuing expenses. Alternatively, adding the continuing expenses plus the operating profit will equal the business income loss. The Possible Business Income Losses exhibit provides examples of business income loss calculations for several companies. See the exhibit "Possible Business Income Losses."

Possible Business Income Losses

	Company A	Company B	Company C
Gross Revenues Lost	$3,100,000	$2,100,000	$ 300,000
Noncontinuing Expenses	600,000	600,000	600,000
Continuing Expenses	2,000,000	2,000,000	2,000,000
Operating Profit	500,000	0	0
Operating Loss	0	(500,000)	(2,300,000)
Business Income Pays	$2,500,000	$1,500,000	Nothing

R. Bryan Tilden, 2002 Commercial Property Policy Changes seminar handout, p. 60. [DA04142]

Based on information from the exhibit, Company A's gross revenue would have been $3,100,000 during the loss period. The noncontinuing expenses of $600,000 would be subtracted from the gross revenue for a net income of $2,500,000, which is the business income loss. An alternative way to calculate the loss would be to use the operating profit of $500,000 and add to that the continuing expense of $2,000,000 for a business income loss of $2,500,000.

Company B has no operating profit during the loss period. Instead, it has an operating loss of $500,000. Any interruption in its business because of a loss will only increase the amount of its operating loss. Gross revenue $2,100,000 minus noncontinuing expenses results in a business income loss of $1,500,000. The same result is obtained by taking the continuing expense of $2,000,000 and subtracting the $500,000 operating loss. This occurs because the insured can recover continuing operating expenses only to the extent that they are earned by the business's operations. If the business is losing money, it is not fully earning the funds to cover its expenses.

Company C is a start-up company. It is estimated that the gross revenue it would have earned during the loss period is $300,000. If the noncontinuing expenses of $600,000 are subtracted from the gross revenue of $300,000, the result is a net loss of $300,000, so there is no recovery. If the net income loss of $300,000 is added to the continuing expenses of $2,000,000, the operating loss is $2,300,000, so there is no business income recovery.

INSURANCE FOR LOSS OF BUSINESS INCOME AND EXTRA EXPENSE

The policy statements of coverage for business income and extra expense are brief and relatively simple, but they must be read carefully. Adjusters handling losses under these coverages should understand both the policy language and basic accounting terminology.

The Insurance Services Office, Inc. (ISO) Business Income (and Extra Expense) Coverage (BIC) Form, CP 00 30, applies to a wide variety of organizations and to the business income losses that these organizations might suffer. ISO also offers a BIC without extra expense coverage and a form that covers extra expense only. Therefore, adjusters handling these losses must determine which coverage an insured has and must understand which losses are covered by each policy form.

Business Income

The insuring agreement of the BIC policy states:

> We will pay for the actual loss of Business Income you sustain due to the necessary "suspension" of your "operations" during the "period of restoration." The "suspension" must be caused by direct physical loss of or damage to property at premises which are described in the Declarations and for which a Business Income Limit of Insurance is shown in the Declarations. The loss or damage must be caused by or result from a Covered Cause of Loss. With respect to loss of or damage to personal property in the open or personal property in a vehicle, the described premises include the area within 100 feet of the site at which the described premises are located.[3]

The BIC form defines business income as:

> a. Net Income (Net Profit or Loss before income taxes) that would have been earned or incurred; and

> b. Continuing normal operating expenses incurred, including payroll.[4]

The references to operations, net income, and normal operating expenses clarify that this coverage is designed to protect insureds from losses resulting from interruption of normal operations. Business income losses are determined by examining operating income and operating expenses. Receipts and expenditures that do not appear on an organization's income statement would not be considered in the analysis of loss of business income.

The operation of the coverage and evaluation of claims is conceptually simple:

- The net income that would have been earned is the gross revenue that would have been earned minus the expenses that would have been incurred to do so had no loss occurred.

- Gross revenue that the business would have earned if no loss had occurred is projected from analysis of the business records of the pre-loss days, weeks, months, or years.

- Expenses that would have been incurred if no loss had occurred are projected from an analysis of the business records of pre-loss days, weeks, months, or years.

- The general operating expenses that continue while the business is shut down are projected or documented as they are incurred and are paid as the second part of the business income coverage provided.

Extra expenses that a business incurs to continue operations while repairs are underway are addressed by the policy separately under extra expense coverage.

Extra Expenses

An important coverage in the BIC policy is for extra expense. The BIC provides:

> Extra Expense means necessary expenses you incur during the "period of restoration" that you would not have incurred if there had been no direct physical loss or damage to property caused by or resulting from a Covered Cause of Loss.[5]

The coverage for extra expense is stated in three subsections. The first extra expense coverage is for continuing operations:

> We will pay Extra Expense (other than the expense to repair or replace property) to:
>
> (1) Avoid or minimize the "suspension" of business and to continue operations at the described premises or at replacement premises or temporary locations, including relocation expenses and costs to equip and operate the replacement location or temporary location.[6]

Subsection (1) provides coverage if the insured tries to continue operations after a loss, but the expenses to do so are greater than those that the insured would have incurred through normal business operations. Expenses covered under this section would include, for example, the cost to rent a temporary selling location to maintain sales levels.

Subsection (2) provides coverage for the cost to minimize the suspension of business operations:

> We will pay Extra Expense...to...(2) minimize the "suspension" of business if you cannot continue "operations".[7]

Subsection (2) responds to situations in which the insured cannot continue operations but incurs above-normal expenses to get back into business. A good example of this would be if the insured incurred travel expenses for extra buying trips needed to secure goods for sale.

The third subsection of extra expense coverage provides:

> We will also pay Extra Expense to repair or replace any property, but only to the extent it reduces the amount of loss that otherwise would have been payable under this Coverage Form.[8]

Normally, the insured is limited to a reasonable value (either actual cash value or replacement cost, as applicable) for the repair or replacement of property. The third subsection allows the insured to incur any extra expense to repair or replace property *to the extent that it reduces the amount of the business income loss* such as the cost of overtime labor to expedite the repair or replacement of a damaged building.

The third subsection may also apply to items of property that are not insured under the property coverages such as temporary repairs to the common area of a business condo to allow access to the insured's business.

Adjuster Tip—Another situation in which duplicate payments may occur is the insured's use of its employees to clean and make repairs. Usually these costs are paid for by the property damage insurers and would not be covered expenses on the business income claim.[9]

Extra expense must reduce the amount of the suspension of business or eliminate the need for any suspension of business under Subsection (1) or reduce the amount of the suspension under Subsection (2), but it is payable under the third subsection only to the extent that it reduces the amount of loss that otherwise would have been payable under the coverage form. Only when dealing with the physical property's repair or replacement or records' restoration must the insured actually reduce the business income loss to at least the extent of the extra expense payment. Expenses that lessen the effect of the business income loss are fully recoverable under Subsection (1) and (2) even if the expenses exceed the reduction of business income loss.

Necessary Suspension of Operations

To recover a business income loss, the insured must show that an actual loss has been sustained or incurred as a direct result of a necessary suspension of operations, either partial or total, caused by direct physical damage to insured property. The BIC defines "operations" as "Your business activities occurring at the described premises. . . ."[10]

The manufacturing industry provides the best counterexample of a necessary suspension of operations. Manufacturing facilities typically have an annual scheduled shutdown of operations to perform maintenance on machinery and equipment. If an insured cause of loss resulted in damage to that machinery, the loss of use of the machinery during the shutdown would not be considered a necessary suspension of operations compensable by the BIC policy. In this case, because the insured had already scheduled a suspension of operations, the suspension was not made necessary *by the physical damage*. It was made necessary by the need for routine maintenance.

The requirement that a suspension be necessary is consistent with the insured's typical duty under property insurance policies to minimize loss. Insurance should not reimburse an unnecessary suspension of operations.

Covered Causes of Loss

The policy provides this regarding the causes of loss:

> See applicable Causes of Loss Form as shown in the Declarations.[11]

The declarations page should show one of the causes of loss forms, Basic, Broad, or Special, applicable to the business income coverage. These are the same causes of loss forms used with the BPP.

The BIC form represents stand-alone coverage for loss of business income, just as the BPP represents stand-alone physical damage insurance. Neither form describes what perils are insured. A separate causes of loss form is used to specify whether coverage is to be on a named-perils basis or a special-form basis. This modular approach provides greater flexibility in designing coverages for a variety of risks. Although some type of property damage must occur for the loss of business income to be covered, the physical damage and loss of business income do not need to be covered for the same causes of loss. Although not common, different causes of loss forms can be used for physical damage and business income.

All of the causes of loss forms that might be attached to the BIC have special exclusions applicable to the BIC. These special exclusions are:

- Loss caused directly or indirectly by a power failure or the failure of another utility service supplied to the described premises, regardless of cause, as long as the failure occurs outside of a covered building. If a covered cause of loss results from the failure of power or utility service, the loss resulting from a covered cause of loss will be covered.

- Loss caused by damaged or destroyed finished stock. Finished stock is defined in the BIC as stock that the insured has manufactured. Thus, this exclusion only applies to manufacturers. For manufacturers, the stock itself should be covered as direct physical damage. If a manufacturer suffers loss to its inventory of finished goods but not to its productive capacity, it may be able to work overtime to make up the lost inventory. This exclusion does not apply to extra expense.

- Loss caused by or resulting from damage to radio or television antennas (including satellite dishes) and their lead-in wiring, masts, or towers.

- Any *increase* of loss caused by or resulting from interference of strikers at the location where repairs or rebuilding is occurring, or caused by loss of a contract, except to the extent that the loss of contract affects loss of business income during the period of restoration.

- Extra expense caused by or resulting from suspension, lapse, or cancellation of any license, lease, or contract, beyond the period of restoration.
- Any increase of loss caused by or resulting from delay in rebuilding, repairing, or replacing the property or resuming operations due to interference at the location of the rebuilding, repair, or replacement by strikers or other persons.
- Any other consequential loss.

Actual Loss

The term "actual loss sustained" is used to describe the extent of financial loss insured by the policy. The intent is to limit recovery to those losses that are real and direct, rather than speculative and remote. Losses must be real in the sense that not every property loss or interruption of operations results in loss of business income. For example, the owners of many small businesses are the chief salespersons. After a property loss, the owner might be occupied with the situation for a week or two, during which time no sales are made. Nevertheless, if the owner can make up sales after he or she returns to selling, it may turn out that no sales are actually lost. The capacity for make-up sales is common in service businesses and in some retail operations and must be considered carefully.

Difficulties might arise in the adjustment of business income losses concerning the degree of directness of the financial loss incurred by the insured. The last listed exclusion from a causes of loss form is for "any other consequential loss." Business income losses are always consequential in relation to direct physical damage to property. The last listed exclusion simply eliminates consequential losses *other than* those described in the BIC form. One common other consequential loss is the long-term loss of customer loyalty or goodwill that could result from a business's extended shutdown.

The causes of loss forms also include an exclusion for a specific type of indirect loss, loss of contract. Direct physical damage can sometimes cause an insured to lose certain contracts. For example, an owner of a shopping mall might lose its tenant leases if the shopping mall is damaged by fire. After the shopping mall is repaired, the owner will continue to suffer loss because the leases terminated, allowing the tenants to depart. At this point, the losses are caused by the loss of contract, not by the physical damage. The causes of loss forms exclude both loss of business income and extra expense that occur after the period of restoration because of loss of contract.

DETERMINING LOSS OF BUSINESS INCOME AND EXTRA EXPENSE

Loss of business income is the net income that would have been earned plus the continuing normal operating expenses.

The coverage provided for loss of business income is conceptually simple. The net income loss is the gross revenue (or sales) that would have occurred minus the expenses that would have been incurred. These must be estimated from pre-loss business records allowing for overall trends in business and seasonal fluctuations. The continuing expenses are determined by a case-by-case analysis of which general operating expenses will continue and at what rate. Both net income and continuing expenses are limited by the time reasonably necessary to complete damaged property's repair or replacement. Extra expenses are also evaluated case-by-case if the insured's policy provides such coverage. Basic spreadsheet programs are used to create trend sheets and business income worksheets that are the tools used by adjusters to evaluate revenue and expenses.

The adjuster must evaluate the revenue and expenses so that the policy does for the business what it would have done for itself had no loss occurred; that is, normal operating expenses are paid and expected net income is received. Although this may not always be possible, given policy limits and other factors, it is the aim of the business income loss evaluation process. This evaluation will be difficult if the insured is in a dynamic business environment of growth, decline, new products, or new competitors. It should also be recognized that the loss settlement is based on the analysis, interpretation, and projection of historical business data. This process is not absolute or exact. The process requires communication and mutual compromise between the adjuster and the insured.

Loss of Business Income

The Business Income (and Extra Expense) Coverage (BIC) form makes this statement regarding loss determination:

> a. The amount of Business Income loss will be determined based on:
>
> (1) The Net Income of the business before the direct physical loss or damage occurred;
>
> (2) The likely Net Income of the business if no physical loss or damage had occurred, but not including any Net Income that would likely have been earned as a result of an increase in the volume of business due to favorable business conditions caused by the impact of the Covered Cause of Loss on customers or on other businesses;
>
> (3) The operating expenses, including payroll expenses, necessary to resume "operations" with the same quality of service that existed just before the direct physical loss or damage; and
>
> (4) Other relevant sources of information, including:
>
> (a) Your financial records and accounting procedures;
>
> (b) Bills, invoices and other vouchers; and
>
> (c) Deeds, liens or contracts.[12]

This loss determination clause emphasizes that many factors can be considered in determining a business income loss. The qualification to the second listed item is included to avoid compensating insureds for loss of windfall business that would have existed only because of the covered loss. For example, an insured building supply company would expect windfall business following a hurricane. However, the BIC form's intent is to place the insured in the same position as it would have been in had no loss occurred.

Normal operating expenses should be included in any determination of business income. The definition of business income clarifies that it intends to cover the insured's expected net income plus *normal* operating expenses that continue. In contrast, only extra expense insurance covers operating expenses above normal. For example, a fire-damaged business may rent storage trailers to hold inventory during reconstruction. The storage trailers' cost is not a normal operating expense. However, the storage trailers would be considered an extra expense.

Extra Expense Loss

Provision b. under Loss Determination in the BIC form makes this provision for extra expense:

b. The amount of Extra Expense will be determined based on:

(1) All expenses that exceed the normal operating expenses that would have been incurred by "operations" during the "period of restoration" if no direct physical loss or damage had occurred. We will deduct from the total of such expenses:

(a) The salvage value that remains of any property bought for temporary use during the "period of restoration", once "operations" are resumed; and

(b) Any Extra Expense that is paid for by other insurance, except for insurance that is written subject to the same plan, terms, conditions and provisions as this insurance; and

(2) Necessary expenses that reduce the Business Income loss that otherwise would have been incurred.[13]

The evaluation of how much extra expense incurred by the insured is compensable by the BIC policy is a two-part process. Initially, the adjuster must determine if the expense is an extra expense, meaning that it exceeds the normal operating expenses that would have been incurred had no loss occurred. If it is not an extra expense, then the adjuster should determine whether it is a necessary expense that reduces the business income loss.

To determine whether the expense reduced the business income loss that would have been incurred had the additional money not been spent, the adjuster must understand the reasons why an expense is incurred. For example, if a damaged piece of machinery would take ten days to replace if shipped by truck, but it would take only two days if shipped by airfreight, the use of airfreight to expedite the repair of damaged machinery would reduce the loss of productive capacity from that machine, as shown in the table:

	Regular Freight	Airfreight	Difference
Freight in	$1,000	$1,500	$500
Income value of production per day ($500)			
Days saved by airfreight			8
Income value saved			$4,000
Difference between income saved and additional airfreight			$3,500

By spending $500 more on freight, the insured would be able to reduce the business income loss by $3,500.

Evaluation of Revenue Trends

Evaluation of revenue trends is essential in calculating a business income loss. **Trend sheets** are spreadsheets created by organizing a business's historical gross revenue data in a series of days, weeks, months, quarters, or years. The choice of what time period to use depends on the facts of the loss. For example, if a restaurant suffers a three-day loss that begins on Monday evening and ends on Wednesday evening, (ignoring, for the moment, the seventy-two-hour deductible in the BIC form) a sequence of gross revenues on previous Monday to Wednesday evenings should give the most accurate picture of the loss period. This approach would certainly be more accurate than taking an average of all days because such an average would include weekend evenings that are typically higher in revenues. There may also be seasonal fluctuations to consider. A typical Monday to Wednesday evening for a beachside restaurant in the winter is likely to be lower in revenue than in the summer. The historical data that adjusters consider should reflect the loss period to achieve the most accurate projection of revenues.

The Trend Sheet With Gross Revenue Data exhibit shows a simple trend sheet for three years before the January 1, XXX3, date of loss for XYZ, Inc., a gift store that does its heaviest business during the last three months of the year. See the exhibit "Trend Sheet With Gross Revenue Data."

The monthly revenue data is taken from the historical business records of XYZ, Inc. Simply arranging the data on a trend sheet provides much of the information about revenue trends. XYZ's busy season is clearly the last quarter of the year because the revenue is highest in October, November, and December and is otherwise flat. Comparing the annual figures from year to year shows steady growth of 5 percent from year to year.

$$\text{Percent Change} = \left[\left(\frac{693,000}{660,000}\right) - 1\right] \times 100.$$

The same comparison applied month to month shows that the 5 percent growth is steady over the entire year. The Trend Sheet With Gross Revenue

Trend sheets

Spreadsheets that show a business's historical gross revenue data in a series of days, weeks, months, quarters, or years.

Trend Sheet With Gross Revenue Data

XYZ, Inc. —Trend Sheet—Date of Loss 1/1/XXX3

	XXX0	XXX1	XXX2	XXX3
January	$ 50,000	$ 52,500	$ 55,125	
February	50,000	52,500	55,125	
March	50,000	52,500	55,125	
April	50,000	52,500	55,125	
May	50,000	52,500	55,125	
June	50,000	52,500	55,125	
July	50,000	52,500	55,125	
August	50,000	52,500	55,125	
September	50,000	52,500	55,125	
October	60,000	63,000	66,150	
November	70,000	73,500	77,175	
December	80,000	84,000	88,200	
Annual Gross Revenue	$660,000	$693,000	$727,650	

[DA04156]

Data and Percentage of Change Over Time exhibit is a trend sheet with additional columns that show the annual percentage change from month to month. Adjusters often create spreadsheets with this type of detail to explain their evaluation to the insured. See the exhibit "Trend Sheet With Gross Revenue Data and Percentage of Change Over Time."

If XYZ will be completely shut down from January 1, XXX3, until April 1, XXX3, the adjuster's first step in evaluating the business income loss is projecting the revenue for the loss period. The loss period is normally the time necessary to repair the physical damage or restore operations. The trend sheet analysis shows that revenue in January, February, and March of XXX3 would likely have been 5 percent higher than January, February, and March of XXX2 if no loss had occurred. XYZ would have earned $57,881 each month ($55,125 × 105% = $57,881) if no loss had occurred. The gross loss of revenue is projected to be $173,643 ($57,881 × 3 = $173,643).

The trend sheet analysis in the Trend Sheet With Gross Revenue Data exhibit is simplistic. Adjusters are cautioned to evaluate revenues carefully. Errors can occur easily in projecting revenue if the trend sheet analysis is not done properly and completely. Consider a claim for XYZ presented based on the previous three months of October, November, and December; or a flat

Trend Sheet With Gross Revenue Data and Percentage of Change Over Time

XYZ, Inc.—Trend Sheet—Date of Loss 1/1/XXX3

	XXX0	XXX1	Percent Change	XXX2	Percent Change	XXX3
January	$ 50,000	$ 52,500	5%	$ 55,125	5%	
February	50,000	52,500	5	55,125	5	
March	50,000	52,500	5	55,125	5	
April	50,000	52,500	5	55,125	5	
May	50,000	52,500	5	55,125	5	
June	50,000	52,500	5	55,125	5	
July	50,000	52,500	5	55,125	5	
August	50,000	52,500	5	55,125	5	
September	50,000	52,500	5	55,125	5	
October	60,000	63,000	5	66,150	5	
November	70,000	73,500	5	77,175	5	
December	80,000	84,000	5	88,200	5	
Annual Gross Revenue	$660,000	$693,000	5%	$727,650	5%	

[DA04158]

monthly average based on the XXX2 annual figure; or an erroneous allegation by XYZ that it is growing at a rate of 14 percent based on a comparison of the last two full months of November and December.

After the loss of gross revenue has been projected, the business's historical expenses must be analyzed to determine the net income and continuing expenses. Income statement worksheets are used to analyze expenses.

Evaluating Expenses

To project or estimate the expense for the business income loss, trend sheets should be created for the various expenses. If expenses are flat throughout the year, this exercise is relatively easy. As an example, if rental expense is $5,000 per month for twelve months, then it is easy to project that a three-month loss will be $15,000. But other expenses may vary each month. Utilities may be based on actual consumption. If the loss occurs in the summer and the doors and windows are open to facilitate repairs, the electric use may increase because of an increased demand on air conditioning. Other factors such as a rate increase can cause utility costs to change from one month to another. Projecting expenses is often quite a complicated process, and a thorough explanation of the process is beyond the scope of this text. Most adjusters rely on accountants to review the insured's books and records to make these projections. However, an adjuster should be able to ask specific questions as to what factors were considered when making the projections.

After the expenses have been projected, the adjuster can begin the loss adjustment. Two methods are commonly used by adjusters and accountants to determine the value of net income plus continuing expenses that is owed under the BIC form:

- Net income plus continuing expense method
- Gross profit less noncontinuing expense method

The best method for a particular loss depends on the size, complexity, and duration of the loss and related circumstances, but adjusters and accountants use any one or a combination of methods.

Net Income Plus Continuing Expense Method and Gross Profit Less Noncontinuing Expense Method

The net income plus continuing expense method most closely matches the policy language and is arguably the easiest method to reconcile with actual incurred expense figures once they are available. The Income Statement Worksheet for XYZ, Inc., Showing Projected Lost Net Income Plus Expenses exhibit demonstrates both the net income plus continuing expense method and the gross profit less noncontinuing expense method. The adjuster must decide which expenses will continue and which will not. For the purposes of this illustration, assume that all expenses are evenly prorated throughout the year and that they did not increase over year XXX2. Wages, insurance, and interest will continue at 100 percent; depreciation will continue at 50 percent. Rent and expenses for utilities will not continue at all. See the exhibit "Income Statement Worksheet for XYZ, Inc., Showing Projected Lost Net Income Plus Expenses."

The Income Statement Worksheet for XYZ, Inc., Showing Projected Lost Net Income Plus Expenses exhibit shows that the continuing expenses will amount to $68,725 and that the net income lost is $19,111. Note that 50 percent of the depreciation expense is continuing and that 50 percent is noncontinuing. Accordingly, the net income plus continuing expense loss amounts to $87,836. The gross profit less noncontinuing expense method also shows a loss amount of $87,836 ($104,186 – $16,350). Note that the $87,836 result is the same under both methods. However, legitimate and substantial deviations in final evaluation amounts are common. It is important to recognize that decimal rounding affects calculations and can be a factor when comparing manual calculations to more precise computer evaluations. Other methods of arriving at loss period expense amounts include turning the annual operating expense figures into daily figures (dividing by 365 days)

Income Statement Worksheet for XYZ, Inc., Showing Projected Lost Net Income Plus Expenses

Assumes that expenses did not increase over the prior year and that the expenses are prorated evenly throughout the year.

					Percent of Gross Sales
Revenue from Gross Sales	$173,643				100.0%
Cost of Goods Sold	69,458				40.0
Gross Profit	$104,185				60.0

Operating Expenses		Continuing	Noncontinuing	Percent Continuing	
Wages	$62,500	$ 62,500	—	100%	36.0
Rent	9,000	—	$ 9,000	0	5.2
Depreciation	2,700	1,350	1,350	50	1.6
Insurance	1,875	1,875	—	100	1.1
Interest	3,000	3,000	—	100	1.7
Utilities	6,000	—	6,000	0	3.5
Total Operating Expenses	$85,075				49.0
Projected Lost Net Income	$19,110				11.0
Total Continuing Expenses		$68,725			39.6
Total Noncontinuing Expenses			$16,350		9.4
Net Income PLUS Continuing Expenses		$87,836			50.6
Gross Profit LESS Noncontinuing Expenses			$87,836		50.6%

[DA04159]

and then multiplying by the number of days in the loss period. This, too, will create variations in final evaluation amounts.

Expenses may be paid daily, weekly, monthly, yearly, or at irregular intervals. However, note that the expenses are generally analyzed and negotiated from an annual figure. Determining which expenses will continue or discontinue and which methods to use in calculating loss period figures are key negotiating points in business income claims.

After XYZ, Inc.'s ninety-day loss period has passed, the insured may find that it did use some utilities or that not all wages continued as expected. The continuing expense figures can be easily adjusted to reflect actual incurred expenses. The process of reviewing actual incurred expenses against the projections done before the end of the loss period is called reconciliation. Reconciliation is almost always done on larger, more complex losses but may be mutually waived on smaller, simpler losses.

Reconciliation: Evaluation of Actual Incurred Continuing Expenses and Partial Sales

Reconciliation is the process of matching the net income and continuing expense projections with the actual sales made and expenses incurred during the loss period. Often, a business maintains partial operations during the loss period. The less-than-normal sales are called partial sales. These partial sales are easily reconciled by deducting the gross amount of partial sales from the gross loss period sales projections before the application of the gross profit percentage or business income percentage. Consider the example of XYZ, Inc. The Income Statement Worksheet for XYZ, Inc., Showing Projected Lost Net Income Plus Expenses exhibit shows a projected gross loss of revenue of $173,643. If XYZ, Inc. had been open for partial operations during the loss period and made partial sales of $20,000, the projected gross sales loss would be $153,643 ($173,643 – $20,000), as shown in the Income Statement Worksheet for XYZ, Inc., Showing Projected Lost Net Income Plus Expenses exhibit. The net income loss would be $7,110. Note that the cost of goods sold has changed to reflect the partial sales and that the net income lost has changed as well. Note also that the difference between the outcomes shown in The Income Statement Worksheet for XYZ, Inc., Showing Projected Lost Net Income Plus Expenses exhibit and the Income Statement Worksheet for XYZ, Inc., Showing Projected Lost Net Income Plus Expenses (Partial Sales of $20,000) exhibit is $12,000, the amount of gross profit on $20,000 of sales. This occurs in this example because all of the expenses stayed the same in the two exhibits. See the exhibit "Income Statement Worksheet for XYZ, Inc., Showing Projected Lost Net Income Plus Expenses (Partial Sales of $20,000)."

Because of disparity between when bills are paid as a matter of cash flow and when expenses are incurred for purposes of the income statement, adjusters or the accountants working for them might have to reconcile expenses. Business income insurance covers expenses as incurred on the income statement, not on the basis of bills paid.

For example, insurance premiums are often paid as a lump-sum amount at the beginning of the policy period. This payment does not result in an expense item on the income statement for the entire amount paid. Instead, insurance expense is recognized gradually throughout the year during the policy period. Therefore, under this payment scheme, it would not matter that the date for paying an annual insurance premium happened to fall within the period of the business income loss or outside of it. Insurance expense would be recognized as the pro rata amount of the annual premium represented by the period

Reconciliation

The process of matching the net income and continuing expenses projections with the actual sales made and expenses incurred during the loss period.

Income Statement Worksheet for XYZ, Inc., Showing Projected Lost Net Income Plus Expenses (Partial Sales of $20,000)

Assumes partial sales of $20,000 and that expenses remain flat throughout the year.

					Percent of Gross Sales
Revenue from Gross Sales	$153,643 ($173,643 – $20,000)				100.0%
Cost of Goods Sold	61,458				40.0
Gross Profit	$ 92,185				60.0

Operating Expenses		Continuing	Noncontinuing	Percent Continuing	
Wages	$ 62,500	$62,500	—	100%	40.7
Rent	9,000	—	$ 9,000	0	5.9
Depreciation	2,700	1,350	1,350	50	1.8
Insurance	1,875	1,875	—	100	1.2
Interest	3,000	3,000	—	100	2.0
Utilities	6,000	—	6,000	0	3.9
Total Operating Expenses	$ 85,075				55.4
Projected Lost Net Income	$ 7,110				4.6
Total Continuing Expenses		$68,725			44.7
Total Noncontinuing Expenses			$16,350		10.6
Net Income PLUS Continuing Expenses		$75,836			49.4
Gross Profit LESS Noncontinuing Expenses			$75,836		49.4

[DA04160]

of shutdown. Real estate taxes are similarly paid as a lump sum but recognized gradually as an expense.

Other expenses might be incurred first and paid later, such as on a quarterly basis. For example, building maintenance expenses or professional fees, such as for attorneys, are generally incurred as expenses first then billed and paid later. Heating oil expense is incurred in the winter but might be billed evenly throughout the year.

Most routine expenses are incurred as income statement expenses and are paid in cash in a consistent, congruent manner. However, failure to distinguish between when an expense is incurred and when it is paid can lead to improper calculation of covered expense, especially with relatively short periods of business interruption.

The reconciliation of expenses must be done on a case-by-case basis with careful attention to a fair evaluation of the insured's loss. Generally, business income coverage should do what the business would have done for itself had no loss occurred. Large losses with a long period of restoration can be reconciled several times, such as at the end of each month. However, on small simple losses, the reconciliation process may be mutually waived because the effect of reconciliation would be minimal.

Negotiating Business Income Claims

It is important to understand that evaluating business income claims is not a math problem with an exact answer; rather, it is an adjusting process. Adjusters should be comfortable developing a range of reasonable settlement possibilities.

Business income evaluations are a combination of interpretations and projections from available pre-loss data. Any figure subject to data availability, interpretation, and projection cannot be exact. The final outcome can be affected by factors as small as the number of decimal points used in a particular calculation. Accordingly, adjusters must make great efforts to ensure that their evaluations are well-reasoned and clearly documented. Some of the variables involved include the period of restoration, gross sales projections, methods of calculation, make-up sales, partial sales, which expenses will continue, coinsurance compliance, and reconciliation, as well as other issues that may arise in the adjustment process. Adjusters handling business income claims directly or indirectly with accountant's assistance should be comfortable with these concepts.

A business income loss could be considered a specialty loss because not all property loss adjusters handle this type of claim. Inland marine losses such as transportation losses, and other property losses such as condominium losses, are also considered specialty losses.

DETERMINING THE PERIOD OF RESTORATION

The Business Income (and Extra Expense) Coverage (BIC) Form covers losses occurring during the period of restoration, defined to end when repairs should be completed. This definition allows adjusters and insureds to settle claims prospectively, before restoration is completed, while allowing for reconciliation of actual sales and expenses after restoration is complete.

Recovery for loss of business income and extra expense is limited to the period of restoration. The period of restoration is distinguished from the loss period. The loss period includes the seventy-two-hour deductible and may include extended business income loss after operations are resumed. Determining the period of restoration can present some complex adjusting issues. This section includes the policy definition of this period and explains the insured's typical duty to mitigate loss.

Definition

The BIC form covers losses of business income and extra expense that occur during the period of restoration. This period is defined in the policy:

> "Period of Restoration" means the period of time that:
>
> a. Begins:
>
> (1) 72 hours after the time of direct physical loss or damage for Business Income coverage; or
>
> (2) Immediately after the time of direct physical loss or damage for Extra Expense coverage; caused by or resulting from any Covered Cause of Loss at the described premises; and
>
> b. Ends on the earlier of:
>
> (1) The date when the property at the described premises should be repaired, rebuilt or replaced with reasonable speed and similar quality; or
>
> (2) The date when business is resumed at a new permanent location.[14]

The beginning date for the period of restoration creates a three-day (seventy-two-hour) deductible for loss of business income. However, extra expense is covered beginning immediately after a loss. In most cases, for the sake of determining the period of restoration, the date of loss is not at issue. However, the parties to the adjustment process might have to make a considerable effort to determine when the restoration period should end. The actual time period in which repairs to the insured property are made is not necessarily the time period in which such repairs should be made.

Due Diligence Requirement

The BIC policy definition of the period of restoration requires the insured to repair or replace the property with that of similar quality as quickly as possible.

The BIC form further includes these loss conditions:

> 3. c. Resumption of Operations
>
> We will reduce the amount of your:
>
> (1) Business Income loss, other than Extra Expense, to the extent you can resume your "operations"; in whole or in part, by using damaged or undamaged property (including merchandise or stock) at the described premises or elsewhere.
>
> (2) Extra Expense loss to the extent you can return "operations" to normal and discontinue such Extra Expense.[15]

The "as quickly as possible" standard, which applies to all business income loss evaluations, is important. For example, if a manufacturer could reduce the amount of his or her business income loss by using a competitor's facilities but would, as a result, reveal to a competitor a trade secret manufacturing process, the insurer would not be entitled to require such action because it would be unreasonable for the insurer to require the insured to give up a trade secret. Likewise, even if a retailer could arrange for delivery of merchandise to a nearby competitor's location, requiring the insured to direct customers to the competitor to continue to sell merchandise would be unreasonable. An insurer cannot ask the insured to sacrifice customers to reduce a business income loss. Nevertheless, an insured cannot remain idle and allow business income losses to accumulate. The insured's duty to mitigate the loss is inherent in all first-party insurance contracts and is especially important in a business income loss. Although an insurer can assist an insured in the repair or replacement of physically damaged property, the insurer cannot step in and run the insured's business.

Time Needed to Repair or Replace

Because the time element portion of an insured loss is measured by the time necessary to repair or replace the damaged property, the adjuster must determine the extent of the physical damage loss. To make an accurate determination, early in the adjustment process the adjuster must speak with the people involved in assessing and/or restoring the damage. Discussions with the insured and his or her representatives, including architects, engineers, contractors, and other consultants, are required as soon as possible to gain an early understanding of the probable duration of the financial loss.

The methods used to repair the damaged property directly affect the extent of the financial loss. For example, overtime labor can shorten the reconstruction period, as can other forms of fast-track construction techniques. The BIC form anticipates this possibility in its treatment of expediting expenses as covered extra expenses.

Obviously, not every possible type of loss and method of repair can be anticipated. Circumstances of the reconstruction, such as delays in the adjustment process itself, weather conditions, availability of materials, labor, alternative sites, and governmental restrictions, all affect the actual time needed for repairs.

Time in Which Repairs Should Be Complete

Because of the circumstances that affect actual repair time, a reasonably projected expected time for repairs, rather than an actual one, is often preferred in determining the extent of a business loss. A reasonable time period is the time in which restoration should be completed, as opposed to the time in which it is completed.

Depending on the circumstances of a given loss, all parties might benefit from the use of a reasonably expected time standard. This is true because:

- The physical damage is sometimes never repaired, or it is repaired in such a fashion that it bears no relationship to the originally damaged property.

- Certain extraneous circumstances not contemplated by the parties might affect the restoration period.

- Loss adjustments can be made prospectively, that is, before the period of restoration is complete.

The fact that the insured, for whatever reason, chooses not to repair or replace the insured property does not prevent it from recovering a business income loss. In such a case, the parties must agree on what time should have reasonably been necessary to accomplish whatever repairs were insured by the property damage coverage. Experts can establish that time frame, depending on the degree of difficulty of the repair work.

Prospective settlement has some disadvantages as well. A reasonably expected time element estimate might be longer than the actual time needed to repair the physical damage, which would be a disadvantage for the insurer. Alternatively, the insured might fear that its actual loss will be greater than anticipated by any projection and that it will therefore be underpaid. Unforeseen events can also arise, such as a delay in the replacement of an essential component, which would lengthen the suspension period beyond the projection, creating a disadvantage for the insured. Any lengthening of the actual time period would be uncompensated, but the insured would still have received a certain sum well before property damage repairs were completed and would have the freedom to use the business income loss proceeds as he or she sees fit. In each claim, the insurer and insured must carefully weigh the advantages and disadvantages of a prospective approach to the adjustment process.

Additional Coverage and Limitation: Interruption of Computer Operations

Prior editions of the BIC Form had a limitation of a business income loss caused by the destruction or corruption of electronic data. In the Insurance Services Office, Inc., BIC form (2001 edition), the limitation on electronic media and data has been removed. The Additional Coverage Interruption of Computer Operations and the Additional Limitation—Interruption of Computer Operations have been added. The limitation is meant to help clarify those situations in which coverage applies. It contains a lengthy description of what electronic data means in the policy. The additional coverage provides $2,500 of coverage for all business income extra expense due to a suspension of operations resulting from an interruption of computer operations caused by the destruction or corruption of electronic data by a covered cause of loss. The $2,500 is an aggregate limit for all losses sustained in any one policy year.

Delays Caused by Strikers

All of the causes of loss forms that might be attached to the BIC form include a special exclusion that states:

> We will not pay for:
>
> (4) Any increase of loss caused by or resulting from:
>
> (a) Delay in rebuilding, repairing or replacing the property or resuming "operations", due to interference at the location of the rebuilding, repair or replacement by strikers or other persons. . . .[16]

This limitation applies only to striker interference at the insured premises. It does not apply to strike activities elsewhere. The last three words quoted could be construed to mean that any delay caused by any person is not covered. However, the sense of this entire clause is to exclude delays caused by strike activities, not every delay. The broad wording of the last three words is necessary because identifying perpetrators during strike activities is not always possible.

ADDITIONAL, OPTIONAL, AND EXTENDED COVERAGES UNDER THE BIC FORM

The Business Income (and Extra Expense) Coverage (BIC) Form provides valuable additional, optional, and extended coverages.

The BIC Form provides valuable additional, optional, and extended coverage for interruptions caused by civil authorities, alterations and new buildings, business income losses that extend beyond the period of restoration for a short period of time, and business income losses that extend beyond the period of restoration for a long period of time. There is also a coverage extension for newly acquired locations.

Civil Authority

The BIC form provides this additional coverage for interruption caused by action of civil authorities:

> We will pay for the actual loss of Business Income you sustain due to the necessary "suspension" of your "operations" during the "period of restoration." The "suspension" must be caused by direct physical loss of or damage to property at premises which are described in the Declarations and for which a Business Income Limit of Insurance is shown in the Declarations. The loss or damage must be caused by or result from a Covered Cause of Loss. With respect to loss of or damage to personal property in the open or personal property in a vehicle, the described premises include the area within 100 feet of the site at which the described premises are located.[17]

This coverage applies in the event of damage to property away from the described premises. The intent is to insure the loss of income that results from, for example, cordoning off an entire city block by civil authorities. This additional coverage is limited to three weeks.

Alterations and New Buildings

Another additional coverage provided by the BIC form is for alterations and new buildings. The policy provides this:

> We will pay for the actual loss of Business Income you sustain and necessary Extra Expense you incur due to direct physical loss or damage at the described premises caused by or resulting from any Covered Cause of Loss to:
>
> (1) New buildings or structures, whether complete or under construction;
>
> (2) Alterations or additions to existing buildings or structures; and
>
> (3) Machinery, equipment, supplies or building materials located on or within 100 feet of the described premises and:
>
> (a) Used in the construction, alterations or additions; or
>
> (b) Incidental to the occupancy of new buildings.
>
> If such direct physical loss or damage delays the start of "operations," the "period of restoration" for Business Income Coverage will begin on the date "operations" would have begun if the direct physical loss or damage had not occurred.[18]

The Alterations and New Buildings coverage parallels the extension of property damage coverage under the BPP policy for the same items. If the adjuster determines that the damaged property is covered, the resulting loss of use of that property is also insured. The BIC policy anticipates that property insured under this section might not yet be income-producing at the time of the loss. In that case, the time element is measured from when the property was to begin generating income to when the property actually does generate income after being repaired or replaced.

Extended Business Income

The additional coverage for extended business income (other than rental value) provides this:

> …we will pay for the actual loss of Business Income you incur during the period that:
>
> (a) Begins on the date property (except "finished stock") is actually repaired, rebuilt or replaced and "operations" are resumed; and
>
> (b) Ends on the earlier of:
>
> (i) The date you could restore your "operations" with reasonable speed, to the level which would generate the business income amount that would have existed if no direct physical loss or damage occurred; or
>
> (ii) 30 consecutive days after the date determined in (1)(a) above.

However, Extended Business Income does not apply to loss of Business Income incurred as a result of unfavorable business conditions caused by the impact of the Covered Cause of Loss in the area where the described premises are located.

Loss of Business Income must be caused by direct physical loss or damage at the described premises caused by or resulting from any Covered Cause of Loss.[19]

This feature of the BIC policy provides up to an additional thirty days after the restoration of the property within which the insured can regain whatever business was lost because of the interruption. This extended business income coverage does not increase the amount of coverage beyond what appears on the declarations page. For example, a retail store whose business is interrupted by a covered cause of loss often continues to lose sales income even after the shelves are restocked and the store has reopened. Once consumers discover alternative stores to shop in, insured storeowners may need to take extra steps to recapture customers. To that end, an insured might offer a grand reopening sale, which would be unnecessary if no loss had occurred. The extent to which the sale negatively affects the income that would have been anticipated for the additional thirty-day period had no loss occurred would be insured under this extension of coverage. Nevertheless, the additional coverage for extended business income does not include loss of income caused by unfavorable business conditions caused by the covered cause of loss. For example, after a catastrophe such as a hurricane, the economy in an entire area might be depressed. Losses caused by such a general business depression are not covered.

Interruption of Computer Operations

This provision allows the insured to extend the Business Income and Extra Expense coverage to a loss caused by an interruption in computer operations caused by the destruction or corruption of electronic data from a covered cause of loss. However, the provision limits the covered cause of loss.

Optional Coverage: Extended Period of Indemnity

This provision allows an insured to select a longer period of indemnity beyond the automatic thirty days granted under extended business income in the BIC form. The extension of the period of indemnity does not increase the amount of coverage beyond what appears on the declarations page. This extension usually applies to businesses with a marked seasonal selling period. For example, a retailer selling Christmas ornaments might have a peak season of approximately sixty days before Christmas. If the normal period of restoration and the normal thirty-day extended period ended shortly before the insured's peak season, an additional amount of time would be required for the insured to regain its share of the seasonal market.

Newly Acquired Locations Coverage Extension

The BIC form provides extended coverage, beyond the stated limits, for newly acquired locations (other than fairs or exhibitions) for up to $100,000. The intent of this coverage is to parallel the property coverages for locations acquired during the policy term. This coverage is limited in dollar amount and in duration, but it is additional to the Limits of Insurance. If an insured acquires a new location, it should report its value to the agent as soon as possible to obtain appropriate coverage.

Limits of Insurance for Additional Coverages

The Limits of Insurance section of the BIC form provides that the most that can be paid for any one loss is the limit of insurance shown on the declarations page. This clause also restricts recovery to the stated limit for these additional coverages:

- Alterations and New Buildings
- Civil Authority
- Extra Expense
- Extended Business Income

COINSURANCE REQUIREMENT AND OPTIONAL COVERAGES

Coinsurance requires the insured to carry a specific limit of insurance that is a percentage of the amount of potential loss "at risk." Under building or contents coverage forms, the amount at risk is the total value of the building or contents. Under business income coverage, the amount at risk is the projected annual net income and operating expenses from the date the policy was written or renewed.

This section details how coinsurance compliance is determined under the Business Income (and Extra Expense) Coverage (BIC) Form. This section also discusses several optional coverages that substitute for coinsurance and explains why coinsurance is not a problem under the Businessowners Policy (BOP).

Coinsurance Policy Language

The BIC form specifies the coinsurance requirement as an additional condition:

> If a Coinsurance percentage is shown in the Declarations, the following condition applies in addition to the Common Policy Conditions and the Commercial Property Conditions.
>
> We will not pay the full amount of any Business Income loss if the Limit of Insurance for Business Income is less than:

a. The Coinsurance percentage shown for Business Income in the Declarations; times

b. The sum of:

(1) The Net Income (Net Profit or Loss before income taxes), and

(2) Operating expenses, including payroll expenses, that would have been earned or incurred (had no loss occurred) by your "operations" at the described premises for the 12 months following the inception, or last previous anniversary date, of this policy (whichever is later).[20]

The policy language is followed by a description of the coinsurance calculation and by a list of expenses that are deducted from all operating expenses for purposes of determining coinsurance compliance. The list generally includes those expenses that are directly related to sales such as returns and allowances, discounts, and bad debts. Adjusters should be familiar with this list. These uninsurable expenses are not, and cannot be, "at risk" and should not be included in required limits of business income coverage.

Evaluating Coinsurance Compliance

To evaluate coinsurance compliance, refer to the Annual Income Statement Received from Insured exhibit and assume that the policy inception date was 1/1/XXX3. The annual net income and operating expenses for the previous year total $436,590 ($96,290 + $340,300 = $436,590). Note that this is also the amount of the gross profit that appears on the same exhibit. More importantly, note that the gross profit is 60 percent of gross sales. Now refer to the Trend Sheet With Gross Revenue Data and Percentage of Change Over Time exhibit. Note that sales are steadily increasing at a rate of 5 percent. Since the annual sales for XXX2 were $727,650, the annual sales from the policy inception date of 1/1/XXX3 are projected to be $764,032 ($727,650 × 105% = $764,032). With a gross profit percentage of 60 percent, the amount of net income and operating expenses "at risk" are $458,419 (764,032 × 60% = $458,419). If the BIC policy form carries an 80 percent coinsurance requirement, the insured must carry business income limits of $366,735 ($458,419 × 80% = $366,735). This calculation is also explained here:

Annual gross revenues XXX2	$727,650
Sales trend projections	× 105%
Projected annual gross revenues XXX3 (policy inception 1/1/XXX3)	$764,032
Gross profit percentage	× 60%
Net income and operating expenses at risk	$458,419
Coinsurance requirement from policy	× 80%
Amount of business income coverage required by policy	$366,735

Using consistent sales projections is important. An insured may argue that sales are increasing when discussing the amount of claim payment and then argue that sales are flat or declining while discussing coinsurance compliance.

Remember also that under the policy, the amount at risk is the projected annual net income and operating expenses from the date the policy was written or renewed. Often, a loss occurs many months after policy inception or renewal. This means that the evaluation will include some actual sales and expense data and some projected sales and expense data. See the exhibit "Annual Income Statement Received From Insured."

Annual Income Statement Received From Insured

XYZ, Inc.—Income Statement 1/1/XXX2 to 12/31/XXX2

Revenue From Gross Sales	$727,650
Cost of Goods Sold	291,060
Gross Profit	$436,590
Operating Expenses	
Wages	$250,000
Rent	36,000
Depreciation	10,800
Insurance	7,500
Interest	12,000
Utilities	24,000
Total Operating Expenses	$340,300
Net Income	$96,290

[DA04168]

All expenses directly related to sales and excluded expenses listed in the policy are deducted from the calculation in the Annual Income Statement Received From Insured exhibit. Suppose that the adjuster learns from the insured that the "wages" listed on XYZ's business records includes commissions of 10 percent of gross sales. Commissions are normally listed as a separate expense item, but it is possible to find deviations from generally accepted accounting principles. Commissions are an expense directly related to sales. Accordingly, the adjuster or accountant evaluating coinsurance compliance would move the commissions expense "above the line," and the Annual Income Statement Received From Insured exhibit would be modified as shown in the Income Statement Worksheet for XYZ, Inc., Showing Commissions Above the Line exhibit. See the exhibit "Income Statement Worksheet for XYZ, Inc., Showing Commissions Above the Line."

Income Statement Worksheet for XYZ, Inc., Showing Commissions Above the Line

XYZ, Inc.—Income Statement Worksheet 1/1/XXX2 to 12/31/XXX2

		Percent of Gross Sales
Revenue From Gross Sales	$727,650	100.0%
Cost of Goods Sold	291,060	40.0%
Wages (10% Commissions)	72,765	10.0%
Modified Gross Profit	$363,825	50.0%
Operating Expenses		
Wages (Salaries Only)	$177,235	24.4%
Rent	36,000	4.9%
Depreciation	10,800	1.5%
Insurance	7,500	1.0%
Interest	12,000	1.6%
Utilities	24,000	3.3%
Total Operating Expenses	$267,535	36.8%
Net Income	$ 96,290	13.2%

[DA04170]

Note that deducting expenses does not change the net income amount. But it does show a modified gross profit amount and the modified gross profit percentage. With a modified gross profit percentage of only 50 percent and a coinsurance requirement of 80 percent, XYZ requires business income coverage of only $305,613 (see calculation).

Annual gross revenues XXX2	$727,650
Sales trend projections	× 105%
Projected annual gross revenues XXX3 (policy inception 1/1/XXX3)	$764,032
Modified gross profit percentage	× 50%
Not incomo and oporating oxponcoc at rick	$382,016
Coinsurance requirement from policy	× 80%
Amount of business income coverage required by policy	$305,613

Implications of Being Underinsured

The implications of being underinsured are the same for all property coverages. If the limits are less than required, the loss payment owed is proportionately reduced. The amount of loss reduction is called the coinsurance percentage of loss and is calculated by the "did over should" formula. Recall the coinsurance calculation showing a required coverage limit of $366,735, and assume that the business income coverage limits carried were only $325,000. Using the "did over should" formula shows that the coinsurance percentage of loss is 88 percent ($325,000 ÷ $366,735 = 88%):

$$\text{Coinsurance percentage of loss} = \frac{\text{Limit Insured Did Carry}}{\text{Limit Insured Should Carry}} = \frac{325,000}{366,735} = 88\%.$$

Applying this coinsurance percentage to the loss evaluation shown in the Income Statement Worksheet for XYZ, Inc., Showing Projected Lost Net Income Plus Expenses exhibit results in a payable loss of $77,296 ($87,836 × 88% = $77,296). See the exhibit "Income Statement Worksheet for XYZ, Inc., Showing Projected Lost Net Income Plus Expenses."

Extra Expense and Coinsurance Calculations

The amount of extra expenses needed to reduce a given business income loss cannot be easily forecast and therefore cannot be included in the insurable values upon which coinsurance is based. The BIC policy follows this reasoning by excluding amounts insured under extra expense from the coinsurance condition.

Optional Coverages Instead of Coinsurance

The BIC policy contains three optional coverages that are available to the insured when certain conditions are met regarding either additional premium or reporting requirements. Each allows the coinsurance clause to be suspended.

Maximum Period of Indemnity

If this option is selected in the Declarations, the coinsurance condition does not apply to this coverage form. Additionally, the most the insurer will pay for the total Business Income loss and Extra Expense is the lesser of the amount of loss sustained and expenses incurred during the 120 days immediately following the beginning of the period of restoration or the limit of insurance shown in the declarations.

Monthly Period of Indemnity

This optional coverage allows the insured to limit coverage to a specific fraction of the total limit for each thirty-consecutive-day period after the

Income Statement Worksheet for XYZ, Inc., Showing Projected Lost Net Income Plus Expenses

Assumes that expenses did not increase over the prior year and that the expenses are prorated evenly throughout the year.

					Percent of Gross Sales
Revenue from Gross Sales	$173,643				100.0%
Cost of Goods Sold	69,458				40.0
Gross Profit	$104,185				60.0

Operating Expenses		Continuing	Noncontinuing	Percent Continuing	
Wages	$62,500	$62,500	—	100%	36.0
Rent	9,000	—	$9,000	0	5.2
Depreciation	2,700	1,350	1,350	50	1.6
Insurance	1,875	1,875	—	100	1.1
Interest	3,000	3,000	—	100	1.7
Utilities	6,000	—	6,000	0	3.5
Total Operating Expenses	$85,075				49.0
Projected Lost Net Income	$19,110				11.0
Total Continuing Expenses		$68,725			39.6
Total Noncontinuing Expenses			$16,350		9.4
Net Income PLUS Continuing Expenses		$87,836			50.6
Gross Profit LESS Noncontinuing Expenses			$87,836		50.6%

[DA04159]

beginning of the period of restoration. For example, a business income limit of $200,000 with a 1⁄4 monthly limit of indemnity would provide up to $50,000 of business income coverage each month. This does not limit the period of indemnity; it only limits the amount that can be paid each month. In this example, the insured could also receive $20,000 per month for ten months, $25,000 for eight months, or any other combination that does not exceed $50,000 in any thirty-day period. As with the first option, the coinsurance provisions of the policy are suspended.

Business Income Agreed Value

This option suspends the operation of the coinsurance provisions of the policy when the insured reports business income values before the policy's inception date. However, the Agreed Value coverage operates like a new coinsurance requirement. The insured can preselect the amount of coverage it must maintain, but Section d. of the Agreed Value coverage applies a factor to any loss settlement determined by the proportion of the actual limit to the values agreed at the policy's inception. In the example given in the policy, recovery is reduced by 50 percent because the business income limit of insurance is half of the agreed value reported at the policy inception date. Therefore, for the insured to recover, it must purchase 100 percent of any insured business income loss, and it must purchase 100 percent of the agreed value as the business income limit of insurance.

Limits Under Businessowners Policies

The ISO BOP provides package property coverages including coverage for loss of business income and extra expense. This coverage is substantially identical to the BIC coverage, except that the BOP has no dollar limit of insurance or coinsurance clause for business income loss. Instead, the BOP limits both the loss of business income and extra expense to twelve consecutive months after the date of loss.

SUMMARY

Any business can experience lost income or increased expenses as a result of property damage or destruction. Business income coverages are used by businesses to cover themselves against this eventuality.

Claims adjusters handling business income losses should understand basic accounting for organizations. The two principal accounting statements for organizations are the balance sheet and the income statement. The balance sheet lists an organization's assets and its liabilities. The difference between assets and liabilities is the organization's net worth. An organization's income statement lists the revenue and expenses for the organization for a given period of time. The difference between revenue and expenses is net income. Damage or destruction of property appears on an organization's balance sheet. However, if such damage or destruction results in loss of income or increased expenses, those effects appear on the income statement. Adjusters should be comfortable analyzing sales and expense figures because these are the building blocks of business income loss evaluations.

The Business Income (and Extra Expense) Coverage Form covers an organization's loss of net income, its continuing expenses, and its extra expenses that result from a suspension of its operations.

Property loss adjusters must be careful when determining losses and evaluating claims because claims are often made for items that are covered under building or contents coverages. In all cases, property loss adjusters must be able to evaluate the separate effects of and coverage for reduced revenue and increased expenses.

The BIC form covers losses occurring during the period of restoration, defined to end when repairs should be completed. This definition allows adjusters and insureds to settle claims prospectively, before restoration is completed, while allowing for reconciliation of actual sales and expenses after restoration is complete.

The BIC form provides valuable additional, optional, and extended coverage for interruptions caused by civil authorities, alterations and new buildings, business income losses that extend beyond the period of restoration for a short period of time, and business income losses that extend beyond the period of restoration for a long period of time. There is also a coverage extension for newly acquired locations.

Coinsurance requires the insured to carry a specific limit of insurance that is a percentage of the amount of potential loss "at risk." There are several optional coverages that substitute for coinsurance. Coinsurance is not a problem under the BOP.

ASSIGNMENT NOTES

1. Property Loss Research Bureau, Duplication of Claims, 2002 Pasadena, Calif., conference.

2. Property Loss Research Bureau, Duplication of Claims, 2002 Pasadena, Calif., conference.

3. Includes copyrighted material of Insurance Services Office, Inc., with its permission. Copyright, ISO Properties, Inc., 2007

4. Includes copyrighted material of Insurance Services Office, Inc., with its permission. Copyright, ISO Properties, Inc., 2007

5. Includes copyrighted material of Insurance Services Office, Inc., with its permission. Copyright, ISO Properties, Inc., 2007

6. Includes copyrighted material of Insurance Services Office, Inc., with its permission. Copyright, ISO Properties, Inc., 2007

7. Includes copyrighted material of Insurance Services Office, Inc., with its permission. Copyright, ISO Properties, Inc., 2007

8. Includes copyrighted material of Insurance Services Office, Inc., with its permission. Copyright, ISO Properties, Inc., 2007

9. Property Loss Research Bureau, Duplication of Claims, 2002 Pasadena, Calif., conference.

10. Business Income Coverage (and Extra Expense) Form, CP 00 30 04 02, Copyright, Insurance Services Office, Inc., 2001.

11. Includes copyrighted material of Insurance Services Office, Inc., with its permission. Copyright, ISO Properties, Inc., 2007

12. Includes copyrighted material of Insurance Services Office, Inc., with its permission. Copyright, ISO Properties, Inc., 2007

13. Includes copyrighted material of Insurance Services Office, Inc., with its permission. Copyright, ISO Properties, Inc., 2007

14. Includes copyrighted material of Insurance Services Office, Inc., with its permission. Copyright, ISO Properties, Inc., 2007

15. Includes copyrighted material of Insurance Services Office, Inc., with its permission. Copyright, ISO Properties, Inc., 2007

16. Includes copyrighted material of Insurance Services Office, Inc., with its permission. Copyright, ISO Properties, Inc., 2007

17. Includes copyrighted material of Insurance Services Office, Inc., with its permission. Copyright, ISO Properties, Inc., 2007

18. Includes copyrighted material of Insurance Services Office, Inc., with its permission. Copyright, ISO Properties, Inc., 2007

19. Includes copyrighted material of Insurance Services Office, Inc., with its permission. Copyright, ISO Properties, Inc., 2007

20. Includes copyrighted material of Insurance Services Office, Inc., with its permission. Copyright, ISO Properties, Inc., 2007

Direct Your Learning

Specialty Losses

Educational Objectives

After learning the content of this assignment, you should be able to:

▷ Explain the coverage provided and the adjusting considerations for transportation and motor truck losses.

▷ Explain the coverage provided and the adjusting considerations for bailee and warehouse legal liability losses.

▷ Explain the interests of the unit owners and the condominium association in the individual units and the common elements and, given a claims situation, adjust a loss under the condominium association coverage form and the unit owner's coverage form.

▷ Adjust a loss under builders' risk policies and explain how subrogation, termination of coverage, and loss adjustment are handled under builders' risk policies.

▷ Describe the extent and limitations of coverage for crime losses under the Building and Personal Property Coverage Form (BPP) and the ISO Commercial Crime Coverage Form.

▷ Given a loss, outline the loss adjustment procedures for computer and computer-related losses.

▷ Describe legal liability for pollution under the Superfund law.

▷ Explain to what extent property insurance policies provide coverage for cleanup of pollution and how they exclude coverage.

▷ Describe the different types of contractors' equipment and their uses.

▷ Explain the causes of loss, the exclusions, and the coverage extensions commonly found in contractors' equipment policies.

▷ Explain the valuation of a total loss claim for a piece of contractors' equipment and the valuation for a business income loss that may also result.

11

Outline, continued

Summary

Specialty Losses

11

INLAND MARINE INSURANCE: TRANSPORTATION LOSSES

Inland marine insurance includes a variety of insurance coverages. These coverages are grouped together as much because of their history as because of any logical relationship. Nevertheless, inland marine coverages share certain characteristics that adjusters must recognize and understand.

The categories of inland marine coverages are defined in the **Nationwide Marine Definition**. The definition was created to delineate the scope of inland marine underwriting. Although modern property-casualty insurers have full legal power to write all types of property insurance, the Nationwide Marine Definition remains important because inland marine business is less regulated and less standardized. See the exhibit "Summary of the Nationwide Marine Definition."

Generally, an inland marine risk must be in transit (such as cargo) or bear some relation to transportation (bridge and tunnels) or communication (radio and TV transmission towers). Inland marine insurance can cover personal property such as cameras, golf equipment, and jewelry or commercial property such as signs, film, photographic equipment, and physicians' equipment. Inland marine insurance usually covers risks of direct physical loss.

Nationwide Marine Definition

Statement of the types of property that may be insured on inland marine and ocean marine insurance forms.

Named-Perils or Special-Form Coverage

Many inland marine policies are written on a named-perils basis, but the special-form approach is the norm. However, an adjuster cannot assume that inland marine special-form coverage is equivalent to the perils of the Building and Personal Property Coverage Form (BPP) with the Causes of Loss— Special Form or to any other familiar standard. Because inland marine policies were developed to meet specialized needs, the coverages are often distinctive. An inland marine policy's special-form coverage might be broader than that of other special-form policies. For example, it might extend to earthquake or flood. Conversely, it might be narrower because of exclusions unique to certain types of property.

Inland marine policies' additional coverages are often broader than those of conventional property insurance policies. For example, many policies include loss of use coverage. Other inland marine policies have attractive extra

Summary of the Nationwide Marine Definition

- *Transportation*, covering the shipper or owner's goods, or the interests of the common carrier
- *Bridges, Tunnels, Instrumentalities of Transportation or Communication*

    Piers, dry docks

    Pipelines

    Telephone and telegraph property, including transmission lines and generating equipment

    Radio and television communication equipment, including towers and antennas and electrical apparatus

    Cranes and equipment to load and unload

- *Bailee—Bailor*

    Garment contractors' floater

    Bailee liability policy

    Bailees' customers policy

    Bailor policy

    Warehouse legal liability policy

    Furrier's customer policy

- *Floater policies (personal)*

    Personal effects

    Furs

    Jewelry

    Silverware

    Fine arts

    Stamps and coins

    Musical instrument

- *Floater policies (commercial)*

    Physicians' and surgeons' instruments

    Patterns and dies

    Theatrical

    Live animals

    Salespersons' samples

    Exhibitions

- *Installment sales, covering the vendor or purchaser of property*
- *Contractors' equipment*
- *Builders' risk*
- *Dealers' policies (floor plan)*
- *Miscellaneous policies*

    Jewelers' block

    Valuable papers

    Accounts receivable

    Fine arts

    Difference in conditions

    Electronic data processing

[DA04174]

features, such as coverage for additional expenses and expanded coverage for property of others.

Adjusters must be aware of the nonstandard nature of many inland marine policies. Policy clauses or conditions that an adjuster might take for granted in other policies might not even exist, or they might be substantially different, in inland marine policies. Therefore, adjusters must read each policy related to a loss.

Multiple Parties

Inland marine losses often include transportation, custody, or use of property by someone who is not the owner. The losses often involve more than one party, even when only one named insured is on a given policy. The involvement of more than one party can result in multiple insurance policies applicable to a given loss. These policies might cover only the respective interests of the various parties in the property, or they might cover the same interest. An adjuster must be alert to these possibilities and must resolve overlapping coverage and loss-sharing problems when they arise.

Need to Consult Contracts and Documents

Because several parties can be involved in inland marine losses, adjusters must often consult contracts or documents to determine interests or property values. These contracts and documents include bills of lading, consignment contracts, warehouse receipts, equipment leases, construction contracts, and sales invoices. These documents might specify or determine who has an interest in property and who must insure the property. Adjusters must also become familiar with various industries' business practices and jargon.

Transportation Losses

Transportation coverages were the historic origin of the inland marine business and still account for a significant amount of the business. Most businesses have some transit loss exposure. Manufacturers receive and ship goods. Wholesalers and retailers receive and ship goods. Any organization that moves from one location to another is shipping goods. These exposures require adjusters to determine legal interests and responsibilities for the damaged property. Because various laws define the responsibilities of rail, air, and ocean carriers, this section deals only with motor carriers, as this is the type of transportation loss that most adjusters encounter.

Parties in Transportation Losses

Transportation losses sometimes involve one party, if the property is being transported by its owner on the owner's trucks to the owner's locations. Usually, however, transportation losses involve three parties.

The shipper, or **consignor**, is the party with whom transportation of property begins. The shipper of property is usually a seller sending property to a buyer. Because the shipper is usually in some business other than carrying goods, it usually hires a carrier to transport goods.

The consignee is the party to whom goods are to be delivered. The consignee is usually a buyer and, depending on the terms of sale, might also own the goods throughout the course of transit.

Consignor
The party who is shipping goods.

Carrier

A person or organization in the business of transporting property of others.

Carriers transport goods. They can operate by truck, railroad, aircraft, barge, or ship. Transportation of a shipment by two or more different modes of transportation is referred to as intermodal transportation. Rail, air, and ship carriers are subject to different laws of liability than are truck carriers, which are often regulated by federal statute. Even truck carriers face different liabilities depending on whether they are common carriers or contract carriers.

Responsibility for Loss

Responsibility for loss to goods in transit depends on the answers to several questions. Who owns the goods? Who agreed to insure them? Was the carrier liable? Did any party limit its liability?

Who owns goods depends on the terms of sale. The seller and buyer can agree to any one of a number of sales terms. Ownership might transfer to the buyer at any point from the seller's warehouse to the buyer's receiving dock. So an adjuster must check the terms of sale to see who owns goods at the time of a loss. See the exhibit "Terms of Sale."

Terms of Sale

FOB (free on board) point of origin—Ownership passes from the seller to the buyer as soon as the carrier picks up the goods from the seller's premises. The point of origin might be named.

FOB destination—Ownership passes from the seller to the buyer when the carrier delivers the goods to the buyer's premises. The destination might be named.

FAS (free along side) vessel at a named port—Ownership passes from the seller to the buyer when the seller delivers the goods alongside a vessel for loading onto that vessel.

C.I.F. (cost, insurance, and freight)—The seller is obligated to pay for the insurance and freight charges for delivery to the buyer. However, ownership passes when the seller has delivered the goods to the carrier. The insurance and freight charges become part of the goods' insured value.

C.F., or C. & F.—The same as C.I.F., except the seller is not obligated to provide insurance coverage and is obligated to provide freight charges.

No agreed terms—If the agreement requires or authorizes the seller to ship by carrier, the risk of loss is like FOB point of origin. If the agreement is silent about shipping terms, the seller bears the risk of loss until the goods are delivered to the buyer.

[DA04175]

Typically, the goods' owner would have the greatest incentive to insure them, but when goods are being transported, the parties involved can agree on any arrangement. The adjuster must check the sales invoice and the bill of lading to see who has agreed to insure the goods. A **bill of lading** is both a contract of carriage between the carrier and the shipper and a receipt for the goods. Although an agreement to insure property does not automatically create insurance coverage, an adjuster who sees an agreement by a party other than the insured to insure the goods should investigate that party's coverage.

Adjuster Tip—The sale document or shipping document provides information on ownership and terms of sale. The document may use the shorthand term "Ex works" or "Ex Factory." "Ex" is Latin for the word "from." So if the adjuster sees the term "Ex factory," he or she will know that the goods were shipped from the shipper's factory.

A carrier is usually legally liable for loss or damage to goods in its custody. A common carrier offers its services to the general public and is liable in all cases, except for losses caused by acts of God, acts of a public enemy, exercise of public authority, shipper's neglect, or inherent vice of the goods. A contract carrier operates under contract with a shipper. Its liability depends on the contract's terms. Its liability might be as strict as a common carrier's or less strict. For example, a contract carrier might be responsible only for losses caused by its negligence.

Carriers often limit their liability by the terms of a bill of lading. Particularly, they often limit their liability to a specified dollar amount. Adjusters should not conclude that a carrier would cover a loss without first checking for such a limitation. The buyer and seller might also limit their liability for loss, although liability between these parties usually depends entirely on ownership. The owner of goods at the time of loss bears the loss.

Transit Policies

Shippers and consignees can insure goods in transit with transit insurance. Transit policies can be annual transit policies (covering all of the goods shipped that year) or trip transit (which covers only one specific shipment). Coverage under transit insurance does not depend on ownership. It certainly covers owned property, but it might also cover property for which the insured is liable or has agreed to insure, or for which the insured is the consignee.

Transit insurance applies only while goods are in transit. For an owner carrying its own goods, transit begins when the goods leave the starting point on their way to the destination. When a carrier for hire is transporting goods, transit begins when the goods have been placed in the carrier's custody, ready for shipment.

Transit claims' adjusting challenge concerns the issue of when the transportation actually ends. Minor deviations and customary stops usually do not signal the end of "due course of transit." However, if the stop is lengthy or the deviation is not work-related, issues could arise as to whether the transit has ceased. Temporary storage for the convenience of the shipper, carrier, or consignee is not an interruption of transit. Generally, transit ceases when the property is delivered to its final destination. But disputes often arise as to what constitutes delivery. Sometimes the truck arrives at its destination too late, and the

Bill of lading

A document acknowledging receipt of goods from the shipper, given by the carrier which includes the terms of the contract of carriage for the goods.

goods cannot be unloaded. Sometimes the truck arrives on time, and the consignee is not ready for the goods. Sometimes the consignee refuses the delivery entirely. An adjuster must thoroughly research each of these scenarios in the jurisdiction of the loss before payment of a claim.

The shipper's/consignee's transit policy usually covers property while in the custody of a carrier for hire or on owned/operated vehicles. It generally excludes contraband or property that is illegal to transport. Some policies are written to exclude high-value items such as money, jewelry, precious metals, and furs.

These policies also cover goods in temporary storage, before delivery to their final destination. The policy does not define temporary. Although the policy is not intended to cover long-term storage, what constitutes temporary is open to judicial interpretation.

Covered Causes of Loss—Transit policies can be written on a special-form basis with few exclusions or on a named-perils basis. Both forms usually contain exclusions for loss caused by governmental action, nuclear hazard, and war.

Theft coverage gets special attention in transit policies. The policies might include an exclusion for the dishonest acts of the insured's employees. They might also include exclusions for voluntary parting, unauthorized instructions, unexplained disappearance, and inventory shortage. These policies often contain an exclusion for theft of property from an unattended vehicle unless the vehicle is locked and has visible signs of forced entry.

Most transit policies exclude breakdown of refrigeration equipment, but such an exclusion applies only to vehicles owned or operated by the insured. If the insured has this exposure, the policy can be endorsed to cover spoilage resulting from refrigeration equipment's breakdown.

Valuation—Transit policies typically use the invoice price as the basis for valuing shipments. This is the good's selling price as shown in the sales invoice. Shipments of goods other than those made between a buyer and a seller are usually valued at actual cash value or the least of these:

- The property's actual cost
- The cost to restore the property
- The cost to replace the property

Subrogation—When a carrier for hire moves goods, that carrier may be legally liable for loss or damage to the goods. The extent of the carrier's liability is governed by the bill of lading. The bill of lading contains a section called "Limitation of Carriers Liability." Unless a greater dollar value is declared by the shipper and stated in the bill of lading, the carrier's liability is limited to the amount stated in the limitation provision. This is commonly referred to as a "released bill of lading." For household-goods movers, this limitation is expressed as XX amount of cents per pound. For other types of carriers, it is expressed as XX amount of dollars per package.

Adjusting Transit Losses—It is essential for any adjuster to begin a transit loss adjustment with the terms of the policy because they might be unique to the insured. The adjuster must gather all of the facts concerning the loss. The shipping documents, such as the bill of lading and the sales invoice, are necessary. If the goods have sustained damage, the adjuster should have the goods and the shipping container or packaging inspected. Prompt inspection also facilitates salvage.

Salvage is an important option in transit losses. If the goods are perishable, they must be moved quickly to maximize salvage recovery. If the bill of lading is released at only a fraction of the actual value of the damaged goods, salvage may be the only way to recoup some of the loss payment.

Motor Truck Cargo Liability Insurance

To protect a carrier for hire's exposure for loss or damage to cargo, the Motor Truck Cargo (MTC) Liability Policy was developed. Despite the fact that it is a liability policy, a property loss adjuster usually handles the claims because, under such a policy, the loss is to property, not to people.

Liability For Cargo—Section 14706 of Title 49, United State Code, describes motor carriers' cargo liability. It applies to any motor carrier, except for agricultural carriers, household-goods carriers, express and package carriers, motor carriage incidental to air carriage, and contract carriage in which the contract's terms allow for specific conditions. Under Section 14706, a motor carrier's liability is strict liability subject to certain defenses and subject to limits agreed on in the bill of lading.

The defenses available to a motor carrier are these:

- Acts of God
- Acts of a public enemy
- Acts of public authorities
- Fault or neglect by the shipper
- Inherent vice or nature of the property

An **act of God** is defined as an event that occurs without human intervention or an act that cannot be prevented by the exercise of human care. Tornadoes, floods, and earthquakes are all classified as acts of God. However, if a carrier ignores a flood warning concerning travel on a particular road and the cargo suffers flood damage, it would be unlikely that the carrier would escape liability for the damage.

Act of God

A natural and unavoidable catastrophe that interrupts the expected course of events.

A **public enemy** is a nation or government at war with the nation in which the motor carrier is domiciled. It does not refer to an individual criminal or to groups of criminals. It is unclear what the status of a terrorist or terrorist organization might have under the exclusion.

Public enemy

A nation or government at war with the nation in which the carrier is domiciled.

Acts of public authorities refers to any act taken by a public official acting within the scope of his or her authority. If a U.S. Customs agent damages cargo while searching for illegal drugs, the carrier would not be held liable unless the carrier could reasonably have foreseen and prevented the damage.

A carrier may avoid liability if the loss is caused by the shipper's fault or negligence. However, the carrier must prove that the shipper's act was the sole cause of the loss and that the carrier did not contribute to the loss in any way. If the carrier is aware that the packaging or loading is improper and it accepts the shipment anyway, the carrier will be held liable for the loss.

Inherent vice

A quality of or condition within a particular type of property that tends to make the property destroy itself.

Inherent vice is a condition that can cause property to deteriorate or destroy itself. This condition can be a defect, disease, decay, or condition that will cause deterioration. For example, wood warps if subject to humidity for a period of time, and fruit decays after several days, especially without refrigeration.

The MTC liability policy covers property in carriers' care, custody, and control, or when loaded or unloaded at a terminal for up to seventy-two hours, excluding Sundays and holidays. The property must be accepted under the terms of a bill of lading or shipping receipt.

The MTC liability policy excludes contraband and high-value items such as money, jewelry, and furs. Live animals are also usually excluded. Breakdown of refrigeration equipment is usually excluded but can be added back by endorsement.

The BMC 32 endorsement can be found on most motor truck cargo liability policies. The U.S. Code, 49 USC 13906, requires motor carriers operating within federal jurisdiction to show evidence of financial responsibility up to a minimum limit of $5,000 for loss or damage to the contents of any one vehicle and $10,000 for aggregate losses at any one time and place with respect to any one shipper or consignee. The insurer files a form with the Federal Motor Carrier Safety Administration, Licensing and Insurance Division, advising that the obligation is met. The BMC 32 endorsement states that the insurer will pay for loss or damage for which the motor carrier can be found legally liable for having caused. Under the terms of the endorsement, the insurer must pay the claim, subject to the limits, regardless of any exclusions or conditions contained in the policy. An example would be loss caused by the theft of goods by a carrier's employee. Although this is not a covered loss, the insurer would pay the claim subject to the limits in the BMC 32 endorsement and then attempt to recover the payment from the insured.

Adjuster Tip—The BMC 32 endorsement is valid until it is canceled by a proper filing made at the policy's expiration or cancellation. Cancellation or expiration of the policy without the proper filing is not sufficient to void the BMC 32.

MTC liability coverage is a third-party coverage that most insurers treat as a first-party coverage. Because the loss is to property, insurers assign these claims to property loss adjusters. These adjusters must determine liability as well as coverage. The investigation must reveal the insured to be legally liable for the damage before the policy will respond.

Coverage verification is the starting point of any claim investigation, and the MTC liability claim is no exception. In fact, it can present new issues to the adjuster. MTC liability is written either on a scheduled-vehicle basis or a blanket/gross-receipts basis. If the coverage is on a scheduled-vehicle basis, then the unit involved in the loss must be listed on the policy. Because of the nature of the trucking industry, the identity of the named insured may also be an issue. There are many types of ownership, trip-lease, and owner-operator agreements used within the trucking industry, so it is important to verify that the legally responsible party is in fact insured under the policy.

The property loss adjuster must determine the facts of the loss, obtain all of the shipping documents, and inspect the loss. Salvage potential is just as important in the MTC liability claim as it is in a merchandise claim.

INLAND MARINE INSURANCE: BAILEE AND WAREHOUSE LEGAL LIABILITY LOSSES

Inland marine insurance includes a variety of insurance coverages. These coverages are grouped together as much because of their history as because of any logical relationship. Nevertheless, inland marine coverages share certain characteristics that adjusters must recognize and understand. The categories of inland marine coverages are defined in the Nationwide Marine Definition. See the exhibit "Summary of the Nationwide Marine Definition."

Losses involving bailments are insured under bailee/bailor policies. Repair shops, jewelry stores, and dry cleaners all need this type of coverage. Warehouse legal liability is another form of bailee insurance. The warehouse legal liability policy covers the warehouse's legal liability for loss or damage to a customer's property.

Bailee Losses

A **bailment** is the transfer of possession of property from one person to another for a specified purpose. Giving cargo to a carrier to transport is a bailment. But many other types of businesses are involved in bailments. They range from warehouses to repair shops, jewelry stores, or consignees of property on consignment. In these situations, title to the property remains with the owner, the **bailor**, and the property is expected to be returned to the bailor once the specific purpose has ended. The person entrusted with the property is the bailee and is responsible for the property while it is in his or her control.

A bailment differs from both a lease or an agency situation. In a lease, the lessee has full rights during the lease to use the property *in any way*, even to the exclusion of the owner. In a bailment, the bailee's use of the property is limited to a specific purpose. If an agent or employee holds property, the law considers that condition as equivalent to possession by the principal/owner.

Bailment

The temporary possession by one party (the bailee) of personal property owned by another party (the bailor) for a specific purpose, such as cleaning or repair.

Bailor

The owner of the personal property in a bailment.

Summary of the Nationwide Marine Definition

- *Transportation*, covering the shipper or owner's goods, or the interests of the common carrier
- *Bridges, Tunnels, Instrumentalities of Transportation or Communication*

    Piers, dry docks

    Pipelines

    Telephone and telegraph property, including transmission lines and generating equipment

    Radio and television communication equipment, including towers and antennas and electrical apparatus

    Cranes and equipment to load and unload
- *Bailee—Bailor*

    Garment contractors' floater

    Bailee liability policy

    Bailees' customers policy

    Bailor policy

    Warehouse legal liability policy

    Furrier's customer policy
- *Floater policies (personal)*

    Personal effects

    Furs

    Jewelry

    Silverware

    Fine arts

    Stamps and coins

    Musical instrument
- *Floater policies (commercial)*

    Physicians' and surgeons' instruments

    Patterns and dies

    Theatrical

    Live animals

    Salespersons' samples

    Exhibitions
- *Installment sales, covering the vendor or purchaser of property*
- *Contractors' equipment*
- *Builders' risk*
- *Dealers' policies (floor plan)*
- *Miscellaneous policies*

    Jewelers' block

    Valuable papers

    Accounts receivable

    Fine arts

    Difference in conditions

    Electronic data processing

[DA04174]

Liability in Bailment Situations

Bailment for the benefit of the bailor

A bailment in which the bailee owes only a slight duty of care to safeguard the bailed property from loss or damage.

There are three types of bailment situations. First is a **bailment for the benefit of the bailor** only, such as when one neighbor agrees to take care of a vacationing neighbor's plants. The property owner enjoys the sole benefit. In such a bailment, the bailee owes only a slight duty of care and would probably be liable to the owner only for intentional wrongdoing and gross recklessness.

The second type is a **bailment for the benefit of the bailee** only, such as when one neighbor borrows another's lawn mower. In this situation, the bailee owes a high duty of care and is presumably liable for any damage.

The third type is a **bailment for the mutual benefit of bailee and bailor (mutual benefit bailment)**. For example, a dry cleaner/bailee receives payment for the service of laundering, and the customer/bailor receives clean clothing in return for his or her payment. This situation is also known as a commercial bailment. The bailee owes a duty of ordinary care for the property in his or her possession.

Bailee Coverages

Coverage purchased by bailees typically falls into two broad categories:

- The bailee liability policy
- The bailees' customers policy

The bailee liability policy covers the insured for sums that he or she becomes legally obligated to pay as a result of loss caused by a covered peril. As the name implies, this is liability coverage, and the insured would have to be legally liable for the loss for the policy to respond.

Under the bailees' customers policy, coverage is provided for property in the bailee's custody with no need to prove the insured's liability or negligence. The coverage is often invoked when bailees want to maintain customer goodwill by replacing the customer's damaged property, even when the bailee has not been at fault. Bailees' customers policies always involve dual interests: both the bailee and the customer have interests in the property and in the claim settlement proceeds.

Bailor Coverages

Bailors do not necessarily rely on the bailees' coverage. Often, when a bailment is created, either the bailee provides no coverage or the bailee's coverage will not respond, such as when the bailee is found not to be legally liable for the loss. Sometimes, bailors insure an exposure despite coverage available from the bailee. Perhaps the property involved is of particularly high value or is hard to replace, or perhaps its loss would interfere with the bailor's regular business.

Most bailors seeking coverage for their property when it is off-premises first check the built-in extensions contained in their own homeowners or commercial property forms. The homeowners policy covers personal property while it is anywhere in the world. The BPP provides tightly limited off-premises coverage. Coinsurance requirements must be met, and the loss must occur at a place that the insured does not own, lease, or operate. Additionally, the covered property cannot be in or on a vehicle; in a salesperson's care, custody, or control; or at a fair or an exhibition. The limit for this extension is $5,000.

Bailment for the benefit of the bailee

A bailment in which the bailee owes a high duty of care to safeguard the bailed property from loss or damage.

Bailment for the mutual benefit of bailee and bailor (mutual benefit bailment)

A bailment in which the bailee owes a duty of ordinary care to safeguard the bailed property from loss or damage.

Because the built-in off-premises coverages are limited and might not be adequate for losses, several types of bailor policies are available. In personal insurance coverages, various endorsements can be added to cover specific property such as jewelry, cameras, and fine arts. These endorsements (often called floaters) cover more than just a bailment situation, but they do apply to losses occurring to property in a bailee's possession. Commercial bailors can also use numerous inland marine floaters and endorsements to provide off-premises coverage. A processing floater, used by businesses that send their goods to other businesses for processing, is an example.

Adjustment of Bailment Losses

Because of the many coverage possibilities, as well as the possibility of overlapping or joint coverage, a bailment loss requires special handling. Adjusters must determine all parties to the bailment and the nature and extent of their specific interest in the property damaged. Adjusters must also examine all documents related to the bailment to determine the parties' contractual rights and whether either party has waived any rights before the loss. For example, the contract might contain a hold-harmless agreement or might require a specific party to insure the property.

Adjusters must also be familiar with industry practices concerning specific types of property. For example, in the jewelry business, retailers typically hold property of others on a consignment basis. While the property is in the retailer's possession, he or she must usually provide insurance.

Adjusters should also be aware of differences in valuation clauses between policies. For example, under a bailee liability policy, the insurer would be liable to cover property on an actual cash value (ACV) basis; under a homeowners form, the coverage could be written either on an ACV or a replacement cost basis.

If a bailees' customers policy insures a laundry or dry cleaner and the loss involves virtually all of the bailor's property in the store, the adjuster could set up a claims operation on the premises. The policy usually covers the ACV of the customer's property. The adjuster might be dealing with 300 or more customers, so a standard procedure would be necessary. The adjuster might require each claimant to complete a claim form, then negotiate the claim and issue a check on site. The adjuster would handle claims involving a few shirts or a pair of slacks in this manner, but if a large value is involved, the adjuster might go to the claimant's home to settle the loss. Alternatively, the adjuster might simply have the insured distribute claim forms to its customers to be completed and then sent to the adjuster's office, after which negotiations are handled by phone.

In some cases, insurers allow the businessowners to settle losses up to a certain dollar amount with their customers, for example, up to $100 or $250. The insurer might believe that the insured knows the customer and the garments and is therefore better able to negotiate a reasonable actual cash value. This method, of course, has its drawbacks. The insured might be only interested in keeping its customers happy and might not subject their claims to adequate scrutiny. Another settlement method is to settle directly with the insured with a policy release, which allows the insured to handle the customers' claims.

Warehouse Legal Liability

Another type of bailment that is significantly involved in the transportation industry is the storage of goods in a warehouse. A warehouse is in the business of receiving and storing others' goods for a price. The Uniform Commercial Code (U.C.C.) regulates the business of warehousing. The U.C.C. is a body of rules that regulate all commercial transactions. Warehouses may be public, private, or bonded. A public warehouse is one that accepts goods for storage from anyone for a price. A private warehouse is usually controlled by a large retailer or manufacturer for the storage of its own goods. A bonded warehouse is one in which goods are stored awaiting the payment of import duty. For the purposes of this text, the discussion focuses on public warehouses.

Warehouse legal liability policies cover the warehouse's legal liability for physical loss or damage to property of customers at specified locations. It, too, is a third-party liability policy handled as a first-party policy.

The warehouse legal liability coverage can be named-perils or special-form coverage. It excludes the same types of causes of loss as the motor truck cargo liability policy. It also excludes loss resulting from processing and war risks.

Generally, a warehouse is not under a duty to insure stored property for the benefit of the owner or depositor. However, state statutes, the depositor's instructions, custom and practice, or a contract may require the warehouse to have insurance for the benefit of the depositor. The U.C.C. Article 7, Section 204, makes a warehouse liable if the loss or damage is caused by its failure to exercise reasonable care.

Investigating a Warehouse Legal Liability Claim

Warehouse legal liability claims present many levels of adjusting challenges. They can be some of the most complex and interesting claims to work on because a warehouse loss rarely involves only one depositor. When a warehouse is damaged by fire, water, smoke, wind, or any other possible cause of loss, the property of many different depositors is often affected. Large quantities of property for each depositor may be involved. Each depositor will require his or her own inventory. The adjuster may have to use different methods of restoration, salvage, and valuation to properly adjust these losses.

The terms of each depositor's warehouse receipt or contract may be different, so the adjuster reviews every contract for its terms. The cause of loss investigation may be hampered by vast quantities of debris, uncooperative witnesses, and bad weather. The cause of loss investigation may lead to the discovery of information that affects coverage, such as the discovery that the insured was storing chemicals on the premises when the policy was written for a general merchandise exposure.

Initial Response to Loss

It is not uncommon for the warehouse legal liability policy to be placed with a different insurer than the insurer handling the building's property coverage. The warehouse may simply be a tenant in the building. If the building coverage is with another carrier, it is a good idea to work with the building carrier's property adjuster to secure the premises and share related expenses.

Keep in mind that the warehouse legal liability interest and the building interests may ultimately be adverse to one another. For example, the building owner may blame the warehouse for causing a fire that guts the building. The warehouse may blame the owner for the fire based on the owner's failure to maintain the building. Nevertheless, until it is established that a conflict exists, it is best to try to work together to secure the site and protect all of the property from further damage.

Analysis of Storage Documents

The storage receipts of each depositor must be reviewed to determine the nature of the relationship between the depositor and the insured. It is possible for the relationship to be that of bailee-bailor, landlord-tenant, or carrier-shipper. Only the storage documents clarify the relationship. The storage documents also define the parties' obligations to each other. It is also a good idea to review correspondence, brochures, and advertisements to determine whether they affect the parties' obligations. This is especially true for losses resulting from extremes in temperature and humidity when the warehouse advertises itself to be climate-controlled.

Limitation of Liability

The warehouse receipt or other storage receipt includes a limitation of liability provision. The U.C.C. allows a warehouse to limit its liability under certain circumstances. To be an enforceable limitation, the terms must specify liability per article or item or a value per unit or weight. The warehouse must give the depositor the opportunity to increase the valuation.

Storage Arrangements

One of the key elements in determining the warehouse's liability and the potential for subrogation against another party is understanding the storage arrangement used by the warehouse. Warehouses generally use these types of storage arrangements, alone or in combination:

- Bulk storage
- Solid piling storage

- Palletized storage
- Rack storage

The commodity can dictate what method of storage is used, and that method affects fire behavior, fire control, and the goods' susceptibility to water damage.

Bulk storage refers to loose granules, powder, or pellets stored in silos, bins, or tanks, or in piles on the floor. Conveyors are usually in the building to help move the material. Automatic sprinklers are essential for this arrangement. Heat sensors are also a good idea because certain types of commodities can ignite while in a pile and the ignition might be difficult to locate deep inside a pile.

Solid piling storage consists of one pallet, at floor level, piled high with cartons, boxes, bales or bags, all in direct contact with one another. Stacking is usually done by hand or with lift trucks. Piling in excess of fifteen feet can be difficult to protect with sprinklers.

A **pallet unit** is usually three or four feet in height and consists of many smaller packages stacked on top of one another. The pallet can be banded or shrink-wrapped to keep the packages in place on the pallet. Pallets are easy to move with a forklift, so they can be stacked very high. Because of the stacking, it is difficult for sprinklers to be effective against a fire occurring within the stack.

A steel shelf unit in one's garage or basement is an example of **rack storage**. Commercial rack storage is made of steel frames. The racks' height is only limited by the vertical reach of the handling equipment. Some rack-storage facilities are highly automated, using computers to track locations and inventory and control the material-handling equipment. Rack storage can have narrow aisles, allowing fire to jump easily from one rack to another. Conventional ceiling sprinklers are not very effective in a rack storage facility. In-rack sprinkler systems provide the best protection.

Liability Assessment

The type of storage arrangement and the sprinkler system within the building can affect the liability assessment. If a warehouse manager knowingly accepts goods for storage that are incompatible with his or her storage system and sprinkler system, then the warehouse's liability may be increased.

Adjuster Tip—Not all warehouses are sprinklered. Check local ordinances to determine whether the warehouse complies with fire regulations and building codes.

A warehouse may unknowingly accept goods that are dangerous. Because the standard of care depends on "reasonableness," the adjuster must investigate what a reasonable warehouse would have done under similar circumstances to determine the goods' exact nature. This becomes particularly important in chemicals' storage. When a chemical is stored in a warehouse, a **Material**

Bulk storage

Storage of loose granules, powder, or pellets in silos, bins, or tanks, or in piles on the floor.

Solid piling storage

A pallet, at floor level, piled high with cartons, boxes, bales, or bags, all in direct contact with one another.

Pallet unit

A wooden base stacked with smaller packages up to a height of three or four feet, which are usually banded or shrink-wrapped to keep the packages in place.

Rack storage

Steel shelving of any height, on which goods are stored.

Material Safety Data Sheet (MSDS)

A document required by the Occupational Safety and Health Administration (OSHA) that describes a property's hazardous chemicals and how they must be handled.

Safety Data Sheet (MSDS) should be obtained from the depositor. The chemical manufacturer writes the MSDS. It describes what the chemical is; who makes it; what ingredients are in it; and how it reacts to heat, cold, and water. It describes the potential for fire and explosion and recommends the method for extinguishing a fire. It also describes how stable the product is, whether it will react to other chemicals stored around it, and whether there are any special handling instructions for it.

Burden of Proof

In the event of a contested claim, the adjuster must ascertain which party has the burden of proof regarding the warehouse's negligence. Unfortunately, there is no uniformity among the states, so it will be necessary to consult with local counsel to learn who has the burden of proof. In states that favor the warehouse, the depositor must show that the warehouse was negligent by a preponderance of the evidence. In states that favor the depositor, the warehouse must show that the loss was not its fault and could not have been prevented by any reasonable action on its part.

CONDOMINIUM LOSSES

Many different kinds of property policies are used for specialized risk exposures. Condominiums are a special form of property ownership that present several unique legal, coverage, and adjusting issues.

A **condominium** is one of the units in a multiple-unit structure, each of which is separately owned. These units can be dwelling or business-type units. Each unit owner receives a deed of record independent of any other unit owner. A single unit often consists of nothing more than a cubicle, or "box of air," of one or more levels of space within the structure's unfinished surfaces of walls, floors, or ceilings. After a developer has sold a certain percentage of the units, it relinquishes authority to the condominium association.

A condominium should not be confused with a cooperative. A **cooperative or co-op** is a not-for-profit corporation that owns the units and the associated property. A tenant buys stock in the cooperative that entitles the tenant to lease a unit.

Common Elements

A **condominium association** manages the condominium complex and is responsible for the **common elements**. The association does not own the property. The common elements, or areas, are jointly owned by all unit owners and include the land on which the building is located as well as other real property, consisting of foundations; roofs; main support walls; halls; stairways; entrances and exits; lobbies; yards; gardens; parking areas; power; light; gas; plumbing; heating and air conditioning systems; elevators; pumps; duct

---

Condominium
A real estate development consisting of a group of units, in which the air space within the boundaries of each unit is owned by the unit owner, and all remaining real and personal property is owned jointly by all the unit owners.

Cooperative (co-op)
A not-for-profit corporation that owns the housing units and the associated property.

Condominium association
An entity composed of the unit owners in a condominium to manage the condominium and to own the common elements.

Common elements
Areas of a condominium that are jointly owned by all unit owners, including the land on which the buildings are located.

work; storage areas or basements; and pools, playgrounds, and other recreation facilities on the grounds.

Because of the complexity of the relationship between unit owners and the association, condominiums are created and defined by legislation in most jurisdictions. These statutes also address insurance requirements. Most states require the association to provide insurance to cover loss or damage to the common elements. A unit owner must insure his or her contents and interest in his or her own unit. Some statutes state that improvements and betterments are to be covered under the unit owner's insurance because the improvements increase the value of the unit itself. Other statutes require improvements and betterments, whether to the individual units or to common areas, to be insured under the association's policy.

Master Deeds and Bylaws

To determine who is responsible for specific property, adjusters must check not only state statutes but also the **master deed** and the unit deeds of the condominium. The master deed might also be called the "declarations of the condominium association" or the "condominium association agreement." The condominium's developer or builder usually draws up the deed or declarations.

Either the master deed or separate bylaws describe the relationship between the unit owners, the duties of the association, maintenance fees, how assessments are to be made, and insurance requirements. The deed or bylaws also describe the transference of properties, how the association is to be governed, and requirements for any modifications or amendments to the bylaws.

Master deed
A document that defines a condominium and specifies the relationship between the unit owners and the association.

Nature of the Unit Owner's Interest

After reviewing a copy of the master deed and bylaws, adjusters can determine insurable interests and which policy is to provide coverage for damaged items. Condominium deeds outline the insurable interests in two possible ways:

*   The **bare-walls concept**
*   The **all-encompassing concept**

For a loss adjustment based on the all-encompassing concept, the condominium association insurer repairs or replaces all original installations. The unit owner's insurer covers damage to improvements and betterments and any personal property involved in the loss and installed by the unit owner.

Bare-walls concept
A concept of condominium ownership in which the association has no ownership interest within the bare walls of each unit.

All-encompassing concept
A condo association's interest when it owns and is responsible for all interior and exterior items within the individual condo unit at the time of the original purchase by the unit owner.

Coverage Forms

Insurance Services Office, Inc., (ISO) provides a separate, simplified commercial property insurance program for condominium associations. Unit owners are protected by a special type of homeowners form or a commercial unit owner's form.

The Bare-walls Concept

Under the bare-walls concept, a unit owner's property consists only of what is within the bare walls, including paint, wallpaper, carpet or flooring, appliances, fixtures (electrical or plumbing), and interior walls. A claim adjustment under an association's policy would not cover these items. Conversely, the unit owner's policy would not provide coverage in the event of a loss for damage to drywall that forms an exterior, or load-bearing, wall; floor decking; joists; studs; rafters; foundations; or roofing.

For a loss adjustment based on the barewalls concept, the adjuster for the association and the adjuster for the unit owner must decide which policy provides coverage for which items. This issue should be decided before repairs are made so that no misunderstanding occurs during the final settlement or payment of the claim. When the structural damage is serious, a unit owner's insurer often allows the condominium association insurer to cover all repairs and reimburses it for the portion of the damages covered by the unit owner's policy.

The All-Encompassing Concept

Under the all-encompassing concept (also known as the "air space concept" or the "single entity concept"), the condominium association owns and is responsible for all exterior and interior items within the unit at the time of its original purchase by the unit owner. When the unit is sold with appliances, flooring, and fixtures already installed, the association is responsible for insuring these items. The purchase contract describes these items.

[DA04179]

Condominium Association Coverage Form

The condominium association coverage form is used in conjunction with the common declarations, common and commercial property conditions, causes of loss forms, and other assorted forms. The condominium association form is similar to the Building and Personal Property Coverage Form (BPP) and contains the same coverages, additional coverages, extension of coverage, optional coverages, and property not covered. The condominium association coverage form provides coverage for the building. It also covers certain types of property within a unit, such as fixtures, improvements, and appliances, if the condominium master deed or bylaws require the association to insure such property. This coverage applies whether or not the unit owner owns these items. Under the unit owner's insurance provision, the insurance for the association is primary. It is not contributory with any insurance carried by the unit owner covering the same property.

Business personal property is covered if it is owned by the association or indivisibly by all unit owners. It is not covered if owned solely by a unit owner. Property under this coverage could include clubroom furnishings, deck or lawn chairs, lobby or hall decorations, and recreational equipment. The condominium association coverage form, like the BPP, provides coverage for personal property of others if shown in the declarations. This coverage includes unit owners' property.

Associations commonly appoint an insurance trustee to act on the unit owners' behalf. The insurance trustee is responsible for decisions regarding the placement of coverage and the settlement of claims. The condominium association coverage form has added a provision under loss payment to state that the insurer may adjust the loss with the association but pay the insurance to a trustee if one has been appointed. Any payment made to the trustee satisfies the claims of all unit owners.

The association is made up of individual unit owners. Accordingly, the right of subrogation by the insurer against individual unit owners has been waived in the waiver of rights of recovery provision.

Unit Owner's Coverage Form

Two types of unit owner's coverage are available:

- Coverage for commercial unit owners
- Coverage for residential unit owners

Commercial unit owner's coverage complements the association policy and has many of the same provisions of the other commercial property coverages. It includes no building coverage because the building is insured under the association policy. It does include coverage for building fixtures, improvements, and alterations owned by the unit owner and not insured by the association. Any settlement on these items is subject to the policy's coinsurance provision. If the same property is covered under both the unit owner's policy and the association policy, the unit owner's coverage is excess over the association coverage. The condominium commercial unit owner's coverage has two optional coverages:

- Loss assessment coverage
- Miscellaneous real property coverage

A **loss assessment** is a charge by the condominium association against the unit owners. The association has the right to make such charges, under certain circumstances, as described in the master deed or bylaws. Loss assessment coverage is limited to liability for assessments resulting from direct physical loss or damage by a covered peril to common property in which all unit owners have an interest. The unit owner purchases loss assessment coverage for protection in case the association's insurance is not sufficient to cover a loss. Loss assessment coverage can be purchased for multiples of $1,000, with a $250 deductible. If the assessment is made to cover a large deductible in the association's coverage, the limit of liability is $1,000 regardless of the amount purchased by the unit owner. Miscellaneous real property coverage is provided under a separate limit of insurance. This class of real property includes property owned by the condominium unit insured only or required by the association agreement to be insured by the unit owner. An example is a storage structure located in the common areas and used solely by a unit owner.

Loss assessment
A charge by the condominium association against the unit owners for the cost of uninsured losses.

Residential unit owner's coverage is provided by a homeowner's unit owner's form (HO-6). The policy insures against all broad-form perils, including fire; lightning; windstorm; hail; explosion; riot; civil commotion; aircraft; vehicles; smoke; vandalism; malicious mischief; theft; falling objects; weight of ice, snow, or sleet; accidental discharge of water or steam; tearing, cracking, burning, or bulging of a steam or hot water system; freezing; artificially generated electrical current; and volcanic eruption. Coverage against these named perils is important for the insured's personal property, but it also applies to building improvements and betterments and other building items owned by the unit owner and not insured under the association agreement. It also applies to other structures owned solely by the unit owner (other than the residence premises) and located on the residence premises. If a loss occurs, insurance provided under this form is excess to the association's policy covering the same property. Loss assessment coverage is an additional coverage under the HO-6 form. When an assessment is made as a result of direct loss to property owned collectively by all unit members and caused by a peril insured against, the insurer will pay up to $1,000.

Adjuster Tip—Do not assume that the occupier of the unit is the unit's owner. Tenants can occupy a condominium unit, and they would have renter's insurance for their personal property. Therefore, determining who all of the parties are when investigating the loss is very important.

BUILDERS' RISK LOSSES

Many different kinds of property policies are used for specialized risk exposures. Property under construction has special loss exposures. Builders' risk coverage responds to these exposures.

Builders' risk coverage differs from standard commercial property insurance. Loss adjustment of builders' risk claims can be accomplished in several ways.

Builders' Risk Exposures

When a contractor or builder is prepared to begin construction of a new building, it faces the difficult situation of insuring a structure whose value and condition are constantly changing. Initially, machinery, equipment, tools and supplies, building materials, scaffolding, fencing, temporary buildings, and sheds might be on the site. Therefore, if the contractor were to secure ordinary commercial property insurance to cover the structure's completed value, it would pay excessive premiums while the building was under construction. As the construction nears completion, the contractor might be underinsured because of increased construction costs.

The contractor might be required to protect not only its own interests in the building but also the interests of the owners and the mortgagees as well as the subcontractors that work on the structure. The contractor might even be required to protect its suppliers' interests. The contractor's obligation to protect these other interests comes from the construction contracts. Although the contractor might not bear each of the preceding obligations, rarely is a contractor obligated to protect only its own interest.

The building also faces special hazards while the building is under construction. Building materials are difficult to protect while on a construction site. They are subject to theft and severe damage by windstorms and by fire. While under construction, the building itself is also exposed to these types of losses and to vandalism or collapse. Protecting the building from loss is difficult because it lacks safeguards such as sprinkler systems or even adequate access to water.

Coverage Forms

The builders' risk form was devised to address the special problem of changing values and the unique exposures to loss of a building under construction. The policy is written for one year but normally terminates when the building has been completed or occupied. A builders' risk policy can be written for basic, broad, or "direct physical loss unless excluded" coverage.

The policy can be written on a builders' risk form, or it can be a manuscript policy.

Commercial Property

A builders' risk form is attached to a commercial property policy and becomes subject to the common declarations and conditions, as well as the commercial property declarations and conditions and the causes of loss form that make up the policy.

Commercial property builders' risk forms do not cover collapse during construction unless it is added back by an endorsement that covers collapse caused by faulty design, plans, or workmanship. Nor do they cover theft of building materials not attached to a building under any causes of loss form. Even the Causes of Loss—Special Form eliminates theft coverage for building materials and supplies and also eliminates any coverage for machinery, tools, and equipment owned by, or in the care, custody, or control of, the insured.

Manuscript Forms

The policy can be written in a manuscript form to cover uncertain or uncommon exposures. The construction might take several years, or the project may be an unusually large and complex structure that requires more coverage than that provided by the standard commercial form. Manuscript forms may also cover the testing and commissioning of equipment installed in the building as part of the project.

Inland Marine Policies

Builders' risk coverage is also provided as an inland marine coverage under a builders' risk policy or an installation floater, usually on an "all-risks" basis. Inland marine builders' risk policies usually have broader coverage than commercial property policies do because they can cover property in transit and at other job sites, they cover collapse and theft, and they can be endorsed to cover earthquake and flood. Most important, inland marine policies may cover increased **soft costs**. Soft costs, such as interest, real estate taxes, advertising, architects' and engineers' fees, legal and accounting fees, and insurance, are incurred when there is a delay in the completion of the project. Adjusters may need professional assistance to identify and evaluate increased soft costs.

Soft costs

Various incidental expenses that may result from physical loss or from a delay in completion of a construction project, such as interest, real estate tax, advertising, architects and engineers fees, and legal and accounting fees.

Property Covered

Builders' risk policies provide coverage for buildings or structures in the course of construction on the described premises, including foundations and materials used for construction. It extends coverage to fixtures, machinery, and equipment that service the building. Inland marine forms cover building materials and supplies owned by the insured; building materials and supplies of others in the insured's care, custody, or control; and temporary structures, including scaffolding, cribbing, and construction forms.

As in most coverage forms, there is no coverage for land, water, or certain outdoor property such as lawns, trees, shrubs, plants, radio or television antennas or towers, and detached signs. Builders' risk coverage forms might also exclude the preexisting part of a building to which alterations, additions, repairs, or renovations are being made.

Handling Changing Values

The builders' risk policy is written on a completed value approach or a reporting form. Insurance is usually written for the completed value of the building or structure. The premium charged is reduced because the policy limits exceed the value at risk to the insurer until the building is completed. The completed value form includes a condition called "need for adequate insurance" that is effectively a 100 percent coinsurance clause. The policy limit must equal the expected completed value or a penalty is imposed.

The reporting form requires the insured to make monthly reports of value. The initial premium is generally determined by computing the actual cash value of the property brought onto the insured premises at the start of construction. As the monthly reports are filed, the limits of liability are increased accordingly, and additional premium is computed. If the reports are late or undervalued, the insured can face severe penalties if a covered loss occurs. Because the coinsurance clause in a full reporting form is 100 percent, failure to report limits the insurer's liability to the actual cash value at the inception

of the policy. Failure to report on time can limit the insurer's liability to the
last reported value.

Subrogation

Because of the various interests covered by the policy and the relationship between these parties, adjusters should check both the policy and the
contracts between the parties to determine whether subrogation is possible. Determining who is an insured, the extent of the interest insured, and
whether subrogation has been waived in writing by agreement before an
actual loss is important.

Many commercial property builders' risk forms require an insured to obtain
the insurer's written permission to waive any rights to recovery before a loss
occurs. The inland marine version of the builders' risk form may limit this
provision to architects or engineers, thus permitting waiver of subrogation
against other contractors or subcontractors. These provisions are especially
important because many form contracts in the construction business, such
as those provided by the American Institute of Architects, require waiver of
actions by the parties. Such waivers might threaten a contractor's insurance
coverage unless the insurer approves them.

Coverage Termination

The coverage of the builders' risk form ends when *any* one of these five conditions is met:

- The policy is canceled, the policy expires, or ninety days have passed
  since the completion of the project.
- The owner or purchaser accepts the property. This acceptance, of course,
  should mean that other specific insurance on the completed building is in
  place.
- The insured no longer has any interest in the property; therefore, the
  insured cannot suffer a loss if the property is damaged.
- The construction is abandoned, and the insured has no intention of completing the building and has given up his or her right or interest in the
  building.
- Sixty days after the building has been wholly or partially occupied, put to
  its intended use, or leased to others.

Loss Adjustment

The investigation of a builders' risk loss usually begins with an inspection of
the construction site and the damaged property. Taking a statement from the
site superintendent or clerk of the works can help the property loss adjuster
obtain and understand the facts of the loss, the parties involved, and the
extent of the damage.

An important part of a claims investigation involves gathering all contracts relevant to the claims handling process. Relevant contracts include the construction contract between the general contractor and the owner, as well as those between the general contractor and the subcontractors.

Construction contracts often require one party to purchase insurance for the benefit of the other party. If this is the case, the adjuster should obtain certificates of insurance verifying that insurance was obtained as required. Additionally, reviewing contracts may help the adjuster determine whether they contain hold-harmless or indemnity agreements that might waive the insurer's subrogation rights against an at-fault party. For example, a hold-harmless agreement between the general contractor and a subcontractor may prevent the general contractor's builders' risk insurer from subrogating against a subcontractor who caused the loss. Several other documents may directly affect the amount of loss recoverable. In the case of physical loss, the receipts, subcontracts, and records of interim payments made by the owner to the contractor can give the adjuster a good idea of the amount of work actually completed at the site before the loss. This information can help to determine the amount of loss payable for a claim.

When handling a claim that includes soft costs, the adjuster obtains critical-path charts, minutes of site meetings, and other documents that help to establish the project's status at the time of loss and the loss's effect on the project's completion date. A critical-path chart is a schedule of the construction project that highlights the steps and stages that are vital to the project's completion. It is used to track job progress and completion. Reviewing the critical-path document enables the adjuster to determine whether the project was on schedule and whether the loss will result in a delay of the project's completion. If a delay will result and the policy covers loss of rental or business income, the adjuster will need to obtain an estimate of the revenue that the completed building would generate. To determine the amount of a soft-costs loss, it is usually necessary for an insured to produce a great deal of financial documentation, including the specifics of the project's financing package, contracts, and income projections presented to lenders when the project was proposed. Sometimes repairs can be accomplished without affecting the project schedule, thereby incurring no soft costs or delayed opening claim.

Determination of the amount payable in a builders' risk claim often requires the use of experts. When adjusting large losses, the insurer normally hires a construction consultant. The construction consultant is frequently an engineer or a general contractor skilled in commercial construction. The consultant helps establish a reasonable amount of loss as well as the length of the delay that will result from the loss. If the claim involves soft costs, the adjuster may also need to hire an accountant. The accountant's role is to analyze the financial documentation and revenue projections and to apply them to the delay estimate prepared by the construction consultant.

In a large builders' risk loss, a significant portion of the adjuster's duties centers on managing the experts and integrating the various opinions and data into a fair valuation of the insured's claim.

CRIME LOSSES

Crime losses are among the most challenging that an adjuster can face. An adjuster must verify coverage thoroughly and must understand the coverage applicable to a given loss.

Crime coverage varies considerably from personal insurance to commercial insurance and from one commercial insured to another. Investigation of crime losses is difficult and sensitive. For example, the perpetrator would have tried to prevent discovery, an insured might have staged a loss, or an insider might be involved.

Types of Theft

Common law and modern criminal statutes define various crimes. Theft is the broadest category of illegally taking property with the intent to deprive the owner of the property. **Burglary** is entry into a building with the intent to commit a crime, usually theft. **Robbery** is the act of taking property from a person, or taking it in the presence of that person, by threatening the person with violence. Burglary and robbery are forms of theft. Insurance policy definitions might not be identical to common-law or crime statute definitions. For example, insurance policies usually define burglary as having "marks of forcible entry or exit," a characteristic that might be absent from crime codes.

Property thefts often occur in office, residential, retail, or warehouse-type occupancies where a quick, secretive act can go unnoticed. Personal property often disappears under a coat, in a shopping bag, or even in an employee's toolbox. Property can be easily disposed of in a pawnshop or kept for the thief's use.

Burglaries account for the largest dollar loss amounts among all thefts. The secrecy with which burglary is accomplished gives a perpetrator ample time to carry off large quantities of merchandise without detection. Notwithstanding burglar alarms, watchdogs, security guards, and other security measures, burglary is easier for criminals to commit than is robbery.

Robberies often occur in establishments that hold cash and have only one or two attendants, such as convenience stores, dry cleaners, and gas stations. Couriers for banks or high-volume retail stores are particularly susceptible to attack. Trucking companies are likely targets for robbery or theft of merchandise because the driver is usually alone. Criminals target high-value stock that is easily disposed of, such as liquor, cigarettes, and appliances.

Burglary

The taking of property from inside a building by someone who unlawfully enters or exits the building.

Robbery

The unlawful taking of property from the care and custody of a person by one who has caused or threatened to cause that person bodily harm; includes situations in which the thief commits an obviously unlawful act that is witnessed by the custodian of the stolen property (such as an observed "smash and grab" theft from a shop window).

Crime Coverages in Personal Insurance

Crime coverage is a standard part of all homeowners policies and is essential to a well-constructed personal insurance package. Crime against a private citizen can take many forms and can cause loss to both personal and real property. When copper was expensive, many homes were stripped of copper gutters and downspouts, which were then sold for scrap. Stained glass windows are also theft targets. Even woodwork, trim, or plumbing fixtures can be taken by thieves. Building materials awaiting installation are favorite and easy targets.

Standard homeowners policies cover an insured's real and personal property against theft losses, but the policies limit classes of property that have an extremely high loss potential, such as firearms, gems, gold, jewelry, furs, and other expensive articles. However, these articles can be scheduled on an endorsement to the policy for an agreed value and for an additional premium. When these articles are listed in the policy, they are said to be **scheduled articles**. They are covered against a broader range of perils and for a wider geographical scope.

Scheduled articles

Personal property specifically listed on a homeowner's policy that is typically covered against a broader range of perils, for a wider geographic scope, and/or at an agreed value.

Crime coverage limited to the home would not completely cover an insured's entire exposure. At times, all insureds leave their residence and travel, often with substantial valuables on their person or in their baggage. For many reasons, the exposure to loss increases substantially when the owner leaves home. Articles are lost or misplaced and believed to have been stolen. Luggage is lost and believed stolen. Articles are left unattended. Travelers often innocently stray into high-risk areas. Insurers recognize this off-premises exposure and provide coverage for the insured's protection. In most policies, coverage extends to losses to personal property anywhere in the world. Coverage is for the named insured and other household members.

Theft of personal property at other locations owned by, rented to, or occupied by an insured is covered only while the insured is temporarily living there. For example, theft from a summer home while an insured is living there would be covered. The status of a student insured is slightly different. The student only needs to establish that he or she was at the temporary residence where theft occurred within forty-five days before the theft. The student's property is thus protected over long holiday periods, but not for a full summer. Theft coverage away from the residence premises does not apply to watercraft, their furnishings or equipment, outboard motors, or trailers or campers.

Homeowners policies usually have an Additional Coverage for losses caused by unauthorized use of a credit card, check forgery, or loss by receipt of counterfeit money. No deductible applies to any loss under this coverage. This coverage does not apply to losses arising out of business use or out of an insured's dishonesty. In the Additional Coverage, the insurer also agrees to settle or defend actions against an insured arising out of fraudulent fund transfer or credit card use. The insurer bears the cost of such a defense, which is not deducted from the available loss coverage. Defense costs are in addition to the policy coverage limit.

Crime Coverages in the BPP

Unlike the homeowners policy, which is a package, commercial insurance coverages are offered separately. Insureds choose the coverages they want. Exposures vary so widely by business that a package approach would not be an efficient way of meeting business insurance needs. A policy is built by selecting various forms that meet a customer's needs.

Nevertheless, the Building and Personal Property Coverage Form (BPP) provides certain limited crime coverages. They are so limited or restricted that a business with any significant crime exposure must consider purchasing crime insurance, such as Insurance Services Office, Inc. (ISO) Commercial Crime Coverage.

The BPP with the Causes of Loss—Basic Form and the Causes of Loss—Broad Form include crime coverage only for vandalism and looting accompanying a riot. They cover only the damage to the building caused by the vandals' breaking in or exiting. This is the extent of the crime coverage provided under the Basic and Broad Forms.

The BPP with the Causes of Loss—Special Form is written to cover all losses that it does not specifically exclude or limit. This form includes crime coverage except to the extent that it is excluded or limited. This form specifically excludes losses caused by a dishonest or criminal act of the insured or employees or by voluntary parting of property caused by a fraudulent scheme, trick, device, or false pretense. These limitations also apply to theft claims:

> We will not pay for loss of or damage to: . . .
>
> d. Building materials and supplies not attached as part of the building or structure caused by or resulting from theft. . . .
>
> e. Property that is missing, where the only evidence of the loss or damage is a shortage disclosed on taking inventory, or other instances where there is no physical evidence to show what happened to the property.
>
> f. Property that has been transferred to a person or to a place outside the described premises on the basis of unauthorized instructions.[1]

These sublimits apply to covered theft losses:

> For loss or damage by theft, the following types of property are covered only up to the limits shown:
>
> a. $2,500 for furs, fur garments and garments trimmed with fur.
>
> b. $2,500 for jewelry, watches, watch movements, jewels, pearls, precious and semiprecious stones, bullion, gold, silver, platinum, and other precious alloys or metals. This limit does not apply to jewelry and watches worth $100 or less per item.
>
> c. $2,500 for patterns, dies, molds, and forms.
>
> d. $250 for stamps, tickets, and letters of credit.[2]

The ISO Crime Program

The crime coverage provided by the BPP and the standard causes of loss forms are inadequate for many businesses. To meet the need for expanded crime coverage, ISO has developed a commercial crime coverage form. The form's crime coverage options can be added to a package policy or written as a stand-alone policy.

Eight options for crime coverage are available under the ISO Commercial Crime Coverage Form. The declarations page indicates which of the eight possible insuring agreements have been selected, along with the limit of insurance and the deductible that will apply.

The eight coverage options are these:

Employee

A person hired to perform services for another under the direction and control of the other party, called the employer.

1. *Employee Theft.* The definition of "employee" found in the policy is important to this coverage. An **employee** can be only a natural person, not a corporate entity. Temporary workers are considered employees, but leased workers are not. Terminated workers are considered employees for up to thirty days after their termination date.

2. *Forgery or Alteration.* This coverage protects the insured if he or she accepts a bad negotiable instrument or commercial paper or if the insured tenders a forged or altered negotiable instrument or commercial paper. It reimburses legal costs, in addition to the policy limit. The deductible does not apply to the legal costs. It covers anywhere in the world.

3. *Inside the Premises—Theft of Money and Securities.* Coverage is provided for theft, destruction, or unidentified disappearance but does not cover accounting or arithmetical errors. Theft by the named insured or partner is excluded.

4. *Inside the Premises—Robbery or Safe Burglary of Other Property.* This agreement provides coverage for other tangible property such as a watch that has been taken in to the insured for repair work and is then stolen from the premises.

5. *Outside the Premises.* This provides coverage for theft, disappearance, or destruction of money, securities, and other tangible property from a messenger or armored car. "Messenger" is defined as the insured, the insured's relatives, partners, members, or any employee while having custody outside the premises. The coverage for other tangible property is limited to loss from an actual or attempted robbery.

6. *Computer Fraud.* This provides coverage for loss to money, securities, and other property that results from the use of a computer to fraudulently transfer property from the insured's premises or bank to someone outside these premises.

7. *Funds Transfer Fraud.* If a fraudulent instruction to a financial institution to transfer funds results in a loss, there will be coverage under this option.

8. *Money Orders and Counterfeit Paper Currency.* If the insured accepts a counterfeit money order or paper currency, the loss will be covered.

Another important definition is "occurrence." For employee theft coverage, an **occurrence** encompasses loss caused by one or more employees in a single act or through several acts. The forgery and alteration coverage also has its own definition of "occurrence." It is all losses caused by any person regardless of the number of instruments involved. For all of the other insuring agreements, an occurrence is an act or series of related acts involving one or more persons or an act or event or series of related acts or events not involving any person.

Occurrence

An accident, including continuous or repeated exposure to substantially the same general harmful conditions.

Exclusions

Acts committed by the insured and acts committed by the insured's employees are excluded unless the employee theft option is selected. Legal expenses are excluded unless the forgery or alteration option is selected. There are the standard exclusions for government action, nuclear reaction and contamination, and war. Indirect losses are also excluded. An example of an indirect loss is the loss of a contract or sale as a result of a covered cause of loss. There is also an exclusion for the cost of proving that a loss has occurred, such as the cost of hiring an accountant.

Also, some exclusions apply to a specific insuring agreement. The employee theft agreement has an exclusion whereby it will not cover any employee who has been previously excluded from coverage because of a prior theft. It also excludes inventory shortage. The inside and outside coverage agreements all exclude loss as a result of accounting or arithmetical errors or loss as a result of the insured's making a mistake about an item's value. Loss by fire is also excluded unless the fire damages the vault or the safe that the goods are stored in.

The computer fraud option has a specific exclusion that states that the insured cannot use an inventory or profit and loss statement to prove that a loss has occurred.

Conditions

The policy's Conditions section is very important because it indicates whether the policy is a Discovery Form Policy or a Loss Sustained Form Policy. The Discovery Form conditions state that the policy applies to loss due to acts or events that occur at any time but are discovered during the policy period. The Loss Sustained Form applies to loss due to acts or events that occur during the policy period and are discovered during the policy period.

Both forms have an Extended Period to Discover Loss Condition. The Discovery Form allows an additional sixty days from the date of termination or cancellation to discover the loss. The Loss Sustained Form allows up to one year from termination or cancellation to discover the loss. Both forms state that the loss must be sustained before the cancellation or termination date. Should the insured replace the coverage with another policy, these extended periods of discovery end on the date of the new coverage.

Additional conditions apply to all of the insuring agreements. One is the condition that cancels coverage for an employee upon discovery that he or she is involved in the theft. However, the policy does not define discovery. This can be a major issue with ongoing theft. Is the discovery the date when the employee is first suspected, or is it the date when the employee is confronted or arrested or convicted? Case law can help provide an answer.

A suit clause in the Conditions states that suit cannot be brought until ninety days after the insured files a proof of loss and it must be within two years of the date of discovery of the loss. An individual state's laws can override this provision.

Loss Sustained Form Conditions

The Loss Sustained Form has some additional conditions. There is a condition that states that the insurer will pay the larger of the amounts covered by this policy or the prior policy for any loss covered partly by this policy and partly by the prior policy. However, this applies only if the prior policy was with the same insurer or an affiliate. There is a condition that if a loss is sustained during a prior policy and the insured did not collect on that loss because the time to discover the loss had expired, then this policy will cover the loss if two conditions are met:

* The loss would have been covered under the prior policy and is covered under this policy.
* This policy became effective upon the prior policy's termination.

There is also a clause that if two or more coverages of this policy cover a loss, then the insurer will pay the actual amount of the loss or the sum of the limits applicable to the coverages involved.

Lastly, the Loss Sustained Conditions has an Other Insurance Clause that is distinctive from the standard clause found in property policies. It states that the policy does not apply to loss recoverable or recovered under any other insurance. However, if the amount of the other insurance is insufficient to cover the entire amount of the loss, then this policy will apply to the unreimbursed part of the loss, subject to this policy's deductible and limits.

Valuation—Settlement

Under the crime coverages, a loss to money is paid at face value. Securities are valued as of the close of business on the day the loss is discovered. Other property is valued at replacement cost if the item is repaired or replaced. If not, then it is valued at actual cash value.

For Inside the Premises—Robbery or Safe Burglary and for Outside the Premises coverages, the policy will only pay for the loss that the insured cannot recover from the insurer of the armored car company. There is also a $5,000 limit, in any one occurrence, for loss to precious metals, precious or semiprecious stones, pearls, furs, or articles containing these items.

Manuscripts, drawings, records, and the cost to restore them are also subject to this limit.

Investigation and Adjustment of Crime Losses

As in most investigations, the adjuster should tour the insured premises, survey the physical conditions of the property to see where the premises were entered and where the property was located, and get a general overview of the circumstances related to the loss. The adjuster should then investigate with the insured or anyone else who knows the most about the circumstances of the loss and the property itself.

For commercial losses, the adjuster should obtain tape-recorded or written statements regarding the type of business; how it operates; how long it has been at the location; its loss history; its financial data, including inventory records, cost of goods, and mark-ups; its customer relationships; and other details of the loss. For homeowners losses, the adjuster should obtain documentation concerning purchase dates, invoices, and the condition of the property. The adjuster must know as much as possible about the property, the insured, and the circumstances of the loss.

Verification of the Event

Under any of the crime coverages, the adjuster's primary goal, after determining that coverage applies for the type of loss and property involved, is to establish that a loss has actually occurred. Staged crime losses are among the easiest types of frauds to accomplish. Unlike other perils, which show evidence of having occurred, a theft might leave no overt sign at all. Even if a fire might be arson, the adjuster would know that a fire occurred. But with a staged burglary or other theft, the insured could move or sell the property to create the appearance that a crime has occurred.

Because suspicion is a natural response to crime losses, adjusters need to be trained to interview insureds and others without offending them and creating an impression of bad faith. Interviews with employees, neighbors, or police might also be appropriate. In staged crime losses, neighbors often inform adjusters that they witnessed the insured carrying large amounts of property from the premises shortly before the alleged loss.

The insured might try to prove a loss by indicating, for example, the absence of three pallets or two shelves of merchandise. The decision to accept that a loss has occurred rests partly on the adjuster's assessment of the insured's integrity and partly on proof. For instance, an adjuster would have little reason to doubt the integrity of three teachers who attest to the theft loss of gym equipment from a high school because they probably would not have a personal interest at stake. In that case, the teachers' statements could be enough proof. Still, each case must be weighed on its merits, and the degree of proof required should be assessed accordingly. Significant dollar losses call for significant investigation. Many crime claims, especially under home-owners policies, are small and can be handled by telephone or inside adjusters. Though ostensibly cost-effective, such investigations are often not as thorough as an on-the-scene investigation and might be confined to securing a police report.

Fraud Indicators

Although some losses are undoubtedly totally fraudulent, fraud usually occurs when a legitimate loss occurs and the insured uses the opportunity of filing a claim to exploit the loss, claiming many times the amount actually stolen. Any of the indicators of a fraudulent or exaggerated claim might also be present on legitimate claims, so the adjuster must interpret them carefully.

Insured's Statement

In most circumstances, adjusters are required to take a signed or recorded statement from the insured or other individuals. When a theft, burglary, or robbery occurs, a statement is almost mandatory except when the claim's value is small. The statement should record facts that are fresh in the insured's or witness's mind. It should also serve as an inventory of what was taken. If the adjuster asks questions logically and chronologically, a statement could evoke other thoughts and facts that might have been overlooked. Taking a statement puts the adjustment process into a more formal atmosphere and might deter an insured from some intended dishonest act. Statements might also be used to identify property or to recall facts years later during litigation. Examinations under oath can also be used to obtain the necessary information.

Employee Involvement

In a commercial setting, after determining that a commercial covered crime loss has actually occurred and that the insured is not involved, the adjuster must then ascertain whether an employee is involved. All policies exclude losses caused by employees, except those specifically written for employee dishonesty or fidelity losses. Unless such coverage is purchased, the exclusions under all other crime coverages will bar recovery for theft by an employee. Employees, by definition, must be employed when the loss occurs. Independent contractors and other associates are not considered employees.

Determining an employee's involvement is often difficult, and the evidence is often circumstantial. If the only way that a loss could conceivably have occurred is through a specific employee's participation, such evidence should be enough to deny a claim. Whether the employee dishonesty coverage (which is often purchased separately from a different insurer) or the crime coverage should pay the loss is often a question. Certainly the insured should not suffer as the two insurers try to discover which is responsible. Complete payment to the insured should be made under an agreement between the insurers to arbitrate their differences. The insurers should agree that any payments made to the insured would not prejudice the insurers' rights at arbitration.

Amount of Loss

After being satisfied that a covered loss has occurred and that neither the insured nor an employee is involved, the adjuster must measure the loss. For many commercial crime losses, salvors and accountants can assist the adjuster in this effort. First to be determined is the type and amount of property that was at the insured's premises just before the loss. Salvors might be needed to count what remains after a loss to tangible property.

An accountant can work backward with records of purchases and sales and with previous physical inventory to prove what existed just before the loss or to show how much money was on hand. Properly kept books and records are helpful. An insured with poor records causes much inaccuracy in this procedure. In fact, the adjuster might encounter a wide variety of accounting records—anything from a shoebox full of receipts to a certified public accountant's formal journals. Nevertheless, the adjuster must deal with whatever records are available. The policy requires that the insured divulge all records, regardless of their nature and quality.

Recovery of Property

Because of the nature of crime coverage, the adjuster is likely to communicate with police about the loss. It is expected that a report of the loss will be made to the police. Often, the police arrest and convict the responsible party. It is important that the adjuster notify the police of the insurer's loss payment to the insured because if an arrest and a conviction occur, the court may order restitution of the funds or property taken. Although this can be an involved process, it can be worth the effort.

COMPUTER LOSSES

Computer equipment needs special handling in the event of a loss. Restoration and computer experts need to evaluate the damage and make recommendations on repairs. Adjusters often have to deal with the issue of obsolescence when handling computer losses. Adjusters can use computer consultants to find cost-effective replacement units.

Handling computer losses is one of the fastest changing areas in loss adjusting. Most people are generally acquainted with various computer types and sizes, but the field is broadening daily. Present computer technology includes, in addition to computers, portable handheld personal digital assistant (PDA) devices, machine control systems, building mechanical control systems, communications relay systems, medical diagnostic tools, and technical test equipment. Telephone and intercom systems are often computer-driven.

Almost all of these systems can be insured. Claims for repair or replacement of these items are surfacing with greater frequency.

Terminology

Here is a review of some terms used in insurance policies and in the computer trade.

Data

Information recorded in a magnetic code that is used in or with a computer.

Hardware

A physical machine and all of its component parts and cables.

Media

Any computer-readable device that can hold information.

Programs (software)

A series of logically connected steps that are loaded into a computer, allowing it to perform a given function.

- **Data** include any information used in or with a computer. They are recorded in a magnetic code that is usable by a computer. Data include programs (software), raw information that has been placed in the system, calculations, and memory system content. Sometimes the term is used more restrictively, to mean only the stored user information, whether input or output.

- **Hardware** includes the physical machine and all of its component parts as well as connecting cables.

- **Media** are any computer-readable devices that can hold information. They include magnetic tapes, optical disks, compact discs (CDs), digital video discs (DVDs), and magnetic disks (hard or floppy) and their carriers. Media are tangible and serve only as vehicles to carry or store information. Some insurance policies define media to include data and programs.

- **Programs** (or software) are a series of logically connected steps that are loaded into the computer, allowing it to perform any given function when directed by an operator. They are carried on a disk or tape. Programs can be proprietary (fully owned and protected by copyright), licensed, or in the public domain. Some are general purpose and sold widely in the market, but others are so specialized that they have no value outside a particular application.

Causes of Loss

Here are several causes of loss that can do the most damage to computers:

- Heat damage (with or without fire)
- Water damage/humidity
- Smoke
- Contamination
- Impact or crushing
- Voltage variation
- Magnetic field intrusion

Heat

A computer is built with many heat-sensitive materials. Plastics distort or degrade at relatively low temperatures. Tolerances change as materials expand. Heat damage might be produced internally because of cooling system failure, or externally, such as when a room heats up unexpectedly. A system's conductivity changes, and some cosmetic discoloration is likely to occur in the system or at the console. Heat caused by fire raises additional concerns about contamination.

Water/Humidity

Water falling into a computer or rising around it is extremely destructive. Excessive humidity can have the same effect. Water cross-conducts between pin connectors and may deposit chemicals whose corrosive action erodes and destroys connectors and circuit boards.

Repairing a water-damaged computer is best left to an expert. The machine should be shut down until it has been cleaned and decontaminated. Any effort to turn it on to determine whether it will work might do new and irreparable damage. If restoration personnel are not available for several hours or days, the cabinet should be opened, and warm air should be blown gently across the wet areas, concentrated particularly on cable plugs and connectors. A dehumidifier should be used to reduce the humidity in the area where the computer is located. These actions will mitigate the loss to the equipment. See the exhibit "High-Tech First Aid."

Smoke

Smoke is made up of carbon and other chemicals that can destroy a computer. When smoke invades a computer and settles onto its connections and circuit boards, the result can be disastrous. Losses include internal and external discoloration, electrical failure through carbon chains, arcing, contact point failure, and varnish deposits.

As with water damage, the system should be turned off and protected against further invasion of smoke. It can be wrapped in plastic. Professionals should be called to dismantle and clean it. The smoke residue must be tested to identify the chemicals it carries and to enable the restorer to select a detergent that will remove those chemicals. Acids in the smoke can etch metal and even cut the trace lines on a circuit board. After twenty-four hours, rapid degradation of the affected areas or systems is likely.

Repairing the damage from smoke contamination is a job for a professional. Fans can eliminate smoke. Protective covers can be arranged. The entire unit might need to be dismantled so that it can be hand-washed with suitable solvents. In any case, the system should not be turned on until a competent restorer has checked it and approved it for use.

High-Tech First Aid

FIRST AID

WHEN DISASTER STRIKES YOUR HIGH-TECH EQUIPMENT	
DO	Disconnect All Equipment From Power Source
DO NOT	Start Up Equipment, Not Even For Testing

FIRE

- Disconnect equipment from ALL power sources, including backup batteries and uninterruptible power supplies (UPS). At power panels, remove fuses and place tape over circuit breakers to keep them in the "OFF" position.
- Open windows and use fans to remove smoke.
- Remove portable equipment to dry, clean area.
- Where building repairs are underway, protect the equipment with plastic drop-cloths and run dehumidifiers beneath the shelter.
- Prevent further spread of smoke, soot and/or water contamination from the fire source to other areas.

WATER

- Immediately disconnect equipment from ALL power sources, including backup batteries and UPS. At power panels, remove fuses and place tape over circuit breakers to keep them in the "OFF" position.
- If water enters through the ceiling, protect the equipment with plastic drop-cloths and run dehumidifiers beneath the shelter.
- Vacuum and wipe water from walls, floors, subfloors, heating ducts, etc.
- Turn on the heating system and/or dehumidifiers to speed drying.
- Critical metallic surfaces or machinery and work-in-progress should be temporarily protected with water-displacement oil.

INDUSTRIAL DUST AND FIRE-EXTINGUISHING POWDER

- Disconnect all dust-sensitive equipment from power sources.
- Do not operate any dust-contaminated equipment.
- Seal off the area from further dust infiltration and eliminate the dust source.
- Change the air filters on any equipment that must continue to operate before decontamination.
- Keep equipment dry wherever fire extinguishing powder is present.
- Fire extinguishing agents are very abrasive and when they mix with moisture in the ambient air will lead to corrosion. Professionally decontaminate as soon as possible.

OES Technical Restoration   Toll Free (866) 637-8324

OES Technical Restoration, Kansas City, Kans. [DA04185]

Contamination

Contamination includes water, smoke, and other airborne particles. The major concerns are dust and dirt, but oil, oil vapor, and other airborne fumes or contaminants can damage a computer.

In any loss by contamination, the machine should not be turned on. Attempts to do so to test its operation can be very costly. The best solution is to have the unit opened by a competent restoration service person and checked for foreign matter. If a contaminant is gaseous, the clean-up routine suggested for smoke should be followed. If the material is solid or fluid, the suggested recovery from water loss should be followed.

Impact or Crushing

Although computers are generally sturdy machines, if a cabinet is struck and bent by a lift truck or other heavy equipment, wires could be pinched, or connections could be stressed or broken. Sealed areas within the computer may be compromised.

Special preparations, as outlined by the manufacturer, should be made before a computer is shipped. Damage to a computer or one of its components can occur during shipping. Most freight carriers recognize the units as special-handling cargo. Even so, units get dropped, overturned, rained on, and otherwise abused along the way. Most physical damage from impact or crushing occurs while the units are in transit.

Voltage Variation

Voltage is the pressure exerted by electricity. If the voltage along a wire is doubled, twice as much electricity will flow through the wire. However, wire has a limit as to how much current it can safely carry. When the voltage increases and causes the current to surpass the wire's capacity, the wire heats up and melts—just like a fuse. Upon melting, the wire cannot carry current. Whatever appliance was receiving current at the output end of the wire would be deprived of power, and the system would be disabled.

This condition occurs when lightning strikes a power line and momentarily increases the voltage on that line. That increased pressure could travel down the line to a computer. The voltage at the wall plug could increase momentarily from 115 volts to 170 volts or to 500 volts, which is one type of line surge. Tiny wires in the computer, some thinner than a human hair, would become overstressed and melt, disabling the computer.

Adjuster Tip—If examination by an expert reveals that the only damage sustained is to the computer's internal modem, the cause is usually lightning. The only connection that the modem has to the outside world is the telephone or communication line and the computer's main board. If the computer is connected to a surge protector, a utility surge would damage something other than the internal modem.[3]

Many computers are fitted with voltage regulators to smooth out line surge. They should also have special grounding to intercept any lightning surges that come in on the power line. If a computer is fitted with these attachments, machine failure caused by lightning will be unlikely. In examining the circumstances surrounding a computer loss allegedly caused by lightning, the adjuster should check the local weather records for the time when the computer failed. Many power companies keep detailed records of their line voltages and lightning strikes to their lines, which are often available to an adjuster.

Magnetic Field Intrusion

Computer data are recorded in magnetic spots on a disk or tape that has an iron oxide face. These disks and tapes could be erased by simply passing them through a magnetic field that would rearrange the electrons in a uniform direction. In such a case, the intelligence encoded on the disk would be lost. The same effect would be produced by bringing a magnetic field near a computer. The magnetic field would also rearrange the electrons in the computer, on disks or on tape, and the intelligence stored in the computer would be lost.

Certain welding equipment generates a magnetic field. Induction heating coils operate through the use of magnetic fields, as do some other systems. Anything with an electromagnet has a magnetic field. Office workers often have magnets or magnetized objects on their desks. These objects can destroy computer disks. If the computer and its media are not shielded from magnetic fields, the data and programs on the disks could be accidentally erased.

Movement of recorded data through a magnetic field and vice versa can be equally damaging. Whenever data are missing or scrambled, the adjuster must consider the possibility that data were exposed to a magnetic field of enough strength to wipe it clean.

Coverage

Generalizing about computer coverages is difficult. This section presents some of the most important features of such coverage. An insured computer owner could suffer various kinds of loss, including:

- Physical loss to equipment or media
- Costs to replace data or programs
- Extra expense to continue computer operations
- Loss of business income

In working with any computer loss, an adjuster must be aware that these systems can be expensive and complicated and also that they might be the center for many other operations of the business. As a result, continuous disablement can have far-reaching effects.

Computer Coverage in the Homeowners Policy

The HO-3 or standard homeowners policies do not specifically deal with computer hardware or software. Computer equipment is considered personal property. Loss to computers would be handled similarly to any other piece of personal property. The issue that arises concerns items' valuation. Actual cash value (ACV) or replacement-cost basis may be difficult to calculate because of the insured computer's technological obsolescence. Even attempting to settle based on like kind and quality may mean that the insured nevertheless gets a better computer than what he or she had originally because of changes in technology that have occurred since the original purchase.

Computer Coverage in the BPP

The Building and Personal Property Coverage Form (BPP) provides valuable coverage for computer losses, but with significant limitations. Coverage for business personal property extends to equipment and all other personal property owned by the insured and used in the insured's business. Nothing in this language would exclude computer equipment and media. Additionally, the BPP provides a $2,500 coverage extension for the cost to research, restore, and replace valuable records, including those on electronic media. The BPP does not cover certain types of property, including accounts, bills, evidences of debt, and other specifically described property that other policies cover. The exclusion of the last type of property is significant because computer data can be covered specifically under inland marine forms.

The BPP causes of loss forms contain exclusions for power failure and for artificially generated electrical current that disturbs electrical devices, appliances, or wires, as well as for mechanical breakdown and changes in temperature or humidity. Thus, some of the most significant computer loss exposures are not covered. Also, the enumerated covered causes of loss in the Basic and Broad Forms might not adequately address computer equipment exposures.

Electronic Data Processing and Electronic Commerce Coverage

For those businesses with a substantial loss exposure to computer hardware, software, data, and loss of business, more specific coverage is available.

Electronic Data Processing (EDP) Coverage is often added to commercial property packages to provide special coverage for hardware, software, and data. It also provides coverage for business income loss that results from direct loss to the equipment. This coverage is usually written as direct physical loss caused by a covered peril to covered property while on the premises described on the declarations, subject to a list of exclusions.

The E-Commerce endorsement is designed to cover loss arising from e-commerce activity conducted on the Internet or another computer network. It provides coverage for electronic data owned, licensed, or leased to the insured that originates and resides in computers located within the United States, its territories or possessions, Puerto Rico, and Canada.

Under this coverage, the insurer agrees to pay for the cost to replace or restore electronic data that have sustained damage from a covered cause of loss. The endorsement also provides business income and extra expense coverage.

The covered causes of loss are modified by adding back coverage for interruption of utility service, for loss caused by artificially generated electrical current, and for mechanical breakdown.

Several exclusions unique to e-commerce activity are added. These include loss or damage caused by a virus, unauthorized use, errors in programming, faulty design or installation of the system, system or network overload, or failure of the Internet.

Computer Loss Adjusting

Losses to computer equipment, media, and data present the adjuster with unique loss mitigation and settlement challenges and opportunities. This section presents several of them.

Initial Assessment and Response

The adjuster's first obligation at the site of a computer loss is to be sure that the entire system is shut down and that it stays shut down until a full analysis of the loss is made and a qualified repair person is on site to monitor and initiate any restart. The adjuster must talk to whoever was present when the incident occurred to identify what systems were running at the time of the loss and the specific cause of loss. Examining the equipment and the loss site often reveals evidence that identifies the reason for failure. Adjusters are not expected to analyze the system's internal failures, but they should take charge, advise the insured of the duty to mitigate the loss, and help the insured to obtain the services of a competent repair technician.

Detailed Identification of Equipment

A precise identification of all of the components and peripherals that are damaged is essential to handling computer losses. The identification should include the make, model, and upgrades to the unit. This information will help the restorer as well as be useful in the determination of ACV or replacement cost.

Backup of Data

In most well-run computer operations, the data in the system are copied at specific intervals. The copy is stored as a backup in anticipation of a malfunction or damage to the computer system. An adjuster should ask the insured whether such a procedure is used, at what intervals the data are copied, and how the backup data are preserved. Are they retained on site? Are they sent to secure off-site storage and, if so, where? How often? For an insured that relies on its computers for business, it is possible that the insured has made arrangements with another facility to run its operations temporarily. The backup data could then be transferred to this facility, and the insured could be back in business with a minimum of downtime.

Settlement Options

An important factor in computer settlements is obsolescence, which results from the speed with which computer technology evolves. As a new model reaches the market, the related older models sharply lose value even if they are unsold. When these units become technically obsolete, they lose their salability. With small units, such as personal computers, new but obsolete models go on sale, and the inventory is quickly absorbed at reduced prices. However, larger obsolete components might remain in warehouses for months or years waiting to be sold. There is also a regular market trading in used equipment from major manufacturers. This inventory can be the adjuster's salvation. Finding and obtaining just the right replacement unit to fit into an existing system take patience but can result in dramatic savings.

Computers often contain a set or group of related items. Even a personal computer is usually made up of three or more components, each of which can be replaced separately. Replacing a single element without replacing an entire system might be possible and economical.

During repair evaluation, the adjuster often discovers that repairs, though possible, might take several weeks because of a delay in obtaining parts. At this point, the insured and the adjuster must decide how to proceed. These are the options:

- Wait for the repairs to be complete
- Purchase a new unit
- Purchase a used unit
- Rent a temporary unit

The analysis of how to make this decision is beyond the scope of this text. However, if the insured has business income loss coverage, the insurer providing such coverage would play a major role in the physical damage settlement. Extra expense coverage pays for the necessary extra expenses incurred to resume or continue operations as nearly as practicable. The adjuster must agree with the insured on a course that will best serve all concerned.

Insureds often lease computer equipment. An adjuster who identifies equipment as leased must review the written lease. Usually, the lessee is required to insure the equipment; however, this is not always the case. Sometimes a lease expires upon the equipment's destruction. In any case, the lessor is usually not named on a lessee's policy, so an adjuster can make settlement directly with the lessee. Software is licensed. By reviewing the licensing agreement, the adjuster can determine whether the insured is entitled to replacement software.

Computer Consultants

Although an adjuster may be able to handle a home computer loss, a commercial loss may require a consultant's services. Computer consultants have access to various sources for units. It is possible to get new units or refurbished units that are warranted to be as good as new. Obtaining a replacement unit can save other components of the overall system. This option might solve the problem of an insured who sees the need for an entirely new system. The

Orion Blue Book is a good source of information on computers for valuation purposes.

Computer consultants have at their disposal several references on the value of used units and components. This valuation is not an exact science, and market conditions must be considered. Valuation is probably best determined by someone who is familiar with the industry, changes that are occurring, the history of any problems, the number of sales made, and the current quantity of unsold merchandise.

Most experienced adjusters can determine the value of a personal computer with an original cost under $3,000. Enough of a market exists in most communities to create a mutually acceptable value. By contrast, valuation of a $200,000 mainframe requires research on a national scale. No one locality will have a sufficiently large market to guide the adjuster. Using a paid consultant is advisable in such a case.

Service Contract

Service contracts protect owners of many computers. Through those contracts, service agencies maintain and repair the units during the life of the agreements. These agreements are generally void in the event of certain casualty losses to the unit. Thus, loss to a computer by fire would likely void the service contract protection.

Equipment Breakdown Coverage

Equipment breakdown coverage, often referred to as boiler and machinery (B&M) coverage, is very specialized. Only a small group of adjusters who regularly handle equipment breakdown claims fully understand the coverage and what is required in the investigation and adjustment of the losses.

Equipment breakdown insurance pays for a loss that results from the accidental breakdown of equipment that operates under pressure or that controls, transmits, transforms, or uses mechanical or electrical power.

Steamboilers, electrical generators, pumps, engines, air conditioning systems, production equipment, and even computers and copiers can be insured under an equipment breakdown policy. The BPP only covers this equipment for the perils enumerated in the causes of loss forms. Electrical or mechanical breakdown and steam boiler explosion are excluded. Equipment breakdown insurance provides coverage for these causes of loss as well. It also covers other property damaged by the breakdown as well as the attendant business income and extra expense loss.

Because the handling of equipment breakdown claims requires specialized knowledge, these claims are usually assigned to specific adjustment companies with the required engineering expertise.

CONTAMINATION CLAIMS AND THE SUPERFUND LAW

Pollution and contamination-of-property claims have become more common in first-party policies.

Both state and federal law may affect the legal rights and responsibilities of both the insured and the insurer concerning any claim for contamination-cleanup damages under a first-party property coverage. The most important of these laws is the federal Superfund law.

This section briefly introduces first-party property insurance coverage and the principles of law as they relate to pollution and contamination cleanup claims.

Contamination Claims

A great number of pollution/contamination claims are presented under property policies and other first-party coverages. These claims include a claim for damages from leaking or overflowed oil tanks, well water contamination, asbestos and lead abatement, herbicides and pesticides in the soil and ground-water, sewer backup, toxic smoke and fumes, mold, mercury, radon, and so on. Other contamination sources arise from the third-party exposures resulting from the use, transportation, storage, disposal, release, or discharge of chemicals and other hazardous substances into the environment.

Any hazardous substance in transit is especially vulnerable to vehicle accidents. Hazardous substances can be transported over water or land in barges, ships, trains, or trucks. Even when these materials are in storage, they can present a contamination threat to the environment. Many are explosive or combustible in nature and produce gases, creating pressure within the containment vessels, which then have the propensity to explode. The container or drum itself might spill, leak, or be damaged, enabling the solvents to seep into soil and groundwater and then leach across or down grades onto other properties, creating both first-party damage and a potential third-party liability situation.

Superfund Law

The Comprehensive Environmental Response, Compensation, and Liability Act (CERCLA), known as the **Superfund** law, was enacted in 1980. It was not the first major federal environmental law, but it has had the greatest effect on the insurance industry regarding both first-party and third-party claims for damages.

Under this law, the Environmental Protection Agency (EPA) is required to identify, investigate, and remediate hazardous sites. The EPA must consider whether a site has shown evidence of a release of a hazardous substance, or

Superfund law

Federal legislation that gave the Environmental Protection Agency (EPA) the authority to identify, investigate, and remediate hazardous sites.

whether a potential release appears to be an imminent threat to the public. The EPA is required to create a list of hazardous sites that need attention in order of priority. This list of sites is referred to as the National Priority List (NPL). The EPA is also authorized to pursue and order Potentially Responsible Parties (PRPs) to eliminate the contaminants and to clean up the sites. If these parties fail to respond, the EPA is authorized to take the necessary remedial measures to protect public health and welfare and to pay for the cleanup efforts out of Superfund money. The EPA then proceeds to take legal action against the PRPs for reimbursement.

CERCLA imposes strict, joint and several, and retroactive liability for the costs of response, removal, and remediation of hazardous sites. The law allows the EPA to impose liability and to pursue those who deposited hazardous substances before the statute became law in 1980. Because of the magnitude of the number of hazardous sites and the huge estimated costs to cleanup the NPL sites and other areas across the country, there has been, and will continue to be, great emphasis on pursuing the recovery of costs from the responsible parties. The state and federal EPA agencies also work with and encourage the PRPs to enter into formal agreements to voluntarily cleanup their owned properties without litigation.

The EPA can seek recovery of its costs from these potentially responsible parties:

- The current property owner
- The past property owner of the facility/property at the time that the hazardous substance was released, or the property operator who may have caused the contamination
- Any person who contracted for, or arranged for, the disposal of the hazardous waste, referred to as the generator
- Any person who accepted the hazardous waste for transportation or disposal, referred to as the hauler

The facility's past owners and operators can be held liable if hazardous substances were released on the property during their ownership. Current property owners become liable for all existing and retroactive contamination as soon as they take title to the land. The statute does not require that the PRP be negligent in disposing of its hazardous substances; rather, the statute has deemed this to be an absolute liability standard, or strict liability.

Only a few defenses can be effective against the strict liability standard. An act of war or act of God may be valid defenses if appropriate. Likewise, the act or omission by an unrelated third party could serve as a defense, provided that the defendant could not foresee that third party's negligence. Additionally, the parties can have no contractual relationship, not even by deed. Although the statutory defenses to liability are limited, the insured ultimately might avoid liability if the EPA cannot prove its case. The EPA's inability to prove a defendant's nexus as a PRP can limit or eliminate CERCLA liability.

The 1986 amendments to the Superfund law created an **innocent landowner defense**. This applies to an owner who may have purchased a contaminated site without knowledge of the problem even though he or she had conducted the required site investigation into its prior use. Most states now require an environmental property assessment be completed before any commercial property can be sold.

COVERAGE ISSUES IN FIRST-PARTY PROPERTY INSURANCE

The most significant effect of the Superfund law on first-party insurance is making the owner responsible for past and present contamination on his or her owned property. Because the owner's property is alleged to be damaged or defective from contamination, many owners have sought recovery from their first-party insurance. (Most of the insurance litigation arising out of environmental claims concerns third-party liability coverage; however, this section discusses only the problems of environmental claims under first-party coverages.)

Coverage for pollution/contamination claims depends on the facts and circumstances of the loss, the specific policy's language, and the law in the applicable state. The more important coverage issues in first-party property contamination claims surround:

- "All-risks" policies
- Debris removal coverage
- Suit limitation

"All-Risks" Coverage

Since 1983, the phrase "all-risks" has been deleted from most property policies, and the phrase "risk of direct physical loss" has been substituted. Even with this policy language change, any loss still must be fortuitous for coverage to apply. Pollution or contamination can involve loss that is "direct" and "physical." The only remaining issues are whether the loss is to covered property and whether pollution/contamination or its cause is covered or not. The most significant type of property *not* covered in a pollution claim is land itself. Exclusions for pollution/contamination are also common.

Since 1987, Insurance Services Office, Inc. (ISO) policies have been drafted to exclude loss by contamination unless that event is preceded by a covered loss. That is, pollution/contamination is now covered only as a consequence of a prior covered loss, and then only within narrow limits of coverage. Some losses (to land, for instance) are typically excluded. The Building and Personal Property Coverage Form (BPP) excludes pollution unless it is caused by a peril specifically named in a causes of loss form.

Innocent landowner defense

A possible defense to Superfund liability; used when a party purchases a contaminated site without knowledge of the problem, despite having conducted the required site investigation before purchase.

The Causes of Loss—Special Form, because of its use of the "risk of direct physical loss unless excluded" language, has a long list of excluded risks, including the following pollution/contamination exclusion stating that the policy does not apply to:

> l. Discharge, dispersal, seepage, migration, release or escape of "pollutants" unless the discharge, dispersal, seepage, migration, release, or escape is itself caused by any of the "specified causes of loss." But if the discharge, dispersal, seepage, migration, release or escape of "pollutants" results in a "specified cause of loss" we will pay for the loss or damage caused by the "specified cause of loss."[4]

The term "specified causes of loss" means fire; lightning; explosion; windstorm or hail; smoke; aircraft or vehicles; riot or civil commotion; vandalism; leakage from fire extinguishing equipment; sinkhole collapse; volcanic action; falling objects; weight of snow, ice, or sleet; and water damage. Water damage means accidental discharge or leakage of water or steam as the direct result of the breaking or cracking of any part of a system or appliance containing water or steam on the described premises.

Debris Removal

Insureds have also sought coverage for pollution cleanup under debris removal coverage. They typically assert that the polluting material itself became debris after it had contaminated the insured property or that the contaminated property itself constituted debris. The merit of this argument depends on the wording of the applicable debris removal clause. The ISO forms have been modified to prevent coverage for pollution cleanup under the debris removal clause. This property coverage issue continues to be frequently litigated in many states.

The additional coverage for debris removal includes the expense to remove debris of covered property that results from a covered cause of loss occurring during the policy period. These expenses must be reported to the insurer within 180 days of the date of loss.

Note that coverage extends only to removal of debris of *covered property* caused by a *covered cause of loss*. Any debris that does not satisfy both of these conditions is not included under this additional coverage. Furthermore, the clause specifically excludes pollution cleanup, such as the cost to extract pollutants from land or water.

The BPP specifically states that it will not respond to pollution claims under the Debris Removal Additional Coverages section. Instead, another type of additional coverage is specifically designed for pollution cleanup:

> d. Pollutant Clean Up and Removal
>
> We will pay your expense to extract "pollutants" from land or water at the described premises if the discharge, dispersal, seepage, migration, release, or escape of the "pollutants" is caused by or results from a Covered Cause of Loss that occurs during the policy period .
> . . .[5]

Here, the policy affirms its intent to pay for pollution that is a consequence of a covered loss that occurs during the policy period. The BPP has an annual aggregate limit of $10,000. Higher limits are available.

Suit Limitation Clause

Another important property policy provision that affects a first-party claim for pollution/contamination damage or cleanup is the Suit Limitation Clause. This is one of the most significant differences between a third-party and a first-party policy as this Suit Limitation Clause is only found with first-party property coverages.

In third-party claims or suits, insureds have been able to pursue coverage on policies that are decades old. First-party policies require that the loss occur during the policy period and that suit commence within one year after the date of loss. Generally, there is no problem with complying with this condition when a loss is easily detected. However, with pollution/contamination claims that lie dormant for long periods of time, the suit limitation period can become an issue and bar coverage on expired policies.

This coverage provision has also been litigated frequently in the courts, and generally it is determined that because a first-party claim is brought by the insured, and the insured is generally aware of all the details surrounding the claim on the insured's property, the courts hold the insured to compliance with the policy condition and bar coverage. However, some jurisdictions have adopted rules that the time limit does not begin until the insured has become aware of the loss or has sufficient knowledge that the insured should have been aware of the loss. Other jurisdictions have ruled that the suit limitation period does not begin until the insurer has actually denied coverage.

TYPES OF CONTRACTORS' EQUIPMENT

Contractors' equipment can be defined as the tools and machinery used in projects involving construction, renovation, earth-moving, and many other activities.

Contractors' equipment can be classified in various ways. The equipment can be self-propelled or in need of transport. If it has to be transported, it may be the type of equipment that can be hauled, such as an excavator, or the type of equipment that can be towed, such as an air compressor. If the equipment is self-propelled, it can be identified by method of travel. It either uses a crawler/ track or tires/wheels.

The equipment can also be identified by its attachment, such as a loader, backhoe, scraper, grader, or dozer. The proper identification of a piece of equipment usually has both the method of travel and the attachment in its title, such as crawler dozer or wheel loader.

Contractors' equipment
The tools and machinery used in projects involving construction, renovation, earth-moving, and other activities.

Adjuster Tip—It is important to use the correct name for the piece of equipment. Otherwise, an adjuster's credibility with the insured or the repair facility may be diminished.

Equipment can also fall into categories based on function, such as one of these:

- Earth-moving
- Site improvement
- Material handling

Earth-Moving Equipment

Earth-moving equipment

Equipment that clears job sites and moves, eliminates, or compresses large amounts of earth, rock, snow, debris, construction materials, and other materials.

Earth-moving equipment serves two basic functions necessary in almost every construction project. First, it provides the power to clear job sites and move, eliminate, or compress large amounts of earth, rock, snow, debris, and similar materials. Second, earth-moving equipment can be used to handle and move construction materials and components within the job site. Attachments can be added to further vary the functions of earth-moving equipment, allowing machinery to handle and place irregularly shaped materials, such as pipes. See the exhibit "Types of Earth-Moving Equipment."

Earth-moving equipment is subject to several perils. Upset and overturn can occur because of rough working terrain, the equipment's large size, the equipment's weight distribution, and carried materials' weight. A high concentration of equipment on a job site can create traffic problems and increase the likelihood of fire and collision. Fire hazards develop from the variety of ignition sources and combustible materials found in equipment and on job sites. The most frequent cause of fire loss involves the breaking of hydraulic lines that operate shovels, buckets, and outriggers. The hydraulic fluid ignites when it is sprayed onto hot engine parts and burns combustible equipment, fuels, and debris allowed to accumulate in or under machinery. Flammable gasoline, oil, and lubricants in construction equipment and the fueling and building supplies stored near equipment increase the fire exposure. See the exhibit "Earth-Moving Equipment."

Site-Improvement Equipment

Site-improvement equipment

Pieces of equipment that prepare and finish asphalt and concrete surfaces.

Contractors bring in **site-improvement equipment** after the area has been cleared and leveled by the earth-moving equipment. Primarily, site-improvement equipment prepares and finishes asphalt and concrete surfaces. Mixers and pavers are often large and difficult to move, making them less prone to theft but more prone to flood or earthquake damage. Additionally, upset, overturn, and vandalism can damage site-improvement equipment. See the exhibit "Site-Improvement Equipment."

Types of Earth-Moving Equipment

	Uses	Attributes
Backhoe/ Excavator	• Excavates below the level of own tracks or wheels for trenching, footing, basement excavation, and similar work. • Handles and places pipes, equipment, and other job site materials.	• Digs by extending hydraulic boom and bucket and then pulling bucket down and toward machine. • Available in different sizes, digging depths, and load capacities. • Attachments available for digging in hard earth, clearing debris from low areas, breaking and loosening rock, and lifting building materials. • Often combined with a front-end loader.
Dozer/Tractor	• Pushes and pulls materials to clear land and remove debris. • Fills in open pits and uneven surfaces. • Prepares ground for paving.	• Available in a number of sizes and horsepower ratings. • Blade attachments available for moving materials of differing weights and densities, ripping imbedded objects, maneuvering in small work areas, cutting trees and low growth, and carrying materials. • Serves as vehicle for attachable or towable equipment such as rollers, trenchers, and forklifts.
Power Shovel	• Excavates material at the face of hillsides or embankments. • Excavates roadbeds. • Loosens and loads material in quarry pits.	• Digs by moving bucket down and away from machine into material and then upward in a lifting motion. • Available in a number of sizes, digging depths, and load capacities.
Loader (Front End, Pay, Scoop, Bucket, Wheel, High Lift, Tractor Shovel)	• Loads and moves loose materials and construction supplies. • Excavates above wheel or track level from level or sloping surface.	• Available in a number of sizes and horsepower ratings. • Variety of bucket sizes and dumping angles. • Attachments available for lifting, debris cleanup, tearing packed materials, removing snow, lifting logs and pipes, etc.
Scraper/ Grader	• Removes or relocates large volumes of earth during ground leveling or cut-and-fill operations. • Prepares surfaces for paving. • Scraper performs rough grading. • Grader performs final stage of fill and leveling.	• Scraping/grading device usually has its own towing unit but may be attached to or towed by a tractor. • Available in a number of sizes and horsepower ratings. • Graders may include laser detector and computer-leveling system.
Roller/ Compactor	• Compacts earth or asphalt in preparation for laying asphalt or concrete. • Sheepsfoot roller (also called tamper) used for loose earth. • Static or drum roller used for finely granulated materials and smoother surfaces.	• May be self-propelled or attached to a tractor. • May have up to three compaction wheels. • Vibratory function to consolidate sand and soil available on most compaction equipment. • Attachments available to create different surface patterns and textures (such as "rumble strips").
Trencher	• Digs trenches for utility lines, drainage ditches, and similar underground structures.	• Uses a number of small buckets to continuously chew and remove material in the direction of travel. • May be self-propelled or attached to a tractor. • Available in different sizes, digging depths, and trench shapes. • Various models can dig in any type of material other than solid rock.

[DA04229]

Earth-Moving Equipment

Dozer

Excavator

Front End Loader

Site-Improvement Equipment

	Uses	Attributes
Batching and Mixing Plant	• Mixes components of paving materials. • Consolidates paving materials for installation.	• Includes automated measuring and mixing systems. • May be stationary or attached to pavers.
Paver	• Applies base, intermediate, and topcoats of asphalt or concrete. • Provides initial compaction of paving material.	• Allows for adjustable paving width and thickness. • Includes microcomputer leveling systems for precision alignment. • May be self-propelled or towed by tractors. • Concrete paver runs on track mountings. • Asphalt paver can be tire or track mounted. • Paver models available for special or smaller jobs such as shoulders, curbs, and sidewalks.
Pavement Planer	• Prepares existing pavement and similar surfaces for repaving. • Removes top layer of earth or pavement to specified depth and texture. • Removes and pulverizes materials for immediate recycling and reuse.	• Uses rotating cutting drum and conveyor to transport cut material for disposal or recycling. • Self-propelled on tracks or wheels. • Available in a variety of sizes from a small version used to create rumble strips to larger machines capable of grinding an entire highway lane.
Finisher	• Creates a smooth surface free from irregularities.	• Different size blades used to cut and scrape raised areas from paved surface. • May be self-propelled, handheld, or attached to a paving machine.

[DA04233]

Material-Handling Equipment

To move large amounts of building materials and heavier objects within the site or into position within a structure, many contractors use **material-handling equipment**, typically lifts and cranes. Lifts raise, lower, and transport supplies and personnel within the job site. Cranes raise and move heavy materials. Cranes' lifting capacity varies according to the angle of the lift and the crane's size, strength, and stability. Tire-mounted truck cranes that can be easily moved from site to site may have a lifting capacity of a few tons, while tower cranes, because they are larger and used for a longer duration at one location, may be able to lift hundreds of tons. Crane services specializing in heavy lifts often use cranes that can lift thousands of tons. See the exhibit "Types of Material-Handling Equipment."

Material-handling equipment

Equipment that raises, lowers, and transports supplies and personnel within a job site.

Types of Material-Handling Equipment

	Uses	Attributes
Forklift	• Loads and unloads trucks, trailers, and similar vehicles. • Transports and raises building materials from ground level to elevated positions. • Handles heavy single units of packaged materials.	• Hydraulic and telescopic attachments allow for high-lift and forward-reach capabilities. • Attachments available for use in rough terrain, snow, mud, water, and other special conditions. • Attachments available for personnel baskets to permit working at elevations.
Hoist/Lift	• Raises personnel and smaller loads of materials above ground level on a platform. • Supplies materials to larger lifting equipment.	• May be mobile or fixed. • Hoist platform travels on extended mast. • Lift platform raises on scissor formation or telescopic boom. • Available in different heights and platform sizes. • Rough terrain models available.
Mobile Lift Crane (Mechanical and Hydraulic)	• Lifts, moves, and lowers materials. • Transports loads across job site.	• May be self-propelled or truck mounted. • Available in different lifting capacities and traveling speeds. • Lifting capacity and distance dependent on length of boom and mast and type of counterweight. • Attachments available to convert lift (hook) crane to an excavation machine include dragline, shovel, backhoe, and pile driver.
Tower Crane	• Lifts, moves, and places materials for high-rise construction or low-rise construction.	• Usually built on a fixed base, but truck-mounted tower cranes are available for short-duration, high-lift loads. • Freestanding or climbing base (raises and lowers height of mast).
Gantry Crane	• Lifts and moves materials within area spanned by the crane bridge. • Used in construction of precast concrete buildings or foundations in limited working spaces. • Used for dock and shipyard operations.	• Moves along rails mounted on an inverted U-shaped structure. • High-lift capacities available. • Can be designed and built to suit specific needs and operations.
Concrete Pump	• Carries concrete from ground to elevated level through a piping system within boom. • Used in larger projects requiring specific placement of concrete.	• May be mobile or fixed. • Available in different boom lengths and pumping capacities.

[DA04235]

Material-Handling Equipment

© Image Ideas, Inc./Picture Quest. [DA04237]

Lifting Crane, Fixed-Boom, Crawler Mounted

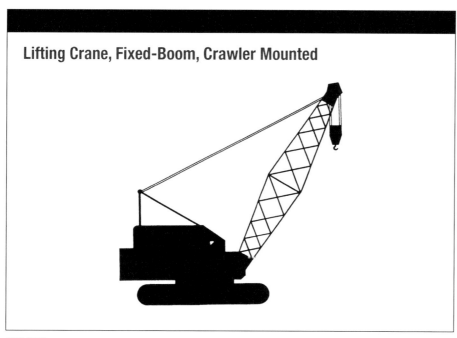

[DA04238]

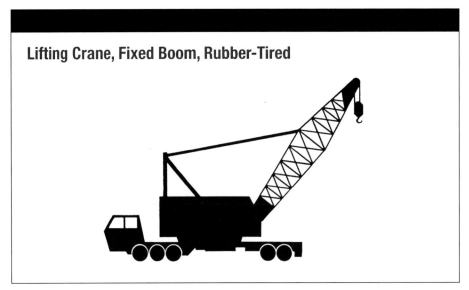

Lifting Crane, Fixed Boom, Rubber-Tired

[DA04240]

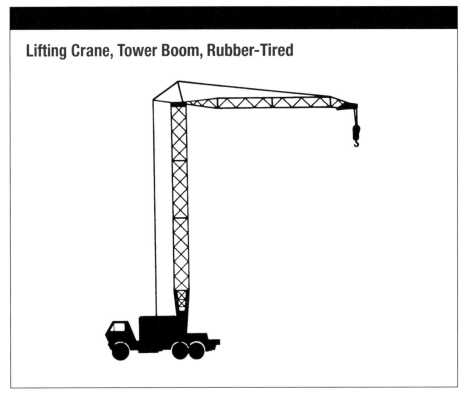

Lifting Crane, Tower Boom, Rubber-Tired

[DA04241]

Tower Crane

A crane is made up of five major components:

- The base is that part of the crane that stays in contact with the ground during normal operation.
- The cab sits on top of the base and contains the controls for the crane.
- The boom is attached to the cab and is the arm that does the lifting.
- The counterweights are at the rear of the cab and keep the crane from tipping over when it is moving a load.
- The outriggers are hydraulic arms that extend down from the base. They, too, provide additional support and stability for the crane. [6]

Another important piece of a crane is the jib. This is a lattice-shaped extension that is attached to the boom. It may be set in line with the boom or at an angle to it. The jib allows the crane a greater range of motion than with just a boom. The crane in the 'Lifting Crane, Tower Boom, Rubber-Tired' exhibit is an example of a jib crane. Inside the cab of the crane is an important piece of information called the load chart. This chart shows what the crane's maximum lifting capacity is in a given configuration and its boom extension. The crane's ability to lift heavy objects depends on the boom's length or extension and the angle that is created by this extension.

The cab also has many indicators in it. A very important one is the load moment indicator. This device warns an operator when a load exceeds a crane's limit.

Adjuster Tip—When investigating a loss involving boom damage that occurred during a lift, the adjuster interviews the operator and asks questions about the load and the load's movement, asks what was the calculated weight of the load, and asks whether it was within the load chart's limits. If the crane is rented, the adjuster determines whether the operator is an employee of the insured or of the rental company and how much experience the operator has.

There are two basic types of cranes:

- A friction crane
- A hydraulic crane

A friction crane uses an open or lattice boom that is made up of several sections. The sections are usually trucked to the worksite and assembled there.

A hydraulic crane has a telescoping boom that does not require assembly. The crane is usually driven to the site, and then the boom is extended. See the exhibit "Hydraulic Crane."

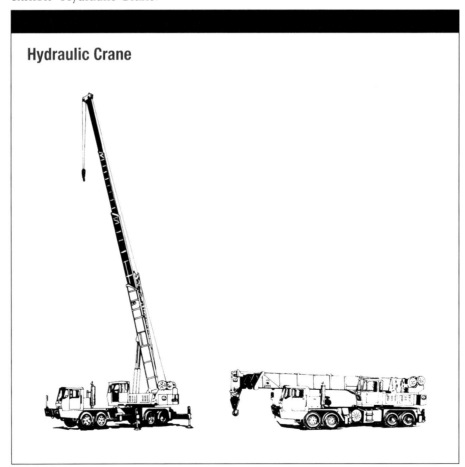

Hydraulic Crane

Reprinted with permission from Grove Manufacturing Co., Shady Grove, Pa. [DA04244]

Booms represent a considerable portion of the crane's value, and collapsed booms generally result in a constructive or total loss. Long booms receive much handling because they are made in sections, erected at the job site, and dismantled when moved to another location. If any of the boom members bend during erection, dismantling, transit, or storage, the boom's structural integrity will be weakened, and it may collapse under a load that it could normally bear. Once a crane is erected, its height increases its exposure to loss by windstorm. Metal fatigue (a weakening in boom members) or weakened cables also contribute to boom collapse.

Booms often sustain damage during lifting operations. Lifting loads in excess of the equipment's lifting capacity or lifting loads in tandem with another crane can bend or twist the boom. Any sudden or uncontrolled movement of the crane, including bumping the boom against adjacent structures, allowing the load to swing into the boom, or releasing the load suddenly, may also cause damage. Upset may occur if crane outriggers or stabilizers are not in use under required conditions.

Other Types of Contractors' Equipment

Other types of contractors' equipment provide supplementary power and support functions to equipment and job sites. Nearly every type of contractor uses a generator, a pump, or an air compressor. In addition to facing loss by the principal perils of fire caused by refueling or poor maintenance, collision during transportation or operation, and flood damage when stored in low-lying areas, miscellaneous pieces of contractors' equipment are prone to theft. The small size, portability, and large market for compressors, generators, and pumps make them prime targets for theft.

Types of Operations

One of the most familiar types of construction operation is that of a building contractor. Building contractors perform a wide range of specialized construction projects such as land clearing, concrete work, framing, and electrical work. The projects use many different types of mobile equipment, small machinery, and hand tools. Values for individual pieces of equipment range from thousands to millions of dollars, depending on the size and scope of a contractor's projects.

The principal causes of loss for building contractors are theft and vandalism. Contractors may leave equipment at unsecured job sites, allowing access by organized crime rings, disgruntled employees, and vandals. Other common perils include fire from poor equipment and site maintenance, overturn during excavation, and collision with other pieces of equipment or the structure being built. In building operations that use cranes, boom damage may occur as a result of overloading, improper operation, collision with nearby structures, upset from unstable footing, and windstorm.

Other types of operations that use contractors' equipment are road-building contractors, utility contractors, logging operations, mining operations, stevedoring operations, and agricultural operations. Each of these operations has exposures unique to its business, so the adjuster should understand what type of operation the insured is engaged in before going to the loss site or taking a statement.

Exposures and Investigation

Theft and vandalism of contractors' equipment account for the largest percentage of loss occurrences and loss dollars. Given the equipment's mobile nature and the ease of accessibility at job sites, this is not surprising. The investigation of an equipment loss is the same as the investigation for a stolen car, with minor alterations. It is a good practice to take the insured's statement and those of any witnesses who can describe the equipment and its last known location. The adjuster should obtain a police report. A report of the theft should be sent to an index bureau such as NICB, ISO ClaimSearch®, and the National Equipment Register (NER). The NER asks equipment owners to register the piece before any loss. If a theft occurs, the equipment can be identified if recovered or if someone other than the owner attempts to sell the piece.

If the loss involves a rented or leased piece of equipment, the adjuster should obtain a copy of the lease/rental agreement. It may be necessary for the adjuster to contact the owner of the equipment to get the complete identification information and the maintenance history, to determine the equipment's actual condition at the time of loss.

Regardless of the type of loss, it is a good claims practice to obtain the maintenance log for the piece of equipment involved. This often helps in determining the cause of the loss in a fire. It also aids in evaluating the equipment's overall condition for actual cash value purposes.

Fire is a frequent cause of loss to contractors' equipment. Many fires result from poor maintenance. This is another reason why it is beneficial to obtain the maintenance logs for the piece of equipment involved. If a third party has done some repairs or maintenance immediately before the loss, there is a potential for subrogation.

In addition to boom collapse, overturn is a frequent cause of loss to cranes. An overturn can result from improper set up, exceeding the lift capacity, or soil collapse underneath the crane. If an overturn results from soil collapse, then it is important to determine whether a soil analysis had been done before the crane's use. The soil analysis would determine if the ground was sufficiently solid to support the weight of the crane under full load. It is common on large construction projects for an expert to perform the soil analysis for the general contractor.

The causes and coverages for boom collapse have been previously discussed. Because of the complexity of this type of failure, hiring a structural engineer or failure analysis engineer to determine the cause of loss is usually necessary. The manufacturer often makes repairs to a damaged boom because the crane must be certified as safe to use once the repairs are completed.

CONTRACTOR'S EQUIPMENT POLICIES

Contractors' equipment coverage is an inland marine form of coverage.

Contractors' equipment can be defined as the tools and machinery used in projects involving construction, renovation, earth-moving, and many other activities. Contractors' equipment insurance protects the insured against direct physical loss to the covered property. Endorsements may be added to contractors' equipment policies to cover time element losses—either loss of income or extra expenses—resulting from physical loss to covered equipment. A contractors' equipment policy tailored to a contractor's unique needs can cover the cost to repair or replace the damaged piece of equipment. Adding rental reimbursement and business income coverage endorsements can then cover the costs of renting substitute equipment and the loss of income from interrupted operations.

The adjustment of a contractors' equipment loss follows the same pattern as an auto physical damage claim. The policy must be reviewed for coverage, the loss must be assessed, and the equipment must be either repaired or replaced.

Contractors' Equipment Policy Provisions

Contractors' equipment is a nonfiled class of insurance in most states, allowing inland marine underwriters to tailor policies to best fit each insured's operation. American Association of Insurance Services and Insurance Services Office, Inc., each offer a form for use, or the underwriter may chose to manuscript the policy completely. A contractors' equipment form can be a stand-alone policy or can be added by endorsement to a commercial package policy. Regardless of the form used, the basic policy provisions remain the same.

Declarations Page

The contractors' equipment policy declarations page lists the named insured on the policy. It also lists endorsements for loss payees, such as a financing company or a leasing company, on the covered property.

What Is Insured?

Contractors' equipment insurance covers the insured against loss or damage to mobile equipment, machinery, and tools used in the insured's business. Policy descriptions of covered property often have two components:

- The applicable coverage basis (scheduled versus blanket)
- The policy definition of covered property

Scheduled Versus Blanket Coverage

Scheduled basis

A basis for insuring each item of insured property by individually describing them in the policy declarations or schedule and assigning a coverage limit to each listed item.

Contractors' equipment insurance can be written on either a scheduled basis or a blanket basis. When written on a **scheduled basis**, each item of insured property is individually described in the policy declarations or schedule, and a limit is assigned to each listed item. A schedule of contractors' equipment also includes a full description of each item so that there is no question of identification or valuation. Information such as the manufacturer, model, model year, and serial number are included with the amount of insurance. This policy excerpt shows an example of schedule language:

> Property Covered
>
> "We" cover the following property unless the property is otherwise covered, excluded, or subject to limitations.
>
> 1. Scheduled Equipment—When Scheduled Equipment is indicated on the "schedule of coverages", "we" cover direct physical loss caused by a covered peril to:
>
> a. "your" "contractor's equipment"; and
>
> b. "contractors' equipment" of others in "your" care, custody, or control; described on the "equipment schedule".

Blanket basis

A basis for insuring all items within a single amount of insurance without specifically identifying each item.

When a contractors' equipment policy applies on a **blanket basis**, the policy is written for a single amount of insurance covering all items. Blanket insurance eliminates the need for a schedule of covered property, allowing insureds to cover all of their contractors' equipment without having to declare new pieces. Many insurers set a per item limit and a per occurrence limit in their blanket policies.

Many contractors' equipment policies offer both scheduled and blanket coverage. Individually listing and describing smaller items and hand tools can be impractical. Insurers, therefore, schedule higher-value items of equipment and establish a blanket amount of insurance for smaller items of lesser value.

Regardless of how the policy is written, be it scheduled, blanket, or a combination of the two, the policy or underwriting file should contain a list of the equipment associated with the policy. In a scheduled policy, the list is on the declarations page or attached to it. In a blanket policy or in a combined policy, the list of equipment that was used to determine the amount of coverage needed is usually in the underwriting file notes. For a blanket or a combined policy, this list provides some information but is not to be used as an agreed amount or as the item's actual cash value (ACV). The list provides background information and should include the make, model, and serial numbers of the equipment to be covered by the policy.

One of the problems associated with handling contractors' equipment losses is that—unlike autos, which have a standardized vehicle identification number (VIN)—there is no standard form of identification for equipment. A serial number or a component part number can be located anywhere on the piece of equipment. Because there is no standard format for the number, it will not reveal any particular information about the piece of equipment as the VIN does for an auto. However, the number will be helpful if an adjuster must contact the manufacturer for information about the piece.

Covered Property

Insuring equipment on a scheduled or a blanket basis may not guarantee coverage for all property used by the insured. Many contractors that own equipment may also loan or borrow equipment for temporary use. Additionally, many contractors rent equipment from dealers for both short- and long-term use. Generally, the covered property in a scheduled or blanket policy includes property of others as covered property. However, property of others is not always included as covered property. Schedule requirements and differences in covered property provisions can create coverage gaps for newly acquired property, miscellaneous property items of lesser value, and property owned or used by a third party. Additional coverages and endorsements can amend such gaps.

Newly Acquired Property

In contractors' equipment policies written on a scheduled basis, newly purchased equipment is technically not covered. To remedy this, scheduled policies usually include a clause that automatically covers newly acquired property up to a specified amount, provided that the insured reports the new equipment within a stipulated number of days. This clause may be in the form of a coverage extension or an endorsement.

The clause for newly acquired property in scheduled policies generally covers the lesser of a specified dollar amount or a stipulated percentage of the total amount of insurance. For example, newly acquired equipment might be covered for no more than $50,000 or 25 percent of the total amount of the policy, whichever is less. Moreover, the clause may apply to accessories added or improvements made to equipment already scheduled. The piece of equipment is then covered for the scheduled limit plus the value of the improvement.

Property Leased, Rented, or Borrowed

Rental and leasing agreements obligate contractors to return equipment in as good a condition as it was—normal wear and tear excepted—when they took possession of it. A contractor that has leased or rented equipment can be held responsible for damage to the equipment that occurs during the rental period. A contractor will likely want its contractors' equipment policy to cover leased or rented property. Contractors' equipment policies may cover property leased, rented, or borrowed by the insured in any of these ways:

- By including property of others in the care or custody of the insured in the Covered Property Provision
- By including nonowned property in the Newly Acquired Equipment Clause
- By including a coverage extension or endorsement for property leased, rented, or borrowed from others

Contractors' equipment policies excluded property loaned, leased, or rented to others more often than they exclude property rented *from* others because greater hazards exist when property is removed from the insured's control. Many policies will cover property leased to others only if the insured provides a trained operator for the equipment.

Miscellaneous Property Items

Even when written on a scheduled basis, contractors' equipment policies often include blanket coverage on unscheduled miscellaneous items and hand tools owned, borrowed, or rented for use in the insured's business. A per item limit and a per occurrence limit typically apply to the coverage. Many contractors' equipment policies offer additional coverage for tools, clothing, and miscellaneous property items owned by the insured's employees, subject to limits separate from those for other unscheduled property.

Property Not Covered

Contractors' equipment policies contain various property exclusions. Many policies exclude these kinds of property:

- Property in high-risk or uncontrolled working environments
- Property more suitably covered by other types of insurance

Property exclusions can be modified depending on the insured's needs and the underwriter's assessment of the risk. The next sections describe the property exclusions commonly found in contractors' equipment policies.

Property in High-Risk Working Environments

The working environment of property directly affects its susceptibility to perils. For example, a loader used in underground mining faces perils, such as ceiling collapse, unlikely to occur if the loader were used in above-ground road-building operations. That same loader in the custody of a party other than the insured may not be protected by the loss control practices—such as operator training and site security—that the insured would provide. Accordingly, contractors' equipment policies often exclude property located underground or underwater; property while waterborne or airborne; and property loaned, leased, or rented to others. Insurers may develop specific forms and endorsements designed to cover property in high-risk working environments. For instance, contractors that use equipment in water—such as a dredge used in quarry operations—may request that the underwriter delete the exclusion of waterborne property after a review of the risk. Therefore, the adjuster must review the policy and all endorsements carefully to determine what is and is not covered by it.

Property Covered by Other Insurance

Contractors' equipment policies generally exclude property more appropriately insured under other types of insurance policies. Coverage may be arranged for such property under additional coverage parts or policies. Contractors' equipment policies often exclude aircraft and watercraft; money and securities; plans, blueprints, design specifications, and similar property; building materials and supplies; and property intended to become part of a permanent structure. Most contractors' equipment policies also exclude automobiles, motorcycles, motor trucks, trailers, and semi-trailers; however, contractors' equipment additional coverages and endorsements exist for certain vehicles. An example of a coverage endorsement directly modifying the exclusion of trailers would indicate where the trailer would be covered, such as at a jobsite or in transit. It would also specify a limit of liability for the coverage.

Covered Causes of Loss

Contractors' equipment policies can be written on either a special-form basis or a named-perils basis. The special-form version typically insures against risks of direct physical loss or damage unless caused by a peril that is limited or excluded. Most contractors' equipment policies today provide special-form coverage.

Underwriters issue named-perils policies less frequently than they issue special-form policies, reserving named-perils policies for insureds desiring lower premiums or insureds posing special risks. Contractors' equipment policies issued on a named-perils basis can be tailored to include coverage for risks specific to the insured's operations. For instance, policies covering mining operations may add coverage for loss caused by slate fall, roof fall, cave-in, landslide, or squeeze.

Exclusions

Contractors' equipment policies usually contain exclusions for war, nuclear hazard, and governmental action but tend not to exclude earthquake and flood. These policies can also exclude mysterious disappearance, inventory shortage, voluntary parting, unauthorized instructions, and dishonest acts of the insured's employees or others to whom property is entrusted. In addition to the general exclusions discussed, a contractors' equipment policy may include some or all of these exclusions, which may be subject to exceptions that allow coverage for the otherwise excluded exposure (under certain conditions):

- *Artificially generated electrical currents.* Contractors' equipment can include complex electrical and computer systems that are sensitive to electrical disturbance. An artificially generated electrical current exclusion typically excludes damage caused by short circuits or electrical disturbances within the covered property. The exclusion often contains an exception stating that damage to covered property caused by fire or explosion ensuing from a surge or shortage is covered.

- *Mechanical breakdown.* Most contractors' equipment policies contain a mechanical breakdown exclusion. The exclusion eliminates coverage for mechanical breakdown or failure—such as a blown head gasket or a broken axle. However, the exclusion typically does not apply to physical loss that results from mechanical breakdown provided that the resulting loss is caused by a covered peril. For example, the cost of repairing a fuel line that ruptures because of mechanical breakdown would be excluded. If this breakdown resulted in a fire, the resulting fire damage to the equipment would be covered.

- *Work upon the property.* Contractors' equipment must be serviced and maintained, but repairs and adjustments may unintentionally damage equipment. Many contractors' equipment policies exclude coverage for work on the property. A "work upon the property" exclusion typically excludes adjustments, servicing, and maintenance operations, unless fire or explosion ensues, and then only for loss caused by such ensuing fire or explosion.

Special Exclusions

Underwriters may attach exclusions for certain types of equipment, operations, or locations subject to unique perils. Crane operation provides examples of such exclusions.

Crane booms are very susceptible to loss, and operator error can easily damage them. Three types of exclusions apply to cranes and derrick booms:

- Weight-of-load exclusion
- Tandem lift exclusion
- Boom operation exclusion

Weight-of-load exclusion

An exclusion that typically does not allow coverage for loss caused by the weight of the load exceeding the manufacturer's rated capacity of the equipment.

A **weight-of-load exclusion** typically excludes loss caused by the weight of the load exceeding the manufacturer's rated capacity of the equipment. Claims involving a weight-of-load exclusion can be very complex to adjust. Should such a loss occur, the insurer would need to refer to manufacturer specifications and the equipment owner's manual, as well as obtain a detailed statement from the equipment operator.

A **tandem lift exclusion** may be added to contractors' equipment policies to address situations in which two or more cranes are used together to perform a single lift. A tandem lift requires detailed coordination and must be engineered before the lift. Despite extensive planning, tandem lifts performed by well-maintained equipment following specific operating instructions have a higher probability of causing loss or damage to lifting equipment. A tandem lift exclusion may be deleted for an additional premium if the underwriter reviews and accepts engineering plans.

If a contractors' equipment policy covering cranes does not contain a weight-of-load or a tandem lift exclusion, it may contain a **boom operation exclusion**. A boom operation exclusion deletes coverage for crane and derrick booms while being operated unless the loss is directly caused by specified perils, such as fire, lightning, hail, windstorm, explosion, riot, aircraft, vehicles, landslide, or overturning. The exclusion is commonly worded so as to prevent payment of claims resulting from such causes as metal fatigue, improper operation of the crane, and a load too heavy for the equipment. Some versions of the boom damage exclusion apply only to booms with a length exceeding a certain number of feet. Other versions preclude payment for a boom loss unless outriggers or stabilizers are extended to their full operating position at the time of loss.

Coverage Extensions and Endorsements

Damage to covered property often results in expenses beyond the equipment's value. Many contractors' equipment policies contain coverage for rental reimbursement and business income and extra expense.

Rental Reimbursement Coverage

Many insurers offer rental reimbursement coverage as an additional coverage or endorsement to contractors' equipment policies. **Rental reimbursement coverage** pays the expenses that the insured incurs to rent substitute equipment for covered equipment that has been damaged or destroyed by a covered peril. Because a loss to a piece of contractors' equipment rarely shuts down operations completely, most contractors can continue operations by renting substitute equipment until the damaged equipment can be repaired or replaced. Rental reimbursement coverage is thus a type of extra expense insurance.

Rental reimbursement coverage requires that the rented equipment be necessary to continue the insured's normal operations. Coverage would not apply if the insured has equivalent equipment that is lying idle. Rental reimbursement coverage is usually subject to a waiting period during which coverage does not apply. A typical waiting period is seventy-two hours following the time that

Tandem lift exclusion
An exclusion that applies to losses occurring when two or more cranes are used together to perform a single lift.

Boom operation exclusion
An exclusion for losses to crane and derrick booms while being operated, unless the loss is directly caused by perils specified in the policy.

Rental reimbursement coverage
Coverage that can be added to a contractors equipment floater to pay the cost of renting necessary substitute equipment to replace covered equipment that has been damaged by a covered peril.

the equipment is physically damaged. Rental reimbursement is usually subject to both a per day limit and an overall limit. Coverage ends when the damaged property has been repaired or replaced or the need for it no longer exists, whichever occurs first. The coverage typically requires the insured to exercise due diligence in having the covered property repaired or replaced. Sample rental reimbursement provisions are shown here:

Provisions

1. We will pay you the actual rental expenses up to the limits shown in the Schedule for renting equipment when all of the following apply:

a. You have a loss to Covered Property;

b. The equipment is necessary to continue as much as possible the normal operations or work in process;

c. You do not have the equivalent, idle equipment available.

2. Payment is limited to expense incurred during the period starting 72 hours after the covered loss occurs and ending when the Covered Property has been:

a. Replaced;

b. Restored to service; or,

c. Is no longer needed;

whichever occurs first.

Our payment will not be limited by the expiration date of this policy.

3. You and we agree that the Covered Property involved in the loss will be repaired promptly.

Business Income and Extra Expense Coverage

In certain situations, physical loss to equipment can cause time element losses that cannot be adequately handled by rental reimbursement coverage. For example, one high-value, customized piece of equipment (such as a conveyor system in an underground coal mine or a special tower crane) may be an essential part of the insured's operations. If this piece of equipment is destroyed, operations may come to a halt until the equipment can be repaired or replaced. If the equipment's repair or replacement takes several months, the insured can lose several months of income. In such cases, the insured can purchase business income and extra expense coverage. Business income and extra expense coverage, usually added by endorsement, covers lost net income, operating expenses that continue during the business interruption, and extra expenses that the insured incurs to continue normal operations.

The extra expense component of the combined form of business income and extra expense coverage would cover the cost of renting substitute equipment, the cost of overtime labor to expedite repairs, and other reasonable expenses incurred to continue operations. Unlike rental reimbursement coverage, this type of extra expense insurance is not limited to paying the costs associated with renting substitute equipment.

Limits

The limits of insurance in contractors' equipment policies typically apply on a per item and per occurrence basis. Loss payments do not reduce the per item or per occurrence limits unless a total loss occurs to a scheduled item, in which case the item is no longer included in the schedule and any unearned premium on the item is returned to the insured.

Application of the per item and per occurrence limits varies between scheduled and blanket contractors' equipment policies. Scheduled policies establish a limit of insurance for each scheduled item. Policies with a large schedule of equipment may also contain a per occurrence limit, sometimes called a **catastrophe limit**. The catastrophe limit sets a maximum amount that the policy will pay for all property losses associated with a single occurrence. Catastrophe limits may be considerably less than the total of the scheduled limits because the likelihood of a loss to more than one piece of equipment is often minimal.

Blanket policies set an overall policy limit that applies to all covered equipment and machinery, often subject to a per item maximum limit. In both scheduled and blanket policies, limits for small tools and miscellaneous items, as well as for other coverages added by endorsement, are payable in addition to the per item and per occurrence limits for contractors' equipment.

Catastrophe limit
A maximum amount that a policy will pay for all property losses associated with a single occurrence.

Valuation

Most contractors' equipment policies cover on an ACV basis. ACV covers the cost to replace or repair damaged equipment and machinery less depreciation and obsolescence. Rather than depreciating based on the number of miles driven, contractors' equipment depreciates based on its age and its hours of use. Construction and contracting operations place a physical burden on the machinery they use, and wear and tear on contractors' equipment can be considerable. ACV valuation for contractors' equipment accounts for this physical depreciation and seeks to replace damaged equipment with equipment of the same physical condition and value.

ACV can be difficult to assess on partial losses because of the wording of the pair or set language in the policy. Many contractors' equipment policies modify their ACV provisions to account for losses to a pair or set or a loss to equipment parts. For example, the boom of a truck-mounted mobile crane may be damaged by a collision with a nearby structure. Although the crane boom is completely destroyed, the truck to which it is mounted sustains no damage. A pair or set provision in a policy usually states that the loss should not be valued at the ACV of the entire truck-mounted mobile crane, but that it should be valued at the cost to repair or replace the crane portion of the equipment because a loss to a part of the unit is not considered a total loss of the pair or set.

Some contractors' equipment policies provide coverage extensions or endorsements that do not adjust losses for depreciation if the loss is less than a certain percentage of the equipment's scheduled value. A waiver of depreciation applies only to ACV policies and provides replacement cost coverage for some partial losses.

Full replacement cost coverage, which replaces lost or damaged equipment with new equipment of like kind and quality at current market prices, may be obtained for an entire schedule of equipment or for specified equipment. Some contractors' equipment policies also offer agreed value coverage by extension or endorsement for scheduled equipment. Agreed value usually applies in two ways:

• Total losses are covered for the amount stated in the equipment schedule
• Partial losses are covered for the lesser of the ACV of the property at the time of loss or the cost to repair or replace the damaged equipment with similar equipment

Coinsurance

Contractors' equipment policies are generally written with an 80, a 90, or a 100 percent coinsurance clause that applies to each separate limit. The coinsurance calculation is:

$$\frac{\text{Did}}{\text{Should}} \times \text{Loss}.$$

Adjuster Tip—With a blanket policy, the ACV/RCV of all the equipment is used in the calculation.

Insurance to Value

As a practical matter, the ACV of contractors' equipment is usually determined as the fair market value of equipment of the same make, age, and condition. Fair market value is "the price that a seller is willing to accept and a buyer is willing to pay on the open market."[7]

Adjusters can use several references to help determine whether the policy limits represent adequate values. The *Green Guide for Construction Equipment* lists current fair market values and specifications for construction equipment and optional attachments up to ten years old. The *Green Guide* also lists approximate resale and replacement cost values that can serve as a basis for determining insurance to value. Adjusters may also gather valuation information from other sources, including local equipment dealers and online equipment brokerage services. Print and electronic trade journals also advertise the prices of new and used construction equipment.

If a contractors' equipment policy requires 80 percent coinsurance, the insurance-to-value minimum for equipment valued for $100,000 at ACV would be $80,000. The replacement cost for the same equipment would be higher, and equipment valued for $120,000 at replacement cost would require a limit of at least $96,000 to meet 80 percent coinsurance requirements. Accurate establishment of insurance to value is important because overvaluing equipment may encourage a moral hazard, and undervaluing equipment can lead to inadequate limits and losses subject to coinsurance penalties.

Deductibles

A deductible may be represented as either a specific dollar amount or as a percentage of the value of the damaged item or scheduled amount. When a percentage deductible is used, minimum and maximum deductible amounts are typically indicated on the declarations page.

In addition to a deductible that applies to covered losses of scheduled equipment, separate deductibles for additional dollar amounts, sometimes called split deductibles, may apply to certain properties or perils. Coverage added by endorsement, such as that for waterborne equipment or employees' tools, may have a separate dollar or percentage deductible. Specific perils may also be subject to a separate deductible. For instance, a deductible provision can show a dollar deductible for all scheduled and blanketed equipment and a separate percentage deductible for losses incurred during boom operation.

Locations Covered

Contractors' equipment policies usually cover property wherever it is located, subject only to the policy's territorial limits. Territorial limits generally include Canada, Puerto Rico, and the continental United States, which includes Alaska. Some policies only cover the contiguous United States, which excludes both Hawaii and Alaska. Property located in those states can, at the underwriter's option, be covered by endorsement.

CONTRACTORS' EQUIPMENT VALUATION

Most contractors' equipment policies cover on an actual cash value (ACV) basis.

Contractors' equipment appraisers, like auto appraisers, are a highly specialized group. If an insurer writes many contractors' equipment policies, a heavy equipment appraiser will probably be on staff. These appraisers are usually certified by a training facility that specializes in heavy equipment. If an independent appraiser is used to inspect losses, the appraiser must be certified.

Total Loss

In the event of a total loss or a constructive total loss, the adjuster must determine ACV. These factors affect ACV:

- Accessories
- Age
- Hours of use and type of use
- Local market demand
- Maintenance
- Manufacturer
- Prior unrepaired damage
- Salvage
- Type and size

Adjuster Tip—Pieces of contractors' equipment are rarely titled and registered with the state. If a total loss occurs, the adjuster must obtain a signed salvage receipt before taking the equipment.

Resources are available to assist in the calculation of the ACV for contractors' equipment. A canvass of local dealers and resellers will garner information on local values. Many Internet sites also provide global search capabilities for both valuation purposes and possible replacement of the equipment. The most relied-on source is the *Green Guide* that is available in print or online. A list of resources can be found in the course guide.

Business Income Loss

If a major piece of equipment sustains a loss, the equipment may have significant downtime while it awaits repair or replacement. If a piece of equipment is unusual or unique, there may be limited availability of repair parts or replacement equipment. The resulting downtime can result in a loss of revenue, contract penalties, and extra expenses. A contract penalty is an amount specified in the contract for failure to complete the project by a specified date. If the policy covers loss of use, then the adjuster will have to calculate the net income per day for the period of restoration, much like it is calculated for a building loss. The property loss adjuster must carefully review extra expenses in light of the policy terms to determine what may be covered.

SUMMARY

Transportation policies provide coverage for the shipper and the consignee of the goods as well as the carrier who transports the goods. The adjuster must ascertain who has the responsibility for loss to the goods. The shipping documents indicate when title to the goods passes. The contract between the shipper and the carrier, called a bill of lading, indicates any limitations to the carrier's liability for loss or damage.

The BMC 32 endorsement included in most motor truck liability policies responds to a federal law requiring carriers to show evidence of financial responsibility up to $5,000 for loss or damage to goods on any one vehicle. The BMC 32 requires the insurer to pay any cargo claim for which the carrier is liable, whether covered by the policy or not. If the loss is not covered by the policy, the insurer would have the right to collect reimbursement from the insured for the loss payment.

Losses involving bailments are insured under bailee/bailor policies. Repair shops, jewelry stores, and dry cleaners all need this type of coverage. The bailee liability policy covers insureds for losses that they are legally liable for and that result from a covered peril. A bailees' customers policy provides that same type of coverage without the requirement of legal liability. Bailors who do not wish to rely on the bailee's coverage purchase bailor coverage. This covers their goods off their premises. Businesses that send their goods to other businesses for processing use this coverage to protect their property while it is being worked on off their premises.

Warehouse legal liability is another form of bailee insurance. The warehouse legal liability policy covers the warehouse's legal liability for loss or damage to a customer's property. Similar to a transportation claim, the warehouse receipt indicates the owner of the property, the condition it was received in, the terms of the storage, and any limitations on the warehouse's liability.

Condominiums are a special form of property ownership. Losses involving a condominium require review of the property deeds to determine ownership. Condominiums have areas called common elements owned by all of the members of the condominium association. The master deed of the condominium association describes what property belongs to the association and what property belongs to the unit owner.

The bare-walls concept means that the unit owner is responsible from the bare walls in. Under the all-encompassing concept, the condominium association is responsible for all exterior and interior items that the unit contains at the time of sale to a unit owner.

Builders' risk has special loss exposures. Because the structure is under construction, opportunities for theft and vandalism exist in addition to added exposure to windstorm and collapse. Various insurable interests may exist as well. The owner, the mortgagees, and the contractors that are working on the structure all have some interest in the structure. The builders' risk policy covers the structure during the course of construction as well as material, supplies, and temporary structures such as scaffolding. Often, the challenge in a builders' risk loss is determining the amount of the loss. Builders' risk policies may cover soft costs and business income loss. The adjuster must become heavily involved in the construction schedule to see whether the loss will affect the project's completion date.

Because the BPP offers limited coverage for crime losses, many commercial insureds purchase separate crime coverage to insure their exposures. Eight options for crime coverage give insureds the ability to tailor coverage to their specific needs. Investigation of crime losses requires the adjuster to have a high degree of tact and sensitivity. Interviews with employees, neighbors, and police are often required. The adjuster must also review the insured's financial statements and inventory records to verify the loss.

Just about every business has a computer system. Individuals have home computers and handheld devices. Special policies have been developed to cover hardware, software, data, and media. Many of the computer coverages insure loss to hardware, software, and data. Computer equipment needs special handling in the event of a loss. Restoration and computer experts need to evaluate the damage and make recommendations on repairs. Adjusters often have to deal with the issue of obsolescence when handling computer losses. Adjusters can use computer consultants to find cost-effective replacement units.

Pollution and contamination-of-property claims have become more common in first-party policies. Most states require an environmental assessment when commercial property is sold. CERCLA of 1980 empowered the EPA to identify, investigate, and remediate hazardous sites.

A property owner can be responsible for the property's past and present contamination. Insureds have attempted to find coverage for the contamination through their property insurance. Coverage depends on the facts and circumstances of the loss, the policy language, and the applicable state law. The BPP offers a $10,000 annual aggregate limit for pollution cleanup and removal, if caused by a covered loss.

Contractors' equipment can be defined as the tools and machinery used in projects involving construction, renovation, earth-moving, and many other activities. Contractors' equipment can be classified in various ways. Equipment can be self-propelled or in need of transport. Equipment can also fall into categories based on its function or attachment.

Contractors' equipment policies can be written on either a special-form basis or a named-perils basis. Contractors' equipment policies usually contain general and specific exclusions. Many contractors' equipment policies contain coverage for rental reimbursement and business income and extra expense.

Most contractors' equipment policies cover on an actual cash value (ACV) basis.

ASSIGNMENT NOTES

1.   Includes copyrighted material of Insurance Services Office, Inc., with its permission. Copyright, ISO Properties, Inc., 2007

2. Includes copyrighted material of Insurance Services Office, Inc., with its permission. Copyright, ISO Properties, Inc., 2007

3. Robert Karbin, "Adjusting Power-Surge Damages," Claims Magazine, July 2002, p. 5

4. Includes copyrighted material of Insurance Services Office, Inc., with its permission. Copyright, ISO Properties, Inc., 2007

5. Includes copyrighted material of Insurance Services Office, Inc. with its permission. Copyright, ISO Properties, Inc., 2007

6. Cranes (Greenfield, Mass.: Douglas G. Peterson and Associates, Inc., 2002).

7. Black's Law Dictionary, 7th ed. (St. Paul, Minn.: West Publishing Co., 1999).

Index

Page numbers in boldface refer to pages where the word or phrase is defined.

C

Calculating Book Value, 9.13–9.16
Carbon dioxide system, **7.9**
Carrier, **11.6**
Catastrophe, **4.19**, 4.27
Catastrophe Environment, 4.24–4.26
Catastrophe limit, **11.69**
Catastrophe Loss Adjusting, 4.29–4.31
Catastrophes: Physical Environment and Loss
    Adjustment Environment, 4.19–4.26
Catastrophes: Pre- and Post-Loss Adjustment
    Procedures, 4.27–4.35
Cause, **6.15**
Causes of Loss, 11.36–11.40
Causes of Mold Claims, 4.12–4.19
Challenges to the Decision, 2.34
Change in Property: Ongoing Promises, 4.32
Changes in or Waiver of Proof of Loss, 2.30
Checking Reported Values, 9.24–9.25
Choice of Estimating Methods, 7.33–7.34
Circuit breaker (fuse box), **8.63**
Civil Authority, 10.35–10.36
Clean water, **4.13**
Code Requirements, 7.41
Coinsurance, **1.14**, 2.18–2.21, 11.70
Coinsurance Examples, 2.18–2.20
Coinsurance Policy Language, 10.38–10.39
Coinsurance Requirement and Optional Coverages,
    10.38–10.44
Coinsurance Requirements, 1.14
Collapse, 1.32–1.33, **1.33**
Commercial Fire Losses, 4.3–4.4
Commercial Property, 11.23
Common carriers, **1.9**
Common elements, **11.18**–11.19
Common Errors, 7.35
Communications With Insureds, 4.30
Compromise, 2.27–2.28
Computer Consultants, 11.43–11.44
Computer Coverage in the BPP, 11.41
Computer Coverage in the Homeowners Policy, 11.40
Computer Loss Adjusting, 11.42–11.44
Computer Losses, 11.35–11.44
Concealment, **4.33**
Concrete, 8.3–8.4
Concrete form, **8.4**
Concurrent causation (concurrent causation doctrine),
    1.36
Conditions, **2.21**,11.31–11.32
Condominium, **11.18**
Condominium association, **11.18**
Condominium Association Coverage Form, 11.20–11.21
Condominium Losses, 11.18–11.22
Conflicts of Interest, 3.26
Consignee, **1.8**
Consignor, **11.5**
Contamination, 11.38
Contamination Claims, 11.45
Contamination Claims and the Superfund Law,
    11.45–11.47

Continuances, 5.16
Continuing expenses, **10.14**
Contract of indemnity, **1.4**
Contractor's Equipment Policies, 11.61–11.71
Contractors, 3.26
Contractors' equipment, **11.49**, 11.61
Contractors' Equipment Policy Provisions, 11.61–11.63
Contractors' Equipment Valuation, 11.71–11.72
Contractual Duties, 5.11
Contrast to Finished Estimate, 7.24
Cooperative (co-op), **11.18**
Corporate veil, **1.7**
Cost Data, 7.34–7.35
Cost of goods sold, **9.12**
Cost of Goods Sold Formula, 9.12
Cost of sales, **9.13**
Cost-to-Sales Ratio, 9.13
Countertops, 8.25
Course of an Arson Investigation, 6.12–6.15, 6.12–6.20
Coverage, 11.40–11.41
Coverage Aspects of Estimating, 7.40–7.43
Coverage Defenses, 4.31
Coverage Extensions and Endorsements, 11.67–11.68
Coverage for Lightning Losses, 1.27
Coverage for Merchandise Loss, 9.3–9.5
Coverage Forms, 11.19–11.22, 11.23–11.24
Coverage Issues in First-Party Property Insurance,
    11.47–11.49
Coverage Review, 9.5
Coverage Suspension, 1.30
Coverage Termination, 11.25
Covered Causes of Collapse, 1.32–1.33
Covered Causes of Loss, 10.20–10.21, 11.65
Covered Property, 11.63–11.64
Crime Coverages in Personal Insurance, 11.28
Crime Coverages in the BPP, 11.29
Crime Losses, 11.27–11.35
Custody Interests, 1.8–1.9
Cutting and fitting waste, **7.27**

D